The Last Hurrah

The American Crisis Series
Books on the Civil War Era

Series Editor: Steven E. Woodworth, Professor of History, Texas Christian University

Titles in the Series

The Last Hurrah

Sterling Price's Missouri Expedition of 1864

Kyle S. Sinisi

ROWMAN & LITTLEFIELD
Lanham • Boulder • New York • London

Published by Rowman & Littlefield
A wholly owned subsidiary of The Rowman & Littlefield Publishing Group, Inc.
4501 Forbes Boulevard, Suite 200, Lanham, Maryland 20706
www.rowman.com

Unit A, Whitacre Mews, 26-34 Stannary Street, London SE11 4AB, United Kingdom

British Library Cataloguing in Publication Information Available

Library of Congress Cataloging-in-Publication Data

Sinisi, Kyle S., 1962–
The last hurrah : Sterling Price's Missouri Expedition of 1864 / Kyle S. Sinisi.
p. cm. — (The American crisis series)
Includes bibliographical references and index.
ISBN 978-0-7425-4535-9 (cloth : alk. paper) -- ISBN 978-0-7425-4536-6 (electronic)
1. Price's Missouri Expedition, 1864. 2. Price, Sterling, 1809–1867. 3. United States—History—Civil War, 1861–1865—Cavalry operations. 4. Missouri—History—Civil War, 1861–1865. 5. Kansas—History—Civil War, 1861–1865. I. Title.
E477.16.S56 2015
973.7'37—dc23
2014049116

Printed in the United States of America

For

Scott T. Sinisi, who shares a love of history

and

Lindsey A. Sinisi, who just loves to get lost on a
Civil War battlefield with her dad

Contents

List of Maps

Map Key

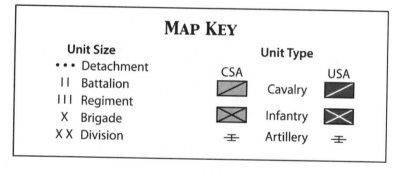

Figure 0.1. Map key

Preface

In the literature of a war that has produced over seventy thousand books, Sterling Price's Missouri expedition of 1864 is a rarity. There are very few book-length examinations of a campaign that ranks among the most unique of the war. Riding at the head of an army that initially numbered twelve thousand poorly armed and ill-disciplined men, Price attempted a deep strike behind enemy lines and the liberation of a state long occupied by Union forces. Price's army marched more than 1,400 miles in three months while fighting several pitched battles and numerous smaller engagements. No other mounted operation of the war, including John H. Morgan's or James H. Wilson's more well-known raids, compares in magnitude to Price's attempt to conquer Missouri in the fall of 1864. In the end, Price failed miserably when two separate Union forces led by Samuel R. Curtis and Alfred Pleasonton converged on him near Kansas City. The subsequent defeat at Westport on October 23rd started a headlong retreat to Texas that saw Price only narrowly avoid annihilation. Beset by cold weather, disease, and malnutrition, Price's threadbare army concluded its long march with less than half the men it had at the outset of the campaign. It was a tactical and strategic disaster that exemplified, perhaps more so than either Jubal A. Early's strike down the Shenandoah Valley or John B. Hood's movement into Tennessee, the unrealistic last-ditch efforts of the Confederacy to survive in late 1864.[1]

While Price's expedition lacks extensive scholarly treatment, many people have indeed written about it. As with just about every Civil War battle or campaign, the participants began publishing their recollections, reminiscences, and diatribes just as soon as the expedition concluded in December

1864. Some of the book-length accounts, but especially those by John N. Edwards and Richard J. Hinton, were written with verve and an eye for the dramatic anecdote. They also reflected well the different biases in the postwar struggle for how the expedition would be remembered.[2]

Outside of primary accounts, the interested reader has always had to piece together the story of the expedition from theses, articles, and books on isolated parts of the campaign. The best of the books were written before the mid-1980s and are now badly in need of revision due either to factual mistakes or more recently discovered sources. The only places to read about the expedition in its entirety have been in the relevant sections of no-less-dated books dealing with the Civil War in the Trans-Mississippi. Even the biographical literature on the major participants is surprisingly thin and unoriginal. Jo Shelby and his Iron Brigade have attracted the most attention, but those works have ranged from the fawning to the uncritical. Generals such as Curtis and Pleasonton, who possess a military significance well beyond the Price expedition, lack full-length biographies.[3]

Given the dearth of relevant scholarly treatments, this book attempts a comprehensive history of Price's expedition based in many heretofore unused or rarely exploited primary sources. It devotes early attention to the strategic decision making and politics that led to the expedition. Of particular interest will be Lieutenant General Edmund Kirby Smith's understanding of Price's intentions in Missouri and the impact of the Confederacy's civil-military politics and Kirby Smith's poor health upon the planning of the operation.[4] Likewise, the book discusses the Union's unpreparedness for the invasion and the attendant failure of Major General Frederick Steele to contain Price in Arkansas. In a departure from most of the extant histories, the book examines the early organization of Price's army and its march through Arkansas in order to address some of the greatest criticisms directed at Price regarding the pace of his march and the logistical requirements of the expedition. As should be expected, a considerable number of pages will be devoted to the major engagements in the vicinity of Pilot Knob, Kansas City, and Mine Creek. But those studies will be with an eye to providing new information and reassessing long-standing interpretations. For example, historians have usually asserted that Pilot Knob was a bloody disaster for Price and that it caused him to steer away from his primary objective of St. Louis. But was the battle really all that bloody, and was Price so diverted from St. Louis? In the battles around Kansas City, our knowledge of the action, and the attendant battle analysis, has relied upon a series of maps that have been passed down and accepted uncritically for nearly 150 years. But here too, should historians have been that accepting? Moreover, for those same 150 years, early-morning actions before Byram's Ford on October 23rd and the escape of Price's trains that same day have been shrouded in vague detail and controversy. Courts-martial records will clarify those events as well as some of the controversy associated with the stand of the 2nd Kansas State Militia at the Mockbee Farm on the 22nd. And at Mine Creek, historians have rarely looked at the battle's casualty figures and asked if a massacre occurred well after Confederate forces tried to surrender. These kinds of questions are but the tip of the examination of the major battles. Other issues to be studied include the impact of partisan politics upon Union command decision making, the consequences of the lack of a formal unity of command within Union forces, the prevalence of poor marksmanship among Union and Confederate forces, the importance of terrain and mapmaking in shaping the battles, and the condition of postbattle casualty care.

No less important, the book explores facets of the Missouri expedition that occurred outside the major battles. In some cases, this translates to extensive treatment of the lesser-known engagements. Included on this list are actions at Union, Herman, Glasgow, Sedalia, Fort Lincoln, the Mounds, Mound City, Marmaton River, and Newtonia. In other cases, the coverage goes beyond the conventional narrative to answer a series of questions about events on the periphery of the expedition. Was there, for example, any linkage between Sterling Price and the Missouri guerrilla uprising in the summer of 1864 as historians have long speculated? Aside from the mobilization of Curtis's Army of the Border, how did Kansans prepare to meet Price within their state? What problems did the Missouri State Militia, whose experience had been largely confined to guerrilla warfare, face in conducting large-scale operations against Price? Were free blacks along Price's route captured and enslaved to a great degree? Did Price irrationally maintain a headquarters train that was too large and ponderous, which readily enabled Federal forces to track him down and rout the Confederate army? In a related fashion, was Price, as so much of the literature would have it, a truly bad and inexperienced cavalryman unsuited to command an expedition that required speed and dash?

Finally, one of the more significant holes in the coverage of Price's expedition has been the treatment of its aftermath. This book hopes to correct that with an examination of several matters. The first studies the return of Union forces to their outposts and garrisons. Although many histories have described the privations of Price's retreat through Arkansas and the Indian Territory, there has been little mention of the corresponding difficulty of the pursuit and its return upon Union forces. Moreover, there has been strikingly little discussion of several Union atrocities that accompanied the journey. The second covers the attempts of at least one thousand men who tried to enroll in Price's army even as it fled Missouri. One of the greatest ironies of Price's disastrous retreat was that as the army lost thousands of soldiers due to malnutrition, disease, and desertion, groups of pro-Confederate Missourians struggled mightily in the cold, rain, and snow to get past Union forces to join Price. Hundreds would die in the process. Third, the book investigates the fate of well over 1,200 Confederate deserters and battlefield captures, many of whom claimed to have been conscripted at gun point. Part of that story details the misery endured by these men. More than 30 percent would suffer and die in prison due to overcrowding and sanitary ignorance. Put another way, it was a mortality rate that far exceeded the 12 percent of Confederate prisoners who died in all Union camps during the war. However, another part of the story pertains to all of those men who alleged conscription. Their declarations of loyalty to the Union, whether real or manufactured, revealed the hard reality of the Confederate cause in Missouri. Despite all of Sterling Price's hopes of sparking a popular uprising against Yankee tyranny, there were simply not enough well-armed true believers to sustain the campaign. If there ever was a lost cause with little chance of success in the Civil War, it was Price's Missouri expedition of 1864.[5]

There is one final point to make, and that concerns the place of Price's expedition in the larger history of the Civil War in Missouri and Kansas. There is a temptation to see the expedition as an anomalous event where large armies fought pitched battles in a region more accustomed to guerrilla war during the preceding three years. More importantly, the nature of the warfare associated with Price's expedition seemed strikingly different as commanders on all sides demonstrated a willingness to forget the savagery of the guerrilla conflict. Indeed, Union and Confederate senior commanders sought actively to observe the laws of warfare and to restrain soldiers conditioned to the brutality of the guerrilla war. One historian, Mark Neely, has even concluded, "The guerrilla war proved an exception, not a learning ground."[6] There is some truth to the argument. Throughout the campaign, certain types of property would be protected, and hundreds of captured soldiers would either be paroled or spared execution. Nevertheless, this book will also demonstrate that Union and Confederate combatants had not quite forgotten the remorseless nature of the guerrilla war and had in fact learned a great deal from it. While commanders such as Sterling Price, Jo Shelby, and Samuel Curtis sought to mitigate barbarism, subordinate officers and enlisted soldiers often displayed no such willingness. Men would be cut down in the act of surrendering, the dead would be mutilated, civilians would be executed, and private property would eventually be stolen, assessed, or destroyed without a second thought. No matter the good intentions of many, the culture of the guerrilla war would accompany Price's army as it moved through the region. It should have surprised no one.

Chapter One

Sterling Price Is the State of Missouri

There was an oft-repeated old adage about Sterling Price and the Civil War in Missouri. According to the adage, Missourians believed there were five different seasons: spring, summer, fall, Price's Raid, and winter. At first glance, there is no small irony in the saying. Following the ejection of Price and his army from Missouri in 1861, Price only made it back into the state once, and that was with his expedition of 1864. Even then, it distorts history to designate the expedition as a raid. Although the campaign would eventually degenerate into a scavenging operation that resembled a raid, Price himself initially had far greater strategic hopes that included the Confederate conquest of the state. Still, the old adage is not without meaning. If Sterling Price did not personally raid Missouri every year, others did it for him. M. Jeff Thompson, John Marmaduke, and Joseph Shelby all made it a practice to strike into Missouri in search of recruits and the simple satisfaction of showing the flag in occupied territory. Unfortunately for the Confederacy, more often than not the raids proved of small military value, and they frequently came perilously close to outright disaster for Confederate arms. It was in this failure, however, that a deeper meaning of the adage can be sensed. The five seasons of Missouri revealed the expectations of the state's Confederates and the faith they placed in Sterling Price to redeem Missouri from Yankee tyranny. After three years of bitter warfare, experience told them that no amount of bushwhacking or small-scale raids could deliver the state. In their darkest hours, Confederate Missourians needed their greatest hero, and Sterling Price was clearly that man.[1]

Price embodied the realities and myths of the Old South in Missouri. He was a native Virginian who had migrated to Keytesville, Missouri, in his early twenties. Handsome, tall, and charismatic, he readily parlayed a smoldering ambition into a successful life as a planter and Democratic politician. Price looked and acted like a leader, and it was only natural that with the outset of the Mexican War in 1846 many Missourians turned to Price to lead their troops. He did not disappoint. Although not without some controversy, especially among Whigs in Missouri, Price's time in Mexico was distinguished. He assumed command of an oversized cavalry regiment and marched it to New Mexico where he used it efficiently to suppress various Mexican uprisings. By the end of the war, Price was a brevet brigadier general and a bona fide hero.

It did not take Price long to translate his enhanced military status to politics. By 1852 he had become a prominent member of the pro-slavery faction of the state Democratic Party, and that same year Missourians elected him governor. He was an able administrator and well attuned to the pulse of his constituents. He avoided controversial decisions and left the governor's mansion in 1856 as perhaps the state's most popular politician. Over the next four years Price maintained and cultivated an almost statesman-like reputation. His pronounced defenses of slavery and states' rights illustrated his attachments to the South, but it did not make him a fire-eating secessionist. Like so many other Missourians, Price embraced a conditional Unionism and sought to steer a neutral course. Rather than tilt in the direction of either the unconditional Unionism of Missouri's ethnic Germans or the secessionism of the Missouri River counties, Price embraced the idea that his state could simply stay out of the impending crisis. Only when Brigadier General Nathaniel Lyon's precipitous actions finally brought the war to Missouri in May 1861 did Price commit to secession and then eventually to the Confederacy. Although subsequently forced from Missouri along with thousands of militia, Governor Claiborne Fox Jackson, and assorted political hangers-on, he easily became the state's most prominent Confederate and the one most Confederate Missourians naturally relied upon to return and liberate their state.

Price understood this near-messianic faith, and he consequently spent the rest of the war trying to live up to the expectation. At first the task looked easy. In the summer of 1861 he gained decisive victories at Wilson's Creek and Lexington that shattered two Union armies and severely rattled Union control of Missouri. Recruits joined his army by the hundreds, and he became known throughout the region as Old Pap for his patrician-like care of his troops. Unfortunately, the arrival of yet another Yankee army quickly dashed these hopes and forced Price to retreat out of the state and back into Arkansas. For the next two years, Price saw events spin far out of his control and along with it the chances of ever getting back into Missouri. First, he and his Missourians found themselves merged into a larger Confederate army commanded by Major General Earl Van Dorn. The impetuous Van Dorn proceeded to lead the Missourians to defeat at Pea Ridge in March 1862. Second, Price's ambitions in Missouri fell victim to larger Confederate war plans that placed greater emphasis upon events east of the Mississippi River. Following the Battle of Pea Ridge, General Albert Sydney Johnston, commander of what was then called the Western Department, ordered Price and his men across the Mississippi to meet a surging Union offensive that had already captured forts Henry and Donelson in Tennessee. None too happy with this development, Price not only crossed the Mississippi but also several other rivers as he raced to Richmond to argue for a transfer back to the Trans-Mississippi.

The trip was a disaster. The only thing Price accomplished was to ignite an open feud with President Jefferson Davis. For Davis, Price's appearance in the capital could not have been more poorly timed. While Price pleaded for a return to Missouri, the very existence of the Confederacy was in doubt as Union forces under Major General George B. McClellan threatened Richmond. If this were not enough, Davis suspected Price's loyalty to the Confederate cause. Davis remembered well that Price was a late convert to secessionism. Making matters worse, wild and unsubstantiated rumors had reached the capital that dissatisfied elements in the government were plotting to overthrow Davis. More importantly, the dissidents hoped to replace Davis with Price! Price's dramatic appearance in the capital with most of his staff in tow sent various tongues to wagging about the possibility of a coup d'etat. Given the circumstances, it is not surprising that the two men fell to arguing when they finally met and that Price angrily resigned his commission. What is surprising is that although Davis initially accepted the resignation, he reversed himself after sleeping on the decision. Davis could not escape the fact of Price's popularity among Missourians, and he did not want to risk a backlash. He chose then to compromise—and to dump the problem off on someone else. Consequently, he instructed General Braxton Bragg, the commander of the newly designated Army of Tennessee, to return Price and his Missourians across the Mississippi River when the military situation permitted. This was hardly what Price wanted to hear, but his extensive conversations with the Missouri congressional delegation and members of the Davis administration must have told him there was no better deal possible. Undoubtedly disappointed, Price withdrew his resignation and departed for Mississippi.[2]

Throughout the summer and early fall of 1862, Price remained remarkably patient on the issue of a return to Missouri. He fought in two battles, Iuka and Corinth, and displayed a basic tactical competence that was exceeded by an ability to inspire his troops in battle. His men followed wherever Price led them, and they performed courageously. The division suffered extraordinary losses, but it was not enough to get the Missourians posted back across the river. Complaints and threats of mass desertion from within the ranks tested Price's patience and tact. He fired off letters to almost anyone he believed could help his cause, and he issued a special order to his troops that not so subtly suggested that they had been lied to and that Price would lead them from bondage if he determined the government had acted unfaithfully. Price resolved not to wait around while others pondered his fate, and he looked for another chance to plead his case in Richmond. That opportunity arrived after Major General Ulysses S. Grant's first attempt to capture Vicksburg, Mississippi, fizzled in late December 1862. Price got leave and traveled to Richmond. When he arrived, Old Pap discovered that the politico-military universe of Confederate Missouri had changed.[3]

For the first two years of the war, Price symbolized the Confederacy to Missourians. He was by no means the only prominent Confederate Missourian, but his large figure and charisma eclipsed all others. This included Governor Claiborne Fox Jackson, who had attempted to create a government in exile at Little Rock, Arkansas. Though possessed of no small personality himself, Jackson had become marginalized. He led no troops, taxed no citizens, and spent only what he could raise through selling bonds and by what Richmond gave him. Making matters far worse, by 1862 he was dying of cancer. His death in early December ushered into the governor's chair Lieutenant Governor Thomas C. Reynolds. This was a pivotal event for Missouri and one that would come to cast a shadow over Price's attempt to get back into the state—and the historical memory of that attempt.

Reynolds was a native South Carolinian. He graduated from the University of Virginia and traveled abroad where he studied the law and learned to speak several foreign languages. Reynolds subsequently served as diplomat to Spain and practiced law in St. Louis beginning in 1850. His arrival in St. Louis also started a meteoric rise within the pro-slavery wing of the Missouri

Democratic Party that seemed to culminate with his election as lieutenant governor in 1860. He was brilliant and indefatigable. He was also petty and overly sensitive to perceived slights. His irritability and sense of honor were legendary, and they inevitably led to dueling. In one notorious episode prior to the war, he dueled Democratic rival B. Gratz Brown with rifles. An expert shot, Reynolds aimed only to wound. Indeed, while Reynolds emerged unscathed, Brown left the field with a bullet in his kneecap.[4]

Such a man was not to be trifled with, especially when he became governor. Reynolds was determined not to fall into irrelevance as had his predecessor. Accordingly, he believed that the basis of relevance was not in Little Rock, but Richmond. He further calculated that Jefferson Davis held the key to Missouri's—and his own—political viability. If Missouri and its interests could be kept before the president, while not alienating him in the process, the state could remain a part of the Confederacy's active plans. To Reynolds, Sterling Price threatened all of this with his almost obsessive pleadings, which also encouraged the state's congressional delegation to equally obsessive and unproductive declarations. More importantly, he agitated Reynolds's already deeply held distrust of the old general. In many ways Price was the antithesis of both Reynolds and the qualities Reynolds deemed necessary in a Confederate public servant. Where Price had been squishy on secession and parochial in his dedication to Missouri's interests, Reynolds had been a strident and committed Confederate. Where Price led a lavish and patrician lifestyle, Reynolds preferred personal sacrifice and self-denial. Where Price cared little for details, Reynolds obsessed over minutiae and pried into any issue that took his fancy. Perhaps most significant, where Price had countless political friends and the popularity of the masses, Reynolds was a backroom politician with a hyperactive imagination. To Reynolds, Sterling Price was therefore, at worst, an obstacle to be overcome and, at best, a figure to be manipulated for the betterment of both Thomas C. Reynolds and Missouri.[5]

So it was that when Reynolds arrived in Richmond in early January 1863 he insinuated himself into what he called the "Price embroglio [*sic*]." He tried to assume the persona of an honest broker who held the trust of all sides. This, by itself, would be a difficult task. Not all sides trusted him. Price and his many friends suspected the governor's ambitions, and the Missouri congressional delegation thought him meddlesome. Perhaps only Jefferson Davis and his cabinet trusted the governor's intentions as they clearly sought help in making Price go away. Reynolds immediately held a series of interviews with members of both the Missouri congressional delegation and Davis's cabinet. The information was disconcerting to Reynolds, and it appeared to confirm all of his suspicions regarding Price's commitment to the Confederate cause. There was, of course, Price's near-mutinous special order to his Missourians. There was also fresh news that Old Pap's son, Edwin, had resigned his commission in the Missouri State Guard and publicly renounced the Confederacy. The implications of this for the future actions of Sterling Price—at least to Reynolds—were loaded with ominous possibilities. But of paramount concern to Reynolds, and apparently Secretary of State Judah P. Benjamin as well, were rumors that connected Price to numerous secret societies allegedly plotting to detach the states of the Old Northwest and Missouri in order to create their own separate republic, or Northwest Confederacy. The ripest of these rumors had Price leading an invasion from the South that would be the signal for a popular uprising. According to the gossip, Old Pap's reward would be the presidency of this new confederacy. Like many conspiracy theories, there was a kernel of truth somewhere deep inside the rumors. Price was indeed connected, though tenuously, to a group called the Order of American Knights (OAK).[6]

Before the war, an obscure self-promoter named Phineas Wright tried to create a fraternity resembling the Masons or the Odd Fellows. He failed miserably. When the war broke out, Wright saw an opportunity to gain political importance. He therefore attempted to transform his still-born fraternity into a paramilitary haven for disaffected northern Democrats, Confederate sympathizers, and other assorted political outcasts. Here, too, he failed. Few joined his ranks, and many who did tended to think that they were joining a completely different Democratic association. As for Sterling Price, there is nothing in the historical record to suggest that he had any formal ties to the OAK. That said, there is also little doubt that full-fledged members of the OAK in Missouri made their way south to Price's camp. As one staff officer noted, "Periodical installments of these well dressed, sleek looking gentry came among the rugged veterans . . . , with mysterious books, innumerable signs, grips, signals, passwords, and incantations sufficient to get up a dozen of Macbeth's witch dances." Apparently nonplussed by such exotic behavior, Price seems to have accepted their news and military intelligence from Missouri in the same way he accepted the news and intelligence from other refugees or spies who traveled between the lines. Their information was usually just another piece of a puzzle that told Price he needed to return to Missouri.[7]

When Price and Reynolds finally did talk in early February 1863, the governor had largely made up his mind about how best to proceed. Price, he concluded, was not imminently in danger of deserting the Confederacy. For the long term, Reynolds could not be as sure. He so informed Secretary Benjamin and adopted what would become his own policy regarding Price for the rest of the war. It was a policy based on three suppositions.[8]

First, Reynolds thought little of Price's military abilities. Price had not scored any victories since 1861, and there were reports that he coddled his troops in the search for their approval. Perhaps more to the point, Reynolds had probably not yet jettisoned his own pretensions to a military reputation. At the beginning of the war, Reynolds had tried, and failed, to get a general officer's commission that would have trumped Price. It was a situation that gnawed at Reynolds, and he subsequently never resisted an opportunity to weigh in on military affairs. Second, Reynolds believed that Old Pap's ego might lead him to wander from the Confederate fold in search of glory and power. Third, and finally, the governor sadly concluded that the general could not be sacked. He was far too popular among his troops and the reputed legions of Southern-sympathizing Confederates left behind in Missouri. Consequently, Reynolds pursued the idea that Price must always be carefully harnessed and watched by skillful officers, while nevertheless keeping Price in a position important and visible enough to rally all Missourians. It went without saying that Reynolds saw himself as the one man most capable of watching and harnessing Price. According to Reynolds, he sought, and gained, from Davis the status of an "unofficial advisor" to both the president and Price's superior in the Trans-Mississippi, Lieutenant General Edmund Kirby Smith.[9]

So it was that Reynolds brokered a deal sending Price, but not his troops, west of the Mississippi River. In language similar to that seen in the deal that kept Price in Mississippi in the spring of 1862, the troops would recross the river only "when existing necessities will allow." Explicit in the orders was the idea that an equivalent number of soldiers from west of the river must be exchanged for Price's troops. Given Ulysses S. Grant's renewed operations against Vicksburg, there was little chance that the Missourians would ever be spared. Price was wary of the agreement but concluded, again, that it was the best deal available. Old Pap then left Richmond for the long ride back to Arkansas and, he hoped, Missouri.[10]

Once Price crossed the Mississippi River, he had entered the Department of the Trans-Mississippi. The department was enormous, encompassing six hundred thousand square miles of all claimed Confederate territory west of the Mississippi River. Largely cut off from the rest of the Confederacy, the department was, in the words of Albert Castel, "as much a semiautonomous nation as it was military theater." Although grossly short of troops, money, and war material, the department was commanded by an officer of some reputation. Lieutenant General Edmund Kirby Smith had assumed his post in March 1863. He did not seek the position, and he never warmed to the department, calling it "a vast empire . . . without means, without troops." Kirby Smith owed his appointment to basic competence and a proper deference to authority so lacking in many Confederate general officers, including Sterling Price. While not obsequious, Kirby Smith got along well with President Jefferson Davis. He had extensive combat experience and a reputation for being an able administrator. He was, in other words, a soldier that Davis trusted to run a department well beyond the president's physical ability, or that of anyone else in Richmond, to control. Pious and even tempered, Kirby Smith seemed well equipped to handle the egos and ambitions that were bound to run rampant in a department so detached from Richmond, Virginia.[11]

Unfortunately, Kirby Smith would still have problems with Price. To that point in the war, Price had demonstrated little ability to get along with his fellow general officers. But making matters even more difficult would be the added presence of Thomas C. Reynolds, who arrived in Arkansas shortly after Price and Kirby Smith. A prolific letter writer and chronicler, Reynolds tried after the war to portray himself as a long-suffering supporter of Price who crossed the Mississippi River willing to give Price every benefit of the doubt on matters personal, political, and military. Reynolds certainly tried to convince Price of this friendship through his letters and conversations with the general's inner circle of friends. Notwithstanding Reynolds's frequent claims of his ability to help Price achieve his "patriotic ambition," the governor was highly agitated about Price and his status as the designated savior of Confederate Missouri. Ever since Reynolds had assumed his office, Price's supporters rarely missed an opportunity to remind the governor of Old Pap's exalted status. According to Reynolds, one such friend, Thomas Snead, went so far as to inform the governor that Price, "in fact, is the State of Missouri," with the not-so-subtle suggestion that Reynolds should either support Price or get out of the way. Needless to say, such commentary made Reynolds seethe, and it had to be with a certain amount of relish, or venom, that when he arrived in Arkansas he presented Kirby Smith with dispatches from Richmond announcing his own privileged status as a military "advisor" and one who must be consulted in all matters concerning Missouri. [12]

Although there was little outward conflict between Price and Reynolds for much of 1863, the calm did not survive the end of the year. Price struggled to get along with his new district commander, the aged and increasingly forgetful Theophilus Holmes. Relations between Holmes and Price disintegrated soon after the disastrous attempt to take Helena in July. Holmes, probably unjustly, blamed Price for much of the defeat, which then caused insults to be hurled back and forth for the rest of the year. The most important consequence of the battle, and the subsequent acrimony, was that Kirby Smith began to sour on Price. Old Pap's reputation in the eyes of Kirby Smith and, if one can believe Reynolds's postwar account, many Missouri Confederates, received another blow in October when Price evacuated Little Rock in the face of Major General Frederick Steele's advancing Union army. As Albert Castel has argued, the evacuation was in all probability inevitable, but Price was nevertheless directly in charge when Kirby Smith saw his Confederacy shrink even further. Consequently, by January Kirby Smith wanted to replace Holmes as district commander with someone other than Price. To Kirby Smith, "Price is not equal to the command, and I would regard it unfortunate were he to succeed to it." [13]

The winter of 1863 to 1864 was a depressing time for Price. Battlefield setbacks had been followed by the inevitable finger pointing, and, worst of all, he was no closer to a return to Missouri than he was in the winter of 1861 to 1862. Still, the general plotted and planned. Writing Reynolds in November, Price noted that he had discussions with Kirby Smith concerning "our common & now immediate interest in the speedy redemption of our state." Suppressing his own distrust of Reynolds, Price went on to say that "I may confer with you upon the military movements which in my opinion are apparently most conducive to that end." [14]

True to his word, Price opened a line of communication with the governor that included forwarding mail and news from Missouri. The news was familiar. Confederate sympathies ran high in Missouri, and recruits by the tens of thousands were ready to flock to the Confederate cause. All that the state needed to channel this enthusiasm and manpower into the Southern army was Price himself. As Price forwarded this sort of information to Reynolds in early January 1864, he also revealed to the governor a basic frustration that went beyond his inability to return to Missouri. Although Price understood his role as deliverer, he had become incredulous that Missourians had not done more to liberate themselves. He simply could not understand how "men who have been free can be made to submit, without a struggle, to that abject slavery which the North is attempting to impose upon the South, nor that they can be so cowardly as to surrender without a blow [for] their liberties, their property, and their honor." In an almost bitter tone, Price went on to bemoan the fact that so many Missourians were waiting for him to arrive before they arose en mass to destroy tyranny. Instead, Price noted, these professed sympathizers needed to perform their manly duty and join him in Arkansas, which would give him an invincible army capable of shoving aside all Yankee opposition and liberating Missouri.[15]

Price did not let his disappointment with the lack of a native uprising deter him. Early in March 1864, the general proclaimed that "if his counsels should be followed . . . they would pass the next Christmas in St. Louis." To his great disappointment, Old Pap quickly rediscovered that, as always, his desire for a return to Missouri was still held captive to other, and more strategically pressing, events. That spring, the Confederate high command in the Trans-Mississippi was in a reactive posture as it tried to divine the Union's next move in its region. For Kirby Smith, figuring those intentions was particularly vexing. He believed that it made little sense for the Union to concentrate any troops in the Trans-Mississippi when it seemed better to assemble all available Yankee manpower in the east where it could prove more decisive. Remarkably, however, all intelligence pointed to a Union effort up the Red River into northern Louisiana and the nerve center of Kirby Smith's Confederacy.[16]

Likewise, it seemed a good bet that Frederick Steele would take his Union army from Little Rock, push aside or defeat Price's small army, and march it south to catch Kirby Smith in his operational rear. In the flurry of consultations and guessing that then took place between Kirby Smith and Price, who by mid-March succeeded against Kirby Smith's better judgment to the command of the District of Arkansas, Old Pap made it plain that, although the Union threatened Kirby Smith in Louisiana, his own operational thoughts concerned Missouri. In a presentation of ideas that he enunciated repeatedly over the next few months, Price suggested that Kirby Smith devote his efforts to raising an army of twenty thousand men in Arkansas that could then eject Steele from the Arkansas River valley. With Steele out of the way, Missouri would be open to Confederate recruiting officers and a subsequent reconquest of the state. Price graciously, though not seriously, left open the possibility that Kirby Smith himself could command the movement. Either way,

Sterling Price remained consistent in his strategic outlook. Missouri must be redeemed. [17]

Unimpressed with Price's arguments, Kirby Smith took time also to consult with the ubiquitous Governor Reynolds, who was then at Kirby Smith's headquarters in Shreveport. Writing on March 15th, Kirby Smith squashed Price's suggestion with the correct observation that Confederate manpower was much too limited to operate in the Arkansas River valley. He hinted also that Major General Nathaniel P. Banks's movements near the mouth of the Red River would necessitate a concentration of Confederate forces in Louisiana. Indeed, just three days after posting this letter, Kirby Smith concluded that Banks was indeed coming up the Red River toward Shreveport and that Price needed to strip his district of what little infantry it had to support Major General Richard Taylor's operations in northern Louisiana. At the same time, Kirby Smith instructed Price to use his cavalry to delay any southern movement of Frederick Steele. [18]

This effectively ended Old Pap's springtime Missouri reverie. Jolted into action, Price performed very well over the next month of campaigning. Tasked to delay a Union pincer from Arkansas that had the potential to trap Taylor and his army against Banks's main body advancing up the Red River, Price accomplished his mission with a limited force of five cavalry brigades. As Robert Shalhope has noted, "Not only did he slow the enemy advance, but he forced Steele to continually concentrate his force, thus depriving him of a desperately needed wide forage front." Before additional troops and Kirby Smith himself arrived to help Price, Old Pap pinned down Frederick Steele's very hungry Union army at Camden. Kirby Smith's arrival on April 19th did not portend greater results. With Price now the head of a provisional corps of infantry, Kirby Smith was unable to turn the inevitable Yankee retreat from Camden into a rout. Steele retreated back to Little Rock, returning a positional status quo to the region that had the Union occupying territory along a line from Fort Smith in the west through Little Rock in the center and onto Pine Bluff in the east. [19]

Despite the failure to crush Steele, Kirby Smith could rightly view the entire campaign a success. Not only had he turned back the Yankee tide in Arkansas, his district commander in Louisiana, Major General Richard Taylor, had performed brilliantly, defeating Banks's push up the Red River. Kirby Smith was not a terribly energetic commander, but he realized that the victory in the Red River campaign gave him an opportunity to seize the initiative and strike north through Arkansas into Missouri. Union forces in

Arkansas had suffered immensely during the recent battles. They had lost over 2,300 men, 635 wagons, and 2,500 mules. Moreover, Union strategy had itself become reactive with most Northern troops concentrated at Little Rock, Fort Smith, Helena, and Pine Bluff. A siege mentality soon infected the commanders of these posts while offensive operations ceased and intelligence gathering withered. As the historian Thomas Belser has noted, Confederate Brigadier General Jo Shelby revealed the weakness of these dispositions when he operated with his cavalry almost at will in northeastern Arkansas from May through September. In Missouri the situation was no better for the Union as volunteer regiments continually marched east to reinforce Major General William T. Sherman, leaving only 3,950 well-trained troops in that state. Union troop movements were not a well-kept secret, and it quickly became a part of the conventional wisdom that Missouri was ripe for the proverbial plucking as the spring of 1864 turned into summer.[20]

Kirby Smith did not want to let this opportunity slip through his fingers. But any decision he made about an expedition would be complicated by personal and political conflicts that had been rubbed raw during the Red River campaign. Despite the Confederate drubbing of two Union armies, Kirby Smith believed that he was both underappreciated and stymied by his subordinates. First, his commander of the District of West Louisiana, Richard Taylor, was beside himself with what he believed was Kirby Smith's incompetence. Just when Taylor thought he was in a position to annihilate Banks, Kirby Smith decided to take the field himself. Kirby Smith then detached two infantry divisions from Taylor's army to accompany the department commander on a march to reinforce Sterling Price then facing Frederick Steele at Camden. Taylor ultimately concluded that Price had already defeated Steele and that any reinforcements were not only unnecessary but also calculated chiefly to puff Kirby Smith's own glory in the campaign. Brilliant yet overly sensitive, Taylor was not one to let such a slight go unnoticed, and beginning April 28th he bombarded a genuinely stunned Kirby Smith with insubordinate letters designed to get Taylor a transfer east. Second, the commander of the Department of the Trans-Mississippi had his own axe to grind with Sterling Price. As he often did, Kirby Smith chose to blame subordinates for any disappointments. He was convinced that Price had inexplicably failed to cut off Steele's line of retreat at Camden and thus forfeited the probable capture of Steele's entire army. Although the historiographical consensus is that Price performed capably, Kirby Smith believed that Price had bungled.[21]

Notably, Kirby Smith chose not to confront Price directly with his criticisms. This could have been the result of equal parts Kirby Smith's own documented personal reticence and a measured way of not aggravating Price and his legion of followers. Kirby Smith chose instead to vent his feelings toward Richmond and Thomas C. Reynolds. In an impassioned letter to Davis dated May 5th, he painted a dismal picture of the command and staff structure in the Trans-Mississippi. Price, in particular, came in for scathing criticism as Kirby Smith concluded that while Old Pap's "name and popularity would be a strong element of success in an advance on Missouri, . . . he is neither capable of organizing, disciplining, nor operating an army, [and] he should not be left in command of the district or an army in the field."[22]

From this moment until the first week in August, Kirby Smith's exact intentions for an expedition, and Sterling Price's role in it, were muddled. There were, however, three things that seemed clear. First, and as Price had suggested back in early March, the operation would be predicated on controlling the Arkansas River valley, which would then serve as a springboard for the movement into Missouri. Second, Kirby Smith would hold nothing back, using all of his available infantry and cavalry in the offensive. Third, Kirby Smith wanted to move quickly. Therefore, on May 16th he ordered the infantry divisions of brigadier generals Thomas J. Churchill and Mosby M. Parsons, then located in northern Louisiana, to head north to the vicinity of Camden preparatory to an expedition. The very next day he directed Richard Taylor to bring his men north. And finally, on May 19th, Kirby Smith provided Price his long-awaited orders to prepare for a return to Missouri and that he needed to start gathering intelligence, "collecting supplies, putting your trains in order, and establishing depots." Unfortunately, no sooner had Price and his fellow officers received these orders than Kirby Smith fell strangely silent. Kirby Smith offered no explanation, and planning for the expedition ground quickly to a halt, leaving the Missourians both anxious and perplexed.[23]

What then had happened to Kirby Smith? Unfortunately, the answer is largely a mystery and one open to speculation, but it appears that two things undermined Kirby Smith's best intentions. First, and as Albert Castel has noted, he may have become unsettled by the logistics of a midsummer campaign. His transportation was a mess, although it had been augmented greatly by animals and wagons captured at Mark's Mill and Poison Springs the preceding month. Even worse, food and forage would still be scarce in June, July, and August over territory that was none too fertile to begin with. It should be noted, though, that there is nothing in the historical record to show that Kirby Smith linked this sort of logistical difficulty with a midsummer campaign. It was only Taylor who raised the problem of food and transport in a reply to his commander's original march order. A second problem to beset Kirby Smith concerned Richard Taylor and the use of his troops in the upcoming operation. Writing on May 24th, Taylor notified Kirby Smith that he was not well and could not take to active campaigning. Kirby Smith could not have been surprised by Taylor's plea of infirmity. At the heart of Taylor's discontent was a belief—and rightly so—that his superior was abandoning Louisiana in favor of a misguided northern adventure. With Nathaniel Banks's army still struggling to extricate itself from the Red River, Taylor could not believe that Kirby Smith was going to miss this opportunity to annihilate a Yankee army in Louisiana. By this point in the war, Kirby Smith understood very well Taylor's strategic preferences and the personal vitriol that accompanied them. Not surprisingly, Kirby Smith had already discounted Taylor's direct participation in the upcoming campaign. In fact, Kirby Smith's letter to Taylor hinted that what was most important to the departmental commander was not so much Taylor himself, but his troops. Kirby Smith's language was tentative, requesting only that Taylor "should accompany the column from your district. Your presence will add to its efficiency and increase the prospects of success."[24]

The wording of Kirby Smith's letter and Taylor's insubordinate behavior make it highly unlikely that Kirby Smith wanted Taylor to take overall command of the expedition, as Albert Castel has also suggested. While Kirby Smith may have thought that Richmond might send him another competent general officer to command the expedition, it is more likely that Kirby Smith expected at this early stage to retain overall command for any operation that included troops brought from outside Price's District of Arkansas. Such a move would have been in keeping for Kirby Smith, who distrusted Price and chose just one month earlier to desert his department headquarters to take command in the field. Given then that Kirby Smith expected little personally from Richard Taylor, what truly must have surprised Kirby Smith was Taylor's revelation that his troops could be of no immediate assistance in the grand expedition. According to Taylor, the recent campaign left him with few combat-ready men and animals. Moreover, Taylor made sure to take a jab at Kirby Smith by implying that the department's bureaucratic inefficiency had contributed to this level of unreadiness. After proffering some scattered advice on the conduct of the expedition, Taylor reemphasized his desire that he be relieved of command.[25]

The effect of Taylor's letter cannot be underestimated. Not only did it help fan a war of words with Kirby Smith, but it also forced him to reconsider his enthusiasm for an immediate push into Missouri. On June 3rd, in what would be Kirby Smith's last communication with Price about the expedition for almost two months, Kirby Smith's chief of staff, Brigadier General William R. Boggs, asked for more detailed intelligence about Missouri, the state of the Confederate resistance, Union defenses, and supply possibilities. But critically, Boggs wanted this information as it applied "during the months of August, September, October, and November next." Only then, Boggs concluded, might there be an "opportunity" to "make a campaign into Missouri."[26]

Kirby Smith's silence and a marked unwillingness to discuss his plans allowed confusion to spread. Writing Price from Marshall, Texas, on June 2nd, Thomas C. Reynolds glumly noted that he was embarrassed by a lack of information on the expedition. Price's response revealed his own frustration. Recent intelligence from Missouri announced that "there are 20,000 men in Saint Louis alone now armed and waiting to join me." Unfortunately, he had "but little encouragement to form opinions or plans for our future military movements." Price also sensed that he was being pushed into irrelevance by what he termed "the promotion of his juniors over me." Here, Price was reacting to Kirby Smith's attempted promotion of several brigadiers to the rank of major general, pending the approval of Jefferson Davis. Included on this list was fellow Missourian John S. Marmaduke, who Price disliked. In reality, Old Pap had overstated the importance of these promotions, as their dates of rank would always be inferior to Price's. Similarly, and Price did not know it yet, President Davis refused to sign off on Kirby Smith's promotion of general officers. The promotion of general officers was a privilege granted only to the government, and Davis balked at delegating it to Kirby Smith, no matter how far away the Trans-Mississippi.[27]

Despite Price's overreaction to being displaced by Kirby Smith's attempted promotion of new major generals, he did have cause for concern because, unbeknownst to him, Richmond had finally sent Kirby Smith a general officer he really wanted. On June 21st, Major General Simon Bolivar Buckner arrived in Alexandria, Louisiana. Buckner was a skilled, yet unfortunate, officer who was most notable for having been abandoned by two superior generals to surrender Fort Donelson in 1862. In early March, Kirby

Smith had officially requested that Richmond replace the increasingly useless Theophilus Holmes as commander of the District of Arkansas. His request listed Buckner as one of three officers who he believed would work
well in the Trans-Mississippi. Kirby Smith took care to send his request by a
trusted staff officer who was also then to discuss the entire command structure with Jefferson Davis and the Secretary of War. These discussions then
resulted in Buckner being dispatched to the west from Virginia. As could
have been expected, Buckner's arrival touched off a guessing game concerning his assignment. Some thought he would command the District of Arkansas, while others concluded he was destined to take Richard Taylor's place in
Louisiana. Thomas C. Reynolds ultimately concluded that the best place for
Buckner was as a "quasi-Secretary of War," which would free Kirby Smith
to take the field.[28]

However, in the midst of all this speculation there was little talk, or at
least none that was recorded, that had Buckner taking command of the Missouri expedition. At most, there was some belief that Buckner would remain
subordinate to Price during the actual campaign, with his Kentucky birth
helping to assuage the feelings of many Missourians who traced their lineage
to the Bluegrass State. For his part, Kirby Smith helped fan the speculation
by his simple absence from headquarters. Early in June he departed Shreveport for a trip to Texas that mixed business with pleasure. His wife had gone
to Hempstead earlier in the spring to escape the possibility of a Yankee
capture of Shreveport. She stayed on through the summer to deliver their
second daughter. Kirby Smith therefore arrived in time to celebrate that birth
on June 9th. He subsequently toured the District of Texas, winding up in
Houston as late as June 22nd. Even upon his return to Shreveport in July, he
remained silent on both the possibility of an expedition and the assignment of
Buckner.[29]

Price and his fellow Missourians could only stew over Kirby Smith's
inaction and simple failure to communicate his plans. Unfortunately, the
prospects for a fully developed campaign took yet another blow on July 15th
when Kirby Smith received the first of many telegrams from Lieutenant
General Stephen D. Lee, commander of the Department of Alabama, Mississippi, and East Louisiana, demanding that Kirby Smith send troops across the
Mississippi. Lee was frantic over intelligence that had Yankee Major General
E. R. S. Canby making a major push from New Orleans to Mobile. He
needed reinforcements badly and began first by citing Braxton Bragg, military advisor to Jefferson Davis, and then ultimately the president himself as

the basis for his demand. It is no exaggeration to say that this information stunned Kirby Smith. Earlier in the spring he had informed Richmond that the Union's control of the waterways made it virtually impossible to cross troops to the east. Moreover, his department was already grossly under-manned for its own defense. Of course, making matters more difficult was the situation with Richard Taylor and the reported poor condition of his troops in Louisiana. In fact, Kirby Smith had already relieved Taylor, who was then awaiting reassignment.[30]

From the moment when he received Lee's first call for troops on July 15th, Kirby Smith hesitated, and while he hesitated to act Missourians of all stripes continued to lobby for an attack. Thomas C. Reynolds did not know about the request for the transfer of troops back across the Mississippi, but he readily divined that the strategic situation in the east had deteriorated to the point that an expedition of Missouri could only be justified as a means of diverting Union strength in that quarter. Accordingly, he wrote Price on July 18th to suggest a change in strategy that would ignore Union forces in the Arkansas River valley and instead press a much smaller cavalry force con-sisting only of Shelby's and Marmaduke's brigades into Missouri if only to relieve Georgia and Mobile. Moreover, Reynolds wondered if initial success with the cavalry could be sustained by infusions of Missouri recruits and infantry support from Arkansas. Reynolds concluded by asking if Price would be willing to lead such a small force of cavalry, as "your name would largely increase it on its entrance into Missouri." Price responded on July 22nd with a note that revealed just how desperate he was to get back to Missouri. He agreed with Reynolds that it was not necessary to control the Arkansas River valley preparatory to the movement and that it was possible to retake Missouri with "cavalry alone." Not surprisingly, Price also noted his willingness to command the operation. Now, more than ever, Price wanted to go. News from Missouri continued to flood into Price's camp that the state was ready for a general uprising, and he believed "the time was never more propitious for an advance of our forces." His troops concurred, and many Missourians began to proclaim loudly "that they would rather die in Missouri than live in Arkansas."[31]

Galvanized into action, Price yet again wrote Kirby Smith, proposing an expedition. He reiterated his most recent intelligence, while now asserting that "the least sanguine" of reports had thirty thousand ready to join his flag. The time had arrived for Kirby Smith to make a decision, not only about Missouri, but also about trying to reinforce Stephen Lee. Paramount for

Kirby Smith was trying to decipher the precise intentions of Jefferson Davis and his military advisors. In fairness to Kirby Smith, this was a difficult thing to do, as it seemed the Confederate command group could not quite make up its own collective mind. On the one hand, there were reports from Missouri congressmen Thomas L. Snead and E. C. Cabell that Richmond thought it best for Kirby Smith to mount some type of movement into Missouri as a means of diverting Union troops. On the other hand, the near-hysterical cables from Stephen D. Lee gave no doubt that Richmond wanted him also to strip his department of infantry to reinforce combat operations in Mississippi and Alabama. There, of course, was no way for Kirby Smith to know it, but Lee's demands for troops were a product of a complete breakdown in communication between Davis and his advisor, Braxton Bragg, and then again between Davis and his departmental commanders. Davis, in fact, had never authorized a further troop draw on the Trans-Mississippi. However, Bragg believed that Davis would support such a move and went ahead and authorized it in Davis's name. Further guaranteeing confusion, Bragg was at that time in Georgia and forgot to send Davis copies of his correspondence with Lee and Kirby Smith.[32]

Ironically, Bragg still forgot to inform Davis of his orders to Kirby Smith when a most unusual proposal arrived in Richmond in early August. At that time, J. Henry Behan, an obscure commissary captain in Meridian, Mississippi, took it upon himself to advise the president on the war's grand strategy. On July 23, Behan boldly mailed Davis a letter proposing a fantastic scheme that would not only throw terror into the Old Northwest but would also disrupt William T. Sherman's operations around Atlanta. The captain believed that Kirby Smith could combine all available troops in the Trans-Mississippi under his command, march through eastern Arkansas and Missouri, capture St. Louis, cross the Mississippi River, sweep up the Ohio River, capture Louisville, and turn south attacking Nashville and Chattanooga. The end result, he postulated, would find Sherman stuck between Kirby Smith's advancing hammer and John B. Hood's anvil. That Davis did not reprimand the captain for violating the chain of command was only a minor surprise compared to the fact that Davis took the proposal seriously and then discussed it with Braxton Bragg and Secretary of War James Seddon. Bragg informed the president that he "maturely considered" the plan and thought it "very comprehensive." Bragg then announced that the plan "might now be contemplated in the Trans-Mississippi," but that he was not optimistic of success simply because of "our limited means on this side." Seddon liked the plan only if Kirby Smith could not cross troops to Mississippi. On August 23rd, Jefferson Davis closed the debate by noting that events in the Trans-Mississippi had overtaken their theorizing.[33]

Davis was quite right. By July 30th Kirby Smith had finally decided on a course of action. In accordance with what he thought were Davis's wishes, Kirby Smith committed to transferring the bulk of his infantry, numbering about ten thousand men in eight brigades, across the Mississippi River in support of Stephen D. Lee. But Kirby Smith would have little to do with the actual, and potentially disastrous, exercise. Wracked by dysentery and rheumatism, he was a physical mess. Kirby Smith's mental state could hardly have been any better as he began taking morphine regularly. The effect was predictable, and Kirby Smith admitted to his wife that the drug "reduced me in flesh and spirit." When Smith could work through the pain and the fog of the morphine, he concluded that the operation was far too risky and that he should take no part in it. Unwilling, then, to lead the crossing, he did the next best thing: he reactivated Richard Taylor and tossed all responsibility for the operation on to his shoulders. What soon followed mixed the comedic with the tragic. Taylor wanted the responsibility even less than Kirby Smith, and he tried to flee across the river with only his staff to accompany him. Many of the troops themselves were none too enthusiastic for the mission, and wild rumors of a mutiny swirled through the ranks. Still, Kirby Smith persisted for much of August in the attempt to get a workable plan for crossing the river. It was, however, all for naught. On August 19th, Kirby Smith received what was probably the most bizarre communication addressed to him during the entire war. Jefferson Davis curtly pulled the plug on the whole business by telling Kirby Smith that he had never ordered a transfer of the troops in the first place. Davis's telegram stunned Kirby Smith, who then needed three days to gather himself before ordering a complete halt to the attempted crossing.[34]

Kirby Smith's ability to withhold the infantry had the potential to change dramatically the course of events in the Trans-Mississippi because Kirby Smith had also on July 30th committed to invading Missouri. He announced this intention in the same telegram to Davis that proclaimed his effort to transfer the infantry across the Mississippi. In keeping with Governor Reynolds's earlier suggestion that the expedition be scaled down, the general informed Davis that while he was "too weak for prosecuting a campaign in the Arkansas Valley," he still intended to "push a cavalry force into Missouri." In a fit of pique, Kirby Smith asserted that the request for Taylor and his troops came at an inopportune time as his "arrangements were perfected for offensive operations in Arkansas and Missouri." To the extent that Kirby Smith might have perfected such plans in his own mind, he could have been telling Davis the truth. But as of July 30th, Kirby Smith had shared these plans with no one. Having now wasted more than two months to coordinate any offensive operation, Kirby Smith called immediately for what one observer termed "a grand powwow" of military commanders and political leaders at Shreveport.[35]

By August 3rd, Price, Buckner, and Reynolds, among others, had gathered. At first glance, there appeared to be little to talk about. At that very moment, Kirby Smith was in the middle of trying to ferry ten thousand infantrymen across the Mississippi, leaving him with no more than twelve thousand poorly armed cavalrymen for any movement into Missouri. Common sense and operational precedent dictated that, at most, Kirby Smith could generate a large, mounted raid into Missouri. Like all such raids, its objectives would be of short-term significance. Property could be either destroyed or captured. Recruits could be raised. And perhaps most importantly, enemy troops could be diverted from other operations.[36]

Governor Reynolds, in particular, advocated a raid into Missouri if only as an attempt to relieve pressure on Atlanta. He had raised this very point in mid July and continued to press it through the meeting. He was, however, quite nervous about any other movement into Missouri, especially one that aimed for a more permanent Confederate presence in the state. In this, Reynolds's old distrust of Sterling Price became evident again. Although Reynolds had softened his attitude toward Price during the summer, the governor sensed anew that Price was involved in some type of dark conspiracy to control Missouri outside of Confederate authority. Writing Secretary of War Seddon on August 6th, Reynolds claimed that Thomas L. Snead was organizing a movement to hold elections in January 1865 to install Price as leader. He ominously warned Seddon that "a singular movement is on foot among the Missouri exiles. With most of them what is called 'just look to Gen'l. Price' is a watch word and cardinal principle." Reynolds's assertion was hardly earth shaking, especially to Seddon. For three years, Missourians had made no secret of their attachment to Price and their belief that he would deliver them back to the Promised Land. But Reynolds's concerns were justified in that Sterling Price wanted to lead far more than a cavalry raid into Missouri.[37]

Price's ambitions for the campaign were, of course, influenced by his own ego. No mere cavalry raid would be able to contain that. More critically, however, Price was influenced by the flood of optimistic intelligence that guaranteed easy pickings in Missouri. The reports were at least partly correct in that they accurately depicted a state denuded of volunteer troops. Union operations east of the Mississippi River had taken thousands of men, leaving the defense of the state in the hands of its militia. Unfortunately for Price, these same reports invariably came with bold attempts to quantify just how many Missourians would flock to Price's colors should he march into the state. The numbers varied, but one thing was certain: they increased over time. In January, the reports forecast that twenty thousand men were ready to join Price. By July, the number had jumped to thirty thousand. By August, even Jo Shelby dared to write Price's adjutant general and claim that "if Gen. Price, at the head of 5,000 cavalry, could penetrate the State he could light such a fire of opposition and enthusiasm that 50,000 loyal Missourians would spring to arms." The high point of what the historian Michael Fellman has called "the Missouri revitalization movement" had arrived. In the midst of such unguarded optimism, how could any commander settle for a raid that aimed only for a temporary presence in the state? The latest estimates simply confirmed Price in his long-held belief that the majority of Missourians were not only ready for liberation but that they were also ready to join his army and purge the state of Yankees.[38]

The time, therefore, had arrived for Kirby Smith to make some decisions. When the meetings finished late in the morning on August 4, Kirby Smith placed Price in command of the movement north. This decision came with the grudging support of Governor Reynolds, who had spent a large amount of time and effort before the meeting trying to decide just who he wanted to recommend to lead the expedition. He even sounded out Buckner as a possible candidate only to have the general squelch the idea, stating that he was better fitted to an administrative job. Only reluctantly did the governor finally recommend Price for the job. Just how much Kirby Smith relied upon Reynolds's recommendation is not known, although Reynolds later asserted he had to work hard to convince Kirby Smith because the department commander still despised Price and thought him "absolutely good for nothing." But what is certain is that Kirby Smith only offered the command to Price. Writing in 1867, John N. Edwards, Jo Shelby's wartime adjutant and postwar hagiographer, suggested that Kirby Smith first tendered the command to Simon Buckner and then John Marmaduke before settling on Price. Although subsequent generations of historians have been quick to accept Edward's assertion, there is no firsthand evidence to support his claim. A brilliant and flamboyant journalist after the war, Edwards was notoriously fond of both alcohol and stretching the truth, especially when it cast his mentor, Shelby, in a more positive light. This tendency coupled with the fact that Edwards was never closer than three hundred miles to Kirby Smith throughout the summer of 1864 casts a great deal of doubt upon his version of events.[39]

Kirby Smith used the opportunity of placing Price in command of the expedition to shuffle his entire command structure. With Price now commanding an army in the field, Major General John Bankhead Magruder transferred from the District of Texas to Arkansas. Meanwhile, Kirby Smith posted John Walker from West Louisiana to Texas, while Simon Buckner received command of the District of West Louisiana. It is more than likely Kirby Smith saw the shuffling as a convenient opportunity to deprive Price of his district command. Yet Kirby Smith was taking a chance in the timing of the change. With Magruder in Texas, it would take a month for the new district commander to tie up old business and make the trip to Arkansas. By the time Magruder arrived, Price would be gone, and so, too, would be the opportunity to reach any kind of understanding about how Magruder would support the movement. It was a potentially disastrous misstep.[40]

Regardless, Kirby Smith proceeded with his plans, and he issued a letter of instruction to Price describing an operation that was unlike any other seen in the Civil War. By August 20th, Price was to head toward Missouri with the entire cavalry force of the District of Arkansas and an additional brigade of Louisiana cavalry led by Colonel Isaac Harrison. Kirby Smith exhorted Price to "rally the loyal men of Missouri, and remember that our great want is men, and that your object should be, if you cannot maintain yourself in that country, to bring as large an accession as possible to your force." Kirby Smith further ordered Old Pap to "make St. Louis the objective point of your movement, which, if rapidly made, will put you in possession of that place, its supplies, and military stores, and which will do more toward rallying Missouri to your standard than the possession of any other point. Should you be compelled to withdraw from the State, make your retreat through Kansas and the Indian Territory, sweeping that country of its mules, horses, cattle, and military supplies of all kinds." In a cautionary note, Kirby Smith instructed Price to "scrupulously avoid all wanton acts of destruction and devastation, restrain your men, and impress upon them that their aim should be to secure success in a just and holy cause and not to gratify personal feeling and revenge."[41]

Kirby Smith's orders represented a triumph for Sterling Price and one that historians have misunderstood. According to Albert Castel, Kirby Smith's orders made recruiting "the principal endeavor" of the operation. Stephen Oates has argued that Kirby Smith viewed the maneuver as "simply a cavalry raid" where "primary consideration was to be given to recruits, horses, destruction of supply depots, and diversion of enemy troops." Anything political, or any attempted reconquest of the state, was something that Castel believes Price "privately added." Other historians, such as Robert Kerby and Scott Sallee, have offered comparable interpretations while concluding that Price was about to freelance in Missouri against the distinct wishes of his departmental commander. However, another reading of the orders is that Kirby Smith gave Price a large amount of latitude to indulge his deeply held and openly stated desire to liberate Missouri. The accession of troops, Kirby Smith wrote Price, became the primary object only if "you cannot maintain yourself in that country." Similarly, Kirby Smith's injunction to retreat through Kansas and the Indian Territory, confiscating its military supplies and animals, came only if Price "was compelled to withdraw from the State." More tellingly, Kirby Smith made no mention of the diversion of Union troops from east of the Mississippi River as a primary concern of the operation. All of this was, of course, in perfect keeping with Price's own unambiguous and openly stated intentions. When Price had written Kirby Smith on July 23rd outlining a plan for a march into Missouri, he made no mention at all of a diversion, as Governor Reynolds had suggested the week previously. Instead, Price emphasized that the purpose of the mission was "military possession as well as to encourage our friends there." Sterling Price planned to conquer Missouri, and Kirby Smith knew it. [42]

Kirby Smith was hardly optimistic about the movement's chances of success. No sooner had Price begun to assemble his force at Princeton than Kirby Smith started to talk freely about the mission among Confederate politicians at Shreveport. To the surprise of Price's supporters, Kirby Smith downplayed the importance of the occupation of Missouri, or what Congressman E. C. Cabell termed "the full sweep of your [Price's] expedition." At most, Kirby Smith talked only of the expedition as ensuring "a diversion in favor of our armies in the East." Such talk also quickly cast doubt upon Kirby Smith's willingness to support Price, leading some of Price's friends to wonder if the expedition would be "frustrated" by Kirby Smith. [43]

Early in August, the question of support was moot as Kirby Smith had nothing more to give Price. But things changed drastically when on August 19th Kirby Smith received word from Jefferson Davis canceling his transfer of Richard Taylor's ten thousand infantrymen across the Mississippi River. Price had not yet started north and would not do so for another two weeks, which left Kirby Smith with two realistic options to incorporate the suddenly available infantry into Price's expedition. First, there was no real obstacle to marching the men two hundred miles north from their camps at Harrisonburg, Louisiana, to join Price's assembling cavalry at Princeton, Arkansas, and accompany it into Missouri. Given Kirby Smith's instructions to Price authorizing the seizure of a fortified city, St. Louis, and the occupation of substantial territory, the infantry was well suited to the task. Second, Kirby Smith now had the chance of using the infantry in the way he had originally envisioned back in late July when he informed Jefferson Davis that his plans for an expedition were "perfected." Smith's subsequent correspondence with Davis indicated his desire to have the infantry "support" the cavalry, albeit in a curiously detached service. Accordingly, Kirby Smith believed that he might be able "to recover the State of Arkansas" if Frederick Steele turned to help defend St. Louis against Price's attack. At worst, he thought he could keep the infantry close enough to help Price should he get into difficulty.[44]

However, in either contingency, Price's cavalry was on its own in Missouri. Assistance was available only if the expedition failed, and even then Kirby Smith implied that help would be located at the Arkansas-Missouri border. In any event, the important issue was that after August 19th Kirby Smith had his infantry back, and many people expected the department commander to integrate it, in some fashion, with Price's expedition. The expectation had even filtered down through the ranks of the infantry, with one foot soldier in late August observing, "We are certainly off for Arkansas or perhaps to Missouri: we hope the latter, at any rate we will take Arkansas in preference to Louisiana."[45]

Unfortunately, Kirby Smith did not meet the expectations. Rheumatism and dysentery continued to punish his body, and by the middle of August he was incapacitated. Too weak even to sit and write, the general expended what little energy he had in dictating a response to Davis's letter canceling the crossing of the infantry, which he interpreted as a rebuke. This effort alone took two days, and only at the end of it did Kirby Smith issue new orders for the infantry then stuck at Harrisonburg. On August 22nd, he directed his new commander in Louisiana, Simon Buckner, to move the infantry first to Monroe, Louisiana, and then to an unspecified point in Arkansas at an unspecified time. Buckner kept the troops in Monroe until the end of the month, passing them onto John Magruder shortly after Magruder had arrived in Arkansas.[46]

Magruder was an energetic officer, but he was also one who needed careful guidance. This was especially true when Magruder unexpectedly received ten thousand infantry with no instructions as to how to use them. Although John N. Edwards in yet another of his fanciful accounts has Magruder chomping at the bit to send everything into Missouri "except the old men, the women and the children," Magruder was far less certain. On August 30, he inquired of Kirby Smith, "I should be pleased to receive written instructions as to what I am expected to do in Arkansas, and what assistance I am to lend to Gen. Price in his expedition into Missouri." Over the next month, Kirby Smith remained strangely quiet. Despite reassuring Price, through Congressman E. C. Cabell, "that all the troops in Buckner's Dist. are being moved to Arkansas to cooperate with you," Kirby Smith did little else besides leave Magruder with an army now numbering in excess of fourteen thousand men of all arms in the vicinity of Monticello with still no idea of what to do with it. For a brief moment, Magruder gave the impression that he was going to take matters into his own hands even without Kirby Smith's explicit blessing. On September 12th, Magruder forwarded 150,000 percussion caps to Price with the terse message that he "was operating on the lower Arkansas to divert the enemy from you." Aside from the percussion caps, Magruder's sudden burst of decisiveness was nothing more than an empty promise. Old doubts and insecurities rushed back to cloud his mind, and he subsequently did little except fret over ill-founded reports of Steele's movements and hold a dress parade. Sterling Price was very much on his own.[47]

Chapter Two

We Suspect Missouri Is the Objective

Before Price could make his return into Missouri, there was much yet to be done. He needed to piece together an army and then make a long march from south of the Arkansas River through rugged and punishing terrain. No less important, he had also to evade Union forces in Arkansas that could easily trap and destroy his fledgling army. It would be a trying experience made worse by several factors. Mutual distrust and suspicion permeated the ranks of the officer corps. Most of the men were either sick or conscripted. Many would have no horses, and those that did often found their mounts in a broken-down condition. There was a host of other problems, including a lack of weapons and worn-out wagons, but nothing would deter Price from his appointed return to Missouri.

Price began his final planning for the expedition when he arrived back in Camden on August 8th. He wasted little time and called for a series of meetings with several high-ranking officers, including two of his three division commanders—Major General James Fagan and Brigadier General John Marmaduke. His third division commander, Brigadier General Jo Shelby, was far behind enemy lines in northeastern Arkansas. By August 11th, Price was ready to unveil his plans, and he began issuing orders to consolidate the army and make logistical preparations. At first, there was a thin veil of secrecy over the operation. Most people sensed that an active campaign was in the offing, but they had no concrete idea of where exactly the army was going. The day Price issued his orders, John W. Brown, a Confederate Treasury agent living in Camden, noted rumors of a movement, but he dismissed it as "our military will as heretofore make such preparations and talk about it so

Figure 2.1.   Sterling Price's Missouri Invasion of 1864

long that the chance will slip of doing anything." At about the same time, and
with a bit more optimism, trooper Henry C. Luttrell of the 10th Missouri
could not help but notice all the orders to shoe the regiment's horses. With
almost breathless anticipation, Luttrell exclaimed that "everyone is on the *qui
vive*, an expedition is on foot, and we suspect that Missouri is the objective
point."[1]

As expectations soared among the Missourians, Sterling Price had to
come to grips with several personnel and logistical problems. The first of

these problems concerned his two ranking divisional commanders, Fagan and Marmaduke. Although these men were really the only available senior commanders in the Trans-Mississippi outside of Simon Buckner, Price distrusted them. Fagan was Price's senior division commander. A native Kentuckian and Mexican War veteran, Fagan had raised an infantry regiment at the start of the war and then led it with some distinction at the Battle of Shiloh. Shortly thereafter, he moved to the Trans-Mississippi where he was promoted and served in the infantry and cavalry. By 1864 he was a major general, commanding a division of Arkansas cavalry that mixed veteran horsemen with several regiments and battalions of recently mounted infantry. However, when finally teamed with Price during the Red River Campaign, he performed erratically. Although he had the great distinction of destroying one of Steele's supply trains at Mark's Mill, he had also violated orders that directed him to other and bigger targets. It was a gaffe that not only strained relations with Price but one that Kirby Smith blamed on Price. Handsome with dark hair and eyes, Fagan was a fairly sociable if moody officer. He could be kind and warmhearted, such as when he gave a complete set of clothes to Colonel William A. Crawford, but he could also be cold and aloof. He feuded with a number of his officers, and some of the troops believed him "an incompetent greeny." Price, too, never warmed to Fagan and preferred giving matters of great responsibility to others.[2]

Unfortunately for Price, he also disliked giving matters of great importance to his second-ranking commander, John S. Marmaduke. A native Missourian, Marmaduke came from one of the state's most prominent families. He attended Yale and Harvard and eventually graduated from West Point in the class of 1857. At the outset of the war he split with his father—a former governor of Missouri—over the issue of secession, and he followed his uncle, Governor Claiborne Jackson, out of the Union. By 1864, Marmaduke had amassed an uneven military record that included successes at Shiloh and the Red River Campaign and two disappointing raids into Missouri. Tall with angular features and swept-back hair, Marmaduke cut an awkward figure, and one that was severely near-sighted. According to one contemporary, "The most partial judge would not be guilty of calling him handsome." More critically, Marmaduke possessed an imperious personality and was prone to arguing with his fellow officers. It was a flaw that led to a duel with Brigadier General Lucius M. Walker at the height of the campaign for Little Rock in 1863. The duel, which left Walker dead, poisoned Marmaduke's relations with a number of senior officers, including Sterling Price.[3]

Animosity between Price and Marmaduke possibly predated the war
when the politics of the 1850s found the Marmaduke family at odds with
Price's faction of the Missouri Democrat Party. The war seems only to have
aggravated the bad blood as far too many allegations of misconduct and
plundering had followed Marmaduke's two raids into Missouri to suit Old
Pap. Although Price saved Marmaduke from arrest and court martial in the
aftermath of the duel with Walker, he looked warily upon his subordinate.
Marmaduke did little to ingratiate himself to Price with an uneven performance during the Camden campaign in the spring of 1864. Marmaduke
sensed the disfavor and more than returned the suspicion, believing Price
might try to make him a scapegoat for any failure in the invasion of Missouri.
Not surprisingly, Price did not suffer for advice as to how to handle Marmaduke. Thomas Snead strongly advocated that Price reduce Marmaduke to a
brigade commander. Otherwise, Snead believed Marmaduke would agitate to
the point of distraction for a promotion to befit his status as a divisional
commander. To Snead, Marmaduke was nothing more than a petty intriguer
and backstabber. Nevertheless, without any other more senior general officer
available, Price had no choice but to keep Marmaduke in charge of his
division.[4]

Price's manpower difficulties went well beyond any squabbles with Fa-
gan and Marmaduke. Price had few troops, and they were widely dispersed.
Ever since the Red River Campaign, Confederate cavalry in the District of
Arkansas had been quite busy. In late May, Kirby Smith had ordered Jo
Shelby to northeastern Arkansas to enforce conscription laws and bring deserters back into the ranks. At about the same time, Kirby Smith posted
Fagan's division to patrol in the vicinity of Monticello and Marmaduke's
division to an area near the confluence of the Arkansas and Mississippi
rivers. While Kirby Smith wanted both Fagan and Marmaduke to interdict
Union traffic along the waterways, he wanted them also to establish a Confederate presence and bring order to regions that harbored skulkers and encouraged trading with the enemy. These would be tough orders for most
commanders, but the task was made more difficult by the small size of
Fagan's and Marmaduke's divisions. In reality, they were nothing more than
reinforced brigades. Fagan's division was the larger of the two, and it consisted of an artillery battery and two brigades of Arkansas cavalry led by
veteran commanders: Brigadier General William L. Cabell and Colonel
William F. Slemons. With over 2,700 men in the ranks, Cabell had by far the
largest brigade in the District of Arkansas, while Slemons's approximately

one thousand troopers gave the colonel less than half his authorized strength. Marmaduke's command justified even less its classification as a division. By July, Marmaduke controlled only the 1,200 men of his old brigade, Robert C. Wood's battalion of cavalry, a battery of artillery, and a pontoon bridge. Most of these troops were veterans, but they were also fairly worn down. Marmaduke's men suffered, in particular, from constant patrolling in swampy terrain that destroyed shoes and clothing and produced a widespread outbreak of malaria. By the middle of August, Marmaduke's old brigade was largely shoeless and had 443 men, or 33 percent of its aggregate strength, listed as sick and not present for duty. As the division was completely destitute of quinine, chills were rampant even among the 888 men present for duty.[5]

It was but the beginning of the obstacles facing Price. Among others, there was a shortage of horses and mules. Despite a windfall of captured animals from the Red River campaign, hundreds of men in Price's army had no horses, and thousands more rode mules. Just as problematical, the overall quality of the animals could only be described as marginal. Active campaigning in the spring had given way to hard riding during the summer, and many animals needed rest before more hard marching. Heavy draft horses used for the artillery were especially worn down and in need of replacement. In fact, Colonel John Burbridge, a temporary commander of Marmaduke's brigade, termed the horses in one of the division's two batteries as being "unfit for active service." Finally, a type of glanders, or nasal infection, swept the camps and proved fatal to a large number of the horses and mules. As the number of healthy animals declined, competition among different military agencies and units became fierce and revealed also a brittle state of discipline even within Price's more veteran units. In June, for example, Colonel John C. Wright's regiment of Arkansas cavalry of Fagan's division had a large number of men mounted with mules as they either rested worn-out horses or waited to buy new ones. Because the army needed mules to haul wagons in the trains, Price's inspector general, Major James R. Shaler, attempted to confiscate the animals. Unfortunately for the inspector general, all he got for the attempt was a public threat of physical violence and the looting of his wagons when Wright spread the word to Marmaduke's old brigade that Shaler was coming. By the start of the expedition the lack of good horses and mules could only be relieved by either capturing enemy livestock or impressing it along the march. In the meantime, hundreds of dismounted men would have to be culled from Marmaduke's and Fagan's ranks and forced to walk alongside the trains when it came time to move north and join Shelby. However, linking with Shelby would by no means alleviate the situation. He, too, had hundreds of dismounted troopers.[6]

A no less daunting, and far more controversial, task facing Price was the assembly of the army's wagon train. Quite simply, the District of Arkansas was no longer capable of manufacturing wagons. Iron supplies were nearly exhausted, and Kirby Smith had diverted what little iron was left to his ordnance shops. The District of Arkansas's principal wagon-making facilities at Washington, which had been making a paltry sixteen wagons a month, were effectively shut down by mid-August. Just as in the case of the horses and mules, Price had to rely upon what the Confederacy could capture from the enemy. Although Price had liberated a large number of wagons during the Red River Campaign, they were, according to Brigadier General John B. Clark Jr. of Marmaduke's division, in poor condition. Nevertheless, Price took what he could get and eventually accumulated a large train of what John N. Edwards later called "wheezy, rickety wagons."[7]

Price's large train has attracted more than its fair share of criticism. To Edwards, not only was it "wheezy" and "rickety," it was also "useless." A veteran of Shelby's Great Raid of 1863 into Missouri, Edwards had no use for a ponderous train. Edwards was not alone in his sentiments. Another observer thought the train "an incubus" that slowed the progress of the army to a crawl and allowed Union forces to concentrate against it. However, at the beginning of the expedition few people thought the train large or unnecessary. Kirby Smith had ordered Price on an expedition behind enemy lines to conquer territory. Failing that, Kirby Smith wanted Price to make a march of over one thousand miles sweeping the land of animals, supplies, and men. With Kirby Smith not committed to ejecting Union forces from the Arkansas River valley, there would be no supply line or depot system for Price to tap into as he headed north. Whatever Price needed he would have either to carry it with him or gather it along the invasion route. Quite simply, he needed a lot of wagons.[8]

Food required the greatest amount of transport. Finding and carrying food for twelve thousand men was a difficult enough task as one wagon could haul only enough food to feed five hundred men per day. Indeed, it was an amount of food the army could never sustain, and the deficiency would force Price to order a reduction in the daily ration before the army marched anywhere. But finding and carrying an equivalent amount of the right fodder and forage for nearly thirteen thousand horses and mules, which also included those animals necessary to pull the wagons, was an entirely different and more complicated matter. By regulations, horses required twenty-six pounds of hay and corn per day. It was a daily requirement that could not be met by merely grazing the animals along a tactical route or picket line at night. This sort of scrounging for grass was possible—and feasible—during a short raid, but even then it was a dangerous practice as grass could never substitute in nutritional value for hay and corn when animals were subjected to hard marching. In fact, every extended cavalry operation of the Civil War was notable for the almost complete destruction of the horseflesh that made the march. It also warrants mentioning that the problem of providing a magical twenty-six pounds of food per day to each horse did not really come close to meeting the actual needs of the animals. As Edward Hagerman has noted, while twenty-six pounds of food was enough for a 1,600 pound horse in camp, the ration furnished only 70 to 75 percent of what that same horse needed in an active campaign.[9]

Therefore, the bottom line for Sterling Price was that he needed a significant number of wagons to accompany his march and scour the outlying countryside for food on a near daily basis. Price's previous experience as a cavalry commander in the spring of 1864 had already left this lesson firmly embedded in his mind. Old Pap's greatest achievement during the Red River campaign had been to stop Frederick Steele's advance at Camden. He did this not so much by defeating Steele's main body in a decisive battle, but rather by destroying or capturing his various support trains. Stuck in a fairly barren part of the state at the wrong time of the year, Steele eventually had no choice but to retreat.

Price was not without blueprints or experience in assembling his wagon train. Throughout the war, North and South had been putting their myriad armies together complete with supporting networks of supplies, wagons, and animals. The rations and prerequisites varied from army to army and from early in the war to late in the war, but one constant remained: neither side shied from using enormous numbers of wagons and horses in support of their operations. Corps-sized cavalry units were particularly reliant upon large numbers of transport, which Union Major General James H. Wilson could certainly attest to when in December 1864 he authorized his corps 555 wagons. Absent such a comparison, Price created his wagon train using a set of calculations mandated by Kirby Smith and the Trans-Mississippi Department. Issued in May of 1864, General Orders #19 provided a mind-numbing method of figuring transport requirements that ultimately authorized Price no less than 239 wagons to support an army whose manpower, once joined with Shelby's division, would more closely resemble that of a corps. By all accounts, Price came fairly close to meeting this number as he started the campaign with no more than 250 wagons. However, his greatest difficulty with the wagons would be in controlling the growth and content of the train as the army acquired more recruits in Missouri and swept it of supplies. Perhaps most important, Price would have to be able to recognize a tactical situation that demanded he either pare back or abandon the train. Failure to do this would indeed turn the train into an incubus. [10]

Although the difficulties of maintaining a large train lay in Price's future, his most pressing need in early August was weapons. When Price issued his first orders announcing the invasion on August 11, almost one-half of the over four thousand men in Fagan's and Marmaduke's divisions were unarmed. Those men who did have weapons were indifferently armed with everything from shotguns to smoothbore flintlock muskets to Enfield rifle muskets. Given this situation, on August 11th, Kirby Smith's chief of staff, Brigadier General W. S. Boggs, authorized Price a shipment of 1,062 shoulder-fired weapons, which included 640 obsolete smoothbore muskets. Although a considerable gain for the army, this authorization was still not enough. While there are no records extant to document the precise numbers of unarmed men in Fagan's and Marmaduke's divisions, the recollection of Brigadier General William L. Cabell of Fagan's division was that his own brigade of 2,500 soldiers marched with at least an additional two hundred unarmed men even after Price distributed the one thousand newly arrived weapons on August 29th. Cabell also believed his brigade among the better armed. [11]

With three other brigades in the two divisions, it is more than likely that at least another seven hundred men were unarmed. The number is astonishing, and even more astonishing was the fact that Jo Shelby was waiting for Price in northeastern Arkansas with another four thousand unarmed men. This situation certainly reveals both the wretched state of Confederate logistics in the Trans-Mississippi and the desperation of the Confederate cause in 1864. But more importantly, it illustrates a fact of life that Confederates in the Trans-Mississippi had more than learned to live with. Most Confederate movements into Missouri since 1861 had been accompanied by a horde of unarmed men. In April 1863, Marmaduke took over 1,200 unarmed men with him out of a force of 5,086 on his Cape Girardeau raid, while Price himself fought at Wilson's Creek in 1861 with no less than two thousand such men.

Price won at Wilson's Creek and then managed to find weapons enough for his unarmed troops. Capturing arms from the enemy was a way of life for Confederate Missourians, and they had no reason to believe that there were any less to be had in 1864.

The shipment of Price's weapons from Shreveport would take time, and it had ramifications for the invasion well beyond arming an additional one thousand men. Price's timetable for starting the invasion had to be pushed back at least one week beyond the originally set launch date of August 20th. The delay did not please Kirby Smith, who was still quite sick and talked little with Price himself. In fact, for much of August Kirby Smith barely talked with his own staff, and it was not until August 23rd that he became aware of troubles in getting Price his weapons. Although both Price and Kirby Smith were frustrated with postponement, there were positive benefits. All during August the weather had not cooperated with Price. Day after day, rain had soaked southern Arkansas, flooding bayous and rivers and turning roads into quagmires. The rain thus helped delay not only Price's ordnance but also the arrival of Marmaduke's division, which became bogged down in its march from the east. Postponing the advance thus gave Marmaduke extra time to join Price and Fagan at Princeton before marching north. [12]

Similarly, the delay allowed extra time for some badly needed money and supplies to make it to Price. On August 22nd, for example, treasury agents from east of the Mississippi River delivered $6,000,000 in currency to Kirby Smith, who then disbursed $1,700,000 to Price to use for food, supplies, and troop pay. In announcing the arrival of the money to Price, Congressman E. C. Cabell hoped the amount would "keep you supplied until your army becomes a self sustaining machine." One day later, Cabell would also proudly inform Price that he was forwarding a large shipment of newly arrived medical supplies, including one hundred boxes of quinine and smaller quantities of morphine and opium. For the malaria-stricken men in Marmaduke's division, the quinine would be vital to achieving operational readiness. [13]

As Price thus waited for Marmaduke and the arrival of the ordnance train, his own headquarters element began to take shape, and a large shape it was. By one estimate, the headquarters numbered about three hundred men, consisting of a bodyguard, brass band, servants, assorted hangers-on, and the military staff. Within this assemblage, the military staff conformed generally to accepted numbers given the twelve thousand men Price would command before leaving Arkansas. Like most staffs during the war, it could be divided into primary and personal sections. In the primary staff, Price counted ten officers including an inspector general, three assistant adjutants and the chiefs of supply, commissary, ordnance, artillery, engineers, and medicine. Of all these men, Price relied most heavily upon his ranking assistant adjutant general, Lieutenant Colonel Lauchlan Maclean. A Scottish immigrant and Mexican War veteran, Maclean was an experienced engineer and a cartographer who did far more than just maintain the army's muster rolls and issue orders in Price's name. By the end of the expedition, Price used Maclean to select the army's camps and make many of its maps. A toddy-loving poet prone to reciting the verse of Robert Burns, Lauchlan Maclean proved quickly to be an ideal staff officer for the equally sociable and toddy-loving Sterling Price.[14]

Outside of Lauchlan Maclean and the primary staff, Price maintained a personal staff consisting of junior and field-grade officers. In no great departure from other such creations, Price filled the personal staff with relatives, friends, and friends of friends. Included in this group were his son, Celsus; the brother-in-law of Kirby Smith, Robert Selden; and former governor Trusten Polk. Also in this collection was an officer with no apparent personal or professional connection to Price, Colonel Charles H. Tyler. Tyler was a West Pointer with considerable cavalry experience in both Virginia and Tennessee. He had been captured in early 1864 but was exchanged to the Trans-Mississippi and Price's army in July. Although members of the personal staff were generally no more than overpaid couriers or political consultants, Price also intended to use these men to run his military courts and command the recruits who entered the army in Missouri.[15]

Where Price could find a number of political friends at his headquarters, he did not have to look far to see a political rival. No sooner had Kirby Smith authorized an invasion on August 4th than Thomas C. Reynolds announced his intention to join it. Governor Reynolds's motivations were only thinly veiled. As Price had proclaimed his intention to occupy Missouri, Reynolds plainly desired to rule his state from the capitol in Jefferson City. No less important, Reynolds wanted to look after his own political fortunes while making sure that Price did not hold sham elections whose only purpose was to remove Missouri from the Confederacy and install Old Pap as its leader. There was also one other reason for Reynolds joining the invasion. Political viability in Missouri depended on the might and good graces of the army, and Reynolds had long realized that he carried little favor with Missouri's Confederate soldiers. It was evident the day he first arrived in Little Rock when not one soldier came to help him with his transportation or personal arrangements. Reynolds therefore knew that he had to earn the respect of the army and that he had to demonstrate not only his physical presence on a campaign but also his physical bravery. Writing in 1863, Reynolds had noted that "a civil officer must look somewhat to appearance, if he wishes to inspire respect in an army: a Governor afoot is a mere camp follower, a sponge & horse borrower." Reynolds would start the expedition stationed firmly in the middle of Price's army headquarters element, but he would eventually bolt to join Jo Shelby's division when it linked with Price. [16]

All waiting to launch the expedition ended on August 28th. The previous day, the long-anticipated ordnance train had arrived in Camden, which then freed Price to start his headquarters element and trains to join Marmaduke's and Fagan's divisions at Princeton, some thirty miles to the northeast. When Price arrived one day later on August 29th, he distributed the newly acquired weapons and ammunition to his division commanders, while also absorbing virtually all of their wagons into the army's centralized trains. Also included in this absorption was Marmaduke's pontoon bridge, which Price believed he might need for crossing the Arkansas River. As the troops shuffled the wagons and equipment, Price met with Fagan and Marmaduke to unveil a change of plans that he had been considering during the previous week. In his initial plan, Price intended to cross the Arkansas River between Little Rock and Devall's Bluff. He would then march north to link with Shelby in the vicinity of Batesville before finally pressing on to St. Louis. However, the delay of his ordnance train made Price suspect the Federals "had been informed of my intended line of march." Accordingly, and with Kirby Smith's after-the-fact-approval, Old Pap now planned a much more circuitous route that crossed the Arkansas River about seventy-seven miles west of Little Rock and then proceeded through Springfield and Batesville where Price still planned to link with Shelby. Although the new plan added 240 miles, and at least ten days, to the march, Price ultimately concluded that the new route had several advantages, including a more secure crossing of the Arkansas River, a masking of his true objective of St. Louis, and the better availability of food and forage. [17]

This was not, however, the only change in plans that Price had to make at Princeton. The shortage of good horses had already begun to show, especially in the artillery that had yet to find enough of the solid dray horses to pull heavy loads. Consequently, Price decided to send back to Camden two pieces of Captain William M. Hughey's artillery from Fagan's division. Price had also to resign himself to the loss of Colonel Isaac Harrison's brigade of 1,500

men, which he had long planned on giving to Marmaduke. Despite Kirby
Smith's promise in his orders of August 4th, Harrison never arrived in time.
It was an ominous development for an army badly in need of trained horse
soldiers.[18]

Nevertheless, after dispatching his change of plans to Shelby, Price
marched his army north on August 30th. Rain fell heavily, and the road
turned quickly into a muddy bog. Consequently, the army traveled only nine
miles by early afternoon when it stopped in the vicinity of Tulip. The next
day, the army continued north at sunrise and advanced to within seven miles
of Benton where Price split his force. Conscious of Steele's ability to wreck
havoc with the crossing of the Arkansas, Old Pap detailed Fagan to march
north and feint an advance against Little Rock, while Price and the remainder
of the army swung to the north northwest toward Dardanelle. The effort,
while sound, was unnecessary. Steele was already terribly confused as to
Price's intentions and posed little threat to the operation. Ever since July,
Steele had been trying to guess what Price would do next. His guessing was
not, however, for the lack of information as scouts, deserters, refugees, and
spies flooded his headquarters with reports. Although much of it, particularly
that processed by General Powell Clayton at Pine Bluff, pointed to Price
crossing above Little Rock, Steele could not be sure. Of particular concern
were persistent rumors of the pontoon bridge that had been sent first to
Marmaduke and then to Price. To Steele, the pontoon bridge meant a crossing to the east of Little Rock, if not Pine Bluff. As the Arkansas River was
fordable above Little Rock, Steele could not see the point of Price carrying it
with him. Utterly baffled, Steele allowed himself to think as late as August
30th that reports of any grand movement of Price were nothing but a "humbug."[19]

Steele's grasp of the situation was all the more unfortunate because in
early September he received considerable reinforcements to deal with Price.
Sitting at Cairo and Memphis and waiting to reinforce William T. Sherman's
operations against Atlanta was about nine thousand infantry and two thousand cavalry commanded by A. J. Smith and officially designated as the
Right Wing of the XVI Corps of the Army of the Tennessee. At the same
time Steele was pronouncing the rumors of Price's movement "a humbug,"
Major General E. R. S. Canby, who commanded the District of West Mississippi, got permission to divert one division of four thousand infantry and
almost all of the cavalry to Arkansas. Led by the newly promoted Major
General Joseph A. Mower, this force reached the White River at Clarendon

and St. Charles by September 8th. Nonetheless, and despite the confidence that such reinforcements should have inspired, Steele remained in a virtually catatonic condition. He would do nothing, allowing Price to pass freely.[20]

Fagan's departure from Price's column lasted only a few days, and in the journey he never wandered more than ten miles from the main body. By the time Fagan rejoined Price at the rear of his column on September 5th, the only notable thing to have occurred to the division commander was to pass by his burned-out home on the Saline River. That same day, both Marmaduke and Fagan sent out advance elements to Dardanelle to grind corn and shoe horses. The next morning the bulk of Marmaduke's division began entering the city. The arrival of the army came as a relief to the Confederate-sympathizing population of Yell County. The war had not been kind to them since Price's evacuation of Little Rock. Subject to the depredations of Yankee foraging and scouting missions and the equally devastating actions of roving deserters, the county was desolated in many places. Price's army offered hope, and, as noted by William H. Trader of Fagan's staff, the women of Dardanelle turned out on a warm and clear day to line the streets, wave Confederate flags, and cheer.[21]

All day on September 6th, unit after unit of cavalry passed through the city and headed toward the river. Curiously enough, the pontoon bridge was not necessary. Although the bridge had caused Frederick Steele much consternation, Price never placed a foot of it over the Arkansas River. Price's chief engineer, Captain Thomas Jefferson Mackey, a graduate of the South Carolina Military Academy in Charleston, had made a reconnaissance of Dardanelle and discovered a ford about one-half mile south of the city that was only three to four feet deep. As elements of the army then forded the river on September 6th, Mackey converted four of his eighteen pontoons into wagon bodies and then burned the remaining fourteen. Mackey retained the wagons for his engineers and a small company of pioneers attached to Fagan's division. During the early crossing of the river, sixteen-year-old Mollie Johnston and her family managed to meet most of the Confederate command structure and their staff. To the young girl, Sterling Price did not present a terribly martial image. He was instead "a fine fleshy looking old gentleman of about 65 years of age," who took the time to socialize after dismounting from a specially outfitted ambulance pulled by two bay horses and two mules.[22]

The local excitement continued on September 7th as the remainder of the army crossed the river. For William McPheeters, Price's chief medical officer, the whole operation was a "grand & picturesque" spectacle as thousands of cavalry and 250 wagons with water up to the beds made their way to the north bank. The entire operation was a success beyond the best hopes of Price and his followers. Only one wagon had capsized, and the Yankees had allowed free passage. It was cause for celebration, and Price's staff threw a party that night with the army camped at Dover.[23]

The early success of Price's expedition was not without its cautionary note. The army had been stunningly slow. Since commencing the campaign at Princeton, Price had averaged not quite seventeen miles per day. This was a number that a commander could readily expect from veteran infantry, if not actually a great deal more. But for cavalry and mounted infantry the pace had to be considered disappointing as horse soldiers were often known to ride more than forty miles per day. More to the point, the slow pace not only made the army an easier mark for Union troops, but it seems to support the legion of critics and historians who saw Price as a doddering politician turned infantryman who had no business commanding cavalry. The "fleshy looking" Price was hardly the beau ideal of a cavalryman, and he would make several costly errors in generalship throughout the campaign, but he was not incompetent when it came to commanding the cavalry. Indeed, it is easy to forget Price's experience with cavalry prior to the Missouri expedition. Not only had he commanded mounted troops during the Red River Campaign, but more importantly, he had led cavalry on an eight-hundred-mile forced march from Fort Leavenworth to New Mexico during the Mexican War.[24]

Given Price's practical experience with mounted troops, it would not have been hard for him to see that there were several obstacles to marching his troops at a rapid pace. First, there was the matter of horses. Hundreds of men had no mounts, and hundreds more rode horses and mules of only fair condition. Second, Price was certainly aware of the rough terrain to be traversed. Hills and mountains covered central and northwestern Arkansas, and they would test even the best-conditioned men and animals. Indeed, the most common refrain among the various diarists in Price's army during the march through Arkansas concerned the rugged nature of the terrain. To William McPheeters, the road to Dardanelle "was exceedingly rough & stony with one mountain, several high hills & numerous streams—all covered thickly with huge boulders." Major James T. Armstrong, a staff officer with Fagan, painted an agonizing picture of the march to Dardanelle as: "We have traveled over the roughest, hilliest & most mountainous road since we left

Princeton I ever saw." Making matters worse to Armstrong, "The country seemed to produce nothing but yellow jackets, chiggers and all sorts of disagreeable insects." A third problem guaranteed to aggravate the first two. Price's Army of Missouri had to travel 350 miles before it even reached the Missouri border. To push the army hard over that distance was to do nothing but risk its disintegration. One final, and obvious, impediment to Price's march was his train and the hundreds of dismounted men that accompanied it. The army, obviously, could not outstrip its train without losing it, and Price was therefore trapped by the wagon requirements of a mission that aimed first to conquer territory and then second to sweep that territory of supplies. [25]

Aside, then, from the pace of the army, Price's handling of the cavalry was remarkable only in his adherence to fairly standard practices and procedures. Shortly after taking command of Fagan's and Marmaduke's divisions at Princeton, Price issued a flurry of general orders establishing basic practices for the army. Some were mundane and pertained to the forwarding of unit musters, the creation of military courts, and the penalties for theft. Others were more operational and addressed ways to prevent straggling and the breakdown of the column. Price, for example, ordered each division commander to establish rearguards to stop stragglers with the injunction that if men did fall behind they were not to gallop forward, which could cause a stampede in the inexperienced ranks. Stragglers who did gallop forward would "be dismounted, disarmed, and court martialed." Another order barred troopers from stopping to water "their horses except by order of Division Commanders." Perhaps the most important of these orders dealt with the configuration of the army on the march. On September 1st, Price directed that divisions, brigades, and regiments alternate their place in the column on a daily basis. [26]

The importance of the order was twofold. First, and like the rest of Price's directives, it represented a grasp of accepted practices and current army regulations. Rotating units through the line was intended to prevent any one unit from continually bearing the stress of leading an advance or fighting a rearguard. But more importantly, the order attracted the ire of Governor Thomas Reynolds, who thought little of the whole exercise and would later use it, ironically, to illustrate his belief that Price did not know how to handle cavalry. To Reynolds, the alternating of units created a "Virginia Reel" of men and horses that served only to slow the army to a crawl and create a host of stragglers who could never quite find their units. Reynolds sarcastically concluded that the whole process was "an enlarged application of the mode in which that renowned warrior, Baron Munchausen, killed the lion by thrusting his arm down the animal's throat, and turning him wrong side out by pulling his tail through his mouth."[27]

There was, however, an element of truth in Reynolds's criticism, and it illustrated a recurring problem for Price. Old Pap's orders and intentions were generally fine, but his implementation left a lot to be desired. Quite simply, Price and his staff failed for a long time to orchestrate the rotation of units effectively. Not until the army had already marched over seven hundred miles to Boonville, Missouri, did Price and his staff begin staggering the reveilles and start times of his different units to minimize delays and eliminate the worst example of the age-old army problem of "hurry up and wait." Until that time, the previous day's rearguard often spent a good part of morning daylight hours in just moving to the van of the army. Although there was very little urgency in Price until he arrived at Boonville, the sloppy implementation of the order did not augur well for when the army would need to quicken its pace.

For now, Price's most immediate concern was linking with Jo Shelby. On August 30th, Price had sent a courier to Shelby notifying him of the change in route around Little Rock while also establishing a meeting place at Batesville. Price had yet to hear back from Shelby, but he pushed on nevertheless. Anticipating a dearth of forage, Price divided his army again into two columns. Army headquarters and the trains would accompany Marmaduke's division along the road to Clinton. Fagan would take a more southerly—and longer—road to Springfield. From both of these very small cities, which were twenty-five miles apart, the two columns would march toward Batesville where Price believed Shelby was waiting. The march to Batesville was fairly uneventful and marred only by rumors of an outbreak of varioloid, or smallpox, and minor skirmishing with various Union scouts and roving bands of what Lauchlan Maclean called Federal Jayhawkers. Of greater concern to both officers and men was the punishing terrain. The roads, according to William H. Trader, were simply "diabolical," as they wound around hills and mountain spurs, fatiguing men and beasts. But more problematical was the utter lack of food, forage, and water. Water, in particular, was most scarce, and the staff struggled to find enough for the many units to camp by at night. Indeed, another of Fagan's staffers, James T. Armstrong, bemoaned the fact that on two consecutive nights the men had to march around until midnight searching for precious water. To Armstrong, the march had gotten progressively more difficult ever since leaving Dardanelle.[28]

For the trains and Marmaduke's division, the road from Clinton to Batesville was probably worse. The road started to deteriorate on Sunday the 11th, but on Monday the 12th it was almost impassable, especially when the column veered off the main road and took another route over Greenbrier Mountain that was ostensibly much shorter. According to Chief Surgeon McPheeters, the road was obstructed by "huge rocks, steep cliffs, and deep cuts," which then played havoc with the trains. Though greatly fatigued by this leg of the march, McPheeters took solace in his understandably biased belief that "in these mountain regions of barren lands the poor[,] ignorant and debased are Union[,] but where we meet with persons of any intelligence they are uniformly loyal to the South."[29]

Price and his staff had left the security of the army on September 12th to ride through Batesville and on to Powhattan, sixty-four miles to the northeast. Old Pap was determined to meet with Jo Shelby as soon as possible, and he pushed it to arrive at Shelby's headquarters on the evening of the 13th. In Shelby, Price had his most capable, and most junior, division commander. At the time of the expedition, Shelby was a thirty-three-year-old cavalryman with quite a reputation. A native Kentuckian, Shelby had moved to Missouri in 1850 and quickly became one of the more prosperous men in the state through his manufacturing of hemp in Lafayette County. Short and weighing about 150 pounds, Shelby was also a combative personality who had participated in the border skirmishes of "Bleeding Kansas." In 1861, he raised a company of cavalry and proceeded to rise through the ranks, fighting in most of the major battles in the Trans-Mississippi. By 1864 Shelby possessed an almost mythical reputation among enemy soldiers, with some believing that Shelby's quick-moving Iron Brigade never ate or slept while on the march. Only after the war did they discover that Shelby had his men feed their horses by hand as they traveled. Recently promoted to brigadier general, Shelby had spent most of the summer of 1864 commanding his own personal Confederacy in northeastern Arkansas.[30]

Price had tasked Shelby with getting men for the army. Shelby pitched into the assignment with gusto and authorized officers on an almost daily basis to raise new companies, battalions, regiments, and even brigades. Shelby was coolly efficient as he directed his various brigade commanders to block all roads leading into targeted villages and then sweep every house looking for slackers and conscripts. Moreover, his single-minded enthusiasm to bring men into the ranks paid no heed to state borders and allowed for little resistance. In one situation, Captain Edgar Asbury ventured into Howell and Oregon counties in Missouri only to discover that his backwoods conscripts would not cross the state line into Arkansas. Decked out in "coon-skin caps, leather breeches, hunting shirts, and . . . armed with squirrel rifles, old horse pistols, flint-lock muskets and percussion cap shot-guns," this motley collection realized at the last moment that they preferred bushwhacking in Missouri to soldiering with Shelby in Arkansas. Shelby's response was to send out two of his veteran companies of cavalry to bring them into his camps.[31]

By the end of the second week of August, Shelby had more than accomplished his mission. One Union scout of several towns in the area concluded tersely: "Country swept of everything; all the men from fifteen to fifty gone to Shelby." Indeed, this was probably not far from the truth as there were nearly eight thousand men in Shelby's camps scattered in the vicinity of Powhattan. Unfortunately, he lacked the wherewithal to arm them. Despite the experience of Captain Asbury in recruiting a haphazardly armed company of men, most of Shelby's newly recruited troops lacked any firearms at all. Just as in the case of Fagan's and Marmaduke's divisions, it is difficult to quantify exactly how many men were without arms. Except for Jackman's and Shelby's brigades, armaments records simply do not exist. Nevertheless, Sidney Jackman's brigade seems representative of the newly recruited units. By the end of August, Jackman, a one-time bushwhacker, had fielded a brigade of 1,696 men. Of this imposing number, 1,155 were unarmed. Even Shelby's old Iron Brigade was not immune to receiving unarmed recruits. By the middle of September, the brigade had 1,445 men, of which 278 were unarmed. Contemporary estimates that Shelby started the invasion with four thousand unarmed men, or over 50 percent of his force, do not seem that far-fetched.[32]

While Shelby struggled to find weapons for these men, he also labored to maintain order. Disciplinary problems with the new recruits were not unexpected. Many of the men he conscripted were deserters and Jayhawkers who had difficulty forgetting their barbaric ways. Shelby responded by boldly proclaiming he would shoot anyone "caught insulting helpless females and plundering starving children." Desertion was just as troublesome. With the vast majority of the Arkansans taken by authority of the conscript laws, the simple proximity of home, or as Shelby put it, "a desire to see Sarah and the children," tempted many to plot desertion. The only solution to this, to Shelby, was an active campaign with Price's army that would take the men far from home.[33]

Shelby's problems did not end with his conscripts. With so many of his officers lacking any military training except that gained through the hard experience of bushwhacking and border warfare, they were not predisposed to bother with military punctilio and discipline. They knew little of drill, failed to hold regular musters, and generally ignored the practice of controlling the movements of their men in and out of the camps. Perhaps most frustrating for Shelby was the constant poaching of recruits, which took place among his various company, regimental, and even brigade commanders. By August 19, Shelby was almost beside himself trying to stop colonels Thomas Freeman and Sidney Jackman from snatching soldiers recruited for other brigades, warning Jackman, in particular, that "these tricks will not be tolerated." Even as late as September 11th Shelby was ordering the arrest of Colonel Thomas H. McCray's assistant adjutant general for "stealing" a company recruited for another brigade.[34]

Price's arrival at Powhattan and meeting with Shelby signaled the beginning of the consolidation of the army before it headed into Missouri. With forage almost exhausted around Powhattan and Shelby's brigades scattered about the area, the army moved eighteen miles to the northwest where it settled down in the vicinity of the almost deserted town of Pocahontas. On Saturday, September 17th, Price began redistributing Shelby's newly recruited brigades and regiments. In this reshuffling, James Fagan gained three battalion-sized units and one brigade of about eight hundred men commanded by Colonel Archibald S. Dobbin and another, much larger, brigade of 1,700 men commanded by Colonel Thomas H. McCray. Although both Dobbin and McCray left much to be desired as commanders, one report listed their troops as "well armed." John Marmaduke was certainly less fortunate than Fagan when Price assigned him Colonel Thomas Freeman's brigade, which numbered about 2,700 men. Of these troops, seven hundred were only "partially armed with pistols and shotguns." The remaining two thousand represented the latest, and generally unarmed, portion of Shelby's recruits. Marmaduke did, however, reacquire Colonel Solomon G. Kitchen's 7th Missouri, which had been operating in northern Arkansas for most of the summer. With the new units now cast about the army, Jo Shelby was left with his own old brigade and that of Sidney Jackman. Shelby also retained an unattached regiment of recruits commanded by Colonel W. O. Coleman, giving him a combined divisional strength of no less than 3,100 men, of whom 1,400 were unarmed.[35]

However, Shelby could probably have taken solace in the fact he retained Captain Richard A. Collins's battery. Collins was an excellent artilleryman, and with four guns he led the largest battery in Price's army. Collins also commanded what had to be the only unit in the Civil War that kept a black bear as its mascot. Nicknamed Postelwait, the bear had been with the battery for more than two years, and he freely roamed the camps at night poking into whatever kettles and plates he could find. However, Postelwait was no mere camp follower as he rode to battle on the footboards of one of the limbers. It was, therefore, not uncommon to see a horribly frightened bear among the guns during any hasty engagement.[36]

Price's reorganization of the army lasted two days, during which time he authorized new recruiting cadres to head into Missouri in advance of the army. By Monday, September 20th, all was ready. Looking at his map, Price determined that his next objective was Fredericktown, Missouri, some 120 miles to the north. He then ordered the army north in three columns. Fagan's division would have the center column as it marched through Martinsburg, Reeves's Station, and Greenville. Marmaduke would march to the right of Fagan and Shelby to the left, each making sure that they never wandered more than ten to twenty miles from Fagan. Prior to departing, Price issued maps to his divisional commanders along with an injunction to prevent straggling and plundering. After only a march of twenty miles, Price, who accompanied Fagan in the center column, crossed the Current River six miles north of Pittman's Ferry and into Missouri. Price and the Missourians were jubilant. Three long years of frustration had finally ended with their return home. To honor the moment, Quartermaster Brinker offered a bottle of Missouri wine to Price's staff at dinner.[37]

And yet, the odds facing Price were still enormous. Now deep in enemy-occupied territory, Price commanded an army that was not only outnumbered, but one that did not even have weapons for one-third of its men. With its daily ration of food already having been reduced at Princeton and still lacking shoes and clothing, the army presented a stark picture of military deprivation. Nevertheless, this litany of problems paled in comparison to an elemental lack of motivation, training, and discipline. There was certainly great enthusiasm for the expedition among the Missourians, but that enthusiasm did not come easily for others. This was especially true for the thousands of Arkansans conscripted by Jo Shelby. Even Price's staff suffered reservations. Chief Engineer Thomas Mackey, a South Carolinian, doubted the legitimacy of the Confederate cause in Missouri and later termed the invasion "a manifest violation of the principle of State sovereignty on which the Confederacy itself was founded."[38] Similarly, when the enthusiasm was strong, it often did not count for much when so many men were either ill-trained recruits or part-time guerrillas burning for revenge. Discipline had been fairly easy for Price to maintain in his march through Arkansas. Veteran soldiers in Cabell's, Marmaduke's, and Slemons's commands saw to that. But Price's army was now an entirely different beast as it crossed into Missouri. Repeated attempts, and Price would make these by the dozen, to rein in stragglers and those who wanted to turn foraging expeditions into exercises of wanton plundering would become increasingly futile. Perhaps most indicative of the difficulties that lay ahead, Price's senior leadership began to fray before it made camp on the first day in Missouri. This was particularly true in Fagan's command where General Cabell bitterly denounced the newly arrived Archibald Dobbin for causing "disaffection" within the ranks. Dobbin's troubles were not surprising given that he maintained two very public and long-running feuds with General Marmaduke and Colonel Thomas McCray. Perhaps worse, Fagan himself suffered the public disobedience of Colonel John C. Wright, who protested Fagan removing his regiment from the advance of the column due to a lack of experience. With Wright thundering that Fagan's orders were a "gross insult" in front of a number of staff officers, a vacillating Fagan chose only to reply by shouting, "Take your d——d regiment and go to h—l!" It was not an auspicious start to the redemption of Missouri.[39]

Chapter Three

To the Arcadia Valley

The titular head of Missouri's military resistance to Price was a relative newcomer to the theater. Following his bitter defeat at the Battle of Chickamauga in Tennessee, Major General William S. Rosecrans had been exiled to Missouri in late January 1864 to preside over a department whose primary purpose was to provide men and material to more active theaters of operation. Although Rosecrans enjoyed the lukewarm support of Abraham Lincoln, there were precious few other men who thought much of him. Secretary of War Edwin Stanton, Chief of Staff Henry W. Halleck, and generals Ulysses S. Grant and William T. Sherman all thought Rosecrans an incompetent windbag that was best ignored. Whether it was Rosecrans's repeated attempts to transfer out of Missouri or his more dire assessments of the situation in Missouri, the Union's military command structure could not have been more dismissive. To Grant, especially, Rosecrans was a nuisance not to be trusted. Much as Sterling Price had been left to his own devices in the conquest of Missouri, so, too, would William Rosecrans be left on his own in its defense.

"Old Rosey" had, with good reason, long feared a Confederate invasion of Missouri. Although the state had recruited 110,000 men for the Union, the Department of Missouri was largely defenseless against any large-scale attack. When Rosecrans assumed command in January, the department was in the middle of transferring over forty-two thousand men, or 67 percent of its aggregate strength, out of state. By September 30, Rosecrans had only 17,559 soldiers and fifty pieces of field artillery to defend a state of sixty-nine thousand square miles. In keeping with the policy of his immediate predecessor, Major General John M. Schofield, Rosecrans scattered these troops about the state in several geographical districts, which were then headquartered at places such as Rolla, Springfield, and St. Louis. From these garrisons, and many outposts in between, the troops attempted to maintain a façade of law and order while suppressing the ever-present roving bands of Confederate guerrillas. It was a nearly impossible task given the limited number of troops, the strength of Confederate sympathy, and the often impenetrable nature of the terrain. Rosecrans well understood the difficulty of the task. Therefore, throughout the spring and early summer of 1864, Rosecrans made repeated calls for reinforcements. His messages, which were often accompanied by plans for great concentrations of troops and elaborate offensive operations, drew nothing but the ire of both Halleck and Grant. Grant, in particular, thought the requests absurd, and in June he caustically informed Halleck that Rosecrans would scream for troops even if he "were stationed in Maine." He also concluded that "Rosecrans should be removed and someone else placed in command. It makes but little difference who you assign." [1]

Halleck did not, however, remove him, and Rosecrans grew increasingly frustrated. A large part of Rosecrans's aggravation went well beyond his lack of troops. Old Rosey, much like Thomas C. Reynolds, fully believed that the mysterious and dangerous Order of the American Knights (OAK) threatened Missouri. Rosecrans came to believe in the conspiracy through the investigations and imaginations of Colonel John P. Sanderson, his provost marshal general. Sanderson had served on Rosecrans's staff through much of 1863 and had followed the general to Missouri. They were also apparently close friends with Sanderson becoming a confidante in the wake of the Chickamauga disaster. When Sanderson arrived in St. Louis, he, too, suffered a severely battered reputation. Widespread allegations of cowardice at Chickamauga had surfaced, and they stalled his promotion in Congress. Nevertheless, after Sanderson assumed the duties of provost marshal, he stumbled upon some old case files left by his predecessor, outlining the subversive activities of alleged secret societies in St. Louis. In a few months' time, Sanderson created a secret police force of his own that combed most of the Midwest and even New York City, tracking down what he thought were the tentacles of the OAK. With the conviction of a Jacobin, Sanderson believed that he had uncovered a massive plot "to overthrow the government," involving hundreds of thousands of Democrats and Confederate sympathizers across the North. Although Sanderson seems to have genuinely believed in the conspiracy, he also saw its unveiling as a way of guaranteeing promotion and a ticket out of Missouri. Consequently, he arrested numerous men in the St. Louis area, including an old friend of General Grant and the Belgian Consul. He also concocted fantastic stories about the OAK and its connection not only to Sterling Price but, more than ironically, to Thomas C. Reynolds. Rosecrans believed Sanderson without reservation and generally viewed the conspiracy as a vehicle to legitimize his claims to men and material for the Department of the Missouri. There is little doubt that he, too, saw the exposé as a possible ticket out of Missouri. Determined to circumvent their known personal enemies, Henry Halleck and Edwin Stanton, Rosecrans and Sanderson began an almost farcical series of attempts to get Lincoln personally interested in the matter. They persuaded governors, congressmen, and judges of the conspiracy and then enlisted them to gain a personal audience with the president in order to present their evidence. However, the most Lincoln would do was to send one of his personal secretaries, John Hay, to St. Louis to view the information. The trip was a disaster, as Hay believed very little of what he saw and heard. Rosecrans would not get any more aid for his department, and he and Sanderson would certainly not get any transfers out of Missouri.[2]

Rosecrans may have been repudiated in Washington, but it hardly stopped his belief in the conspiracy. Guerrilla activity burst upon the state with a ferocity that it had never seen before, and Rosecrans tied it directly to the OAK and Confederate recruiting officers who Price had sent into the state to stir up trouble in anticipation of an invasion. Every day seemed to bring forth new reports of bushwhackers running amok. On June 14th, Colonel W. E. Moberly proclaimed from Brunswick that "the Union men of our County are being murdered in their beds." In Westport, Jonathan B. Fuller noted on June 20th that "everybody is under arms" in fear of an imminent attack. From Warrensburg, a soldier wrote on June 25th that "the Bushwhackers are very troublesome up here and we have been out after them nearly all the time for the last 4 weeks." On July 2nd, separate bands of guerrillas succeeded in burning a 150-foot bridge across the Salt River, while failing to ignite another near Pilot Knob. That same day, an estimated four hundred guerrillas swarmed near New Madrid, "stealing, murdering, [and] cutting the wires." Three days later, Colonel John F. Williams informed Rosecrans that Boone, Howard, and Randolph counties were "full of outlaws and marauders, bent on pillage and plunder." By August, one Union soldier in Warrensburg glumly noted that "the Union People down here Are not doing Much at farming as Thay [sic] have to Lay out to Keep from being killed by The Secesh."[3]

For many, there was not even enough safety in staying indoors. Countless Missourians chose instead to flee the state and, in the words of one refugee, "escape from the discomforts and disorders of the coming invasion." All such turmoil left Rosecrans in an unenviable position. His troops were spread too thinly, and what he did have in the way of volunteer troops was not terribly good. Scattered about northern Missouri and St. Louis, for example, was the 17th Illinois Cavalry, which, according to Rosecrans, had been "demoralized" and was "festering in service without cavalry arms or horses." Under such circumstances, Rosecrans had to rely upon various exotic forms of militia to try to keep the peace. Since the beginning of the war, Missouri had struck a number of different bargains with Federal authorities to maintain a viable home defense force. The first offshoot of this was the Missouri State Militia (MSM), which mustered men into a federally subsidized long-term active duty with a guarantee of service only within Missouri's borders. As befitted locally raised units in a guerrilla conflict, the MSM more often than not engaged in a tit-for-tat blood war with the bushwhackers. Such a struggle engendered lawless behavior, and MSM units rarely hesitated to apply a scorched-earth technique to Southern sympathizers. The 1st MSM Cavalry exemplified the worst of this behavior when Rosecrans accused its commander, Colonel Bazel Lazear, in September 1864 of "causing a reign of terror in La Fayette and Saline Counties" and allowing his men "to murder peaceable citizens, . . . while the pursuit of the bushwhackers is abandoned by loading the troops with the plunder."[4]

Although the service of the MSM was characterized, in part, by these sorts of outrages, the MSM tended also to be well equipped—with many of its cavalry units outfitted with some form of repeating rifle—and tactically proficient. By the summer of 1864, the MSM had experienced two years of almost nonstop small-unit patrolling and combat. Its greatest tactical weakness would be in operating in anything beyond company strength as the various regimental commanders rarely, if ever, took the field at the head of the entire regiment. Limited by statute to no more than ten thousand men, the MSM nevertheless accounted for about one-half of all active Union soldiers in Missouri in 1864. It should also be noted that the ranks of the MSM were thinned that summer by a smallpox vaccination program gone strangely awry. No less than one-quarter of the 9th MSM Cavalry, responsible for much of central Missouri, was incapacitated by a vaccine tainted with what many thought was a "syphilitic poison." While it is most unlikely that syphilis actually tainted the vaccine, there was little doubt as to how the vaccine affected the men. At outposts from Sturgeon to Glasgow, vaccinated troopers suffered a multitude of side effects, including chancre sores, rheumatism, and diarrhea, that all resembled syphilis. The command at Lafayette was so weakened by the inoculation that on June 26 its commander reported no men available for duty.[5]

In theory, the MSM counted on another kind of militia for assistance during a time of crisis like that of the summer and fall of 1864. Established in the summer of 1862, the Enrolled Missouri Militia (EMM) registered all able-bodied males not already serving in a military force. It thus provided a readily available list of troops that could be trained and activated to guard depots and suppress local disorders. If measured only by the raw numbers of men registered, the EMM was a great success. Initially, over fifty thousand men enrolled into a militia that, when activated, was well supplied and armed by the Federal government. However, the EMM was a considerably more elusive force because by 1864 it rarely mustered more than four thousand men for active duty in a given month. Additionally, the EMM often proved more of a liability than a benefit. While many units could be counted on to serve loyally, others were riddled with all manner of ex-Confederate veterans, Southern sympathizers, and bushwhackers.[6]

This was especially the case in northwest Missouri where two regiments of the EMM mobilized in early July only to join a force of three hundred Confederate recruits in the short-lived capture of Platte City. Just as problematical, and in a fashion similar to that of the MSM, even when loyal units of the EMM could be activated there was a great risk of violent revenge seeking. Units rarely served beyond their own county, or neighboring counties, and Southern-sympathizing citizens—long identified and listed on military rolls—proved easy marks for ill-disciplined soldiers.[7] This habit was also especially true in Platte County as the local district assistant adjutant general had repeatedly to warn the EMM to stop the "wanton violation of orders in pressing arms, horses, and other property."[8] In some cases, members of the EMM did not bother to discriminate against Southern sympathizers. When describing the situation in Moniteau and Miller counties, Franklin Swap, the assistant provost marshal of St. Louis, decried the fact that EMM soldiers "rob and plunder the peaceful & law abiding citizens," while taking "advantage of the present state of the country to settle their private difficulties & quarrels."[9]

Difficulties with the EMM, and the open disaffection of some units, could not have come at a worse time. With the guerrilla uprising in full swing and Confederate recruiting agents swarming the state, rumors ran wild that Price and his cohorts were ready to invade. Indeed, paranoia swept the state, and it was perhaps best revealed by the *Liberty Tribune* of July 5th, which fantastically proclaimed: "Shelby with 3,000 in Lafayette. Marmaduke coming up the line between Missouri and Kansas with 5,000. Quantrill in Jackson with 3,500. Col. Thomas McCarty on Hannibal R.R. with 26,000. 20,000 troops from Illinois to join Quantrill. The main column, 240,000 strong, on way to capture St. Louis." In the midst of this hysteria, Rosecrans called for the mobilization of yet another kind of local defense force. In General Orders 107, Rosecrans appealed for the Union men in every township and county to elect "committees of public safety" which would, in turn, collaborate in the selection and mobilization of loyal companies from the EMM. Rosecrans's actual hopes for this militia are not known, but the general was bound for disappointment. In some areas, the committees of public safety were invariably politicized with most conservative Democrats complaining that the committees were nothing more than adjuncts of the Republican Party. In other areas, especially those most in need of Union defense forces, the committees never met due to an overawing presence of Confederate sympathizers. Regardless, this latest iteration of home defense militia never amounted to anything of great military significance. The guerrilla uprising persisted through the rest of July and August.[10]

For Rosecrans, the guerrilla attacks were a planned precursor to Price's invasion. He continued to believe that there was a vast network of OAK lodges scattered throughout Missouri, and that they were in contact with Price and privy to his plans of invasion. In this scenario, Rosecrans was convinced that Price had forwarded word to his loyal Knights in the spring that he would be launching an invasion and that he "expected the co-operation" of the order. According to Rosecrans, the OAK then responded by helping orchestrate the guerrilla insurrection with Price's recruiting officers when they arrived in seemingly unprecedented numbers. Rosecrans's beliefs were supported, if not formed entirely, by a few vague confessions John P. Sanderson extracted from avowed members of the OAK in the St. Louis area. However, any connection between Price, the OAK, and the insurrection was more than tenuous. Sanderson continued to hear only what he wanted to hear from the evidence, while ignoring countless testimony that denied a link to Price. More importantly, Sanderson and Rosecrans habitually overestimated the strength of the OAK and its ability to organize anything. In fact, its so-called national leadership had disintegrated the previous year amid personal infighting, and the OAK lacked any grassroots structure at the local level. Despite Rosecrans's fears, a more impotent group could not have been imagined. [11]

Unlike the OAK, pro-Confederate bushwhackers were very real, and many of them professed some vague loyalty to Price. In November 1863 William C. Quantrill, the most famous bushwhacker of them all, had relayed word to Price that he would be willing to serve under the general's flag should he return to Missouri. Price believed this encouraging news, much as he believed all encouraging news from Missouri, and he wanted to exploit the military possibilities. Soon after getting his original orders from Kirby Smith, Price dispatched several riders into Missouri with the hopes of contacting the bushwhackers. One such courier was Captain John Chestnut, who bore special instructions for George Todd to commence operations north of the Missouri River. Another courier, Private Jeremiah Moore, was the only one of five messengers dispatched by Price who actually found Quantrill. Moore caught up with Quantrill on September 12th only after a harrowing dash to the Missouri River in which he was pursued by large numbers of Union cavalry. [12]

Despite these connections, historians have overstated Old Pap's coordination of guerrilla activity. Albert Castel, for example, has noted that John Chestnut "met with the principal partisan leaders early in August and soon afterwards the bushwhackers were riding rampant through the northern and western counties." More recently, Ronald D. Smith has stated that "guerrillas north of the Missouri River tried to confuse the federals as to Price's ultimate objective." Unfortunately, there are three problems with this interpretation of coordination between the guerrillas and Price. First, according to John N. Edwards (the only near firsthand source concerning Chestnut's mission), the captain never met with any guerrilla leaders aside from George Todd. Second, there is a simple problem of chronology. The uprising had started in June, three months before any of Price's couriers allegedly established contact with the bushwhackers. Third, and perhaps most important, little chance existed that the guerrillas would take any direction from Price. Possessing a militant sense of independence, the bushwhackers had fought among themselves in the spring and were thus bitterly fragmented, with only Bill Anderson leading a large and active group throughout the summer months. As

Anderson had long been on a psychopathic binge of violence, he needed no further inducement from Price to attack Yankees.[13]

Sterling Price was therefore lucky in the timing of the guerrilla uprising. He could perhaps take some credit in unsettling Missouri on the eve of his expedition by his willingness to dispatch recruiting officers and "advance agents" to scout the state and report on the military situation. Their presence and the rumors they spread probably did more to spook the Union population about a potential invasion than anything else. But even here, Jo Shelby deserves more credit as most of the officers belonged to him and operated outside of any knowledge of the expedition. Still, the recruiting officers did not account for the bulk of the mayhem, which ultimately can be attributed to the simple lack of Union troops in the state. William Rosecrans had lost over 60 percent of his available manpower in January, and the bushwhackers needed neither directions nor encouragement to take advantage of the situation.[14]

There is some irony when evaluating the condition of Rosecrans's military intelligence. He suffered an overload of information on all matters pertaining to the OAK, guerrillas, and rumors of Price invading the state. But actual knowledge as to the whereabouts of Price and his army was almost completely missing as August turned to September. Taken within the context of modern military analysis, Price may well have long lost the principle of surprise at the strategic level, but he most assuredly retained it at the operational level. In this regard, the Union botched the opportunity to take advantage of Price's agonizingly slow movement through Arkansas. Indeed, what was notable about Price's march was not its lethargy, but rather the Union's inept reaction to it. Here, too, Rosecrans was ill served by others. In Arkansas, generals Frederick Steele and Powell Clayton failed miserably in either resisting or scouting Price's movements. Steele deserves special censure. Absolutely befuddled by Price's movements in front of Little Rock, Steele inexcusably allowed Price to slip across the Arkansas River. Steele then proceeded to magnify the error by losing contact with him. He was thus never in position to provide Rosecrans with even a basic idea of where the Confederates were headed. Not until September 10th, three days after Price had crossed the Arkansas River, did Steele write Rosecrans and inform him of the event. In that message, Steele took time also to rationalize his poor performance. He noted that he had only recently received reinforcements in the shape of a division of four thousand infantry and about two thousand cavalry led by Major General Joseph Mower. Had "the troops reached me sooner," he claimed, "I could have easily defeated Price's Missouri movements, if such are his plans."[15]

The only valuable intelligence to reach Rosecrans during the early stages of Price's march came not from Steele in Arkansas, but rather from Major General C. C. Washburn, who commanded the District of West Tennessee at Memphis. Indeed, it was Washburn who had been critical in getting Major General A. J. Smith to divert Mower's troops to Steele on September 1st. By September 3rd, Washburn was even more concerned with Confederate movements in Arkansas, and he wrote Rosecrans that Shelby was at Batesville, preparing for the arrival of Price. Furthermore, Washburn informed Rosecrans that A. J. Smith had still more veteran infantry at Cairo, Illinois, awaiting transportation to sail to Nashville and then move to join William T. Sherman in his operations against Atlanta. Washburn was a shrewd and unselfish commander, and when a talkative Unionist refugee from Batesville arrived at the general's headquarters he realized immediately the importance of the refugee's news. Rosecrans then seized upon Washburn's not-so-subtle hint that A. J. Smith was readily available, and he telegraphed Henry Halleck in Washington on September 6th to have Smith and his remaining troops rerouted to the defense of Missouri.[16]

Halleck assented to the request, but not before issuing orders that were guaranteed to anger Rosecrans. Acting upon advice from General Grant "to give A. J. Smith the problem of catching Price," Halleck authorized Smith on September 9th to assess the situation and to operate independently of Rosecrans if there really was an emergency. Halleck then followed this with another message instructing Smith to consult with Rosecrans and others only in "regard to the assistance and cooperation they can give you." Rosecrans easily detected the insult, and with some measure of relish, he would later note that Smith's professionalism led him not into eastern Arkansas but rather to St. Louis where he placed himself under Rosecrans's command on September 13th. By September 17th, one division and three batteries of artillery from Smith's Right Wing of the XVI Corps numbering about 4,500 men were at Jefferson Barracks just south St. Louis.[17]

A. J. Smith fit the image of a hard-charging general in the western Union armies. Short, bald, profane, and a heavy drinker, "Whiskey" Smith was a charismatic old army Indian fighter. He also cared little in disciplining his own troops. This was never more evident than in the recently concluded Red River Campaign where Smith's men laid waste to the Louisiana countryside along their march. Despite Smith's distinct lack of social skills and his indifference to discipline, his appearance provided great relief to Rosecrans and much of St. Louis's Unionist population. Prominent citizens organized reception committees, and Frank Boehm's notoriously off-key City Post Band marched to the docks to greet the troops. Official St. Louis feted Smith personally as a savior of the city and presented him with an expensive gold sword on September 20th. According to one of Smith's German-speaking soldiers, the impressive ceremony was capped by the speeches of "General Schmit and officer Rosencraus."[18]

Although Smith's presence was a comfort to Rosecrans, he was still largely unaware of Price's location and objectives. Even when he finally received some concrete information from Steele on September 23rd that Price had indeed crossed the Arkansas River and was then near Batesville, Rosecrans could hardly be sure of where Price was going. Despite Price's march to the northeast, conflicting reports and captured letters revealed that Price could take any one of several routes into the state. One route would have Price track back to the northwest through Cassville and then to the Kansas border where he could march to the Missouri River. A second path could take Price through Cassville, Springfield, and Sedalia before reaching the Missouri River. A more central route could take Price from Batesville to West Plains and then to Jefferson City. As Rosecrans looked at his maps, he also considered the possibility of Price moving through Pocahontas and into southeast Missouri. Lacking troops to plug each of the routes, Rosecrans guessed first that Price would head either for Springfield or Jefferson City, while dispatching raiding columns to southeastern Missouri. Accordingly, Rosecrans moved quickly to protect the enormous depots the Union had created at Springfield and Rolla by instructing his district commanders to improve their fortifications and to confiscate their district's already harvested crops. He also concentrated about two thousand men of the EMM at Sedalia.[19]

The biggest problem with Rosecrans's assessment was that he believed Shelby would operate separately from Price's main body as it headed toward the central part of the state. Rosecrans had held this view since at least the middle of the month, and all the reports that then filtered into St. Louis did little to disabuse him of the notion. When a reinforced scouting party from the 3rd MSM encountered Confederate troops at Doniphan early on the morning of September 18th, the men they encountered were advance elements of Shelby's division. Although the scout succeeded first in dispersing Shelby's men and pursuing them to the Arkansas border, the Confederates soon turned the tables in great force as they surrounded and nearly captured or killed the entire Yankee detachment. The commander of the scout, Lieutenant Erich Pape, submitted his report of the action on September 20th, but he concluded that he had faced only Shelby and that Price was nowhere in southeastern Missouri. Two days later, Rosecrans received information from Brigadier General John B. Sanborn in Springfield that only confirmed Pape's assessment. Sanborn had captured the personal correspondence of several Confederates in Shelby's division, and all predicted Price would march on Jefferson City.[20]

Price was not without luck in all of this deception. At Pocahontas, Marmaduke had detached Colonel William Jeffers's 8th Missouri to move well in advance of his column. By the 22nd, Jeffers's column brushed aside a company of Lieutenant Colonel Hiram Hiller's 2nd MSM cavalry at Bloomfield. Unfortunately for Hiller, he could not identify the troops in his front. Reports from Cape Girardeau nevertheless assumed the Confederates belonged to Shelby and that he possessed anywhere from eight hundred to eight thousand men all ready to invest the city! While Marmaduke had no designs on Cape Girardeau, Jeffers's push into Bloomfield coincided with Shelby's rout of a Federal garrison at Patterson on the 22nd and his march into Fredericktown on the evening of the 23rd. With reports then of Shelby seemingly everywhere in the southeast, Rosecrans became anxious for the safety of the Iron Mountain Railroad, which ran eighty-six miles from St. Louis to its terminus at Pilot Knob. The only north-south railroad in the area, the Iron Mountain line was vital to the logistics and communications of the region.[21]

Demonstrating his concern, Rosecrans late on September 24th ordered Brigadier General Thomas Ewing Jr. to secure the line with a brigade of A. J. Smith's infantry. Ewing was to report directly to Smith, who was also to follow Ewing down the railroad on the 25th. Despite the fragmentation of his command, Smith was filled with confidence. As the men prepared to embark on the trains, one of Smith's soldiers, Monroe J. Miller, overheard Smith exclaim that he was ready to give Shelby "a damned good thrashing and then come back and go and elect Old Abe President." More than ironically, Smith's irreverent confidence did little to inspire the pious Miller, who then sadly concluded that all "of our Generals, without scarcely a single exception, are such profane, dissipated, wicked wretches. If they were God fearing men, we would have nothing to fear from the Rebellion."[22]

If Monroe Miller sought some divine confirmation of his assessment of the Union's leadership, he might have got it later that morning. Ewing departed hastily with only six hundred men out of the 1,700 effectives in the detailed brigade. As Ewing traveled south, he scattered some of his men to guard various bridges along the line. By the time Ewing reached Mineral Point, nearly forty miles south of St. Louis, he had only four hundred infantry left. Ewing then paused there to assess the situation and determine if Price was actually in the vicinity. Throughout the night, reports trickled into Ewing that Price was indeed in the area and concentrating his force at Fredericktown. Although Ewing continued to doubt this possibility, he nevertheless determined to ride on to Pilot Knob in the northern portion of the Arcadia Valley at mid-morning accompanied by only 134 men of the 14th Iowa.[23]

When Ewing arrived at Pilot Knob around noon on September 26th, a more controversial Union commander could not have been found in the Trans-Mississippi. Born in 1829, Ewing was the son of a prominent and wealthy Ohio politician. After studying law in Cincinnati, he moved to Kansas in 1856 and quickly assumed a highly visible role in the abolitionist movement. By the outbreak of the war, he was the first chief justice of the Kansas Supreme Court. A year later he commanded the 11th Kansas Cavalry with some distinction at the battles of Cane Hill and Prairie Grove. But it was in 1863 that Ewing became a notorious figure among Confederates and conservative Democrats in Missouri. He commanded the border area between Kansas and Missouri at the time of William Quantrill's massacre at Lawrence, Kansas, and he responded to the attack by ordering all rural inhabitants in four Missouri counties from their homes if they could not prove their loyalty. A draconian measure, Ewing's order depopulated most of Jackson, Cass, Bates, and Vernon counties, prompting many a Confederate Missourian to burn with hatred for Ewing. Although a fairly competent soldier, Ewing owed his presence in the St. Louis area in 1864 more to family connections than military ability. Two of his brothers were high-ranking officers, and his family had raised William T. Sherman as a child, with Sherman eventually marrying Ewing's sister, Ellen. It was this connection to Sherman that William Rosecrans sought to exploit when he asked Ewing to command the Federal District of St. Louis, especially in the matter of the OAK.[24]

Ewing could not help Rosecrans sway Sherman, or anyone else for that matter, about the OAK, but he was now well positioned to inform Rosecrans once and for all if Sterling Price was in southeast Missouri. At Pilot Knob, Ewing took command of an odd assortment of troops and an equally odd fortification at just about the same time Sterling Price decided to march in the direction of Pilot Knob. As Ewing later noted, four small mountains encircled the mining village of Pilot Knob and its two hundred residents. Cedar and Rock (Depot) mountains lay almost directly north of the village, while Shepherd and Pilot Knob mountains loomed to the south and east. Littered with rocks, trees, and heavy underbrush, each mountain was between five hundred and six hundred feet in elevation. The village itself was tucked almost in the middle of a plain of nearly one thousand acres. The military focus of the area was, surprisingly, not on any one of the mountains. Instead, and dating back to 1861, Union commanders had placed a small hexagonal fort about three hundred yards from the base of Pilot Knob Mountain and about one thousand yards from Shepherd's Mountain. There was nothing terribly elaborate about Fort Davidson. Soldiers and laborers had shoveled enough dirt to create walls that were 150 feet in length and about five feet high and five feet thick. Just outside the fort, the troops had dug a moat no less than ten feet wide and eight feet deep. In addition to the moat, there were two rifle pits, or trenches, one extending 190 yards to the north and the other about 150 yards to the southwest. Inside the fort a fairly shallow cellar served as a crude magazine. For ordnance, the fort mounted several pieces of heavy artillery, including four 32-pounder siege guns, three 24-pounder howitzers, and two 24-pound Coehorn mortars. Additionally, the fort would soon claim eight light artillery pieces from units attached to the fort. Although a succession of post and district commanders had armed the fort well, they had nevertheless created an installation that could not possibly withstand even a brief siege, or for that fact, a well-prepared assault. Surrounded by mountains, the fort could be enfiladed by not only artillery but by rifle fire as well. Inspection reports in 1864 readily admitted this weakness but ultimately could not propose a better site in the area that could be erected with the available manpower and resources. [25]

Its many weaknesses to the contrary, Fort Davidson stood as the headquarters of what was known as the Third Sub-District of the District of St. Louis. Commanding the post and the district was Major James S. Wilson of the 3rd MSM Cavalry. One of the more infamous guerrilla fighters in southeast Missouri, Wilson also came from a family divided by the war. His wife's family hailed from Virginia, and most of its men were then fighting in the Confederate army. Wilson's brother, John, also served the Confederate cause. In the days leading up to Ewing's arrival at Pilot Knob, Wilson had consolidated at Fort Davidson most of the detachments that were normally posted at Patterson, Centreville, Fredericktown, and Farmington. By September 26th, Fort Davidson had thus become home to six companies of both the 3rd MSM and the 47th Missouri Infantry and one company each from the 2nd MSM Cavalry, the 1st MSM Infantry, and the 50th Missouri Infantry. Other units packed into the fort and its immediate environs included Captain William C. F. Montgomery's battery of the 2nd Missouri Light Artillery, a detachment from the 14th Iowa Infantry that Ewing brought with him, and finally a hastily recruited company of local militia that contained a group of fifty blacks commanded by one of their own, Charles Thurston. All told, Wilson—and then Ewing—counted about 1,450 men to oppose the approaching Confederates. However, it was not lost upon Ewing that many of these men were ill trained. The 47th Missouri and the 50th Missouri were newly recruited from local EMM units and were not well trained. Indeed, the 50th had yet to muster into actual Federal service. Despite some close order training in the days preceding Price's advance, the men of both these units spent most of their time clearing trees and brush off Pilot Knob and improving the rifle pits so that a man could stand erect and shoot. The level of training in the 1st MSM Infantry and in Montgomery's battery was not much better as both units had no combat experience. Aside from the small detachment of veterans in the 14th Iowa, Ewing's most experienced men were in the six companies of the 3rd MSM and the one company of the 2nd MSM. Unfortunately, that experience was both limited in scope and of a kind that made these units notorious in the eyes of many of Price's men.[26]

The 2nd and 3rd MSMs were regiments guaranteed to attract the visceral hatred of Missouri's Confederates. They were locally recruited and had long been responsible for policing and patrolling southeast Missouri. Their mission was difficult as bushwhackers and Confederate partisans, but especially those led by Timothy Reeves, operated freely due to the large number of Southern sympathizers in the area and its close proximity to the Arkansas border. Though they were not without their tactical successes, the 2nd and 3rd MSMs were largely ineffective against the bushwhackers, and both units, instead, became synonymous with the worst features of ill-disciplined militia in the Department of the Missouri. Problems were most noticeable in an officer corps that could control neither itself nor its men. Between January and June 1864 alone, disciplinary boards for the 3rd MSM dismissed two officers for "incompetence," another for "contracting a loathsome disease," and yet another for drunkenness, consorting with prostitutes, and "exposing himself publicly." One year earlier, the commander of the 3rd MSM, Lieutenant Colonel R. G. Woodson, tried to resign his commission when he could not discipline two officers and twenty-seven men for "misbehavior before the enemy." There was then little surprise that the 2nd and 3rd MSMs proved more adept at plundering and destroying property than fighting the enemy. Remarkably, these units directed much of their lawless behavior toward Union loyalists. As Price advanced into the area, Brigadier General James R. McCormick, who commanded the EMM in the southeast, ruefully concluded that "the lack of discipline in the M.S.M. of the Southeast MO has worked great evil to our cause during the past season. I candidly believe that the law abiding people of the Dist have sustained greater loss of life and property from them than from Bushwhackers."[27]

Although a frequent scourge to Unionists, the 3rd MSM was notorious among the men of southeast Missouri who first joined Shelby and then Price in 1864. For the previous two years, the 3rd MSM had laid waste to countless homes and villages suspected of Southern sympathies. In April 1863, one company of the 3rd went on a rampage in the vicinity of Patterson after losing a skirmish with guerrilla forces. According to one Yankee trooper, before retreating through the village, they "burned everything that would burn." In late October 1863, columns of the 3rd MSM entered the area around Doniphan and informed the families of suspected guerrillas that if their husbands and sons did not surrender, "their houses, stock, &c., will be given to the flames, and the families all sent down the Mississippi River, to be imprisoned at Napoleon, Ark." In like fashion, Erich Pape's ill-fated reconnaissance through Doniphan in the middle of September 1864 witnessed his troopers burning much of the village because of its Southern tendencies.[28]

But most important to sparking a Confederate desire for revenge were two events that occurred in 1863. In the first, Captain William T. Leeper and a company of the 3rd MSM captured and executed six men of an independent company being recruited by Timothy Reeves. The second incident also involved Reeves. In December 1863 Reeves led a battalion-sized unit in a campaign through the area that netted more than one hundred Yankee prisoners. Unfortunately for Reeves, he paused for Christmas at Pulliam's Farm in southwestern Ripley County without establishing proper guards. Consequently, a hard-riding column of the 3rd MSM led by Major James S. Wilson tracked Reeves down and surprised him in the middle of his dinner. Reeves barely escaped while losing nearly two hundred men killed and captured. Reeves had suffered an acute embarrassment and the loss of a great many men. It was enough to produce a powerful desire for revenge that could end only with the death of Wilson.[29]

The opportunity for revenge became a distinct possibility when Price's army began reassembling in Fredericktown. Shelby's column arrived first on the 23rd. Fagan—with Timothy Reeves and his newly reconstituted 15th Missouri in tow—followed on the 24th. While Shelby, Fagan, and Price then waited for Marmaduke's division to arrive, four hundred recruits rode into camp. In a rarity among Price's new recruits, these men were well armed as most had deserted the EMM carrying their weapons with them. As the recruits trickled into the camps, the officers and men of the army also discovered quickly that Fredericktown abounded in food and luxury items that they had long forgotten existed. For many, then, this was a chance to purchase goods at costs established by Price and his staff when they first entered the state. As Chief Surgeon William McPheeters recorded, "Officers & troops were as thick as blackberries & as busy as bees about town in securing whatever was for sale." However, for others this was a chance simply to take whatever they needed. Fagan's Arkansans were particularly tempted by the possibilities, and James T. Armstrong described an abundance of goods including china, cosmetics, skirt hoops, and children's shoes that were seized and parceled out to the men. At that moment, Price's glorious attempt to redeem Missouri began to look strangely like a free shopping spree for the women back home.[30]

The interlude drew to a close late on September 25th when Marmaduke's division encamped about eight miles from town. Marmaduke could be well pleased with events to that point. His division had easily sown confusion among the enemy, and on September 24th it had just received a large number of badly needed recruits when Colonel Alonzo Slayback rode into his camp at the head of a freshly recruited battalion of four companies. Marmaduke himself rode on to Price's headquarters where a meeting then ensued between Price and all of his division commanders. Of paramount concern to the commanding general were reported concentrations of enemy forces in the Arcadia Valley and at St. Louis. By the time of the meeting, Price had been well apprized of A. J. Smith's transfer to St. Louis. However, the reports exaggerated Smith's available manpower, estimating that he commanded eight thousand troops. Shelby also reported to Price that advance elements of Smith's corps were at Sulphur Springs, twenty-four miles south of the city. The information on the Arcadia Valley was more encouraging as it accurately depicted a concentration of 1,500 men, albeit at Ironton two miles to the south of Pilot Knob.[31]

A critical moment in the campaign had thus arrived. Smith's large body of infantry was clearly something that Price had not counted on meeting with his loose collection of ill-trained cavalry and dismounted recruits. Although St. Louis had long been the intended objective of the operation, Price was now willing to postpone its conquest until he had acquired more recruits and was in more of a position to take on Smith and the city's defenses. He therefore solicited the opinions of his division commanders. Writing twenty-three years after the event, Shelby left the only record of the meeting. According to Shelby, he went first and argued strongly for marching hard to St. Louis and disregarding the collection of troops in the Arcadia Valley, believing them too well entrenched to break.[32] However, Shelby's account is more than a bit self-serving. At the time of the meeting, all available information showed the Union force not within the walls of Fort Davidson, but rather out in the open at Ironton with no indication that it would seek protection at Fort Davidson. More importantly, Shelby's recollections never reveal how he would have proposed to break through Smith's reported eight thousand infantry with ill-trained cavalry and then penetrate the fortifications of St. Louis. In contrast, Marmaduke and Fagan saw correctly that Smith's presence in the vicinity of St. Louis—no matter the exaggeration of his numbers—had changed the focus of the campaign, at least in its early stages. Any push for St. Louis would have to be delayed, and in the meantime a more manageable prize lurked twenty miles to the west in the Arcadia Valley. Marmaduke and Fagan thus voted to move west, and Price concurred.

Price therefore determined to isolate Union forces in the Arcadia Valley. After the conclusion of the meeting, he ordered Shelby to the northwest to destroy a series of bridges along the Iron Mountain Railroad. Early the next morning on the 26th, Shelby marched his division through Farmington and encamped that night about five miles from the railroad. At daylight on September 27th, Shelby detailed three regiments of the Iron Brigade to destroy the bridges. Colonel Benjamin F. Elliot's regiment rode to Irondale, while Colonel Frank Gordon took charge of two regiments and hurried to the north to burn three bridges in the vicinity of Mineral Point. Shelby kept the remainder of the division with him to rip up the track between Elliot and Gordon. When Gordon completed the destruction of his first bridge, he headed up the railroad to destroy another bridge at Mineral Point. Upon arrival, Gordon ran into three regiments of A. J. Smith's corps commanded by Colonel James K.

Mills that had followed Ewing down the Iron Mountain Railroad. By this time, Federal intelligence gathering had broken down completely, and Smith believed himself confronted by thousands of Confederates. After only limited skirmishing, he ordered the infantry, which easily outnumbered Gordon's cavalry by at least two to one, to retreat back to DeSoto where it would join nine other regiments and await further developments. Emboldened by Smith's passivity, Gordon burned the South Big River Bridge and pressed on in the direction of DeSoto and burned yet another bridge over the Big River before turning back toward Shelby. For his own part, Shelby had been quite busy, destroying five miles of track between Irondale and Mineral Point. With military precision, Shelby arrayed his men by the hundreds alongside the track, and "with one vast exertion of concentrated strength and with a might of upheaving [*sic*], the entire bed of the road was torn from its firm foundation and hurled—grinding, crushing, [and] crashing, down steep embankments into the mud and water below." Not content with just destroying track, Shelby demolished "telegraph poles, wires, cattle-stops, bridges, trestle-work, depots, cars, cord-wood, ties, and heavy timbers."[33]

For almost five hours Shelby wreaked havoc on the main line of the Iron Mountain Railroad. By noon, however, he turned his attention to a spur of the railroad that connected Mineral Point with Potosi. Shelby rode west on the spur and into Potosi, where he encountered some resistance from a detachment of twenty-six men from the newly recruited 50th Missouri and about 130 citizens. Shelby quickly chased the Unionists into the local courthouse, which briefly stymied the Confederates. However, the skirmish ended when Shelby brought up Richard Collins's battery of Parrotts, and they pumped ten or twelve rounds in the building. After producing a white flag, the men in the courthouse surrendered. The act of surrender itself was not without drama as Shelby's men ordered one of the prisoners to cut down the Union flag and run up the Confederate banner. Loudly proclaiming that he would rather die, the man grabbed the flag pole, whereupon a group of Confederates readily obliged his willingness to die for the flag. When the Confederate battle flag finally did ascend the pole, Shelby unleashed his men upon the railroad and its depot, which also included seven rail cars that were quickly consigned to the flames. Shelby made sure to send out several patrols, and they reported back throughout the day with captured prisoners and booty, including one wagon train that had departed from Fort Davidson. Despite their success in destroying public property and gathering prisoners, Shelby's patrols also began to demonstrate a problem endemic to warfare in Missouri. Cut free from larger units and operating under orders that proscribed the destruction of private property, Shelby's roving detachments did not take long to engage in revenge killing and the theft of private property. At least three prisoners were executed, and numerous houses and barns all went up in smoke. Even Shelby's medical staff showed few signs of restraint. Two doctors, Brown and Fulkerson, discovered in Potosi both medicine and whiskey. Each doctor handled this embarrassment of riches in his own way. Brown got "dead drunk," and Fulkerson began prescribing canteens full of whiskey for his patients. With drunken soldiers and cast-off plunder now filling the streets of Potosi, Shelby waited anxiously for word from Price. It never came, and Shelby decided to spend the night of the 27th at Potosi. Early the next morning he would march his division south toward Pilot Knob and Price.[34]

Chapter Four

General, My Brigade Never Flickered

Sterling Price well understood that heavy combat lay ahead at Pilot Knob. On the 25th, he distributed most of the Army of Missouri's trains to each of the divisions, while ordering the division commanders to issue two days of cooked rations to the men. The next day, he broke camp at Fredericktown, heading first for Ironton in the Arcadia Valley. Fagan's division had the lead. After marching eleven miles, Fagan paused outside the Arcadia Valley at the St. Francis River. Accompanying Fagan was Price's chief engineer, Thomas Mackey, who then scaled a ridge overlooking the southern entrance into the valley. In what must have been a great surprise, he detected no large Union presence in the lower valley at Ironton. Especially noteworthy was the fact that James Wilson had erred greatly and not placed any troops at Shut-In Gap, which served as the gateway into the valley. Fagan, realizing that his passage was now unobstructed and with the permission of Price, ordered William F. Slemons's brigade to move through the gap along its gravel road and to seize Ironton. Slemons, however, did not make the march. He was ill, and command of the brigade fell to the disputatious Colonel John C. Wright. [1]

By 1:00 PM Wright advanced cautiously into the valley with perhaps only one-half of Slemons's brigade of five hundred men, surprising a Federal outpost at the small village of Russellville, which managed yet to remain undetected. In an attempt to spread the word of the Confederate advance, the outpost commander dispatched two riders toward Ironton and Pilot Knob. When the first soldier quickly headed for the brush and hid in fear, the commander sent another messenger, Corporal Azariah Martin. A Confederate deserter turned Yankee soldier, Martin had reason to fear what would become of him should he be captured. He thus rode hard into Ironton, where he began bellowing: "The Rebels are on us!" and "Rebels Coming!" He halted only long enough to warn a small detachment of the 47th Missouri Infantry guarding Ironton. Martin then spurred his horse northward, warning anyone who would listen, until he finally pulled up in Fort Davidson. Because the newly arrived General Ewing was elsewhere at that moment, Martin delivered his breathless report to James Wilson. Major Wilson believed that Martin exaggerated the threat, but he nonetheless dispatched a patrol of about eighty men from the 3rd MSM to investigate. Unfortunately for the Confederacy, John C. Wright displayed no great sense of urgency in advancing through the valley. Wilson's patrol found the Confederates in almost the same spot where Martin had left them. A relatively bloodless firefight then ensued and ended only when Wright outflanked the MSM, scattering it about the lower valley. Wright stopped only when the detachment of the 47th Missouri deployed in line across Ironton's main street and delivered a withering volley into the Confederates. Stunned, Wright's troops dismounted, sought cover, and then watched the Yankee detachment fall back into Ironton's courthouse.[2]

The heavy firing from Ironton could be heard at Fort Davidson at just about the same time scattered troopers of the 3rd MSM came riding headlong into the fort. It thus stirred both Wilson and Ewing to action. Wilson hastily assembled the remaining cavalry from around the fort, numbering anywhere between two hundred and three hundred men, and advanced toward Ironton. Ewing followed shortly thereafter with men from the 14th Iowa accompanied by two cannons from the 2nd Missouri Light Artillery. By 3:00 PM both Ewing and Wilson had arrived in Ironton. The highly visible approach of these columns prompted Wright's troops to withdraw south to the village of Arcadia. Pausing only briefly to incorporate the rescued men of the 47th Missouri into their ranks, Ewing and Wilson formed a line of battle. Ewing then decided to remain behind in Ironton, leaving Wilson to lead the combined force toward Wright's line. Wilson performed capably and forced Wright east from Arcadia and through the valley toward Shut-In Gap. At the gap, Wright picked up the remainder of his brigade and began a counterattack that once again pushed the Unionists in the direction of Arcadia. By nightfall, Wilson's line had retreated to a point midway between Arcadia and Ironton. For all of the riding and shooting that had taken place during the day, there were few casualties to report, with perhaps the most significant being Major Wilson, a bullet having creased his temple. More importantly,

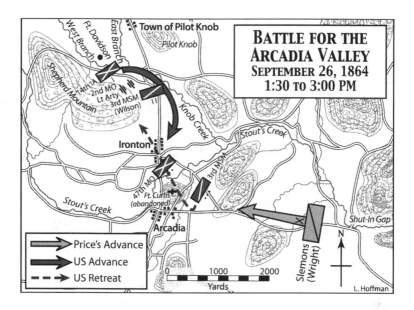

Figure 4.1.   Battle for the Arcadia Valley, September 26, 1864, 1:30 to 3:00 PM

Ewing remained in a fog of doubt as to Price's whereabouts. Despite the daylong action, he did not even know that he was engaged with Slemons's brigade of Fagan's division. The best Ewing could tell, he faced the advance units of Shelby's division, which he believed numbered between three thousand and five thousand men. By nightfall, nothing had occurred to change his assessment. Ewing therefore ordered Wilson to maintain his position, and the general then returned to Fort Davidson to better assess the situation.[3]

Ewing arrived back at the fort by 8:00 PM and just in time to help quell the panic that had been building since his departure. Rumors ran wild proclaiming that Ewing had been killed and one hundred thousand Confederates were bearing down on Pilot Knob. S. D. Carpenter, medical director of the Department of the Missouri and both a friend and relative of Ewing, had arrived at the fort from St. Louis only one hour before Ewing, and he was stunned to find the streets "full of people, loaded with plunder." Upon his return to the fort, Ewing exuded confidence. He called out for food, whereupon an orderly immediately produced coffee and a few pounds of bacon. What Ewing did not eat he stuffed into his uniform pockets and began writing dispatches. Among the dispatches was a telegram destined for A. J. Smith and Rosecrans, announcing that he still did not know Price's whereabouts and he had thus decided not to evacuate Fort Davidson. He would stay and fight what he believed were the no more than five thousand men in Shelby's division. Ewing began redoubling his efforts to prepare the fort for the upcoming attack. Realizing that he could not defend the Pilot Knob railroad terminal and the fort, Ewing also determined to send three trains north toward A. J. Smith loaded with fifty thousand rations and excess supplies. As Ewing was short of available staff officers, he directed Surgeon Carpenter to coordinate the loading of the trains.[4]

No sooner had Ewing made his decision to stay and fight than he began to have second thoughts. By 9:00 PM Ewing had received a panicked message from Major Wilson in the lower Arcadia Valley. Wilson and Captain William J. Campbell of the 14th Iowa had become unnerved as Fagan's division poured through the Shut-In Gap and proceeded to establish camp. Literally thousands of campfires dotted the valley, leading both men to conclude that they faced all of Price's army. They therefore hastily sought permission to withdraw their troops to at least Ironton. At first, Ewing was skeptical of the report, and he merely dispatched two more pieces of artillery to Wilson. But by 10:30 he relented when one of his staff officers provided a firsthand confirmation of the large number of Confederates. Shortly thereafter, Wilson withdrew his force across Stout's Creek and formed it east of Ironton. When rain began to fall, Wilson allowed many of the men to leave the formation and sleep in the Ironton courthouse. Fortunately for Wilson, this ill-advised decision to weaken his line did not come back to haunt him. Marmaduke's division was still not up, and Price chose not to rush things in the valley.[5]

Still, Ewing was sufficiently concerned to delay sending his freight trains to A. J. Smith. They might be needed for troops instead of supplies. Furthermore, he exchanged a series of telegrams with both A. J. Smith and Rosecrans about the latest developments and requested reinforcement. The important result of these telegrams was twofold. First, Rosecrans properly deferred all matters related to the defense, or evacuation, of Pilot Knob to Smith, who was much closer to the action and in the best position to make the appropriate decision. Second, around midnight Smith informed Ewing there would be no reinforcements from Mineral Point. This news threw Ewing into a quandary as he began to consider evacuation. He had arrived at Pilot Knob just a scant twelve hours previously and was thrust immediately into a crisis situation. He was unfamiliar with all of his troops and had only a rudimentary knowledge of Fort Davidson and its environs. Perhaps even worse, he was personally isolated, with few trusted subordinates to turn to for advice. One of those subordinates was S. D. Carpenter, a surgeon who had never before been near combat. Another was Colonel Thomas C. Fletcher, commander of the 47th Missouri Infantry. Like Thomas Ewing, Fletcher was not only new to the fort and its men, but he was also a readily identifiable and reviled figure among Missouri's Confederate population. Although an experienced regimental commander and one-time prisoner of war, Fletcher was more widely known in 1864 as a radical Republican politician and gubernatorial candidate. It was only chance, however, that put him at Pilot Knob. At the time of Price's invasion, Fletcher was on medical leave from Sherman's army. Nevertheless, Rosecrans persuaded him to take command of the 47th Missouri Infantry during the crisis. After traveling first to Cape Girardeau in anticipation of Shelby striking there, Fletcher only rode into Pilot Knob at 7 PM on the same train as S. D. Carpenter. Ewing eventually assigned him command of all 598 infantrymen at the post.[6]

Shortly after midnight, Ewing sought out Fletcher and walked with him to the railroad terminal where Carpenter was assembling wagons to haul surplus goods from the fort. A most unusual council of war then took place as Ewing solicited opinions from Carpenter and Fletcher about what to do next. Fletcher spoke first and recommended evacuating the fort. Carpenter, on the other hand, argued for remaining to fight the Confederates. The good doctor assessed the available intelligence and concluded that only Shelby lurked in the darkness. Besides, and no less important, Carpenter believed a retreat would be political suicide for both men. Fletcher "could not be elected governor . . . nor could the General ever expect to be a senator."[7]

As might have been expected, Carpenter's and Fletcher's conflicting advice only confused matters more for Ewing. He wanted yet another opinion. He left both men and traveled back to the fort where he met Lieutenant David Murphy. The most colorful figure at Fort Davidson, Murphy was technically the assistant adjutant general of the 47th Missouri. But Murphy's experience as an artilleryman at Prairie Grove and Vicksburg had led Ewing to place him in charge of Fort Davidson's artillery. In this role, Murphy had labored hard throughout the day and night creating platforms for four pieces of William Montgomery's field artillery to be placed inside the fort. When Ewing finally peered into his eyes and asked his advice, the combative Murphy argued forcefully to stay and fight. As Murphy later recalled, he proclaimed it necessary to "develop" Price's army. Moreover, a retreat at that late moment could be disastrous with inexperienced recruits. "If suddenly attacked on the march," he argued, "they would be like a flock of pigeons and flight would be their first thought." The only alternative was for the recruits to fight behind thick, earthen walls. Murphy concluded by amplifying Carpenter's earlier comments. A retreat would leave everyone "disgraced forever." When Ewing voiced the very real concern about what would happen if the Confederates got artillery on Shepherd Mountain, Murphy reassured the general that Fort Davidson could hold at least until the next night when an escape could be made. At that moment, according to Murphy, Ewing made the decision to stay. With but little pause, Ewing told Murphy, "Get ready then for a fight." Ewing shortly thereafter ordered his trains away filled not with troops, but with supplies and about two hundred civilian refugees.[8]

By any objective standard, Thomas Ewing had just made the wrong choice. He occupied a position dominated by mountains. He commanded untrained recruits and a state militia that was best characterized by ill discipline and a lack of battlefield success. He could not be sure of the identity of the enemy in front of him. He did not even know its strength. Indeed, while Ewing continued to talk of being able to defend against Shelby and his four thousand to five thousand men, he kept receiving reports that indicated Price was very much in the area with not only nineteen thousand men but a brass band to boot. Just as important, Ewing still had the ability to get his force out of the Arcadia Valley with relative ease. Three freight trains waited at the Pilot Knob terminal precisely because Ewing might want to load them with troops. This fact certainly contradicts David Murphy's belief, or at least his fantastic recollection of a belief, that any retreat meant a forced march by green troops in the darkness. Nevertheless, Ewing resolved to stay if only because, as he later reported to Rosecrans, "the advantages of delaying the enemy two or three days in his march northward" outweighed the consequences of possibly losing "much of the garrison." This was a bold rationale and one not really supported by either the military situation or Rosecrans's orders. Rosecrans had tasked him to locate Price and defend the Iron Mountain Railroad, not sacrifice 1,500 troops in the needless delay of Price's already snail-like advance. Given Price's true strength and the fishbowl of a fortification that Ewing chose to defend, Ewing's odds of military success were not high, although—as both Carpenter and Murphy noted—his personal honor and political viability would be enhanced.[9]

It was now up to Sterling Price to exploit the opportunity Thomas Ewing had handed him. During the night, Marmaduke had come up to the Saint

Francis River with his division, while Fagan had concentrated his division south of the village of Arcadia. At daybreak, Price ordered Fagan to press through the lower part of the valley. Fagan, in turn, rotated his troops at the front so that now Cabell's brigade took the lead. Undeterred by intermittent rain and fog, Cabell forced Wilson and Campbell back through Ironton toward the one-quarter-mile-wide Ironton Gap between Shepherd and Pilot Knob mountains.[10]

Campbell's infantry fell back first as Wilson deployed his cavalry to cover the retreat. When both Campbell and Wilson had finally reached the gap, the Union troops formed a line that was anchored by both mountains. Although Cabell had pursued Wilson fairly closely throughout the early morning, by 9:00 AM the line had stabilized enough for Ewing to send to the gap a sutler's wagon filled with breakfast. At about the same time, Campbell received permission to sidestep his infantry from the floor of the gap to the west and to a spur of Shepherd Mountain. Campbell had wisely cleared the way for Fort Davidson's 24-pound guns to engage the Confederates gathering in the lower valley. By 9:15, the artillery commenced a cannonade, which scattered the Confederates who had begun to mass north of Ironton. Unfortunately for the defenders of the gap, the situation deteriorated quickly. First, some of the artillery fire from Fort Davidson began landing near Campbell's position. Second, Colonel James C. Monroe's regiment got in close to the south face of Shepherd Mountain and attacked Campbell in his front and right flank. Third, and finally, Wilson's detachment of the 3rd MSM, which was then positioned to Campbell's left at the base of Pilot Knob Mountain, believed that the Confederates had overrun Shepherd Mountain. Naturally, they began firing into Campbell's men. The total effect was too much. At 10:00 AM, Campbell and his exhausted 14th Iowa stumbled into Fort Davidson.[11]

As Fagan forced Campbell from Shepherd Mountain, the Confederate general sent a demand for surrender under a white flag to Wilson. Major Wilson promptly forwarded it to Ewing, who thought the offer a trick to mask Confederate maneuvers. Ewing refused to meet the Confederate emissary, and Fagan responded quickly by ordering his artillery then positioned just north of Ironton to fire canister into Wilson's detachment. The fusillade was largely ineffective. But Wilson did not hold the position much longer anyway, and he retreated over the top of Pilot Knob Mountain and back down the northeastern slope, arriving at Fort Davidson around 11 AM. Though Wilson and his men were most assuredly upset by their loss of the

mountain, their disappointment was nearly matched by that of a partner in the
Iron Mountain Company, which ran the iron works on Pilot Knob Mountain.
Demonstrating the precept that business should not stop for a battle, James
Harrison exhorted his men to keep working as the battle raged over and
through their machines and furnaces. In testament to either his iron will or
fuzzy thinking, Harrison somehow managed to keep one of the furnaces
working even as ordnance exploded all around him and his men. [12]

While Harrison thus stuck to the mountain and Wilson abandoned it,
Fagan's artillery shifted its target to Fort Davidson. The resulting salvos of
round shot and shell, much like the canister directed at Wilson, proved remarkably useless. Most of the balls fell at least thirty-five yards short of the
fort, with some having only enough momentum to roll slowly up to the edge
of the south rifle pit. The weakness of this bombardment allowed the defenders of Fort Davidson to concentrate most of their attention upon Confederate
skirmishers who then began to flow down and around the bases of the mountains. At Pilot Knob Mountain, Fagan's troops swarmed into a row of railroad workers' log houses that extended north to an iron furnace in the gap
between Pilot Knob and Rock, or Depot, Mountain. Whatever discipline
these troops possessed broke down immediately when they burst into the
houses and a store near the furnace. Many of the Confederates took to stealing whatever they could lift. Artillery fire from the fort soon forced these
troops out of the buildings and into the brush at the base of Pilot Knob
Mountain and eventually back over its summit. Atop Shepherd Mountain,
John Marmaduke's division had finally arrived on the battlefield and occupied the southern face of the mountain. Confederate sharpshooters soon crept
over the crest of the mountain and began harassing the south rifle pit whose
terminus was no more than 140 yards distant. [13]

While these preliminary actions flickered, Price sent his chief engineer,
Thomas Mackey, to the top of Shepherd Mountain to survey Fort Davidson
and the upper valley. Union sharpshooters at the fort quickly targeted Mackey, which led Mackey to stay no more than two minutes. The South Carolinian then scrambled back down the mountain and reported to Price just north
of Arcadia. Mackey's arrival at Price's headquarters coincided with that of
Fagan, who had just returned from his own personal trip to the top of Pilot
Knob Mountain. Although Marmaduke was absent conducting a reconnaissance of Shepherd Mountain, an impromptu council of war took place, last-
ing until no more than 11:30 AM. Using an older map of the area to illustrate
his observations, Mackey recommended taking advantage of the heights sur-

rounding Fort Davidson to bombard it into submission. Price, he suggested, should "place six or eight field pieces on the crest of Shepherd Mountain" and that this could be done within two hours. He then recommended that Fort Davidson "be invested by the remaining troops of the two divisions of Gen.'s Marmaduke and Fagan, with the remaining four pieces of artillery." A logical plan, it nonetheless had no other supporters. Lauchlan Maclean, Price's adjutant, wanted a quick strike into the fort if only because it contained the hated Ewing and Fletcher. Fagan called for a quick attack because the garrison was small and reinforcements from St. Louis likely. The attack, Fagan believed, should take only twenty minutes. Even Marmaduke, who was not physically present, supported a hasty assault. According to Mackey, Marmaduke sent word by a staff officer that with two guns atop Shepherd Mountain, "he could take the works in a few minutes." Price, who had initially favored Mackey's suggestion, now began to lean toward an assault. He then made up his mind to a direct attack when a group of local citizens pleaded with him not to shell the fort because they believed, incorrectly, that Ewing had coerced an undetermined number of "Southern residents," including young boys, into the fort.[14]

Price had therefore just squandered the gift Ewing had given him. Although Fort Davidson was entirely vulnerable to a cannonade, Price determined, instead, to try a frontal assault across open ground. It was a baffling decision. Price went against his first judgment and acceded to the wishes of two division commanders whom he distrusted greatly. One can only assume that the unreliable report of Southern sympathizers in the fort weighed heavily with the chivalric Price. There is also one other point. Price had become far too reliant upon his subordinates when he failed to get a firsthand look at the situation. Here, for the first time during the invasion, Price's age and physical condition had caught up with him. He could not scale the mountain and assess the situation for himself.

Lacking personal knowledge of the terrain and enemy dispositions, Price blindly made his plans for action. He determined that the battle would commence at 2:00 PM with four separate, but simultaneous, attacks that would nearly encircle Fort Davidson. Coordination of the assaults was critical, and Price emphasized it repeatedly to his commanders. From the east, McCray's and Slemons's brigades from Fagan's division would attack over Pilot Knob Mountain. To their immediate left, Cabell would press through the Ironton Gap toward the fort. Forming on Cabell's left and extending down the spur of Shepherd Mountain would be John B. Clark Jr.'s brigade of Marmaduke's

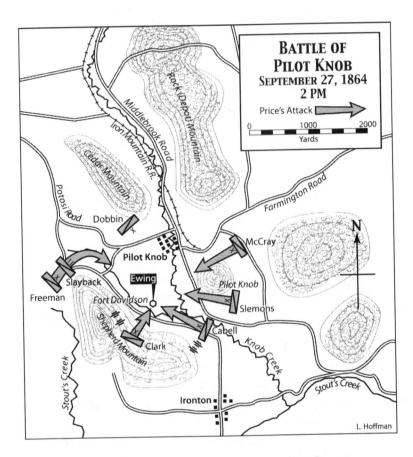

Figure 4.2.   Battle of Pilot Knob, September 27, 1864, 2 PM

division. Finally, Alonzo Slayback's battalion—which had been only recently recruited and attached to the Army of Missouri—and Freeman's brigade of
Marmaduke's division were to ride around the western perimeter of Shepherd Mountain and form up north of the fort near the Potosi Road. Price then
desired that they attack south from this isolated position. Further to the north,
and also astride the Potosi Road, Price placed Archibald Dobbin's brigade to
act as a reserve and block the garrison's escape. Although Price had decided
to forgo a heavy artillery bombardment, he ordered four artillery pieces to the
top of Shepherd Mountain to support the assault. As something of an insu-
rance policy to prevent Ewing's escape should he somehow evade Dobbin,
Price also sent a courier to Jo Shelby, ordering him south from Potosi.[15]

All told, Price would have about 4,700 men available for the assault as one of every five troopers were detailed as horse holders to remain behind the mountains. Ironically, these dispositions did not degrade Price's combat power. The horse holders were unarmed and could not have materially aided the assault. Still, many Confederates dreaded their prospects. Aside from Marmaduke and Fagan, there were a number of officers who argued against the plan. Objections were particularly strong in Fagan's division where Cabell and colonels John C. Wright and William A. Crawford protested strenuously, while arguing in favor of a massive bombardment from Pilot Knob Mountain. Wright was so incredulous of the order that he believed Fagan drunk. In the end, however, Crawford could only murmur that "it is General Fagan's orders and I must obey them."[16]

Between 11:30 and 2:00, the division commanders marshaled their troops to positions behind the mountains and out of the sight of Union cannoneers at Fort Davidson. During this period, the artillery had the most difficult maneuver. On Shepherd Mountain two pieces each from Hynson's battery and Harris's battery labored up steep and often obstructed trails to reach the summit. It was a Herculean task that was completed only when the gun crews hitched eight horses and six mules to each cannon. Nevertheless, two of the guns never made it to the top. One hour into the pull up the mountain they received orders to return down the mountain and report to Fagan's artillery chief at Ironton. All told, the Confederate struggle to haul their guns did not go unnoticed by the troops at Fort Davidson. During lulls in the exchanges of small arms fire, David Murphy heard the sounds of the Confederate artillerymen wielding picks and shovels in order to level off firing positions.[17]

Ewing did not stand idly while Price made his placements. After receiving and rebuffing yet another surrender demand, Ewing deployed two separate detachments outside Fort Davidson. Once again, Ewing turned to Major Wilson and Captain Campbell. Campbell's mission was the easier of the two as Ewing wanted him to scout in the direction of Shepherd Mountain. Although Campbell still thought it suicidal, he led the 14th Iowa to the base of Shepherd Mountain where he readily detected Cabell's brigade massing just beyond the Ironton Gap. After taking considerable fire and acting as something of an artillery forward observer for Murphy's heavy guns, Campbell succeeded in hustling his men back to the fort a little before 2:00 PM. Major Wilson was considerably less fortunate in his task. Ever since Wilson had retreated from the Ironton Gap, Ewing had him remain outside the fort in the vicinity of the iron furnace. At about 1:00 PM, Ewing ill advisedly provided

Wilson reinforcements and orders to establish a skirmish line on the northern slope of Pilot Knob Mountain and to hold the town of Pilot Knob. It was a senseless order that meant Wilson and his men could be easily overrun and sacrificed to no purpose at all.[18]

Regardless, at 2:00 PM Price's main effort began. Artillery fire from Shepherd Mountain signaled the attack, with one of the first shells entering the fort and blowing off the head of a Yankee gunner. Hearing the salvo, Clark's brigade became the first to move. Aligned four regiments abreast with one trailing in reserve, the brigade moved down Shepherd Mountain and almost immediately ran into trouble. The mountain was steep and littered with boulders and fallen trees that sent most of the men sprawling. Heavy artillery fire from the fort quickly added to the pandemonium as the brigade literally tumbled to the bottom of the mountain. There was, however, little time to sort the brigade out and dress its line because Cabell's brigade now poured through Ironton Gap. The right of Clark's brigade, consisting of Wood's battalion, Colonel Robert Lawther's 10th Missouri, and Colonel Cotton Greene's 3rd Missouri, pulled to the east to link with Cabell. This sidestep left a yawning gap of about 150 yards with the rest of Clark's brigade as the Confederate line now charged toward Fort Davidson. It also helped cause the left of Clark's brigade to begin lagging far behind the pace set by Cabell.[19]

Casualties soon mounted. Rifle balls and artillery shells blew holes through the ranks that, for Henry C. Luttrell of Lawther's 10th Missouri, created "a panorama, ghastly, horrible, yet sublime." Men by the dozen fell in clumps upon the plain. However, Cabell's brigade and the linked regiments of Clark's brigade continued the charge, yelling like "incarnate fiends."[20] Within minutes, they crossed over the dry bed of Knob Creek and then advanced another one hundred yards where the regiments stopped to deliver their first volley into the fort. With officers shouting frenzied commands, the wavering Confederate line charged the remaining two hundred yards to the fort. Despite Ewing having recalled the men in the south rifle pit, the defenders poured a devastating fire into Cabell's and Clark's brigades. With over 1,300 defenders now jammed into a fort designed to hold five hundred men, Ewing was able to create a nearly continuous chain of rifle fire as hundreds of men loaded weapons and passed them to shooters who were packed four deep on the parapet. Smoke hung thickly about the fort as Cabell, Lawther, Wood, and Greene led their men to the moat where they delivered one more volley up and into the fort, shredding numerous sandbags but hitting few Yankees. Cabell, whose horse had been shot forty yards from the fort, tried to exhort his men for one final push, but it was to no avail. The men turned and fled with many of Clark's brigade jumping into the creek bed, seeking cover. No doubt to the disgust of some, they jumped nearly on top of the troops from John Burbridge's 4th Missouri and William Jeffers's 8th Missouri, who never got past the beckoning safety of the creek bed.[21]

Burbridge and Jeffers were not the only Confederates to falter in the face of Fort Davidson's guns. Most of Fagan's right wing consisting of McCray's and Slemons's brigades cascaded down Pilot Knob Mountain and met with initial success when they captured the hated Major Wilson and dismantled his exposed command. While Wilson had just survived the battle, he would not survive the war. Six days later, Timothy Reeves discovered Wilson and six other men of the 3rd MSM among the prisoners in Price's trains. In the typical fashion of Missouri's guerrilla war, they would be executed. Not surprisingly, William Rosecrans later ordered the execution of seven of Price's captured soldiers. But for the immediate battle, Confederate success at Pilot Knob was short-lived. No sooner had the troops of McCray and Slemons spilled onto the base of the mountain than they came under a blistering direct fire from the fort. Within minutes, most of the Confederates had scattered. However, and contrary to T. J. Mackey's later testimony, some of Slemons's men did press on to the fort. Here, too, Cabell was the key. Just as Cabell and his veteran troops acted like a magnet drawing three regiments of Clark's brigade into the attack, so, too, did they draw the men of Colonel John C. Wright's regiment. Posted to Cabell's right, Colonel Wright stayed with his fellow Arkansan for most of the first charge. Wright, too, rode into the battle only to have his horse take a cannonball that eventually passed through the horse's chest and between Wright's legs. When Wright's men finally broke near the moat, Wright wound up carrying his severly wounded second-in-command, Lieutenant Colonel James W. Bowie, to the rear.[22]

The aggressive Cabell was hardly through. He rallied his veterans in the Ironton Gap and turned them around for a second charge. Henry Luttrell, who remained stuck in Knob Creek with the rest of the 10th Missouri, could only watch in awe when Cabell's dismounted cavalry marched forward as if they "were on parade battalion drill." This time, Cabell was supported by two artillery pieces (probably from Hughey's battery) that had taken position in Knob Creek near the Ironton Gap during the first attack. As Cabell went forward, the artillery followed him up the creek where it finally took a position one hundred yards from the fort. The gun crews then proceeded to hurl several rounds into the fort. The increase in morale that came with working the guns lasted only momentarily. Ewing and David Murphy, who at one point threw rocks at the Confederates, led an inspired defense of the fort that repelled Cabell's advance at least fifty yards from the fort, throwing it back once again in the direction of Ironton Gap. [23]

Sterling Price's plan had gone awry, and there was no better evidence of that than the sudden appearance of Alonzo Slayback's and Thomas Freeman's units just as Cabell's men retreated for the second time. According to Price's plan, these two commands were to have ridden around the western slope of Shepherd Mountain, aiming for the Potosi Road. They were then to attack south toward the fort at 2:00 PM in conjunction with all of the other units. For reasons never explained, Slayback and Freeman were now two hours late in hitting their start point for the attack, almost two hundred yards north of the terminus of the north rifle pit. No less perplexing, Slayback and Freeman allowed themselves to be distracted when they peeled off about two hundred men to continue northeast and strike at wagons and horses Ewing had left on the Middlebrook Road between Depot and Cedar mountains. It was then with a dramatically reduced command that Slayback and Freeman charged at nearly a right angle to the rifle pit. While unable to bring most of their weapons to bear upon the attacking Confederates, the defenders of the rifle pit, mostly men of the 3rd MSM, nevertheless repulsed the attack with the help of artillery and small arms fire from the fort. [24]

Even when the 3rd MSM abandoned the rifle pit, Slayback and Freeman could not penetrate the fort. With no other Confederate pressure on the fort at that time, Ewing was able to concentrate his available firepower against these charging Confederates. With commands made up almost entirely of recruits and conscripts, Slayback and Freeman quickly disengaged from the battle and headed north toward the base of Cedar Mountain. All that remained to finish the battle was for Cabell to try one more time to crack the fort. As proof of his leadership ability, if not his common sense, Cabell rallied his men in the Ironton Gap just as the action north of the fort petered out. He then formed his brigade in three long lines, each four ranks deep. As Clark's men looked on in paralyzed fear from Knob Creek, Cabell somehow got his soldiers moving one more time in a charge that swarmed up to the fort and down into its moat. It was a critical moment. Cabell's men had overcome the daunting specter of the moat. Although under normal circumstances it could have easily been traversed, the pressure and fears of combat turned the moat into an almost impenetrable void, which had previously forced them back without attempting to cross it. With Confederates now spilling into the moat, discipline began breaking down among the defenders. Dozens of Ewing's new recruits cowered in fear beneath the parapet. Near the gate of a sally port, another forty or fifty men charged the soldier guarding the gate in order to bust free. There were still several others who had managed to help themselves to a barrel of "medicinal whiskey," leaving them well nigh sloshed. Once again, however, the battle-tested Captain Campbell of the 14th Iowa recognized the danger of the situation and acted quickly. Commandeering a number of noncombatant blacks, he started ferrying hand grenades from the magazine to the soldiers still manning the parapet. In moments, the defenders had tossed enough of the grenades into the moat to kill and wound the Confederates caught there. The assault was thus finally broken, and Cabell's survivors fled first to Knob Creek and then to Ironton Gap. At that point, night began to fall, and only with a covering darkness did most of Clark's troops abandon the comforting walls of the Knob Creek for the exposed run to the gap. Scattered sniping and artillery fire continued for some time, but the day's fighting had ended. "All was hush," one Unionist remembered, "save the groans of the wounded and dying and the low hum of the men and officers as they became united again as companies."[25]

Further to the south, however, there was considerably more noise. Sterling Price, who had played little active role in the execution of the battle, now tried personally to rally his troops as they streamed to the rear. When the exhausted Cabell finally joined Price, he could only mutter, "General my Brigade never flickered—by G—d, Sir, she never flickered." Dismayed and perhaps humiliated, Price plotted to resume the attack at daybreak in the morning. By 8:00 PM he had formulated a new plan, but it hardly presaged victory. Although Price intended to haul six more pieces of artillery to the top of Shepherd Mountain, he did not intend an extended bombardment of Fort Davidson. Instead, he projected using the artillery for close support of yet another dismounted assault and one that would eventually include Shelby's troopers. Convinced of the necessity of a frontal attack, Price concluded that the only obstacle to success was the moat, and this he proposed to surmount with the lead troops carrying scaling ladders. As Chief Engineer Mackey and his men settled in at Ironton Cemetery for a long night of ladder making, disaffection began to brew within the ranks. Curiously, it was a disaffection that seems not to have blamed Price directly. Among those who left any account of the battle, there was talk of "unreasonable blunders," condemned commanders, and staff officers scorned. But strangely, there was little mention of Price as the root of the problems. James Fagan was, however, not so lucky. Cabell and Colonel Crawford were disgusted with him, and Colonel Wright still thought Fagan drunk. Some within the artillery discussed the battle that night and concluded Fagan was incompetent, while "Old Pap Price would direct the movements on the morrow and give us victory."[26]

Price, however, never got the chance to get that victory. At 9:00 PM, Ewing convened a wide array of his officers in a council of war. Much as it was the night before, Ewing solicited opinions about whether to attempt an evacuation of the fort. Ewing also noted to stay at this point meant that the garrison would eventually have to surrender if Price used his artillery effectively. Ewing's assessment assumed too much of Price's learning curve, but it did sufficiently spook his officers. When Thomas Fletcher and the men of the 3rd MSM pondered their potential fate as POWs, they voted to evacuate the fort. Once again, it appeared that Ewing had made the wrong decision. Price's troops completely surrounded the fort, and the area was going to be remarkably well lit as a large pile of coal at the furnace had caught fire and glowed eerily through the night. At first, Ewing made his preparations assuming that Price blocked all roads from the fort and Pilot Knob. According to Ewing, his only option was to abandon his wounded, horses, and artillery and slip out between the roads for Mineral Point, twenty-three miles to the north. But in a mysterious and last-minute twist, Union pickets around midnight ushered into Ewing's presence a boy who lived two miles up the Potosi Road. The boy then reported that Price had miraculously left the road unattended. The intelligence was flimsy, but it seemed Slayback and Dobbin had camped west of the Potosi Road about nine hundred yards from the fort. Astounded, Ewing modified his plan. He would now leave the fort through the north rifle pit, taking eighty mounted troopers and a section of light artillery, and then march to the Potosi Road that skirted the base of Cedar Mountain. As the men assembled for the escape, Ewing disabled his heavy artillery and piled any excess powder and ordnance in the garrison's magazine. By 1:00 AM, the garrison was ready to march, and one hour later the fort stood empty except for five men who had—unbeknownst to their comrades—fallen asleep amid the debris of the ramparts and a detachment of soldiers left behind to fire the magazine. Tense moments passed as the column snaked its way through a biting north wind to the Potosi Road where it then marched past the sleeping camps of Slayback and Dobbin. Somehow, Ewing's column drew little notice as it passed within eighty yards of the campfires to their left. Groggy Confederate sentries merely dismissed the column as fellow Southerners changing their positions. By 3:30 AM Ewing had made good his initial escape, and the fort erupted in a multicolored explosion that was heard at least twenty miles distant.[27]

While the explosion blew in windows throughout the town of Pilot Knob and debris rained down all around the fort, Sterling Price and the entire Confederate command structure remained oblivious to the importance of what had just happened. Price, who spent the night at Ironton, and his subordinate commanders ultimately concluded that the explosion signified nothing important. Within the Confederate ranks, some simply assumed that one of the fort's big guns had exploded, while others speculated that the Yankees had fled. What mattered, however, was what Price thought of the explosion, and he chose to ignore it. Only at daylight did Confederate pickets report the fort abandoned.[28]

By that time Ewing had already a four-hour head start, and it threw a stunned Price into a quandary. On the 27th, Price had received confirmation of A. J. Smith's presence near St. Louis and had therefore already decided to avoid that city entirely. He would seize the state capitol at Jefferson City instead. But the humiliation of Pilot Knob made Price more than willing to chase Ewing and delay the march on Jefferson City. To that end, by midmorning Price dispatched Marmaduke in pursuit of Ewing, minus Freeman's brigade that would remain behind to guard Price's trains and headquarters. In like fashion, Price kept Fagan's division in Pilot Knob to refit and clean up a mess that included sixteen pieces of heavy artillery, bales of blankets, and a large quantity of flour, bacon, and coffee. Price, who had yet to hear from Shelby in two days, also forwarded yet another set of orders to his junior division commander. This time Shelby was to join Marmaduke in the pursuit.[29]

As Price made these hurried dispositions, burial details fanned out around the area to collect bodies and inter them in a mass grave just south of the fort. Their work was grim, but it could have been a whole lot worse. For the Union, there were only twelve men killed from an army that numbered nearly 1,500 soldiers. By any measure, Ewing had escaped lightly. Assessing Confederate casualties, however, is more difficult. The tendency among historians has been to portray the battle as a bloodbath that, in the words of Richard Brownlee, "destroyed the combat effectiveness of two of the three divisions of Price's army." This seems hardly the case. The best estimate of Price's casualties shows that he lost, at most, five hundred killed and wounded from an army of over nine thousand men assembled in the Arcadia

Valley. At 6 percent, this casualty rate was remarkably low for an army that
had just attempted three frontal assaults of a fixed position. Even the losses in
the more exposed units were relatively small and certainly not crippling of
future actions. Colton Greene's 3rd Missouri, which had an aggregate
strength of 290 men, reported only three killed and twenty-six wounded.
More strikingly, Cabell's highly exposed veterans suffered 275 total casualties, yet this number was only 10 percent of a unit that had an aggregate
strength of 2,700 men. The casualty rate in these units would certainly be
much higher if detached personnel and horse holders were subtracted from
the aggregate strengths, but that is largely beside the point as those men
would be readily available for duty in future engagements. Ultimately,
Price's losses were comparatively light in the hard calculus of a war where
units frequently suffered casualty rates in excess of 50 percent.[30]

Although burying the dead occupied Price's men in the immediate aftermath of the battle, so, too, did some other matters. Several hundred wounded
from both sides needed attention, and Union and Confederate surgeons
worked together on soldiers scattered in houses about the town. Price posted
guards at the doorsteps of the wounded Yankees, prompting one such soldier
to later proclaim, "All honor to old Pap Price." The degree of cooperation
between Union and Confederate medical personnel was large. It was eventually best exemplified by S. D. Carpenter and a Confederate surgeon traveling
together to St. Louis in order to procure medical supplies for 215 badly
wounded Confederates and a far smaller number of Yankees left behind at
Pilot Knob. Before the two men reached St. Louis, Rosecrans had arrested
the Confederate surgeon, but there is no indication that Union authorities
mistreated the Confederate wounded once Price departed the Arcadia Valley.[31]

That the wounded Confederates were unmolested was something of a
minor miracle. Price's passage through the Arcadia Valley had inflicted
much damage upon the local population. Price had tried scrupulously to
avoid wanton destruction. He appointed a temporary provost marshall. He
placed countless guards on various homes and stores, and he directed his
officers to pay for whatever was confiscated. Much of this, however, was for
naught. While some officers took great care to pay for what they took, others
cared little. Similarly, the guards were too few and the opportunities for
plunder too great, especially when curious Confederates discovered Fort
Davidson's medicinal whiskey. It became open season on the inhabitants of
the valley as soldiers swarmed into homes and lifted all manner of bedding,

carpeting, clothes, and food. In Ironton, Fagan's men proved more adept at storming a guarded store than they had been in storming Fort Davidson. Adding to the confusion, local Southern sympathizers eagerly helped themselves to the bounty of their Northern neighbors, taking everything from horse collars to tea sets. The pillaging of the valley continued right up until the last of Fagan's troopers left on the evening of the 28th. Colonel John C. Wright, who had been charged with policing stragglers and—ironically—protecting private property, found a saloon basement filled with alcohol as his regiment marched out of town. He immediately halted the unit in front of the establishment and ordered "some of the boys into the cellar." In short order, and much to his later personal regret, Wright and his entire regiment were soused, which then made for a rollicking ride to Caledonia. Although Price was not aware of Wright's misadventures, reports of disorder filtered back to him as he rode north. Just as important, Thomas C. Reynolds and Trusten Polk had also either observed or heard of depredations and began agitating Price to take action. By Price's encampment at Richwoods on the 30th, Old Pap responded by creating a permanent Provost Marshal Department, consisting of fifty men from each brigade. Price placed the recently wounded Lieutenant Colonel John Bull of Cabell's brigade in charge of the Department, and only time would tell if these were measures enough. [32]

In the meantime, Price had to catch Ewing, and much depended upon Jo Shelby. By daybreak on the 28th, Shelby had already begun marching south from Potosi. None of Price's couriers had reached him, but Shelby nonetheless headed for the Arcadia Valley, which he knew to be Price's last known objective. At Caledonia, fourteen miles north of Pilot Knob, Shelby's scouts blundered into Ewing's advance. Ewing was no less surprised, but he immediately altered his plan. Instead of continuing his march to Mineral Point, Ewing now intended to lead his little army west to the fortified Union army depot at Rolla via the small town of Webster (modern-day Palmer). For his part, Shelby was slow to react to the skirmishing and believed that A. J. Smith had somehow gotten in front of him. He thus delayed pushing into Caledonia for a couple of hours, and only at that time did he get word of the affair at Pilot Knob and Price's orders to link with Marmaduke. [33]

While Shelby hesitated, Ewing marched hard for Webster, which was a small hamlet containing nothing more than a blacksmith shop, a store, and some militia. Ewing's exhausted and famished men arrived there just after sundown and a total march of almost thirty miles. Over the next few hours and as a cold rain fell, the men alternately ate, slept, and stole each other's

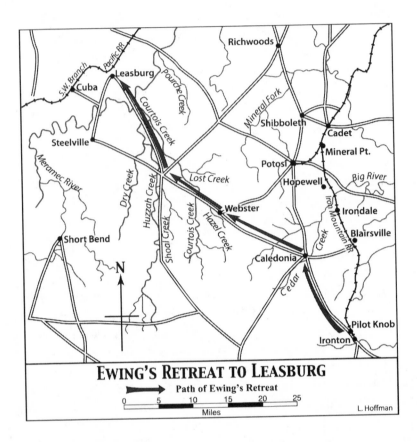

Figure 4.3. Ewing's Retreat to Leasburg

horses. No man's animal was safe as the dismounted men took what they could find unguarded. By 11:00 PM, however, Ewing ordered his belea-guered army forward again. Ever conscious that the Confederates would soon catch up with his largely dismounted force, Ewing not only kept march-ing but also he yet again changed course. From Webster, he had planned on continuing his march along the substantial Caledonia to the Steelville Road, but it was one that would have left his army susceptible to various Confeder-ate flanking and turning movements. Ewing then looked at his maps and discovered a ridgeline just to his west that ran sixteen miles to the northwest, ending about seven miles from Leasburg. No more than a hotel doubling as a railroad station on the Southwest Branch of the Pacific Railroad, Leasburg was just thirty miles up the track from Rolla, and it could be readily rein-forced. Ewing could not have chosen a better route. Carved out of the waters of the Huzzah Creek and the Courtois River, the ridge offered a fairly secure, if rocky and forested, avenue for Ewing's retreat. All that he needed to do was keep marching. [34]

Nevertheless, progress was miserably slow. Darkness, poor roads, and a cold, driving rain punished the men. The army tottered to a crawl. A lantern had to be carried at the head of the column and candles placed alongside of the road so the following units could remain in the road. The pace of the army was now further exacerbated by the presence of a large number of civilian refugees and EMM who had attached themselves to the column as it fled. As soldiers literally held onto the clothing and equipment of the men in front of them so as not to get lost, the army sloshed west to Hazel Creek and then northwest to a point where the creek joined the swollen Courtois River. The bedraggled men then crossed the Courtois before it had to stop due to the darkness and the increasing number of stragglers. Ewing had marched only five miles, but the relative security of the ridgeline lurked ahead. By daybreak, Ewing had his men moving again, and they started climbing the ridge around 8:00. [35]

Ewing had made it to the ridge just in time. Marmaduke and Shelby had finally arrived. Throughout the pursuit from Caledonia, Marmaduke's division had taken the lead, riding at a "trot march." During the daylight hours, tracking Ewing had been fairly easy. The Unionists had not only left a trail of debris, but stragglers littered the road unwittingly leading the Confederates on. Although Lawther's 10th Missouri ran headlong into Ewing's rearguard on the morning of the 29th, Marmaduke failed to take advantage of some initial confusion in the Union ranks that created a chain reaction of panic first within the 3rd MSM and then the 47th Missouri Infantry. Much as it had been at Pilot Knob, the 14th Iowa stood as a bulwark around which the other units, and the artillery, could rally. For the entire sixteen-mile length of the ridgeline, Marmaduke's troops charged ineffectually into Ewing's rearguard. By the late afternoon and about the time the Yankee column descended the ridge onto flatter and more open terrain, Marmaduke exchanged places with Shelby, who then had no more luck in forcing Ewing's rearguard back upon the main body. [36]

Nightfall on the 29th found Ewing's army rushing wildly into Leasburg. It was an army on the verge of collapse. Exhaustion had created apathy among many of the men that led them either to straggle or simply to desert. Of the 1,300 men who had begun the march there were between six hundred and seven hundred left. [37]

Consequently, Ewing's officers now threatened to shoot any man who attempted to desert, which then resulted in at least one soldier being gunned down. The lead element of the army was an almost weaponless mob and totally unsure of what was taking place to its rear. Rumors ran wild, and when the advance stumbled into the hotel and railroad cut at Leasburg, soldiers and refugees alike began shouting that Ewing and the artillery had been captured. Ewing's arrival shortly thereafter stabilized the situation, and he ordered the troops to improve breastworks that a unit of the EMM had started and only recently abandoned. Made of railroad ties, the breastworks sat atop a ridge that had been cleared of timber for at least two hundred yards to the south and east. Although Shelby made one small push against the Union line that night, he postponed further action until he could consult with Marmaduke. As Shelby then pulled back, a train mysteriously rolled into the depot from the northeast. The train was headed for Rolla and filled with ammunition, shovels, picks, food, and three barrels of whiskey. Ewing's first response was to take this unexpected gift and load it with as many of his men as possible and steam to Rolla. Mounted troops and artillery would march beside the train on roads parallel to the track. As units thus began loading the train in the darkness, Ewing and his staff spotted fires above and below Leasburg. Concluding that the Confederates had cut the track, Ewing reversed his decision. To the painful dismay of the troops, Ewing ran from the Lea Hotel and shouted, "For God's sake, boys, get back to your places behind the defenses, for we are all likely to be killed at any moment." In a move that aggravated a number of troops even more, Ewing also ordered the destruction of the three barrels of whiskey aboard the train. Some soldiers were hardly deterred by the sight of the whiskey flowing along the tracks. With canteens hurriedly emptied of water, soldier after soldier scraped his canteen along the gravel and mud trying to get some of the precious liquid. One blue coat was even spied lapping up the drink from a hoof print in the mud.[38]

Ewing thus passed a nervous night waiting for the expected attack on the morning of the 30th. Although the army had overcome a great deal to reach Leasburg, physical exhaustion and the steady erosion of manpower led many to lose all hope and talk openly of surrender. However, and as if by divine intervention, a big Confederate push never happened. Despite some scattered probing actions and skirmishing, Marmaduke and Shelby had decided against pursuing Ewing anymore. With their own troops and animals rapidly wearing out and Ewing ensconced behind his railroad ties, the Confederate generals thought it best to leave Ewing just where he was and instead rejoin Price heading north into the heart of Missouri. To that end, the Confederates began withdrawing late on the morning of the 30th while Colton Greene's regiment started a noisy series of demonstrations against Ewing's breastworks. A little after 12:30 and four wounded Confederates later, it was all over. With no Federal pursuit possible, Greene pulled slowly away from Leasburg and eventually overtook the main column at Sullivan's Station near midnight.[39]

As the Confederates marched northeast along the railroad, they were also rejoined by John Q. Burbridge's 4th Missouri. The previous day, Marmaduke had dispatched Burbridge on a side raid to Cuba, about eleven miles south of Leasburg along the railroad. By 2:00 PM, Burbridge had returned from a foray that had begun to seem typical of the invasion. While Burbridge had successfully burned the depot at Cuba and ripped up over four hundred yards of track, an entire platoon of his men had conducted an even more successful attack upon a saloon and millinery store. Within a short period of time, every one of the men emerged from their conquest drunk, wearing ladies' hats and wraps.[40]

Marmaduke's and Shelby's disengagement from Ewing brought an inglorious end to this stage of the campaign. The attack on Ewing in the Arcadia Valley had been filled with promise and was squandered by Price's ill-conceived plan. Making matters worse, a simple lack of vigilance had allowed Ewing to start an escape that turned into a nearly epic chase and ended in complete failure. Although most of Ewing's men lauded their general for getting them out safely, Captain William Leeper provided a more sober assessment when he addressed his fellow officers and concluded, "Gentlemen it[']s my candid opinion we all got away by good luck and damned awkwardness."[41]

If Price could take comfort in anything at that point, it was in the fact that his army remained a potent threat. Pilot Knob was a setback, but it was not debilitating given his relatively slight losses. Moreover, Price now headed for Jefferson City and the Missouri River valley where Confederate support was strongest and potential recruits most plentiful. Sterling Price's dream of retaking the state was still quite alive.

Chapter Five

For God's Sake, Give Me Authority to Do Something

Confederate defeat at Pilot Knob and A. J. Smith's presence at St. Louis had not yet changed Sterling Price's intention to reclaim Missouri for the Confederacy. These events only altered the fashion in which he would achieve the goal. Price originally desired to take St. Louis, the state's most populous and economically important city. Although St. Louis still remained the grand prize of the expedition and the key to staking a legitimate claim to the state, Price realized he lacked the strength to attack the city. His dreams then rested upon the tens of thousands of men he hoped to recruit and the military hardware he planned on capturing. Unfortunately for Price, the process of scouring the countryside for men and equipment allowed for a breakdown in discipline that the Confederate cause in Missouri could not afford. Furthermore, the acquisition of men and equipment was clearly incompatible with rapid movement. Subsidiary columns needed to break off from Price's main body, and such operations required time to reach objectives, suppress enemy resistance, and then return to the main body. These operations would bring the Union time to concentrate troops against Price and thus eventually jeopardize his ability to stay in Missouri.

Absent a first strike to St. Louis, Price concluded that his army should move to Jefferson City. There were two reasons for this. First, Price believed that Jefferson City contained a wealth of military supplies and that it was guarded by inconsequential militia. Second, and more important, the capture of Jefferson City carried with it the political hopes of the entire expedition. Price desired the reclamation of Missouri for the Confederacy, and there

could be no better assertion of Confederate resolve and power than to occupy
the state capital. For Thomas C. Reynolds, the occupation of Jefferson City
would mean governing legitimacy. For Price, the occupation of Jefferson
City would be of incalculable value to persuading potential recruits that he
meant to stay and that their enlistment would be a good investment of time
and effort. Just as Price had intuitively calculated the benefits of striking
Jefferson City, he wanted to move quickly.[1]

But as Price moved north along the Potosi Road on the morning of September 28th, it became evident that he could not march with the quickness he
desired. Just as he had determined to capture Jefferson City, so, too, had he
made the decision to send both Marmaduke and Shelby chasing after Ewing
in a westerly direction. By the afternoon of the 28th, Price had marched
twelve miles to a point just south of Caledonia with the consolidated trains of
the army and most of Fagan's division. On the 29th, and by the time Marmaduke and Shelby had finally given up their chase of Ewing, Price's main
body had moved another twenty-two miles northward, camping in the vicinity of Shibboleth. Price resumed the march on the 30th, but he chose riskily
to divide his army once again despite lacking any concrete news from Marmaduke and Shelby. After marching only ten miles and stopping at the small
crossroads town of Richwoods, Price dispatched Lieutenant Colonel J. F.
Davies's battalion of three hundred men from Fagan's division east to DeSo-

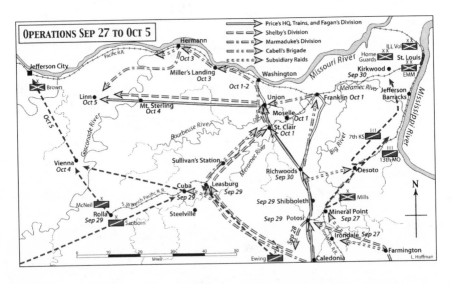

Figure 5.1. Operations, September 27–October 5, 1864

to with instructions to destroy its depot along the Iron Mountain Railroad. He also ordered Cabell's brigade to continue marching north until it hit and destroyed a section of the Pacific Railroad east of the town of Franklin. Although both subsidiary raids were successful, Cabell's was not without moments of caution. First, local militia resisted Cabell's entry, leaving six Confederate casualties and causing Cabell's staff to believe that A. J. Smith's corps of infantry was in the area. Second, and in a situation that seemed to foreshadow the breakdown of discipline even within one of Price's veteran units, a number of Cabell's men somehow got drunk and were unable to complete the physical task of destroying the railroad. Cabell could only rip up the track with the help of captured railroad workers.[2]

Unaware of Cabell's difficulties, Price remained headquartered at Richwoods for the rest of the 30th. Here he awaited Slemons's brigade, which had been detailed to police the battlefield at Pilot Knob, attend to the dead and wounded, and then herd prisoners, volunteers, and conscripts northward. When Slemons did catch up to the army's headquarters, Price started a process of shedding many of his prisoners. Hundreds of men had been captured or conscripted ever since the army had entered the Arcadia Valley, and Price now tried to sort through the mob and determine who would be a reliable, or at least semireliable, soldier for the Confederacy. Uniformed enemy combatants were generally paroled, while a senior officer, including General Cabell, personally interviewed the conscripts and civilian prisoners. Typical of such interviews was one with Cyrus Russell. Russell had been pulled from his home in the eastern Arcadia Valley on the 26th and had marched along with the army in the rain and mud until the morning of the 29th when he and several others appeared before Cabell. In a strikingly short interview, Cabell asked each one, "Are you a Union man?" Russell's simple, though anxious, response of "yes" got him quickly released from the army, while the others who answered "no" disappeared into the Confederate ranks. Russell had correctly guessed that the Confederates did not want men "whose guns would have been more ready to shoot backwards than forwards."[3] For Price, however, the difficulties of sorting through prisoners and conscripts would be a never-ending task throughout the life of the expedition.

On a much less vexatious note for Price, the halt at Richwoods allowed a small, yet critical, wagon train containing 150,000 percussion caps to catch up to the army. John Magruder had sent this badly needed shipment from Camden on September 15th, and its arrival was fortuitous because Price had yet to capture a substantial amount of Yankee ordnance. Nonetheless, the real significance of the shipment was in Magruder's accompanying letter to Price. In it, Magruder unequivocally—though far too optimistically—informed Price that he "was operating on the lower Arkansas to divert the enemy from you."[4] This information Price received with no small amount of satisfaction as rumors had begun circulating that Frederick Steele's army was fast approaching from the south. Magruder's news thus emboldened Price with the implication that Steele was either pinned down or in the process of being chased from the region. Either way, Price had just been given a greater sense of security to loiter in Missouri. Fortunately for Price, Magruder did not need to campaign actively in order to immobilize Frederick Steele at Little Rock. Steele had been frozen in place ever since the spring, and it would take a near act of God to pry him from his fortifications.

When Price resumed his march on October 1st, rain fell throughout most of the day. With mud thus clogging the road, Old Pap and the trains slogged about twenty miles west to St. Clair. Only here, along the Southwest Branch of the Pacific Railroad, did Price finally link up with the long-absent Marmaduke and Shelby, whose division now included Alonzo Slayback's new battalion of recruits. Price then directed them to march northwest for Union, the seat of Franklin County.[5]

The appearance of Price's army in Franklin County set off a panic among the predominant Unionist population. Hundreds of citizens fled across the Missouri River to Augusta and were followed shortly thereafter by most of the 54th EMM, which William Rosecrans had ordered to defend the area's bridges. The flight of the 54th EMM surprised few people in Washington County. The 54th, to one observer, was composed overwhelmingly of Southern sympathizers with "a decided aversion to guns."[6]

Still, not all of the EMM fled. No less than three companies of General Orders 107 militia, which had been hurriedly incorporated into the EMM, stayed behind to defend the towns of Union and Washington. Shortly before noon on October 1, the militia defending Union was roused to action when two riders galloped into town warning of Price's advance. Showing no small amount of pluck, two companies totaling about two hundred men quickly erected breastworks in some woods southeast of the town. By four o'clock, John B. Clark Jr.'s brigade appeared in their front. Clark quickly deployed his troops by bringing up a section of Major Joseph H. Pratt's artillery and dismounting all of his men except Lawther's and Jeffers's regiments. As Jeffers moved to the left, or south, of Clark's line and Lawther marched to the right of the line to block any possible Yankee retreat toward St. Louis, a skirmish ensued. Clark's dismounted advance was met with two volleys of musketry from the militia, which then fled once Pratt's artillery lobbed a few rounds into their works. Lawther's regiment inflicted most of the damage upon the militia when it then charged into Union and effectively ended the engagement by capturing the courthouse filled with militia. Brief though the skirmish may have been, it had cost the militia severely. Thirty-two men were killed and seventy were captured, while the Confederates reported only one man wounded. It was, in other words, a skirmish in which Price's troops had killed almost three times as many Yankees as they had at the Battle of Pilot Knob.[7]

For the next several days, Price shepherded his army west toward Jefferson City. Though Price and his major commanders were briefly reunited at Union, Old Pap divided the army once again for the push on the capital. Beginning on the 2nd, Marmaduke headed northwest to Washington and then proceeded west along a line that hugged both the Pacific Railroad and the Missouri River. Price attached himself and his trains to a column including Shelby's and Fagan's divisions. Marching generally in a cavalry column of twos stretching seven miles, this group took a more direct approach to Jefferson City along a road that measured nearly eighty miles and passed through Mount Sterling and Linn. For both columns it was a continuation of the veritable happy times that had attended their march since Price had left Pilot Knob on the 28th and Marmaduke and Shelby had finally turned from Ewing on the 30th. William Rosecrans had as of yet been unable to mount a serious opposition to Price, and the Confederates easily brushed aside various militia while destroying numerous railroad bridges and depots.[8]

Of Price's two columns, Marmaduke's had the most eventful march. On the 2nd it entered the town of Washington and then followed that up the next day by marching over thirty miles along the Pacific Railroad to Miller's Landing. There, Marmaduke's troopers had the good fortune to meet up with an eastbound train filled with, among other things, four hundred weapons, including Sharps carbines and Austrian muskets. Marmaduke did not, however, pause to disburse the weapons. Almost immediately he ordered his division toward Hermann, another twelve miles up the Missouri River. After a hard ride in a rainstorm, Marmaduke approached the outskirts of Hermann late in the afternoon of the 3rd. Colton Greene's regiment took the lead, and three miles from Hermann it ran into a small militia outpost, which it then drove into the center of town. After a short pause, Marmaduke ordered Greene to charge into Hermann and take a thinly held militia position that included one iron 6-pound cannon. Greene then stampeded into town, scattering the militia and capturing their cannon. With night then falling, Marmaduke stopped the advance, leaving the bulk of his troops outside of Hermann.[9]

At daylight on the 4th a cold and heavy rain continued to fall. As the rain turned the streets of Hermann into a quagmire, Marmaduke marched his troops through the town and south toward Linn where he hoped to rejoin Price, Fagan, and Shelby. While at Hermann, Marmaduke tried to take advantage of the train he had captured at Miller's Landing. Late the previous night, the train with its two freight cars and one flat car had rolled into Hermann. Not only did Marmaduke then distribute its valuable cargo but also he jammed Wood's battalion aboard with all of its horses and one piece of artillery for a trip up the road to the mouth of the Gasconade River where they hoped to burn the bridge. Perhaps fortunately for Wood's tightly packed troopers, the ride was short-lived. Two companies of the 34th EMM guarded the bridge over the Gasconade, and they hurriedly ripped up a large chunk of track on the approaches to the river before fleeing in the direction of Jefferson City. Forced to dismount the train a few miles from their objective, Wood's battalion proceeded onto the bridge and burned it before heading to Linn.[10]

Despite the lack of any great Union resistance on the march to Jefferson City, Price was greatly disappointed in the behavior of his army. Again and again, Price attempted to enforce discipline on his widely flung soldiers. On October 4th, two soldiers from Fagan's division were executed for desertion. On October 9th, four officers and one NCO from Shelby's division were reduced in rank and their horses taken away for straggling. On October 14th, Price ordered Fagan to use unit funds to pay for his men's hog thieving. So it was that despite a series of orders prohibiting theft, the activation of a sizeable army-wide provost marshal detachment, and several well-publicized punishments, Price's men still found it easy to commit depredations. As recollected by one of Price's generals, M. Jeff Thompson, the army "left in its track a line of robbery, almost as bad as that of Sherman's bummers." In many cases, the depredations were indiscriminate; Price's men were not terribly picky about whom they plundered. According to Gert Goebel, a Washington County Unionist, "The logic of the rebels was short and conclusive: 'We will take from our enemies but expect our friends to give and if they won't do it, we will take also.'" At Linn, one Southern sympathizer woke up to find all of his fences burned and his entire stock of sheep, hogs, and cattle eaten. After viewing the devastation of Richwoods, Unionist Bates Frissell happily noted, "I think that some of the rebs that wanted Price to come through the country have their full of the rade [*sic*] as their property was taken with the Unions." Writing from Big River, Frissell's sister, Carrie, described a similar tendency with Price's men treating Southern sympathizers "worse if anything than the unions [*sic*]."[11]

Nevertheless, the propensity of Southern sympathizers to suffer damage generally paled in comparison to that of their Northern sympathizing neighbors. Marmaduke's Missourians, in particular, viewed this segment of the invasion as a glorious opportunity to mix revenge with a sense of entitlement when it came to acquiring food, clothing, and fresh transportation. For the men of Lawther's regiment, the plundering of the town of Washington was "great fun." As recorded by Henry Luttrell, Lawther's troops smashed in the doors and windows of stores and took whatever they wanted. One nearby resident, W. G. Tate, found himself caught in this maelstrom, and he later glumly noted the personal loss of $762 in Greenbacks, two mares, nine head of cattle, three suits of clothes, two saddles and bridles, ten acres of corn, four thousand bushels of oats, and the "boots taken off my feet." Although this sort of activity was evident all along Price's march, the town of Union was perhaps hardest hit. As one Federal soldier observed on October 4th, "the Rebs have been thru this place like a dose of salts." Confederate Lieutenant Frank Barnes, a former resident of Union, was particularly anxious to settle old grudges. He singled out the homes of Yankee Lieutenant Colonel A. W. Maupin and his mother for destruction. Other Confederates went on a rampage in Union when it was discovered that two storeowners in town had removed all of their goods to St. Louis in advance of the raid. The soldiers promptly shredded the stores and the proprietors' homes. Not surprisingly, some Confederates were willing to do far more than just plunder hapless Northern sympathizers. By one estimate, twenty-eight civilians lost their lives in Franklin County alone. Much of this violence can be attributed to the army's passage through a stretch of territory containing a large and much demonized German population. Upon entering the town of Union, William M. McPheeters tartly noted that all true Missourians were more than anxious to be "rid of Dutch and Yankee domination." Sadly, Confederate malfeasance—or xenophobia—did not stop with simple murder. Shortly after Marmaduke's division moved through Union, allegations surfaced of sexual assault against two German women, Mrs. Charles Schmidt and Mrs. Frank Scheyver.[12]

Although the allegations could normally be dismissed as the typical hyperbole of the fiercely anti-Confederate *Missouri Democrat*, which reported the incidents, the newspaper's willingness and ability to name the victims of a sexual crime cast little doubt upon their existence. The episode itself raises at least two points. First, and what is perhaps most striking, was the essential rarity of sexual assaults during the expedition. These were, in fact, the only credible allegations of a sexual crime made against Price's generally ill-disciplined men. Second, the rarity of sexual assaults confirmed the simple calculation of many Union men who fled the region in advance of Price's army. They believed that while the invading Confederates would readily execute or conscript them, a prevailing notion of masculine honor would protect their women from any physical abuse. That their own behavior might have stood as an abandonment of masculine honor was well nigh lost in the flood of male refugees to St. Louis and points beyond. As Willard Frissell of Desoto concluded, it was simply "a general thing" that "females & their property [were] left to the mercy of Rebs."[13]

The unruliness of Price's soldiers was not without other qualifications. First, the Confederates did not destroy all that they came across. Price had issued several injunctions against the plundering or destruction of private property, and many of his men seemed to obey the orders, albeit with a notable inclination to forget that stores and businesses were a species of private property. Carrie Frissell noted with satisfaction that "the Rebs did not treat [us] as bad as some of the merchants[.] They never came in our house." In like fashion, officers and men chose to exempt horses from the category of private property and either stole them outright or simply "exchanged" their broken-down nags for healthier stock. Nonetheless, there was a demonstrable attempt by Price's officers and men to avoid the ransacking of private dwellings, which then provoked a sense of disbelief among Northern sympathizers. More than a little bit shocked, Willard Frissell could only conclude that the Confederates either did not have enough time to plunder or "that they were gorged & could not carry more." While Frissell may well have been correct, a number of Price's units retained a sense of discipline and actively sought to protect private property. In Desoto, Davies's battalion of Fagan's division put out fires that spread from the railroad depot to private homes. In Washington, a nearly identical situation occurred when a Confederate officer ordered his troops to douse a fire that threatened several homes. In Franklin County, Gert Goebel believed that some Confederate authority had issued orders against the burning of private property if only because the Confederates believed that they had retaken the state. [14]

A second qualification concerning the destructiveness of Price's army is that not all depredations can be attributed directly to his men. Various bands of bushwhackers and outlaws traveled on the fringes of Price's army, and they more than took advantage of the situation to better plunder and intimidate the citizenry. Gert Goebel took note of this when guerrillas rode through his neighborhood in advance of Price's army. After the guerrillas lifted everything that could be carried away, they were followed into town by what Goebel called "real soldiers." Goebel managed then to entertain a number of officers, noting that "they were as courteous as in a ball room" and left with "a compliment for my daughters." Similarly, some of the murders of the local German population in Franklin County can be better attributed to bushwhackers than troops associated with Price. This was unquestionably the case when EMM from St. Louis finally rode into the vicinity of Washington a few days after Price had left the area. At that time, one soldier later recalled riding up to a house filled with weeping German women and discovering that bushwhackers had just recently executed one of their men. Although Price and his troops were nowhere near Washington at the time of the incident, they were irrevocably, and unfortunately, linked to its occurrence. It was a situation repeated throughout the invasion, and there was little desire on the part of Northern sympathizers to separate Price and his men from the acts of the bushwhackers. The *Missouri Democrat* captured this sentiment neatly when it proclaimed Price the "father of all outrages committed, even by the bushwhackers and guerrillas in his track." [15]

The bushwhackers were not the only group outside of Price's army to participate in the general mayhem associated with the expedition. Thousands of claims filed against the state after the war bear witness to a Unionist population looted by its own troops. In county after county, the EMM especially chose to plunder and forage liberally. In Monroe County, for example, a company of the 50th EMM visited Darius Alverson's farm and cleaned out both his fields and pantries, taking eighty bushels of oats, ten barrels of corn, twenty turkeys, five chickens, and twenty gallons of molasses. Near Vienna, men from two separate companies of the 63rd EMM masqueraded as bushwhackers to better steal from the locals. As might be expected, Southern sympathizers tended to suffer more as even official directives sanctioned stealing from them. On October 16th, Rosecrans's chief of staff, Colonel John V. Dubois, ordered one hundred wagons to head from Rolla to Jefferson

City with the terse command to "forage on the rebel sympathizers." Under such circumstances, horses, saddles, and food were all favorite targets of the EMM, particularly when they could be seized in advance of Price's approach. The wonder, then, was not so much what the Confederates themselves took or destroyed as they marched through Missouri but rather that there was often anything left for them to plunder.[16]

With parts of Missouri then being picked clean, William Rosecrans struggled to divine Price's route and intentions. It was only late on September 25th that he had concluded Price was indeed in Missouri and that Governor Willard P. Hall needed to activate the EMM throughout the state with orders to report to the various U.S. district commanders. The following day, Rosecrans issued a proclamation, exhorting Unionists to resist "Price and his recreant Missourians." Although Old Rosey called for all able-bodied men to join a militia—any kind of militia—and "bring arms, if you have any, horses if you can," he hardly knew where to point them. Even after the Battle of Pilot Knob, all that Rosecrans could be sure of was that Price was definitely in southeast Missouri. Price's and Fagan's march north toward Richwoods and the presence of Shelby and Marmaduke along the southwest branch of the Pacific Railroad only confused matters more. Was Price headed toward Jefferson City or St. Louis? Or, perhaps, were his recruiting efforts successful enough so that he might try attacking both cities simultaneously? Rosecrans thus played it safe by continuing to concentrate troops for the defense of Jefferson City and St. Louis.[17]

Within St. Louis and its environs, Rosecrans counted about six thousand experienced troops, which included A. J. Smith's 4,500 infantry and 1,500 cavalry from the 7th Kansas, 13th Missouri, and Merrill's Horse. Far less reliable was a hastily assembled conglomeration of militia, consisting of 4,400 EMM under the command of Bridadier General E. C. Pike, five thousand "Home Guards" commanded by Senator B. Gratz Brown, and five regiments of one-hundred-day volunteers from Illinois. Though not terribly reassuring, the availability of the militia freed Rosecrans to post A. J. Smith's troops to Kirkwood, about twelve miles west of the city along the Pacific Railroad, when he discovered Price at Richwoods on the 30th. As most reports continued to show that Price possessed an army of at least twenty thousand men, Rosecrans was content to remain on the defensive around St. Louis while awaiting the arrival of even more veterans in the form of Mower's four thousand infantry and two thousand cavalry from Arkansas.[18]

All the while Rosecrans assembled this force around St. Louis, another motley collection of troops coalesced at Jefferson City. On September 23rd, Rosecrans had started this concentration of manpower when he ordered Brigadier General Egbert B. Brown, commander of the District of Central Missouri, to forward a mixture of MSM and volunteer units totaling 2,500 men to Jefferson City. The very next day, Brown got authorization to call out all the available EMM in the area, which then added about 1,500 men to the budding defense of the capital city.[19]

By October 1st, Brown's troops began flowing into the city and were immediately put to work alongside the local citizenry—and convicts from the penitentiary—digging a line of entrenchments three miles long and containing five fortifications. The line was based on the city's original defenses started in 1861 by John C. Fremont. That line began west of Wears Creek at College Hill and then largely followed the outer trace of the creek as it curled around the city, first to the south and then to the east. The line then terminated near the penitentiary. However, Brown decided wisely to shorten the southern face of the line by bringing it back across Wears Creek and running it along High Street. Brown and his men got some much-needed useful intelligence on September 30th when Rosecrans located Price marching north at Richwoods. At that time, Old Rosey ordered the commander of the District of North Missouri, Brigadier General Clinton B. Fisk, to reinforce the capital "with all dispatch."[20]

It was, however, a difficult order. While Fisk had upward of 6,500 men under his command, they were scattered all about the northwest, but particularly between the Hannibal and Saint Joseph Railroad and the Missouri River. Distance thus presented Fisk a problem in concentrating his force, but it was by no means the only one. Guerrilla activity remained high north of the Missouri River, and Fisk hesitated to pull all of his troops from that quarter. More problematically, hundreds of EMM refused to budge through either fear or Southern sympathies. It was a situation that on October 4th provoked one Unionist near Brookfield to write Fisk and fulminate: "For God's sake give me authority to do something regardless of these milk-and-water commands, who [*sic*] dare not move an inch from their block-houses." Against such difficulties, Fisk succeeded only in concentrating about 1,800 men in Jefferson City by October 7th. Unfortunately, the majority of these men were no more trained than the EMM and local citizen-volunteers Egbert Brown had already accumulated. According to Fisk, at least one thousand of his freshly arrived troops "had never been drilled an hour."[21]

Of considerably more value and perhaps the critical element in the defense of the capital was the arrival of a cavalry force of 2,400 troopers and eight pieces of artillery commanded by the combative Brigadier General John McNeil. Of medium height and a powerful physique, McNeil possessed a brusque personality that ingratiated few people. A notorious guerrilla fighter, McNeil was behind the Palmyra Massacre in 1862 where he had summarily executed ten prisoners. McNeil's status as a butcher and black-flag Yankee was ensured when he also publicly took credit for executing an additional seventeen prisoners. [22]

Although McNeil's tactical incompetence would be revealed later in the campaign, his march to Jefferson City was prescient and daring. Commanding the District of Rolla, McNeil had ordered a relief column for Ewing at Leasburg and then correctly guessed on October 3rd that Price was heading for Jefferson City. With the telegraph lines to St. Louis severed and lacking any orders from Rosecrans, McNeil determined to send as many troops as possible to the capital. Setting off from Rolla early on the 4th, McNeil also directed Brigadier General John B. Sanborn, then camped at Cuba with a brigade of cavalry from Springfield, to join him at Vienna before then marching to the relief of Jefferson City. A lawyer and Republican politician before the war, Sanborn had raised a regiment of Minnesota infantry in December 1861 and then advanced to command a division in the Vicksburg campaign. Despite extensive combat experience with the infantry, this was Sanborn's first time commanding a large force of cavalry in the field. No matter his relative inexperience with the cavalry, Sanborn tended to the vainglorious, and he resented being subordinate to McNeil. Only time would tell if Sanborn's ego matched his cavalry skill. But on the afternoon of the 5th and after a march of seventy miles through rain and mud, McNeil's and Sanborn's combined force entered Brown's lines in Jefferson City. [23]

The arrival of McNeil and Sanborn was timely. Not only did it add 2,400 troops to the city's defenses, but it came just as Price began bearing down on the city. Price's army, which had been divided into two columns as it approached Jefferson City, had reconstituted itself early on October 5th in the vicinity of Linn, about twenty miles to the west of the capital. It was, however, a fairly curious move. Although Price cannot be faulted for wanting to mass his army before assaulting the city, there really was no need at that point. The process of marching Marmaduke to Linn slowed Price's westward advance, and it allowed Union commanders at Jefferson City to focus their attention on a single axis of advance from the southeast. Nevertheless, with

Marmaduke's division now serving as a rearguard, Shelby led the army on a ten-mile march to Westphalia through yet another cold and driving rain. After nightfall on the 5th, Shelby dispatched Colonel David Shanks and his brigade ten miles north to destroy the Pacific Railroad Bridge near the mouth of the Osage River, which would thus prevent any large-scale Yankee escape from Jefferson City. It was a wise decision, but it was also a decision made necessary by Price ordering Marmaduke to abandon his separate axis of advance along the Pacific Railroad. Shelby would now have to wait at Westphalia for Shanks to return before crossing the Osage and attacking the capital from the south. This delay permitted the Union position to grow stronger by the hour. For his own part, Shanks did all that he could. After marching most of the night, he had the good fortune to find the bridge guarded by a less than inspired company of the 34th EMM. He then attacked at daylight on the 6th and quickly gained the bridge and its protective block-houses. After capturing fifty-one nervous militiamen, Shanks fired the bridge, a warehouse, and a mill and then headed back to Shelby. [24]

Without Shanks, Jo Shelby hesitated to cross the Osage River. Federal scouting and resistance had increased since the army passed through Mount

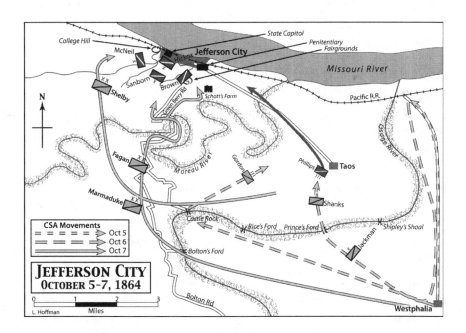

Figure 5.2.   Jefferson City, October 5–7, 1864

Sterling the previous day, and Shelby began to hear rumors that Thomas Ewing's long-lost army had resurfaced in the vicinity of Jefferson City. At this point, Shelby's scouts had not been terribly effective, and by sunrise on the morning of the 6th, he had very little sense of what actually lay in front of him. He decided then to stay put until David Shanks returned to Westphalia. When Shanks finally did arrive at camp just before noon, Shelby ordered a careful crossing of the Osage. He posted Frank Gordon's 5th Missouri six miles west to the ford at Castle Rock where it was to divert Union attention away from Shelby's main crossing at Prince's Ford. Shortly after posting Gordon, Shelby splashed two mounted regiments through Prince's Ford while using two dismounted regiments and his artillery to scatter one company of the 1st MSM that had been guarding the ford. The sudden shock of the attack had surprised the defenders, who lost at least four men drowned in the river.[25]

Shelby's success, however, was short-lived. Positioned all along the river was a mixed force of about 1,500 MSM cavalry under the able command of Colonel John Philips. The gunfire at Prince's Ford quickly attracted Philips's attention at his headquarters near Taos, about three miles north of Prince's Ford. He then hurriedly dispatched Major Alexander Mullins's battalion of the 1st MSM to block Shelby's advance. A critical moment in the action had therefore arrived. Mullins ran into Shelby about a mile north of the river and drove the Confederates back toward the Osage. In response, Shelby deployed the remaining two regiments of Shanks's Iron Brigade across the river. Shanks then forced Mullins back, but only gradually. By nightfall the Iron Brigade had advanced only three miles from the river to the vicinity of Taos. Over at Castle Rock, Gordon's regiment was only marginally more successful, having moved north to the Dixon Plantation near the banks of the Moreau River.[26]

The entire affair did not reflect well upon Shelby, and it had large consequences for the army. Shelby had frittered away much of the day waiting for Shanks to return to Westphalia. While Shelby was certainly correct in believing that the operation required more troops, he failed to marshal manpower that was close by and readily available to him. Jackman's brigade of his own division and Fagan's troops stood idle while Shelby waited nervously for Shanks. This was an error that Shelby compounded throughout the remainder of the day as the outnumbered Alexander Mullins fought his skillful delaying action. Shelby lost contact with Gordon's regiment and inexplicably never ordered Jackman into battle. Sterling Price himself bears no small amount of responsibility for the conduct of this action. At daybreak on the 6th, Price was eighteen miles behind Shelby and obviously in no position to either reinforce his junior division commander or hurry him along. The physical cost of the day's action had been relatively light as both sides suffered no more than twenty casualties apiece, but it was the Confederacy that paid the stiffest penalty aside from the precious time lost. David Shanks, the army's most capable brigade commander outside of William Cabell, had taken a bullet through the chest and would be captured by the Federals. [27]

Mullins's rearguard action bought more time for the defenders of Jefferson City to prepare and for the bulk of Clinton Fisk's 1,800 troops to arrive. Commercial activity ceased while all able-bodied men joined an already diverse collection of military units digging rifle pits and shoring up fortifications. By virtue of his seniority, Fisk succeeded Brown as commander on the afternoon of the 6th, and he promptly reorganized his approximately eight thousand men into four brigades commanded by generals Brown, McNeil, and Sanborn and Colonel Franklin W. Hickox of the EMM. Fisk then posted McNeil to the western portion of the line beginning at the fortification on College Hill on the Missouri River. Sanborn occupied the center of a line that looped around the city to the fairgrounds. Brown filled the eastern third of the defenses with his brigade anchored at the penitentiary on the Missouri River. Hickox's brigade acted as a reserve. Although Sanborn and McNeil were to maintain most of their men within the city's entrenchments, Fisk directed them to advance some of their cavalry toward Castle Rock in order to resist Shelby from that quarter. Fisk also ordered Mullins and Philips to continue resisting Shelby's main thrust that ran along a line from Prince's Ford through Taos and the Moreau River. [28]

That night, Sterling Price encamped at Prince's Ford along with his headquarters. Although there is no record of Price's thoughts, he most certainly had to have been discouraged by the day's events. Shelby had been unable to drive the enemy, and there was the failure to confirm reports that the Yankees had amassed large numbers of troops in the area. Price was not yet willing to abandon the idea of taking Jefferson City, but at the same time he would continue to proceed cautiously in his approach to the capital on the 7th. Indeed, he would not deploy the entire army, choosing instead to rotate Fagan's division to the front merely for the purpose of developing the enemy's forces and driving his pickets across the Moreau River and into the city's line of entrenchments. Fagan's advance would also take him along the Bolton Road and well to the west of Shelby's axis advance, which had taken him to Taos and hinted at a crossing of the Moreau much closer to the Missouri River. Marmaduke's division remained to the rear of Fagan's advancing units, and Shelby marched in an arc to the south and west of the city, well within view of its fortifications. Aside from the occasional Federal shell thrown at Shelby's troopers, the only action Shelby saw occurred when Price ordered a detachment of one hundred of his men to head further north and destroy three small bridges over Graves Creek and a nearby water tower along the Pacific Railroad. With Price's forces thus scattered about Jefferson City, Fagan was virtually guaranteed a slow advance against the reinforced Yankee resistance at the Moreau River.[29]

Fagan, unlike Shelby on the 6th, got an early start in the push toward the Moreau. By 6 AM he had juggled his units for the attack, putting Wright's cavalry of Slemons's brigade in the lead. Heavy skirmishing then ensued as Wright and Slemons attempted to shove aside a series of dismounted Yankee companies that were hidden among tree lines and ravines. Northern resistance, now spearheaded by the 6th and 8th regiments of the MSM, was strong as Slemons had frequently to dismount his command and call for artillery support to root out the enemy. Just before noon, Wright finally crossed the Moreau. Wright and the rest of Slemons's brigade marched another one mile north when stiffening Yankee resistance forced a halt to the advance. Only at this point, and much to the chagrin of Wright, did General Fagan press the remainder of his division to the forward area, which finally encouraged the Yankees to seek the protection of the city's entrenchments.[30]

It was then about 1 PM, and Price had to make a decision about what next to do. All Union forces had been pushed into their works, and the city was now in the plain sight of both Fagan and Price. Price, however, chose to delay a decision on any attack until later when he had a chance to talk with his generals. In the meantime, the last gasp of the day's fighting took place to the southeast of the city at the fairgrounds. There, in a stretch of woods, Fagan had attempted to place Hughey's battery of artillery and begin shelling the city's fortifications. However, after shooting only a few rounds, Hughey was himself the recipient of Union counterbattery fire from three separate units located on the left and center of the Yankee line. When a Yankee round hit and dismounted one of his cannons, Hughey withdrew to safer ground.[31]

For the remainder of the afternoon, the two sides faced each other in a pregnant silence. While the Federals prepared for what they thought was a certain assault of their position, Sterling Price convened a meeting of his general officers at his headquarters in Frog Hollow a few miles west of the city. There was little to encourage the Confederate leaders. Intelligence reports had alerted Price to the recent arrival of McNeil's and Sanborn's brigades, and other reports inflated Union manpower to at least twelve thousand men with three thousand more ready to cross the Missouri River. Given Jefferson City's well-designed fortifications and three miles of entrenchments, all of which was in plain view of just about everyone in the Confederate army, Price and his generals had little choice but to give up the idea of storming the capital. Only at this point, and with night fast approaching on October 7th, did Price also abandon his dream of conquering Missouri for the Confederacy. From this point forward, Price would reorient the Missouri expedition to more conventional raiding objectives. This did not mean, however, that Price intended on leaving the state any time soon. In keeping with Kirby Smith's original orders, Old Pap would march west toward the Kansas border seeking men and ordnance to take back to Arkansas. Accordingly, Price directed Fagan and Marmaduke to begin redeploying that night and to encamp about two miles south of Jefferson City. The next morning, the army headed for Boonville, with Shelby in front followed by Fagan and then Marmaduke. [32]

Chapter Six

D—n the State, I Wish I Had Never Seen It

While the failure to capture Jefferson City may well have spelled the end of Price's dream of retaking the state, Old Pap had reason to be optimistic as he headed toward the Boonslick, the most pro-Confederate region of Missouri.[1] Price was about to receive the outpouring of support and affection that he had anticipated ever since the beginning of the expedition. The welcome was intoxicating, and it would almost blind Price to a changing dynamic in the Union's opposition to his expedition.

Price's movements after he left Jefferson City were very typical of the expedition to that point in time. The straight-line distance covered by the main body of the army would be small. On the 8th, Price traveled west fourteen miles to Russellville. On the 9th, he continued for several miles in his march to the west before turning north at High Point, headed for the small railroad town of California. He concluded the day's march along the banks of the Moniteau Creek, having traveled twenty-six miles. The next day he proceeded another sixteen to Boonville. Price also continued to dispatch subsidiary raids from the main column. As the army marched along the Russellville Road, Price ordered Shelby to send yet another column north to burn bridges and destroy railroad track between Jefferson City and California. Heading out on the morning of the 8th, Colonel Moses W. Smith's 11th Missouri hit the railroad and wrecked it for miles before finally encamping at California and liberating the town of its food and clothing. Smith then awaited the arrival of the remainder of Shelby's division on the 9th.[2]

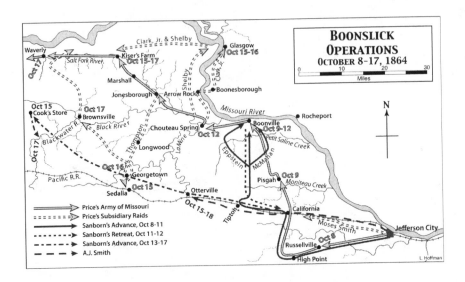

Figure 6.1. Boonslick Operations, October 8–17, 1864

Despite these continuities in Price's conduct of the campaign, all was indeed not the same after Jefferson City. For the first time since the Confederates had entered Missouri, Union forces actively probed and attacked Price's army. While previously the enemy had sought to escape Old Pap's advance, it now started to nip at the flanks and rear of the Confederate army. No sooner had Shelby begun his march toward Russellville along the Jefferson City and Springfield Road on the morning of the 8th than Union forces under John Sanborn drove in Lieutenant Colonel John A. Schnable's battalion, which protected Shelby's right flank at a crossing of Moniteau Creek. A series of charges and countercharges ensued for the remainder of the morning that spread from the flank of Shelby's division to the rearguard of the army commanded by Cabell. For ten miles, the action flickered as Cabell, especially, struggled to disperse the Yankees. The terrain was fairly open, but numerous fence lines stitched the land, which limited Cabell's ability to deploy most of his regiments against Sanborn. Ultimately, Cabell repelled Sanborn when he succeeded in forming his entire brigade, including Hughey's artillery, on a ridge near Garner's Mill. With night falling, Cabell's frustration boiled over in the waning moments of the action when he shouted above the din: "Here is your uprising in Missouri; here is your forty thousand men with guns in their hands; d—n the State, I wish I had never seen it."[3]

The invigorated Union pursuit of Price had everything to do with the arrival of Major General Alfred Pleasonton in Jefferson City. A West Pointer and one-time commander of the cavalry of the Army of the Potomac, Pleasonton was yet another high-ranking officer posted to the Trans-Mississippi because he had fallen out of favor with the Union high command. Hard charging and fast talking, Pleasonton had put the much-maligned cavalry of the Army of Potomac on a professional level with J. E. B. Stuart's Confederates. This achievement was not, however, enough for him to keep his job. Pleasonton was self-aggrandizing, petty, and xenophobic. By the spring of 1864 he found himself on leave in Pennsylvania, pending reassignment to the army's personnel scrap heap, the Department of the Missouri. Price's entry into Missouri prompted William Rosecrans to end Pleasonton's leave and recall him to St. Louis. Pleasonton arrived there on October 6th, and Rosecrans then posted him immediately to Jefferson City to take command of the pursuit of Price. His arrival in the capital city early in the morning on the 8th established an immediate contrast with the informally mannered and loosely disciplined militia and western volunteer officers already present. Pleasonton was the embodiment of the regular army officer. He carried a riding whip at his right wrist and wore his uniform impeccably. He surrounded himself with like-dressed staff officers and orderlies, who, according to one observer, all looked as if they had just stepped off the parade ground. With buglers and snapping guidons at his side, Pleasonton assumed command of all forces in the vicinity of Jefferson City and organized them into a provisional cavalry division. It consisted of four brigades commanded by generals Brown, McNeil, Sanborn, and Colonel Edward F. Winslow of A. J. Smith's XVI Corps. With Winslow's troops not yet arrived at Jefferson City, and in accordance with Rosecrans's instructions, Pleasonton waited to activate the division formally and instead ordered Sanborn's newly designated 3rd Brigade "to proceed as a corps of observation after the enemy, to harass and delay him as much as possible until other troops could be brought forward."[4]

Despite the irritation that Sanborn caused General Cabell on October 8th, Old Pap chose to minimize the significance of the Federal harassment. The Confederate army was headed to the Boonslick and the heart of Southern sentiment in Missouri. While Price knew that the Boonslick could not provide enough men to reconquer the state, Old Pap fully expected the region to furnish a large number of men. To that end, Shelby remained in the lead of the army on the morning of the 9th when Price ordered his division from Russellville to California. Riding in the van of Shelby's division and now commanding the Iron Brigade in the place of the captured David Shanks was Brigadier General M. Jeff Thompson. Like so many of his fellow Missouri Confederates, Thompson was a striking and colorful figure. Almost entirely self-taught, Thompson drove himself to become, at varying times, a civil engineer, inventor, railroad president, and mayor of St. Joseph, Missouri. He was also an ardent states' rights champion who owned no slaves. A natural leader bearing a commission in the Missouri State Guard, Thompson readily distinguished himself in the first two years of the war fighting in the swamps of southeast Missouri while brandishing a white-handled Bowie knife and accompanied by a war-painted Indian orderly named Ajax. Widely known and feared as the "Missouri Swamp Fox," Thompson had been captured in 1863 and bounced around numerous Union prison camps and ships throughout the North before finally gaining his exchange outside Charleston, South Carolina, on August 9, 1864.[5]

Thompson's journey to Price's army was arduous. After gaining freedom, Thompson traveled to Selma, Alabama, where he heard rumors of Price's upcoming expedition. With no hesitation, he determined to be a part of the grand movement. Over the next six weeks Thompson rode, swam, and paddled across the remainder of the Confederacy before finally catching up with Price at Ironton the day after the Battle of Pilot Knob. Thompson, who had never actually been commissioned in the Confederate States Army, subsequently rode as an escort to Governor Reynolds until Shanks had been unhorsed at Jefferson City. On October 7, Price appointed Thompson to succeed Shanks. Although the men of the brigade readily accepted Thompson as their new commander, they were far less trusting of other newcomers. Battlefield success had created a sense of elitism within the Iron Brigade, and it had become accepted practice among the men to try to drive out newly transferred officers through insults and insubordination. As Thompson later noted, the troopers "thought a private in this Brigade was better than an officer in any other."[6]

It would take Thompson about a week to notice this situation, but for the immediate time being he focused on pushing his brigade to California where he would link up with the advance party led by Colonel Moses W. Smith. Once in California, Thompson did not have long to wait for Shelby—and Price himself. Shelby was now in very familiar territory, and his blood was up. According to Thompson, Shelby "begged permission" from Price to go and capture Boonville much as he had done the year before in his swashbuckling raid through Missouri. Price readily assented, and Shelby rode at a "swinging trot" at the head of Jackman's brigade with Thompson following. Around 4 PM and after a hard ride of almost thirty miles, two of Shelby's lead companies drove in a group of fifteen pickets two miles east of the town. This unfortunate set of Unionists belonged to three companies of General Orders 107 militia. Commanded by Captain Horace Shoemaker, these three companies mixed infantry and cavalry, totaling about three hundred men. Shelby's appearance caught Shoemaker by surprise. Shoemaker had received at least two reports claiming that Price was retreating along the Pacific Railroad headed for Tipton, over twenty miles to the south of Boonville. At worst, Shoemaker and his comrades believed that Bloody Bill Anderson might strike the town, and they posted pickets to guard against the notorious bushwhacker. Although Shelby had killed and wounded several of the pickets, a number of survivors made it back to town and spread word that Anderson had indeed attacked. Determined to resist Anderson to the last, Shoemaker herded his militia down Vine Street and into the Thespian Hall and some outlying breastworks made of railroad ties. Only after firing one ineffectual volley at the approaching Confederates did Shoemaker discover that the enemy horsemen belonged to Shelby and not Anderson. With Shelby's troops now pulled up in front of the imposing two-story brick building, the Confederate commander paused momentarily to parley and offered to protect the militia should they surrender. Noting his untenable position, Horace Shoemaker quickly accepted. [7]

The remainder of Price's army pulled into the vicinity of Boonville throughout the next day. For Marmaduke's division, the ride had not been pleasant. Assigned to the rear of the army on the 9th, Marmaduke engaged in a near daylong running battle with John Sanborn's brigade. By 5 PM that evening, the two forces were skirmishing heavily at California. While Marmaduke chose to hurry the bulk of his force toward Boonville, he entrusted John B. Clark Jr. to organize some of Pratt's artillery with Lawther's 10th Missouri to parry Sanborn's annoying thrusts. For about one hour, the Confederates ably resisted the more numerous Yankees, which also allowed the army time to separate itself from Sanborn and to destroy a large quantity of railroad track to the west of town. Lawther's rearguard defense did, however, end on a more troublesome note when several squads broke ranks as the regiment began withdrawing through the town at dusk. Tempted by the idea of free whiskey, these wayward men stumbled through a saloon only to be quickly scattered by several rounds of incoming artillery. Fortunately for Lawther's thirsty troops, no one was hurt in the saloon, and the regiment managed to break free from Sanborn and encamp that night about eight miles north of California with only a few total casualties.[8]

The next morning, Fagan's and Marmaduke's divisions switched positions in the army's column with Fagan once again assuming the rearguard. Price's Confederates then proceeded on to Boonville. The line units set a moderate pace, but it was not quite fast enough for many in the army's headquarters' element. They knew Boonville was filled with numerous old friends and hundreds of people sympathetic to the cause. Several staff officers therefore spurred ahead of Fagan and Marmaduke to be a part of what was sure to be a joyous celebration. They were not disappointed. As various units rolled through the town, the citizenry took to the streets to cheer and cry for their heroes. Amid the outpouring of emotion, few Confederates paused to notice, or later recollect, that a good chunk of Main Street had been leveled by a recent fire. All that seemed evident were cheering crowds. Surgeon McPheeters was almost overcome emotionally by the greeting and could only bemoan a fate that kept his wife and children from being a part of such a joyous welcome. By 11 AM, Old Pap rode into town, and what had been a spontaneous celebration now turned into near bedlam. "The citizens," McPheeters wrote, "flocked to see him and for the rest of the day the scene baffle[d] description." With no great exaggeration, Price recalled that "old and young, men, women, and children, vied in their salutations and in ministering to the wants and comforts of my wearied and war-torn soldiers." Price then established his headquarters in the City Hotel, while posting his divisions in a semicircle about the town with Shelby four miles to the west, Marmaduke less than a mile to the south, and Fagan further to the southeast and east. Even with most of the troops placed on the periphery of the town, an almost circuslike atmosphere prevailed. This was perhaps best illustrated by the men of Collins's battery, who used their pet bear, Postelwait, to entertain the citizenry and attract contributions of chickens, hams, biscuits, pies, and cakes. That evening, Confederate Boonville continued the celebration with an exuberant and alcohol-drenched party at Old Pap's headquarters.[9]

By nightfall, some of the Confederates had become a bit too exuberant and had forgotten they were in the midst of a friendly population. Some of Shelby's troopers, in particular, felt the urge to plunder and began loading down their horses with what Jeff Thompson sarcastically called "their rights." Thompson's men were partial to new clothes, and they paid special attention to William Johnson's store, lifting over $1,500 worth of clothes shortly after arriving in town. Perhaps hardest hit of all was the local Mason- ic Lodge and Odd Fellows Hall, which both lost their jewels and ceremonial regalia. There was no small amount of frustration among Fagan's men when they finally marched into the town and found only limited quantities of clothing still available. Fagan's saving grace in this instance was, at least, that his quartermaster, Benjamin Duval, paid for most of what he took. Nevertheless, an orgy of plundering does not appear to have taken place. Some ex post facto accounts seem to have confused damage caused by Price with that caused by the fire that ravaged the city just before Price's entry.[10]

However, the following morning the war in Missouri reintroduced itself to Price. After breakfast on the 11th, Old Pap, and an entourage that included Governor Reynolds, moved to the steps of the city hall where Price continued to receive and greet guests. Below him, several of his officers worked through the process of questioning and paroling the prisoners captured the previous day. No sooner had Price delivered a speech to the assembled pris- oners when a large body of about three hundred darkly clad horsemen, all with several pistols shoved into their belts, clattered into the middle of town and reined up before city hall. Almost immediately the newcomers drew their pistols and started for the prisoners, shouting, "Shoot the sons of bitches!" Bloody Bill Anderson had arrived in Boonville. While most of the Confeder- ates seemed paralyzed by the presence of the infamous Anderson, who was fresh from massacring more than 120 Yankees at Centralia, Price and Re- ynolds rushed down the steps and confronted Anderson before the bush- whackers could shoot the prisoners. At the same moment, Price and Re- ynolds noticed a multitude of human scalps attached to the bridles of Ander- son's mounts. Repulsed and taking no small chance given Bloody Bill's unbalanced reputation, the two leaders ordered Anderson away until he re- moved the barbaric relics. For the moment, Anderson's craving for official recognition and acceptance outweighed his blood lust. He turned his men away, removed the offending scalps, and returned to present Price with a brace of handsome, silver-mounted pistols. Just as Anderson had suppressed a contrary impulse, it was now Old Pap's turn to do likewise. Smiling, Price thanked Anderson for the pistols and proclaimed to a tense crowd, "If I had fifty thousand such men, I could hold Missouri forever."[11]

As Albert Castel and Thomas Goodrich have noted, Price was desperately short of fighting men and he was thus in no position to be picky when bona fide fighting men appeared within his ranks. Price did, however, hope to tame Anderson to his own purposes. Accordingly, he had Lauchlan Maclean write out a set of orders for "Captain" Anderson, detailing him "to destroy the North Missouri Railroad, going as far east as practicable." Price hoped Anderson would make it to a bridge near the limit of St. Charles County, which, if destroyed, would interdict rail traffic between St. Louis and the Hannibal and St. Joseph Railroad indefinitely. In like fashion, Price tried— and failed—to contact William C. Quantrill and order him to operate against the Hannibal and Saint Joseph Railroad. Price's attempt to harness the two guerrilla chieftains served little purpose. William Rosecrans, in organizing his pursuit of Price, had already disregarded the northern lines in favor of a more direct approach along the south bank of the Missouri River. Moreover, even if Price had succeeded in contacting Quantrill, there was very little Quantrill could have done. His power had long been eclipsed, and he exercised control over few men. For Bloody Bill, who had supplanted Quantrill as the preeminent bushwhacker, there was little incentive or desire to destroy bridges and railroad track to the east. Though Anderson did indeed burn two depots along the North Missouri, he quickly reversed himself and headed west, preferring instead to travel on the fringes of Price's army where there was no discernible organized force to prevent robbery and butchery. In the words of Castel and Goodrich, Bill Anderson never "had it so good, so easy, so safe." In a postscript regarding Anderson, Bloody Bill's guerrillas left town on the evening of the 12th with a violent flourish. Somehow Anderson's men got word that Horace Shoemaker had been paroled to his house where two of Shelby's men provided protection. As Shoemaker carried a reputation of never offering quarter to bushwhackers, Anderson's men determined to grab him. Masquerading as a detail from Shelby, they duped the guards into surrendering him. The guerrillas then executed Shoemaker before dumping him into the Missouri River and heading out of Boonville. [12]

Bloody Bill's appearance was but the first event to throw cold water on the festivities surrounding the Confederate capture of Boonville. No sooner had Anderson and his men marched out around noon than the sounds of an artillery exchange south of town reverberated over Price's headquarters. Soon pickets from Marmaduke's and Fagan's divisions reported a strong enemy attack that converged near the intersection of the roads from Tipton and Pisgah. For the Union, the timing of an attack could not have been better. Throughout the 10th and 11th, Price had paid little attention to an enemy threat from the direction of Jefferson City. The attitude clearly trickled down to Marmaduke and Fagan, who occupied positions astride any probable enemy advance from the south and east. Consequently, both commanders failed miserably when they lost contact with advancing Union forces and then magnified the error by posting weak pickets along the main avenues of approach. Despite Cabell's later claim that he had made every preparation to deal with an enemy attack, his brigade was no more strongly posted than the others. The stage was thus set for a potential disaster when on the morning of the 11th Price summoned many of his senior officers to town for a reception of local notables. The sound of nearby gunfire, however, quickly put an end to the socializing as Price returned the officers to their units with instructions to "drive the enemy back." Fearing for his trains, Price ordered his wagons to park just west of town along the Georgetown Road. [13]

John Sanborn had once again caught up to Price. After Marmaduke had shaken free of Sanborn at California on the evening of the 9th, the Yankee commander did not pursue Price directly north to Boonville. Instead, he continued west along the path of the Pacific Railroad to Tipton, guarding against any potential move of Price either to the south or west. Once he was confident that Price was headed to Boonville, Sanborn turned north at Tipton and eventually encamped about nine miles outside of Boonville on the evening of the 10th. Price's merrymaking commanders were completely unaware of his location. Early the next morning, Sanborn split his brigade into thirds. One column under Lieutenant Colonel Joseph Eppstein rode fifteen miles west where it then turned northeast along the Georgetown Road. A second column commanded by Lieutenant Colonel John F. McMahan marched east a much shorter distance to the east before it pivoted back to the northwest along the Pisgah Road. Sanborn commanded the center in a fairly direct march to the north along the Tipton Road. It was not a terribly ambitious operation as Sanborn wanted merely to reestablish contact with Price's army. He and Colonel McMahan were therefore astonished when their columns crossed the Petit Saline Creek and trotted to within three miles of town before meeting any resistance. Within minutes, the Federals drove about one hundred surprised pickets from the 4th Missouri back into the outer streets of Boonville. Fortunately for Price, Marmaduke and Fagan were able to rally their troops. The division commanders maneuvered their men into a ragged line that mixed mounted and dismounted units and extended almost two miles from the Tipton Road east and north to the Missouri River. Their subsequent counterattack was brief, but effective. Confederate artillery drove McMahan's men from the protection of the houses, and Fagan succeeded in curling some troops around McMahan's right flank, which then precipitated Sanborn's gradual withdrawal south. Near dusk, Shelby also entered the fray.

Earlier in the morning, Jackman's brigade had skirmished heavily with Joseph Eppstein's Federals well to the southwest along the Georgetown Road. As that action died out by midafternoon, Shelby ordered Jackman to pivot and march east in order to fall on Sanborn's left and rear. Difficult terrain delayed Jackman's march, and he reached Sanborn only in time to watch the Federals cross the Petit Saline Creek safely. Jackman would pursue no more that night. The next morning, Price ordered Slemons's brigade of Fagan's division to reinforce Jackman. The reinforcements did not, however, inspire decisive action. After a series of charges and countercharges at the Petit Saline, Jackman and Slemons allowed the Federal commander to completely disengage his brigade from the contest, burning the bridge across the river as he retreated. By nightfall on the 12th, Sanborn had countermarched over twenty-five miles back to California, where he gained reinforcements and resupply.[14]

The physical cost of the episode had been light. Sanborn sustained only a few casualties, while Price lost in excess of fifty men killed and wounded. However, the engagement was not without greater significance. Although John Sanborn was certainly outnumbered and under no orders to develop a battle, he had missed a major opportunity to damage Price's unprepared army. Sanborn had divided his force one too many times, posting Eppstein's column far beyond its ability to support the other two should contact be made. Not surprisingly given the distance he had to travel, Eppstein finally arrived at the southwest corner of Boonville on the 12th just as Sanborn and the rest of the brigade were backpedaling to California. After some scattered skirmishing with Shelby, Eppstein pulled out and headed to California as well.[15]

In the actions of the 11th, Sanborn had been a victim of both the fog of war and his own bad decision making. He had committed to battle early on the 11th based upon the report of a citizen that Price had moved one-half of his army north of the Missouri River. If his postwar recollections are to be believed, he intended his attack only as a means to draw Price back across the Missouri River. By noon he thought Price had done precisely that, which justified his own disengagement. Sanborn then compounded his error by taking his brigade entirely out of the area of operations in his retreat to California. Sanborn later tried to rationalize this abandonment of Price on logistical grounds. His brigade had little food and forage for the previous thirty-six hours, and Sanborn concluded that he needed to rest and resupply before continuing the chase. While it is true Sanborn's men and animals had gone without the prescribed rations for over one day, Sanborn the infantry-man appears to have underestimated the endurance of his cavalry brigade. It was far from exhaustion. The brigade could have readily maintained contact with Price while waiting an extra day for the supplies to come to them in the field. This was indeed exactly what Alfred Pleasonton wanted, and he tried belatedly to get word to Sanborn to stop his retreat at Pisgah where supply trains could then be routed. Sanborn, to the detriment of the cause, got the order much too late. Instead, by retreating to California Sanborn gave Price two additional days of operational freedom. [16]

By the time Sterling Price chose to leave Boonville late in the evening of October 12th, elements of his army had spent over three days in the town. It was an extraordinary amount of time given Sanborn's probing actions and the gathering of Pleasonton's command at Jefferson City. Why, however, Price chose to linger in Boonville was no great mystery. There was, of course, an element of vanity involved. In Boonville, Price finally got the reception he had come to expect. There were too many friends to greet and too much applause to receive for Price to leave quickly. But more important-ly, Price's personal reception was part of a larger outpouring of Confederate sympathies that netted the army hundreds of recruits. Heretofore, recruiting for the army had been nothing less than a disaster. Not even the dubious proclamation of John W. Taylor, the supposed Supreme Commander of the OAKs in Missouri, had helped the situation. On October 1st, Taylor had issued a grandiloquent statement appointing Price "military commander of the OAKs" and ordering the knights to "seize all arms and munitions of war within your power" and report to Price. [17]

Unfortunately for Taylor and Price, there is no evidence of the proclama-tion having any circulation beyond that of Taylor's own desk. If any member of the OAK actually did rise up and join Price's army, it remained a secret befitting the secret pretensions of the order. No less elusive than the number of OAK enlistments are Price's total manpower accessions during his march toward Boonville. Although Price's trains had swelled, by one Yankee esti-mate, to include five thousand men, there were few reliable—or motivated—recruits in the bunch. As the army marched through Missouri, the trains came to include not only the usual teamsters, bodyguards, staff sections, and sick troops, but also an assortment of volunteers, conscripts, prisoners, and politi-cal hangers-on. Nevertheless, with no muster rolls extant there is simply no way to determine how many men belonged to each category. What can be stated impressionistically is that most of these people belonged to an ever-changing group of conscripts forced at gunpoint to follow the army. For many conscripts, their stay in the army would last until they were either killed, ran away, or the war had ended. For a great many others, their time in service was much more limited and generally confined to the amount of time it took for a senior officer to conduct an interview and then announce a parole. The only thing that can be noted with finality is that by the middle of October Price had been able to create only two new battalions for his army, and those belonged to Alonzo Slayback and Rector Johnson.[18]

In the Boonslick, Price's frustrations over recruiting began to change. Hundreds of Southern sympathizers who had long waited for Price to liberate their state now willingly left farms and families to be a part of the grand expedition. Other, less enthusiastic, Southerners, when faced with the prospect of being conscripted by Union militia, chose finally to join the cause of the South. Still, such men needed to be encouraged, organized, and brought to the army. For this Price relied upon a host of recruiting officers who had infiltrated the state in advance of the expedition. A majority of these men were part of a wave of recruiters sent by Jo Shelby in August and September with explicit instructions to raise whole units and then report back to the army when it passed nearby. As listed in the special orders, the destinations of these recruiters could be found in all parts of Missouri, though most were headed in the direction of the Boonslick. Among the more successful was Major James Searcy. Dispatched by Shelby on September 20th to recruit in the Boonslick counties, Searcy raised a regiment in short order and presented it to Price after the army departed Boonville.[19]

Captain George S. Rathbun was another successful recruiter. A native Ohioan and one-time state legislator from Lafayette County, Rathbun departed Shelby's camps at Batesville, Arkansas, in mid-September. By October 14th he reached his hometown and final destination, Lexington. The local EMM fled, leaving the city as easy pickings for the anxious Rathbun. Over the next three days, Rathbun conscripted no less than five hundred men between the ages of seventeen and fifty. Although Rathbun's battalion of recruits was hardly the most motivated group of men, they were probably the best armed. Somewhere along his journey through Missouri, Rathbun had managed to acquire hundreds of shotguns. Indeed, by the time Rathbun departed the area on the evening of the 16th headed east toward Price, he had to leave behind at least thirty weapons and one thousand rounds of ammunition.[20]

Specially designated recruiters such as George Rathbun and James Searcy were not the only Confederates out scouring the countryside for men. There were a number of other recruiters not tied directly to Price's Army of Missouri. These leaders were either guerilla chieftains conscripting men for their own bands or commissioned officers seeking troops for independent units. Price's arrival in central Missouri encouraged the more orthodox of these men, such as Colonel Caleb Perkins, to join the "regular" army. Dating back to the early summer, Price had dispatched Perkins to Missouri to recruit as many men as possible and wait for the arrival of the army. Should Price not be able to make the expedition, Perkins bore orders to come south with his new soldiers. Perkins then faithfully recruited in Audrain, Calloway, and Boone counties throughout much of the summer, keeping some men with him while leaving others safe at home with instructions to wait until he spread the word to rally together. The wait for Price proved too much for several bands of Perkins's recruits, and they took readily to bushwhacking. Nevertheless, by the end of September, Perkins called for his men, and about eight hundred gathered in northern Calloway County. While most of these men were completely unarmed, some of the more organized bands had managed to outfit themselves quite well with everything from shotguns to pistols. Perkins subsequently led his recruits southwest through Boone County where they crossed the Missouri River at Rocheport and finally joined Price at Boonville. On October 12th, Price christened Perkins's unit a regiment and eventually united it with Searcy's and Colonel John T. Coffee's regiments of unarmed men to form a brigade under Colonel Charles H. Tyler.[21]

Given the pro-Confederate outpouring of emotion seen in the Boonslick, Price quickly saw the opportunity for recruiting beyond what the infiltrated cadres had already accomplished. Accordingly, Old Pap dispatched other officers into the countryside, especially across the river into Livingston, Carroll, Chariton, Boone, and Callaway counties. Among those dispatched was Lieutenant Colonel D. A. Williams from Jackman's brigade. He departed Boonville sometime between the 12th and 14th with about 150 soldiers from his self-named battalion and almost immediately found dozens of recruits ready to join his ranks. By October 18th, Williams had combed Livingston and Carroll counties and came up with a force numbering anywhere from three hundred to eight hundred men. Of these recruits, at least one hundred had ridden with either Bloody Bill Anderson or the somewhat less notorious Cliff Holtzclaw. Emboldened by his recruiting success, Williams concluded that his force was strong enough to take the town of Carrollton in south central Carroll County and its garrison of two hundred militia from the 65th EMM. On the 18th he divided his men into two separate columns and approached the town from both the north and south. Once his troops were in position on the outskirts of town, he demanded its surrender. Major George Deagle, who commanded the post, thought himself outnumbered by more than one thousand men. Deagle promptly surrendered when Williams guaranteed terms including parole and protection. However, shortly after Deagle and his men put down their arms it became evident that Williams had ulterior motives for taking the town. For the next forty-eight hours the Confederates remained in Carrollton, liberating its merchants of every conceivable item and its bankers of all their money. Although Williams did eventually parole the officers and men, it was not before pulling six of the Unionists from the ranks. These men stood accused of assassinating three Confederates, who a month earlier had been recruiting in the area. Among those assassinated was Monroe Williams, the brother of Lieutenant Colonel Williams. The accused, according to one witness, "were taken a few miles from town and after listening to an eloquent talk . . . from Colonel Williams were summarily executed." Only after this did Williams and his recruits make their way back to Price's army.[22]

The efforts of Williams and the other recruiters inserted in advance of the expedition did not mark the end of Price's efforts to acquire men in the Boonslick. Throughout the invasion, Price, Marmaduke, and Shelby granted liberal furloughs to their soldiers. While Price, especially, was sympathetic to letting his soldiers see long-missed families and friends, the primary purpose of the furlough was to recruit among those same family and friends. The practice of granting furloughs along the march only increased the closer the army came to the Boonslick. With the chief purpose of the expedition now all about recruiting and gathering supplies for transport south, Price was gambling that the consequent short-term destabilization of the army's manpower would be well worth the men gained in the long term.

The gamble produced mixed results. For some soldiers, the furlough was an opportunity, much like that presented to D. A. Williams, of exacting revenge. Such was indeed the case in Saline County for the killers of William Howerton. Howerton had the misfortune of being labeled a Yankee informant. A small group of furloughed Confederates dispatched Howerton as soon as they arrived home. For other soldiers, such as George Cruzen of Gordon's 5th Missouri, the furlough meant home-cooked meals, the chance to kiss a bevy of girls, and a jaunt back to the army at the head of a platoon of new recruits. For still other soldiers, such as Phineas Woods, the furlough was the last pleasant thing they ever did. Union militia, tipped off to Woods eating lunch at his family's house in Platte County, captured and shot him. Finally, and for a very large number of men, the furlough meant that they would be irrevocably separated from the army and eventually captured. Typical of such men was Thomas W. Westlake, who managed to get a ten-day pass to visit his home once the army rode into Boonville. With signed paperwork in hand, he crossed the Missouri River and spent a few days at his home twenty miles north of the river before trying to rejoin Price. For the next several days, Westlake wandered around central Missouri with what he called "quite a little army of unarmed men" trying to pass through a countryside filled with Yankee patrols. With Price then far to the west and south, Westlake never made it. Union militia eventually captured him in Randolph County and shipped him off to Gratiot Prison in St. Louis where he joined dozens of other recruits and furloughed soldiers who had become separated from Price's army. [23]

Despite the loss of men such as Thomas Westlake, Price still managed to add no less than 2,500 men to his army from the Boonslick counties. At this point in the campaign, the value of these recruits was clearly in their future potential as soldiers. But these men needed first to be brought safely out of Missouri and into Arkansas where they could be trained and equipped for the anticipated battles and campaigns of 1865. However, as Price traveled through the Boonslick that safe passage seemed unlikely, and the odds were strong that the recruits would have to fight long before they made it to Arkansas. Given their lack of training, weaponry, and horses, these much-sought-after men could yet prove to be more of a burden than benefit to the Army of Missouri. [24]

Chapter Seven

You Are Home Boys, and I Do Not
Want to Hurt You

Price's decision to leave Boonville did not mean the Army of Missouri would accelerate its pace to make an escape from the state. On the contrary, over the next several days Price prolonged his march through the Boonslick in order to continue recruiting. During this time he also mounted the largest subsidiary actions of the expedition. Using the most disciplined brigades from Shelby's and Maramaduke's divisions, Price succeeded not only in garnering a large amount of food, clothing, and weapons, but he did so in a fashion that avoided the excesses of Missouri's internecine war that had heretofore marred the expedition. But once again, there would be a consequence to Price's deliberate loitering. Even more Union troops began to gather in Price's rear and flanks. No less ominous for Price, these men were not militia, but veteran infantry and cavalry.

Although Price had attracted hundreds of recruits in his slow passage through the Boonslick, many of these men were unarmed, which aggravated the Army of Missouri's great shortage of weapons. Almost serendipitously for the Confederacy, no sooner had Price ridden out of Boonville on the evening of the 12th than he got word of the supposed existence of a Union depot at Glasgow containing five thousand weapons. A small town of just a few hundred residents, Glasgow was located alongside the opposite bank of the Missouri River as it twisted and flowed south in Howard County, about twenty miles in straight-line distance from Boonville. By the end of Price's first day's march out of Boonville on the 12th, he stopped at Chouteau Springs having marched less than eleven miles and dispatched a column to seize Glasgow. John B. Clark Jr. commanded the column, which consisted of both Clark's and Sidney Jackman's brigades. Harris's battery, commanded by Lieutenant Thomas J. Williams, would support the cavalry. At first glance, Price's choice of units for the independent operation was somewhat odd. Clark and Jackman commanded brigades from two separate divisions, and neither unit had really distinguished itself to that point. Left unstated in the assignment, however, was the simple fact that both Clark and Jackman were natives of Howard County, and Price readily hoped to capitalize on their name recognition. To that end, Price ordered the column to Arrow Rock on the near bank of the Missouri River. At Arrow Rock, Clark ferried the 1,700 men of his command across the river. He then proceeded the remaining sixteen miles almost due north to Glasgow by daybreak on the 15th. However, when Clark arrived at Arrow Rock he received a report that the Yankees at Glasgow possessed an armed "tin-clad boat" tied along the wharf. Concerned with this unexpected addition of Yankee firepower, Clark requested that Price send some cavalry and a section of artillery to the south bank of the Missouri River and "drive the gunboat from its position." It was an inspired bit of tactical thinking as the Missouri River at Glasgow was less than three-tenths of a mile wide, putting the entire town and its wharf well within the range of any Confederate field artillery. Price concurred, and he ordered Jo Shelby on the evening of the 14th to take about 125 cavalry and a section of Collins's artillery to the Missouri River. Shelby responded ably, and after a cold, hard ride he had his men in place an hour before daybreak.[1]

In Glasgow, the Unionists were completely unaware of either Shelby's presence on the opposite bank of the river or the advance of Clark from Arrow Rock. The garrison and its commander Captain John E. Mayo of the 13th Missouri Cavalry were highly agitated, but it had little to do with any fear of Price's advance. Much like the garrison at Boonville the previous week, the defenders of Glasgow believed Price was moving away from their town. Mayo had reports of Price's defeat at Jefferson City, and he thought there was no way for Old Pap to transport a large number of troops across the Missouri River. What Mayo did fear were bushwhackers and the big concentrations of Confederate conscripts on the north side of the river. Commanding no more than one hundred men from different militia organizations and having the telegraph lines out of town cut, Mayo sent dispatch riders in search of reinforcements on October 13th. To his great relief and luck, Mayo almost immediately found six understrength companies of the 43rd Missouri

Infantry under the command of Colonel Chester Harding Jr. temporarily grounded aboard two steamers less than ten miles up the Missouri River.

Unfortunately for Mayo, Harding's troops would be all the reinforcement he could find. Although Alfred Pleasonton had correctly used his cavalry in the harassment of Price's main army, the Union general fumbled badly in the handling of his infantry when he took command at Jefferson City on October 8th. One day after arriving in the city, he ordered three of his best volunteer infantry regiments up the Missouri River to garrison Lexington and Boonville. With Price then headed toward Boonville, and Pleasonton generally unsure of what Confederates lay ahead on the Missouri River, the Union infantry stood a greater chance of getting ripped to shreds in the river shallows by Price's artillery than it did of reaching either Boonville or Lexington. William Rosecrans realized this and tried, belatedly, to get Pleasonton to stop the mission. Clinton Fisk, who Pleasonton placed in command of the two regiments heading to Lexington, also objected to the undertaking and requested an alternate assignment should the river be blocked before reaching Boonville. Fisk wanted the flexibility to disembark on the north side of the river and march overland to Glasgow. Fisk, with no small amount of foresight, argued that at Glasgow he would be in a good position to interdict any attempts by Price to operate on the northern side of the river. With little apparent belief that Price could operate north of the river, Pleasonton refused and merely ordered Fisk to hold fast on the north side of the river and await orders if he found the Missouri blocked to Lexington. By October 10th, and one day into his journey up the river, Fisk called a halt to the expedition at Rocheport when he received reports that Price had taken Boonville. Still perceiving Glasgow as a vital strategic point north of the river, Fisk requested permission to march on the town. For the next three days, however, Fisk could do little but turn down the appeals of nearby towns for assistance and vent his frustrations by mail to Missouri congressman James S. Rollins. Finally, on October 13th, Pleasonton dispatched orders to Fisk, refusing his request to march for Glasgow. Instead, and just as Mayo's riders searched for all available reinforcements, Fisk had to turn his infantry around for an overland march back to Jefferson City and away from the impending battle. John E. Mayo would have to rely upon Chester Harding and his six companies to defend Glasgow.[2]

For Harding, the stop at Glasgow was but the latest delay in a trip that had begun eight days earlier in St. Joseph. At that time, Fisk had ordered Harding and his 450 men to Jefferson City as a part of the hurried defense of the capital. But Harding's trip down the Missouri River was fraught with difficulty as the two steamboats, the *Benton* and the *West Wind*, had to dodge both sand bars and guerrillas. Consequently, the Union commander spent time either stuck in the river or simply stopped at a levee, giving chase to bushwhackers who swarmed around the river towns and reveled in taking pot shots at the lumbering steamers. When Harding did receive Mayo's frantic appeal for help on the 13th, he determined to rush on to Glasgow as soon as possible, eventually arriving at 3 PM. After being treated to a lavish dinner by a local dignitary, Harding decided to stay in town until he could receive further instructions. As Jefferson City had already been saved, Harding saw no reason to leave. The next morning, troops unloaded onto the dock all supplies from the steamers, which then allowed the shallow draft *Benton* to start a return trip to Leavenworth. The heavier *West Wind*, which was neither "tin clad" nor armed, remained with Harding.[3]

Harding was now the senior officer on site, and he assumed command of all 550 troops in the vicinity of Glasgow. The son of a portrait artist and a personal favorite of William Rosecrans, Harding was a competent and experienced officer who had served in a number of important staff and regimental commands in the MSM. In at least one respect, Harding now occupied a very favorable position. Glasgow sat upon a hill that rose precipitously from the banks of the Missouri River. Any attacking force would have a difficult slog up that hill if it were to take the town. In most other respects, however, Harding would have a tough time resisting anything beyond a band of guerrillas. Although the local militia had in recent weeks started construction of two fortifications atop the hill and facing to the south and east, both forts were neither terribly imposing nor large enough to accommodate all of Harding's men. At most Harding could jam forty troops in each of the forts, while also emplacing about two hundred soldiers in the rifle pits that connected them. Harding tried to expand the length of his line by anchoring its southern face at some freshly dug rifle pits near Second Street and its eastern face at a schoolhouse where the Huntsville Plank Road entered town. The line now extended over eight hundred yards, but it was highly porous with woodpiles, stables, houses, and commercial buildings substituting for connected entrenchments. Given the state of these defenses, Harding deployed most of his troops well outside the line and astride the various roads that emptied into the town from Keytesville, Huntsville, Fayette, and Boonville. Harding took care also to push patrols two miles out on each of these roads to forestall any surprises.[4]

Despite the preparations, Harding was rudely shocked at 5 AM on the 15th when Jo Shelby opened up with his artillery and sharpshooters. Shelby concentrated his fire on the *West Wind*, the streets above the levee, and the still-burning campfires of several units encamped around town. While the incoming rounds sparked an exodus of citizens and isolated the *West Wind* from the rest of Harding's troops, the cannon fire was not terribly deadly. A handful of Yankees and their horses were killed, but perhaps the most notable casualty was William G. Caples, a Methodist minister who had served earlier in the war as a Confederate chaplain. As Shelby's rounds fell within

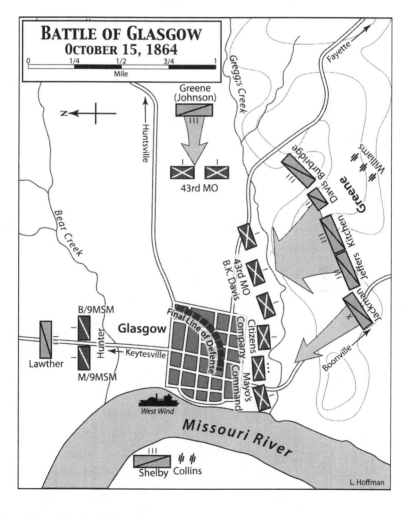

Figure 7.1.   Battle of Glasgow, October 15, 1864

the town, Caples refused to seek shelter, exclaiming that "God had put a band
of iron around him, and the shell of his friends . . . would never harm him."
Unfortunately, the good chaplain's confidence was misplaced. To the shock
of those near him, a cannonball soon blew off one of his legs, wounding him
mortally. Caples's death notwithstanding, Harding was able to send a number
of sharpshooters to the houses facing the river. They quickly neutralized the
much more exposed Confederate sharpshooters, forcing them into brush well
back from the river. An even bigger problem for Shelby was that John B.
Clark Jr. was nowhere to be found. Clark's crossing of the Missouri River
had not gone according to plan as the landing at Arrow Rock could not
readily accommodate large numbers of men. Only at midnight had Clark
succeeded in getting his command across. By the time Shelby commenced
his bombardment, Clark was still three miles south of Glasgow. Harding was
thus unaware of Clark's advance when he received a frantic report from his
pickets north of the town along the Keytesville Road that nine hundred
Confederates were fast approaching. Harding seems to have doubted this
report and sent only a token force of independent militia from Saline County
to reinforce the pickets on the Keytesville Road. The militia rode out of town
and promptly fled to Macon City without ever realizing that the report of
nine hundred Confederates was false.[5]

While Harding was therefore occupied looking west across the river at
Shelby and north for a phantom regiment of Confederate cavalry, pickets
from the south came racing in with the news of another big force of Confederates advancing on the town. Clark had finally arrived, and he rapidly deployed his troops about Glasgow with an eye to cutting off all escape. He
arrayed most of his men and Williams's artillery along a ridge that extended
east from the Missouri River for more than two miles to the Fayette Road.
Astride the road from Boonville, and thus closest to the Missouri River,
Clark placed Jackman's brigade. To its right, he positioned his brigade then
commanded by Colton Greene. That brigade formed from west to east with
the units of Jeffers, Kitchen, Davies, and Burbridge. Clark also arrayed Colton Greene's 3rd Missouri, then commanded by Captain Benjamin Johnson,
directly east of the town, while swinging Robert Lawther's 10th Missouri all
the way around to the north, blocking the road to Keytesville. As Clark made
these dispositions, he drafted two local townsmen and sent them into Harding's lines with a gentle request to surrender, noting, "You are old home
boys, and I do not want to hurt you." Harding was befuddled by the request,
as it came not through a commissioned Confederate, but rather civilians. The

Union commander chose then to deny the request. Consequently, by 8 AM Clark signaled the beginning of the attack with a number of salvos from Williams's artillery. Williams directed his fire at a hastily formed line of Yankees positioned behind Gregg's Creek, which ran across the main axis of advance. To Clark's good fortune, the creek was readily fordable and not a major obstacle, especially when the defenders were outgunned by more than three to one. Still, a mixture of local citizen guards and elements of the 43rd Missouri resisted the Confederate advance with a series of volleys and even a countercharge against Jackman's brigade along the Boonville Road. By 10 AM, however, the Confederates had pushed across the creek and forced Harding's troops through town and into their predesignated defensive line. At this time Jo Shelby's artillery became a factor in the battle as it swept the streets not only hitting several of the buildings along Harding's line but also pinning down troops and hindering their movements. Frustrated by his somewhat detached role in the battle, Shelby moreover determined to make a bold attempt to seize the *West Wind*, and he sent a handful of volunteers across the river in a large skiff. Having called for reinforcements from Price, Shelby intended to use the *West Wind* to ferry his column over the river. It was, however, all for naught. Despite attracting the attention of seemingly every blue-coated sharpshooter in Glasgow, the volunteers made it to the *West Wind* unscathed only to discover the engines disabled. The daring volunteers had to return to Shelby minus their steamboat.[6]

No matter his success in repelling Shelby's amphibious dreams, Chester Harding's situation rapidly deteriorated. Despite a failure of Robert Lawther's 10th Missouri to drive from the north and collapse Harding's rear, the Confederates were by noon close to breaching the Union line at a number of points. Fighting had become house to house with combatants now only separated, in some cases, by a few yards. Already having suffered eleven killed and thirty-two wounded, Harding held a council of war with several officers and concluded he would surrender if Clark offered honorable terms and guarantees of protection. Not wanting any valuable supplies to fall into Confederate hands, Harding ordered the burning of the City Hall, which contained fifty thousand rations, if not the reported five thousand small arms. To the chagrin of many in Glasgow, a brisk wind caused the fire to spread to several other buildings. By the time the fire had been extinguished, Glasgow had lost at least fifteen buildings valued at $130,000.[7]

Whatever disappointment John B. Clark Jr. must have felt in not getting the weapons, he was anxious to avoid any more casualties of his own. Clark made no official report of the numbers involved, but his losses most certainly exceeded those of Harding. With little haggling, he therefore offered liberal terms of surrender, which included a parade, the ability of officers to retain their side arms, horses, and private property, and a parole to Harding's location of choice. True to his word, Clark the next day ferried Harding and his men across the river and escorted them with fifty troopers to the nearest Federal force on the Lamine River. It was a gentlemanly, and atypical, end to a battle in Missouri. It was an ending made even more atypical by the matter-of-fact report of Harding's adjutant, George A. Holloway. Writing just three days after the surrender, Holloway took pains not only to praise the behavior of Shelby and Clark but also a series of lesser officers, including, of all people, the infamous William C. Quantrill. Unbeknownst to Clark, Quantrill and a small band of his men had indeed joined the attacking Confederates and had somehow managed to behave themselves in the immediate aftermath of the victory. Only after Clark and Harding had departed on the 16th did Quantrill revert somewhat to form and rob the Thomson and Dunnica Bank of $21,000.[8]

Sterling Price's foray to Glasgow had been a success. There were, of course, disappointments. The rumors of five thousand weapons stored in the City Hall had proven false, and the burning of fifty thousand rations was nothing to take lightly. Yet there was reason to be happy. Jo Shelby and John B. Clark Jr. had executed a complicated plan of attack fairly well. Clark's late arrival on the battlefield was inconsequential, and the subsequent performance of his troops did much to wipe away the memory of their disastrous attack at Pilot Knob. More importantly, Clark and Shelby rode away from Glasgow with a heavy load of supplies and ordnance that had escaped the flames. When Clark's quartermasters made the final accounting, the victory at Glasgow yielded over 1,200 small arms and one thousand uniforms for Sterling Price's ragtag army.[9]

Price's willingness to initiate large-scale subsidiary raids while marching through the Boonslick did not end with the attack upon Glasgow. Indeed, no sooner had Price sent Shelby riding toward Glasgow on the evening of the 14th than he had also determined to try a raid of equal scale to seize Sedalia, which sat about twenty-six miles south of the army's camps at Jonesborough. In Sedalia's case, however, the lure was not weapons or prisoners. Instead, Price had received some information that the Union army had stockpiled both mules and cattle by the thousands in Sedalia. This was news that Price could hardly ignore. His quartermasters had long struggled to mount and feed the army, but the march through the Boonslick exasperated the problem, as Price was suddenly faced with thousands of new recruits who needed both food and horses. Any move to take Sedalia came with large risks. Not only would the operation further delay Price's westward march, but it represented an even greater fragmentation of an army already spread dangerously thin. Nevertheless, and despite vague reports of Federal troops marching west from Jefferson City, Price directed Jeff Thompson to attack the small Federal post at Sedalia and bring back the "drove of cattle and mules said to be in that neighborhood." He would be accompanied by the remaining section of Collins's battery commanded by Lieutenant David Harris.[10]

Thompson readied his brigade throughout the night of the 14th and 15th. It was a far more difficult task than it should have been. Most of the men of the Iron Brigade were natives of the Boonslick, and both Shelby and Thompson had been more than lenient in granting furloughs. In fact, when Thompson mustered his brigade at 3 AM on the 15th, he counted only 1,200 troopers out of an aggregate strength of more than two thousand men. According to Shelby, six hundred soldiers were "scattered about at their homes in Saline and La Fayette, many with leave and many without." Undeterred, Thompson departed from Jonesborough and stopped first at Longwood, about thirteen miles to the south. There Thompson met up with Alonzo Slayback's battalion, which Price had previously ordered to the south of the army in order to scout for the Federal troops rumored to have marched from Jefferson City. Slayback did not bring comforting news. Patrolling a bit further south that day, Slayback had observed a large body of Yankee cavalry passing to the west. Thompson was properly concerned about this development, but he chose to continue the march. The brigade moved cautiously after daybreak, reaching the outskirts of Georgetown around 9 AM. There Thompson's scouts cornered two stragglers from the Federal column that had passed through the previous day. The stragglers were ex-Confederates who claimed to have been impressed into the Union ranks from Gratiot Prison. They readily offered a gold mine of intelligence that momentarily aborted Thompson's mission. The stragglers belonged to John Sanborn's cavalry, and they not only provided Thompson with confirmation that Sanborn had passed the previous day, but that twelve thousand to eighteen thousand Federal infantry under A. J. Smith had massed at Jefferson City. Worse yet, the stragglers claimed that at least ten thousand of the infantry were already at California and due to march toward Georgetown. They also reported the news that the Federals were concentrating an army at Kansas City to dispute Price's west-

ward march. Thompson was more than troubled by all of this, and he immediately dispatched a note to Sterling Price, relaying the information and
telling Price that he would not ride on to Sedalia. Thompson did not want to
march any further south while leaving two large enemy forces in his rear that
had the potential to close off all avenues of return to Price. Instead, Thompson wanted to march northwest toward Sanborn with the intention of harassing the Yankee and drawing him away from Price's main body.[11]

Thompson remained near Georgetown until noon when new information
from his scouts altered the plan once more. Thompson believed that Sanborn's brigade was encamped too far to the west to stop his advance upon
Sedalia. No less important, Thompson thought, erroneously, that the Federal
infantry was headed north toward Price and not west toward Georgetown.
Much as he had determined earlier to divert Sanborn from Price, the Missouri
Swamp Fox now concluded that an attack upon Sedalia would draw the
infantry south, toward him, and away from Price's main body. Thompson
then crafted a simple plan of attack. Sedalia was stuck in the middle of an
expansive prairie with few trees and even fewer terrain features to mask the
Confederate approach. Two small redoubts connected by rifle pits housed a
garrison of nearly eight hundred EMM and local home guards all commanded by Colonel J. D. Crawford of the 40th EMM. Given these circumstances, Thompson believed surprise was the only way to crack the town.
Accordingly, he ordered his brigade into a column of fours with Elliot's
regiment in the advance. With most of Elliot's troopers decked out in captured blue Federal coats, Thompson hoped to advance quickly upon a garrison fooled into thinking friendly troops had arrived. Although the garrison at
Sedalia was on alert for a Confederate attack, Elliot got within pistol shot of
some pickets stationed one mile outside of the town before the Federals
recognized their foe, fired a harmless volley, and then galloped for the town.
As Thompson then described it, a kind of steeplechase ensued for one mile as
the Iron Brigade ran down the pickets and burst into the Federal defenses.
Elliot's cavalry had separated itself from the rest of the brigade and quickly
pounded into, over, and through the earthworks, scattering many of the home
guards and EMM, including their commander, Colonel Crawford. However,
a large number of troops rallied around a detachment of thirty men from the
7th MSM who had only recently arrived in Sedalia after escorting a wagon
train. This act of resistance stunned Elliot's Confederates, and they beat a
quick retreat out of the works. The setback was only temporary. In less than
ten minutes, the rest of the brigade and Harris's artillery deployed in line

before the fortifications. Harris then showered the Federals with several rounds, prompting the remainder of the EMM to flee and leaving the plucky soldiers of the 7th MSM to surrender the works. For the militia that attempted to escape, yet another steeplechase followed as the Confederates ran them into the prairie, killing and capturing an undetermined number.[12]

Thompson's cavalry soon turned around and headed back to town. Once there, the men commenced a brief celebration capped by one trooper removing the Union flag from its pole and then riding around the area with the flag draped around his shoulders. This diversion aside, Jeff Thompson chose not to linger. The Confederate commander hoped that the noise of his attack, as well as any reports that might leak out, would soon divert Sanborn and A. J. Smith to Sedalia and away from Price. The trick, then, for Thompson was to not actually be there should the Federals move in his direction. For Thompson, the capture of Sedalia also represented the first time in the campaign where he commanded the initial capture of a town or depot. He was thus determined that the impressment of captured goods be done by regulations and not by indiscriminate looting. No sooner had the Federals surrendered than Thompson ordered his regiments into line to await the orders of the various commissary officers and quartermasters. Some within the ranks did not know quite how to take this and chose to ignore the order as they had ignored most attempted restraints since their arrival in Missouri. Thompson, however, gained some control over the situation when he spanked a few looters with his saber while shooting the mule from underneath another. Still, with a brigade numbering 1,200 soldiers Thompson was unable to stop all plundering, but that which did take place followed a familiar pattern seen throughout the expedition. Private homes escaped unscathed, while numerous stores were ransacked.[13]

Just before dark, Thompson was ready to leave. But before Thompson could depart with a booty that included nearly two thousand cattle and mules, he had also to dispose of his prisoners. With over three hundred frightened Federals milling about the captured fortifications, Thompson easily concluded that he could neither take them with him nor offer them a traditional written parole. Time was simply too scarce. Desperate to ride, Thompson hurriedly assembled the Yankees and verbally paroled them, but not before delivering what he called a "spread-eagle speech" filled with bombast and ominous threats should the prisoners violate their parole. Thompson ignored the protests of several Yankee officers, who deemed the parole illegal, and promptly marched out of town with his bellowing herd of animals in tow.

Dumbfounded, the abandoned Federals waited the night in Sedalia before most departed the next morning for Jefferson City in search of friendly forces. Thompson's return march to Price was no easy thing. Sanborn's scouts had to be avoided, and the march was painfully slow as the animal herd often slowed the pace to a crawl. Nevertheless, Thompson safely linked back with Price on the evening of the 18th near Keiser's Farm on the Salt Fork River.[14]

As Price anticipated the arrival of Thompson, the extended march through the Boonslick seemed to offer renewed hope for the idea of liberating the state from Yankee rule. The outpouring of Confederate sympathies had been overwhelming. Recruits had streamed into the ranks, and tactical victories at Boonville, Carrollton, Glasgow, and Sedalia had finally bagged the large quantities of prisoners and ordnance that the Confederates had always desired. But Price's flush time in the Boonslick masked dramatic events taking place further to the east and west. Large numbers of Union troops had finally mobilized and were now massing all around Price's army.

For Price, his most immediate concern was reports of newly arrived Union infantry and cavalry that had begun concentrating around Jefferson City. For William Rosecrans, the very fact that he could concentrate any fresh troops at all was a minor miracle. Sterling Price had systematically destroyed huge chunks of the Pacific Railway and most every bridge between Kirkwood and Jefferson City. Indeed, it was not until October 20th that Union work gangs had entirely repaired the railroad to Hermann. Making matters worse, Rosecrans could rely little upon river transport. Despite what had been a wet October, the Missouri River remained shallow, stopping a number of the available ferries and troop transports, especially between Washington and Jefferson City. By October 9th, no boat drawing more than three-and-a-half feet could make it to the capital city. In practical terms, there were few such steamers on the Missouri, and those that did exist could only move at a sloth's pace of no more than five miles per hour. Most reinforcements to the militia already congregated in central Missouri would, generally speaking, have to march to get there.[15]

Leading that march would be 4,500 infantry from the 3rd Division of A. J. Smith's XVI Corps and the three regiments of volunteer cavalry that had spent the last days of September guarding St. Louis. In a move befitting the military emergency, Rosecrans chose also to send Brigadier General E. C. Pike's division of inexperienced EMM infantry that had been organized in the early panic to defend St. Louis. By October 6th Pike took two of his brigades and joined Smith's 3rd Division at Port William, about ten miles to the east of Union. The next morning, both divisions started for Jefferson City. However, it quickly became obvious that the EMM would have difficulty in completing the mission. In the march to Union, the militiamen were strung out all along the road with most of them having overpacked their food and clothing. Blisters and simple exhaustion nearly decimated the ranks. The story was only slightly better on October 8th. Although straggling decreased, Pike's infantry labored to make a thirteen-mile march to John's Creek where they halted for the night. The agony for Pike and his men continued one more day when on the 9th Rosecrans halted their march and ordered them back to St. Louis.[16]

The 3rd Division resumed the march on the 10th as the weather grew progressively colder. Over the next few days, Smith's infantry averaged more than eighteen miles per day with the only remarkable event being the crossing of the waist-deep Gasconade River on the first day out. According to George Swain of the 58th Illinois, the crossing of the division drew the wide-eyed attention of four or five German girls who watched the men strip down from the waist and carry their clothing across the river. Once through the cold water the men pressed on to Jefferson City, arriving October 12th through the 13th. Unfortunately for the now exhausted troops, there was little time to rest. Some of the units marched straight through to California, while others waited for a series of trains to carry them to the same place. With Sterling Price's headquarters then only thirty miles away near Jonesborough, Smith got orders to pause and rest his men.[17]

Smith's pause had less to do with exhaustion than it did with simple numbers. William Rosecrans did not believe Smith's 3rd Division, and the three cavalry regiments that had accompanied it, were enough to deal with Price. Rosecrans could now count on more than eleven thousand soldiers in the area, exclusive of the unreliable EMM, but he chose instead to remain in a defensive posture that took advantage of a pocket formed by the bend in the Missouri River. While the main body of Price's army stayed well within the pocket, Rosecrans pushed his newly arrived infantry and cavalry to the west along the entrance to the pocket. At best, Rosecrans hoped he could contain, or restrict, Price's movements to the river counties between the Lamine and Lexington. Any more aggressive action, Rosecrans believed, would have to wait for reinforcements in the shape of Smith's 1st Division of infantry under James Mower and about two thousand cavalry commanded by Colonel Edward F. Winslow. Given the numerical disparity of troops, the course of the

Missouri River, and the anticipated arrival of Mower, Rosecrans made the right choice. It was, however, just the type of decision that had frustrated Rosecrans's powerful critics in the Union high command. By mid-October, Edwin Stanton, Henry Halleck, and Ulysses Grant had concluded that Rosecrans should have already caught and disposed of Price. In keeping with Grant's earlier impulse to just sack Rosecrans, Edwin Stanton on October 16th suggested to Lincoln that either Major General John A. "Black Jack" Logan or Major General Joseph Hooker should be sent west to take command in Missouri. For the time being, Lincoln ignored the request, and Rosecrans remained oblivious to the backroom machinations. Old Rosey was thus free to tie his offensive hopes to the arrival of Mower's troops. Nevertheless, the appearance of these troops would only occur after an extraordinary march.[18]

Mower's and Winslow's active campaigning had started back on September 1st. Previous to that, Mower and Winslow had been in Memphis preparing to join Sherman in his Atlanta campaign, much the same as A. J. Smith's 3rd Division had been doing in Cairo, Illinois. However, at the prodding of Major General C. C. Washburn in Memphis, the commander of the Division of West Mississippi, E. R. S. Canby, diverted Mower and Winslow into Arkansas to help Frederick Steele track down Sterling Price. It was a waste of valuable assets. After marching 150 miles into central Arkansas, the troops did little of anything except get sick. Steele had lost all contact with Price and then made little effort to determine his location or route. Only by September 16 did Steele trace Price to northeastern Arkansas and send Mower and Winslow in pursuit. It was futile. The Yankees were ninety-five miles behind Price, and they never got close. By October 2, the chase exhausted itself at Greenville, almost fifty miles north of the Arkansas-Missouri border. Mower and Winslow turned to the east and the safe haven of Cape Girardeau. They had just marched nearly 320 miles to seemingly little purpose.[19]

Notwithstanding the futility of the march and the exhaustion inflicted upon these troops, the Union war machine would ensure that those same soldiers did not remain combat ineffective for long. By October 7, and just two days after Mower and Winslow arrived at Cape Girardeau, steamboats arrived to transport their men to St. Louis. Three days later, the infantry and cavalry were at Benton Barracks where they peeled off their filthy uniforms, bathed, and received treatments of rubbing alcohol to rid their bodies of lice. Quartermasters issued new clothing and boots, and the cavalry turned in unserviceable horses. Within two days, Winslow had received five hundred new horses, five ambulances, and five wagons plus complete teams. It was, in other words, a material rejuvenation that would have been alien to any Confederate commander—especially one in the Trans-Mississippi. [20]

From St. Louis, Rosecrans tried to hurry these valuable reinforcements to the front. With Price then at Jefferson City, Rosecrans pushed the infantry and more than seven hundred cavalry onto steamboats for the journey up the Missouri River on the 8th and 9th. For some of the troops, but especially the cavalry, the trip went quickly and smoothly. Due more to simple luck than precise logistical planning, the boats carrying the cavalry drew less water and therefore easily navigated the unusually shallow Missouri River between Jefferson City and Hermann. Mower's infantry did not fare so well. Even with many of the soldiers stationed around the decks of the boats to look for sand bars and snags, the vessels ran aground several times. The only way to refloat the boats was for the troops to disembark. It was a time-consuming process that left officers and men fuming. It was also an exceedingly cold process as more often than not the troops were dumped ashore at night with no blankets. With little to ward off the freezing temperatures, it became common to see the men burrowing into haystacks for whatever warmth they could find. Efforts to get the troops upriver were also upset by one regiment of Missouri infantry that refused to make the trip. As their enlistments had expired, these troops thought it well within their rights to boycott the defense of Missouri. At Washington, the regiment disembarked from their boats and refused to go any further. However, the protestors were not terribly committed to staying at the wharf. On October 13th, the 4th Iowa rode into the area and then easily herded the Missourians back onto their boats. Given such delays, the transports bearing the infantry only reached Jefferson City on the 15th and would not complete their mission for another three days when the 3rd Brigade of the 1st Division pulled ashore. Indicative of just how slow the journey upriver had been, Winslow and his remaining 1,200 cavalry, which had never boarded the boats, galloped into Jefferson City on the 16th after having ridden 138 miles from St. Louis. It was a tough march and one that especially jarred its commander. Winslow, long bothered by a severe pain in his left leg, made the trip reclined in an ambulance. [21]

As Mower's infantry first came ashore at Jefferson City, they discovered two things. First, Joseph Mower was in fact no longer their commander. On the 11th, he had been ordered to William T. Sherman's army in Georgia, leaving Colonel Joseph J. Woods of the 12th Iowa in command of the 1st Division. Second, and only after being hurriedly marched out of the city toward California, the men realized that there still would be no immediate offensive. With the 1st Division still strung out along the Missouri River, William Rosecrans, who would himself arrive at Jefferson City on the 17th, wanted to wait still longer in order to concentrate his forces. But more importantly, the 1st Division even when reunited with A. J. Smith's 3rd Division quickly ran into a natural barrier that slowed the westward pursuit of Price. Before Jeff Thompson's raid on Sedalia, Jo Shelby had sent a detachment to the south of Price's main body to burn the Pacific Railway Bridge over the Lamine River. Located one mile to the east of Otterville, the bridge was completely destroyed. Making matters far worse for the Union, the best fords were about twelve miles to the north of the bridge. With the blue-clad infantry heavily dependent upon its wagons and the railroad for logistical support, movement ground to a halt. The men of the XVI Corps now began to pile up on the east bank of the Lamine River. Not all of the 1st Division's men were disappointed by the delay. For many, the encampment was a welcome lull after their forced march through Arkansas and Missouri. According to trooper Socrates Walmsley of the 2nd New Jersey Cavalry, "the rest was like heaven, and no bugs." The respite did not, however, cause Walmsley to forget the important things in his life as a cavalryman. Each night on the Lamine he went to bed praying for his family, squad, and horse.[22]

There was one other consequence in the destruction of the bridge. Not only did it stall the advance of the XVI Corps, it also degraded John Sanborn's ability to stay close to Price's main body west and north of the Lamine River. Sanborn, who had disengaged from Price at Boonville on October 12 due to a concern over forage, found himself in a similar situation on the 17th. Two days earlier, he had marched to Cook's Store about seventeen miles to the southwest of Price who was then stopped at the Salt Fork River; however, Sanborn once again fretted about his available forage while struggling to determine Price's exact whereabouts. Despite Old Pap's almost glacial movements, Sanborn thought the Confederates were eight miles further west at Waverly. Sanborn's original intention had been to attack Price in his flank should the Confederates march west toward Lexington, but the Union cavalryman concluded that his need for supplies outweighed the benefit of finding and hitting Price. Moreover, he feared engaging Price, with no nearby bridge over the Lamine guaranteeing resupply and reinforcement. On the afternoon of the 17th and at the suggestion of A. J. Smith, Sanborn decided to retire about five miles south to a position on the Blackwater River and await a supply column from Sedalia.[23]

Sanborn's withdrawal came at a most opportune moment for Sterling Price. For the three previous days, Old Pap had been fretting about his decision to dispatch the subsidiary expeditions to Sedalia and Glasgow. He had dispersed his army greatly, leaving the main body to consist only of the trains, Fagan's division, and Freeman's brigade of Marmaduke's division. Just as problematic, Price had to slow the westward march of the main body so that Thompson, Clark, and Shelby could more easily rejoin him. Accordingly, on October 15th Price marched just twelve miles to the northwest from Jonesborough to Kiser's Bridge on the Salt Fork. Only upon encamping for the night did Price receive word of the triumph at Glasgow. Though elated, Price then hurriedly dispatched orders to both Shelby and Clark to return without delay, while also ordering Marmaduke to investigate the reports of both Alonzo Slayback and Jeff Thompson that Sanborn's cavalry was advancing from Georgetown to Lexington. Price then sat and waited anxiously at Kiser's until the night of the 17th when Clark rode ahead of his brigade and reported back for duty. The next day, Shelby and the remainder of Clark's brigade arrived at Kiser's, and the newly reunified army headed west. It would stop at Waverly after a twenty-two-mile march. [24]

Although Price had become increasingly concerned about the vulnerability of his army in the final passage through the Boonslick, an air of invincibility, or perhaps unreality, still circulated among the troops. The army's officer corps continued to entertain civilian relatives and guests, including Old Pap's long-exiled son, Edwin. More importantly, Price was determined to take advantage of the lull to recruit still more men, and he reissued what had become a fairly standard appeal to the citizenry "to throw off the shackles which have bound you for nearly three years" and join "the army I have brought for your redemption." With no small amount of satisfaction, William McPheeters could note that Price's siren call continued to resonate in the Boonslick as men by the hundreds poured into the army's ranks. "The people of Mo [*sic*] are thoroughly aroused," McPheeters exclaimed on the 14th, and "it is evident that the great heart of the people are thoroughly with us." [25]

Unfortunately for the Confederacy, "the great heart of the people" secured neither health nor discipline for the army. Officers and men persisted in going AWOL to visit family and friends. Some of the more egregious examples occurred among Marmaduke's own staff. Fagan's division was hardly better. Ever since they had entered the Boonslick, the men from Arkansas had become something akin to second-class soldiers within Price's army. Married to Price's headquarters and trains, Fagan's men received neither morale-boosting furloughs nor opportunities to engage in adventurous and profitable independent operations. Some officers fell to quarreling among themselves, with two even finding time to fight a duel on the morning of the 18th. The duel itself was more farce than tragedy. After a dispute whose details have been long lost to history, the two officers, Major Albert Belding and Major William F. Rapley, faced off at fifteen paces with revolvers. According to the terms, both men could advance upon firing the first shot. When the duel commenced, Rapley held his ground while Belding advanced. Belding was soon hit, but he continued toward Rapley, firing at every staggering step. Fifteen paces later, Belding fell at Rapley's feet not having hit his opponent at all. Bloody and in great distress, Belding could only toss aside his revolver and exclaim, "My God! I ought to be killed for not hitting a man as close as this." Though Belding most certainly should have been killed, he somehow survived his wounds.[26]

With considerably less drama, yet far more significance for the army, Price's quartermaster and commissariat could not maintain Fagan's division. Dropping temperatures magnified food shortages, particularly in breadstuffs, and the men suffered greatly from a lack of blankets. It was thus with no small amount of frustration that Fagan's divisional surgeon reported an enormous sick list composed of soldiers having "catarrh, bronchitis, pneumonia, rheumatic affections, and glandular swellings."[27]

No less indicative of the condition of the army as a whole, many men continued to plunder whenever they could get away with it. This was certainly the case at Marshall where some of Price's troops managed to ransack the post office and pilfer $136,000 as the army moved through the town. It was also the case when the army pulled into Waverly. This small Missouri River town was most notable as the home of Jo Shelby. The town had thus long been marked by Unionists and pillaged throughout the war. Most of the homes of the town's Confederate sympathizers had been trashed or burned out with even their trees uprooted in revenge. Jo Shelby had been a particular target, as the Unionists well nigh obliterated his house and hemp factory. Despite such ruination, there was no shortage of Confederates who were willing to add to the damage. Colonel John C. Wright, yet again of Fagan's division and one who had long revealed himself to be more adept at plunder than combat, candidly admitted to allowing his "men to go into the stores and help themselves to whatever they needed." Not unexpectedly, Wright's men hit at least one store owned by a Southern sympathizer. The surprise for this storeowner was not so much that he had been looted by avowed Confederates, but rather the simple fact that Wright's foot-sore Arkansans had exchanged their tattered footwear with his stock of ladies shoes.[28]

There is one final note to make regarding the passage of Price's army through the Boonslick. In recent years, historians have focused attention upon the Confederate army's treatment of blacks in its marches through Union-controlled territory. This is especially so in the Gettysburg campaign where historians have taken General Robert E. Lee and his army greatly to task for their enslavement, or capture, of blacks in Pennsylvania. It is an issue that prompts a similar inquiry in Price's march through Missouri. The evidence is frustratingly thin, but it seems certain that Price's army, or the many bands of men recruiting on behalf of the army, grabbed an undetermined number of blacks, free and slave. There are a few primary accounts that attest to this. Governor Thomas C. Reynolds in his scathing post-invasion criticism of Price noted that a rabble, including "stolen Negroes on stolen horses," followed the army. Jo Shelby in his report of the campaign referenced the capture of twenty-three Negroes in the vicinity of Potosi. On the other side of the conflict, Captain A. J. Hart of the Morgan County Provisional EMM described an encounter on October 12th, whereby his unit captured five "Negroes, which the rebels had stolen and were taking South." The *Missouri State Times* in its rendition of Price's passage near Jefferson City reported that Price's men conscripted men, "both white and black, and negro boys not more than twelve years old." However, complicating any precise assessment of those blacks forcibly taken in Missouri was the presence of hundreds of slaves who had accompanied their masters on the expedition. Further complicating the assessment was the practice of temporarily impressing blacks to perform fatigue details such as grinding corn. Ultimately, however, there was considerable ambiguity within the army's leadership about the possible theft of blacks. James Fagan illustrated this during the passage through the Boonslick when rumors reached him that some soldiers had confiscated slaves. Fagan was aghast at this possibility, and he promptly ordered an assistant adjutant general to inspect his division's camps for any such thing. Remarkably, the inspection turned up one slave woman in the possession of a regimental quartermaster in Cabell's brigade. Fagan then promptly arrested the quartermaster. All of this does not directly address the confiscation of slaves in the other divisions, nor does it say anything about the potential enslavement of free blacks. However, in the absence of any other evidence it does suggest that official policy mitigated the extent to which Price's army actually seized black Missourians.[29]

Chapter Eight

Men of Kansas, Rally!

Sterling Price's expedition did not stop partisan politics in either Kansas or Missouri. However, the outcome of the Union's national and statewide elections in Missouri could offer no surprises outside of Price's ability to occupy and hold the major population centers. Loyalty oaths had effectively marginalized the state Democratic Party, giving the Republicans a stranglehold on elective office. Although there was considerable dispute between the radical and moderate factions of the Republican Party, the radicals had relatively clear sailing to maintain control of both the legislature and the governor's mansion. Consequently, Price's expedition would not greatly affect the outcome of the election, and neither would the election shape the state's military reaction to the invasion. Such was not the case in Kansas. Indeed, with Price's army pointed toward Kansas, state politics and military operations would soon be intertwined to a remarkable degree and with potentially disastrous consequences for the Union.

The root of this politico-military entanglement lay in the bare-knuckle nature of Kansas politics and the complete supremacy of the Republican Party in the state. Given the lack of party opposition in Kansas, it was hardly surprising that Republican Party factional chiefs controlled the state's politics. Of all such chiefs, none dominated Kansas quite like James H. Lane. A veteran of the state's bloody territorial period, Lane had become the de facto leader of a militant Radical Republicanism that tended to express itself with cries of abolitionism and violent guerrilla, or Jayhawking, raids into Missouri. Elected senator upon Kansas's admission into the Union in 1861, Lane held a vicelike grip on the state's government through a magnetic personality and a willingness to reward his friends with the spoils of political corruption, army contracts, and booty from Missouri. Shrewd like no other politician in Kansas, Lane ruined the reputation of the state's first governor, Charles Robinson, through a trumped-up impeachment and then subsequently used his political machine to help elect the successor. Lane exercised his influence, and accumulated still more power, through the auspices of Abraham Lincoln. Dating back to March 1861 when Lane and his self-appointed "Frontier Guard" of federal patronage seekers provided armed security for the skittish president in Washington, Lincoln entrusted Lane to handle most matters in faraway Kansas. The resultant federal patronage, which included both a commission as a brigadier general and the ability to overrule the governor in appointing officers to state regiments, was unprecedented. The collection of such power in Kansas was guaranteed also to stir opposition, and by the time of Price's campaign in 1864 it was an opposition located squarely in the state's governor, Thomas Carney.

Stocky, prematurely bald, and aloof, the governor was the physical and political antithesis of Jim Lane. Carney had come to Kansas during the territorial period to sell groceries, not fight pro-slave southerners. While Lane toiled for years to gain popular favor among Kansans, Carney systematically built the largest wholesale grocery in the territory. But Carney's business acumen soon propelled him into politics as a state legislator in January 1862. Less than one year later, Carney found himself elected governor by virtue of his business reputation and the sheer disinterest of Senator Lane, who viewed Carney as a political nullity. Carney was, however, an ambitious man, and his sense of gubernatorial power did not allow for any interference by Senator Lane. No sooner, then, did Carney become governor than he began a political war with his fellow Republican for control of the state government. This political struggle defined much of Kansas's wartime history, and by the fall of 1864 it sucked most soldiers associated with the state into one of the two competing political camps.

Although Governor Carney had a lock on the loyalty of most militia commanders in the state, Senator Lane retained the allegiance of several senior officers among the volunteer units in the region. Of these men, none were as important as Major General James G. Blunt. Short and powerfully built, Blunt's deep-set eyes and shaggy beard gave him, according to Howard N. Monnett's memorable description, the look of "a fanatic—a dark and dangerous man." A common seaman in his youth and a doctor by training, Blunt arrived in Kansas in 1856 and soon dropped any pretense of practicing medicine. He chose, instead, to devote most of his time to following both John Brown and Jim Lane on an assortment of raids against pro-slavers in Kansas and Missouri. By the start of the Civil War, Blunt had become a member of Lane's inner circle of friends. Under Lane's guiding patronage, Blunt began a meteoric rise through the volunteer ranks, reaching major general in March 1863.[1]

Fearless in battle, Blunt was also personally debased in much the same fashion as Jim Lane. His sense of the truth was elastic, and he cared little for anyone who got in his way. He manipulated government contracts to his own benefit. He used the army payroll to lard his headquarters with female servants and other self-pronounced "exceteries" he could never quite explain in official correspondence. Perhaps most ominously, Blunt possessed a highly strung personality that would eventually land him in an insane asylum at the end of his life. But in the fall of 1864 James Blunt commanded the newly created District of Upper Arkansas in the Department of Kansas. In this position, Blunt was a very busy man with little real military responsibility. As he had throughout 1863 and 1864, the general spent prodigious amounts of time chasing rogue Indians, skimming profits from government contracts, and feuding with various political and military figures. With a list of enemies that included generals Henry Halleck, Thomas Ewing, and John M. Schofield, Blunt considered Thomas Carney a particularly heinous scoundrel. Beginning in the summer of 1863, the governor had openly aired charges of corruption against Blunt, while also seeking to remove a series of volunteer officers appointed by either Blunt or his benefactor Jim Lane. Carney's attacks pushed Blunt into a frothy rage. In a letter to Carney, he denounced the governor as nothing more than the leader of "secret assassins in my rear." Blunt was, however, only warming up. In a tirade addressed to Abraham Lincoln, Blunt thundered that "a greater thief and corrupt villain than Thomas Carney does not live, and all that he lacks to make him a finished scoundrel is his stupidity and want of brains."[2]

Blunt's alliance with Lane was thus no surprise. They were two men motivated just as much by power and the spoils of war as they were by any ideological concern. The same thing, however, could not be said of Major General Samuel R. Curtis, another important ally of Senator Lane. Grim faced and portly, Curtis was a hard-bitten West Point graduate of the class of 1831. A veteran of the Mexican War, Curtis led a varied life after graduation that included stints as a lawyer, civil engineer, railroad promoter, and politician. By 1861, Curtis was a prominent Republican congressman from Iowa notable primarily for his strident abolitionism. Considered briefly for a spot in Lincoln's cabinet, Curtis resigned his seat in Congress to take command of an Iowa infantry regiment in 1861. Over the next three years, Curtis drew attention to himself not only for his victory at the Battle of Pea Ridge but also for his vocal advocacy of abolitionism while a commander of the Department of the Missouri. That advocacy led to a very public feud with Missouri's governor, Hamilton Gamble, which in turn got Curtis fired. The only thing left for the Lincoln administration was to move him even further west to lead the newly created Department of Kansas in the fall of 1863.

Commanding the Department of Kansas was a thankless experience. In an area covering Kansas, the Indian Territory, Nebraska, and Colorado, Curtis could count on less than six thousand men present for duty. With scattered bands of Indians forever oscillating between peace and war, the general had to perpetually guess how best to use his limited assets. The constant threat of Confederate, or bushwhacker, incursions did little also to settle Curtis's mind. What little Curtis could take solace from included his alliance with Lane. Curtis and Lane had forged a friendship that dated back to the territorial period and through the early days of statehood when Curtis supported his fellow radical during the senator's recruiting and patronage battles with Kansas's first governor, Charles Robinson. Lane thus encouraged Lincoln to send Curtis to the Department of Kansas, and the old general rewarded Lane by turning a blind eye to the shady military supply contracts that lined the pockets of Lane and General Blunt.[3]

Given Curtis's linkage to Lane, it was hardly surprising that Governor Carney distrusted Curtis. This distrust only grew in the late fall of 1864 as the election season approached. Neither Lane nor Carney would actually stand for election. They instead would fight it out through their surrogates and political machines. Carney, in fact, had withdrawn from the gubernatorial race to better position himself for a future run at the U.S. Senate. He was content in the immediate election to sponsor an "irregular" Republican ticket led by Solon Thacher for governor and Brigadier General Albert Lee for the state's only congressional seat. Opposing this ticket were Jim Lane's "regular" Republicans, which included Colonel Samuel J. Crawford for governor and Sydney Clarke for Congress.

Although there is no definitive way to determine the political strengths of Carney and Lane heading into the fall election, most evidence suggests that Carney held a decided edge. Carney's repeated charges of Lane's corruption had scored well, and the senator's reputation and machine had certainly

suffered since the last election in 1862. Even when Carney fumbled politically, the governor emerged unscathed. Writing on October 1st, Charles Robinson concluded that "it is generally thought the Thacher [Carney] ticket will
be elected." Only a colossal blunder could prevent Carney from sweeping
both the election and Jim Lane into political oblivion. [4]

That colossal blunder began to unfold on September 13th when Samuel
Curtis, then in western Kansas chasing Cheyennes and Arapahoes, received a
report that Sterling Price and fifteen thousand men had crossed the Arkansas
River. Over the next four days and as Curtis traveled back to his headquarters
at Leavenworth, he continued to receive information that Price had indeed
crossed the Arkansas. By the time Curtis arrived at Leavenworth on the 17th,
the news of Price's movement had already begun to spread throughout the
general population. Much as Missouri had been on edge with rumors of a
Price raid throughout the summer of 1864, so, too, did Kansas wait with
anticipation. Concerns over Price were also more than matched by fears of
another large-scale guerrilla attack into the state. By late August, Governor
Carney expressed the sentiment of the times when he nervously wired
William Rosecrans: "Our citizens are much alarmed about a raid from Missouri. Have you any information of gathering guerrillas on the Western Border?" Nevertheless, amid this general uneasiness, the initial reports concerning Price were vague, and they implied that Price's army was headed toward
Fort Gibson as part of a general Confederate uprising in the Indian Territory.
Curtis was incredulous. He knew that it would be nearly impossible for Price
to lead an army from Dardanelle through desolate regions of Arkansas and
the Indian Territory. The terrain, particularly in northwestern Arkansas, was
exceedingly difficult, and food and forage would be hard to find. Still, Curtis
had to take the reports seriously, especially when news filtered in on September 20th that Confederate General Stand Watie had overcome a large Union
wagon train at Cabin Creek in the northeast corner of the Indian Territory.
Curtis could only conclude that Price was headed for Fort Scott, 110 miles to
the north of Cabin Creek. As Curtis relayed this information to Thomas
Carney, the governor's first reaction was one of support. On September 21st,
Carney informed Curtis that he was calling out the militia in the eastern
counties so that they could man a string of outposts along the Kansas-Missouri border. Such a mobilization, Carney believed, would free Curtis to
deploy his five regiments of volunteer cavalry to the south and meet Price's
anticipated invasion. [5]

Curtis welcomed Carney's call for the militia and also readily accepted his proposal that the militia go into garrison. But unfortunately for Curtis, the governor almost immediately had second thoughts about the whole thing. The news concerning Price's whereabouts was simply too sketchy, and as more information arrived on September 25st that suggested Price was actually in southeastern Missouri, Carney began to smell a rat. With the fall election then rapidly approaching, Carney sensed that Curtis, at the behest of Jim Lane, had overinflated the threat to Kansas. The rumors of invasion were, in the rhetoric of the day, a political humbug. The governor drew his greatest electoral support from the eastern counties, and any mobilization of the militia meant that his largest bloc of supporters might not be anywhere near a polling station when it came time to vote in November. Making matters more ominous, most of Carney's political advisors and stump speakers filled the senior ranks of the militia. Service in the field would take them far from their appointed political duties. All of this led the governor to change his mind about mobilizing the militia. In a perverse twist to this about-face, Carney chose also not to tell Samuel Curtis of the decision. Carney's unwillingness to communicate with Curtis was certainly not affected by distance or difficulty in sending messages. Both men had taken up residence in Leavenworth. Ultimately, Curtis would have to find out the hard way on October 3rd, as his commander of the District of South Kansas, Major General George Sykes, began to wonder why only a handful of militia in Bourbon and Linn counties had mustered. The perplexed Sykes could only telegraph Carney in Leavenworth and ask: "Is there any hitch?"[6]

Whether Sykes's telegram finally prodded Carney to talk to Curtis is unknown. What is known is that Carney did meet with Curtis at his headquarters the next day. During the ensuing discussion, Curtis admitted to knowing very little of Price's whereabouts or intentions. It was an intelligence blackout made worse by downed telegraph lines on October 3rd and the loss of communications with all points in Missouri. As for Carney, he lamely explained his unwillingness to mobilize the militia by noting that his citizen soldiers had mustered repeatedly during the summer and that they were thus in little condition for yet another mobilization. The meeting broke up when Curtis pledged to try to find out more regarding Price. Only when he had that news did Carney promise to call out the militia. There was one other point made evident in the meeting. Carney emphasized to the general that any new call for militia would fall heavily upon the state's interior counties. Curtis, without any comment to the contrary, accepted Carney's explanation that this would merely balance the books among the militia in all counties. Not mentioned was the simple fact that Jim Lane drew his strength from the interior counties and that it would therefore be his supporters—and not Carney's—who might be stuck in the field at the time of the election and unable to vote.[7]

Regardless of the lack of militia, Curtis continued to prepare for a defense of Kansas. Wanting both to contain Price south of the Missouri River and to bolster his own logistical transport, Curtis began to commandeer and fortify all available steamboats and ferryboats then operating around Kansas City. However, the lack of information concerning Price forced Curtis to keep his relatively small number of troops fairly well dispersed. North of the Kansas River and headquartered at Leavenworth was the District of North Kansas and about six hundred troops commanded by Brigadier General T. A. Davies. South of the river and scattered all along the Kansas and Missouri border was George Sykes's District of South Kansas and its 2,700 soldiers. Although a significant number of men, the units were not among the best. The nature of the area's guerrilla fighting and a climate of poor senior leadership had taken its toll. The 15th Kansas Cavalry exemplified the problem. Colonel Charles R. "Doc" Jennison, whose reputation as a plundering Jayhawker was second only to that of Jim Lane, commanded the regiment, and he devoted little time to either training or discipline. Diminutive, scowling, and possessing an angular set of features, he resembled what one newspaper editor called "an enraged porcupine." Jennison's lack of interest in military regimen led to a scathing report by an inspector in September. His companies were scattered about the district, and they were overrun with camp followers and wives. Officers were quartered far away from the men. Nonregulation uniforms permeated the units. The quality of drill, discipline, guard duty, and area police were poor. And not surprisingly, there were far too many reports of "violations of the private rights" in the district.[8]

With quality manpower thus at a premium, Curtis was fortunate that William Rosecrans on September 29th provided him Colonel James H. Ford's 2nd Colorado Cavalry. A rough-and-tumble regiment drawn from the mining areas of the Colorado Territory, the 2nd Colorado had been assigned to the Department of the Missouri since February 1864 and had proven quite effective in dealing with bushwhackers in Jackson, Cass, and Bates counties. Well trained and led, the unit's biggest problem was its weaponry. Equipped with Starr carbines and pistols, the regiment could not have had weaker ordnance as the single-shot carbine often misfired and the barrel-heavy pistol usually undershot its intended target. These difficulties aside, Curtis was glad to have the regiment. In like fashion, Curtis was glad to have some militia assistance from the Missouri side of the border. The municipal leadership of Kansas City showed none of the political trepidation that afflicted their brethren in Kansas. On October 4th, Mayor Robert T. Van Horn mobilized the Kansas City Guards militia and ordered it into a larger organization known as the Sixty Days Regiment, commanded, conveniently enough, by Van Horn. For those militia lacking weapons, Curtis quickly provided muskets.[9]

This militia soon became responsible for the defense of the city as Curtis ordered the 2nd Colorado eastward to conduct reconnaissance. By October 5th, Curtis stationed elements of the 2nd Colorado at Independence, ten miles to the east of Kansas City, and Pleasant Hill about thirty miles to the southeast. The yawning gap between Independence and Pleasant Hill worried Colonel Ford to no small degree, eventually leading him to fret that Price might slip between his companies and hit Kansas almost undetected. Curtis shared Ford's worry, and to assist him in gathering information the general turned to a number of privately contracted "secret" scouts, or spies. Given the nature of their work and the desperation of Curtis for any information regarding Price, these scouts did not come cheap. The commanding general soon found himself paying at least one scout the sum of $125 per month, which was considerably more than the $17 per month the army was then paying its privates.[10]

Although Curtis's scouts and the 2nd Colorado detected little more than normal bushwhacker activity during the first week of October, by the 5th Samuel Curtis believed that he had accumulated enough information on Price's location to convince Governor Carney to call out the Kansas militia. The telegraph lines to the east had been repaired, and a torrent of reports had begun to flow into Leavenworth. The news, which Curtis hurriedly forwarded to Carney and the Leavenworth newspapers, placed Price just fifteen miles to the south of Jefferson City on the Osage River. In accordance with what he thought was the agreement with Carney from the previous day, Curtis asked the governor "to suspend business and labor" and "call out the entire militia" for thirty days. Curtis then requested that the governor concentrate his militia at Olathe before marching "to aid our comrades in Missouri in destroying these rebel forces before they again desolate the fair fields of Kansas."[11]

Not surprisingly, Governor Carney was unmoved by both the news of Price at Jefferson City and Curtis's mobilization request. His thinking on the matter was reflected perfectly by the *Leavenworth Times*, a newspaper that he owned and controlled editorially. Despite Price's documented presence at Jefferson City, the *Times* wanted some demonstrable proof that the Confederates were still headed toward Kansas. With some degree of accuracy, the paper, and Carney, could rightly claim that "the telegraph furnishes no adequate conception of the enemy's operation." The *Times* could therefore only guess that Jim Lane was at the root of the whole mess. "We understand that Gen. Lane has requested Gen. Curtis to order out the Kansas militia, and have them marched as a reinforcement to Gen. Brown at Jefferson City. Big thing. It won't work." Indeed, the governor proved that Lane's alleged machinations would not work by refusing to call the militia and suggesting instead that Curtis merely request Federal reinforcements from the Department of Arkansas in the form of the 9th Kansas Cavalry. [12]

The next few days witnessed much confusion. At first all new information seemed to confirm Governor Carney's worst fears of a Lane conspiracy. On the evening of the 6th, General Curtis made a speech before Leavenworth's Union Republicans that called not only for the mobilization of the entire militia but the necessity of sending it into Missouri—and far away from election polling stations. The next day Lane himself returned to Kansas from an extended stay in Washington accompanied by rumors that he brought authorization for Curtis to replace George Sykes, a well-known McClellan Democrat, with the much-reviled General Blunt as local district commander. That same day, Sidney Clarke did not ease any of Carney's worries when he proclaimed in Lane's political mouthpiece, the *Leavenworth Conservative*, that Blunt was the only man who could "save Kansas." Through all of this, General Curtis remained oblivious to the governor's concerns, and he bombarded Carney with several telegrams that indicated his frustration with the hesitant governor. Curtis made the oft-repeated call to "hurry up the militia," while relaying the latest news from his scouts: "You see[,] they seem moving steadily westward. Delay is ruinous." Still, Carney was not persuaded. His trust of Curtis had long evaporated, and he wanted confirmation of Price's whereabouts from independent sources. Only on the night of October 8th did Carney finally begin to get that confirmation when a friend and business associate, Peter Ridenour, arrived in Leavenworth after a hazardous journey from St. Louis. Carney, nearly frantic for information, peppered the weary traveler with several questions, and Ridenour confirmed most of Curtis's reports. By noon the next day, the 9th, Carney called out the militia in dramatic fashion:[13]

> Men of Kansas, rally! One blow, one earnest, united blow will foil the invader and save you. Who will falter? Who is not ready to meet the peril? Who will not defend his home and the State? To arms then! To arms, and the tented field until the rebel foe shall be baffled and beaten back![14]

It was a stirring call to arms. It was also one that Carney did not thoroughly believe himself. He was still not convinced that Price posed a threat to Kansas. Tellingly, no sooner had Carney called out the militia than he telegraphed William Rosecrans with a stark demand for news: "Are we in danger here from Price? Inform me." As long as Jim Lane remained in the area, Carney would always fear the worst from his political meddling. Indeed, the governor did not have to wait long for the apparent proof of his fear. On October 10th, Curtis announced that he was replacing George Sykes with Blunt as commander of the District of South Kansas. To Carney, this change clearly indicated the influence of Lane upon Curtis—especially when on that same day Curtis appointed Lane a member of his staff. Fanning suspicions even further, Lane decided that evening to brag publicly about his role in the switching of generals.[15]

No less disquieting to the governor, Curtis declared martial law on the 10th. The order itself was curious in that Curtis did not suspend the operations of the civil courts, which, historically, was the primary purpose in declaring martial law. Instead, Curtis chose, in a directly contradictory fashion, to invest all troops "with the powers . . . prescribed in the Articles of War," while also keeping the courts and their magistrates in operation. How exactly unit commanders, let alone ordinary soldiers, were to balance the powers of martial law and sitting courts was anybody's guess. But more importantly, and where the declaration of martial law stepped directly on Governor Carney, Curtis decided to supersede Kansas state law in determining who exactly should be in the militia. Realizing that the state militia law did not include blacks, Curtis in General Orders 54 declared that "all men, white or black, between the ages of eighteen and sixty will arm and attach themselves to some of the organizations" then forming. Curtis's bold racial egalitarianism had the potential to provoke a reaction from the ever-suspicious Governor Carney and his supporters, but it did not. Instead, they reacted not at all. Much the same as the people had supported the enlistment of blacks in volunteer regiments from the beginning of the war, so, too, did they support the idea of black service in the militia at the moment of the state's deepest peril. By the time the crisis had passed, Curtis's call for black militia netted fourteen separate company-sized units, totaling almost one thousand men and several officers. [16]

The sum total of Curtis's actions on the 10th was, however, enough for Carney to seek a personal interview with Curtis. Sometime the next day, Carney met with the general in Leavenworth and, according to Curtis, expressed his vivid concern that the mobilization "might be a political scheme gotten up by some around me to transport the people beyond the convenient exercise of their elective franchise." Curtis dutifully expressed shock while trying to reassure the governor that partisan politics did not register in his brain. Curtis also addressed Carney's foremost concern when he pledged his "honor that the militia should go no farther than necessary to repel or avert the approaching danger to the State." The old general was probably being forthright in his protest. His contemporary correspondence and actions reveal no particular political malice. But more importantly, that same correspondence and actions reveal a man remarkably tone deaf to the political ramifications of his orders. Ultimately, what was so obvious to even the most obtuse observer of Kansas politics—namely the pernicious influence of Jim Lane—never even suggested itself to Sam Curtis. [17]

For the moment, however, Governor Carney accepted Curtis's protestations. The governor focused then on mobilizing his militia. For the operational and logistical details of the mustering, Carney deferred to George Washington Deitzler, his militia general-in-chief. Fortunately for Carney, Deitzler was an experienced officer who had previously done everything from running "Beecher's Bibles" during Bleeding Kansas to commanding a regiment at Wilson's Creek and a brigade during the Vicksburg campaign. Deitzler resigned from the army in August 1863, only to be coaxed back into military service in 1864 when Carney commissioned him a major general in the Kansas State Militia (KSM). In the immediate crisis, Deitzler ordered the militia from the various counties to march to collection points at Atchison, Olathe, Wyandotte, Paola, Mound City, and Fort Scott, where the units would be organized into regiments and brigades. [18]

Kansans reacted with grim determination. The people of the state had waited nervously for Price's long-rumored invasion, and, according to Erasmus Manford of Leavenworth, they "expected no mercy." In Lawrence, one observer noted a popular consensus that "the desolating of Kansas was a part of the rebel plan." Also in Lawrence, J. S. Sands simply concluded that

"Kansas never saw so gloomy a day." The citizenry had thus but little choice to rally and repel the attack. Throughout the state, all commercial activity ceased, save that related to the mobilization, as most able-bodied men gathered in their local militia companies. These same companies clamped a tight control over towns and cities as outposts, guard houses, entrenchments, and redoubts sprang up along main roadways. In Leavenworth, most of the city's daily activity shifted from the wharves to Delaware Street, one of its main thoroughfares. By October 12th, a seemingly endless line of ill-equipped and unarmed men had begun marching through the city with bands playing and flags flying, which in turn left the city's levees virtually deserted and cargo lying in piles. A number of the gathering units paused on the outskirts of town for a grand review and inspection before heading south to Olathe on the 14th. Inspecting officers were appropriately horrified by what they found. The men were destitute of most items required to survive in the field. One officer noted sadly that "many of these militia are too poor to own overcoats, blankets, or stockings, and will suffer unless supplied." Things were, however, better in Lawrence. The governor's call for the militia arrived in town shortly after noon on Sunday and the close of most church services. By the next morning five militia companies and the Lawrence Brass Band had assembled just west of town and readied for the march to the east. These companies were probably among the best trained and armed units in the state. The trauma of Quantrill's massacre just one year earlier had led not only to an increased willingness among the militiamen to train more seriously, but also a desire to get the best weaponry possible. While military officials in the Department of Kansas had taken special care to offer the men of Lawrence rifle muskets, most chose instead to buy their own Spencer repeating rifles.[19]

Not all of the mobilized militia departed for the various points selected by Deitzler. The four hundred men of the 15th KSM, raised primarily from Davis County, mobilized but remained in the western portion of the state headquartered at Fort Riley. Hostile Indians had attacked a mail coach in the vicinity of Salina, and local and state officials did not want to take a chance by dragging the militia out of the area. Also standing fast was the 17th KSM in Marshall, Washington, Republic, and Clay counties. The Indian threat created a significant amount of confusion among militia commanders in the west and led one, Brigadier General S. N. Wood, to retain several other companies at home in various western counties.[20]

Further to the east, a large number of mustered regiments and companies remained behind to defend some of the prominent cities and towns should

Price break through Curtis's mustering army. At Leavenworth, the 7th KSM joined several other volunteer and militia detachments to turn the city into a virtual citadel complete with six 24-pounder guns, one 8-inch mortar, two brass field pieces, and four smaller rifled guns. At Topeka, Lawrence, and Paola, the stay-behind, or home guard, militia was able to take advantage of a military construction program that Curtis had started in July. For Topeka, this meant that the city had a ten-foot-high circular stockade planted at the intersection of Kansas Avenue and Sixth Street. The men of the city also dug out a series of outlying trenches, or rifle pits, in support of the stockade. The fortification itself was open on one side, but the standing walls contained numerous rifle ports to allow men to fire from both the standing and kneeling positions. To man these works, Topeka kept one company each of infantry and cavalry in addition to a section of artillery and one company of black infantry. In Lawrence, two militia companies of infantry remained in the city to occupy five roofless blockhouses. These troops augmented another two companies of volunteer cavalry stationed at a partially completed blockhouse sitting atop Mount Oread. Over the next three weeks in both Lawrence and Topeka, a martial routine permeated the air. The militia drilled constantly, though not very well. Target practice took place regularly as Curtis somehow managed to funnel a plentiful supply of ammunition to the cities. Military authorities closed all businesses and saloons, and sentries interrogated all strangers. In Topeka, the post commander, Major Andrew Stark, ordered all militiamen to sleep in their company areas. The total mobilization of Topeka was ultimately reflected in the fact that Stark even ordered men exempt from military duty into a company and provided them light tasks.[21]

While most Kansans found themselves doing something for the Union war effort, many did not serve willingly. In Riley County, the 20th KSM failed to account for a number of men who were thus left behind when the regiment marched for the border. To the eternal dismay of those who marched during that "corn-making" season, the skulkers were the only ones to get in a good crop of corn in the fall of 1864. For the most part, however, militia commanders were not content to let men dodge their duty, which then meant that armed details scoured the countryside looking for shirkers. In Leavenworth, one discharged veteran resisted the call to arms by pulling a pistol on his would-be comrades. Leavenworth was also the home of one shirker who boarded himself up in the garret of his house with enough food, coffee, newspapers, and books to last what he thought would be the duration of Price's sojourn near Kansas. It took a company of the 19th Kansas Cavalry to uproot him from his lair. In Lawrence, the older men of the city were grouped into two companies of self-proclaimed "graybeards" and given the task of searching the countryside for accursed "sneaks." Back in Topeka, the home-guard militia spent a fair share of its time rounding up what post commander Stark called "delinquents." Being delinquent in the capital area also knew no racial barrier as Stark detailed one detachment to bring in "colored men" not yet enrolled for duty. Among those who chose not to enter the ranks were a small number of men who were committed to waging a very familiar Jayhawking border war with Missouri. As early as October 12, no less than eighty men from Leavenworth crossed the Missouri River, according to one Union officer, with the sole "intention of plundering the Missourians."[22]

Though reliably informed of these sorts of activities, Samuel Curtis gave them little attention. He was determined to take the field at the head of an army. Shortly after meeting with Carney on the 11th, Curtis organized his headquarters element complete with cavalry escort and departed Leavenworth for Olathe, which Curtis had now selected as the primary rallying point for the militia. Despite Curtis having passed several columns of militia on the march, none of the militia actually arrived at Olathe before him on the afternoon of the 12th. When the militia did begin arriving that night, they were a sorry lot. In a startling yet misguided effort, Colonel C. H. Robinson of the 1st KSM ordered his regiment of citizen-soldiers to make the thirty-mile march from Leavenworth in one day. It was a fiasco, as the regiment quickly broke down, leaving men scattered all along the road. Curtis had then to send all of his headquarters wagons and ambulances plus impressed civilian transportation to round up and then haul the 1st KSM into Olathe. For those militia that staggered into Olathe, there was little access to water and fuel, which then led Curtis to direct most of the weary militia to concentrate much closer to the Missouri border at Shawnee Mission. For the state troops marching from points around Atchison, the general ordered it to concentrate at Wyandotte where Curtis would establish his headquarters in what he would soon call the Army of the Border. Before finally going to bed on the night of the 12th and 13th, Curtis also decided to concentrate and bring forward the bulk of his volunteer troops now commanded by General Blunt.[23]

Moving with alacrity, Blunt began massing his volunteer cavalry almost fifteen miles south of Kansas City at Hickman Mills on the morning of October 14th. As the units arrived, Blunt brigaded the various regiments and detachments to form a cavalry division that Curtis labeled the right wing of his Army of the Border. It was a force that carried with it all of the political and personal baggage that had become the essence of public life in Kansas. For the 1st Brigade, Blunt placed Doc Jennison in charge of his own 15th Kansas Cavalry and a detachment of the 3rd Wisconsin Cavalry. Jennison was hardly a personal favorite of Blunt. Although the two men were unscrupulous Jayhawkers of long standing, Jennison had fallen out with Blunt's patron, Senator Lane, and had become a vocal supporter of Governor Carney.[24]

Much more congenial to Blunt was his 2nd Brigade commander, Colonel Thomas L. Moonlight, who now rode at the head of 11th Kansas Cavalry and elements of the 5th and 6th Kansas cavalries. A Scottish immigrant and one-time noncommissioned officer (NCO) in the regular army before the war, Moonlight had been Blunt's chief of staff in the campaigns of 1863. Competent yet irascible, Moonlight eventually became embroiled in his very own political war with Carney. The governor had long ago challenged Jim Lane's military appointment privileges by commissioning his own officers into the 11th Kansas. Carney met with only occasional success as Blunt protested all the way to the War Department, claiming that Carney was attempting "to prostitute the Regiment for his own base purposes." Where Blunt—and Lane—could revel in the retention of Moonlight as commander of the 11th Kansas and thus the 2nd Brigade, they were yet again politically less fortunate in the commander of the 3rd Brigade. The next senior colonel in the District of South Kansas was Charles W. Blair. An officer of long service in the Trans-Mississippi, Blair had commanded the 2nd Kansas Infantry at Wilson's Creek and then occupied an assortment of post and artillery commands before Governor Carney appointed him commander of the 14th Kansas Cavalry in January 1864. Though Blunt and Moonlight knew Blair to be a competent and fairly apolitical officer, the appointment nevertheless galled them: Blunt because he wanted to exercise special commissioning powers delegated by Lane, and Moonlight because he wanted the command at that time. Thus distrusted by Blunt and Moonlight, Blair would command elements of the 14th Kansas Cavalry and the 5th, 6th, and 10th KSM in the coming campaign.[25]

Unfortunately for Blunt, the addition of the militia brought further headaches. The commander of the 6th KSM, Colonel James D. Snoddy, was also the vitriolic editor of Mound City's *Border Sentinel*. Notoriously opposed to Lane and Blunt, Snoddy did not depart for Hickman Mills until he had blasted Lane in print one last time, accusing him of "unblushing licentious-ness everywhere" and "the prostitution of public trusts." Making matters even worse, Snoddy and the other militia commanders retained a state bri-gade organization and reported first to Brigadier General William Fishback, yet another Carney loyalist. Perhaps the only positive news for Blunt was that he could attach one battery of artillery to each of the three brigades with the 3rd Brigade getting one extra section of guns.[26]

Although Blunt's volunteer troopers were generally well equipped prior to their march to Hickman Mills, the same could not be said of the Kansas State Militia. At the outset of its mobilization, the militia lacked everything from uniforms to weapons. But this did not last long, as Curtis succeeded in eliminating critical deficiencies. When a militia unit arrived at Shawnee Mis-sion, it began a material transformation that, while not perfect, allowed the unit to function in a cold-weather campaign. This transformation was due in no small part to Curtis impressing into military service all ferries and steam-boats operating in the vicinity of the border area. Not only did Curtis thus deprive the Confederates of any potential craft to ferry their men across the Missouri or Kansas rivers, he also greatly enhanced his own transport capa-bility. The Union could now quickly ship the enormous quartermaster and ordnance stockpiles available at Fort Leavenworth to the men in the field. By October 15, company commanders at Shawnee Mission were drawing a wide variety of quartermaster items. This list of supplies included everything from frying pans, coffee pots, blankets, and kettles to axes, eating utensils, tents, and canteens. More importantly, there were plenty of new rifles and ammuni-tion to be had. Indeed, the widespread availability of new weapons allowed many a citizen-soldier to trade in a poorly functioning or obsolete piece and then get in some target practice as well. About the only significant item army quartermasters could not provide was uniforms. This prompted Curtis to order the men to affix something red to their caps or blouses as a means of differentiating Unionist from Confederate. With the fall season then turning tree leaves red, many of the troops turned to the sumac tree for their badge. It was not long then before the men began to refer to themselves as the "Sumac Millish."[27]

There was one other element to supplying Curtis's gathering Army of the Border. When it came to gathering food, horses, and wagons, unit quarter-masters could always resort to a piece of paper with nearly magical proper-ties, the voucher. Beginning with Governor Carney's call for the militia, state officials clearly suggested that the U.S. government would reimburse the citizenry for the costs of repelling the invasion. It was a promise, or at least a perceived promise, that unit quartermasters embraced fully. On a daily basis they headed out into the countryside in search of food and forage armed only with vouchers to give farmers in return for what was taken. Though readily accepted by farmers, the vouchers had the potential to be a financial time bomb. There was no guarantee in October of 1864 that the U.S. government would indeed honor any of the vouchers.[28]

Nonetheless, the militia got fed, equipped, and armed as it prepared to meet Sterling Price. Samuel Curtis deserves no small measure of credit for the efficiency of the mobilization as he, in stark contrast to Price, attended to administrative matters large and small. Between October 14 and October 21, Curtis rooted himself in the house of an old family friend in Wyandotte where he organized a staff befitting his new field army and fretted over every logistical detail until that staff could actually begin work. Prior to the beginning of his sojourn in Wyandotte, Curtis was hardly optimistic of his chances to fend off Price. On October 13, for example, he feared the worst and privately instructed his wife, who had remained in Leavenworth, to pack their belongings and get out of town, while cautioning her not to tell anyone else for fear of starting a stampede. With each passing day, however, Curtis grew more confident of his ability to beat Price should he actually arrive at the border. It was a confidence bred of daily reports that the militia was, in fact, arriving at Shawnee Mission and his simple realization that the bushy and hilly terrain in the vicinity of Kansas City would be ideal for defensive operations.[29]

In spite of his frenzied preparations, Curtis was not focused entirely upon logistical and operational readiness. Other issues crowded his brain. First, there was the matter of his son, Major Samuel S. Curtis. The younger Curtis had, the previous week, set off with the ill-fated Colonel Chester Harding and the 43rd Missouri Infantry to reinforce Jefferson City aboard the steamer *Benton*. Curtis and his wife worried daily about his son as the boat disappeared from view and rumors of Price's advance placed the Confederates all along the path of the *Benton*. Making matters worse for the general, he had lost another son, H. Z. Curtis, the previous year in William C. Quantrill's bloody victory at Baxter Springs. Only by the evening of the 17th did the general discover that Samuel had successfully returned up the Missouri River, but only after seeing his steamer riddled with three hundred bullet holes delivered by bushwhackers lining the banks of the river.[30]

A second issue facing Curtis was one of longer standing. The partisan political bickering that had previously haunted the general's efforts to call out the militia surfaced again with a fury. Part of the problem was Curtis's continued ham-handed approach to Kansas politics. Curtis could not have made a clumsier political move than when he loaded his volunteer staff with an array of anti-Carney politicos. Among the general's new aides was the devil himself, Jim Lane, as well as Lane's two top candidates in the upcoming election: Colonel Samuel J. Crawford and Sidney Clarke. Curtis's appointments only magnified the deep divide that had begun to affect the assembling Army of the Border. George Deitzler, who commanded the militia and what Curtis designated the "left wing" of his army, countered Curtis's appointments by creating a personal staff populated by what seemed every anti-Lane politician in the state, including former governor Charles Robinson and Thomas Carney's candidate for governor, Solon J. Thacher.[31]

A bigger part of Curtis's political problem was that Sterling Price had once again disappeared from the view of anyone in Kansas. Despite Price lingering in the Boonslick between October 10 and 20, John Sanborn and Alfred Pleasonton had failed to maintain any consistent contact with him. This tactical failure and downed telegraph lines to points east left Kansans completely blind as to Price's whereabouts. Lacking any substantive news regarding Price's movement, the pessimists in Kansas were renewed in the faith that Jim Lane and James Blunt had snookered Curtis into a deep conspiracy to throw the upcoming election. By October 16th, former Governor Robinson, then encamped with Deitzler, expressed the conventional wisdom when he wrote his wife: "It is beginning to be thought that our being called out is all a sham & a trick of Lane & Curtis to make political capital. We think that we are kept in ignorance of the true condition of affairs in order to keep the people out as long as possible." Robinson, like so many others, firmly believed that Price had given Pleasonton and Sanborn the slip and "had gone South [*sic*]." Even in Lawrence, which had become rightly paranoid about its physical safety, a citizen noted that "some few began to think the whole thing was a gigantic hoax practised [*sic*] on them for some political purpose." The anti-Lane press, but particularly the *White Cloud Kansas Chief*, the *Oskaloosa Independent*, and the *Lawrence Journal*, picked up on the charge of conspiracy and began a loud campaign to bring the militia home. Headlines in the *Leavenworth Times* screamed "Lane's Last Fraud," and a reporter infamously described the whole episode as "an egregious humbug." If this were not enough, a series of wild rumors began sweeping the border area. In one, Lane was about to be made Supreme Commander of all forces. In another, Blunt was preparing to place his artillery behind all militia units so as to drive them into Missouri. Ten days into the news blackout concerning Price, the campaign to bring the militia home reached a crescendo. The *Times* proclaimed Lane a "Thing of Evil" and "His Satanic Majesty," while thundering in a bold headline: "Price South of the Arkansas in Full Retreat!"[32]

It did not take long for the bombast and fears to start affecting operations. Of concern to Carney was not just his belief that Sterling Price was nowhere near the Kansas-Missouri border. No less important, he believed that the northeast section of the state, with its militia drawn south of the Kansas River, was in grave danger of guerrilla attack. Accordingly, Carney and George Deitzler ordered mobilizing militia in Doniphan and other northern counties to stand fast. By the 17th, they had also ordered the 9th KSM, which had been raised in the vicinity of Atchison, to return home after having already marched to Leavenworth. In like fashion, Carney ordered the 8th KSM to Atchison as well. To the disgust of the governor and his supporters, General Curtis immediately revoked Carney's directives while ordering the 9th KSM to march on to Wyandotte. Only after some initial hesitation did the 9th board steamers to reinforce Curtis.[33]

Even more troubling were events that unfolded on the 16th at Hickman Mills. For the previous three days, the 5th, 6th, and 10th regiments of the KSM had stewed in their camps. Posted in advance of Deitzler's other militia, they had not been equipped and fed in near the fashion of the militia encamped at Shawnee Mission in Kansas. Stomachs growled and men shivered as they slept in hog pens and haystacks. More importantly, the senior officers boiled with resentment that they had been marched across state lines and placed in a division commanded by the hated James Blunt. With no actual sighting of Sterling Price, the officers and men feared that the Confederates had sidestepped the Kansas City area and were headed for the southeastern border of the state—and their homes. At first, Colonel Snoddy of the 6th KSM simply requested that Blunt allow them to return home. General Fishback, the overall commander of the militia regiments, followed this up by refusing to turn his militiamen over to Blunt's command. It was only predictable that on the night of the 15th and 16th the regimental commanders and General Fishback "resolved to call Blunt's hand and go back to Kansas." Although Thomas Carney had no direct role in dictating the retreat, the officers used Carney's and Deitzler's order that the militia converge in Kansas as their legal justification. So it was that shortly after breakfast on the 16th, the three regiments of KSM assembled for the march west. Fishback directed Snoddy and the 6th KSM to take the lead. Unfortunately for Snoddy, the column got no further than a mile west of Hickman Mills when Blunt got word of the movement. He quickly gathered up his headquarters staff and a section of 12-pound Napoleons and raced along the column from its rear to the front, scattering militiamen in all directions. Blunt's mad dash took him past Snoddy and to a place where the road crossed a small stream. He faced the artillery about and then waited for Snoddy and the militia. When Snoddy came face to face with Blunt, the general hurled several insults toward the colonel and promptly placed him under arrest. Although General Fishback was, at that moment, nowhere to be found, Blunt subsequently arrested him, too. After marching the 6th back to its camp, Blunt assembled the regiment and loudly informed the men that Snoddy needed to be "tried by a drum-head court martial and shot." Blunt did not carry out his threat, but the dramatic affair profoundly affected the regiment. That night, the 6th KSM elected a new commander, the infamous Jayhawker, Colonel James Montgomery, who had recently returned to Kansas from plundering much of the Georgia low country at the head of the 2nd South Carolina Colored Volunteers. Unlike Snoddy, Montgomery would have no qualms about fighting in Missouri.[34]

Anti-Lane sentiment was not confined to Blunt's division. Back across the Kansas border, a tidal wave of conspiracy allegations flowed through the camps. The men and officers drilled frequently, but there was little to disguise the fact there was no enemy in sight. As the men sat around their camps, they noticed also that martial law applied only to Kansas. A soldier need only cross the border into Missouri to find all businesses open and men, apparently, just going about their daily, normal lives. Further aggravating the situation was the simple desire of so many farmers to get home and tend to their fall plowing. It should have thus been no surprise that, one day after Snoddy tried to return his command to Kansas, Curtis struggled mightily to send any militia at all into Missouri.

Despite the lack of intelligence concerning Price, Curtis determined late in the evening of the 16th to push most of his army into Missouri with the idea of establishing a defensive line as far east as Lexington. He then ordered Blunt, minus his militia brigade, to march east from Hickman Mills toward Warrensburg in search of Price. If Blunt did not detect Price, he could pivot to the north and move on Lexington. Showing great enthusiasm, Blunt marched quickly to Holden albeit without Blair's militia-heavy 3rd Brigade, which was ordered to Kansas City to draw supplies. More awkwardly, Curtis ordered Deitzler to send three regiments of mounted militia and some artillery to join James H. Ford's 2nd Colorado at Independence. A howl of protest greeted Deitzler when he tried to assemble the militia for the march into Missouri. Only after personally addressing the troops and promising that they would not be "ordered too far into the State" did he succeed in getting two regiments, the 12th and 19th, to go. Deitzler then followed this up with a brash telegram to Curtis, informing him that the men "knew their rights under the militia laws of our State and will not submit to an effort to move them far from the homes unless the necessity is great and apparent." The movement of these two regiments, and subsequently that of the 4th KSM, did not mean that many of the militiamen were sold on the idea of being in Missouri. No sooner had the militia arrived at Independence than several hundred men simply decided to desert with little apparent fear of consequence.[35]

Back in Kansas, matters turned worse. Governor Carney and his political surrogates fanned popular discontent with Curtis and Lane by turning the Shawnee Mission camps into one big pro-Carney political jamboree. One day after Snoddy's failed attempt to head home, the camp of the 1st KSM was the scene of a large Carney rally that numbered more than two thousand officers and men, representing two-thirds of the militia then assembled at Shawnee Mission. The 1st KSM Regimental Band serenaded the governor and gubernatorial candidate Solon Thacher. Thacher then promptly responded with a stump campaign speech against a backdrop that included the hanging of Jim Lane in effigy. If there was any doubt as to the men's attitude toward the senator, they attached a sign proclaiming, "Jim Lane, the Curse of Kansas."[36]

Circumstances did not muzzle Lane and his supporters. They were hardly content to let Carney have a political field day. Reports flowed quickly to Curtis about the politicking in the militia camps and the wariness of the rank and file to cross into Missouri. Lane's friends were also quick to blame Governor Carney's political organ, the *Leavenworth Times*, for most of the discontent. The paper, according to Leavenworth's provost marshal general, "should be temporarily suspended, and editors and writers arrested as enemies to the public and cause." In one sense, the recommendation made sense. The *Times* had become the primary vehicle for Governor Carney to shape not only popular opinion but military action as well. The paper had the largest circulation base in Kansas, and it was widely distributed among the troops at

Shawnee Mission. Curtis was not entirely unmindful of the power of the *Times*. Ever since the beginning of the crisis he had tried to ingratiate himself to the paper—as well as Governor Carney—by sharing many of his dispatches. Such openness backfired. William Rosecrans was suitably horrified to find his telegrams being printed in the *Times*, and, even more importantly, the paper chose always to interpret the telegrams differently than Curtis. Nonetheless, it probably would have done Curtis no good to have closed the paper. Governor Carney could easily funnel information and opinions to other sympathetic papers in the area. But more importantly, it was simply not possible for Curtis to shutter a newspaper literally owned by the governor. The political fallout from such a move would have been more lethal than any of the editorials ever published in the *Times*. Because Curtis had lost the ability to influence the reports of the press, he encouraged the pro-Lane forces to attempt their own politicking in the camps. Despite Curtis's later claim to the contrary, the effort was a spectacular failure. Lane and friends were simply drowned out by the governor's political machine and the reality of citizen-soldiers just sitting in the camps waiting for a mysterious Confederate army that no one could find.[37]

Once again, there was obvious military fallout from the governor's political triumph in the camps. Many militia regiments, but particularly those from Leavenworth, began to hemorrhage men. By October 19th, more than half of the 1st KSM left camp and headed home. The Leavenworth Mercantile Battery followed shortly thereafter. Although opposition to crossing the state line was strongest in those units raised, ironically enough, in the border counties, some regiments from the interior, such as Douglas County's 3rd KSM, demonstrated a similar reticence to enter Missouri. Finally, there was an equal amount of trepidation among black militiamen. Captain Richard J. Hinton, who at this point in the crisis commanded all black troops, lamented a large number of desertions from what was known as Leavenworth's Colored, or Independent, Battery. The battery itself was already among the most unique units in the entire Union army as it was commanded and officered entirely by blacks. Among the section officers was Lieutenant Patrick H. Minor, who had once served as a private secretary to Lieutenant Colonel George Hoyt of the 15th Kansas. Hoyt had achieved his greatest fame before the war defending John Brown for his attack upon Harpers Ferry. No less interesting were the travails of a black company of Oskaloosa militiamen. While the company made it to the vicinity of Shawnee Mission, most of the men simply stopped marching at the border. When queried after the war, the commander of the company, Captain Wilber C. Ball, offered a different set of reasons for not venturing into Missouri. First, the men feared being returned to slavery should they be captured. Second, "wicked and designing persons" had gained influence over the troops and persuaded them that their unguarded homes were in a greater danger than that posed to white militiamen.[38]

The failure of militia, both black and white, to not only cross the border but also actually go deep into Missouri and establish a defensive position was about to have a profound effect upon the campaign. Around 4 AM on the morning of October 20th, messengers from General Blunt arrived at Curtis's headquarters, which had been moved forward to near Independence the previous day. Nearly breathless, the couriers brought confirmation of what Curtis had expected for the previous two weeks. Earlier in the evening, lead elements of Price's army had attacked Blunt at Lexington.[39]

Chapter Nine

A Beautiful and Exciting Scene

In the next phase of the campaign, Sterling Price would fight two major battles at Lexington and the Little Blue River. These battles represented yet another shift in the campaign. Previously, operational initiative had rested with Price's Army of Missouri. Although John Sanborn's brigade of cavalry had jabbed the Confederates in the Boonslick, Price had been allowed to move slowly and without great resistance. All of that would change beginning at Lexington where, for the first time since Pilot Knob, Price ran into an aggressive and capable commander who insisted upon fighting the bulk of the Confederate army.

In the prelude to these battles, Samuel Curtis would come to rely upon James Blunt to find Price's army. No matter his many vices, Blunt was aggressive and experienced in commanding large numbers of men. Blunt would then be the key to finding Price. On October 16th, Blunt received orders from Curtis to break camp at Hickman Mills and scout to the south and east, marching no further than Pleasant Hill. Leaving behind Charles Blair's 3rd Brigade of militia with orders to head to Kansas City where it could receive badly needed equipment (and avoid any deeper penetration of Missouri), Blunt departed in the early evening on the 16th with the remainder of his division. He thus marched with about two thousand men and eight 12-pound mountain howitzers. Shortly after midnight he arrived at Pleasant Hill. Finding nothing there, Blunt decided immediately to go beyond the limits of Curtis's order. The next morning he marched for Warrensburg. Along his route, Blunt ran into a parade of detached scouts, refugees, and militia, including a battalion of General Orders 107 troops commanded by Major Emory Foster. The hard-luck loser of the Battle of Lone Jack in 1862, and a postwar duelist with John N. Edwards, Foster brought with him four hundred men, many of whom were extraordinarily armed with Henry repeating rifles. Foster also brought news that the Confederates had captured Sedalia and that they were about to gobble up Warrensburg as well. Blunt was skeptical. He halted the advance of the division at Holden, seven miles from Warrensburg, but he ordered Foster to return to Warrensburg with one-half of his men and report back by telegraph the true state of affairs.[1]

By 5 PM Blunt received and processed a torrent of startling information. The Confederates had not captured Warrensburg. Shelby was with Price near Waverly. John Sanborn was in the vicinity of Dunksburg, and A. J. Smith lurked in supporting distance. Blunt did not hesitate. He determined to confront Price at Lexington and have both Curtis and Sanborn support him. He dispatched couriers to Sanborn and telegrams to Curtis announcing his plans while requesting that both generals forward troops to Lexington. Blunt did not wait for any replies, and shortly after darkness fell on the 17th, he pointed his division, which now included about two hundred of Emory Foster's militia, commanded by Captain George Grover, north toward Lexington. Late the next morning, Blunt's advance led by Thomas Moonlight pulled into the city and dispersed a small group of bushwhackers. The rest of Blunt's division rode into the city throughout the morning and into the afternoon.[2]

Lexington was hardly an ideal spot to defend. Missouri's fourth largest city with a population of about four thousand, Lexington had little high ground save where the Masonic College sat near the Missouri River. More troubling, there were no nearby tributaries of the Missouri River that might force a bottleneck in Confederate movements. Instead, Lexington sat on fairly open terrain with roads running into the city from the south to the east. Blunt understood the situation and thus also understood that he needed reinforcements if he were to offer a credible defense against the twenty thousand to thirty thousand men then rumored to be in Price's army. While Blunt waited on the 18th for his reinforcements, he positioned Moonlight's 1st Brigade at the Masonic College, the exact site of Price's great victory in 1861. A few miles to the south of the college at the fairgrounds, Blunt planted his 2nd Brigade commanded by Doc Jennison. However, Blunt's energy and decisiveness waned soon after his arrival in Lexington. Blunt— and a staff that now included Senator Jim Lane—had gotten very little sleep in the preceding forty-eight hours, and there was a noticeable lack of defensive preparation during the afternoon and early evening of the 18th. It would not be until the following morning that Blunt proclaimed martial law in Lexington and tried to mobilize all men—white and black—to begin digging fortifications.[3]

Indeed, Blunt only roused himself to place battalion-sized pickets well after dark on the 18th. At that time, Blunt ordered Captain Louis Green and two companies to the south of the city where they would patrol the road to Warrensburg. About three miles east of the city and straddling the Dover Road, Blunt placed Captain H. E. Palmer at the head of a battalion-sized element drawn from the 11th Kansas and the 2nd Colorado. By this point, Palmer and his detachment of men from the 11th Kansas were probably the most exhausted troopers in Blunt's division. They alone had penetrated the Boonslick in a patrol during the previous week and skirmished almost non-stop with all manner of Confederate recruits, bushwhackers, and regular troops. Regardless, Palmer got his orders near midnight on the 18th and soon proceeded to his position after loading his men down with ammunition and two days of rations of bacon and crackers. After breakfast on the 19th, Palmer's men began the arduous task of dismantling fences and clearing fields of fire. Blunt's last words to Palmer were to hold his advanced position for as long as possible.[4]

With pickets such as Palmer's now firmly situated, there was little more for General Blunt to do than wonder when his reinforcements would show. By 11 AM, Blunt had his answer. A courier arrived at his headquarters, delivering bad news from Samuel Curtis. There would be no reinforcements. The unwillingness of the militia to cross deep into Missouri, according to Curtis, meant that no force could be spared to buttress Blunt's defense at Lexington. Blunt would have to fall back past the Little Blue River and Independence to a defensive line along the Big Blue River. It was no doubt the correct decision. Although Curtis had at his disposal several regiments willing to go deep into Missouri, they were only a fraction of the total force he wanted to bring to the battlefield. Blunt would have to come to him. Blunt would also receive no aid from John Sanborn. Unbeknownst to Blunt at that time, his dispatches had only begun to arrive at Sanborn's headquarters on the morning of the 19th. Sanborn promptly fired off a series of messages, imploring Blunt to hold as long as possible. Sanborn's efforts were to no avail. Blunt never got the communications. More importantly, it was already much too late for Sanborn to do anything. Just after Blunt read Curtis's message at 11 AM, gunfire echoed around the fringes of Lexington. Sterling Price had arrived.[5]

Price's western thrust had been long in the making. His rate of travel had slowed greatly in the Boonslick as he waited for a seemingly endless parade of recruiters, furloughed men, and detached raiders to make their way back to the army. The reconstitution was almost complete by the evening of the 17th when most of the major units of the army had rendezvoused with Price at Kiser's Bridge. The reconstitution of the army and the ability of Price to make a western push could not have come at a better time. All available intelligence revealed that large, if not greatly exaggerated, numbers of Unionists were closing in all around Old Pap. Price was particularly struck by the information passed by one of his trusted spies, a man who had been posted to St. Louis before the army had even left Pocahontas in Arkansas. The spy arrived in Price's camp at Waverly on the 18th and informed Price that he was being chased by a total of thirty-nine thousand men from both Jefferson City and Saint Louis. The news only got worse when Price received scouting reports claiming that the accursed Jayhawkers Blunt, Lane, and Jennison had occupied Lexington with no fewer than three thousand troops. The accumulated intelligence persuaded Price to move quickly. It also convinced Old Pap for the first time to stop active recruiting. He had now come to the realization that he would not be able to protect and feed any more recruits.[6]

Therefore, at daybreak on the 19th, Price had his army in motion toward Lexington along the Dover Road. Jo Shelby was in the front. The army's initial movements were fairly impressive and well disciplined. This was especially so given the large numbers of raw recruits that had just flooded Price's camp. As one Union informer noted at the time, "The whole army was moving in a compact body, the trains in the center, wagons moving two abreast, about 250 in number," and those followed by Thompson's captured drove of one thousand cattle. What is striking about this observation is not so much the assessment that the army moved in a "compact body," which was surprising enough, but rather the informer's quantification of the wagons. Contemporary critics and historians were quick to inflate, albeit without direct observation or attribution, the number of wagons in Price's trains. With estimates sometimes reaching six hundred wagons, it has always been easy to conclude that Price had allowed the trains to become a plunder-laden and bloated drag on the army. One early historian, William E. Connelley, exclaimed that Price's "train of loot was the longest ever gathered by an army in America." However, even if one were to believe that the informer had undercounted by one hundred wagons, which is unlikely based upon the

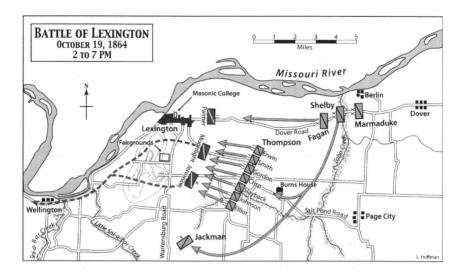

Figure 9.1. Battle of Lexington, October 19, 1864, 2 to 7 PM

accuracy of several of his other observations, there is a simple matter of context. For an army that numbered over seventeen thousand men in its ranks with a corresponding number of horses, Sterling Price needed more, not fewer, wagons to sustain the march.[7]

Regardless of the size of Price's trains, the army made excellent time toward Lexington. Of primary concern to Price was that Federal cavalry and infantry might reinforce Blunt from the southeast. Therefore, once he crossed Tabo Creek, about eight miles to the east of Lexington on the Dover Road, Price decided to change his route. He now directed what he called a "flank march" to the south and east of Lexington in order to interpose his army between Blunt and any Federal reinforcements that might arrive from either the south or southeast. The orders also took into account his very real desire to bag Blunt and his entire division in Lexington. Shelby was to remain in the lead and take his division across the Warrensburg Road and ride almost completely around the city to the Independence Road, which entered Lexington from the west. Shelby's movement did not, however, go undetected. No later than 11 AM, and about four or five miles to the southeast of the city, Shelby ran headlong into some federal pickets near the house of Mary Burns along the Salt Pond Road. In the lead of Shelby's division at this time were Thompson and the Iron Brigade. The initial contact, however, did not provoke an immediate attack. Over the next three hours, Thompson redeployed his brigade astride the Salt Pond Road into two wings with Elliot, Johnson, Slayback, and Crisp on the left and Gordon, Smith, and Erwin on the right. Although the left of Thompson's line contained a larger concentration of newer recruits, those units commenced the attack at about 2 PM. Leaving Thompson to handle this attack, Shelby sidestepped the developing battle and continued west until he hit the Warrensburg Road with Sidney Jackman's brigade. Shelby met no resistance when he finally arrived at the road, but he was in a good position to see "a vast herd of horses, mules and cattle being rushed at tremendous rate of speed into Lexington." Marveling at the sight, Shelby later recalled "the fondness of Col. Jennison's men for such earthly and substantial things" and "surmised that our friends of the Fifteenth [Kansas] were in close proximity."[8]

Although Blunt had indeed acquired quite a collection of horses and buggies in the vicinity of the Fairgrounds, the Union general devoted his considerable energies to readying his men for the fight. Unfortunately, he would not be able to use any of the civilians he had ordered mobilized under his declaration of martial law. Blunt's declaration had come too late, and it designated a time, 2 PM, well after Shelby made his appearance. Blunt's would-be trench diggers could only mill about the streets of Lexington as Blunt, with Jim Lane in tow, headed out of the city and organized a line of battle that faced Thompson and ran through what he called "open and undulating country" just to the south of the Fairgrounds. Blunt very carefully kept the road to Independence to the rear of his formation should he have to evacuate the city. As Blunt then deployed his units, he posted Jennison's brigade to the right, or west, of the line and Moonlight's brigade to the left. While Blunt made these dispositions, he directed Jennison to deploy a skirmish line and buy some time. The Union skirmishers, taken from the 3rd Wisconsin and 15th Kansas, were supported by one howitzer, and they soon enough engaged Thompson's own skirmish line. Yankee resistance proved stout, especially when Blunt directed his available artillery to fire into Thompson's line.[9]

Jennison and Moonlight were not the only commanders to slow the Confederate advance. Over on the Dover Road, Captain H. E. Palmer stood his ground. Throughout the late morning and early afternoon, Palmer and his battalion-strength detachment, which had been reinforced by George Grover's company of militia wielding Henry repeating rifles, engaged an equal number of Confederates who tried to press down the road. Three times the Confederates assaulted Palmer's position, and three times he and his men managed to hold. It was close-quarters combat, and in the mix of one melee the Yankees captured fifteen very surprised Confederates. As the afternoon wore on, Palmer realized that he could not stay indefinitely. He then sent a series of messengers to Blunt asking to be relieved. No reply ever came back to Palmer. By 3 PM, Palmer could plainly hear the main battle off to the southeast reaching a crescendo as Richard Collins's Confederate battery joined the fray. Two hours later, Palmer was still stuck in his besieged position, and he was now faced with the chill-inducing possibility that General Blunt had either forgotten about him or had simply abandoned him to the Confederates. The sound of gunfire had all but dissipated to the southeast, leaving Palmer to conclude that he was cut off from the main part of the army.[10]

Palmer had good cause to be worried. Things had not gone well for the Union on the main battlefield. Thompson had shoved Blunt inexorably north and west. In this engagement, Collins's battery proved the decisive element. Although only two guns to Blunt's eight, Collins's artillery had a considerable advantage in effective range over that of the Yankee mountain howitzers. Blunt thus decided that he needed to disengage and head west to Independence. To cover the retreat, Blunt turned to Thomas Moonlight. Doc Jennison and his brigade dropped back to the Old Independence Road, while Moonlight, with about five hundred men and four pieces of artillery, initially anchored his rearguard on a hill about one mile from Lexington and southwest of the Fairgrounds. Despite the pressure on Moonlight, the situation was not desperate. For all the success that Shelby had in pushing Blunt backward, it was a thoroughly lackluster performance. Shelby and Thompson made first contact at 11 AM, but Thompson did not deliver his main attack until 2 PM. No less troubling, Shelby failed to spur Jackman's brigade in its drive to cut off Blunt's escape along the Old Independence Road. Shelby and Jackman never got in position to interdict Blunt and instead could only watch from a distance as Jennison evacuated through the Fairgrounds to be followed by Moonlight. Sterling Price performed no better. Price, who had originally designed the advance into Lexington to cut off Blunt from both support and escape, pulled back from a total effort as the afternoon wore on. Price certainly had the opportunity to either reinforce Shelby or simply direct Fagan or Marmaduke to turn Blunt's line. As it was, Fagan and Marmaduke marched slowly from the east, and Price contented himself to advance to the front with his friend, Surgeon William McPheeters, and observe the Yankees retreating in a "beautiful and exciting scene."[11]

Price's lackadaisical handling of his army late in the afternoon detracted only somewhat from Thomas Moonlight's performance as a rearguard commander. Moonlight initially formed his brigade on the heavily wooded southern face of the hill. He then waited until nearly the last moment of the Confederate assault before ordering his troops to scramble over the hill and down its northern face. With Shelby's men in close pursuit, this first delaying action produced a hair-raising close call for Moonlight's successor as commander of the 11th Kansas, Lieutenant Colonel Preston Plumb. Plumb and several other men retreated down the hill toward the Lexington Road, taking to a lane flanked by six-foot-high walls. As Plumb and another officer ran down the lane, they were pinned to the wall by a fast-moving caisson that nearly overturned. The situation quickly grew grim for Plumb as the Confederates closed in and pistol shots began clanging off the caisson's wheels. Fortunately for Plumb, Thomas Moonlight somehow realized that he was about to lose a regimental commander, and he quickly mounted a counterattack that froze the Confederate advance and freed Plumb. [12]

For about the next six hours, Moonlight covered the retreat in an aggressive fashion. According to one Union trooper, Moonlight's brigade made a stand every two to three hundred yards. Jo Shelby had a significant amount of trouble attacking the Yankees as Moonlight took advantage of all the heavy fence lines and ravines near the Old Independence Road. Perhaps most important, Moonlight continually integrated his four howitzers into the retrograde movement by repositioning the artillery first and thus allowing it to provide covering fire for the retreating cavalry. Only by flanking the Union lines was Shelby able to sustain the attack and push Moonlight westward. As darkness fell, Shelby's pursuit weakened. Even then, however, some Confederate units persisted. The last significant contact occurred near midnight when the tail elements of the rearguard reached the Sni-a-Bar Creek, about six miles to the southwest of Lexington. Here Preston Plumb made a last-minute attempt to burn the old covered bridge that crossed the creek. It was to no avail as Shelby's troopers came up to the bridge just in time to put out the fire. The failure to burn the bridge aside, Moonlight had succeeded in his mission. Shelby would pursue no more that night, leaving Blunt's division to continue its march. By 2 AM, Jennison's brigade encamped about one mile to the east of the Little Blue River. The total cost to Blunt's division had been light with an estimated forty casualties of all types. That the casualties were this light was something of a minor miracle, especially given the details that had been left behind or cut off from the division when Blunt ordered the retreat. Throughout the night of October 19th and 20th, these groups trickled into Moonlight's lines carrying breathless tales of close-run escapes. One such group was that led by Captain H. E. Palmer, who had been left behind on the Dover Road. To get back to the army, Palmer simply led his men through the heart of Confederate-occupied Lexington posing as bushwhackers.[13]

Sterling Price's handling of the engagement had been uninspiring. His initial battle plan included the objective of taking Blunt's division within the city. But when it came time to press the opportunity, he committed less than one-third of his troops in a drawn-out frontal attack that consumed no less than eight hours of daylight and allowed Blunt to retreat safely. The cost to Price, much as it had been to Blunt, was minimal. Price recorded no official list of casualties, but he later blandly reported them as being "very slight." Given the indecisive nature of the battle, Price had yet another choice to make. All available intelligence revealed that Rosecrans's troops were closing in from the west and southeast and that Curtis was staging a powerful blocking force directly to the west. Logic and self-preservation seemed to dictate that Price should now try to evade the closing vice grips by slipping to the southwest. Such a march had not been practical before his arrival at Lexington. There were too few roads leading to the southwest, and those leading to the south were invariably covered by Union cavalry. At Lexington, however, the gods of war appeared to have provided Price a slim opportunity to escape. By October 19, the combined wisdom of William Rosecrans and Alfred Pleasonton had ordered all of the available infantry and most of the cavalry in the Department of the Missouri to converge on Price's route as it moved near the Missouri River. The only cavalry not headed north toward Price was Sanborn's 2nd Brigade, which was then marching slowly westward toward Warrensburg.[14]

There has been no shortage of critics of this disposition of the Union force, especially as it concerned A. J. Smith's infantry. The critics have a point. Given the slow-moving nature of the infantry and the absolute necessity that Price would have to turn south to get home, some have argued that William Rosecrans should have ordered Smith west, or at least southwest, from Sedalia to head off Price's eventual retreat. No less important, but generally missed by the critics, was another problem. With most of the Union force congregating near the Missouri River, Price could finally take advantage of a road system that exited the Boonslick to the southwest. More specifically, Price's army could move from Lexington to the southwest and head first for Cool Spring and then to Lone Jack and Pleasant Hill. Price also had the opportunity to turn south and west even after the flow of the Battle of Lexington carried his lead elements to the crossing of the Sni-a-Bar Creek. Near that crossing, Price could access the Wellington to Cool Spring Road and still head in the opposite direction from his pursuers. All of this is no doubt counterfactual history. It is also counterfactual history with no guarantee of success for Sterling Price. His margin of error was slim, and Union cavalry would at some point—and barring a complete mishandling of the pursuit—turn about and fall upon his rearguard. But this was a scenario infinitely more promising than what awaited the Army of Missouri when Price decided on the night of October 19th to continue the march west toward the Little Blue River and Samuel Curtis's waiting army. [15]

Despite the danger that continued to multiply around the Army of Missouri, Price headed west in deliberate fashion. He was in no apparent hurry. No sooner had Shelby's men pursued Blunt's fleeing division to the Sni-a-Bar on the evening of the 19th than they returned to Lexington for an encampment along the wharf. The next morning, Shelby's division dropped back to second in the line of march. Fagan's division would now take the lead. For the men of the Iron Brigade, there was little fire in their movement. According to Jeff Thompson, he allowed his officers to slow the rate of travel "so the men could see their friends." With no hint of recognition of the impending menace, Thompson went on to note that "several hours were spent thus pleasantly." The lack of a sense of urgency was not the only thing afflicting the army. The weather had turned very cold. Daylight temperatures plunged into the thirties, and a light rain changed to a dusting of snow by the evening. For many soldiers this was but the beginning of their misery. Various camp fevers had begun to sweep through the ranks, and smallpox broke out in Marmaduke's division. With many soldiers falling by the wayside sick, the army plodded about twenty miles onto the Fire Creek Prairie where it then encamped for the evening. Here Price received word that Blunt's division had fallen back to the banks of the Little Blue River. [16]

Although not wide, the Little Blue was a fairly significant obstacle to Price's westward march. It was deep, and the banks on both sides were heavily wooded, steep, and slippery. The most desirable crossing was a covered wooden bridge along the Lexington to Independence road. There were several fords in the area, but, as Jo Shelby later remarked, the fords were "belly deep" with water. Better yet for any defender, the terrain gradually increased in elevation to the west of the river. But most important, this land was crossed by a number of hollows, ravines, and fence lines running perpendicular to the road.[17]

Blunt understood how the terrain would provide a tactical advantage, and he wanted to make his stand at the Little Blue. He then sent a messenger to Curtis back at Independence to forward not only rations and ammunition but also reinforcements in the shape of the 16th Kansas, the 2nd Colorado, and Captain William D. McLain's Independent Colorado Battery. Blunt additionally implored Curtis to concentrate his other troops further south so they could link with Rosecrans's forces at Lone Jack. Curtis would, however, have little to do with the suggestions. After stating that he had no time to explain, Curtis promptly explained in some detail that provisions were already available at Independence and that, more importantly, the Kansas militia still refused to go deeper into the state. Any final defense must start at the Big Blue River, not the Little Blue. Curtis therefore ordered Blunt to retire to Independence with the bulk of his command, suggesting that Moonlight remain behind yet again as a rearguard with four hundred troopers and a couple of howitzers. The rearguard, Curtis noted, was to delay Price, not start a battle.[18]

With no small amount of disgust, Blunt complied with Curtis's orders. But it was with a twist. Instead of leaving just four hundred men to act as a rearguard, he posted Moonlight with the 11th Kansas and four pieces of artillery. He then instructed Moonlight that upon Price's arrival he should send word back to Curtis, burn the bridge over the river, and resist as much as possible. Blunt took the rest of his command on the eight-mile march west toward Independence where he fully intended to persuade Curtis to change his mind. As for Moonlight, he placed two companies under Major Martin Anderson at the bridge with orders to burn it when Price arrived. At a little less than one mile north of the bridge, he put Captain James E. Greer and Company I with orders "to hold the enemy as long as possible." He relayed similar instructions to Captain Joel Huntoon and Company H, which he positioned at yet another ford about four miles south of the bridge. The only problem with these dispositions was that there were other fords much closer to the bridge both to the north and south. It would be an easy task for Price to cross the river and avoid Greer and Huntoon.[19]

By 7 AM on the morning of the 21st, the Unionists had to wait no longer. About one mile east of the bridge on a dividing ridge between Fire Prairie Creek and the Little Blue, Anderson's skirmishers ran into the advance of Price's army in the form of John Marmaduke's escort, a company-sized

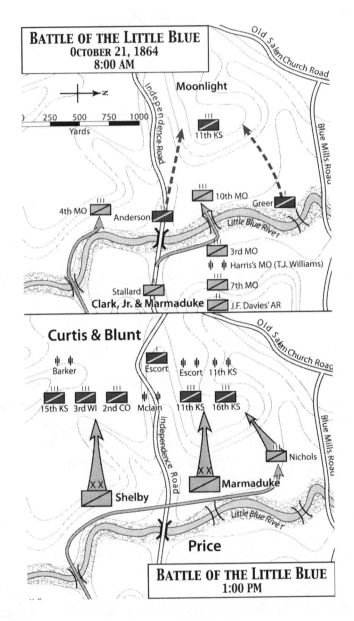

Figure 9.2.   Battle of the Little Blue, October 21, 1864

detachment commanded by Captain D. R. Stallard. For H. E. Palmer, the clash had come much too early in the morning. Stationed at the bridge with Anderson, Palmer was still trying to recover from his harrowing ride of the previous day. More particularly, he was in the middle of sewing his ripped pants when the attack commenced. Having no time to either finish the repair or put the pants on, Palmer threw his pants over his saddle and rode toward the action in his drawers. Palmer's and Anderson's companies then provided a stout defense of the bridge. The Unionists held on for about one hour when it became evident that the weight of the Confederate attack would soon prove irresistible. Anderson then fired the bridge using a burning wagon of hay.[20]

Anderson's defense of the bridge, and its eventual burning, forced John Marmaduke to seek another way across the river. With John B. Clark Jr.'s brigade following Stallard's advance, Marmaduke ordered Clark to deploy the 4th Missouri, then commanded by Lieutenant Colonel William J. Preston, to secure a ford about one mile south of the bridge, and Lawther's 10th Missouri to grab another ford one-half mile to the north. As Lawther's men poured across the river, they flanked James Greer's company of the 11th Kansas positioned less than one-half mile further north. Greer abandoned his ford without a fight. Given this quick success, Clark chose not to wait for a status report from Preston. Clark instead ordered the remainder of his brigade to the ford controlled by Robert Lawther. It was a fateful decision. Clark had just ordered no less than two thousand men to one very narrow choke point marked by freshly constructed abatis, steep banks, and waist-deep water.[21]

No sooner had Clark personally ridden to the ford than he discovered things were not going well. Horses and men struggled to negotiate the clogged crossing, but making matters worse was the simple fact that Robert Lawther had been lured away from the ford and any possible support from the rest of Clark's brigade. Thomas Moonlight had certainly not attempted a deliberate deception of the Confederates. His retreat from the river had been precipitous. Greer's panicked flight from the lower ford along with Martin Anderson's withdrawal across the bridge forced Moonlight to order the 11th Kansas to retreat from the river to a stone wall about two miles to the west. It was an order that never reached Joel Huntoon's Company H, which guarded the southernmost ford. Confederate forces never really threatened that ford for most of the morning, and Huntoon would remain at his post until much later in the afternoon when the battle had clearly moved beyond the river. All of this mattered little to Lawther, who decided rashly to pursue the remainder of the 11th Kansas up the steep terrain to the stone wall. Not only did the 11th have repeating rifles, it also possessed some superior field-grade leadership, which steeled the men for the Confederate charge. Major, and future U.S. Senator, Edmund G. Ross lost two horses in this battle, and he chose to inspire his men by slowly and deliberately saddling a new horse in the open field. Preston Plumb, the commander of the 11th Kansas, was no less dramatic as he led the regiment in singing "Rally around the Flag, Boys" just as Lawther's men pushed toward their position. Lawther charged headlong into a cauldron of bullets pouring from the well-protected Yankee line. [22]

While still at the ford, a now concerned Clark heard this raging fire fight. He then spurred Colton Greene's 3rd Missouri toward Lawther, leaving orders for the other regiments to hurry forward. Clark and Greene broke free of the banks of the river and formed north of the Independence road. About this time, D. R. Stallard's company had somehow made it across the river and joined the effort to support Lawther. As Greene then sorted his men and advanced about one mile west of the river, he ran straight into a confused and retreating mass of Confederate soldiers. These men belonged to Lawther, and they would not stop running until they hit the river. A desperate moment had arrived for the Confederacy. With his 150 men, Colton Greene stood to battle with his back nearly to the Little Blue with all potential help struggling through the bottleneck of the ford. Fortunately for Greene, three pieces of artillery commanded by Lieutenant T. J. Williams rolled into place just fifty yards to the rear of Greene's dismounted troopers. No sooner had Williams set his guns than the 11th Kansas charged down the sloping terrain toward the Confederate lines. With no more than six hundred men, the 11th Kansas spilled around Greene's flanks. The crisis at hand, Greene reacted coolly. He ordered his wings to "fire by the right and left oblique," while personally directing two cannons to fire on the different flanks. When the two lines of men came within but a few yards of each other, and Greene's artillery could no longer realistically fire for fear of hitting Confederates, Greene ordered the gunners to rapid fire blank cartridges if only to make the Unionists believe there was a terrible weight of iron coming their way. As Colton Greene later dryly noted, "It produced the desired effect." Moonlight retreated. [23]

Not content simply to hold his ground, Greene energized his command for its own charge toward the retreating Kansans. Burdened now by fatigue, both mental and physical, and the simple fact that they were outgunned, the Confederates made little headway across the tree- and ravine-lined field. The pattern was therefore set for much of the rest of the early afternoon. In attack followed by counterattack, neither Moonlight nor Greene could budge the other from the battlefield. By 11 AM, the battle took another turn as Yankee reinforcements poured onto the battlefield. James Blunt had returned. True to his promise when he had left Moonlight, Blunt had worked to persuade Samuel Curtis to make some sort of stand at the Little Blue. On the evening of the 20th when Blunt had marched into Independence, he pleaded and cajoled Curtis for a return to the Little Blue. It was no easy task. Powerful elements worked against Blunt. Governor Thomas Carney and his staff had moved to Curtis's headquarters at Independence in order to argue against any further penetration into Missouri. Since early that morning, the Kansans had greeted Blunt's dispatches from the front with a mixture of disbelief and derision. They no doubt contributed to Curtis's unwillingness to allow Blunt to make a stand at the Little Blue. But now Blunt's physical presence and domineering personality emboldened Curtis to support his divisional commander. To the chagrin of Carney, Curtis allowed Blunt to return to the Little Blue the next morning with Jennison's brigade, which still included a few hundred of the General Orders 107 militia, as well as all the units Blunt had requested as reinforcements the previous day. These units—two companies of the 16th Kansas, the 2nd Colorado, and the Independent Colorado Battery—were now designated the 4th Brigade of Blunt's division and were led by Colonel James S. Ford, formerly the commander of the 2nd Colorado. All told, Ford's brigade added nine hundred men, five 3-inch howitzers, and one 12-pound mountain howitzer to Blunt's division. Blunt could now march to the Little Blue with about 2,500 men.[24]

When Blunt assembled his force after daylight the next morning, the officers included a highly agitated Major Nelson Smith, who now commanded the 2nd Colorado. For most of the previous night, Smith suffered with premonitions of impending death. While Doc Jennison and many other field-grade officers stayed up late playing cards, Smith spent the night pacing in his hotel room and writing farewell letters. A depressive cloud hung over Smith, and he did not hesitate to tell several friends of his forebodings throughout that night and the next day. Nevertheless, Smith was more than functional when at 9 AM General Curtis received his first news of Moonlight's battle with Price. Using the telegraph, Moonlight informed Curtis he had engaged Price but had not yet succeeded in burning the bridge. Spurred to quicken the pace, Curtis and Blunt hoped now to reach Moonlight before the Confederates pushed him completely away from the Little Blue. Moonlight's telegram also apparently inspired Curtis to go see for himself. He, too, would head for the Little Blue accompanied by his headquarters escort, which included two pieces of artillery commanded by Lieutenant Edward Gill. With Blunt's troops in the advance, the column started for the Little

Blue by 10 AM, and it took one hour for the reinforcements to link up with Moonlight.[25]

Moonlight was more than a bit surprised by the new arrivals. He had not seen his telegraph operator for most of the morning and did not know that Curtis and Blunt were on the way. Upon Blunt's appearance, he assumed tactical control of the Union forces. A new consolidated line eventually took shape that ran parallel to the Old Salem Church, or Atherton, Road. McLain's battery anchored the center of the line and was joined, from north to south, by Major Nelson Smith's Second Colorado, Lieutenant J. B. Pond's detachment of the 3rd Wisconsin, and Lieutenant George Hoyt's 15th Kansas. To the north of McLain's battery stood Plumb's 11th Kansas. Lieutenant Henry Barker's battery of artillery acted in support of the 15th Kansas, while Major Robert Hunt, Curtis's chief of artillery, initially directed the actions of Captain Edward Johnson's four guns from the 11th Kansas and Gill's escort artillery to the north of the Independence Road. Blunt completed his dispositions by swinging Lieutenant Colonel Samuel Walker's two companies of the 16th Kansas well north of the Independence Road such that they eventually attached themselves to Moonlight's left flank and extended the Yankee line.[26]

The freshly reinforced Yankee line then advanced toward the Confederate line. McLain's artillery ably supported Blunt's cavalry, and the gunners moved no less than eight hundred yards from the Little Blue where they began emptying shell and canister into Greene's formation. Hard-pressed yet again, Greene received some initial help when Lieutenant Colonel Robert Wood's small battalion crossed the river, dismounted, and ran to an apple orchard on Greene's right flank. Within minutes of having deployed his skirmishers, Wood was beset by the 11th and 16th Kansas regiments. The attacking Yankees got within thirty yards of the Confederates when both sides sought as much cover as the various trees and fences could offer. Individual duels now took place with different sets of semiconcealed enemy soldiers pairing up and expending numerous rounds from rifles and pistols in determined efforts to bring each other down. During this melee, Colonel Wood was unhorsed when a Yankee bullet slammed into his mount.[27]

Yet another critical point in the battle had arrived. The Yankee attackers shoved Greene and Wood back toward the river. Making the situation even more dire, the Confederates were now almost out of ammunition. Consequently, sometime after noon the line began to decompose. Able-bodied men and wounded alike streamed to the rear. Among the able-bodied was Private

James H. Campbell, who exemplified the biggest problem of relatives fighting side by side in this war. When a Yankee bullet smashed through his brother's hips, Campbell reacted in a predictable fashion. He carried both himself and his brother right off the battlefield. At that moment, the Campbells were certainly not the only ones headed away. Even more important, T. J. Williams decided to hook his cannons to their limbers and join what appeared to be the final retreat. Price's army would not, however, go down to defeat at the Little Blue. Just as John B. Clark Jr. began to think that "the day seemed lost," two more elements from his brigade arrived on the field, running at the "double quick": Colonel Solomon J. Kitchen's 7th Missouri and Lieutenant Colonel J. F. Davies's battalion (although for reasons never explained to his commander, Davies—formerly a surgeon for the 7th Missouri—was not present with his battalion). The addition of these units stabilized Clark's line. More importantly, Jeff Thompson's Iron Brigade had forded the river to the south of the bridge and drew near to Clark's left flank. It was about 1 PM, and Jo Shelby's division was now on the battlefield.[28]

Shelby's appearance was something of a surprise. Fagan's division was next in the army's column, but Price evinced little trust in Fagan and instead ordered Shelby forward and into the attack. There was naturally some delay to this maneuver as Shelby's passage forced Fagan's division—as well as the thousands of new recruits and the headquarters' wagons and personnel—to move to the sides of the road and watch Shelby's men trot to the sound of the guns. Once across the upper ford secured by the 4th Missouri, Shelby positioned Thompson to the left of Clark's line, which was now anchored by Kitchen's newly arrived regiment near the Independence Road. Once Thompson's brigade cleared the ford, it was Sidney's Jackman's turn to cross. While Shelby ordered the bulk of Jackman's troops to dismount and move to the rear of Thompson's formations, the division commander also directed Lieutenant Colonel C. H. Nichols to ride his regiment of cavalry to the far north of the Confederate line, and he therefore protected Clark's right flank.[29]

The tide of the battle had made its final turn. Where for most of the fight Union forces had constantly pressured both Confederate flanks, now the situation was reversed. The weight of Thompson's brigade on the left and Nichols's regiment on the right proved too much for Blunt's division. Taking station behind Colonel Frank Gordon's 5th Missouri on the northern flank of the brigade, Thompson ordered his men forward through the cornfields and open pastures to his front. Yankee troopers soon gave way. Aggravating matters for Blunt, it was also the Yankees' turn to run short of ammunition. Blunt and Curtis had operated at cross purposes with Blunt, expecting his wagons to remain in the forward area of the battle and Curtis ordering the ammunition wagons away to Independence. It seems that Samuel Curtis anticipated a much quicker retreat than Blunt was willing to allow. Indeed, despite the press of Confederate numbers, especially that of Nichols on Blunt's left flank, the Union soldiers fell back slowly.[30]

Four things aided the Yankee retreat. First, the nature of the terrain continued to affect the course of the battle. Ravines, limestone ledges, and the ubiquitous stone walls all gave ideal defensive positions to the retreating Federals. Second, there was the ever-present combat multiplier of the repeating rifle. With most of the men in Blunt's division, save those of the 2nd Colorado, firing some type of repeating rifle, the Yankees were able to deliver a galling volume of fire against the swarming Confederates. Third, and in like fashion, the Union retreat benefited greatly from a relatively large number of artillery pieces (sixteen guns for just over three thousand cavalrymen). Fourth, Union commanders handled the rearguard with great skill. Although Blunt designated Colonel Ford to command the rearguard, he shared the post with Moonlight over the course of the retreat. In Ford's case, he divided his command into two separate lines, with each line taking turns covering the withdrawal of the other. Here, too, the artillery played an important role as time after time the big guns covered the withdrawal of the different lines. However, it can be noted that in at least one episode it was the cavalry that had to cover the movement of the artillery when five guns attached to the 2nd Colorado proved too heavy for a recently plowed field and became stuck. The omnipresent Captain H. E. Palmer of the 11th Kansas, still fighting in his underwear, led a company-sized charge that momentarily stopped a Confederate advance including the notorious Confederate bushwhacker George Todd, who had joined up with Price's army at Boonville. However, in this same action Palmer and his company eventually became isolated and needed support of their own, necessitating a rescue effort by Nelson Smith and two battalions of the 2nd Colorado. Although Smith succeeded in extracting Palmer and temporarily delaying the inexorable Confederate advance, he also fell at the head of his column shot through the heart. His premonition had come true. Smith was a popular officer, but many a grieving Yankee could take some solace in the fact that George Todd met his end in the same attack.[31]

Sustained combat lasted until around 4 PM when, according to Blunt, the Union rearguard formed a defensive line on the eastern outskirts of Independence. About one hour later, Blunt continued his retreat to the west, marching his men in columns another six miles to the Big Blue River. It was during this march that Blunt's troopers could clearly hear a large artillery barrage coming from the Big Blue. More than a bit confused, the men would later discover that Samuel Curtis was celebrating the telegraphic news of Phillip Sheridan's victory at Cedar Creek in Virginia. For the more pressing business at hand, isolated skirmishing continued through the streets of Independence. Throughout the remaining daylight hours, Shelby's troopers, now supported by Thomas Freeman's brigade from Marmaduke's division, probed the Union rearguard. But by midnight, both armies had settled into their camps—Curtis on the western banks of the Big Blue and Price all around Independence.[32]

Price's Confederates found Independence mostly deserted. An earlier scare had led to a partial evacuation of the citizenry, and rumors of Price's impending arrival the previous night left only women and children to watch the unfolding drama. Despite the fears of many remaining Unionist families, the Confederates behaved themselves in the short time they would remain in the town. Although some readily identifiable bushwhackers took advantage of the opportunity to loot the stores, most of the Confederates who roamed the streets had better things to do than pillage. In the midst of this relative quiet, the busiest man in Independence might have been William McPheeters, Price's chief surgeon. Upon his arrival in town, McPheeters established a central hospital at the Jones Hotel where he tended to thirty wounded Confederates. Later in the evening he provided assistance to a group of forty badly wounded Yankees, who had been left behind in a bank under the care of their own doctor. It was grim work, and McPheeters knew that it would be the Confederacy's turn to leave men behind the next day.[33]

The events of October 21st were notable for a number of reasons. First, for all the sound and fury of almost twelve hours of combat and the apparent near loss of Clark's brigade, the casualties for both sides remained light. The records are yet again fragmentary, but neither side appears to have lost more than forty men killed. Given the quantity of troops engaged and the duration of the fight, the numbers are striking and reveal either incredibly poor marksmanship or the ready availability of stone walls and ravines for protective cover. In the Union camps, the 11th and 15th Kansas and the 2nd Colorado could only count twenty men killed. For the Confederacy, the losses were equally small, with the records from Greene's, Davies's, and Lawther's regiments showing a total of only seven men killed. To be fair to the role of Greene's 3rd Missouri, that unit lost twenty-seven men wounded, which when added to his four killed produced a casualty rate of 20 percent. This was not an insignificant number considering the battles to come in the next few days.[34]

Perhaps no less important, there is a ready comparison of the commanders on both sides. The Union had its fair share of difficulties. Blunt and Curtis, for example, displayed little cooperation. Blunt had to beg and plead with Curtis to let him return to the Little Blue, and even then Curtis managed to aggravate his impetuous division commander by withdrawing the ordnance trains from the battlefield. Nevertheless, Blunt's division had performed admirably throughout the affair. Moonlight's defense of the river had been tenacious, and James Ford's leadership of his brigade had been sure handed. Even Doc Jennison, who paid little attention to the camp discipline or training of his men, can be said to have done well. In stark contrast, the Confederate high command remained consistent in its clumsy tactical management of a battle. Aside from the performance of Colton Greene, who Thomas C. Reynolds would later rightly call the hero of the fight, there was little to celebrate. Sterling Price, much as he had at both Pilot Knob and Lexington, remained fairly aloof from the combat and contented himself with making one primary decision, and that was using Shelby rather than Fagan to support Marmaduke. For no apparent reason other than his distrust of Fagan's capabilities, Price wasted precious time in bringing Shelby from the rear near Lexington when he had Fagan so much closer to the Little Blue.[35]

Even John Marmaduke deserves criticism in the affair. The division commander crossed over to the western bank of the river very early in the battle, and he thus found himself in no position to shape the combat. Marmaduke fought bravely and had at least two horses shot from under him, but he was a useless cog on a battlefront whose primary tactical commanders were John B. Clark Jr. and Colton Greene. Marmaduke should have been on the eastern bank of the river expediting both reinforcements and ammunition. Because Marmaduke was not in a position to manage these assets, badly needed troops and cartridges just trickled over to the western side. Thomas Freeman's brigade, in particular, spent most of the battle doing nothing on the wrong side of the water. With an understanding of the perils of engaging in counterfactual history, one can speculate that Jo Shelby would not have been needed if Freeman had been more gainfully employed. Although the eventual tactical consequence to Price's army was minimal and the Confederates did succeed in chasing Blunt from the field, another whole day had been lost in Price's return to Arkansas.[36]

Major General Sterling Price. Courtesy of the Library of Congress, Prints and Photographs Division, LC-B813-6765 A

Lieutenant General Edmund Kirby Smith. Courtesy of the Library of Congress, Prints and Photographs Division, LC-B813-2013 B

Major General Frederick Steele. Courtesy of the Library of Congress, Prints and Photographs Division, LC-B813-6525

Major General Richard Taylor. Courtesy of the Library of Congress, Prints and Photographs Division, LC-B813-2113 A

Major General John B. Magruder. Courtesy of the Library of Congress, Prints and Photographs Division, LC-USZ62-62496

Brigadier General James F. Fagan. Courtesy of the National Park Service, Wilson's Creek National Battlefield, WICR 31441

Brigadier General John S. Marmaduke. Library of Congress, Prints and Photographs Division, LC-B813-1979 A

Brigadier General William L. Cabell. Library of Congress, Prints and Photographs Division, LC-DIG-cwpbh-00472

Colonel William F. Slemons. Courtesy of the Library of Congress, Prints and Photographs Division, LC-DIG-cwpbh-04868

Brigadier General Joseph O. Shelby. Courtesy of the National Park Service, Wilson's Creek National Battlefield, WICR 31493

Colonel Archibald S. Dobbin. Courtesy of the National Park Service, Wilson's Creek National Battlefield, WICR 31455

Major General William S. Rosecrans. Courtesy of the Library of Congress, Prints and Photographs Division, LC-B813-2001 A

Major General Andrew J. Smith. Courtesy of the Library of Congress, Prints and Photographs Division, LC-USZ62-90950

Brigadier General Thomas Ewing. Courtesy of the Library of Congress, Prints and Photographs Division, LC-B813-2054 A

Brigadier General John B. Clark Jr. Courtesy of the National Park Service, Wilson's Creek National Battlefield, WICR 31453

Colonel Thomas C. Fletcher. Courtesy of the National Park Service, Wilson's Creek National Battlefield, WICR 11509

Brigadier General Egbert B. Brown. Courtesy of the National Park Service, Wilson's Creek National Battlefield, WICR 31447, Wilson's Creek National Battlefield, National Park Service

Brigadier General John McNeil. Courtesy of the Library of Congress, Prints and Photographs Division, LC-B813-1653 A

Brigadier John B. Sanborn. Courtesy of the Minnesota Historical Society, used with permission.

Major General Alfred Pleasonton. Courtesy of the Library of Congress, Prints and Photographs Division, LC-B813-2215 A

Brigadier General (Missouri State Guard) M. Jeff Thompson. Courtesy of the National Park Service, Wilson's Creek National Battlefield, WICR 31454

Thespian Hall, Boonville, MO. Courtesy of the Library of Congress, Prints and Photographs Division, HABS MO,27-BOONV,1—18

Captain Benjamin S. Johnson. Courtesy of the National Park Service, Wilson's Creek National Battlefield, WICR 12192

Colonel Colton Greene. Courtesy of the Memphis and Shelby County Room, Memphis Public Library and Information Center, used with permission.

Senator James H. Lane. Courtesy of the Library of Congress, Prints and Photographs Division, LC-BH82-4185 A

Governor Thomas Carney. Courtesy of the Kansas State Historical Society, used with permission.

Major General James G. Blunt. Courtesy of the Library of Congress, Prints and Photographs Division, LC-B813-6316 A

Major General Samuel R. Curtis. Courtesy of the Library of Congress, Prints and Photographs Division, LC-B813-2075 A

Colonel Charles R. Jennison. Courtesy of the National Park Service, Wilson's Creek National Battlefield, WICR 31691

Colonel James H. Ford. Courtesy of the National Park Service, Wilson's Creek National Battlefield, WICR 12326

Colonel Thomas Moonlight. Courtesy of the Library of Congress, Prints and Photographs Division, LC-USZ62-44452

Colonel John F. Philips. Courtesy of the Library of Congress, Prints and Photographs Division, LC-BH832-703

Captain Richard J. Hinton. Courtesy of the Kansas State Historical Society, used with permission.

Chapter Ten

I Can Stop Price at This Crossing

On October 22, Sterling Price was finally faced with the worst possible tactical situation. He would have to fight enemy forces in both his front and rear. That Price had bungled things to be in such a position is a given. However, in the combat that followed, several things stood out aside from Price's poor appreciation of the location of Samuel Curtis and Alfred Pleasonton. First, Price was not the only senior commander to have a poor sense of the enemy's position. Despite the close contact Curtis's rearguard had maintained with Price's army on the 21st, Curtis would guess wrong as to where he would strike next. Second, and compounding this error, Curtis's prebattle preparation of maps and knowledge of the local terrain left a lot to be desired. Curtis's mapmakers made serious mistakes in marking the route of the Big Blue River, its fords, and the adjacent roads. These cartographic mistakes would have a near-catastrophic effect when Price attacked on the morning of the 22nd. Third, the learned savagery of the guerrilla war would become all too evident in the aftermath of the stand of the 2nd KSM at the Mockbee Farm. New Confederate recruits and former bushwhackers could not resist the opportunity to kill men who had surrendered. Fourth, and finally, the superiority of Union firepower would now be felt on the battlefield; however, the sheer weight of the ordnance thrown at the Confederates did not necessarily translate into large numbers of men who were killed or wounded. In at least that regard, the combat on the 22nd would seem very much like that witnessed in most battles of the war.

With the Confederate Army of Missouri heading toward Kansas City and Kansas militia refusing to go deep into Missouri, Samuel Curtis had decided to make a stand at the Big Blue River. It was as good a place as Curtis would find. Joining the Missouri River five miles to the east of Kansas City, the Big Blue ran about twenty miles to the south before it hooked west into Kansas around Little Santa Fe, which one Union soldier labeled a "squalid little town." Much to the liking of the Union defenders, the west bank of the river in some places stood twelve feet above the water. No less important, the land to the west of the river often rose precipitously in limestone and sandstone ledges that could easily control the ground below it. Fairly open terrain on the eastern side of the river also boded well for Curtis's efforts to discover the exact approach of Price's dusty troops. [1]

Thus presented with a natural defensive position, General Curtis ordered it fortified. As early as October 14, Curtis requested "maps of all localities, rough and general." In the days leading up to the battle, he employed large

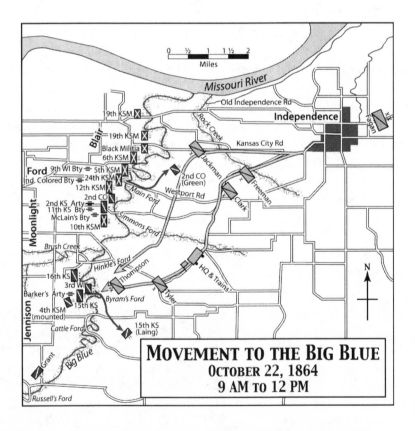

Figure 10.1.   Movement to the Big Blue, October 22, 1864, 9 AM to 12 PM

numbers of his staff, engineers, and the Kansas militia to dig rifle pits and litter important fords with abatis. The return of Blunt's division from the Little Blue on the evening of the 21st helped Curtis finalize his preparations. By daylight the next morning his main line of defense ran ten miles south along the river and counted roughly fifteen thousand men in the ranks. To control these troops, Curtis organized his army into two wings. George Deitzler of the Kansas State Militia commanded the left wing and Blunt the right. Deitzler's control of the left was, however, nominal. Charles Blair's 3rd Brigade of Blunt's division constituted all of the troops in the left wing, and Blair made all of the dispositions. Accordingly, Blair placed one battalion of Colonel A. C. Hogan's 19th KSM at a narrow ford near the mouth of the Blue and then clumped the bulk of his brigade three miles south at the Main Ford through which the Westport Road (the alternate Oregon/Santa Fe Trail) passed. Running from north to south, Blair's line consisted of the remainder of Hogan's 19th KSM, six companies of black Kansas militia, James Montgomery's 6th KSM, Colonel G. A. Colton's 5th KSM, and finally Lieutenant Colonel George Eaves's battalion of militia from Bourbon County, Kansas. At the center of this line and just to the rear of the ford on some high ground were two sections of artillery from the 9th Wisconsin and two Parrots from the Independent Colored Battery.[2]

General Blunt's right wing of the army linked up with Deitzler no more than half a mile south of the Main Ford. Beginning at that point, the 2nd Colorado and the 12th KSM extended the line another half-mile south to Simmons Ford and stood in support of William McLain's battery. At Simmons Ford, Curtis had already placed Colonel William Pennock's 10th KSM and the 2nd Kansas State Artillery. Shortly after the 2nd Colorado arrived, Colonel James Ford, the 4th Brigade commander, directed six companies across the Blue to act as skirmishers. For some of the Coloradans who remained behind, there was trepidation with having to rely upon so many Kansas militia. According to one Colorado volunteer, H. A. Seiffert, the militia had come "not to fight, but to look on and steal the spoils of the battlefield if they could."[3] Fortunately for Seiffert and his comrades, more seasoned reinforcements arrived early in the morning with Thomas Moonlight and the 2nd Brigade. They quickly took up position to the south of the 2nd Colorado. Given this collection of manpower and artillery, Simmons Ford looked impregnable. There was, however, one problem. Moonlight was not supposed to be at Simmons Ford. General Blunt had instead ordered Moonlight to Hinkle's Ford, about two miles further south. Given the apparent mistakes in labeling the fords on contemporary maps and a pervasive confusion about the distances between the fords, both then and since, it was no wonder Moonlight got befuddled. Time would tell if the mistake would haunt the Federals.[4]

Meanwhile, Blunt ordered his final brigade, Jennison's 1st, to Byram's Ford, about three miles further upriver from Simmons. At the ford, Jennison found a battalion of the 4th KSM that had arrived in the early morning hours. Jennison would, however, have to defend the ford without some much-needed firepower. First, there was the loss of George Grover's well-traveled battalion of Missouri militia, which had been fighting with Jennison's brigade since October 17th. The night before, General Curtis had detailed Grover and his men to act as one rather large, and heavily armed, bodyguard for Kansas governor Thomas Carney. Second, Jennison diluted his defense at the ford by dispatching one battalion of the 15th Kansas Cavalry under Major John M. Laing to scout west and south of the Big Blue. Now missing about three hundred men, Jennison concentrated the 15th Kansas and a section of mountain howitzers on the high ground beyond the ford. He moved the 4th KSM beyond the 15th and in the rear. Finally, he placed four companies (which averaged about fifty men each) of the 3rd Wisconsin at the ford itself where they commenced cutting more timber to obstruct the crossing. By daylight on the 22nd, Byram's Ford was yet another significant obstacle should Price choose to cross the river there. The big difficulty though, much like that difficulty afflicting Thomas Moonlight, was that there were still more fords to cover. The right flank of Curtis's army was hardly secure.[5]

Samuel Curtis was not unaware of the existence of other fords or even the possibility that Price might try to turn his army to the south. As early as October 20th, Curtis, through George Deitzler, dispatched two regiments, Colonel George Veale's 2nd KSM and Colonel Sandy Lowe's 21st KSM, across the Big Blue at Russell's Ford about three miles upriver from Byram's Ford. They were then to scout southeast in the direction of Hickman Mills. Notwithstanding his placement of the two regiments of KSM, Curtis was still gambling on the predictability of Sterling Price. For weeks, Old Pap had clung to the Missouri River and had not tried seriously to turn to the south. Although Curtis fully expected that turn, he did not think Price would make it before Kansas City. Furthermore, he chose to believe that should Price make the turn at the Big Blue either Alfred Pleasonton or A. J. Smith would soon be there to block the attempt. By 5 PM on the 21st, and as Blunt's rearguard fell back through Independence from the Battle of the Little Blue, Curtis was convinced enough to telegraph William Rosecrans: "I am confident I can stop Price at this crossing, [i.e., the Main Ford] and hope you will come up in his rear and left. He cannot get out by Hickman Mills. If you can get that position we will bag Price."[6]

Curtis's confidence mattered little to James Blunt. At some point on the night of the 21st after Blunt had shepherded his division to the Big Blue, the two generals met to discuss the placement of the army. When Curtis unveiled his plan to concentrate at the Main Ford, Blunt was incredulous. He refused to think that Price would be so wooden as to assault Curtis's prepared defenses at just one narrow choke point. Blunt's uneasiness over the coming battle was more than shared by countless cold and shivering militia. This was especially the case for those militiamen who watched Blunt's ravenous and wounded troops pass by that night. Shock over the sight of torn bodies led to a constant questioning of the veterans as to Price's whereabouts and just how many rebels were coming toward the Big Blue. The responses were never reassuring, and an imminent sense of doom hovered over some soldiers as it has always hovered over soldiers preparing for battle. One old Kansas farmer had three separate dreams that he would be killed the following morning. This sort of worry pushed the citizen-soldiers to pin a great deal of hope on the arrival of Rosecrans and Pleasonton. As James Hanway of the Miami County militia later recalled: "The question was asked a thousand times,— 'Where is Rosecrans? Why cannot we hear from him?'"[7]

Rosecrans, or at least Pleasonton, was very much close by, but those commanders would not yet prevent Sterling Price from moving on the Big Blue. By the morning of the 22nd, Price made ready for the continued advance. Price understood that Blunt and Curtis were now together in a fairly strong position, although scouting reports vastly underestimated their total strength at no more than eight thousand men. It was nonetheless enough men to finally persuade Price to break away from the Missouri River and indeed head south along the Kansas-Missouri border. To get to the border, Price ordered the main body of the army to head southwest along the Westport Road, heading for a crossing of the Big Blue. Suffering no small amount of fatigue from the previous day's dismounted fight, the army got a late start at 9 AM. Shelby would be in the lead followed by Marmaduke, then Fagan. Despite once again being in the forefront of the army's advance, Shelby's troopers could have taken some solace in reinforcements that arrived late on the 21st. Lieutenant Colonel D. A. Williams finally returned from his recruiting efforts north of the Missouri River in Livingston and Carroll counties. He was accompanied by at least six hundred fully armed men.[8]

Price's movements involved some deception. While Shelby led the bulk of the army southwest along the Westport Road, he pointed Sidney Jackman and his brigade west along the Kansas City Road hoping to fix Curtis along the lower portion of the Big Blue. Shortly after commencing the march outside of Independence, Jackman made contact with elements of the 2nd Colorado. The two forces engaged in some desultory skirmishing for about one hour. When the firing faded, and in accord with Shelby's instructions, Jackman screened the army's passage further south along the Westport Road. There was, however, one final deception (whether intended or not). About two miles from Independence, the Westport Road made a hard turn to the west where the road then crossed the Big Blue at the Main Ford. This was precisely where Curtis had stacked much of his army in anticipation of Price's crossing. Instead, Price chose, in the words of Jeff Thompson, to take a "left-hand road," which pointed the army toward crossing the Big Blue at Byram's Ford. By 11 AM, Price made it to the ford unmolested. The impossible, or at least the improbable, for Samuel Curtis had just happened. The Confederates were now going to make a concerted push on the Big Blue well south of the Main Ford.[9]

During the night of the 21st and 22nd, Curtis had spent a large amount of effort trying to persuade James Blunt that Price would attack at the Main Ford. Nevertheless, as the night wore on and day broke, Curtis began to have second thoughts about the whole thing. He was restless and prowled his defenses near the Main Ford. By 9 AM, he was nearly beside himself with concern. Jackman's skirmishing in his front was too tentative. One hour later, signal officers atop a tower one-half mile north of the Main Ford could pick up little activity along the Kansas City Road. Curtis then fired off orders to Blunt and General Melvin S. Grant, whose two regiments of KSM guarded Russell's Ford and Hickman Mills, to be on guard for a turning movement and to report back to Curtis at thirty-minute intervals. At 11 AM, and just as Shelby began to poke around Byram's Ford, Curtis became even more worried. Signal officers in a tower two miles upriver from the Main Ford spied dust clouds out on the prairie to the south, but more importantly scouts from the 2nd Colorado reported that "heavy columns" of Confederates were heading for the fords occupied by Moonlight and Jennison.[10]

Still, and inexplicably, Curtis could not yet bring himself to alter his dispositions. He remained glued to the northern part of his line and looked for dispatches from Blunt, Jennison, and Moonlight. For the next three hours, Curtis waited, and all the while Shelby's troops continued to ride away from him and spill around Jennison at Byram's Ford. The Iron Brigade was the first large unit to arrive, and Jeff Thompson quickly found that the Yankees had done their work well. The ford was a perfect mess with felled trees blocking passage. A section of mountain howitzers supported by most of Jennison's dismounted troopers on a hill beyond the eastern bank further disputed the crossing of the Confederates. There was perhaps only one thing that worked to the disadvantage of the defenders. In order to obstruct the river, the militia had originally cleared the west bank. The eastern bank remained very wooded and therefore provided the attacking Confederates with far more cover than Jennison's defenders. Notwithstanding this mistake, Thompson struggled immediately with Jennison's troopers. Despite the historian William E. Connelley's later assertion that the defense of the ford should have been entrusted to a better officer, Doc Jennison proved remarkably tenacious. Jeff Thompson would have to flail at the Yankees for three more precious hours during which time Jackman arrived with two of his regiments (Nichols's and Schnables's), having left the other two (Hunter's and Coleman's) to continue the screen to the north.[11]

Finally, around 2 PM and as the army's trains began to approach the ford from the west, Thompson and Shelby determined that it would be better to try to envelop Jennison's position by crossing at fords above and below Byram's. For the upper ford, Shelby turned to Frank Gordon and his 5th Missouri, which had been detached from Thompson for most of the day. Shelby ordered Gordon to find a ford no more than two miles to the south and cross over onto the prairie heading for Wornall Road, about three miles from the river. Gordon was then to pivot to the north and ride along the lane heading for Westport. If Gordon was successful, Jennison would be cut off completely from any reinforcement. For the lower ford, it is not certain who Shelby selected for the operation. Whoever it was, by 3 PM they had found the unguarded Hinkle's Ford. Thomas Moonlight's failure to protect the ford now proved near disastrous. Confederates swarmed around Jennison's flanks, and he had no choice but to fall back. As Jennison retreated, Thompson's troopers splashed into Byram's Ford. Once in the water, and to their great joy, the men found a number of axes that the retreating Yankees had left behind. Wasting little time, the Confederate cavalrymen—who were also joined by Thomas Mackey's pioneers—began swinging the axes and clearing the ford of its obstructions. Following about one hour of heavy labor, the

Figure 10.2.   The Big Blue, October 22, 1864, 1 to 8 PM

cavalry and artillery started to move again. The chase was on with Doc Jennison riding hard for the Kansas-Missouri border.[12]

At first, Jennison tried to pull back in a northwesterly direction toward Westport. But the Confederates who had poured through Hinkle's Ford kept up enough pressure to force Jennison in a westerly path well to the south of Westport. Brush Creek, which ran west to east and emptied into the Big Blue south of Simmons Ford, also served to funnel the 1st Brigade toward Kansas. Though Jennison's troopers contested most of the ground, they soon found themselves four miles to the rear and just beyond the state line near Shawnee Mission, Kansas. Here, Jennison's harried cavalry finally found help. Although General Blunt, upon hearing the cannonade at Byram's Ford around 1 PM, had ordered Moonlight to ride to Jennison's assistance, Moonlight never got the order. Instead, one of Moonlight's own scouts informed him that

Jennison had been turned, which prompted the colonel to action. He wheeled his 2nd Brigade to cross Brush Creek at the Harrisonville Road where he quickly discovered that Jennison had already passed that point. Moonlight and his brigade then galloped to Westport and swung back toward the south-west and Shawnee Mission. Upon his arrival near the state line, the 2nd Brigade formed up on Jennison's left, facing Shelby. Preston Plumb and the 11th Kansas would anchor the extreme left of the brigade's line, while Moonlight took charge of the two battalion-sized detachments of the 5th and 16th Kansas cavalries positioned to their right. [13]

Despite the increased numbers, the Yankee line continued to fall back into Kansas. Not helping matters was the fact that neither Jennison nor Moonlight assumed command of the unified force. Jennison was the senior officer, but he displayed no willingness to push the issue. This potentially calamitous situation was alleviated by the sudden appearance of Major Robert Hunt, General Curtis's artillery chief. Curtis had originally ordered Hunt to lead his personal escort to Byram's Ford and reinforce Jennison when the general finally understood the Confederate turning movement. Hunt got only to the outskirts of Westport when he received a message from Jennison reporting his retreat. Minutes later, Hunt joined Moonlight's column as it rode through Westport heading to the state line. Once Hunt and Moonlight joined up with Jennison, the artillery chief turned over the command of Curtis's escort to a more junior officer. With Jeff Thompson's Iron Brigade pushing the Unionists beyond Shawnee Mission, Hunt took the initiative and cobbled together a heavy skirmish line of eight companies from both brigades. Hunt's new command quickly pressed forward and tossed Thompson's troops into some disarray. As darkness fell, the Confederates began a withdrawal back across the battlefield and past Westport to its south. Hunt, followed by Moonlight and Jennison, did not pursue much further and broke contact for the night, with Jennison making his headquarters at A. B. H. McGee's property just north of Westport. [14]

Hunt's leadership had been impressive, but it was hardly decisive. Similarly, Moonlight had also performed well, but his postwar claim that he stampeded the Confederates with a flank attack on their left was more than an exaggeration. Indeed, by the time either Hunt spearheaded the counterattack or the 11th Kansas charged the Confederate left, the Unionists faced only one Confederate regiment, Lieutenant Colonel William H. Erwin's 12th Missouri. Jo Shelby had mysteriously recalled the remainder of the brigade. The key to this strange turn of events was an accident of war known as the

2nd KSM. Recruited from Topeka and Shawnee County, the 2nd KSM was part of a brigade that had taken shape in the vicinity of Russell's Ford and Hickman Mills. Commanded by General Melvin S. Grant, the brigade was a hodgepodge of various county militias, and it included bits and pieces of the 2nd, 3rd, 13th, 21st, and 23rd regiments of the KSM. The 2nd KSM was a hybrid regiment consisting of five companies of mounted infantry, two companies of dismounted infantry, and one battery of artillery—or really just one old 24-pound howitzer. However, before the 2nd KSM had even marched into Missouri, it left the two dismounted companies behind to be attached to another regiment. All told there were about three hundred citizen-soldiers in the 2nd KSM who marched to the Big Blue. Though mounted like cavalry, the majority of the Topekans carried newly issued Enfield rifle muskets. The men were not well trained, the ammunition for their Enfields did not fit properly, and most had never even heard the report of their own howitzer. At the head of this column was a one-time merchant and county sheriff, George W. Veale, who was also something of a militia anomaly. He had military experience, having spent the first three years of the war as a junior officer in the 4th Kansas Cavalry. Although he had seen his fair share of combat during that time, there was little that prepared him for what was about to happen.[15]

At daybreak on the 22nd, Veale and the men of the 2nd KSM awoke to temperatures that hovered around freezing and were made worse by a stiff, northerly wind. Enervated by the cold, the militia prepared a leisurely breakfast. By 9 AM, however, the men were roused to "boots and saddles" when Samuel Curtis became concerned for his right flank and issued orders to General Grant to scout in the directions of Independence and Pleasant Hill. Grant responded by dividing his force. He kept the 2nd KSM's howitzer, the 3rd KSM, and the battalions of the 23rd and 13th KSMs at Russell's Ford, while sending the 2nd and the 21st KSMs on the desired patrols. In making his dispositions, Grant took two big chances. First, he had just sent regiments on a mission more suitable to companies, which deprived Russell's Ford of several hundred soldiers. Second, Grant accompanied the 2nd KSM in its reconnaissance. Grant's mistakes were those of the amateur soldier. But to the general's credit he had, at least, previously acknowledged that he was in over his shoulders commanding the brigade. According to Thomas Moonlight, Grant, a wholesale grocer by trade, "begged by letter to Gen. Curtis to send him some officer of experience to take command."[16]

Notwithstanding Grant's inexperience or his relative lack of confidence, there appeared to be no immediate consequences to the general's decisions.

Neither the 2nd nor the 21st KSM found much of anything on their patrols, and they began their marches back to the eastern side of Russell's Ford. Similarly, things had been fairly quiet at Russell's Ford. But around 3 PM circumstances changed dramatically. With faint echoes of the battle at Byram's Ford echoing up the river, a messenger arrived spreading the word that Jennison was fighting at Byram's Ford and that the militia should withdraw to Westport "as fast as possible." The word reached the battalion and regimental commanders one by one at Russell's Ford, and one by one they promptly wheeled their units about and headed northwest toward Westport with not one commander alert enough to pass word on to General Grant. A mile later they ran into Frank Gordon's Confederates. In short order, the Confederates scattered the 3rd and 13th KSMs, with many of the Unionists running for the state line and still others seeking shelter in the trees and brush lining the Big Blue. The only Yankee resistance left on the battlefield was the solitary howitzer of the 2nd KSM. The twenty-one men who manned the gun had been abandoned at the outset of the action when the 23rd KSM fled to the west faster than the gun could follow. The gun crew was commanded by a bookish and, heretofore, reticent lawyer named Ross Burns, who then made the fateful decision to fight rather than surrender. [17]

To the relief of the Yankee gunners, no sooner had Burns issued his order than the remainder of the 2nd KSM appeared just to their south. The troops of the 2nd KSM had made the ride from beyond the eastern bank of Russell's Ford, where they had stopped to eat a meal. The meal was, however, interrupted by yet another messenger who brought word of the original skirmishing between Gordon's Confederates and the main body of Grant's militia. The regiment immediately remounted and headed north in the direction of Burns's howitzer. Now aware of the approaching help, Burns unlimbered his gun in the middle of a lane flanked by stone and rail fences. The lane itself ran through the middle of Thomas Mockbee's farm. Before Veale's men even reached the gun, Burns gave the order to fire upon the Confederates then congregating in a grove of locust trees on a hill off to the west. It was a disappointing fusillade. The first shell exploded harmlessly, about one hundred feet above the enemy, provoking the Confederates to laughter as they hallowed and pointed up in the air. The next few rounds were no better as they either exploded too high or failed to detonate at all. But soon enough, the howitzer found both the range and working ordnance. A shell exploded head high among the Confederates, which forced them to seek cover in a ravine. About this time, Veale and his advance galloped up to the gun, having knocked down a fence and ridden across an uncultivated cornfield. With Veale in front, the regimental commander formed a mounted line to the right of the gun that extended to a shallow gully. He also positioned two units, Captain A. J. Huntoon's B Company and Captain H. E. Bush's G Company, to the west in the orchard. The Kansans then delivered a volley of musketry that helped stall the gathering Confederate charge. Though momentarily successful, Colonel Veale was not optimistic of future prospects. He did not want to give battle at this location, fearing that the Confederates would soon bring far superior, if not more well trained, numbers to the field. [18]

General Grant would, however, have nothing to do with a withdrawal. He had accompanied the Shawnee County men to the Mockbee Farm, and he did not believe the enemy to be in great strength. The messenger who had brought the initial word of the fight at the Mockbee Farm led Grant to think that he could force his way through to Westport. Grant also thought reinforcements would be arriving soon from Hickman Mills. This was not wishful thinking. Sandy Lowe's 21st KSM, which had returned from its own scout, was just east of Russell's Ford. Furthermore, Grant knew of another unit in the same area. In the course of that morning's reconnaissance, Grant had bumped into Major John M. Laing's battalion of the 15th Kansas Cavalry from Doc Jennison's brigade. Ever since that morning, Laing had been out scouting in the vicinity of Hickman's Mill. When Grant and the 2nd KSM first returned across the river and rode to the proverbial sound of the guns, the general sent a message back to both Lowe and Laing directing them to ride toward Westport—and him—"as fast as possible." Once the 2nd KSM made contact with Frank Gordon's Confederates, Grant sent another message telling Lowe and Laing to reinforce him at the Mockbee Farm. [19]

As Grant waited for his reinforcements, he could not have known that, already, the action at the Mockbee Farm had thrown the Confederate command into some confusion. More specifically, the skirmishing had caused their pursuit of Doc Jennison to falter. Gordon's engagement with the first three regiments of the KSM had been unexpected. Gordon's 5th Missouri had crossed the Big Blue and stormed up the bluffs of the west blank only to run into the 3rd, 13th, and 23rd KSMs moving toward Westport. In the time that it took Gordon to scatter this militia, Jo Shelby arrived on the scene and began ordering troops to the Mockbee Farm. Shelby's call made it first to Sidney Jackman, but it would still be a while before he rode to the field. In the meantime, and after Ross Burns delivered the initial salvos from the 24-pound howitzer, Frank Gordon advanced his skirmishers and then pushed a column of cavalry down the lane. Burns, especially, was ready for the assault. He pivoted his gun, and it now faced north in the lane. Nevertheless, Gordon's charge initially threw Veale's line into confusion. Veale had not yet dismounted his men, and this proved too much of a temptation for some of the militia. The line began to waver, and a number of men fled. Veale realized his mistake and ordered his troopers to dismount with horses and horse holders to the rear. Somehow, the line held, delivering a stinging volley into Gordon's onrushing ranks and driving them back. At about this time, Colonel Veale could then be seen on horseback riding in front of his line, waving his saber, and shouting, "Hurrah, Boys! We've got them whipped!" Emboldened, Veale advanced his own skirmish line about 150 yards up the hill to a stone fence north of the Mockbee Farm. Veale and the rest of the militia quickly followed their skirmishers to the crest of the hill. The Confederate response was not long in coming as Gordon, and probably elements of Jackman's brigade, attacked yet again. This assault came more from the west, necessitating the Yankee line, and the howitzer, to pivot correspondingly. As one militiaman later noted, Ross Burns and his crew now "did some of the finest work with the gun," using canister to great effect in busting the Confederate assault.[20]

Within the Confederate ranks there was a growing consternation over the inability to break this Union resistance. Jo Shelby did not realize yet that it was militia to his front. Instead, Shelby thought he was facing the advance of Alfred Pleasonton's cavalry. Consequently, Shelby made further calls for reinforcements. This time he sent a messenger to Jeff Thompson, recalling the Iron Brigade from any further pursuit of Jennison. Well within sight of what Shelby called the "domes and spires of Westport," the Iron Brigade returned to Shelby, leaving only Erwin's regiment to deal with Jennison and his reinforcements. The action at Mockbee's Farm was then forty-five minutes old and about to reach its climax. Before Thompson could arrive on the field, Jackman and Gordon marshaled their regiments for a third mounted attack. This attack included a large number of newly conscripted and unarmed men in Jackman's ranks. Jackman was, however, undeterred, and long bugle notes rang out, preparing the men for the charge. A brief silence followed. Seconds later, the eerie Rebel Yell penetrated the air. Charging Confederate cavalry then broke from their wooded line and galloped down upon the 2nd KSM. This time, the Confederates vastly outnumbered their foe. Hard-pounding cavalry spilled over both militia flanks.[21]

Ross Burns, much as he had done at the beginning of the engagement, stood to his gun. As Jackman and Gordon sped toward the Yankees, Burns's howitzer got off two salvos of canister, which opened significant holes in the Confederate line. But when Burns called for a round of double canister, the captain found his gun crew decimated. One gunner fell dead while loading the first can, and another barely had time to ram home the second. At the last possible moment, the howitzer belched forth its final round, killing and wounding several Confederates. It was, however, not enough. The 2nd KSM now disintegrated as the Confederate attack blew through their line. "We scattered like sheep," P. I. Bonebrake recalled, "every man for himself, each running for his horse." Not so surprisingly, most of the men did not find their horses. The horse holders were caught up in the panic and readily let all the animals loose, or at least those animals they could not mount in an attempted escape. Abandoned, the horseless men threw down their weapons. Some attempted to surrender, and most tried to make a run back to the trees and underbrush along the banks of the Big Blue.[22]

The battlefield at the Mockbee Farm was a smoky mess. Most of Gordon's Confederates just milled about in the simple pursuit of food as they scrounged bacon, flour, and hard tack from Yankee wagons abandoned earlier in the afternoon. Black servants and teamsters, who traveled close behind in Shelby's trains, descended upon the Mockbee fields and began picking as much corn as their wagons could carry. Amid this scene of plunder, there was no small amount of confusion as both Yankees and Confederates were dressed in a mix of Union blue and homespun. The lack of uniformity led to one incident in which one homespun-wearing militiaman, John Freeland, was captured and disarmed only to be mistaken for a Confederate and given a shotgun to guard his compatriots. Needless to say, Freeland ran away at the earliest opportunity.[23]

The humor in Freeland's situation was not to be found with several other captured Yankees. It took little time for many of Sidney Jackman's men to revert to their bushwhacker ways by stripping, looting, and executing their prisoners. Merrick D. Race was one such Kansan who surrendered to a promise that he would be spared. Moments later, his captors took his clothes and rings and then shot him in the lungs and legs. Race lingered in agony for the next two days before finally dying. Fortunately for large numbers of captured Yankees, Jo Shelby followed Jackman onto the battlefield, and his presence helped forestall a massacre. As he rode about the scene, Shelby observed about twenty captured militiamen who had been lined up for execution. As described by one of the prisoners, Guilford Gage, Shelby galloped over and harangued Jackman's horsemen, calling them "thieves and cowards." He then sent for veteran soldiers to guard the Yankees with instructions to shoot any of Jackman's men "as you would a dog" if they came around to harm the prisoners. Shelby's influence was pervasive, and this incident was not isolated. Along the banks of the Big Blue, Lieutenant Colonel Henry Greene, already shot in the head and hip after surrendering, was spared at the last minute when his would-be executioners got the word that Shelby wanted the shooting of prisoners stopped. It should also be noted that Jo Shelby was not the only Confederate officer who put a stop to the murder of prisoners. John Kemp and a black teamster were captured by an officer mounted upon a white horse. Despite the protestations of many who wanted to kill "the nigger," the officer guaranteed the safety of both men and ordered them guarded to the rear.[24]

Although about fifty men of the 2nd KSM were now killed or wounded with another sixty-eight having been taken prisoner, all was neither in vain nor lost. Shelby paid a high price for his victory. Forty-three Confederates had been killed or wounded. Moreover, the remainder of the 2nd KSM managed to escape to Russell's Ford where the militiamen found a part of their long-awaited reinforcement, the 21st KSM, on the eastern bank of the river. Although the Shawnee County men kept right on running through the ranks of their relief and caused a small panic, the core of the 21st KSM stood its ground against a weakened Confederate assault. Too many of Jackman's men had peeled off to plunder or murder during the one-mile race from the Mockbee Farm. Nevertheless, sporadic fighting continued in the vicinity of the ford for about another thirty minutes until the sun set and Jo Shelby pulled his division back toward Brush Creek. Melvin Grant was then free to lead the 21st and the remnants of the 2nd KSM on a roundabout march to Little Santa Fe and thence to Olathe, Kansas, and safety.[25]

The final stage of the militia's fight at the Big Blue was not without its controversy. While the 21st KSM readily came to the aid of the shattered Shawnee County regiment, John Laing's battalion of the 15th KS Cavalry was strangely absent. Despite his battalion's location on a hill just across the eastern bank of the river, Laing never made it to the fight. By the time the Confederates ran into Lowe's regiment, Laing had received no less than two messages from Grant asking that he come to his assistance. Making matters worse, Lieutenant Cyrus M. Roberts, an aide to General Curtis, had personally tried to get Laing to cross back over the river and into the fight. Curtis had originally sent Roberts to Hickman Mills to get reinforcements for Jennison at Byram's Ford. Not once but twice did Roberts deliver the orders to Laing, who kept his troopers ensconced and eating on the eastern bank of the Big Blue. Roberts never made it a third time as he joined Lowe's 21st KSM in the final defense of the ford. When Roberts did eventually have a chance to look back for Laing, the wayward cavalryman had vanished. As panicked remnants of the 2nd KSM washed over the ford and into the ranks of his own soldiers, Laing calmly mounted his troopers and ordered a countermarch by the right flank. The battalion retreated to Hickman Mills and turned west for a long ride that took them first to Little Santa Fe, then to Olathe, and finally to Shawnee Mission.[26]

As things stood on the western bank of the Big Blue, Sterling Price had himself a victory. The right flank of Curtis's army had been crunched during the day's fight, which then led to a general withdrawal of General Dietzler's left wing back toward Kansas City. Only by nightfall was Curtis able to stabilize a line guarding Westport along the northern banks of Brush Creek. Old Pap even had two captured battle flags to show for his efforts. The problem for Price, however, was that he was now faced with more than just Samuel Curtis's army. As Jo Shelby had forced his way across the Big Blue during the day, so, too, had Alfred Pleasonton finally concentrated his Yankee cavalry for an attack on Price's rearguard, starting at the Little Blue.[27]

There is no doubt that Pleasonton's appearance was a pivotal moment in the campaign. But it is highly debatable if indeed this was the best place for Pleasonton to be with his entire division. The question here is whether Pleasonton, or at least the bulk of his force, should have ridden to the south and west where they could have interdicted Price's eventual return home. A similar question looms over William Rosecrans's deployment of A. J. Smith's infantry. They, too, were headed for Independence right behind Pleasonton. Although Rosecrans could be faulted for not anticipating Price's turn to the south and reacting accordingly, an even greater mistake was in letting Alfred Pleasonton get too far ahead of his headquarters without explicit instructions to hold off committing all of the cavalry to the direct chase of Price. Acting on his own, Alfred Pleasonton could readily present Rosecrans with a fait accompli. Such indeed was the case on the evening of October 21.[28]

For the previous two days, and ever since Pleasonton assumed field command of the cavalry, Rosecrans had ordered both his infantry and cavalry toward the rear of Price's army. It was a path that took the combined force on a northwesterly march from places such as Sedalia and Cook's Store headed for Lexington. Pleasonton's advance entered Lexington on the afternoon of the 20th, and the rest of the army followed the next day. By the time Rosecrans entered Lexington late on the 21st, Pleasonton had already departed the town in pursuit of Price with his entire division. It was a rash movement and one that Rosecrans dearly wanted to stop. An early afternoon telegram from Curtis persuaded Rosecrans that the time had arrived to head south and cut off Price. He issued orders to Pleasonton to head south, leaving only one brigade to pursue Price directly. A. J. Smith also got orders to march to the southwest and Chapel Hill. All of this was, of course, too late to pull Pleasonton back. He was almost in contact with Price's rearguard, and he smelled battle. By 7:10 on the morning of the 22nd and with Pleasonton already moving across the Little Blue, Rosecrans rubberstamped Pleasonton's actions by giving him discretion to pursue Price as he thought necessary. A. J. Smith, who had already begun his march to the southwest and Chapel Hill, would now have to beat back to the north toward Independence and support Pleasonton.[29]

John McNeil led Pleasonton's advance on the morning of the 22nd. McNeil's 2nd Brigade reached the Little Blue shortly before sunrise. The crossing would be somewhat difficult as the bridge on the Independence Road had been destroyed and Price's rearguard now loomed on the other side. These particular Confederates were led by the perpetually disgruntled Colonel John C. Wright of Slemons's brigade and Fagan's division. Wright's men had been among the last to pull into Independence on the night of the 21st when Wright received orders to return to the Little Blue and guard the rear. It was cold and raining, and Wright felt, much as he had since the beginning of the campaign, that Fagan was singling him out for arduous duty. Claiming that he had "too much pride to gratify Fagan by complaining," Wright headed back east and camped near the Little Blue without rations for men or horses. McNeil's appearance on the eastern bank found Wright's men dismounted and enjoying much the same cover that Moonlight's Yankees had the previous day. For about thirty minutes, Wright held McNeil at the river. McNeil, however, moved some of his brigade to the ford below the bridge where John B. Clark Jr. had crossed the previous day, and therefore succeeded in turning Wright from his original position. While Wright fell back slowly, Alfred Pleasonton rode onto the field and began the process of constructing a temporary bridge across the Little Blue at the crossing of the Independence Road. By 11 AM the rest of Pleasonton's division, including its artillery and trains, began to cross the river in support of McNeil.[30]

About this time, Pleasonton finally got some long-awaited news from General Curtis's army. A courier informed Pleasonton of Curtis's exact position, manpower, and armament. It was all the information that Pleasonton needed to redouble his efforts to pursue Price. Pleasonton's task would not be easy. Between 11 AM and 2 PM, Wright, who was supported by the rest of Slemons's brigade and Captain William Hughey's two-gun battery of James rifles, conducted an efficient rearguard during the seven miles to Independence. News of the action with the Federals passed eventually to Sterling Price and James Fagan, who then ordered William Cabell to bring his brigade to the aid of Wright. As Wright fell back within sight of Independence, McNeil's pursuit slackened somewhat, and it allowed Slemons and Wright to pass through Cabell's brigade, which now assumed the responsibility of the rearguard. During this changeover, Cabell stopped Wright and queried him about the day's fight. Cabell also presented Wright with a watch he had borrowed earlier in the campaign. As the two officers talked, Wright in-

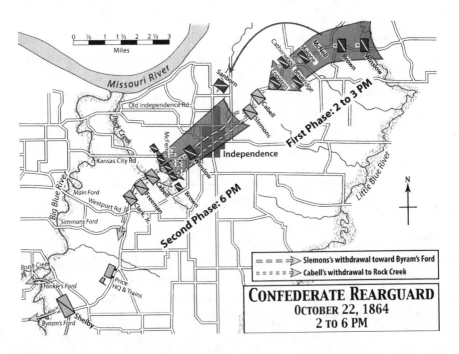

Figure 10.3.   Confederate Rearguard, October 22, 1864, 2 to 6 PM

formed Cabell that he thought "General Price will soon be called on to solve the difficult problem of the man between two impassable fires, which way will he jump." Cabell emitted a strange laugh and replied, "Yes, d—m him, unless he jumps pretty soon, it will be too late to jump." With that Wright took his men through the town and out of action for the rest of the day.[31]

In stark contrast, Cabell's day was only beginning. Cabell initially positioned his brigade about three miles to the northeast of town astride the Independence Road. Included in the brigade's defense was Hughey's battery. Sometime around 2 PM, McNeil renewed his push on the town, dismounting two regiments abreast: Colonel John C. Beveridge's 17th Illinois and Colonel E. C. Catherwood's 13th Missouri. Beveridge was to the extreme left, or south, of the line. Much of Joseph Eppstein's 5th MSM acted as skirmishers in advance of the attack. Although McNeil shoved Cabell inexorably toward Independence, Hughey's artillery served the Confederacy well in slowing the Federals. Yet by 3 PM, Hughey's shelling had stopped. Beveridge and Catherwood pushed west, forcing Cabell back into the streets of the town itself. Around this same time, Alfred Pleasonton arrived on the battlefield. He quickly realized Cabell was in a precarious position because of the many streets and avenues that ran into the city from the flat prairie beyond. Pleasonton ordered John Sanborn's 3rd Brigade forward and to the right of McNeil's command. Sanborn was now in position to flank Cabell from the north and northeast. In accordance with Pleasonton's orders, Sanborn dismounted his brigade and formed it into two lines with Colonel John Phelps's 2nd Arkansas in the lead. As Sanborn later recalled, the Yankees then charged into the town through "gardens, door-yards, streets, and alleys," catching Cabell by surprise. Arkansans now fought Arkansans as the Confederates mounted some resistance to the right and front of Phelps's advance, but the Unionists pressed on, stampeding Cabell's men to the west and southwest. Despite the success, Phelps's attack stalled. The Unionists had charged across several hundred yards, and fatigue gripped their bodies. As Phelps's dismounted troopers gasped for their breath, the Union offensive shifted to the east.[32]

Just as Phelps's charge ground to a halt, Alfred Pleasonton ordered John McNeil back into action. McNeil then directed Catherwood's 13th Missouri to make a mounted charge into Independence. Starting from a point about one-quarter mile from the town, Colonel Catherwood piled his seven companies into one long column of fours. The 13th then raised a yell and charged down the macadamized road into Independence followed by the rest of the brigade. As the charge gained momentum, Catherwood's cavalry benefited from the quick work of a sympathizing citizen. Cabell's troops, before abandoning the western outskirts of Independence, had strung a chain across the road and tied it with ropes to two blackjack trees. If undetected by the galloping Yankee cavalry, they would be toppled into a large jumble of men and horses. Fortunately for the troopers, an old woman ran from her house and loosened the chains to the ground right before the lead company made contact. Catherwood's grateful men now sped unhindered into the town. They did not, however, ride straight into the heart of Independence. Instead, the Unionists rode west, then turned to the south, and then finally west again, carrying "everything before them, sabering, and pistoling [*sic*] those who resisted." In moments, the 13th Missouri made it to the southwestern portion of town where they ran into Hughey's two cannons and their supporting troops. To Mrs. Robert Hill, who observed the charge from her upper porch, the "far-off flash of red fire coming out of the guns and pistols . . . was one of the most sublimely thrilling sights that one could imagine." With sabers flashing, Catherwood's men wasted little time in running over the artillery. The Yankees killed most of the team horses and captured both guns, plus at least three hundred Confederates. Catherwood's regiment suffered only ten men wounded. While many of the captured Confederates had defended their position valiantly, there were, according to Colonel Wright, more than a few who were nothing but "stragglers who had stopped in town and were drunk on Yankee whiskey." General Cabell himself was caught up in this final melee and only escaped the onslaught, as he later recalled, by mounting his horse and "jumping over a piece of artillery and running through the passage of a double log cabin and jumping the yard fence." The general then rode through a number of other lots before galloping hard for his command to the west. It was a close-run escape, and the general could be happy with only losing his saber to the enemy.[33]

Remarkably, Union forces could not immediately follow up their success. Fatigue and confusion permeated McNeil's and Sanborn's victorious ranks, which prompted General Pleasonton to hurry forward his remaining two brigades: General Egbert B. Brown's 1st and Colonel Edward Winslow's 4th. Winslow had been the last to arrive at around 4 PM. He reported to Pleasonton, who was then headquartered in the second story of the city Court House. Pleasonton was brief and to the point. After stating that he "had delayed vigorous action until his militia commands could be supported by experienced and seasoned troops," the general ordered Winslow to move out and support an attack led by Egbert Brown's brigade. Brown's action developed slowly, and Cabell and the Confederates took advantage of the lull and regrouped perhaps a mile southwest of town along the Westport Road, using hedges, fences, and a brick farmhouse for cover and concealment. Sterling Price was now very aware of the threat posed by Pleasonton, and Old Pap ordered Marmaduke's division back to help Cabell.[34]

On the evening of the 22nd, Marmaduke had encamped about two miles to the southwest of Independence along the Westport Road and behind the western bank of Rock Creek. Marmaduke's order of battle found Thomas Freeman's brigade along the creek bank supported by John B. Clark Jr.'s brigade one-half mile to the rear. About an hour before sundown, General Brown's 1st Brigade moved to the western outskirts of Independence and engaged Cabell's reconstituted line. The attack was neither properly supported nor bravely led. General Brown, riding near the front of his column with Colonel James McFerran's 1st MSM, had lost track of the remainder of his brigade. Unbeknownst to Brown, Colonel Nelson Cole, Rosecrans's chief of artillery, had detached a section of Charles Thurber's Company L, 2nd Missouri Light Artillery, from the brigade. The section came to a halt in the streets of Independence, which also had the unintentional effect of stopping the cavalry right behind it: Brown's 4th and 7th MSMs. When Brown thus ordered Colonel McFerran to make an attack down the Westport Road supported on the flanks by the 4th and 7th MSMs, he was really sending McFerran alone to charge Price's rearguard. Brown's attack stumbled even more because Colonel McFerran picked this time to leave the battlefield and lurk about one-quarter mile to the rear with the horse holders.[35]

Consequently, the actual management of the attack descended to Lieutenant Colonel Bazel Lazear. Sensing an impending Confederate counterattack, Lazear dismounted the 1st MSM in a single line of three battalions. Lazear was right. The Confederates gathered off to the left behind a hedge in a stubble cornfield and commenced an artillery barrage. For less than an hour, the 1st MSM fended off a series of weak Confederate advances. Compounding the isolation was Brown's displacement from the front. By this point in the engagement, he was about five hundred yards outside of the town and beyond sight of the action. When Winslow arrived on the field and reported to Brown in accordance with his orders from Pleasonton, Brown replied that "there was nothing to do at present." Taken aback, Winslow scouted ahead with his staff and eventually found Lazear's men engaged in static skirmishing with no orders to advance.[36]

In short order, that situation changed. Confederate pressure upon Lazear increased, which then prompted calls to Brown for reinforcement. Now realizing the situation, Brown finally found Thurber's artillery and elements of the 4th and 7th MSMs, which he hurriedly placed to the left of Lazear with George Kelly's 4th MSM being the southernmost unit. Thurber's guns were placed in the middle of Lazear's line. About the same time, Lazear's and Brown's calls for help resulted in the arrival of two now unidentified companies from Edward Winslow's brigade. Brown likewise fed them onto the flanks of his brigade, creating a line about one-mile wide. He then ordered the entire line forward with thirty minutes of daylight left. In the perpetual seesaw of battle, it was now the Confederates' turn to retreat as Brown's and Winslow's troopers attacked down the Westport Road and the prairie to the southwest.[37]

The momentum of the attack carried the Unionists to roughly the eastern bank of Rock Creek. Despite the success, Brown's brigade was almost spent. Although casualties were exceedingly light with the 1st MSM suffering about five killed and fifteen or twenty wounded, the men were exhausted from the sustained actions of the day and a distinct lack of food. The men had eaten twice during the previous forty-eight hours. More significantly, their ammunition was almost gone. The lack of ammunition was, by itself, hardly unusual. Countless units in countless wars have exhausted their supply of bullets in battle. But Brown's brigade must have certainly set some record for futility in marksmanship. This was especially so in McFerran's 1st MSM. There were 490 men in the regiment, and each, according to McFerran, started the battle with between thirty and forty rounds apiece. Subtracting one hundred horse holders and assuming that each man fired thirty rounds, the regiment had just expended no less than 11,700 rounds in about two hours of combat. The other regiments of the brigade were no less profligate, as all commanders reported having little ammunition on hand after the battle. Although there is no record of Confederate casualties in this particular action, Price's losses were slight and could not have been more than fifty of all kinds. It is only a slight exaggeration to state that perhaps the safest place to have been in the Confederate Trans-Mississippi on October 22nd was directly in front of Egbert Brown's 1st Brigade.[38]

Fortunately for the Federals, the bulk of Colonel Winslow's 4th Brigade had followed in the wake of Brown's attack, and it quickly passed to the front to continue the assault across Rock Creek at sunset. Brown's troopers stood by the side of the Westport Road and in the adjoining fields to wait for their ammunition to arrive. Winslow's men were more than primed for the fight. As Winslow later explained, his cavalry had ridden over the preceding seven weeks a distance the equivalent of a trip from Chicago to New York without so much as hearing a hostile shot. The men were eager to get out of Missouri, and they wished nothing more than "to finish this trans-Mississippi [*sic*] affair." Winslow therefore wasted little time in deploying his small brigade. He dismounted Major Benjamin Jones's 3rd Iowa astride the Westport Road, while moving the 10th Missouri to the left. The 4th Iowa would remain on the Westport Road to support the main thrust of the 3rd Iowa. The 4th would have its advance battalion dismounted and in open order and the remaining companies mounted in column of fours. The 10th Missouri, commanded by Lieutenant Colonel Frederick Benteen, was the trigger for the attack. Once Benteen found the enemy's right flank, his men commenced firing their carbines, which included just about every type found in the Union army. The cacophony produced by the Spencers, Halls, Gibbs, and Sharps carbines signaled the 3rd Iowa to rush the Confederate rearguard concealed in the woods along Rock Creek. Within moments, the Union advance shattered the remnants of Cabell's brigade, which then fell back into Thomas Freeman's brigade. Freeman proved no more able to resist the Unionists than Cabell. Winslow's movement tossed Freeman's troops back, leaving only Clark's brigade to provide any coherent resistance to the Federal offensive. Clark recognized the urgent need to slow the Yankees, and he responded well. With Joseph Pratt's artillery well to the front, Clark organized his rearguard by columns of regiments with Wood in the lead, followed by Burbridge, Lawther, Kitchen, and Jeffers. The Yankee line then ran headlong into Pratt's artillery, which finally slowed the Yankee advance.[39]

Darkness had fallen, but Alfred Pleasonton would not end the battle. It had taken Pleasonton a long time to catch up with Price, and he was not about to disengage. In what was certainly the exception to the rule in Civil War combat, Pleasonton chose to press the battle into the darkness. For at least the next four hours, the 3rd Iowa led a dismounted attack that shoved each of Clark's regiments through the one behind it. For Lieutenant Curtis Ballard of Kitchen's 7th Missouri, "the confusion in the night was terrible." At times the Iowans came within twenty paces, "and we could see nothing but the blaze of their guns." "Notwithstanding the almost impenetrable darkness of the night," General Clark later reported, "they rushed upon us with a reckless fierceness that I have never seen equaled." With the 3rd Iowa pushing the attack, Clark directed the withdrawal of his brigade to the southwest and off the Westport Road. Clark aimed to cross the Big Blue at Byram's Ford. By about 10 PM he had succeeded, while leaving only Jeffers's 8th Missouri on the other side to continue the fight. No more than thirty minutes later, Edward Winslow finally stopped the offensive about three miles to the west of Byram's Ford. Pleasonton wanted Winslow to continue the attack, but only after a moonrise, which would provide more illumination. With clouds rolling in, that illumination never came, and the general advance ceased. Winslow's men had been riding and fighting for almost twenty-four hours. But even then, skirmishing and panic firing filled the night air. Stationed near the west bank of the Big Blue, Henry C. Luttrell of Lawther's 10th Missouri had never experienced anything like it. "This is truly a night of horror," he wrote in his diary. "The enemy, not content with the day's fighting, is feeling our line to find a weak point through which he can make a dash. The shish of a brush or the snapping of a stick is the signal for a fusillade [*sic*] or volley of musketry. Through the darkness, the flash of the enemy's guns is like lightning bugs." For Luttrell and many others, daylight would bring new horrors.[40]

Chapter Eleven

A Desperate Stand at Brush Creek

Things had not gone well for Samuel Curtis on the 22nd. He had guessed entirely wrong that Sterling Price would strike his defensive line well to the north of Byram's Ford. Throughout the day, he clung to that idea even as the battle flowed around his southern flank at Byram's and Russell's fords. Almost as if paralyzed, Curtis remained planted in the north at the main ford, waiting for an attack that would never come. No less striking was Curtis's passivity even with the troops (Dietzler's wing of the army) directly to his front. Curtis was inactive to the point that it was James Blunt who, at about 3 PM, ordered Dietzler's withdrawal from the Big Blue and into the entrenchments at Kansas City. Samuel Curtis's most aggressive behavior that day was, perhaps, firing off situation reports to militia units in Kansas and William Rosecrans in Missouri. On the 23rd, things changed for Curtis. By the end of the day's combat, Curtis emerged, in distinct contrast to Price, as an active commander who led from the front and exercised direct tactical control of his troops in battle.[1]

Throughout the late afternoon and evening of the 22nd, the fortunes of Curtis's Army of the Border looked bleak. The move to Kansas City was chaotic. Although Price's army had been largely inactive along the Westport Road, that inactivity did not prevent the Confederates from prodding the retreating Unionists. The probes met with little success as Colonel A. C. Hogan's 19th KSM held firm and even managed to bag a handful of prisoners. Hogan's capable performance belied a scene of near pandemonium among the first militia units to enter the entrenchments guarding Kansas City. As described by Richard Hinton, now an aide to General Blunt, "The labor of placing the militia was of an onerous character. Not appreciating the importance of position, a large number of the companies sought to pass into town and obtain food. The scene grew animated. Staff officers galloped here and there, shouting hoarsely; portions of the militia obstinately insisting upon their right to do as they pleased; amusing colloquies and expostulations occurred, but at last the long line of works was occupied, and affairs began to assume a business shape."[2]

The early confusion in Kansas City rippled quickly across the state border into Kansas. It did not take long for the news of Curtis's defeat on the 22nd to spread to Kansas's population centers and then cause panic. All rumors pointed to Price rampaging into Kansas and exacting a cost beyond anyone's imagination. In Leavenworth and Topeka, Home Guard militiamen rushed to their stations and began a cold, nighttime vigil. The citizens of Leavenworth thought their city to be Price's first objective given the vast military stores in the fort. The citizens of Lawrence were no less sure that Price was headed straight for them. But unlike Leavenworth, Lawrence had no telegraphic link with Kansas City during the battle to sort fact from rumor. Cut off from any official military contact, the city had to get its information on the 22nd through army deserters and stragglers. It was hardly an ideal situation, and as Richard Cordley later recalled, "These croakers found abundant employment in exaggerating every rumor, and expatiating on every fear."[3]

Notwithstanding the unfolding pandemonium in Kansas City and most points to the west, General Curtis did not alter greatly his passive performance. He chose, for the most part, to remain at his headquarters in the posh, four-story Gillis House Hotel along the Missouri River. The closest he came to trying to see the battle for himself was around 4 PM. At that time he rode several miles to the northern outskirts of Westport to attend the funeral of Major Nelson Smith, the lately lamented commander of the 2nd Colorado who had been killed at the Little Blue. Curtis did not stay until the end of the service, preferring instead to return to the Gillis House before 6 PM. Upon his arrival, Curtis received some badly awaited news. For the first time in the campaign, a courier brought word from Pleasonton. Better yet, the courier informed Curtis that Pleasonton had recaptured Independence and was then continuing the assault upon the Confederate rearguard. Another turning point in the long campaign had been reached.

Curtis was now emboldened. Not only would he continue the battle on the 23rd, but he would, in fact, take the offensive. In an excited telegram to army Chief of Staff Henry Halleck in Washington, D.C., Curtis declared he was "preparing to renew the attack and pursue it at daylight with all my available cavalry." As Curtis considered his options for the next morning, he had to take into consideration the local topography. It would be critical in shaping the battle. Westport stood relatively high in the timbered and brush country of Kansas City. South of Westport, the terrain was dominated by an unnamed hill. A little further south, the land plunged sharply into Brush Creek, which flowed from west to east and emptied into the Big Blue. On the southern bank of the creek, the land rose sharply to a rocky hill in a belt of timber and brush extending another one-half mile. Once out of the timber, the terrain assumed the character of the southern uplands, which Jonathan B. Fuller, a local minister, described as being "open prairie broken by nothing but rail fences and low stone walls put up without mortar." There was, however, one other salient topographical feature of the area. A small, but wooded, tributary (Town Fork Creek) fed into Brush Creek less than one mile east of the Wornall Road and traced back to the south and west with a number of other shallow creeks feeding into it. The consequence of all these creeks and trees was that the looming battle would be squeezed into an open area south of Brush Creek that was really no more than a mile-and-a-half wide.[4]

By 3 AM, Blunt and Curtis had agreed on a plan of battle that would accommodate the terrain and take the army from its varying campsites surrounding Kansas City into a line of battle just south of Brush Creek at daylight. While ordnance officers from the recently discovered and redirected trains hurriedly issued ammunition, Curtis ordered all cavalry in the Kansas State Militia out of Kansas City to Westport, leaving behind the KSM infantry and various Home Guards to man the entrenchments under the command of General Dietzler. The cavalry remained under the brigade command of Charles Blair and consisted of the 4th, 5th, 6th, 10th, and 19th KSMs, the 9th Wisconsin Volunteer Battery, and the section of colored artillery commanded by Lieutenant P. H. Minor. Curtis wanted Blair's untested units to act as an army reserve. Closer to the front, the Union battle plan called for Colonel James Ford's 4th Brigade to cross Brush Creek and anchor the line in the east where the smaller, unnamed stream fed into Brush Creek. Once fully deployed, Ford's line extended about one-half mile to the west to Wornall Road. At that point, Doc Jennison's 1st Brigade occupied the center of the Union line. Like the other brigades, Jennison's 1st Brigade was really no more than a glorified battalion. Due to various company detachments and casualties, it numbered about four hundred men from the 15th Kansas and the 3rd Wisconsin. Jennison's brigade front, much like that of Ford's, probably stretched another half mile as Blunt ordered Thomas Moonlight's 2nd Brigade to a place, according to Moonlight, "a little south of Westport."[5]

Moonlight's original line thus also extended yet another half mile to the State Line Road, which ran perpendicular to Brush Creek. A final piece of the plan was Captain William D. McLain's six-gun Colorado Independent Battery. Blunt had detached it earlier from Blair's brigade and sent it down Wornall Road where it would cross Brush Creek and support the center of the Union attack. There were at least two potential problems with the plan. First, at no point did Blunt or Curtis meet collectively with their brigade commanders. All communication took place individually or by courier. The consequence of this form of mission briefing was that the brigade commanders could not be sure of the placement of the other units, especially where unit boundaries started and ended. A second problem would be the Union's ability to get across the creek without attracting any Confederate attention, let alone artillery fire. Most of the creek's fords would be of little use for cavalry in the wooded terrain. That left only two north-south running roads, which had the easy potential to create bottlenecks for an extended period of time.[6]

South of Brush Creek, Jo Shelby and James Fagan prepared to do more than just block Curtis's Army of the Border. Instead, and in a style especially befitting Shelby, they would attack. The decision to attack was no doubt Sterling Price's, but, as was typical of Price, he did not formally delegate tactical command of that part of the battlefield. This was troublesome as Price, himself, started the day at Boston Adams's house near the intersection of the Harrisonville and Byram's ford roads. Even more to the point, Price appears never to have personally crossed west of the Harrisonville Road. It would be up to the two division commanders to sort things out and coordinate their attacks. The resulting order of battle was a jumble of divisions, brigades, and regiments with little of anything that bespoke an identifiable chain of command or even coherent responsibilities for divisions and brigades. The opening shots of the battle found the Confederate line centered on the Wornall house about two miles south of Brush Creek on Wornall Road. Shelby's division straddled the road, with Richard Collins's artillery either in or near the road itself. At the far left of the division, Shelby placed the bulk of Sidney Jackman's brigade. To the right of Jackman was Jeff Thompson's Iron Brigade, which lined up from left to right with Moses Smith's and Frank Gordon's regiments on the western side of the Wornall Road. Thompson posted Alonzo Slayback's and Rector Johnson's battalions just to the rear of

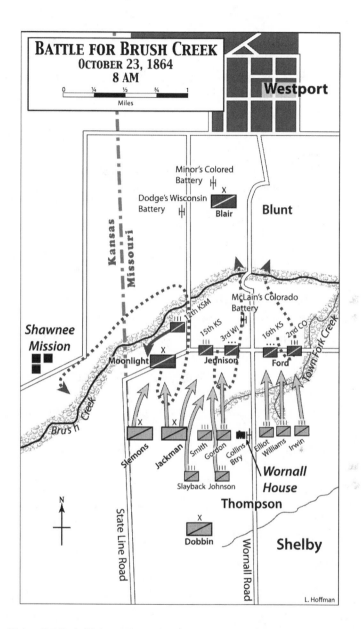

Figure 11.1.   Battle for Brush Creek, October 23, 1864, 8 AM

Smith and Gordon. To the right, or east, of the Wornall Road, Thompson ordered the regiments of Benjamin Elliot and D. A. Williams, who had been detached from Jackman's Brigade. William H. Erwin's 12th Missouri was

probably also with this group east of the road. Initial Confederate disposi-
tions were completed with an inexplicable fragmentation and dispersion of
Fagan's division. William Slemons's brigade fell into place to the left of
Jackman, with John C. Wright's Arkansas Cavalry linking with the Missourians. Archibald Dobbin's brigade marched to the rear of Thompson's Iron
Brigade as something of a reserve for this section of the battlefield. William
Cabell's and Thomas McCray's brigades had already long departed the area
to escort the army's trains. The scattering of Fagan's division left General
Fagan with little clear responsibility. At contact, he would be far from the
action, leaving Slemons's brigade to fight under the inspiration, but not actual control, of Jo Shelby.[7]

And so it began. Daylight brought near-freezing temperatures with a light
crust of ice on parts of Brush Creek. There was a cloudy sky, and an early
morning mist hung near the ground. A light breeze filtered in that would soon
dissipate the mist. Shivering and apprehensive, Jennison's and Ford's men
moved well before the Confederates, and they started crossing Brush Creek
primarily on the Wornall Road. Any Yankee worries about being caught in
the creek bed were not realized. The trees, the mist, and the depression in the
terrain masked all Yankee movements. The troopers therefore moved unhindered. Once across they pushed up the tree-covered heights before disgorg-
ing into the open area south of the creek. The blue-coated regiments promptly formed skirmishers and marched another mile through cornfields and pastures and over stone fences. Near 8 AM, the main line passed through A. B.
H. McGee's property on the Wornall Road when it finally ran into Shelby's
skirmishers and artillery. About thirty minutes later, McLain's battery
wheeled into position just beyond the belt of trees covering Brush Creek.
McLain then divided his artillery, sending one section of two guns under
Lieutenant George Eayre forward up Wornall Road to a place on the hill
overlooking both Brush Creek and the prairie to the south. Eayre engaged
Richard Collins's battery of Confederate artillery, while also lobbing a number of shells into the rear of the advancing Confederate cavalry. As Jeff
Thompson later recalled, one of the "first shells knocked off the head of a
man in Slayback's Battalion as smooth as a guillotine could have cut it."
Despite the effectiveness of Eayre's opening salvos, his section remained on
station for only a short time before having to withdraw and replenish its
ammunition. McLain then ordered Lieutenant Caleb Burdsal's second section to take the place of Eayre in the cannonade.[8]

For at least the next thirty minutes, Unionists and Confederates contented themselves with a long-range artillery duel. As both sides deployed more skirmishers and jockeyed units for the impending clash of cavalry, the artillery duel became heated as Burdsal's section exchanged fire with Collins's battery at a distance of about 1,300 yards. For the most part, the Unionists got the better of this part of the engagement. Eayre's section eventually rearmed and joined Burdsal's section, and together they emptied a galling fire into Collins, who was forced to displace not once but three times. Worse yet, the metal in one of Collins's aged and well-worn pieces finally gave out and shattered, leaving Collins with just three serviceable guns.[9] For more than a few moments, and as it sought a safer spot from counterbattery fire, Collins's artillery was silenced, and that silence allowed the Coloradans to redirect their fire to the Confederate cavalry then massing to their front on Wornall Road. Despite the telling effect of McLain's artillery, the early moments were not without suspense for General Blunt. As Jennison and Ford deployed their brigades in the open area south of Brush Creek, Thomas Moonlight and his 2nd Brigade were initially nowhere to be found. Only after Blunt hurriedly dispatched an aide in the direction of Moonlight did the missing brigade break out from the belt of trees and into a wheat field.[10]

Due to the winding nature of the creek, Moonlight's brigade advanced with timber to its rear and right flank. To the left of the brigade, there was a swell in the terrain that masked Moonlight's sight of that part of the battlefield. Undeterred, and believing Jennison's 15th Kansas just on the other side of the swell, Moonlight pushed ahead. For almost one mile, Moonlight drove Slemons's men south. Eventually, though, the attack lost steam. Jo Shelby miraculously had appeared before Slemons's brigade, shouting encouragement in the absence of Fagan, their actual division commander. But more important, Moonlight had made a critical error. Doc Jennison's brigade was not just on the other side of the swell to the left. The 15th Kansas was, in fact, considerably to the rear, leaving Moonlight's left flank highly exposed. Confederate cavalry did not take long to notice the mistake, and then hurled a deafening fire into the naked flank. Moonlight had seen the horsemen approach his flank but had assumed they were Jennison's 15th Kansas. His surprise at the true identity of the cavalry notwithstanding, Moonlight reacted coolly. He bent back two companies (A and I) on his left to face the oncoming Confederates. More importantly, Lieutenant Colonel G. M. Woodworth's 12th KSM, which had been attached to Moonlight's brigade and held in reserve, rushed on to the field and Moonlight's right flank and thus helped stem the Confederate onslaught. The surprising ability of the raw 12th KSM aside, the relief was only temporary. The combined weight of Slemons's and Jackman's troops continued to push Moonlight inexorably back into the woods and then north of Brush Creek.[11]

Closer to the center of the battlefront, a similar seesaw of events had taken place. By 9 AM, Jeff Thompson had started his mounted forces west of the Wornall Road toward Blunt's line. The movement was slow as there were far too many stone fences to cross, especially with Jennison's skirmishers and main body providing stout resistance. After some initial success, Thompson's forward progress stopped when Moses Smith's horse took a bullet and crumpled to the ground. With the regimental commander dismounted, confusion ran through Smith's 11th Missouri. The regiment rumbled to a halt and then reversed its course. The 11th's precipitous withdrawal left Frank Gordon's 5th Missouri alone and highly exposed, no more than four hundred yards from Jennison's line. Jennison's troopers took advantage of this happenstance to pour a dramatic, if long-range, fire into Gordon's left flank. In stark contrast to Smith's 11th Missouri, Gordon's regiment remained firm. Perhaps inspired by Thompson who rode near the regiment, the 5th would not retreat. But no less important, it would not advance. The 5th sought cover behind a stone fence, commencing what Doc Jennison called a "desperate stand." All the while, Confederate commanders tried to stabilize the line. First, Sidney Jackman, who was himself exposed on his right flank by Smith's withdrawal, redirected at least one of his regiments to the right to plug the gap. Jennison's brigade repelled Jackman's foray, which then prompted Jeff Thompson to commit his reserve battalions led by Alonzo Slayback and Rector Johnson. This last gambit appeared to turn the battle in the Confederacy's favor. Thompson's brigade gradually shoved Jennison, and ultimately James Ford's 4th Brigade, back toward the timber skirting Brush Creek and McLain's artillery.[12]

The situation for General Blunt was now perilous. He had already witnessed the withdrawal of Moonlight's brigade across the creek and clear into Westport. Fortunately for Blunt, Jackman did not pursue Moonlight, choosing instead to prop up Thompson's attack on Jennison and the Union center. This turn of events encouraged Blunt, who came more to fear a potential Confederate maneuver entirely around his right flank. Daringly, he ordered Moonlight out of Westport and to the Line Road south of Brush Creek where the 2nd Brigade would face to the east creating a blocking force. Woodworth's 12th KSM, which had so ably supported Moonlight's withdrawal, would march back to the hill south of Westport and thence all the way over to support Ford's 4th Brigade on the Union left. To fill the gap caused by Moonlight's departure, Blunt had no choice but to turn to his untried Kansas militia in Charles Blair's 3rd Brigade, which had been waiting anxiously on the hill just to the south of Westport. Leaving his horses behind, Blair moved two regiments, the 6th and 10th, down into the creek and up to the line at the edge of the timber. The men of 6th KSM showed all the outward appearances of being ready for the fight, but the Kansans were also famished; they had not eaten in more than twenty-four hours. The hungry 6th formed between the 10th and Lieutenant Colonel George Hoyt's 15th Kansas, thus securing the right of the Union line facing south. [13]

Most of Blunt's men managed to find effective cover behind stone fences and timber. The men of 6th and 19th KSMs, especially, reveled in the protection of their defensive positions and acquitted themselves well in the ensuing firefight. Although both sides kept up a fairly heavy volume of small arms fire, there was no further Confederate attempt to press the issue with a frontal attack. They did, however, achieve the desired result when the omnipresent Richard Collins managed to roll his second section of guns over to the Line Road and in a position that allowed it to enfilade a good portion of the Union line. Blunt therefore chose to order his division across the creek and into the protection of its timber. It was an orderly retreat, and one lacking a substantial Confederate pursuit. Most of Thompson's units had to stop for about one hour and wait for a resupply of ammunition. [14]

It was a significant delay and one that many a Confederate and future historian tended to see as not only a failure of Sterling Price's generalship but ultimately as that moment when Price lost the Battle of Westport. But of course, neither was true. Jo Shelby and Jeff Thompson bore just as much responsibility for the positioning of their ammunition resupply as Sterling Price. Even more to the point, no amount of ammunition and its immediate availability would have changed the outcome of the battle. The truly decisive area of the battlefield was at Byram's Ford where John Marmaduke was then locked in a struggle with Alfred Pleasonton. Shelby's pause along the southern bank of Brush Creek was largely irrelevant for three other reasons. First, any Confederate pursuit across Brush Creek would have been glacial and confused given the tangled and elevated terrain they had to navigate. Second, Blunt's division was hardly in disarray. Its retreat across the creek had been orderly, and the division was now being reinforced by additional regiments of KSM. Third, Blunt could muster twenty-six pieces of artillery in any field north of Brush Creek. Compared to at most eight pieces of artillery for Shelby, it was a decisive advantage for the Union. In what was also a boon to the Union cause, Samuel Curtis began to assert control over the action. [15]

Curtis had arrived at Westport sometime around 7:30 AM. Accompanied by his ponderous staff of military aides and assorted Kansas politicians, Curtis established his new headquarters at the Harris Hotel. From the rooftop, Curtis gained a commanding view of the battlefield and its challenging terrain. He could see not only the dispositions of his own army but also that of the Confederates, whom he described as being "deployed in endless lines on the open prairie." For the first time since the early morning hours, Curtis met with Blunt, who had also ridden to the hotel. The ability to see the unfolding battle animated Curtis, and the old general displayed none of the self-doubt or hesitation marking his earlier performance. Probably helping Curtis's self-confidence was the observable reality that the Army of the Border had not suffered terribly. As recalled by one of a slew of aides on the rooftop, Judge W. R. Bernard, the battle seemed almost harmless. "With powerful field glasses I could see little bunches of men skirmishing about." The men would rush up the hill, fire a volley, and then come scampering back. "I did not see many men killed, and it looked as if a lot of lead was being wasted." Observing the same scene, Curtis determined to counterattack pending the arrival of some more of the militia. As staff officers scurried down from the rooftop with the orders and the troops prepared for the movement, the battlefield had hardly gone silent. Skirmishers from both sides filled the woods with a fairly constant exchange of gunfire. The Confederates, despite the general lack of pursuit, made at least one substantial probe of Curtis's lines. Far to the Union right, an undetermined number of Confederates pushed across the creek in an attempt to flank that part of the line occupied by the 6th and 10th KSMs. The incursion did not catch the militia napping. Before the Confederates had even begun their pursuit, Charles Blair had grown wary of waiting in the woods with musket fire seemingly all around him. Moreover, camp rumors spilled into Blair's headquarters that the Confederates were slipping around his right flank. Unable to sit still, Blair decided, without orders, to extend his line at least two times his existing front through the brush to the right. While Blair's men executed the difficult maneuver among the trees and dense underbrush, they came into contact with two other regiments, the 5th and 19th KSMs. General Blunt, anticipating the same Confederate march, had ordered the 5th and 19th from Westport to bolster the Union right flank. Serendipity and skill placed these units at the proverbial right place and right time. Less serendipitous and more a function of Unionist wealth and industry, at least one company of the 19th, Captain James L. McDowell's, possessed Wesson breech-loading rifles. These weapons helped mitigate the militia's lack of training. Thus well armed, Blair's combined force ran into the Confederates and easily flushed them from the creek bed and then beyond the woods to the south. By the time the enterprising Blair had completed his attack, his brigade of militia was well ensconced on the south bank.[16]

It was then about 11 AM, and the moment had thus arrived for a general advance of the Union line. For the first time in the battle, Samuel Curtis took to his horse and the front line of the attack. He galloped toward the right flank and Charles Blair's militia. Accompanying the commanding general was his escort, which included Company G of the 11th Kansas and Lieutenant Edward Gill's two mountain howitzers. On his journey to the front, Curtis also picked up the six guns of Captain James H. Dodge's 9th Wisconsin Volunteer Battery. Once across the creek, Curtis threw Blair's militia forward and up the heights with the artillery following. A heavy Confederate fire met the attempt, and Curtis's militia scampered back down and into the belt of trees. With the trees and the odd stone fences offering life-preserving cover for the militia, Curtis's attack appeared to be stuck in Brush Creek. In order to get the militia moving, Curtis needed something of a miracle. That miracle arrived shortly thereafter in the form of a seventy-five-year-old man with a thick German accent. George Thoman owned a farm about 2.5 miles to the southeast of the raging battle. The day before, misfortune struck Thoman as the Confederates visited his farm and conscripted his mare. Despite the old man's pleadings, the horse-deprived Confederates mustered the animal into their service. By Sunday morning, an anguished Thoman had left the farm and ventured into the Union lines at Brush Creek with revenge on his mind. Thoman found Curtis and told him of a way to get around Shelby's flank undetected. Having few other alternatives, Curtis allowed Thoman to take the lead on foot in a column consisting of Curtis, his escort, and the aforementioned artillery. What Curtis had found was Swan Creek, which emptied into Brush Creek from the southwest about three hundred yards from Wornall Road. When Curtis and the artillery finally exited the creek bed, they occupied a position near the Bent House to the west and rear of the Confederate line. When the artillery unlimbered and began its cannonade, the Confederates all along the heights south of Brush Creek believed they had no choice but to withdraw. As the Confederates pulled back, George Thoman fell to his knees, letting out a shout of joy. [17]

Thoman's exultation to the contrary, the battle was not yet finished. The Confederates rode south and reconstituted their lines in the vicinity of the Wornall house as Richard Collins continued to throw shells into the Union troops. Nevertheless, any Confederate attempt to retake the lost ground would be more than difficult. For the first time in the morning-long action, Curtis had succeeded in getting most of his artillery across Brush Creek. The massing of the guns was imposing as Curtis possessed twenty-six pieces anchored by McLain's and Dodge's batteries on both flanks of a line that ran just to the north of William Bent's house. Over the next few hours of battle, the artillery batteries would be mixed and matched as the various gun sections bounced from position to position, often with no apparent regard for unit integrity as different battery commanders took charge of any gun lined up nearest to them. This was particularly true when the 9th Wisconsin's Captain Dodge personally sighted a gun of the Independent Colored Battery. A subsequent shot destroyed the carriage of a Confederate gun (probably Blocher's 3-inch rifle) near Wornall Road. General Blunt himself warmed to the task of personally sighting the artillery when he assumed direction of most of the guns on the Union left and center. [18]

As evidenced by Dodge's disabling of Blocher's gun, it did not take long for the Union artillery to help turn the tide of battle. Particularly galling to the Confederates was the rapid fire of McLain's battery. In about thirty minutes of work, Lieutenant Burdsal's two-gun section alone fired 128 rounds from its position in Wornall Road. The situation for the Confederacy was thus fairly clear. The Colorado battery needed to be removed, especially Burdsal's two guns in the middle of the road. At this time, James Fagan finally made his appearance on the battlefield and apparently assumed control of the Confederates' line. Accompanied by his escort, he galloped up to Shelby near the Wornall Road. Shelby saluted Fagan and announced, "General, I am ready to obey any order you may give." After scanning the Yankee position with his field glasses, Fagan announced, "Shelby, I propose to take that battery." In an almost casual fashion, he then instructed Shelby to charge a regiment of cavalry up the lane by mounted platoons. Fagan also wanted the charge supported by dismounted troops. Given the fairly compressed nature of the battlefield, Shelby turned quickly to Colonel James H. McGhee's (or Magee's or McGehee's) Arkansas Regiment from Dobbin's brigade of Fagan's division. McGhee commanded about three hundred men recruited largely from northeast Arkansas. Poorly dressed, ill trained, and exhausted, McGhee's regiment was nevertheless ready for the charge. [19]

It was then around 11:30 AM. As per Fagan's orders, McGhee formed his men by platoons in columns of four, thus filling the road with what John Wright called "a living mass of cavalry." Portions of Dobbin's and Thompson's brigades dismounted and took their places on either side of the road to support the attack—Dobbin's men in a bluegrass pasture and Thompson's in a plowed field. With McGhee's bugler sounding the charge, the Confederates gave out the Rebel Yell and sped at a gallop down the road toward the Colorado artillery and the Union line. It was, as one Union observer called it, "a bold and dashing charge." But McGhee's rampaging Arkansans took no one by surprise. To the west of the artillery, Doc Jennison sniffed out the attack and readied one company from the 16th Kansas, Curtis Johnson's E Company, to pivot from its line and charge the left flank of McGhee's column. To the east of the artillery, the 2nd Colorado was no less adaptive. Captain William H. Greene wheeled his company and raced toward the head of the Confederate attack. As McGhee's column charged toward the Union line, Burdsal's gunners emptied one last round of canister into the Confederates before excitedly hooking the guns to their limbers in an attempt to get back into the woods and across the creek. [20]

Burdsal's artillery exacted a terrible cost. It cut down a number of McGhee's men and horses, piling the narrow road with bloody and eviscerated bodies. At fifty yards from Burdsal's guns the Confederates ran into the massed fire of dismounted cavalry who had taken positions behind the stone fences on either side of the artillery and running perpendicular to Wornall Road. With even more casualties now littering the road, McGhee still continued the charge until he finally reached Burdsal's position. Yet the guns were no longer there. Burdsal had made his escape to the north. Instead, McGhee slammed straight into Johnson's and Greene's converging companies of Yankee cavalry. It was a melee of the worst kind as carbines, revolvers, and sabers all exacted a deadly toll at close range. Among the combatants were Doc Jennison and Colonel Samuel Walker of the 16th Kansas, both of whom had accompanied Johnson in his charge. As the battle broke down into deadly individual fights, none was as dramatic as that between Colonel McGhee and Captain Johnson. Both men galloped straight for the other. As legend would have it, McGhee fired first, hitting Johnson just above the left wrist with the ball traveling up his arm and exiting near the shoulder. Suffering terribly, Johnson continued his ride toward McGhee when at close range he finally fired, dropping the Confederate from his horse with a ball to his chest. Despite the severity of his wounds, each man survived the battle, although rumors of McGhee's death quickly spread far and wide and down through the years.[21]

No matter the condition of McGhee, the fury of the Union countercharge proved too much for the Arkansans. In less than ten minutes of action, it was over. Many Confederates simply surrendered; most turned their horses around and raced back up the hill. The precipitous retreat gave no time, or chance, for the dismounted support to be a factor in the battle. McGhee's regiment was simply back in their midst before the support had an opportunity to move forward. Although the lack of dismounted support contributed heavily to the failure of the charge, perhaps an even greater factor was the lack of mounted reinforcement, which might have given the attack the decisive weight it needed. Whatever the explanation, the charge had failed, leaving about seventy-five killed, wounded, and captured in its wake. In but one postscript to the charge, many Confederates came to believe that Jennison and his officers immediately executed dozens of prisoners. Jeff Thompson was adamant that "every prisoner captured in the fruitless charge . . . had been brutally murdered." Evidence does not support the accusation. Following the battle, at least thirty-four men from McGhee's regiment found their way onto Union prisoner rolls.[22]

The disintegration of McGhee's command did not stop Jeff Thompson—and Sidney Jackman to his left—from pressing a mounted attack west of Wornall Road. There was some immediate success as elements of the Iron Brigade, but especially the 5th Missouri, advanced about two hundred yards. But the Confederates could go no further as two sets of fences caused the troops to dismount while also impeding any further movement. Thompson and the 5th Missouri were then about one-fourth mile west and south of McLain's battery. Other units lagged further south. More important, many throughout the brigade were yet again without ammunition, resulting in a general halt until resupplied. That resupply took perhaps an hour, and during that time the Confederates huddled behind their fences and endured a constant bombardment from Curtis's combined artillery. In between the incoming Union rounds and the less frequent responses from Collins's three remaining cannons, Thompson's men might have been able to hear the rising staccato of gunfire to the south and east. Alfred Pleasonton's provisional division of cavalry had just burst through John Marmaduke's thin line of defense at Byram's Ford.[23]

Chapter Twelve

Rebels, Rebels, Fire, Fire!

For all of the drama and importance of the battle around Brush Creek, the decisive action of the day was about to occur a few miles to the east at Byram's Ford. Though inevitably a smashing Union victory, the struggle for the ford revealed a fissure within Alfred Pleasonton's cavalry. Pleasonton greatly distrusted the Missouri State Militia, and before the battle had even begun he arrested two senior MSM commanders and placed all of the MSM under the tactical direction of a volunteer officer. Pleasonton's removal of one of the commanders, General Egbert Brown, was predicated on several wrong assumptions, but the subsequent performance of the MSM at Byram's Ford showed it to be not quite ready for major combat. Before Price's expedition, the primary experience of the MSM had been in fighting isolated bands of guerrillas. Now they were involved in an action that required a coordinated charge across a river and up a steep hill defended by more than one thousand Confederates and their supporting artillery. Not surprisingly, the MSM's initial attacks met with failure. Union success at Byram's Ford thus depended upon the inspirational leadership of the volunteer officers, the discipline of their men, and the superiority of Union firepower in the assault. When coupled with Price's failure to make a coordinated battle plan, these things guaranteed that the Confederate Army of Missouri would be racing for its very survival by nightfall on the 23rd.

In preparation for the battle at Byram's Ford, John Marmaduke readily ceded the tactical initiative to his Yankee counterpart, Alfred Pleasonton. Marmaduke preferred to defend in place and make Pleasonton come to him. Although a desire to continue offensive operations certainly suited Pleason-

231

ton's combative nature, his division was not well positioned to make an immediate attack. Due to the previous night's extensive and generally chaotic fighting, his division was strung out along seven miles of road running from Independence to Byram's Ford. At the head of this long column lay Edward Winslow's 4th Brigade. Winslow had fought hard through the evening of the 22nd and had stopped three miles northeast of Byram's Ford. Winslow's brigade was stacked up for almost one mile and included a section of Thurber's artillery at the tail of the column. Following Thurber's guns was Egbert Brown's 1st Brigade, which then extended the column for another three-fourths of a mile to the northeast. It was here, well past the rear of Brown's brigade and five miles from Byram's Ford, that Alfred Pleasonton stuck his headquarters. John Sanborn and his 3rd Brigade made their camp just to the north, or rear, of Pleasonton along the Westport Road. [1]

Aside from occasional panic shooting, combat had ceased on Pleasonton's front around 10:30 on the 22nd. Pleasonton was more than disappointed by the inability to press forward, and he refused to accept the verdict of night. Earlier in the evening he therefore instructed Winslow to press on as soon as there was either moonlight or daylight to see. Despite Pleasonton's obvious preference, Winslow chose to wait for daylight. The decision to stop led Egbert Brown, whose brigade had been following Winslow, to ride forward around midnight to discuss matters with Winslow. Brown offered to take the lead for the upcoming assault, but Winslow declined pending further orders from Pleasonton. The meeting then broke up with Brown heading back to his headquarters for a night of little sleep. [2]

No later than 5:30, the brigade commanders had their orders in hand. For Brown, Pleasonton gave him what he initially desired: the responsibility of leading the attack. At daybreak Brown was supposed take his brigade, which consisted of the 1st, 4th, and 7th MSMs, and pass to the front of Winslow's brigade, which had also been ordered forward, and assault the Confederates at Byram's Ford. These were fairly straightforward instructions, but there was something else in Pleasonton's orders that took Brown by surprise. Pleasonton couched the formal language of the orders in a sneering fashion, asserting Brown's "command has as yet done no fighting" and that he would accept "no excuse for the non-fulfillment of this duty today, but hold you responsible, as every other brigade had done so well." Because Brown's brigade had indeed fought on the 22nd, Pleasonton's message let it be plainly known that the divisional commander had somehow become more than dissatisfied with Brown's performance over the preceding two days. As Pleasonton later recalled, he believed Brown a whiner who "was continually making excuses rather than attempting to do his duty." Even more to the point, Pleasonton believed Brown was prone to complaining about needing ammunition when he should be fighting. With this sense of Brown fixed firmly in his mind, the division commander was in no mood for any such excuses on the 23rd.[3]

Brown was stunned by the tone of the orders. When John Sanborn rode into camp at 5:30 to discuss his supporting role in the upcoming assault, all Egbert Brown could initially do was talk about the censorious nature of Pleasonton's orders. The two generals were then joined by Colonel John Philips, commander of Brown's 7th MSM. For Philips, whose camp was just across the road from Brown, the meeting was a small accident. The colonel had been unable to sleep, and he wandered over to Brown's campfire in search of coffee if not camaraderie. Although Philips had participated in the previous day's fighting, he resented Brown for originally placing James McFerran's 1st MSM at the head of the column and Philips 7th MSM at the rear. Philips thought it a deliberate snub. Philips's agitation aside, the assembled officers talked and then talked some more. Finally, by 6:15 the gabbing stopped. Brown broke free from his lassitude and roused his chief of staff, Captain C. H. Little, with instructions to get the brigade mounted and ready. Events then moved quickly. No more than fifteen minutes later, Brown had his chief bugler sound "to horse," which was then repeated by the buglers in the nearby 4th and 7th MSMs. Meanwhile, Captain Little rode northeast in search of the 1st MSM. Although McFerran's regiment was no more than a mile from Brown's headquarters, Little could not find it. Even as the sun rose in the eastern sky, the search for the 1st MSM proceeded, and all the while Egbert Brown did not budge. He was then officially late and four miles away from Pleasonton's appointed spot of attack.[4]

To Alfred Pleasonton, there was little to disguise the absence of an attack. Arising just before daybreak, Pleasonton gathered up his escort for the roughly five-mile ride to the ford where he would witness the proceedings. About one-fourth of a mile into the ride, the divisional commander grew agitated. Not only did Pleasonton fail to hear the sounds of a battle, but he passed through a regiment that showed no signs of battle preparation. Indeed, he thought the regiment in complete disarray. According to Pleasonton, "Some [of the men] were on the right of the road; some of them on the left; some were going for forage; some were going in small parties of 8 or 10; and some were cooking. There was no order or regularity." The general had

discovered James McFerran's heretofore lost 1st MSM. In short order, Pleasonton arrested McFerran and replaced him with Lieutenant Colonel Bazel
Lazear. He then ordered Lazear to march to the front. For Lazear it must have
been a moment of some redemption. A radical Republican, Lazear loathed
the Democrat McFerran and long resented being subordinate to him. McFerran later claimed that the 1st MSM's lack of readiness was due primarily to
the necessity of distributing ammunition. To be sure, McFerran could argue
that a member of Pleasonton's staff (Major Henry Seuss) had appeared earlier in the morning and ordered the resupply. All of the ammunition would not
be distributed, and the regiment was thus ready to march until nearly 8 AM.
Unfortunately for McFerran, the resupply explained little of the generic disarray of his regiment and the fact that he had lost contact with the remainder
of his brigade that night.[5]

Sacking McFerran did not really satisfy Pleasonton. McFerran's lack of
readiness merely reinforced what Pleasonton had come to expect of Brown's
brigade. He sent a courier in advance to find Brown and get the attack going.
Pleasonton then pulled together his staff and continued at a gallop toward
Byram's Ford. For nearly two miles, he found few troops and even fewer
indications of battle. However, as Pleasonton got closer to the ford he came
into a jumble of disorganized Union cavalry and its associated pack train,
most of which appeared to be doing nothing. In a case of misidentification
that would soon bear consequences, Pleasonton believed most of these men
belonged to Brown. The reality was that they belonged to Winslow's brigade. The confused combat of the previous evening had left many a straggler
in Winslow's rear, which already contained not only his own support troops
but also detachments of the 2nd New Jersey and 4th Missouri that served
under Winslow's command. Nevertheless, by 8 AM Pleasonton had forced
his way through the mess and came into contact with the head of Brown's
brigade about four hundred yards from the ford. Pleasonton was by this point
irate.[6]

During all the time Pleasonton rode west across the broken woodland,
Brown had moved the 4th and 7th MSMs to the front. Philip's 7th MSM led
the way in a column of fours and had some difficulty passing through much
of what frustrated Pleasonton's trip to the ford, Winslow's brigade. Also
impeding Philips was at least one of his squadrons that lagged behind, which
then forced the entire column to slow. But Philips was ultimately able to get
to the head of Winslow's brigade about one mile from the ford. Philips then
advanced at the double quick about one-half mile through broken terrain and

thick brush. When the Missourians came to a halt, they could plainly hear Winslow's 3rd Iowa skirmishing with the Confederates one hundred to two hundred yards in advance of the line and still east of Byram's Ford. As Brown, who had accompanied Philips, prepared to issue the order for the charge toward the ford, Alfred Pleasonton stormed onto the scene. Here Pleasonton found Brown astride his horse just off the road, and the divisional commander immediately launched a verbal assault. "You have disgraced your brigade sir; they are scattered for miles." Taken aback, Brown sputtered, "I have obeyed your order[,] general." But Pleasonton would not listen and interrupted: "You have not obeyed my orders this morning. You have acted most disgracefully. You have some men who would fight if you would give them an opportunity, but you have not given them an opportunity." Brown tried yet again to explain, but Pleasonton would still have none of it. He put Brown under arrest, sent him to the rear, and placed the next senior officer, Colonel Philips, in command of the brigade. Pleasonton then sought out T. T. Crittenden, who had been elevated to command the 7th MSM, and demanded he "clear those people of the bottom, and that instantly." Pleasonton also put Winslow in command of the general assault. Pleasonton apologized for continuing to burden Winslow, but the general claimed it could not be averted. Winslow, somewhat stoically, responded, "Well, we will do the best we can."[7]

In many ways, Brown's sloppy handling of his brigade had justified the arrest. Clearly miffed by the insulting tone of Pleasonton's orders, he had delayed his planning for the attack, which he compounded by further delaying the quick distribution of his own attack order. He was thus not ready to move at dawn. Brown had also lost track of McFerran's regiment, which was in a badly disorganized state. The bottom line was that Brown was at least ninety minutes late to make an attack with only two-thirds of his available force. And yet, for all of Brown's problems, Alfred Pleasonton was a bit too anxious to sacrifice him. Pleasonton was predisposed to not trust the MSM. It can be recalled that on the afternoon of the 22nd and upon meeting Edward Winslow for the first time, Pleasonton let it be known that he had theretofore avoided "vigorous action" on account of having no volunteer cavalry. No less telling, as early as 5 AM on the 23rd, Pleasonton had vented in a telegram to William S. Rosecrans: "My difficulty is that the militia cavalry cannot fight as old troops, [*sic*] and lose too much time." While the performance of the various MSM troops throughout the campaign would indeed pale in comparison to that of the volunteer regiments, Pleasonton had little to base this upon at that moment, just two days into combat operations. More troubling was Pleasonton's testimony in the subsequent courts martial of Brown and McFerran. It was fraught with errors and exaggerations. In other words, it fit a pattern whereby Pleasonton had rid his earlier commands of people he had prejudged. Such was the case in 1863 when Pleasonton, in a fit of xenophobia, sabotaged the careers of Brigadier General Julius Stahel and colonels Alfred Duffie, Luigi Palma di Cesnola, and Percy Wyndham while serving in the Army of the Potomac. Regarding Brown and McFerran, especially suspect were Pleasonton's claims that he did not see Brown make any attempt to attack and that Brown was "two or three hours" late. In a war where many officers did not carry watches, and planned attacks were seemingly forever late (see Stonewall Jackson during all the battles of the Seven Days and even Chancellorsville and James Longstreet in every battle he ever fought), Brown's delay of ninety minutes was unremarkable. Perhaps even more relevant was Pleasonton's confusion concerning the troops who were "scattered for miles." While McFerran's regiment was indeed disorganized, it was actually Winslow's troopers who were more scattered about the battlefield, particularly as Pleasonton got closer to Byram's Ford. The court that would eventually sit in judgment of Brown beginning in November got it right when it acquitted the general of disobeying Pleasonton's orders.[8]

With Brown's day of judgment still far off, the Second Battle of Byram's Ford proceeded. Edward Winslow surveyed the area and found the terrain not very favorable. Along the eastern bank of the Blue there was a series of hills that towered over the ford, leaving about two hundred yards from the bottom of the hill to the river itself. Those two hundred yards would be fairly open and the attacking troops exposed to Confederate fire. According to William Forse Scott, the Adjutant of the 4th Iowa, "The only road to the ford descended by a long slope along the rocky face of one of these hills."[9] The ford itself was a significant obstacle to crossing the river. Despite the fact that Price's army had crossed at that location the previous day, the ford remained cluttered with felled trees. Perhaps the one great advantage afforded by the terrain was a wooded ravine that ran perpendicular to the Blue and emptied into the river about 250 yards north of the ford. Troops moving in the ravine would not be seen by Marmaduke's men on the western bank, and the Confederate left flank could be readily turned. Winslow then wisely pushed the one hundred men of Captain Edward W. Dee's Third Battalion of the 4th Iowa into the ravine and toward the river. They would support the main—and very visible—assault of Philips's brigade at the ford itself.

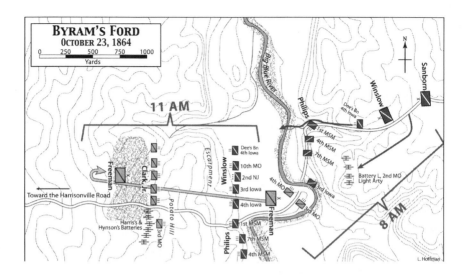

Figure 12.1.   Byram's Ford, October 23, 1864

Given the cramped area around the ford, Philips ordered his brigade to attack on a regimental front. It was about 8 AM.[10] T. T. Crittenden's 7th MSM remained dismounted and led the rush toward the ford just to the left of the road. George Kelly's 4th MSM and Bazel Lazear's newly arrived 1st MSM followed the 7th up the road still mounted on their horses. Operating to the right of Philips was a detachment of the 4th Missouri Cavalry then commanded by Captain Charles P. Knispel. Trumpets then sounded, and the Missourians advanced. As they reached the bottom of the hill amid some gunfire, Philips's men passed through the 3rd Iowa, which was skirmishing with the Confederates on both sides of the road. As Crittenden moved forward, he received an ominous warning. Major Benjamin S. Jones, commander of the 3rd Iowa, intoned, "If you take your men down there they will all be killed." Crittenden disregarded the prophecy and pushed toward the river, where his troopers forced Marmaduke's skirmishers to the western bank, at which point the attack stalled. Marmaduke had not intended to exert his primary defense at the ford, but skirmishers from Freeman's brigade and Colton Greene's and John Burbridge's regiments had proven surprisingly effective in slowing the initial Union advance. The presence of two artillery pieces just off the ford helped matters considerably as the cannons swept the river with a frightening, if not terribly deadly, fire.[11]

The delay at the ford lasted about twenty-five minutes. No sooner had the attack faltered than Colonel Winslow decided to lead the men across the river. He unbuckled the cape from his shoulders to better reveal his rank to the unfamiliar militiamen. He then spurred his horse to the ford where he exhorted Philips and his Missourians to get moving. Even more important, at about that same time Dee's battalion of Iowans exited the ravine to the north of the Byram's Ford road, which caused Marmaduke's skirmishers on the western bank to fall back about two hundred yards across an open field to an escarpment, or limestone ledge, twelve to fifteen feet in height. A small number remained at the ledge, but most continued on to Marmaduke's main line another several hundred yards further to the rear across an open field or plateau. This defensive belt ran south to north for about four hundred yards along the crest of what was then known as Potato Hill. Seeking any and all possible cover on the lightly wooded hill, Marmaduke's men, or more appropriately Clark's brigade, dismantled adjacent fences to create piles of rails among the trees. Marmaduke's left rested near two log houses, and he positioned a number of sharpshooters in the houses as well as in some nearby treetops. The right of Marmaduke's line was anchored by the combined guns of Harris's and Hynson's batteries located astride the Byram's Ford road. Colton Greene's 3rd Missouri, which had been among the skirmishers at the ford, was posted in support of the artillery. Marmaduke's decision to load up his artillery on this part of the battlefield was a wise one. For Union forces to gain the heights, they would most certainly have to come up the road. [12]

That attack did not, however, materialize immediately. There would be no piecemeal assault of the Confederate high ground. Instead, Winslow tried to move most of his available force across the river before attacking. This was a difficult task as Byram's Ford was a congested mess that forced the units to cross single file at various points above and below the road. The delayed passage was further complicated by horses pausing to get water (which Winslow authorized) and the harassing fire of the Confederate artillery. It was then no small achievement that most of these troops got over the river in about thirty minutes. Once over, they deployed with Philips's brigade to the south of the road. Just to the north, Winslow placed, from left to right, the 4th Iowa, 3rd Iowa, 10th Missouri, 2nd New Jersey, and Dee's battalion. Winslow, much like Marmaduke, believed the Byram's Ford road the key to the battle. He wanted to take it quickly and therefore turn Marmaduke's position. Winslow thus instructed Philips to charge his cavalry up the road. Winslow's brigade to the right of the road would "act as soon as he [Philips] had well advanced." Given the small width of the path and the narrow defile by which it passed through the escarpment, Philips thought he could squeeze only one mounted regiment up the road. He therefore ordered Bazel Lazear's 1st MSM to charge in a column of fours. It would not be a cavalry charge in the classical, or perhaps mythical, sense. There was nary a saber to be found in the entire regiment. Similarly destitute of edged weapons, the 7th and 4th MSMs remained dismounted to the left of the road and would support the charge with rifle fire and a linear advance. The plan failed, and it failed badly. Lazear's men rushed up the road twice, and each attempt ended about one hundred yards from the escarpment. Confederate rifle and artillery fire (most coming from the main line of defense) emptied just enough Yankee saddles to force the 1st MSM all the way back to the riverbank. It was not an impressive performance. Despite John Philips's later report that a storm of lead "insured utter destruction to every horse and its rider that ascended" the hill, the 1st MSM suffered no more than three killed and nine wounded during the entire battle. Edward Winslow would have to find a stouter unit and another way to defeat Marmaduke. [13]

The solution came from Winslow's own brigade positioned to the right, or north, of the road. Their first objective would be the escarpment, using several defiles and gorges to get to the top. Winslow planned for an assault using a concentrated regimental front near to the right side of the road. He ordered the 4th Iowa to initiate the assault and to be followed closely by the 3rd Iowa and the 10th Missouri. Except for some officers, the attackers were dismounted. Sharpshooters from the 2nd New Jersey were placed in the middle of the attacking Unionists, according to trooper Socrates Walmsley, "with orders to break the center of the Confederate line." At about 11 AM Winslow ordered the attack, and this time it worked almost perfectly. As Winslow's brigade rushed forward, Union artillery and sharpshooters effectively suppressed the Confederate response. Perhaps more important, Winslow's troopers were armed with just about every type of breechloader or repeating rifle known to northern industry. Representative of the entire brigade was Benteen's 10th Missouri, which charged up the hill with one-third of its men firing Spencers and the rest shooting Gibbs, Halls, and Sharps carbines. This weaponry in the hands of disciplined troops allowed the Unionists to advance quickly while also laying down a heavy volume of fire. Also benefiting from Winslow's charge and firepower was Philips's brigade. Once the 4th Iowa began its movement, Philips pushed his troopers up the hill as well. After a brief hand-to-hand struggle among the rocks, any remaining Confederate skirmishers had retreated to, or through, Clark's brigade at the crest of the ridge.[14]

At this point in the attack, there was very little delay. Led by the 4th Iowa, Union forces clambered to the top of the rocks, reorganized themselves, and pressed further up the hill and toward Marmaduke's line. Some Union regiments now began to suffer significant losses as Clark's brigade let loose a heavy fire. Among the more prominent men hit was Lieutenant Colonel T. T. Crittenden of the 7th MSM. A Confederate bullet struck him in the side, inflicting, according to Paul Jenkins, "great sickness, pallor, and agony." Thinking Crittenden mortally wounded, John Philips rushed to his side and began plying his stricken friend with peach brandy. Upon closer inspection, though, Philips determined that Crittenden was neither mortally wounded nor punctured at all. The Confederate bullet had merely ricocheted off the ground and struck Crittenden either in his belt buckle or a waistcoat pocket full of paper fractional currency. Battered and bruised, yet fortified with the brandy, Crittenden rejoined his command.[15]

Other men were less fortunate, including some junior officers in Philips's brigade. In fact, the Confederate response was heavy enough to stop, yet again, Bazel Lazear's 1st MSM. The safety of some log houses built along the road beckoned, and the regiment sought cover among them. In a questionable, though ultimately successful move, Lazear personally left his command and raced back down the road to seek reinforcements. Somewhere along the riverbank, he ran into Frederick Benteen, who already was in the process of supporting the assault toward the escarpment. Benteen also gathered with him a number of troops (probably including Captain Charles P. Knispel's detachment from the 4th Missouri) and proceeded up the road. "By dint of great urging and exertion of authority," Benteen later reported, and no doubt to his own self-aggrandizement, that Lazear's Missourians tumbled out of their protective shelter and up the hill, trailing the other units to their left and right. By the time of the arrival of the 1st MSM at the crest, the Confederates had, in an almost anticlimactic fashion, once again retreated. This time, it would be a continuous withdrawal one mile to the west and the open prairie. There had been some close combat along the Confederate line, which allowed Company A of the 3rd Iowa to capture a Confederate flag from an unnamed unit; however, Marmaduke's troopers displayed no great willingness to engage in a desperate last stand upon the high ground many a Unionist would soon call "Bloody Hill."[16]

And yet, just how bloody was this, the Second Battle of Byram's Ford? For Marmaduke, the exact cost will never be known as only three of his six regiments reported their losses for the engagement. But for the three (the 3rd, 7th, and 10th Missouris), there were only twenty-five killed and wounded. It can therefore be estimated there were probably fifty casualties of all types, including the wounding of Colonel Solomon J. Kitchen of the 7th Missouri. This number is very low given the duration of the combat (at least four hours) and the number of rounds expended (one postwar recollection pronounced one of the log buildings riddled with five thousand bullet holes). Determining Union casualties is no less difficult with few units reporting their losses. Those that did—especially in Philips's brigade—help disclose the disparity of who actually bore the brunt of the combat. While the 1st MSM's twelve total casualties reveal a unit that took few chances and repeatedly sought cover, the 4th MSM's fifty-one killed and wounded show a disciplined regiment that pressed its attacks in the open fields. In Winslow's brigade, Edward Winslow estimated a total of twenty-five killed and wounded, but this was a figure that included the heavy fighting on the previous day as well as the combat to follow on the 23rd. All told, Union casualties were probably less than one hundred, which is also one hundred fewer than all other estimates. Ultimately, Alfred Pleasonton had conquered Byram's Ford at a small cost. This is especially true given Union charges across open fields and, once again, the long duration of the battle and the incessant rifle fire. But the small cost should not be unexpected. As in Civil War battles everywhere, soldiers with rifle muskets, or even Sharps carbines, tended very much not to realize the parabolic trajectory of their weapons. Consequently, they shot high at ranges between one hundred and three hundred yards. With most Confederate rifle fire directed down the slope of Bloody Hill at those ranges, it is hardly surprising that so many Union cavalrymen lived to fight another day.[17]

With his command thus not greatly bloodied, Alfred Pleasonton exhorted his division to keep pushing the fleeing Confederates. It was a pursuit done without Edward Winslow. In the final push past the rock ledge, Winslow had been hit with a nonfatal wound to his left leg. Although no bones were broken and Winslow remained on the field until well after the final Confederate line had been broken, he eventually ceded command to Frederick Benteen. Subsequently, Benteen's and Philips's brigades kept a running contact with Marmaduke for about one mile. Also joining the pursuit was John Sanborn's 3rd Brigade and Thurber's section of the 2nd Missouri Light Artillery. Sanborn had spent much of the morning trying to enter the battle. Pulling up the tail end of the division, Sanborn reached Byram's Ford about the same time that Winslow made his crossing. Rather than pile further into the congestion of the ford, Sanborn tried to negotiate the terrain both above and below the ford to no avail. Only after Winslow had made his dash to the plateau beyond the ford did Sanborn make his crossing. As the chase then moved west, Pleasonton's division arrayed itself with Sanborn on the left, Philips in the middle, and Benteen to the right. Pleasonton himself hovered near to Philips and the artillery, where he was almost overcome with the excitement of delivering a knockout blow to the retreating Confederates. Over the din of battle he could be heard shouting: "Rebels, Rebels, Fire, Fire, You damned Asses!" Notwithstanding the scattering of Marmaduke's division and Pleasonton's desire to keep pushing his division, Benteen and Philips both had to pull their brigades from the chase. Cartridge boxes needed to be filled and horses fed. Benteen, having stopped his regiments in and around a cornfield, hoped the halt would be long enough to feed his hungry horses. While Benteen and Philips thus attempted to rest, Sanborn pushed another mile to the Harrisonville Road, which ran south toward Russell's Ford on the curving Big Blue. [18]

There at the Harrisonville Road, Marmaduke had finally made good his escape, now almost directly south. Another Confederate force had arrived to check Pleasonton's pursuit. The appearance of these reinforcements, Sidney Jackman's brigade from Shelby's division, was more than fortuitous. While Jo Shelby had heard the noise of battle at Byram's Ford throughout the morning, he had received no official word from Marmaduke of his collapse and retreat. Marmaduke's couriers never found their target, which left Shelby to guess what had happened based upon the frantic reports of stragglers and distant observers. With his own division stalled out along sundry fences awaiting ammunition, Shelby therefore pulled Jackman from his place in line after 12 PM and ordered him south to James Fagan at the Mockbee Farm, the site of Jackman's rout of the 2nd KSM on the preceding day. Before Jackman even reached the farm, however, Fagan sent orders posting the brigade along the Harrisonville Road where the Confederates ran smack into John Sanborn's 3rd Brigade. [19]

At this point on the Harrisonville Road, Jackman was able to take advantage of a steep embankment surmounted with one of the ubiquitous stone walls seen throughout the area. He was also fortunate to have one piece of Richard Collins's artillery follow him into the line. Sanborn's pursuit to this point had been near chaotic, but Thurber's Missouri artillery had somehow managed to keep pace. As Sanborn paused briefly before Jackman's line, Thurber's guns went into action and promptly delivered some short rounds into the midst of the Union cavalry. With confusion then spreading among his troops, Sanborn became flustered when Pleasonton bombarded him with orders to continue pressing the attack. As Sanborn later admitted, "I gave the order in two or three instances to the regimental commanders without designating the points of attack. Indeed I did not know these points and I had no time to ascertain them. My orders were something of the Donnybrook Fair style: 'Charge! And wherever you see a Rebel go for him.'" The result was predictable. Lacking coordination, Sanborn's regiments veered toward the left of the Confederate line, which allowed Jackman to quickly advance some units on the right and thus pour an enfilading fire into the charging Yankees. The attack stalled, and as trooper Gene Greer of the 16th Missouri (Union) laconically recalled, "We was [*sic*] ordered to fall back to the brigade."[20]

The repulse caused Sanborn great anxiety. Pleasonton's orders still rung in his ears; he believed Jackman behind a near impregnable position; he knew his men were running low on ammunition; and he feared a possible counterattack. In the middle of this consternation, Thurber's artillery came to the rescue, as it had moved forward and began pumping double canister into Jackman's line. While Thurber did his work, two things happened. First, Sanborn straightened out his squadrons in preparation for another charge. Second, Sidney Jackman abandoned his position. Jackman's retreat was orderly as he displaced Collins's cannon and most of the brigade heading south for Russell's Ford. In due course Sanborn followed, but Jackman's rearguard regiments resisted at every stone wall and ravine, including the ford itself. Jackman eventually made it to the ford where Sanborn—then joined and aided by the 2nd Colorado on his right flank—finally stopped his pursuit in the face of determined resistance. Jackman's decision to leave his first position had little to do with either Sanborn or the aggressive actions of Thurber's artillery. From his location along the Harrisonville Road, Jackman could plainly see the collapse of all Confederate hope in Missouri. Shelby's and Fagan's commands had crumbled and were streaming to the rear in pandemonium. It was then about 2 PM.[21]

The disintegration of the Confederate force south of Brush Creek began when Sanborn burst upon the scene, running down Harrisonville Road. Now caught directly between Pleasonton and Curtis, Shelby decided to withdraw. Shelby first posted one of his aides, Captain Oliver Redd, to Thompson calling for the retreat. For whatever reason, the order to retreat did not come with an explanation. Thompson did not know Pleasonton had crashed Shelby's flank. Thompson refused to withdraw and instead began issuing orders to attack the Union artillery to his front. Incredulous, Redd spurred his horse down the Confederate line, telling one regimental commander after another to retreat. For the most part, they needed no further encouragement and began to pull back. Thompson and Frank Gordon, nevertheless, stood fast until Shelby's adjutant John Edwards appeared in their midst to repeat the order. At first, the withdrawal proceeded in an orderly fashion as Thompson had only to compete with incoming artillery. But the situation deteriorated rapidly when Samuel Curtis ordered a general advance to the south. On the Union left, James Ford's 4th Brigade, freshly reinforced by the hard-marching 12th KSM, encountered little opposition. Just to the west of Ford and the Wornall Road, some Confederates (probably Thompson and the 5th Missouri) tried to defend a slight hill. General Blunt spotted the Confederates and quickly ordered Doc Jennison to attack using whatever troops were at hand. In moments, Jennison put together a mounted charge with Blunt's personal escort and elements of the 15th Kansas, 3rd Wisconsin, and 2nd Colorado. The suddenness of Jennison's attack and Shelby's orders to retreat meant that there would be no firm opposition here. With a small number of defenders scattering to some woods to the east, most of the Confederates galloped pell-mell a mile to the south where Shelby had fashioned a defensive line. It took only a matter of minutes for Jennison to dismount a detachment of troopers to pour an intimidating, if not exactly lethal, volume of fire into the woods. The Confederates chose not to return fire and abandoned the woods as quickly as they had entered.[22]

Despite the overwhelming success of the Union advance, it was not without its tense moments. One such moment occurred prior to Jennison's charge. As the Union line initially rushed forward from the trees encasing Brush Creek, General Blunt remained behind to exhort and direct reinforcing militia to the front. While so doing, Blunt found one of Jennison's mountain howitzers just to the left of the Wornall Road and near to a farmhouse. Aside from the gun crew, there were no troops left behind to support the gun. This circumstance became readily apparent when a Confederate column emerged from some heavy woods surrounding Town Fork Creek to the east, heading straight for the artillery and what was then Curtis's rear and left flank. Both the gun crew and Blunt reacted capably. The howitzer pivoted to the east and belched loads of double canister into the Confederates, while Blunt, with revolvers at the ready, and his cavalry escort spurred their horses toward the enemy. The effect of all this was much the same as Jennison's charge. The Confederates evinced no desire to contest the ground. They fled south. The identity of these particular Confederates has been long lost to history, but it seems more than likely that these wayward troopers were refugees from John Marmaduke's division. [23]

While Blunt dealt with this incursion, the forward edge of his battle line swept south. Consequently, Jeff Thompson's initial withdrawal took him about one mile to a line that Shelby had formed to prevent the retreat from becoming a rout. But this attempt would be short-lived. No sooner did Thompson arrive than Shelby sent new orders. This time, there could be no mistaking the dire situation for the army. Despite the advance of Curtis's regiments from the north, Thompson was to abandon the line, face his brigade to the east, and meet a new Yankee threat. As Thompson began moving his regiments, Shelby galloped up and said, "General, charge yonder line and break it or the army is lost." In all probability, "yonder line" of Yankees belonged to Philips's and Benteen's brigades. When last seen both brigades had paused earlier in the contest to replenish cartridge boxes and feed their horses, which left Sanborn to pivot on the Harrisonville Road, move south, and then engage Sidney Jackman on Shelby's right and rear. Seeing Shelby's main line of defense on the open prairie, Philips and Benteen continued their drive to the west. The pace of events was then much too fast for Thompson. He did not have time to get his whole brigade on line and could only charge the oncoming Yankees with Benjamin Elliot's regiment. The initial charge shocked the Yankee movement, but a supporting group of Unionists proved too much for Thompson and his solitary regiment. Philip's and Benteen's columns lapped around the right of Thompson's thin line, threatening to cut him off from further retreat. Fighting desperately, Elliot's regiment somehow managed to extricate itself, but there was no organization in the retreat. [24]

It was now a stampede. While Thompson and Elliot fought Pleasonton's two brigades, Jo Shelby used Gordon's 5th Missouri to try to organize another line of resistance further south, behind a ditch. There was only a momentary respite, as the onrushing Unionists easily ejected the remnants of the Iron Brigade. For the men of the Iron Brigade, the path to survival was fairly narrow. The 2nd Colorado had joined on the right of Sanborn's brigade in closing off Russell's Ford. About three miles to the west, Thomas Moonlight's brigade prevented any movement into Kansas. That left only a narrow stretch of prairie near the Kansas border where they could negotiate the steep

banks of Indian Creek, a tributary of the Big Blue running about 2.5 miles
north of Little Santa Fe. Singly and by groups, the Confederates raced for
Indian Creek. "It was impossible to rally the men as a body," Thompson later
reported, "but many brave fellows took advantage of positions to delay the
enemy and let the others escape." Here and there significant pockets of
resistance did indeed form. Among the most conspicuous of which was one
led by Alonzo Slayback. About three-fourths of a mile from Little Santa Fe,
he managed to temporarily stun the enemy when he turned and charged with
one company, shouting "Hurrah for Todd and Quantrell." He could not,
however, keep the company together, as it came apart before arriving in the
village. After pausing momentarily to get some water, Slayback moved into
some brush where he first found one squad of men and then another mass of
troopers from an assortment of regiments. Jeff Thompson, Frank Gordon,
and Major Rector Johnson were also in this bunch, and Thompson subsequently ordered Slayback to organize a rearguard of about sixty-five men so
that everyone else "could get out of the way." About two miles further south,
Thompson and his group finally chased down Shelby and what amounted to
the remainder of the division.[25]

The Army of Missouri had faced long odds at the Battle of Westport. The
Confederates had to fight on two fronts with an army burdened by large
numbers of new recruits and conscripts who were generally unarmed and
dismounted. These new men were not all congregated in the trains, but were
instead present even in the more veteran brigades led by Jeff Thompson,
John B. Clark Jr., and William Cabell. While untrained militia would be
found throughout the Yankee ranks, more experienced and better-armed volunteer cavalry would do the bulk of the fighting for Samuel Curtis and Alfred
Pleasonton. Even more telling was the overwhelming superiority of the Union artillery, which far outnumbered and outweighed the available Confederate ordnance. But for all of these kinds of advantages, there was no inevita-
bility to the scale, or completeness, of the Union victory. Price's army contained enough veteran cavalry and capable commanders to mount a more
effective rearguard action and thus prevent the disaster of the 23rd. The only
thing missing, however, was a plan, and in this Sterling Price had failed his
army miserably. On the night of the 22nd and 23rd, Price had made no
apparent prebattle plan to extricate his army from Curtis and Pleasonton. If
Old Pap had a plan, detailed or otherwise, neither Shelby nor Marmaduke
understood it. The division commanders simply did not know in what way
they were supposed to coordinate a withdrawal from the area. This absence

of instruction also led Shelby to try an attack that would take him across Brush Creek and into Westport itself. With Shelby thus positioned, how was Marmaduke ever to disengage from Byram's Ford without uncovering Shelby's flank and rear? Price's failure to disseminate a plan at night was made even worse on the morning of the 23rd when he would become preoccupied with his trains and depart the battle area, leaving no one in charge to coordinate the actions of Shelby and Marmaduke. In the tactical universe of Sterling Price, a growing obsession with the trains now threatened the very life of his army.

Chapter Thirteen

Lost Opportunity at Hart Grove Creek

The retreat of Price's trains has long been one of the most misunderstood, or controversial, aspects of the battles around Kansas City. Because of the trains, the Army of Missouri was nearly lost and the military reputation of a Union general would be tarnished. This saga starts with a realization that historians have not only exaggerated the size of the trains, but they have never properly noted their route and the attendant combat actions.[1] The problem of locating the trains dates to the event itself. Despite the obvious fact that both armies were filled with natives of the general area, it was the rare two people who could agree on what to call the various roads in the vicinity of the battlefield. This was never so true than when describing the passage of the trains along a road that was called, alternately, the Harrisonville Road, the Military Road, the Fort Scott Road, the Little Santa Fe Road, the Kansas City to Pleasant Hill Road, and the State Line Road. Making matters worse for both soldiers and historians, there was the difficulty of the Big Blue River and determining if what one crossed was actually the river itself or a tributary. The net result of all this has seen one historian after another, from Paul Jenkins down through Howard Monnett, generally show the trains traveling southwest from Independence and passing in the vicinity of Hickman Mills until reaching Little Santa Fe, where they then pivoted to the south on what was either called the Military or Fort Scott Road. Needless to say, it did not happen this way.

The odyssey of Price's trains began along the Westport Road. At mid-morning on the 22nd, the trains departed Independence heading to the southwest. However, and unlike the narrative found in so many books, the trains followed Jo Shelby's turn to the west near Raytown and headed to Byram's Ford by early afternoon. As soon as Jo Shelby secured the ford, the trains then passed over to the western side and on to the Harrisonville Road where they remained for the rest of the night. The trains were large, and when spread out in one column they stretched for at least three miles. There was, no doubt, a large number of plunder-laden wagons, but they hardly dominated the lumbering formation. Of the approximately 250 wagons counted by a firsthand observer at Independence, most were filled with food, forage, ordnance, quartermaster supplies, surgical equipment, and iron forges. Many other wagons found themselves stuffed with the wounded and sick. Even with these wagons—and assuming there were more than a few loaded with booty—the bloated length of the trains was in its collection of over two hundred prisoners, one thousand head of cattle, and the gaggle of three thousand new recruits brigaded under the command of Charles Tyler. It was this column, then, that Price ordered directly south on the morning of the 23rd. Although Price in his official report referred to their route as along the Fort Scott Road, the general had gotten his roads confused. The trains rolled first along the Harrisonville Road to the south, crossing the Big Blue yet again at Russell's Ford. The trains then proceeded another three miles, keeping Hickman Mills to their left before deflecting along an unnamed road to the southwest. Only after moving several more miles would the trains finally strike the Fort Scott Road well below Little Santa Fe.[2]

Price assigned two brigades from Fagan's division to protect the column. Thomas McCray's brigade rode in the front, and Cabell's brigade pulled up the rear. Cabell assumed the overall command of the column, which then crossed the Blue at Russell's Ford at daybreak on the 22nd. By 9 AM and just as the column had advanced a little more than a mile to the south, Cabell detected a large Union force a few miles off to the east. It was John McNeil's 2nd Brigade of cavalry, and it was in a perfect position to slam into the vulnerable flank of the Confederate column.[3]

Alfred Pleasonton had placed a great deal of hope in John McNeil. Just after dark on the 22nd, Pleasonton rode to McNeil's headquarters in Independence and ordered his subordinate to move forward on the Little Santa Fe Road, cross the Big Blue in the vicinity of Little Santa Fe, and attack the enemy "if possible." General McNeil then passed the order on down to the different regiments with instructions to start the march at 9 PM. Things went awry quickly. McNeil's staff could find no local guides, and E. C. Cather-

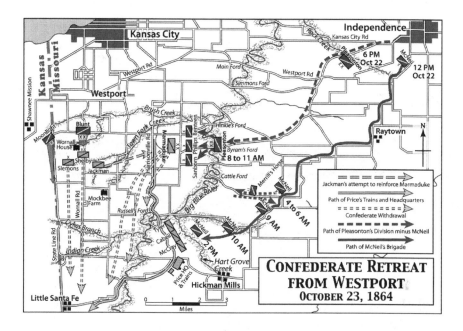

Figure 13.1.   Confederate Retreat from Westport, October 23, 1864

wood was inexplicably three hours late in getting his 13th Missouri Cavalry
to the head of the column to start the march.

The night was cold and crisp, but the presence of a nearly full moon
allowed for plenty of illumination. McNeil and his roughly 2,500 men made
fairly good time as they rode nine miles before halting around 4 AM. Although McNeil believed he was now directly east of Byram's Ford, he was in
reality well south of Byram's and closer to the cattle ford used by Frank
Gordon in his crossing of the Blue on the 22nd. It was not a planned stop.
McNeil noticed an imposing number of campfires burning a few miles off to
the right. This spooked McNeil into thinking that he might be cut off from
Pleasonton's main body of cavalry and was in danger of being attacked. He
reacted accordingly, and first sent some scouts and then a battalion of Merrill's Horse to see if the enemy was moving toward his position. The rest of
his brigade either collapsed from the exertions of the past two days or sought
badly needed water and forage. Within ninety minutes the scouts reported
back that the enemy was preparing to move, but that it did not look as if they
were coming back toward McNeil.[4]

It was now around daylight, and McNeil heard the sound of battle off to his right. That combat unsettled McNeil, leaving him concerned about his isolated position. Consequently, he delayed in starting the brigade toward Little Santa Fe, and when he did the brigade hardly moved at all. By 9 AM the column came within eyesight of the Harrisonville Road, which intersected the Little Santa Fe Road just beyond Hart Grove Creek. To McNeil's dread, he saw a massive body of enemy troops and wagons heading south along the Harrisonville Road, just three miles away. However, the head of the Confederate column was still well north of the intersection with the Little Santa Fe Road. As General McNeil pondered what to do over the next hour, the retreating Confederates took action to deal with the new threat that loomed off to their left.[5]

Word of McNeil's menace reached Sterling Price at his headquarters near Westport. Old Pap wasted little time and issued orders to Shelby and Fagan that they should fall back to the trains when "they could do so with safety." This, of course, was entirely vague, while also providing no coordinating instructions. Instead of remaining at the Boston Adams house to superintend the withdrawal, Price chose instead to lead the defense of the trains. Dressed in civilian attire, which included a white plug hat, Price mounted a horse and rode immediately for the front of the trains accompanied by his headquarters escort. He arrived by 10 AM and set about creating one of the better tactical deceptions seen in the war. He deployed Charles Tyler's brigade of unarmed men to the left of the Harrisonville Road, and still north of the intersection with the Little Santa Fe Road, in a line that screened the rolling wagons and beef herd. He culled about one hundred armed men from Tyler's ranks and joined them with the one hundred men of his escort to form a line of skirmishers. This group then advanced from the main line a few hundred yards toward Hart Grove Creek. Price also ordered Cabell and his brigade forward from the rear of the column to form a line just to the east of the intersection of the Harrisonville and Little Santa Fe roads. Price finalized his dispositions by directing elements of Thomas McCray's brigade back to form on Cabell's right flank. Although Price succeeded in deploying Tyler's brigade within a short period, it would still take some time to get Cabell and McCray into position. However, when all of the screening units were in place, the Confederates would be arrayed in varying locations two to four lines deep, numbering an estimated four thousand men.[6]

Fortunately for the Confederacy, John McNeil was in no great rush to attack. As the hours mounted and the wagons passed, the growing numbers of Confederates began to worry McNeil. In fact, McNeil began to think that the force in front of him was Price's entire army, rather than the trains protected by generally unarmed men. No earlier than 10 AM, McNeil could only bring himself to nudge his brigade, most of it still in column, forward another mile. He then halted atop a ridgeline that looked across Hart Grove Creek and toward the Harrisonville Road, which by then ran atop an undulating ridge parallel to the creek. Almost two miles separated the combatants. McNeil was now almost paralyzed. Aside from ordering one battery of mountain howitzers from the 5th MSM to find a position and commence firing, McNeil and his brigade sat piled up on the Little Santa Fe Road for yet another three hours. All the while, a gaggle of Union officers peered across the valley with their spy glasses, watching the Confederate column trundle south like one big accordion of straggling men, beasts, and wagons alternately bunched and spread out. At 2 PM, McNeil finally decided to try to poke the mostly unarmed screen protecting Price's trains. The brigade descended in bits and pieces from the ridge and deployed dismounted in Hart Grove Creek, which was really a dry, shallow ravine filled with brushwood and tall trees. A section of 3-inch Rodman Rifles from William C. F. Montgomery's battery of the 2nd Missouri Light Artillery occupied a hill behind the left center of the line. Not surprisingly, the brigade clung to the banks of the ravine, while Confederate artillery began to lob shells into their midst.[7]

Shortly after his brigade moved into the ravine, McNeil ordered a heavy skirmish line to advance consisting of several companies from several different regiments. The skirmishers then popped out of the ravine and advanced, in some places, to within five hundred yards of the Confederates. During this brief and lightly contested engagement, the Yankee skirmishers had to deal not only with Confederate sharpshooters but their own artillery as more than a few rounds from Montgomery's artillery landed in their ranks. Despite the friendly fire, McNeil grew a bit bolder and passed an order to Major Frank Malone, commanding the 7th Kansas, to lead his entire regiment into the Confederate line. Malone, who was sick and rode to the battle in an ambulance, was more than a bit incredulous at the order. He sent word to McNeil that he could probably break through the Confederate line and ride to Blunt and Curtis's troops well to the north, but that there was no way he could return alive to McNeil's ranks.[8]

This was not the only bad news that McNeil processed about that time. Confederate artillery, which some Yankee observers incorrectly believed numbered at least ten guns, began to fire heavily on both flanks of the Union line. Worse still, McNeil detected the arrival of Thomas McCray's cavalry on his left. McNeil originally posted Joseph Eppstein's 5th MSM to that portion of the battlefield to take advantage of the rapid-fire capability of their Wesson rifles. Moreover, Eppstein had extended his line and bent it back along a stone wall to meet the new threat. General McNeil, nevertheless, quickly concluded that all of this would be of no use. McNeil believed it only a matter of moments before Price rolled up his entire line. McNeil could stay no longer. Within an hour of his brigade entering the ravine, he ordered its withdrawal to the east and just outside the range of the Confederate artillery. It was an emotional moment for McNeil when Major L. C. Matlock of the 17th Illinois rode up to the general. Reflecting no small amount of frustration as well as complete ignorance of the enemy to his front, McNeil could only murmur to Matlock that this was the first time he had ever turned his back to the Confederates, but that he had little choice because he "could not fight Price's whole army." Indicative also of the acrimony that would surface immediately after the battle, McNeil felt the need to tell his subordinate that General Pleasonton had deliberately deprived him of additional artillery for this mission. Pleasonton, McNeil railed, had sent him to Little Santa Fe to be "used up" and "overwhelmed." Thus overburdened, McNeil maintained his brigade in line and watched Price's trains, soon to be joined by remnants of Marmaduke's and Fagan's retreating commands, ride past until there was simply no more light left to see them.[9]

With McNeil stuck east of the Harrisonville Road, Price and his trains pivoted to the southwest and kept moving toward Little Santa Fe. Not far south of the village, the entire gaggle had finally reached the Line Road where it now turned directly south. Price fled for another twenty miles until finally stopping around 9 PM at the Middle Fork of the Grand River in the southern part of Cass County. For the most part, Union forces did little to disrupt the retreat after Little Santa Fe. Thomas Moonlight's brigade stayed in the saddle for most of the evening but avoided contact with Price and stayed on the Kansas side of the border. Moonlight was content to guard against isolated incursions into Kansas and eventually stopped his march at Aubrey, about ten miles from Price's camps. The most vigorous pursuit of Price belonged to Doc Jennison. Despite his own personal viciousness, or perhaps because of it, Jennison pushed hardest. Jennison believed that A. J. Smith and his infantry were marching for Harrisonville, and the Jayhawker wanted to link with the infantry there. He did not make it. By sundown, Jennison was only four miles south of Little Santa Fe where he could still see all of Price's army rolling away. He ultimately advanced his brigade to within six hundred yards of the enemy when Confederate artillery, probably Collins's, joined with a more organized rearguard to push Jennison back north about one mile. With darkness enveloping the battlefield, Jennison gave up the idea of joining with Smith's infantry. He decided to make camp for the night. The rest of the Union forces had already stopped in the vicinity of Little Santa Fe. Most of the cavalrymen anticipated a quick call to the saddle and therefore, according to Edwin Carpenter of the 17th Illinois Cavalry, caught "snatches of sleep lying in front of our horses with their halters tied to their persons." Trooper Jacob Gantz of the 4th Iowa later gave voice to the thoughts of probably every soldier in the area: "I rested splendid after fighting so hard."[10]

As early as 2:30 PM on the 23rd, generals Curtis and Pleasonton had finally met each other face to face when their units converged at a farmhouse near Indian Creek. The meeting also attracted most of the political potentates of Kansas who had been lurking about the periphery of the previous few days' military action. Thomas Carney, Jim Lane, Samuel Pomeroy, and George Deitzler all assembled to offer their advice on what next to do. For perhaps the only time during the war, all of these men agreed on the first order of business: Curtis must disband the Kansas militia. The great need for the ill-trained citizen-soldiers appeared over, and, besides, the politicians wanted these men home to vote. Pleasonton was the lone dissenter. His opposition reflected a surprising desire to shift the burden of combat to the militia while allowing his own troops to return to their garrisons. As an incredulous Curtis noted one week later, "Pleasonton was especially satisfied after we whiped [*sic*] the enemy Sunday last that we had done enough and ought to stop." Pleasonton thus suggested taking his division to Harrisonville where the men could rest and the Missourians could be furloughed to vote in the upcoming elections. However, Curtis did not quite see the job as being done. Price could still inflict considerable damage along the state line. To prevent that, Curtis retained Pleasonton, while releasing only the Kansas militia mustered from north of the Kansas River. Curtis designated Blunt's remaining troops the 1st Division and Pleasonton's the 2nd Division. Curtis and a disgruntled Pleasonton then departed. The two met again later that night at Little Santa Fe. This time General Blunt was in attendance, and he was most enthusiastic to start the chase. According to Blunt, he pleaded with Curtis to march at 2 AM when the moon rose. Curtis refused, setting the departure time to sunrise. For Blunt, Curtis's refusal to rush was another act of a timid man determined to ignore all of the opportunities presented to destroy Price. Blunt seethed, but Curtis's decision was probably correct. The nearly continuous action of the previous few days had exhausted man and beast. Some rest was necessary. Furthermore, the confusion of the action of the 23rd mandated some time for the different units to sort themselves out. As events shortly proved, there was time yet to catch Price.[11]

While the marching and fighting would still go on, Westport and its environs had to recover from two days of battle. Even before the last shots had been fired near Little Santa Fe, the citizens of Kansas City and Westport trickled out of their homes to view and inspect the battlefield. They were not prepared for what they saw. In one spot near the Wornall House, there was a horse that lay lifeless in the forks of a low-lying tree. Dead and wounded men were "strewn and scattered" about the battlefield and "lay buried in hollows and ravines, or concealed in the brush and timber." The Wornall House, the focus of so much action, was especially grim. Eight Confederates lay side by side in a field next to the house, while dead horses and accoutrements of all kinds could be found at every step. In the vicinity of the Mockbee Farm, wild hogs began to roam the battlefield and, in some cases, feed on the dead of the 2nd KSM who had been lying unattended for two days. Elsewhere, a curiosity-seeking citizen found a dead Confederate with a Springfield rifle, half cocked and double loaded, lying by his side. "The fatal shot had passed through under the hammer grazing the stock of the gun, and striking the rebel in the breast. Carved in the butt of the musket is the name of the owner, John Murdock, Co., B, 15th Arkansas CSA." To one patriotic Unionist reporter, the carnage of the battle confirmed all of his prejudices. On the Harrisonville Road he found a Confederate with "the top of his head shot off by a cannonball. He was the very image of a bushwhacker, and had on three pair of pantaloons." After viewing other dead and captured Confederates, he noted the "stolid, ignorant, degraded appearance of the whole of them. They seem to belong to a different race from ours, and most certainly an inferior one." He concluded by calling them "miserable, degraded, [and] hungry wretches."[12]

Other local citizenry, but especially the area women, flocked to a number of temporary hospitals. While some dressed wounds and cooked food, others simply wrote letters or copied the names of wives and sweethearts. Mary C. Haverty, who operated a school for girls in Westport, kept classes running throughout the battle only to dispatch her girls at the end of the day to help the wounded of both sides. Mrs. H. S. Millett was among several women who served as nurses in the Southern Methodist Church and Lockridge Hall along 5th Street in Kansas City. For a week, these women tended to men stacked up on pews, tables, and floors. The Harris Hotel in Westport became perhaps the largest collection point for the wounded, as one young observer watched wagon after wagon bringing in bodies eventually to be put down on cots or blankets. Doctors from the surrounding towns, but especially Leaven-worth, posted to the Harris Hotel where they treated about forty casualties, mostly Union. Dr. W. Booth Smith visited other hospitals after working the Harris Hotel. He was ever keen to note differences in the combatants and concluded that the wounded Confederates did not fear death and "maintained a stoical and sullen silence." In fact, "One said he wanted to die; he had been driven about long enough." Further to the east and closer to Byram's Ford, another hospital sprouted up in the Boston Adams house. Sterling Price had left behind his most grievously wounded to be cared for by Jo Shelby's chief surgeon, Major Caleb Winfrey. But it was the Wornall house that saw the most drama. During the morning's action, Shelby turned it into a field hospital. Beds were knocked down and pallets placed on the floor. As the casualties accumulated, all members of the family—save father John B. Wornall who was in Westport—cooked food, boiled water, and generally assisted the Confederate attendants. When the Confederates retreated past the house, they left behind twelve wounded soldiers from Dobbin's brigade. All were in the care of three young boys. Of those who would, or could, be interviewed by their Union captors, only one declared he had volunteered for Confederate service. The rest claimed the misfortune of being conscripted. In short order, though, the Unionists evicted those who could be moved and replaced them with Union casualties. It might then have been the Wornall house that George Swain visited when his division of A. J. Smith's XVI Corps passed through the Kansas City area on Monday, the 24th. Swain saw all the horrors of a Civil War hospital, including one young surgeon who he believed "had never cut a leg off before, for it seemed as if theory and practice was with him a stranger." He also saw one Confederate shot through the head who could neither speak nor see. The mangled soldier "crawled upon the floor his features distorted, his limbs drawn up in almost every shape and [emitting] low pitiful wailings and moans from his lips." Swain became nauseous and almost vomited.[13]

The final accounting of casualties will never be known with any certainty. Record keeping was inconsistent across the units of the different armies; many Union regiments did not even report their casualties; and, most disabling of all, numerous Confederate records were destroyed during and after the war. That disclaimer offered, it can be noted that all published accounts of the battles around Kansas City have inflated the casualties. Mark Lause's estimate in the *Encyclopedia of the American Civil War* is the highest at 2,500 Union and as many as 2,800 Confederate. Howard Monnett's influential work is no less wrong when he speculates that both sides lost a combined 3,500 men killed and wounded for the three days of fighting between October 21 and 23. This he believes a "conservative figure." For the combat of October 23 alone, Monnett believes both sides lost a total of 1,500 men killed and wounded. Monnett's conclusions have proven durable and have been repeated throughout the secondary literature since 1964 when he first published his results. The ubiquity of his numbers can also be found throughout the Internet and even on the National Park Service's summation of the Battle of Westport. Barring the discovery of any new unit returns, the best estimation of casualties can be found in Bryce Suderow's meticulous, yet unpublished, research, and it details 510 Confederates and 361 Yankees killed, wounded, and captured on the 23rd. [14]

Chapter Fourteen

Musketry Like Swarms of Lightning Bugs

Sterling Price's defeat on October 23 had been near total. Just barely escaping encirclement, his army had scattered in a headlong retreat south along the state line. Here and there, groups of men stopped long enough to face the pursuing Federals and to try to reconstitute their units. But for the most part, the Confederates retreated in confusion. On October 24, Union pursuit gained strength, and it pressed the Army of Missouri hard. However, the pursuit was not without its problems as several Union commanders began, or continued, feuds that did not stop until the end of the campaign. For the Confederates, Price and his officers eventually restored some order to their army, but discipline within the ranks was largely shattered. No matter the best intentions of Price and Jo Shelby, the learned savagery of the guerrilla war once again became evident all along their retreat. It was hardly surprising that Union troops would be no less primed for butchery.

After the Confederates succeeded in sorting out a jumble of men, artillery, and wagons on the morning of the 24th, the army proceeded south along the Line Road in three columns. The trains moved in the road itself, and the cavalry got pushed to both flanks. The tabletop nature of the prairie helped ease the army's path, but it was nonetheless a forced and hurried march. Teamsters and quartermasters attempted to lighten their loads by shedding the excess baggage and plunder the army had accumulated in its trek across Missouri. Bales of rope, animal harnesses, grindstones, barrels of assorted merchandise, clocks, and a spinning wheel soon littered the prairie. However, it was only the beginning of what needed to be done. As the day passed, worn-out horses and cattle, broken wagons, and even the limber and caisson of the 2nd KSM's captured howitzer all fell by the side of the road. Most telling, the men themselves began to fail. Stragglers and the sick were left behind by the dozen with many readily executed by the pursuing Union forces. Despite the calamity that befell the army, morale had not fallen completely. Senior commanders such as Jeff Thompson understood the army faced daunting odds in its safe return to Arkansas, but many in the rank and file believed help was close. More particularly, a rumor spread through the companies that generals Stand Watie and Richard Gano were driving up from Oklahoma with a relief column and a large supply train. [1]

Suitably inspired, the army marched along the Line Road for about twenty-six miles until it reached West Point, a place Union captain Richard Hinton later described as a "deserted and half-burnt village upon the state line." At West Point, Price veered off the Line Road, heading southwest along what was known as the Old Military Road. Price was now marching toward what he hoped to be the last significant action of his campaign: the capture of Fort Scott. Tucked just inside the border and about thirty miles from West Point, Fort Scott housed tons of ordnance and quartermaster supplies; its capture would also go a long way to removing the embarrassment of defeat at Kansas City. Price therefore continued his drive along the Old Military Road for another nine miles before coming to a halt at nightfall along the Marais des Cygnes River. He had arrived at the small hamlet of Trading Post. The town itself was just to the east side of the river, which at that point was running almost north to south. Just to the north of Trading Post were two large natural mounds that rose up from the prairie. The mounds were separated by about three hundred yards with the Old Military Road running between them and through the town to the river. The mound to the west was the larger of the two with a length of almost four thousand feet, while the eastern mound was less than half that size. Both mounds towered about 140 feet above the prairie. The army apparently divided itself along the river with the trains and Marmaduke's and Shelby's divisions encamped on the west bank. Fagan's division remained posted as a rearguard. Oddly enough, however, Slemons's small brigade of three hundred men found itself on the much larger western mound, while Cabell's two thousand troopers manned the smallish eastern heights. Fagan ordered Arch Dobbin's brigade artillery, two 2-pound Woodruff guns captured from Fort Davidson and commanded by Lieutenant Jesse V. Zimmerman, into the gap between the mounds. [2]

Among those who accompanied the trains on the south bank of the river were about one hundred prisoners. For the most part, these were men from the 2nd KSM who were taken at the Mockbee Farm on October 22nd, although their number included at least one trooper from the 7th Indiana. These prisoners were in the midst of what one author would eventually call "The Long March." Captives in an army struggling to survive and outrun its pursuers, the prisoners suffered greatly. Ever since Price fled Westport the dismounted prisoners had to keep up with their mounted captors. The pace was brutal, and it wrecked the feet of the farmers, mechanics, merchants, and doctors who were unused to the marching. They were footsore and perpetually thirsty and hungry. Only when the army made it to the banks of the Marias des Cygnes did most of the prisoners get their first substantial food (corn and raw beef) in over forty-eight hours. Some prisoners were ordered not to use fires, and the famished prisoners thus ate their rations raw. The sufferings of the Union prisoners would continue, but it could have been worse. They had fallen under the control of Jo Shelby, and Shelby went out of his way to ensure the prisoners were not abused. This became readily apparent when a prisoner overheard one of the Confederate lieutenants conveying orders to the guards to "treat these prisoners as kindly as possible, but let no man get away."[3]

When not dealing with these prisoners, the Confederates attended to some pressing business. The men had to care for the wounded, grind corn, scrounge food, and visit retribution upon the Kansans. Because the path of the Confederate army had now turned to the Kansas side of the border, the experience did not go easy for the local population. More to the point, ever since Price's army had entered into Linn County, Kansas, both foragers and stragglers committed all manner of depredations. They shot men indiscriminately, made boys prisoners, burned farms, and dumped dead livestock into wells. All of this was hardly surprising. It was the nature of the border war. The Confederates were, indeed, reminded of it the previous day when they saw firsthand the Jayhawking-inspired desolation on the Missouri side of the border. Magnifying the problem even more at Trading Post, many units in Price's army nearly disintegrated on the evening of the 24th. In the words of one soldier, half of his battalion spent the night "skirmishing for something to eat." With the bonds of discipline thus frayed and bands of hungry and vengeful men roaming the area, bad things were bound to happen. Therefore, when Price's army began piling into the area of Trading Post around 4 PM, gunfire prompted some of the merchants to flee into the countryside shouting the alarm. There they joined farmers and old men hiding in ravines. For some of these men, even this precaution did not work. At least seven locals were eventually reported murdered. As word spread of Price's arrival, women and children congregated in some of the local farmhouses. One such place was the Huff house where Hannah Gordon, her sisters, grandmother, and Mrs. William Baugh took refuge. A group of Price's men soon entered the house and promptly consumed all of Mrs. Huff's fresh biscuits and buttermilk. "Next, they took everything eatable from the house and all the men's clothing and then asked what we were crying for." Mrs. Baugh soon became hysterical as she could see Confederates swarming around her own home about one-half mile in the distance. In a moment of either exasperation or pity, the Confederates at Huff's house told Baugh to go save her home. It was, however, too late. As Hannah Worden later recalled, "We found it broken into and almost every moveable thing taken out or destroyed. The fields were full of men, some digging potatoes, some pulling cabbage and corn, some killing hogs and chickens." When Gordon later returned to her own family home, she saw "the sides of the house torn down and every hog and chicken killed and the fences destroyed."[4]

The Confederate passage through Linn County was not without its moments of compassion. One case involved Mrs. Amos Tubbs and a handful of children and women who were found on the prairie one mile from Trading Post. An officer provided a guard of four men to escort the group back to their boarding house and farm another mile southwest of town. Once back at the house, however, the group discovered one hundred Confederates getting ready to ransack the place. A Major Phoebe commanded many of these Confederates, and Phoebe recognized Tubbs from having boarded at her house before the war. A conflicted Phoebe then said, "Mrs. Tubbs, if I could help it, not one thing should be taken, but the boys are nearly starved." And so they ate. According to Tubbs, "A big platter of chicken and dumplings my mother had prepared for her family disappeared almost instantly." Soon thereafter, "one man was eating pork right out of the brine and another raw pumpkin." By the time the Confederates left the house, they had also taken four hundred pounds of milled flour and all the available pork. In a parting act of kindness, though, Phoebe intervened when a soldier attempted to shoot one of the boys for his boots. The major also made sure the family retained some food for their own use. In one other besieged household, a Confederate officer confronted a wounded soldier who announced that he wanted to kill all the women and children. It was a tense moment, but the officer somehow overawed the vengeful soldier by proclaiming, "But you don't have your way. Old Pap Price is the commander of this army and you know that he expects every man to be not only a soldier but a gentleman as well." The officer then helped the family hide some food beneath a baby's bed.[5]

While Price's army thus paused at the Marais des Cygnes River, Samuel Curtis's Army of the Border attempted to make up lost time. Just as the Confederates faced confusion in starting the day's march, so, too, did the Unionists. It was well after daylight before Blunt's 1st Division lurched forward with James Ford's 4th Brigade in the lead followed by Doc Jennison's 1st Brigade and Charles Blair's 3rd Brigade. By the time Blunt's division cleared Little Santa Fe, and Pleasonton's took up its march, it was after 10 AM. Curtis's late start left Union forces about fifteen to twenty miles in the rear of Price. In an attempt to further delay the Union pursuit, the Confederate rearguard under William Cabell tried to light the prairie grass in order to create a firestorm. The efforts amounted to nothing as Price's thousands of horses had beaten the prairie grass flat and churned up the moist terrain, leaving grass that would simply not burn. So the Union cavalry rode unimpeded, following a trail that was strewn with the castoff debris of Price's army. Broken wagons, dead horses, and wounded Confederates all dotted the landscape, but most important for the hungry Unionists was the cattle from Price's beef herd that could not keep up with the rapid retreat. Some of the cattle wandered around loose on the prairie, while others had already been slaughtered by the retreating Confederates. Union troopers paused occasionally by such carcasses only long enough to pull any remaining meat to eat it raw.[6]

As hunger gnawed at the soldiers in the Union ranks, animosities grew among the general officers. Blunt, ever aggressive, pushed his division hardest, and it opened up about a six-mile lead on Pleasonton's column. By 6 PM, Blunt had marched forty-seven miles to West Point. To Blunt, this feat of arms was squandered when Curtis sent orders to halt until he and Pleasonton arrived at West Point. Blunt fumed, but he also sought to make the best of the situation. First, he ordered Companies E, I, and K of the 2nd Colorado, commanded by Captain Ezra Kingsbury, to scout forward and determine Price's whereabouts. Kingsbury eventually made that contact near to Trading Post and confirmed what Blunt suspected: Price was camped along the Marais des Cygnes and was probably headed toward Fort Scott. Second, Blunt hunted around the 6th KSM and found some men who knew the local area well, especially the existence of a ford about three miles upriver from Trading Post and Price. As Blunt then waited impatiently for Curtis and Pleasonton to arrive, the night sky darkened with storm clouds, and a misting rain soon fell.[7]

For some of the units in Blunt's division, the march to West Point had been calamitous. This was particularly true of Blair's brigade, which was composed mostly of the remaining Kansas militia in the Army of the Border. As Blair later remarked, the brigade disintegrated during the forced marches of the 23rd and 24th. Men and horses either fell by the side of the road exhausted or the men simply went home as they passed through their native counties. All that was left for Blair to command was James Montgomery's 6th KSM, George Eaves's battalion of Bourbon county militia, and some artillery. That any of the 6th KSM was still around was a surprise. Montgomery's men had marched all day on the 23rd without their horses. Only that night did the horse holders finally catch up to the unit. Having little to command aside from the 6th KSM, Blair left his brigade in the charge of an adjutant and volunteered as an aide to Curtis.[8]

Around 8 PM, Curtis and Pleasonton finally arrived at West Point. The ensuing consultation saw Blunt propose a dynamic turning movement around Price's army. Believing the mounds too much of an obstacle, Blunt suggested a feint against the mounds with a few squadrons of cavalry, while most of the army marched to the ford upriver from Trading Post. The Unionists would cross and then pivot to the east, completely blocking Price's path south and pushing him back against the Marais des Cygnes. Pleasonton uttered some support for the plan, but Curtis rightly dismissed it. The plan involved a risky fifteen-mile march around Price's army and a nighttime river crossing, all preparatory to forming up for a daylight attack into what Blunt hoped was a stationary Confederate army. No less important, Blunt did not really consider the terrain south of the Marais des Cygnes. Big Sugar Creek and Little Sugar Creek were tributaries of the Marais des Cygnes, and they were obstacles that would prevent the quick maneuvering Blunt envisioned. Consequently, Curtis held firm against Blunt, and he ordered Pleasonton to make a nighttime frontal attack into the mounds. Pleasonton, battling sickness, begged off the assault and ceded command to John Sanborn, who volunteered for the job, pledging to bring "the enemy to a stand."[9]

Sanborn advanced with his brigade followed by Philips, McNeil, and Benteen. J. J. Gravely's 8th MSM took the lead, and it groped its way through the dark and an increasingly strong rain. Around midnight the column ran into Kingsbury's battalion of the 2nd Colorado. Sanborn, who earlier expressed great enthusiasm for the chance to bag Price, now felt that enthusiasm wane. Gravely's regiment inaugurated a skirmish that spooked the general. To Sanborn, the musketry seemed like "swarms of lightning bugs." Worse yet, Sanborn heard a "noise on our left resembling that of ten thousand voices speaking at once." With strange and ominous sounds to his flank and the foreboding mounds looming ahead, Sanborn wanted little to do with a night attack. Instead, he feared a Confederate assault and withdrew about one-half mile from the mounds and deployed the division in an arc with Benteen to the far right, his brigade in the middle, and McNeil swung to the left. Philips became the divisional reserve. Sanborn then concluded that if all remained calm for the night, he would attack in the morning. To carry out the attack, however, Sanborn mixed and matched regiments from his own brigade and that of Benteen. While Benteen deployed one regiment to Island Ford, which was several miles north of Trading Post along the Marias des Cygnes to guard against any possible Confederate turning movement, Sanborn directed Gravely's 8th MSM to lead the attack on the eastern mound supported by Major William Plumb's 6th MSM. Abial Pierce's 4th Iowa would be responsible for taking the western mound. After informing his brigade commanders of the plan, Sanborn grabbed a blanket and tried to get some sleep at Elder Williams's house, some two miles north of the mounds. [10]

Although Sanborn had a roof over his head on a cold and wet night, the general did not sleep so well. By 1 AM, emissaries from General Curtis rousted Sanborn from his slumber. Curtis, too, was not sleeping, and he grew restless waiting for the sounds of an attack. Contributing to Curtis's anxiety were the high-powered Kansans who traveled in his headquarters and pestered him with demands of immediate action. Jim Lane, Colonel Samuel J. Crawford (Lane's surrogate candidate for governor), and Charles Blair (one-time commander at Fort Scott) all insisted on some type of movement to spare Linn County from the rapacious rebels (and perhaps the recriminations of angry voters). Just how much these men influenced Curtis can only be guessed, but Curtis did send his aides to prod Sanborn into the attack. To Clarence W. Rubey of Sanborn's staff, the aides "seemed disposed constantly to arouse and annoy" the general, especially after he told them he would not make a night attack unless given written orders. [11]

Curtis dealt with Sanborn's insubordination in a curious way. He did not relieve him. He did not even order his compliance. Instead, Curtis seemed at first to back off the demand for immediate attack by simply ordering Sanborn to begin an artillery bombardment of the mounds no later than first light so as to harass the Confederates. But in reality, Curtis—or at least his staff—tried to bypass Sanborn in getting the attack to move early. By 3 AM, Curtis's aides, including Richard Hinton and R. H. Hunt, found Kingsbury's battalion of the 2nd Colorado and instructed it to attack the western mound immediately. In Hinton's words, they were "to carry the mounds under the cover of rain and darkness." Passing the 8th MSM's camp en route to the 2nd Colorado, the aides informed Colonel Gravely of their intentions and thereby spurred Gravely to start his preparations for the attack on the eastern mound. However, these machinations were largely for naught. There was simply not that much time left before daylight to greatly alter Sanborn's original plan. In reality, the only substantive alteration to Sanborn's plan involved the 2nd Colorado. That detachment was actually in the process of leaving the skirmish line headed for the rear when Hinton ordered its attack upon the northwestern and northern faces of the western mound. Despite any confusion or fatigue, the Coloradans turned their column around and commenced an attack no earlier than 4 AM. They drew fire about one hundred yards from the base of the mound and slowly pushed up the slope. A group of men attempted to get around the westernmost side of the mound, but it met an intimidating flash of musketry and was forced back toward the main body. [12]

As the 2nd Colorado moved up the mound, the 4th Iowa, in accordance with Sanborn's original instructions, moved slowly through cornfields on both sides of the Old Military Road in preparation for their attack through the gap and up the northeastern face of the mound. For the men of the 4th, there was some added incentive in making the assault. Word filtered through the cold and wet ranks to Sergeant James O. Vanorsdol that "if we would clear the hills in front of us we could stop and get breakfast." [13] Adjutant William Forse Scott described what happened next:

> Nothing was seen, nothing was heard but the rustling of the wet corn as it was brushed aside or broken down by the horses. Suddenly a line of flashes burst across the front, and there was a rattle of small arms which seemed very near. But the flashes were surprisingly high in the air, and no balls were heard to whistle. Again and again a line of fire high in front, but not *z-z-zip!* of bullets. [14]

The 4th continued a slow advance through the cornfields toward the base of the mound when the early glow of daylight finally revealed the outline of the mound to the soldiers. For men who had grown used to the sight of

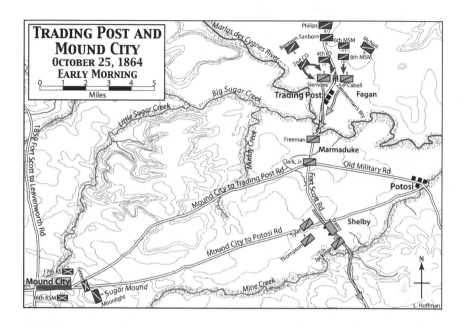

Figure 14.1. Trading Post and Mound City, October 25, 1864, Early Morning

limitless prairie, the mound was a very strange sight. Nevertheless, the Iowans vaulted a fence and pressed up the hill in the face of a galling, if wildly high and inaccurate, defensive fire. The incoming fusillade lasted for most of the climb, but by the time the line of Federals made it to the crest of the mound there were no Confederates to be found. Slemons had evacuated the mound. The only person left alive was a small girl, no more than six years old, who had been cut off from her family and somehow hid on the top of the hill throughout the engagement. With daylight now peeking over the mound, Union artillery shells began falling near the triumphant cavalry. Thurber's and Montgomery's units of the 2nd Missouri Light Artillery had finally commenced the bombardment that Curtis wanted started three hours earlier. In a matter of moments, however, the gunners lifted their fire with no casualties inflicted upon either side. [15]

The story was only slightly different on the other mound. Gravely's 8th MSM, supported by the 6th MSM, jumped off in a dismounted attack just before dawn. The eastern mound was a bit steeper and more barren than the other, and Cabell's much larger brigade protected it. In a dramatic moment before the attack, several officers approached Sanborn seeking confirmation that they had to charge the mound. Once the order was confirmed, some of the officers told Sanborn "goodbye," with a shake of the hands that only foreshadowed doom. Initially, their fears seemed real; the charge fizzled, and the dismounted troopers quickly resorted to crawling up the hill. But as Sanborn later recounted, the Missourians kept moving "steadily forward, loading and firing as they advanced until within a few yards of the crest, when, with ringing cheers and a rattling volley of musketry, they dashed forward, driving back the enemy and gaining the position." Sanborn's breathless account to the contrary, the final assault was not nearly so dramatic. The Confederates had abandoned their positions before the final assault. Neither Sterling Price nor William Cabell were interested in a last-ditch rearguard action at the mounds. Union and Confederate casualties, though never reported, appear to have been almost nonexistent.[16]

Union forces paused only briefly. Alfred Pleasonton awoke that morning and rode unaccompanied to the western mound where he joined John Sanborn in a moment of triumph. Both Sanborn and Pleasonton gazed down from the mound and saw the bulk of Fagan's division piled up around the heavily wooded ford at Trading Post, making its escape across the river. The Union generals wanted very much to hit Fagan before he crossed the river, but the muddy roads and spread-out dispositions of the regiments did not bode well for pressing the attack. Only Captain Kingsbury and his battalion of the 2nd Colorado and the 2nd Arkansas managed to continue the chase toward the ford. They were indeed too late. Fagan got his men across the ford and still had time to obstruct it with two felled trees, preventing an immediate Union pursuit.[17]

While Sanborn organized his brigade and Pleasonton worked to bring the rest of his division to the ford, the Federals assembling in and around Trading Post were amazed by what they saw. Richard Hinton surveyed Fagan's hastily abandoned camp and wrote:

Clothing, blankets, parts of tents, camp utensils, mess chests, etc., all betokened the hasty evacuation. The picture was hideous in its filth. The *debris* of a camp is never a sightly object, but the peculiar features thereof were enhanced by the knee deep mud, the remains of slaughtered cattle, the broken equipments, and the disgusting effluvia which greeted the nostrils. The little hamlet looked woe-begone.[18]

One of the Woodruff guns had been abandoned, and about one hundred cattle roamed the evacuated camp. More importantly, Fagan had to leave behind many of his sick and wounded. Every house in town seemed to hold one of these men. Unfortunately for them and several stragglers captured around Trading Post, the Army of the Border took its own retribution. Hinton believed many "were hung by our troops in the rear."[19]

The Federal seizure of Trading Post was not the only significant action to take place on the night of the 24th and 25th. More drama occurred just eleven miles west at Mound City. The seat of Linn County, Mound City had been in a state of great anxiety for the previous week. Ever since Price closed upon Kansas City, the people of Mound City expected the Confederates to turn south along the border. The citizens naturally feared the worst, and the *Border Sentinel* trumpeted the news that "Price and his imbruted hordes of robbers and murders" were approaching. With most of the able-bodied men of the county already enlisted in the 6th KSM and marching with Curtis, the defense of the city would depend on an odd assortment of armed men. Captain Samuel W. Greer of the 15th Kansas Cavalry commanded a small number of men who had not joined their regiment in time to march with Jennison. He also soon found himself in charge of about two hundred local militiamen (white and colored), boys, and old men exempt from service. Throughout the last week of October, Greer drilled these men at least four hours daily in anticipation of Price's arrival. Despite their preparation, the citizens of Mound City were more than surprised when Robert G. Gibbons and Miles Lamb, two "independent scouts," tumbled into the city around 4 PM on the 24th with the news that Price was at Trading Post. The city had already received telegraphic word of the victory at Westport, but most did not believe Price capable of marching the seventy miles so quickly. Captain Greer then put scouts out toward Trading Post and set up defensive positions just outside the city. Meanwhile, anyone not in uniform joined in a full-scale panic, including one young man who "crawled into a hollow log and remained there till hunger drove him out, long after all danger had passed." Merchants packed up what they could and fled to the interior of Kansas. A group of ladies filled eight to ten wagons with their family possessions and headed west with one man, Preacher J. R. Marr, to accompany them. Sadly, the ladies were hardly inspired by the preacher because he "was so frightened as to be almost worthless." Those who could not leave feared for the worst. Colonel J. D. Snoddy, who had been relieved of his command of the 6th KSM when he refused to take it into Missouri on the eve of the battles of Kansas City, led a scout of twenty men in the direction of Trading Post. They eventually ran into a large body of Confederates at Muddy Creek six miles west of town. Predictably, Snoddy's men scattered at contact and raced back toward the city. Another scout later that night collected an escaped prisoner and a deserter who promptly informed them that Price intended to attack in the morning and that he "would give no quarter." While this news brought still more panic, a ray of hope arrived about the same time when Colonel Thomas Moonlight telegrammed the city that he was racing in their direction with the seven hundred men of his 2nd Brigade of Blunt's division.[20]

Moonlight's journey was longer than that experienced by the rest of Curtis's Army of the Border. Ever since the Confederate collapse at Westport, Moonlight operated well to the west of the main Union army with the mission of blocking Price from moving too deeply into Kansas. At noon on the 24th, he had marched hard enough to run into Price at Coldwater Grove, twenty-six miles from Little Santa Fe. There Moonlight was joined by Colonel Andrew Jackson Mitchell and his 11th KSM, which had been stationed at Coldwater Grove. Thus reinforced, Moonlight's brigade occupied a slight ridge and looked down upon what Sergeant Archer Childers termed "the grandest sight it was my privilege to see the whole three years I was in the army." Price's entire army was in view, traveling in columns along the Line Road. It did not take Price terribly long to detect Moonlight. Old Pap deployed a battery of artillery and lobbed several shells in Moonlight's direction. After some scattered return fire, Moonlight determined it best to withdraw out of sight and to continue paralleling Price's march down the state line. Realizing that Price's route could take him to Mound City, Moonlight pushed his command hard to beat the Confederates there. Captain Greer tried to hurry Moonlight along by dispatching scouts Lamb and Gibbons to serve as guides. For the rest of that "terrible night," as later reported by the *Pleasonton Observer*, "everybody watched and waited, not knowing what moment the enemy would be upon them."[21]

To the everlasting gratitude of the citizens of Mound City, Moonlight and his exhausted men finally arrived around 12:30 AM, having ridden all night on the 1859 Leavenworth to Fort Scott Road. "Gloom gave place to rejoicing, and never did women work more willingly than those who prepared rations that morning for tired soldiers." The grateful women of Mound City stood out in the streets most of the night "with large pans and bread bowls filled with bread and biscuit that the men might take a piece in their hands as they rode by."[22]

The men of the brigade tried to get some sleep only to be awakened near dawn with news that eight hundred Confederates were bearing down on the town from the vicinity of Trading Post. In hindsight, the report of eight hundred men seems a great exaggeration. Price did not have eight hundred men to spare for such a sideshow to Mound City. Marmaduke and Fagan were busy fending off Sanborn's crossing of the Marais des Cygnes, and Shelby was superintending the advance of the trains along the Old Military Road. Nevertheless, the news of the approach of the secessionists renewed the town's panic, although that was somewhat allayed at 7 AM by the arrival of two companies of the 17th Kansas Infantry and a detachment of the 16th KSM. These units had just made a forced march of thirty-five miles from Paola. Probably because of their jaded condition, Moonlight left them behind in Mound City as something of a last-ditch guard. He then marched with his brigade and the other local militia about three-quarters of a mile from the city courthouse and ensconced his men atop and around Sugar Mound. Among the militiamen was an Irish immigrant, Edward Richards, who, upon hearing some scattered rifle fire to the front, thought the Battle of Mound City had begun. It was 8:30 AM. But as Richards and his fellow townsmen waited for the attack, none ever came. Looking over the crest of the hill, they could plainly see the heads of the Confederates "within easy range." Unbeknownst to the defenders of Mound City, these Confederates were a hodgepodge of stragglers and foragers. To Edward Richards's great surprise, the enemy did not fire and, instead, simply disappeared. For all the panic and their trouble, the militia suffered two skirmishers wounded and one dog killed. Richards's dog, Pluto, seems to have been killed, though, by friendly fire. [23]

In the aftermath of the alarum around Mound City, controversy erupted when James Blunt authorized Moonlight to inscribe battle honors on the flags of the 2nd Brigade. Some wondered if any combat had actually occurred near Mound City. Blunt's honors were thus seen as merely an act of political favoritism typical of Blunt and his patron James Lane. The bare-knuckle nature of Kansas politics had long pitted Moonlight and Blunt as enemies of local hero J. D. Snoddy and his newspaper, the *Border Sentinel*. It was therefore no surprise that the editor of the *Border Sentinel* eventually concluded: "The only battle Moonlight ever fought here was the paper fight he had with us." The paper went on to note that the only real fighting around Mound City happened much later on the 25th when a group of Confederate stragglers attempted to raid a town they thought unprotected. With Moonlight's troops, in fact long gone, Greer's militia rose to the occasion and ambushed the stragglers two miles outside of town. At the cost of one man wounded, the militia succeeded in taking at least twelve prisoners. Moonlight's own recollections of the day's events are fuzzy in their detail, but they do conclude with the confident assertion that he appeared "just in time to save the place."[24]

Although Moonlight and his brigade may well not have fired too many hostile shots near Mound City, there is a measure of truth in the belief that he saved the place. On the night of the 24th and 25th, Sterling Price contemplated moving toward Mound City. However, John Marmaduke, who at that point was posted in Price's advance, reported the skirmishing that took place with various Mound City scouts and militia during the evening. More disconcerting, Marmaduke also reported the capture of a dispatch from Captain Greer to one of his scouts detailing the expected arrival of Moonlight's brigade later that evening. Helping complete Price's tactical picture of the Yankee dispositions, several recruits had followed Price for fifteen miles before finally making it into the Confederate camp that night. Claiming they had traveled on the same road as Price, these men somehow reported no Yankee cavalry in the Confederate rear. All of this information led Price to believe Curtis's entire army was traveling parallel to him. He therefore expected battle possibly on his western flank or in front, but certainly not in his rear. It is not evident just what Price thought of Sanborn's skirmishing in and around the mounds later that night. What is certain, however, is that Price chose to ignore it in a situation eerily reminiscent of his decision to ignore the late-night demolition explosion of Fort Davidson just one month earlier. The bottom line was that Price would make no effort to capture Mound City because of the enemy force he believed congregating there. As daylight broke on the 25th, he feared little to his rear and concentrated mostly on driving south.[25]

Chapter Fifteen

I Don't Give No Quarters Nor Will I Ask Anny

By 11 AM on October 25, 1864, nearly ten thousand soldiers gathered in a field just to the north of Mine Creek in Kansas. Within moments, bugles sounded and two small brigades of Union cavalry galloped hard with sabers drawn toward the trapped divisions of John Marmaduke and James Fagan. Thirty minutes later, it would be over. Several hundred men from both sides lay dead or wounded, and over five hundred Confederates, including generals Marmaduke and Cabell, had just become prisoners of war. The Army of Missouri had been badly mauled yet again. Though almost fleeting in duration, the Battle of Mine Creek stands as one of the most decisive cavalry actions of the Civil War. It is also a battle that seemed to have few mysteries after Lumir Buresh wrote *The Battle of Mine Creek* in 1977. However, in the years since Buresh completed his book, several new sources and new research have necessitated revising many things about the battle, including the location of key roads and fords, the placement of units, and the analysis of various decisions on both sides of the battle line. More importantly, the revised narrative needs also to address the possibility that Mine Creek was just as much a deliberate massacre as it was a classic cavalry battle.

The Confederate move to Mine Creek began shortly after midnight when troops on the north bank of the Marais des Cygnes began clearing camp. Shelby's division led the way and guarded the trains as they moved south on the Old Military Road. Jackman's brigade had the advance, while Thompson's Iron Brigade rode on the western flank of the trains near the front with Tyler's brigade of unarmed recruits following it. Thompson's and Tyler's dispositions reflected Price's concern of an attack from the western quarter. Marmaduke's division, set to become the army's rearguard, divided itself, with Freeman's brigade remaining at the ford and Clark's brigade following the trains. To Trooper Henry C. Luttrell of Clark's brigade, the progress of the trains was "fitful and spasmodic," which left Luttrell sitting stationary in his saddle for one hour in the rain waiting for the trains to begin leaving the camp. By 5 AM and the first rays of daylight, a thick fog covered the land, and Cabell had finally cleared the north side of the river and marched through Clark's brigade on the path south. It had been a close-run affair as Cabell's men made it to the far bank of the river just before the 2nd Colorado and the 2nd Arkansas reached the ford. [1]

As the Confederate army rolled south, John Sanborn retained control of the lead elements of Pleasonton's pursuit. He therefore kept the 2nd Colorado and the 2nd Arkansas at the ford clearing the felled trees. The Unionists were not completely alone as Thomas Freeman had not yet given up the area. Some of his men still lurked on the wooded banks of the river north of the ford. To remove these skirmishers, Sanborn directed the 7th Provisional Enrolled Missouri Militia to cross the river about four hundred yards to the north of the ford. The militia then swept south back to the ford at about the same time the 2nd Arkansas was able to splash across the river unimpeded. With the ford secured, Sanborn formed his brigade in a heavy column with the 6th and 7th provisional militias deployed as skirmishers followed by the 2nd Arkansas, the 2nd Colorado, the 6th MSM, and 8th MSM. No sooner had the brigade left the belt of timber bordering the river than it spied Confederates forming in a defensive line about one mile to the southwest of the ford. At first, Colonel John Phelps of the 2nd Arkansas thought these troops might be friendly. Colonel Charles Blair, brigade commander in Blunt's division and now volunteer aide to Curtis, thought otherwise, and so persuaded Phelps. These Confederates belonged to Clark's brigade. Union pressure at the ford prompted Marmaduke to countermarch Clark's brigade to the rear. Clark then formed his troops in two belts. The first consisted of the 7th, 8th, 10th, and 14th Missouri cavalries. Clark arrayed them across the Old Military Road with Henry Hynson's three pieces of artillery (two 12-pound Napoleons and one 6-pound smoothbore) posted in support to the right near to a cabin. About one mile further along the road as it headed southwest, Clark placed Colton Greene's 3rd Missouri and John Q. Burbridge's 4th Missouri. If measured strictly by the number of regimental and company flags present in these lines, Clark's force was imposing. But the reality was that many soldiers were not present for duty. Commanding officers in some units had sent out at least half of their men to forage the previous night. Many of these soldiers had yet to return.[2]

Regardless of the actual number of Confederates in the ranks, the appearance of the Confederates in battle formation gave John Sanborn considerable pause. Not knowing quite what to do, he wanted further orders and reinforcements from Pleasonton. For unknown reasons, Sanborn chose not to send staff officers or couriers and instead went himself. Making matters potentially worse, the general abdicated responsibility for the actions of his brigade by ordering Phelps "not to attack by charge (unless he was certain that he could break it [the Confederate line] and capture the artillery) until reinforcements came up." Sanborn promptly wheeled his horse about and rode one-half mile back to the ford where he found Pleasonton trying to funnel, in order, the 1st and 4th Brigades of his division across the river. Pleasonton quickly ordered Sanborn to return and continue the attack against the Confederate line. While Sanborn was thus engaged in the search for tactical wisdom, Colonel Phelps attacked with the urging of Curtis's aides Samuel Crawford and Robert Hunt. The 2nd Arkansas, which mustered no more than two hundred soldiers, advanced with Kingsbury's battalion of the 2nd Colorado to the right, and the 8th and 6th MSMs, dismounted, to the left. The Union tide swept the Confederate skirmishers back to their line, but the attack soon stalled. After the action, there was no shortage of finger pointing to explain why the attack failed as the different regimental and staff officers all blamed each other. However, it mattered little. Thurber's section of 3-inch artillery arrived, and the Union line advanced again. This time, Clark withdrew before any close combat occurred, although Hynson inexplicably abandoned his 6-pound field piece on the Confederate left.[3]

Now about 10 AM, Clark's first line continued through Greene's and Burbridge's regiments and rode southwest, following Fagan. Hynson's two Napoleons remained behind with Greene and Burbridge. For the Union, John Sanborn found confidence in numbers. Philips's 1st Brigade and Benteen's 4th had come up, first at a trot and then a gallop. They subsequently deployed in a line facing southwest with Philips to the far right, Benteen in the center, and Sanborn to the left. This impressive display of cavalry then shoved off toward the Confederate line. Once again artillery popped on both sides, but the Confederates would still have nothing to do with close-quarters action. The Federals got no closer than eight hundred yards when Greene and Burbridge retreated further down the Old Military Road. It was about this time that John Marmaduke realized his division could not hold back the Union advance by itself. He dispatched a staff officer to William Cabell, requesting help.[4]

Marmaduke's retreat took him another mile to a three-pronged road junction. There, the Old Military Road (sometimes called the Wire Road) veered southeast several miles to the hamlet of Potosi, Kansas, before turning south toward Fort Scott. An undetermined number of men from Price's headquarters, probably including Price himself, actually stopped at Potosi for the night of the 24th and 25th. The second road at the junction headed southwest to Mound City. At Mound City it linked with the 1859 Fort Leavenworth to Fort Scott Road. Thomas Moonlight had ridden to Mound City on this road and would continue his journey on it to Fort Scott. The middle road of the junction represented the most direct route to Fort Scott, and predictably, was best known as the Fort Scott Road. All three paths joined together several miles north of Fort Scott, just inside the Kansas border. Because Sterling Price still desired to capture Fort Scott, he chose the Fort Scott Road; it gave him the most direct line to his objective, although the road brought him closer to the attack he expected on his western flank. Unfortunately for Price, the road also descended to what had become a significant obstacle for an army with a lot of wagons and ambulances, Mine Creek.[5]

If measured entirely by the progress of its advance elements, the Army of Missouri had made relatively good time on the morning of the 25th. By 11 AM, Shelby's division and the lead wagons of the trains had marched nineteen miles south to the banks of the Little Osage River. At that moment in time, Price grew optimistic and increasingly desirous of attacking Fort Scott; he therefore prepared to march on the isolated outpost he believed defended by only "1,000 negroes under arms." The only problem was that the Confederate trains had become exceedingly spread out for most of the eight miles between Mine Creek and the Little Osage. Mine Creek had proven a bottleneck as the trains approached its heavily wooded banks on the Fort Scott Road. Under more dry conditions this might not have been an issue, but on October 25, Mine Creek was swollen with rainwater rushing toward the Marais des Cygnes twelve miles distant. Much as the Old Military Road had divided into a number of different roads three miles south of Trading Post, so, too, did the Fort Scott Road less than one-quarter of a mile from the creek. At that point, the road forked into three separate branches. Each road then ran down the gently sloping terrain to the creek where they crossed at fords separated by no more than one-quarter mile. To the dismay of the

Confederate wagon masters, the two flanking roads tended to be passable only in dry weather. Only the rock-bottomed center, or main, ford would work. Nevertheless, this ford was hardly perfect. The banks at the ford were twelve to fifteen feet in height. Even more challenging, the ford did not provide straight passage across the creek. Instead, once travelers entered the creek from the north, they had to turn left and proceed in the creek bed itself about twenty-five yards before turning right and exiting up a steep bank. Making matters still worse, the condition of the ford deteriorated throughout the morning as thousands of worn-out livestock and hundreds of overburdened wagons, caissons, and ambulances sloshed up and down its muddy banks, making the passage slower by the minute. A more perfect bottleneck could not be imagined. The end result of crossing the trains at the main ford was that by 11 AM, nearly a dozen wagons waited to pass on the northern side of the creek. Even more telling, the bulk of Fagan's division had yet to cross. Only Thomas McCray's brigade had made it to the southern bank. The rest of the division was clustered within a few hundred yards of the ford.[6]

Throughout the daylight hours, Clark's brigade had steadily retreated at a trot toward Mine Creek. All the while, Clark had no idea the army had stalled. He was therefore more than surprised when he came within a mile of the creek and gazed south. The men in the ranks were equally as stunned. Henry Luttrell marveled at the "mob of our baggage wagons jammed up at the fords of the creek." The teamsters and troops could sense that Curtis's army was closing the gap. Just south of the crossing, Barbara Jane Palmer witnessed a steady worsening in the Confederate ranks as they fled. After "marching in some order" early in the morning, "they seemed to be in more and worse confusion, and traveling faster, until as the last wagon train passed they were in a great confusion and going at a dead run." Perhaps the only solace for Clark at this time was the presence of Fagan's division on the north side. Marmaduke's earlier request for help had prompted Cabell to turn his brigade around at the ford and deploy it to the west, or left, of the Fort Scott Road. With Union cavalry separated from Clark's rearguard by no more than five hundred yards, Clark hurriedly found and met both Fagan and Marmaduke. The brief consultation found all in agreement. A stand must be made at the creek. There was simply no time left and no place else to go. Even if they could abandon the remaining wagons on the north side of the creek, they would be unable to get the roughly six thousand men of both divisions across the wooded banks with any semblance of order. Besides, as Marmaduke later recalled, he "preferred to fight."[7]

The decision made, Confederate commanders set about placing their troops in three separate lines. Marmaduke occupied the far right of the battlefield. Burbridge's 4th Missouri anchored the right flank at a ravine that ran several hundred yards southeast before emptying into Mine Creek. The rest of the brigade filled in between the 4th Missouri and the Fort Scott Road. Although the evidence is fragmentary, it appears that Robert Wood's battalion marked the left flank of Clark's main line, which was then joined run-

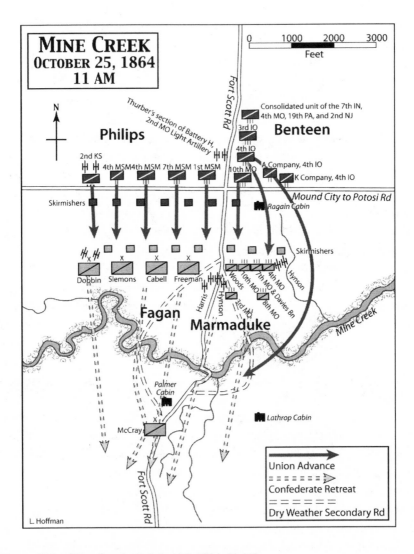

Figure 15.1. Mine Creek, October 25, 1864, 11 AM

ning west to east by Robert Lawther's 10th Missouri and a consolidated unit
of the 7th Missouri and J. F. Davies's battalion. With Solomon Kitchen
wounded at Westport, Davies now led the 7th. Greene's 3rd Missouri stood
in reserve to the left rear of the formation about eighty yards behind the
center, or main, line with Jeffers's 8th Missouri just to his right. Another line
of skirmishers stood about twenty yards in advance of the main line. Who
commanded these troops cannot be proven definitively. To the left of the Fort
Scott Road in the center line was Thomas Freeman's brigade. Elements of
Cabell's brigade overlapped Freeman to his left front and left rear. Joined to
Cabell's left was William Slemons's brigade. Arch Dobbin completed the
line.[8]

Eight pieces of artillery augmented the Confederate formation. On the far
right, near to the ravine, were Hynson's remaining two 12-pound Napoleons.
Astride the Fort Scott Road in the center of the Confederate line and just to
the left and front of the 3rd Missouri, Marmaduke placed four cannons (two
6-pounders from Harris's battery, another 6-pounder from Hynson's battery,
and probably one 3.8-inch James Rifle from Harris). Two pieces of artillery
(one 1.5-inch breechloader and one 2-pound Woodruff) supported the left of
the line in the middle of Dobbin's brigade. The entire Confederate line thus
ran for about eight hundred yards with much of that distance fronting a
pocket formed by Mine Creek. Only Dobbin's and Slemons's brigades extended the line beyond the pocket.[9]

As Marmaduke and Fagan hurried to organize their units, the Union pursuit came over the slight ridge in front of Mine Creek. John Philips's brigade
was the first to appear. Benteen's brigade followed in the distance. Sanborn's
brigade had, by order of Pleasonton, remained several miles to the rear to
feed and rest its horses. Philips had pushed Bazel Lazear's 1st MSM to the
front with the remaining regiments following in three separate columns. Lazear aggressively chased Marmaduke and was well ahead of the remainder of
his brigade. Lazear therefore halted about six hundred yards from the Confederates and deployed into a line with its left flank on the Fort Scott Road.
He ordered his skirmishers forward and waited anxiously for the rest of the
brigade to arrive. Twenty minutes later, Philips galloped onto the scene, and
he began funneling his regiments into the line. T. T. Crittenden's 7th MSM
pulled up on Lazear's right, and George Kelley's 4th MSM formed to the
right of Crittenden. Now supported, Lazear ordered his skirmishers to open
fire on the enemy pickets, which provoked Dobbin's artillery to the right of
the Union line to commence firing. Philips was none too satisfied with this

situation. His brigade was alone on the field, facing two divisions of Confederate cavalry supported by eight pieces of artillery. As of yet, he had no artillery of his own. More disturbing, Fagan's line easily overlapped his three-regiment front. Philips responded "by opening files and swinging off one squadron [of the 4th MSM] some sixty yards" to extend his front. Philips also pushed a small detachment of the 2nd Kansas (about 150 men who had joined the brigade at Trading Post) and its two howitzers to the far west of the line. All told, Philips's line stretched for more than one-half mile and held about 1,500 men. During all of this maneuvering, Philips dispatched an aide to Pleasonton, requesting help. [10]

Philips did not have to wait long. Benteen's troops galloped toward Mine Creek in a stacked column of about 1,200 men. The 10th Missouri led the way and were followed, in order, by the 4th Iowa, 3rd Iowa, and a consolidated unit consisting of detachments from the 7th Indiana, the 4th Missouri, the 19th Pennsylvania, and the 2nd New Jersey. Riding hard among the ranks of the 7th Indiana was Captain John Moore, an officer detailed to command a part of Pleasonton's trains. Sensing battle ahead, Moore abandoned his command to a sergeant and rode with his comrades in the 7th Indiana. As Moore and the rest of the brigade drove south, Benteen deployed skirmishers, and they reported the Confederate lines forming in front of Mine Creek. Almost simultaneously, one of Samuel Curtis's seemingly omnipresent staff officers, Major Henry Hunt, galloped up to Benteen and provided greater detail on the Confederate dispositions and the fact there was an unknown Union brigade already in position. Somehow, Benteen did not know it was Philips who had the divisional advance. Benteen's brigade rode the remaining few hundred yards and formed to the left of Philips and a short distance from the Fort Scott Road. The Confederate line, situated as it was at the bottom of the gently sloping prairie, now came into Benteen's view. Benteen wasted little time. With the brigade still in its marching columns, Benteen ordered all of his regiments "left-front into line." Using the first company in a regiment as a base, each of the remaining companies formed to the left of the base and thus created a regimental front of about four hundred yards in length. Perhaps the only problem with the disposition was that the order left a considerable gap between Philips's and Benteen's brigades. [11]

Whatever problems there were with these evolutions, what unfolded was among the most sublime spectacles of the war. Almost 2,700 massed Union cavalry on an open prairie were about to make a charge. It was a sight that John Philips would never forget. "The sun was just coming above the fog of the river bottom and spreading its golden light over the plain. It gleamed on thousands of guns and sabers being drawn for carnage." Within the Yankee ranks, Corporal Socrates Walmsley of the 2nd New Jersey tried gamely to reassure his nervous comrades by reminding them to "keep a slow gallop and snap-shoot on the rise. Hug tight with your knees! The Lord be with you." Walmsley and his men did not have long to think about the situation. Bugles sounded quickly, and the men of Benteen's 4th Brigade raised a loud yell and rumbled toward Marmaduke's line. Just prior to the charge, Benteen dispatched a courier to Philips imploring him "to charge with me, for God's sake." Benteen's sudden attack caught Philips off guard, and the courier surely did not arrive before Benteen's cavalry surged forward. All of this produced a momentary delay in Philips's charge. Consumed with the business of leading his own attack, Benteen saw the initial delay but not the subsequent movement of the other brigade, which later fanned a war of words between Benteen and Philips over credit and glory at Mine Creek. Nevertheless, in a matter of moments, both brigades thundered toward the enemy. It was a cavalry charge that stirred the chivalrous soul of many a Union cavalryman. To William Lyman, "it was a splendid sight." For Bazel Lazear, he recollected to his wife that "it is worth a lifetime to see and live through such a fight." A trooper in the 10th Missouri (United States) concluded, "it was a pretty sitee to see all the cavalree dash along the prary[.]"[12]

James Fagan and John Marmaduke probably did not share these reveries. Indeed, Fagan may not have even been on the northern side of the creek by this point. There is no evidence to prove he participated in the looming action. Regardless, some of Fagan's and Marmaduke's regiments were fully formed in line, while others still shifted positions. When issuing their original orders, Fagan and Marmaduke had agreed to keep the men mounted. There just was not enough time to move the regiments into position, dismount, and then displace the horses and horse holders to the rear. Notwithstanding the logic of the plan, a number of men in at least one regiment, Lawther's 10th Missouri, dismounted anyway. Not only did they dismount, but they assumed a seated firing position with their rifles resting on a knee. Company G of the 10th Missouri was filled with new recruits. According to Henry Luttrell, there were probably no more than "a dozen of the old veteran boys" on the line, and they were all clumped at the center of the company. With the Federal cavalry now charging in their direction, Captain Thomas B. Murray rode up and down the ranks of his company, encouraging the new men to "Keep cool, boys, and aim low—remember that the eyes of a veteran regiment are upon you."[13]

Murray's efforts, and no doubt those of many other junior officers, seemed to bear immediate dividends. The forward momentum of Benteen's charge lasted all of about 150 yards, or roughly half the distance it needed to cover before reaching the Confederate line. As soon as the Unionists started to charge they received incoming rounds, including canister from Hynson's and Harris's artillery. Captain Richard Hinton described the scene in his usual vivid way: "The rattle of musketry, mingled with the roar of artillery, the shouts of the soldiers, the scream of the shells, the crash of small arms, the hissing sound of canister, and the cries of the wounded as they fell about us, filled the air." For Socrates Walmsley, it was almost too much. Screams came "from below and around us, as we saw limbs blown away, with sounds of great pain, extreme fear, or even hope for death. Yes, the screams sounded like they were coming from the very gates of hell." As the Unionists toppled, the Confederates saw horses bolting "rider-less across the prairie." John Philips believed the "the rattle of small arms fire was fiercer than the thunders of heaven." In the 10th Missouri, one of the old veterans, trooper John McKenney, kept count of his hits and shouted out that he had "dropped two of the enemy's color bearers." McKenney's boast was an exaggeration, but Confederate resistance stopped Benteen's lead regiment, the 10th Missouri (United States), abruptly in its tracks. When the remainder of the brigade piled into the back of the regiment, the attack suddenly ground to a halt. Making matters worse, Philips's brigade stopped as well. Thinking Benteen was about to withdraw from the battlefield, Bazel Lazear halted and dismounted his 1st MSM, which then also stopped the regiments adjacent to his right. What had started as a sublime spectacle now began to look like an awful disaster, especially as Confederate artillery on both flanks began to throw canisters into the stationary Unionists. In the midst of the growing cacophony of Confederate small-arms fire and artillery, the commander of the 10th Missouri (United States), Major W. H. Lusk, and Benteen tried to urge the Missourians onward. Within minutes Benteen rode to the front of the regiment and waved his hat, beckoning the men to move. Buglers continued to sound the charge, and while some horsemen staggered forward, the massed line would simply not budge.[14]

In the middle of this confusion at the head the brigade, Union forces found a savior. Major Abial Pierce, commander of the 4th Iowa, quickly saw a way to keep the attack moving. The 4th Iowa was second in the brigade formation, and Pierce rode on the extreme right flank of the regiment. From this position, Pierce moved to the left flank and then ordered his regiment to follow him to the left, or east, bypassing the stalled 10th Missouri. Within minutes, the well-disciplined Iowans executed the maneuver. Companies A and K swung around the 10th Missouri, while the other companies somehow managed to pass directly through the tangled Missourians in columns of four. Once in the clear, the Iowans resumed the charge toward the Confederate line. The 4th Iowa's maneuver suddenly freed the 10th Missouri from its paralysis. Lusk's Missourians renewed their charge, followed, in order, by the 3rd Iowa and the consolidated unit led by Major Samuel Simonson. The forward movement was contagious. Bazel Lazear, although he could not discern all that had happened with Benteen's brigade, readily understood they were moving again. He had been stalled for ten to fifteen minutes but was now ready to go. No doubt providing Lazear some measure of psychological reassurance was Charles Thurber's newly arrived section of Missouri Light Artillery. Positioned just to Lazear's rear, Thurber's rifles opened on the Confederate right. Thus emboldened, Lazear remounted the 1st MSM, which naturally got the rest of Philips's brigade back in the saddle. In such a fashion, the 1st Brigade pressed home its attack on the western side of the Fort Scott Road.[15]

A pivotal moment in the battle had just passed. Strangely enough, the Union benefited from the momentary disarray within Benteen's 4th Brigade. When Pierce's 4th Iowa sidestepped to the left, it altered the main thrust of Benteen's attack from the center of Marmaduke's division to its right and into John Burbridge's 4th Missouri. Even more fortuitously, Companies A and K of the 4th Iowa found themselves veering across the wooded ravine, which provided some concealment from the Confederates on the right and thus allowed elements of these companies to get behind Burbridge's flank entirely. However, other portions of Companies A and K were the first to slam directly into Burbridge's regiment. The other companies hit Clark's brigade in sequence from the Confederate right to left. Moments later, the rest of Benteen's brigade swept into and through the Confederate formations. Charging at a gallop, the Unionists were able to cover the three hundred yards to Clark's brigade in no more than one minute's time. The ability of the Union to cover that ground at such a pace exploited one of the great weaknesses of Price's army, its weaponry. With single-shot muzzle loaders proliferating throughout the ranks, Clark's troopers would, at best, have been able to get off four rounds from the moment Pierce spurred the attack forward to the time it crashed into the Confederate line. Perhaps most galling for the Confederates was the simple fact that even had they possessed repeating rifles it would have probably made no difference. Far too many Confederates had already exhausted their ammunition. Just as Pierce's attack crumpled the right flank and Robert Wood's battalion began to fall back on the brigade's left, Lawther's 10th Missouri (CSA) could barely resist as their ammunition "dwindled down to a mere nothing." Nevertheless, the officers still exhorted the men to stand their ground, with some offering promises that a reserve was marching to their aid.[16]

As the Union brigades collided with the Confederate lines, close combat ensued. Although it "surpassed anything" Benteen had ever seen, the combat was anything but even. Confederates up and down the line had brought long rifles to a fight better suited to sabers, pistols, and short-barreled carbines. As the Unionists slashed and stabbed with sabers, near helpless Confederates could only parry the blows with their rifles. Abial Pierce of the 3rd Iowa, alone, claimed he cut down eight of the enemy with his saber. With the exception of the troops in Lazear's 1st MSM, the Unionists brought a host of weapons to the battle that were more suited to mounted close combat. Pistols, Henry repeaters, Colt revolving rifles, and Spencer, Gibbs, Hall, Smith, and Sharps carbines all further tilted the balance of the melee in favor of the Unionists.[17]

The result was not surprising. In Clark's brigade, Burbridge's 4th Missouri quickly disintegrated. To its left, both Davies's consolidated command and Lawther's 10th Missouri held their ground briefly, while Robert Wood's battalion began falling back along the Fort Scott Road. The real trouble for the Confederates was, however, west of the Fort Scott Road. Thomas Freeman's brigade in the center of the line seemed to collapse even before John Philip's Yankee brigade made contact. As Freeman's men fled south toward the wooded banks of Mine Creek, Fagan's division unraveled. John C. Wright, on the far left of the line, had begun to make his own preemptive charge when he noticed the chaos to his right. Wright did not hesitate to change the plan. "Facing the regiment about, I moved rapidly to the rear and in a few minutes was in the midst of a disorganized mass of fleeing men pursued by and mixed up with the Federal cavalry." The situation was only marginally better on the eastern side of the Fort Scott Road. Lawther's 10th Missouri became entangled with Jeffers's 8th Missouri, which led to further confusion when Lawther ordered an advance while Jeffers ordered a retreat. The result was that only one of Lawther's companies advanced; the rest retreated with Jeffers. That one company was soon surrounded, leaving the individual troopers to try to shoot their way out and back to the creek. By this point, all that was left standing for the Confederates was Colton Greene's 3rd Missouri. Originally positioned in the rear just to the east of the Fort Scott Road, Greene saw the Confederates on his right front give way. Within moments, Greene also witnessed the destruction of his eight rightmost companies as they joined the headlong dash for Mine Creek. Only B Company remained. Greene then pivoted that company to the right in order to shoot at the exposed flanks of Benteen's cavalry, which then rampaged toward the creek. The effort was only successful in buying some time to get two of Harris's three artillery pieces stationed along the road limbered and moving toward the rear. Once those pieces began to move, Greene realized "the impossibility of staying the panic-stricken mob" and ordered the remnants of B Company to escape as best as they could. Harris's third field piece was abandoned, much like Henry Hynson's nearby 6-pounder. Too many horses and too many gunners had been killed.[18]

Chaos had enveloped the battlefield as some Union cavalry raced for Mine Creek to cut off further Confederate retreat, while still other Yankees sought to eliminate groups of Confederates who refused to surrender or flee. Among those who did not join the dash for the creek was John Marmaduke. He tried desperately to stop the retreat, but he only managed to find himself isolated on the battlefield. In an instant, Marmaduke came under fire from the rear. Private James Dunlavy of the 3rd Iowa, who had been wounded in the arm and fell behind the rest of his company as it sped to the creek, had been heading for the rear, or north, when he spotted several dismounted and running Confederates. Dunlavy used his Spencer carbine to squeeze off several rounds, all of which Marmaduke witnessed. With Dunlavy clad in blue and so many Confederates wearing confiscated Union blue, the badly near-sighted Marmaduke readily believed Dunlavy a Confederate and rode hard for the Iowan in order to berate him. Dunlavy realized the mistaken identity and allowed Marmaduke to approach within thirty feet. He then leveled his carbine at Marmaduke's chest and demanded the general's surrender. Stunned, Marmaduke offered no resistance. He simply handed Dunlavy his revolver, announced his identity, and asked to be taken to General Pleasonton.[19]

Marmaduke was not the only Confederate officer to suffer misfortune from mistaken identity. After his own regiment collapsed, Colonel William Jeffers tried to save Harris's battery, which had already been captured by the

Yankees. A fellow soldier, Buck McManus, described what happened next when Jeffers pulled up to the blue-clad soldiers at the guns. "He waved his sword and ordered them to go away or they would be captured in five minutes." McManus had tried in vain to warn Jeffers of the true identity of the soldiers, but "he either did not understand me or thought I was mistaken, for he went on. As he stopped his horse, one [Yankee] grabbed his sword, one his bridle, and some his legs. He then saw his mistake. He looked back at me and said, 'Oh, hell!'"[20]

There was still more misfortune for high-ranking Confederates. William Slemons had made it across Mine Creek only to have a change of heart when he saw his artillery battery axle deep in the mud at a ford. Slemons rode back to the ford where the Unionists shot his horse. The falling animal pinned Slemons underneath, which made him an easy capture. William Cabell suffered a similar fate. Throughout the brief battle, he had stood firm as his brigade evaporated. With only thirty men of Anderson Gordon's regiment standing around him, Cabell ordered a color bearer to wave the battle flag one last time and his men to then charge south through the Unionists and scatter across the creek as best they could. Cabell mounted his horse and rode hard for the creek only to have the animal stumble in jumping to the opposite bank. The horse rolled over Cabell, and he found himself at the gunpoint of several men in the 7th MSM. Thus started a mini odyssey in which Cabell escaped, was captured, escaped again, and was collared for the final time within what could have only been twenty minutes. Only when Cabell realized that his captors were from the 3rd Iowa and Alfred Pleasonton's command did he reveal his identity and ask to be taken to Pleasonton.[21]

Marmaduke and Cabell were among the fortunate. As Price's men attempted to surrender by the hundreds, many Yankees were in no mood to take prisoners. Major Samuel S. Curtis, the son of General Curtis and a staff officer who rode hard to join the battle, gave testament to just how much the surrendering Confederates feared for their lives. Desperate Confederates beseeched him—as an officer—to not let the Kansans kill them. Colonel John C. Wright was one Confederate who very much planned on surrendering when he first bolted for the rear and saw hordes of Federals blocking his escape. He changed his mind quickly after watching "men shot down while holding up their hands in token of surrender." John Philips tried hard to justify the killing of prisoners in his official report by claiming only those Confederates caught wearing Union blue were summarily executed in accordance with the policies of the Department of the Missouri. However, one trooper in the 10th Missouri (United States) expressed the situation in a much more cold-blooded fashion. "I my salf haf takin but 1 privet after I had no means of cilling him[.] I had shoot him the back with the last load and faild cilling him[.] I had the sattisfaction to try my carbine on an Reb [. . .] I don't give no quarters nor will I ask anny if I should ever happen to git in a foul place[.]"[22]

Among those Confederates who had made it safely across the creek was Wright. The colonel's flight had been ignominious, and he showed no great willingness to stop running. He witnessed others try to rally troops, but to no avail. Finally, at about one-half mile from the creek, he pulled up beside a trooper with a flag. Wright persuaded the color bearer to slow his gallop, which then helped start a line of cavalrymen who, though still retreating, were in a military formation. Wright and countless other officers, probably including James Fagan, now had the remnants of a line that they shortly turned about and faced Benteen's and Philips's brigades. The line was just to the south of a tree-lined, spring-fed creek that crossed the Fort Scott Road. In writing about this action, Lumir Buresh concluded that Confederate resistance first coalesced around Colonel Charles Tyler's brigade of unarmed volunteers and conscripts about three hundred yards south of Mine Creek. Unfortunately, Buresh confuses Tyler's appearance south of Mine Creek with Tyler's future rearguard performance below the Little Osage River, six miles south of Mine Creek. Tyler operated near the head of the trains (which were then south of the Little Osage) under Jo Shelby's command and had not the time to double back, and drive past, Jeff Thompson's well-armed brigade of veterans. It is, however, distinctly possible that the Confederate rallies were based in stands by Thomas McCray's brigade of Fagan's division. There is little evidence to place McCray north of the creek during the battle, and the casualties he suffered on this day (an estimated twenty-nine killed, wounded, and captured) were more indicative of participation in a rearguard effort than fighting near the main line of battle.[23]

The rearguard, such as it was, did not come under immediate attack. Although large numbers of Philips's and Benteen's brigades had made it across the creek, hundreds of troopers remained either on the north side of the creek or among its wooded banks, flushing out countless Confederates who sought cover in the trees. Philips's efforts to gain control of his brigade were further hampered by a wound to his right eye. He was in great pain from what were probably bits of an exploded percussion cap. Regardless, Philips and Benteen eventually managed to get the bulk of their brigades across as cohesive units. They then charged, mostly dismounted, and drove the rallying Confederates from the spring-fed creek. Once shoved back, the Confederates retreated another one mile to a set of mounds that straddled the Fort Scott Road. The mounds rose about two hundred feet above the prairie and were largely devoid of trees. Fagan, or some other officers, concentrated those men who would rally upon the westernmost mound. It was at this time that Alfred Pleasonton reappeared on the battlefield. Tactical control of the battle had largely slipped his hands since his division crossed the Marias des Cygnes earlier in the morning, but now he had forded Mine Creek and pushed the Unionists forward as far as the McAuley house, a few hundred yards short of the mounds and to the east of the Fort Scott Road. Here, Benteen's and Philips's advance stalled for a moment as it awaited reinforcement from John Sanborn's brigade, which had finally joined the battle. In short order, though, Sanborn's men appeared on the Fort Scott Road, and they were accompanied by the sound of Yankee artillery, which began to shell the mound. Almost simultaneously, Philips and Benteen made their ascent up the mound. However, and in predictable fashion, the Confederates had little stomach for continued resistance. By the time the attackers made it halfway up the hill, the defenders scattered down the other side headed further south.[24]

The Battle of Mine Creek had ended. It was a frightful defeat for the Confederacy. Two of Sterling Price's divisions had been shattered with at least 1,280 killed, wounded, and captured. The cost for the Union was no more than eighty total casualties. The numbers are striking and indicative of one of the more lopsided battles of the Civil War. Even more striking is an anomaly within the Confederate figures. In a war where the number of wounded was usually eight times greater than those killed in action, Mine Creek produced no less than three hundred Confederates killed and 250 wounded. More in keeping with the statistical norms of the war were the Union figures of eight killed and seventy-two wounded. The action was far too brief and the impact of Yankee artillery relatively minor to account for the large number of Confederates killed. Even the close nature of the combat and thus the enhanced accuracy of the weaponry cannot account for the numbers. Other mounted cavalry melees during the war simply did not produce more killed than wounded. Brandy Station, for example, saw sixty-nine Yankees killed with 352 wounded. Trevilian Station, though less of a direct-mounted melee, concluded with ninety-five Yankees killed and 445 wounded. A breakdown of Confederate killed and wounded is not possible for these engagements, but the point remains that close-quarters, mounted action was not synonymous with a high kill rate. The only real explanation for the high number of Confederates killed at Mine Creek is that the vast majority were killed while trying to surrender. There is no possible way to know the exact numbers who were thus killed, but it is safe to say that Mine Creek ended more as a massacre and less than a battle. It was a massacre and orgy of blood that compares only to the more infamous, and racially tinged, massacres at Marks Mill, Poison Springs, and Fort Pillow in the annals of the Civil War.[25]

Chapter Sixteen

We All Experienced Tribulation This Day

By 11:30 on the morning of October 25, 1864, it had become apparent that disaster had befallen Sterling Price's Army of Missouri. Two shattered divisions gave ample testament to it. But unfortunately for Price, the day was still very young. An even greater potential disaster lurked ahead as the remainder of the Confederate army struggled to avert complete annihilation. Whether that happened would depend upon how well Jo Shelby's division conducted itself and just how much Alfred Pleasonton wanted to finish the job.

The end of combat at Mine Creek meant that all of the loose ends of a battle needed attention. First, there were the prisoners. Despite the fact that the victorious Unionists had gunned down dozens of Confederates in simple cold blood, several hundred managed to escape the massacre and were taken into custody. The most remarkable feature of the collecting of prisoners was that the rival Union commands fell quickly to squabbling over who actually controlled them. Near the battle's conclusion, generals Curtis and Blunt had ridden to the Ragain cabin, about one-half mile north of Mine Creek. Once there, Curtis ordered all prisoners to be placed under the control of his acting provost marshal, Lieutenant Colonel J. J. Sears. General Pleasonton, and his staff, did not like it. Major Henry Suess and another officer rode to the Ragain cabin and issued their claim that the prisoners belonged to Alfred Pleasonton, who wanted to ship them immediately to St. Louis in the Department of the Missouri. The argument became heated even while combat still raged south of Mine Creek. At stake was something more than the prisoners. The unfortunate Confederates were merely the symbols of battlefield glory that Pleasonton did not want to share. Pleasonton would not win the argument. Curtis was the senior officer present, and the prisoners would follow the army in its pursuit of Price toward Fort Scott.[1]

An even more difficult problem than the prisoners was the wounded. They were scattered everywhere. They were in the main combat area north of the creek. They were in the creek bottom itself, and they were littered about the prairie for miles. This was especially the case with wounded Confederates who tried in vain to keep up with their retreating countrymen. According to one Linn County resident, every "few roads we came upon wounded men unable to walk or even crawl, dying of hunger and thirst." Just south of the creek stood the Palmer house where wounded men had fallen all around and then "crawled to fence corners or brush." Union ambulances soon began to arrive and transport the Yankee dead and the wounded of both sides to the Lathrop cabin, which was due east of the Palmer cabin. By the end of the day, the ambulances took the wounded to Mound City where the army turned three buildings into hospitals. When these buildings overflowed, the wounded trickled into many private homes. The army impressed beds and bedding, while also asking for volunteer doctors, female nurses, and medical-related supplies. The strain on the local population was enormous, especially when so many had been either burned out or dispossessed of every scrap of food. On October 27, Captain Samuel W. Greer, who commanded at Mound City, let Leavenworth know just how bad things were when he wrote the *Leavenworth Conservative*: "Your citizens must help us, give us clothing, bedding and food. Call meetings, and collect those articles, and we will have a committee appointed here to receive and distribute. All our women are busy in taking care of the wounded and dying. Help us, help us, in this hour of need."[2]

Remarkably, Greer was right. Many of Linn County's citizens answered the call to serve, which provided even more of a shock when they saw, firsthand, the near primitive nature of mid-nineteenth-century casualty care. Barbara Jane Palmer pronounced the field hospital "a sickening scene." "Men wounded in almost every way imaginable. Some were bearing their pain without murmur, some groaning, some crying, some praying and dying." To the horrified Palmer, at least one surgeon showed little regard for his patient as he probed the chest of a dying man for an elusive bullet. Palmer begged the surgeon to stop, but he persisted right up until the soldier died in agony.[3]

The Union army had a difficult time keeping up with the casualties. Because the army continued its pursuit of Sterling Price, not all medical and commissary staff remained behind to care for the wounded and bury the dead. It would take time, especially to attend to the large numbers of Confederate dead. Magnifying this problem was the simple fact that much of the adult male population was absent in the army, leaving too few hands to dig graves. Five days after the battle, trooper Socrates Walmsley of the 2nd New Jersey passed back over the area, and it was an experience he would never forget. With countless bodies still unburied, Walmsley "could now smell the sour dreadful stench of rotting bodies." Flies hovered so thick that they sounded like hornets. "From the sight and smell," Walmsley noted, "we all experienced tribulation this day. Even our horses were skittish and apprehensive. I heard a couple of brave young men in my squad, gagging and vomit, and I felt the rise of sickness in my own throat. So many wasted in too short a life."[4]

No matter the carnage and its general assault upon the bodily senses, the victorious Union army never totally cleaned up the battlefield. Almost seventy days later, Lyman Bennett, a mapmaker on Samuel Curtis's staff, visited Mine Creek in order to prepare maps to accompany Curtis's official report of the campaign. What Bennett found shocked him. As he poked around the creek, he came upon a dead Confederate "laying [*sic*] beside the trail. The body was frozen[,] and the feature[s] were preserved as fresh as though he just died. Wolves or hogs had eaten some of the flesh from the thighs and body." Bennett then came across four other Confederates, all of whom, he believed, "by their appearance indicated a low ignorant class." Still, he was not unmoved. "I do not approve of their dead bodies laying [*sic*] on our prairies as food for hogs and wild animals. I shall report this to Genl Curtis and ask that they be buried."[5]

While Curtis would have time to deal with Bennett's letter in January 1865, on October 25, 1864, the general was trying to finish off Sterling Price. At the same time Benteen and Philips had attacked the Confederates north of Mine Creek, Curtis and Pleasonton were trying to bring up the remainder of the army to the main line of battle. In this regard, both generals failed. The failure was, in small measure, due to their own inability to control their units. Both Curtis and Pleasonton let their supporting brigades lag far behind the lead elements of the army. Nevertheless, Curtis and Pleasonton were ill served by the subordinate commanders, all of whom displayed no initiative in riding to the proverbial sound of the guns once they echoed through the prairie. John Sanborn rested his brigade three miles south of the Marias des Cygnes for most of the battle before eventually deciding to ride toward the action. John McNeil was even more negligent as he lounged about the northern bank of the Marias des Cygnes while the battle raged. McNeil later claimed to have received orders to remain above the river, but he distinctly heard the action and did nothing until a courier found the brigade commander and ordered him across the river. Perhaps even worse in terms of deliberate negligence was James Blunt. The mercurial division commander appears to have sat out the battle in a petty reaction to Curtis placing Pleasonton's division in the lead. Blunt made no effort to squeeze by, through, or around McNeil's brigade at the Marias des Cygnes.[6]

Around noon and shortly after Benteen and Philips had driven the Confederate rearguard from the mound south of Mine Creek, Curtis's army reconstituted itself for the continued pursuit. It was a remarkable sight. Two brigades formed up in columns of regiments with Philips's one thousand men on the right, facing south, and Sanborn's five hundred men on the left. Major Henry Hopkins led the 150 men of his 2nd Kansas Cavalry in the front as skirmishers. "The formation," noted Richard Hinton, "was perfect, and the level prairie to their front allowed the whole extended line to move unbroken. In the front and centre rode the two Generals, Curtis and Pleasonton, with their respective staffs and escort, forming themselves an attractive feature of the pageant." As the formation approached the Little Osage at a walk, John McNeil's brigade of 1,500 troopers finally joined the procession to the left of Benteen. McNeil soon reported to Pleasonton, and a heated, but brief, conversation ensued. McNeil somehow mollified Pleasonton with his claims that he had received no orders to join the force earlier. Still seething, Pleasonton ordered McNeil to lead the formation in its drive to the Osage.[7]

The march was brisk and the formation imposing. Still, the land they traveled bore witness to almost all of the horrors of total war. The wanton destruction of people and property that had so characterized Price's march on the 23rd and 24th continued without abatement on the 25th. For an army that had little time to escape, Price's troopers and recruits managed to find the time to loot and burn their way south. James Hanway, an elderly Kansas politician, described the scene in a letter to his brother. "It is true that there is not much property to destroy on his route, but now it is desolation." Shelby's adjutant, John Edwards, recalled with a tone of deep satisfaction that "Shelby moved this day with his division in advance, making desolate a broad track through the fertile fields of Kansas, and leaving behind him long trails of fire and smouldering [*sic*] ruins."[8]

As Pleasonton's command traversed a land scorched by Shelby, they finally ran into Sterling Price and Jo Shelby about one mile from the Little Osage. Old Pap had very little warning about the collapse of Fagan and Marmaduke at Mine Creek. Indeed, those two generals had posted a courier to Price at about 10 AM, requesting help. The courier himself barely outraced the rest of the fleeing divisions to the south bank of the Little Osage where Price had paused to rest his trains and plot the proposed attack on Fort Scott with Shelby. Price immediately jettisoned the attack and ordered Shelby to reverse the Iron Brigade and Slayback's battalion for a gallop back to aid Marmaduke and Fagan. Jackman remained with the trains. No sooner had Price issued the order than he, too, rode north. Curiously, Price had no contact with Colonel Charles Tyler, whose brigade of largely unarmed men marched ahead of and to the right of the trains. Tyler, however, witnessed the flood of refugees that came from Marmaduke's and Fagan's divisions. He rightly concluded there had been a disaster to the rear and set about forming a defensive line just south of the Little Osage.[9]

Shelby and Price did not have to go far to see the refugees themselves. Somewhere north of the river and amid a confused swirl of panicked men and horses, Price tried to stop his fleeing troops and query them about what happened. Among the refugees was Colonel John C. Moore, a staff officer and long-time friend of Marmaduke. According to John Edwards, Price questioned Moore in rapid-fire fashion and found out the worst:

"Where's Marmaduke?"

"Killed or captured."

"And the troops?"

"Captured or dispersed."

"The artillery?"

"All gone, General, all gone, sir."

As Price then tried to digest what had happened, all that was left of his army depended upon the actions of Jeff Thompson and the Iron Brigade.[10]

Thompson would be aided somewhat in the coming struggle by the sudden appearance of a small column of about 150 men of the 5th Missouri commanded by Captain A. C. McCoy. Earlier in the morning, McCoy and his band had split off from the main body in order to attack Fort Lincoln, a small outpost situated about three miles west of the action at the Little Osage. McCoy readily captured the fort and its one hundred militiamen. He then burned everything he could not carry back to the main column. This was but the latest indignity inflicted upon Fort Lincoln. Just five days earlier, and before the arrival of the militia, a band of bushwhackers burned several homes at the fort and robbed a store, killing one man in the process. The bushwhackers faced little resistance, and it would not be very different for A. C. McCoy. Thomas Moonlight did, however, offer some Union hope of attacking McCoy. Last seen riding to the protection of Mound City, Moonlight had departed that place along the 1859 Fort Leavenworth to Fort Scott Road (also called the Telegraph Road) and parallel to Price's retreat. Although Moonlight's arrival occurred after McCoy had already taken the fort, he and his 2nd Brigade did little to cover themselves in glory. With almost the entire brigade available, Moonlight merely skirmished with McCoy's 150 men. "After vainly trying to dislodge" McCoy, Moonlight then contented himself to leave a battalion "to engage his attention," while he took the rest of the brigade on a ride to Fort Scott. It was a poor showing. Not only had Moonlight failed to annihilate an enemy he outnumbered by more than six to one, but he had also missed a great opportunity to drive east and slam into an exposed Confederate flank at the Little Osage. It was much the same scenario as had played out at Mine Creek. Moonlight's too literal interpretation of his orders to bar Price from penetrating deep into Kansas had paralyzed his ability to take the initiative and strike the enemy a decisive blow.[11]

Jeff Thompson was largely unaware of what took place at Fort Lincoln with McCoy and Moonlight. He concentrated on setting up a hasty defensive line one mile north of the Little Osage, and he promptly discovered three brigades of Union cavalry arrayed in a linear formation. Sanborn's brigade stayed largely in the middle of the Fort Scott Road with Philips to his west and McNeil to his east. Benteen, who had paused after the dismounted assault on the mound to wait for their horses, remained far to the rear. Thompson's appearance gave pause to the advancing Yankees. It was the first truly organized resistance the Unionists had seen in almost seven miles of pursuit. Thompson even managed to threaten Philips by posting Slayback's cavalry to the far left of the line, thus endangering the Yankee flank. Shortly after making these dispositions, Thompson received orders from Shelby to pull back across the river. Thompson withdrew the regiments of his line from left to right and reestablished his brigade in three lines designated by Shelby, beginning about one-half mile south of the woods of the river. The withdrawal, given the circumstances and the flood of refugees through Thompson's forces, was remarkably easy and quiet. [12]

For about one hour Thompson heard few shots fired. Thompson was nevertheless surprised that Shelby began arraying the lines so far to the rear, which then caused Thompson to try to use his headquarters and staff as a skirmish line at the river's edge. By now it was to no avail. McNeil had passed to the front of the Union formation, joining a skirmisher line consisting of the 2nd Kansas and 2nd Arkansas. Together they easily pushed across the river and its wooded banks, forcing Jeff Thompson and his staff back toward the first line established by Shelby and his staff. One-half mile from the river, the line formed at the edge of a field on the east side of the Fort Scott Road. Benjamin Elliot's and Rector Johnson's regiments manned the line. When McNeil's brigade fully cleared the banks of the river, the Union troopers paused in the face of the organized Confederate line. McNeil then moved decisively by dismounting the 5th MSM and ordering it to tear down a fence that separated the opposing forces. He then shouted a few inspirational words and started the brigade toward Elliot and Johnson. The Confederates had not dismounted, but they delivered one volley from their position before falling back and toward the second line of defense. This line was located several hundred yards further south, but on the west side of the Fort Scott Road. Frank Gordon's 5th Missouri and Moses Smith's 11th Missouri cavalries formed the core of this line, which was augmented by D. A. Williams's newly recruited regiment from Jackman's brigade. As Thompson headed toward the second line, he and countless other men experienced the genuine fear of being fired upon not so much by the enemy but by their comrades. Well before Thompson reached the second line, its troopers unleashed a blast of musketry toward Thompson and his men. Thompson was somehow spared, but making matters still worse, the second line evaporated soon after unleashing its ill-timed volley. [13]

Thompson and his men galloped another several hundred yards south to the third line, which Shelby placed on the edge of a small depression. There, Thompson found William Erwin's 12th Missouri and Alonzo Slayback's battalion. The retreating mass of troopers from the previous two lines hurriedly passed through Slayback's and Erwin's men and showed little disposition to slow or stop. As these men rode south, Thompson saw the ineffectiveness of D. A. Williams as he tried to threaten, insult, and browbeat his men into rallying. Thompson quickly chased the young colonel down and ordered him to get in the lead of the retreating mass so that he could, in a less panicked manner, cajole them into stopping. About one mile south of the third line, Williams succeeded in stopping the horde and turning it to face the enemy. Meanwhile, Thompson had finally orchestrated a significant stand with the men of the third line. They were quality troops placed in a relatively strong position. Helping matters, the Union assault had become frayed by the charges through the previous defensive belts. For at least twenty minutes, there was a halt in the pursuit as Erwin's and Slayback's men exchanged long-range fire with McNeil's reforming brigade. [14]

McNeil eventually sorted things out and got his brigade moving again. Important to the renewal of the attack was the arrival of the remaining Yankee brigades. Sanborn, Philips, and Benteen began to ford the river in large numbers. At this point, Thompson did not want to tempt fate. He tried briefly to contact what appeared to be the remnants of Arch Dobbin's brigade in order to have them form a line to his rear, but that was fruitless. Thompson then signaled yet another retreat before the Unionists even got close to his line. For the next mile, the Confederates galloped until they ran into a vast hodgepodge of cavalry organized into a few lines by Fagan, Clark Jr., and Shelby. Organized units had largely ceased to exist in the stampede across the prairie, but clumps of men began to rally around battle flags and shouts for company and regimental identification. [15]

It was during this part of the flight south that Charles Tyler's brigade made an attempt to buy more time for Price. Largely unarmed, Tyler's brigade of new recruits had been assigned escort duty for the trains since their last foray into combat on October 23rd. On that day they had formed ranks and helped bluff John McNeil, preventing his assault upon the trains as they rolled south on the Harrisonville Road. Now on the 25th, Price called upon Tyler to repeat the performance. However, Tyler would not yet risk his unarmed recruits. He separated the unarmed men and sent them south. He then formed the armed men into ranks and charged the approaching Yankees. In moments, Tyler's lines quickly became a clustered mass of frightened humanity no less than fifty men deep. As described by J. W. Halliburton of Searcy's regiment, Tyler stopped the charge, reformed the men, and proceeded again with "the boys shooting the best they could with the arms they had." The action lasted no more than fifteen minutes before Tyler withdrew.

For all the drama of the episode, Halliburton believed no "Federals were hit from our fire." More importantly, the Yankees took little note of the charge and were more concerned with trying to keep their own ranks together in the near continuous rout of Price's army. Colonel John Phelps of the 2nd Arkansas (United States) in Sanborn's brigade was frank when he remarked that his army was "scattered pell mell over two miles of ground, without order, without commanders, without any point to rally upon but the small squad that had stood the work so well." Still, and despite the relative disorganization among the pursuing Unionists, they were not vulnerable to counterattack from the more disorganized Confederates. Even when Thompson was able to get some of his men to raise a yell and feign a charge, the Yankees were unimpressed and unfazed. As Thompson noted, "The Enemy didn't scare a cuss." A tactical pattern was nevertheless set. For the next several hours the line broke and reformed over and over again, which provided Sterling Price some breathing space to get his headquarters and trains across the next significant obstacle, the Marmaton River. After the war, John Sanborn refused to concede that the Federals had been slowed at all by the rearguard efforts of Price, Shelby, Tyler, and Thompson. The results belie his claim. Price's army was there for the taking, and neither John Sanborn nor three other brigades had been able to finish the job. The Marmaton would, however, provide yet another opportunity. [16]

The Marmaton River stood about eleven miles from the Little Osage, and Price initially headed toward it along the Fort Scott Road. However, several miles into the retreat Price veered off the road to the southeast and toward the Missouri border. For the pursuing Yankees, the route of the enemy was not hard to track. The prairie grass, though generally damp, caught fire from the combined musketry and cannonade. "Everywhere over the bare stretches of prairie," John Edwards wrote, "vast waves of fire skirted the horizon as far as the eye could reach . . . and threw tufts of burning grass and sods upon the tired, worn, and veteran ranks." Union forces, although badly scattered, followed the smoke and fire with McNeil still in the lead. Benteen trailed about two miles behind McNeil with Sanborn and Phillips further yet. Confederate resistance stiffened two miles from the Marmaton. It had to. Predictably, Price's wagon train had gotten bogged down in crossing the river four miles east of Fort Scott and just inside the border. [17] As the Confederates headed toward the river, the land rose in elevation and then dropped into a draw that ran between Shiloh Creek to the east and an unnamed creek slightly more than one mile to the west. The trains would cross at a rocky ford near to the

unnamed creek. From bank to bank, according to Jeff Thompson, the ford
was no less than fifty yards in width with the water itself being no more than
thirty feet wide. At two feet deep, the Marmaton was shallow, but the problem for Price and his wagons was steep banks rather than deep water. The
train crawled to a halt as jaded horses stopped for water and then struggled
mightily to crawl up the slick southern bank. Dozens of wagons thus remained on the northern side of the river as Pleasonton's division approached
near to 3:30 or 4 PM. [18]

The panic that had overcome Price's army subsided at the Marmaton. For
the first time in a very long day, most of the retreating mob had been stopped
and formed into lines, albeit with mostly jumbled units. Before the terrain
started its descent to the Marmaton, Shelby placed Jeff Thompson's brigade
to the left with Slayback's battalion mooring that line near to the creek.
Surviving elements of Marmaduke's and Fagan's divisions filled in to the
right with Dobbin's brigade closest to Thompson. The largest, and most
intact, unit next to Dobbin appears to have been Clark's brigade, whose
command had devolved to Colton Greene. It numbered, at most, four hundred men. In the rear of the main line and behind the stone fence, a reserve
line took form with Jackman's brigade on the left and Charles Tyler's brigade on the right. Still more scattered pieces from Marmaduke's and Fagan's
divisions settled in between Jackman and Tyler. The three remaining guns of

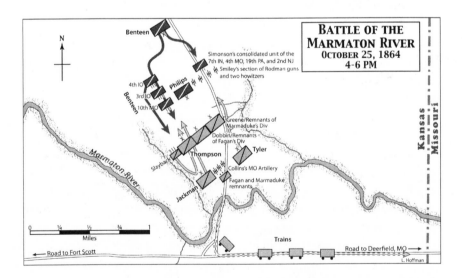

Figure 16.1.   Battle of the Marmaton River, October 25, 1864, 4 to 6 PM

Richard Collins's battery stood near to the center of the line. This was the only artillery left in Price's Army of Missouri.[19]

There is no way to say for sure how many men Price had in these lines at what became known as the Battle of Charlot (Marmaton River), but estimates of nearly eight thousand appear correct.[20] Jo Shelby's delaying action throughout the afternoon had allowed the army this one last opportunity to stand and fight. Given the men available, the Confederates severely outnumbered McNeil's approaching brigade. As McNeil pulled up about eight hundred yards from the Confederates, he readily saw that their line overlapped his own brigade on both flanks. McNeil thus paused and dismounted his brigade, prompting the combatants to exchange long-range small arms fire for at least fifteen minutes. While he waited, McNeil posted Senator James Lane, who had ridden with the advance for much of the afternoon, back to Pleasonton with a plea for reinforcement. Pleasonton responded by returning a staff officer with promises of reinforcement and orders to attack.[21]

What transpired next was stirring, but anticlimactic. Before McNeil could make the attack, Price ordered Tyler's brigade on a movement around Colton Greene on the Confederate right and toward McNeil's exposed left. Price directed Tyler to support the rearguard "by an ostentatious display." Tyler then turned to both armed and unarmed recruits and shouted that Price "looked to them alone for the safety of the train. . . . they must charge the enemy and check him." As Tyler's men had already done on two other occasions, they exceeded all possible expectations. "Yelling like devils," they rode hard toward McNeil's line. As they bore down on the Yankees, Tyler discovered that two Union mountain howitzers and Philip Smiley's two Rodman guns from the 2nd Missouri Light Artillery had arrived on that portion of the line. Their combined firepower thus told quickly on Tyler's charging brigade, hitting men and horses. Although it appears that Tyler had no real intention of taking his unarmed men into the Yankee line, the incoming rounds forced Tyler to stop his charge about four hundred yards from the enemy and retreat quickly to his start point. The entire action could not have taken more than fifteen minutes, but it cost Tyler eleven killed and twenty-four wounded in his brigade. That Tyler's command had not disintegrated was a significant achievement, but more importantly, Tyler had nevertheless accomplished his mission. His attack froze McNeil.[22]

At about this time, Alfred Pleasonton's promised reinforcements arrived in the shape of Benteen's brigade. This much-fatigued unit arrived on the battlefield at a trot, and it formed to the right of McNeil. Benteen lined the brigade in a column of regiments with the 10th Missouri in the lead followed by the 3rd and 4th Iowas. Pleasonton had previously detached Major Samuel E. W. Simonson's consolidated command to support Smiley's section of Rodman guns, which stood to the rear of the formation. With little hesitation, Benteen ordered his brigade into a galloping charge at least one-half mile from the Confederates. It was ill advised. Given the condition of the horses and prairie turf that often found the animals almost fetlock deep in mud, the charge abruptly exhausted itself. None of the weary animals ever reached a gallop. Incoming artillery from Richard Collins's battery and then additional small-arms fire from Thompson's brigade churned up the ground and compelled the attack to halt. Incredibly, no one was yet hit. In a fashion similar to what had happened earlier in the day at Mine Creek, Benteen's brigade stalled in some confusion until Abial Pierce once again ordered the 4th Iowa to sidestep the paralyzed mass of cavalry. This time, Pierce moved the 4th to the right of the line and continued the charge for a few hundred yards, spreading confusion on the Confederate left. Pierce's attack succeeded in throwing back much of Thompson's brigade without even coming into close-quarters combat. Pierce's good fortune would not, however, last. The rest of Benteen's brigade moved no further, despite the visibly advanced and exposed position of their comrades in the 4th Iowa. Making matters still worse for Pierce, the Confederates mounted a last-minute attack by Sidney Jackman's brigade, which had been augmented by Slayback's battalion. Slayback had retreated earlier in the engagement to a position in the Confederate rear. While Jackman and Slayback moved toward Pierce's center and right, Benjamin Elliot's regiment came to their assistance. Elliot had held in the face of the original attack and now pivoted to counterattack into Pierce's left and rear. Pierce's casualties were light with only five wounded, including Pierce himself, but he made the rational decision to withdraw to the remainder of Benteen's stalled brigade. Confederate pursuit was nonetheless brief. Smiley's Rodman guns and the mountain howitzers laid down an intimidating barrage into Jackman's and Elliot's Confederates. Notwithstanding several rounds that fell short and near to the Union troopers, Jackman dared go no further. He was satisfied with stopping Pierce at a cost of only four killed and ten wounded. Jackman therefore called off the fight and headed back toward the Marmaton. That was it. The battle was over.[23]

Darkness was now about to fall. With Price still trying to shepherd his wagons across the Marmaton and the bulk of his men on the north side of the river, odds never appeared more in favor of a Yankee annihilation of the

Confederate army. Notwithstanding the near exhaustion of both McNeil's and Benteen's brigades, Union reinforcements now piled into the battle area. Sanborn and Philips lurked within a mile, and even more decisively James Blunt's division neared the area, too. None of this, however, really mattered to Alfred Pleasonton. Earlier in the battle when Charles Tyler made his demonstration on the Union left, McNeil sent back yet another courier to Pleasonton requesting help. Pleasonton was, by this point, in a position to observe most of the events on the battlefield, and he had made up his mind to disengage. The question for Pleasonton was not really if he would pull back, but where. He was tired and in pain from being thrown from his horse at some point in the campaign. Moreover, he personally despised Curtis, Blunt, the Kansans, and just about any soldier who was not mustered into a volunteer regiment. He believed there was already glory enough for his command, and he prepared for a withdrawal to the Little Osage where his men could rest and feed.[24]

The only thing affecting this plan was not McNeil's courier, but rather the appearance of another officer, Lieutenant Marshall Ehle. The lieutenant had just arrived from Fort Scott and informed Pleasonton that the post was just two-and-a-half miles away. Although Ehle was probably three miles off in his navigation, this news proved decisive. The lure of Fort Scott with all of its quartermaster and ordnance supplies was simply too much for a general who wanted to quit. Despite the protestations of at least one of Curtis's staff officers who had accompanied the lead units, Pleasonton ordered Benteen, Sanborn, and Philips to ride to Fort Scott. John McNeil, still apparently suffering Pleasonton's animus, would be left to his own devices on the battlefield. He was to hold fast until Blunt arrived, assuming, of course, the Confederates did not counterattack and destroy that lone brigade in the meantime.[25]

It did not take long for Pleasonton to issue the orders and then watch their execution. In the falling light of the day, Samuel Curtis would have the same privilege. The commanding general arrived on the battlefield in time to see large numbers of Union cavalry moving off toward Fort Scott. His reaction was, at first, one of satisfaction. He assumed Pleasonton had wisely ordered a flank attack. As Sanborn's troopers faded into the horizon, Curtis immediately sought answers at Pleasonton's headquarters. The meeting was tense, and it revealed that although Curtis had the right plan, which was to keep the troops in the field and simply have the supplies brought to them from Fort Scott, the general lacked the confidence to assert himself over Pleasonton.

The problem was that no one had ever given Curtis actual command of Pleasonton. William Rosecrans, Pleasonton's departmental commander, referred to Curtis in correspondence as "commanding," but he never formalized the designation. Curtis was senior, but heretofore he relied upon consensus in his decision making. He would not do any differently now. Curtis chose to request, cajole, and persuade without actually demanding obedience. In the end, Pleasonton stood firm in his belief that "we had done enough and ought to stop." Curtis acquiesced.[26]

The folly of the situation was not yet complete. Somehow, neither Pleasonton nor Curtis managed to get any instructions to Blunt. When that mercurial general finally arrived near the Marmaton well after sunset and found no orders, he promptly abandoned McNeil and headed for Fort Scott as well. Deserted in the presence of an enemy that outnumbered them by eight to one, McNeil's troopers fell asleep by their horses. For any cavalryman who did not tie the bridle of his horse to his wrist, daylight could find him without a horse as many a trooper sought a replacement for his worn-out mount. In the final indignity inflicted upon the brigade, Curtis promised McNeil a wagon train of rations. Unfortunately, the wagon master met Blunt on the road and believed those were the only troops supposed to get the food. The wagons therefore returned with Blunt to Fort Scott. Perhaps the only solace for John McNeil and his men was that they were not actually alone. Although Pleasonton gave Benteen leave to march to Fort Scott, he declined to move. His brigade had marched over one hundred miles in two days and been in nearly constant combat the whole time. "The exhausted soldiers," William Forse Scott of the 4th Iowa later recalled, "dropped upon the frosty grass to sleep, holding their horses by the bridles."[27]

With Curtis's army either sleeping or marching away from the battlefield, Price continued to withdraw across the Marmaton. Near to midnight, Jeff Thompson finally crossed the river when he received orders that were a long time in coming: Sterling Price had ordered the destruction of a portion of the train. The orders were precise. Old Pap's staff designated what could be kept by the different units and staff functions. Army headquarters kept half of their rolling stock. Each division and brigade headquarters retained one vehicle. Likewise, each division saved a medical wagon, while the ordnance department preserved wagons that were "absolutely required." Otherwise, the staff proscribed any ambulance or buggy not actually carrying the wounded or a private family still tagging along with the army. No more than fifty wagons would remain to continue the flight south. With Sidney Jackman appointed to superintend the destruction, the men began throwing some of the ordnance down two or three wells in nearby Deerfield, Missouri, while leaving the bulk of the excess powder, cartridges, and shells in the abandoned wagons. By 2 AM, the exhausted army took up the march, and in short order Jackman set his fires. What followed was a series of terrific explosions that lit the night sky and frightened anyone either sleeping or not privy to the planned destruction. For James Campbell of Clark's brigade, "it was a sight never to be forgotten by anyone that [*sic*] saw it." For anyone else who cared to look, Price let go of a great deal more than just his wagons. Unemployed horses and mules by the hundreds soon wandered the prairie. Dozens of cattle lay dead, while at least ninety cows and three hundred sheep miraculously survived to be captured and eaten by the Yankees. The ground was also covered with unexploded ammunition, shotguns, muskets, powder kegs, old iron, boxes, clothes, and even dead bodies tossed from ambulances. Perhaps most dishearteningly, about 125 sick and wounded had to be left for the enemy.[28]

It took hours for the entire army to vacate the Marmaton camp. Price himself did not leave his headquarters at William Modrel's house until 4 AM. The Confederates first headed east, crossing the Big Drywood Creek at three different fords. Even this exercise proved painful and time-consuming. The remaining wagons still managed to clog the fords, thirsty horses always paused to drink, and, most embarrassing, Price got lost trying to cross. Adding more chaos to the operation, a light rain began to fall, and then a false rumor spread that the Unionists were advancing. When the army finally untangled itself on the other side of the creek, the march proved just how disorganized things had become. Curtis Ballard of the 7th Missouri recalled how you could hear the continual cries of "'Where is Clark's Brigade? Where is Freeman's Brigade? Where is McCray's Brigade?' Or this or some other regiment." When calls for comrades could not be heard, a strange quiet gripped the exhausted men. R. L. Brown later scribbled in his diary, "Slowly and silently we wended our way over hills and through vales in the direction of Arkansas."[29]

Chapter Seventeen

There Is Not an Enemy in a Hundred Miles

That the Army of Missouri had escaped complete destruction on October 25 was something of a miracle. On three separate occasions, large segments of the army had been isolated and attacked with a river or creek to their rear. Somehow, when daylight broke on the morning of the 26th the army still survived. Needless to say, it was hardly secure. Sterling Price was well over two hundred miles from any potential crossing of the Arkansas River and a return to Confederate-occupied territory. The next few days would be critical as Price sought to gain separation from a Union army that had displayed little unity of command and a festering lack of resolve in one of its senior commanders. The slackening Union pursuit could only be saved by the actions of a tenacious commander. James Blunt would quickly fill that need and promptly bring Price's army to bay on October 28. However, Blunt's tenacity bordered on the rash and thus also managed to give Price the chance of a decisive battlefield victory that he had been denied since the battles around Kansas City.

In starting this phase of the campaign, the Confederate army did not get off to an auspicious start. The entire army took a wrong road, which then consumed at least one or two hours to redress. The command eventually sorted itself out, deploying in four columns with guards stationed between each column to prevent straggling. Thus began a sixty-mile march of misery that took the defeated, hungry, and bedraggled army toward Carthage, Missouri. There was very little of the accordion effect of waiting and hurrying up because the army was able to negotiate most creeks and ravines with relative ease. But all was not smooth riding. The sheer distance and pace of the march fatigued the men and destroyed many a horse and mule. The lack of forage added to the army's problems, making it, according to surgeon J. H. P. Baker, "a fateful day to horse flesh."[1]

Price intended his march to Carthage to put as much distance as possible between his army and that of Curtis. Price also knew that Carthage was about the only place on the prairie south of Deerfield where he could find badly needed forage for his horses and mules. Although the town itself had been burned and ransacked throughout the war, Price did indeed find the badly needed forage. Better yet, his men were able to beg and steal flour and beef, albeit without salt. However, the availability of food and forage did little to arrest the erosion of whatever discipline the army ever possessed. This sad condition was well illustrated when at some point after dark commissary clerk Orson Davis lost $267,280, which amounted to half the army's operating cash. The army's chief commissary officer, Major Henry W. Tracy, had carried the cash in a guarded wagon throughout the campaign. But he became fearful for its possible capture on the 26th, causing him to distribute the money in sacks so that his two clerks could carry the money with them on their more mobile horses. Unfortunately for Davis and the army, just outside Carthage the road narrowed, forcing the clerks into a press of stragglers and roadside confusion. The stragglers "were ungovernable," and Davis struggled to mask the saddlebags with his shawl. Davis eventually escaped the jostling only to discover the bags missing. Then in an entirely different form of panic, Davis tried to find the money. The money was never found, and no one was ever held liable for the loss.[2]

Price's encampment at Carthage was notable for one other thing. At long last, Price began paroling his Union prisoners. Old Pap really had no choice. He could not feed these men, and the many walking scarecrows proved a further drag on his progress. The paroling was also probably a simple recognition that he could no longer guard the prisoners. At the Marmaton encampment, men such as Samuel Reader of the 2nd KSM simply wandered down to one of the creeks and commenced walking west. For others, including P. I. Bonebrake, the Confederates simply turned them loose on the empty prairie. The condition of these men was truly wretched. Guilford Gage noted that by the time they had reached Big Drywood Creek, they were "barefooted, hungry, thirsty beyond the power to describe, worn out, desperate, our feet like pounded meat, our jaws hollow, our bodies worn to mere skeletons covered with yellow parchment." Some of their Confederate captors took pity. Colonel John C. Wright recollected the captives had been the recipients of "the most inhuman and cruel treatment of prisoners by Confederate soldiers that I knew during the war." Interestingly enough, not everyone agreed with him. Samuel Curtis seemed to understand the difference between malicious mistreatment and the shared privation of captive and captor alike. As some of the wandering POWs entered his lines on the 28th, Curtis recorded: "It is proper to say the charges of cruel treatment are exaggerated." It is important to note also the Confederates did not release all of their POWs by Carthage. For unknown reasons, several POWs continued with the army for two more days before they would be paroled on the night of the 28th just south of Newtonia.[3]

On the morning of the 27th, though, Price began his march around 9 AM after taking some additional daylight hours to feed and rest his horses. He then drove the army about twenty miles due south before encamping on the southern bank of Shoal Creek. Despite the less hurried pace of this day's march, the army still suffered. Desertion, particularly among the Arkansans and the new recruits, became rampant. Henry Luttrell noted that increasing numbers of men began to die of their wounds or exposure to the elements. R. L. Brown, a rare surviving member of Marmaduke's escort company, noted plaintively that "we have nothing to eat and have not seen any bread for 6 days. Our horses have not eaten anything for two days and have been constantly under the saddle." Particularly graphic in his description of the march of the 27th was Jeff Thompson. His brigade and Shelby's division continued to cover the rear of the army. Hours were lost when the army crossed a creek that could not have been more than ten feet wide. As a frustrated Thompson recollected, "No mortal can imagine the delay occasioned by the smallest obstruction in a long column of men." The banks of the creek had been worn by the passage of thousands of horses, and most of the men usually paused midstream to let their animals drink. "Shelby cursed himself hoarse and then sent for me to come and finish the job, which being in my line I can do as glibly as anybody." Despite the vocal efforts of both Thompson and Shelby, their troops continued to labor across the creek; it would be well past nightfall when they finally entered camp.[4]

Although Samuel Curtis faced the same physical obstacles as Price, he struggled with other issues as well. Two things, especially, bedeviled the Union commander. First, there was the matter of the captured Confederate artillery and prisoners. Upon his arrival at Fort Scott on the evening of the 25th, Alfred Pleasonton had not given up on the idea of laying claim to all the Confederates rounded up at Mine Creek and beyond. He wanted them shipped to St. Louis as trophies of war. Such a plan competed with Curtis's more utilitarian notion that the Confederates would soon be exchanged for Union POWs and that Fort Leavenworth was better situated to facilitate the exchange. In fairness to Pleasonton, he had reason to doubt Curtis's complete sincerity. Pleasonton saw the omnipresent James Lane and his retinue of Kansas politicians (colonels Cloud, Ritchie, and Crawford) and believed Lane wanted to parade the prisoners as some kind of political freak show in the upcoming election. Between the 25th and 26th, the issue slipped into absurdity as Pleasonton's and Curtis's staff officers nearly came to blows. Throughout the squabble, however, Pleasonton retained control of the prisoners. This was galling to Curtis's Kansans because Pleasonton had housed Marmaduke, Cabell, and five captured colonels in a comparatively posh hotel at Fort Scott.[5]

The second, and more important, issue confronting Curtis was his ability, as he put it, to keep Pleasonton "on the warpath." Pleasonton believed wholeheartedly that he and his troops alone had inflicted a near mortal blow to Price. Pleasonton further believed any additional pursuit should be the task of the rabid and relatively well-rested Kansans. After Pleasonton and Curtis arrived at Fort Scott on the night of the 25th, the generals met and discussed the prisoners and future operations. Still loath to declare his seniority, Curtis allowed the meeting to break up without Pleasonton's submission. After a few hours sleep, Curtis decided not to confront Pleasonton personally, but instead to send a letter asserting his right to command. Curtis then ordered Pleasonton to requisition supplies and march against Price. Left unstated was anything having to do with the prisoners. It appears Curtis believed there was no further problem at this point. Well before daylight, Curtis departed Fort Scott with Blunt's division, thinking all matters resolved. The prisoners would go to Leavenworth, and Pleasonton would follow Blunt. Satisfied also that Price no longer posed a threat to Kansas, Curtis rescinded martial law in the state, which also prompted Governor Carney to order the militia home.[6]

Blunt and Curtis marched in pursuit of Price along a direct road from Fort Scott to Lamar. That road bypassed the Marmaton River, Big Drywood Creek, and Price's encampment of the 25th and 26th. Thomas Moonlight, whose 2nd Brigade had arrived at Fort Scott at 4 PM on the 25th, now moved in advance of Blunt's division. Doc Jennison's 1st Brigade and John Ford's 4th Brigade followed. Charles Blair's 3rd Brigade of militia had been left behind at Fort Scott to muster out of service. The Colorado and Wisconsin batteries accompanied the cavalry. The combined force halted for the night of the 26th at Shanghai, almost twenty-five miles from Fort Scott. John McNeil's brigade joined them at Shanghai near 9 PM after spending hours earlier in the day trying to cross the Big Drywood Creek, which Price had effectively blocked with felled timber and broken wagons. Not having the benefit of the rest and supplies available at Fort Scott, McNeil's men and horses were greatly fatigued and hungry. Nevertheless, McNeil joined the rest of the column when it resumed the pursuit on the morning of the 27th.[7]

Meanwhile, Pleasonton appeared finally to obey, or at least cooperate with, Curtis. Early on the 27th, and about the same time Price departed Carthage, Pleasonton dispatched a message to Curtis announcing the prisoners would be moved to Fort Leavenworth and the cavalry would march in accordance with Curtis's wishes. In fact, the cavalry did depart that morning with Benteen riding south along the Line Road and Sanborn along a different road heading southeast and more directly for Newtonia. Philips's brigade, now numbering approximately 750 men, followed Curtis's path on the road to Lamar. Philips himself still suffered great pain from his eye injury and had to command his brigade from the back of a buggy. With the brigades riding to Curtis, there was only one anomaly. Pleasonton himself was not coming. Pleasonton's message to Curtis contained this news and a medical officer's certificate testifying to his physical incapacity. Pleasonton thus appeared to get what he most wanted, which was to have nothing else personally to do with the continued pursuit of Price.[8]

With Pleasonton now departed from the campaign, Curtis's army had an unremarkable march on the 27th save for the column running into a trickle of escaped Union POWs. The emaciated and threadbare condition of the POWs shocked many of Curtis's men, which in turn further primed them for vengeance upon any and all things Confederate by the time the exhausted and emotionally spent Yankees reached their encampment at Carthage after midnight on the 28th. Price had left behind an undetermined number of sick and wounded in the ruins of the town and further along the trail south. Things did not go well for these men. In the words of Richard Hinton, "Instances of barbarous cruelty were not unfrequent [*sic*]." Mrs. C. C. Warner, who lived on a farm four miles south of Carthage, gave more explicit meaning to this when she described taking in one of Price's stragglers who was unable to go any further. "Within a half day," Curtis's men found him and then hung him from a tree in an orchard.[9]

While Blunt's men satisfied their desire for revenge, early morning on the 28th found the two armies separated by no more than twenty miles. For Price and the Confederates, a sense of safety had spread. The brutal trek of the 26th seemed to have put an insurmountable distance between the opposing forces. The much-slower-paced march of the 27th coupled with no apparent sightings of the Yankees led some to think the danger had passed. Price therefore felt comfortable in starting the army on its march near to mid-morning on the 28th. Shelby's division, which had the rearguard the previous day, now took the lead in a route to the southwest through Granby and toward Newtonia. Fagan's division became the rearguard with Lieutenant Colonel Thomas L. Gunter's Arkansas battalion at the tail end of the army.[10]

For Shelby, the trains, and the remainder of Marmaduke's division, which was now commanded by John B. Clark Jr., the morning and early afternoon were largely uneventful. R. L. Brown described the march as "leisurely." The greatest excitement came with the army's approach to Newtonia, which was then garrisoned by Company K of the 15th Missouri Volunteers. Lieutenant Robert H. Christian commanded the Yankee company, which had become infamous among many in Shelby's division for its punitive forays in and around southwest Missouri. Particularly anxious to get at this Yankee garrison was Lieutenant Samuel Moore from Alonzo Slayback's battalion. Moore believed Christian personally responsible for his father's death and other brutalities committed upon Confederate sympathizers. Moore thus successfully pleaded to join the advance with his partisan company of about fifty men. In a strange twist of events, Christian had word of Price's movement, and he had evacuated his garrison to the east in enough time to avoid any difficulty. However, Christian chose to ride back to town to observe Price's approach. He may also have been motivated by the fact that he had left his wife behind, and unprotected, in Newtonia. Unfortunately for Christian, he got much too close. Moore's group, and one other column, reached the outskirts of Newtonia and drove pell-mell for the garrison. It was too late for Christian to escape, and he was overtaken by Moore, who proceeded to kill and scalp him. The event was not complete until Moore paraded the scalp around Newtonia to the horror of the ladies who remained in town. While Moore displayed his grisly trophy, the remainder of the army traveled through Newtonia and headed directly south along the road to Pineville for about two miles. It then encamped for the night in the woods surrounding Indian Creek and its tributaries in what Price described as the "edge of the prairie." Price's army had traveled no more than eleven miles that day.[11]

Price's sense of security was, of course, ill founded. Despite the confusion of the battles of the 25th and the subsequent best efforts of Alfred Pleasonton to call off the pursuit, Samuel Curtis and James Blunt had engineered a dogged chase that only intensified on the morning of the 28th. Shortly after daylight, Curtis ordered one of his staff officers, Major Thomas I. McKenny, to take a party of about thirty men and to accompany Major James Ketner's 16th Kansas Cavalry in the advance. McKenny's purpose was less tactical than humanitarian. With bedraggled POWs wandering into his ranks, Curtis wanted McKenny to initiate negotiations for an exchange of prisoners. Moreover, Curtis thought there might also be an opportunity to persuade Price to surrender.[12]

Carrying a white flag of truce, McKenny rode no more than ten miles from Carthage when, at about 10 AM, he ran into Price's rearguard just north of Shoal Creek. This was Gunter's battalion of about two hundred men. McKenny immediately sent a courier to the rear to apprize Curtis of the contact. The courier apparently never made it to Curtis and instead gave his dispatch to James Blunt, who traveled forward of Curtis. In what should have been a surprise to no one, the high-strung Blunt would have nothing to do with flags of truce and a discussion of surrender. Blunt had been denied any role in all the combat since the battles around Kansas City, and he yearned to attack the accursed Confederates. Consequently, Blunt ordered McKenny to remove his white flag and, along with Ketner's 16th Kansas, pursue and develop the Confederate rearguard. McKenny and Ketner then pushed the Confederates eastward through the lightly wooded terrain toward Granby. The dismounted pursuit lasted about three miles and garnered only three Confederate prisoners. Exhausted, McKenny and Ketner paused just beyond Granby around noon, at which time they realized Blunt was still nowhere near the skirmishing. McKenny then retraced his route only to find Blunt halted about three-and-one-half miles distant. The fog of war had descended upon Blunt, and the general had not quite realized the extent of McKenny's contact with Price. McKenny now personally rectified that impression, prompting Blunt to shove the remainder of Ford's brigade (the 2nd Colorado) and Jennison's brigade eastward toward Price. It was a potentially disastrous decision. Near to 1 PM, and not yet cognizant of just how close he was to Price's main body, Blunt had allowed Thomas Moonlight's brigade to fall out from the march in order to rest and feed in a cornfield. Blunt's willingness to let one brigade take an extended break stemmed, in some part, from his belief that John McNeil's brigade was close by and would therefore provide the necessary support should combat develop. However, Blunt never communicated this idea to Curtis, who was then traveling well behind Blunt and the brigades of Moonlight, Jennison, and Ford. When Curtis then galloped up to Moonlight's resting brigade after Blunt had already departed, he assumed that Blunt was resting the entire division. Into this early afternoon siesta also rode John McNeil's much fatigued and famished brigade. Curtis naturally ordered it, too, to rest. In the meantime, James Blunt pushed toward Newtonia.[13]

Blunt's eventual arrival at the northwestern outskirts of Newtonia came with some element of surprise, which had more to do with poor communication on the part of the Confederates in Fagan's division than anything else. Thomas Gunter's rearguard battalion had separated itself considerably from Fagan's division and the remainder of Price's army. Throughout the morning and early afternoon, it showed no inclination to engage McKenny's and Ketner's advance column of Yankees. Instead, Gunter dutifully retreated, while providing a careful screen of the Confederate main body. Better yet, Gunter sent several couriers throughout his retrograde movement to Fagan, sounding the warning that the Federals were in force and pushing him. Fagan, however, did not believe the warnings. But at some point between 2 and 3 PM, Fagan was finally moved to action. He found John C. Wright, who was then near the timber of a branch of Indian Creek, and informed him of Gunter's several warnings. Fagan, according to Wright, then mused, "Gunter is ordinarily a brave officer[,] and I can't imagine what has come over him, for I know that there is not an enemy in a hundred miles of him." Fagan's sudden grasp of the situation showed when he ordered Wright to march his regiment back into town from the south. Wright was then to send a company (Lieutenant Henry Burks's) back to relieve Gunter, while the remainder of his regiment ground flour in the town.[14]

Word that the Yankees were nearby spread fairly quickly. Jo Shelby got the message from a courier as he peered into a supply wagon, asking for some sugar. "In a moment," recollected a Union POW who happened to be close by, "Shelby was at his horse and without stopping to put on a blanket of any kind, he threw on the saddle, mounted, and commenced giving orders." Shelby thus prepared to make a stand with some elements of Fagan's division, while the rest of the army made its escape. Shelby's initial call to action was not met with any type of enthusiasm. For what may have been the first time during the entire campaign, a mutinous feeling ran through the ranks. Hamp B. Watts in D. A. Williams's battalion had just started a fire when the

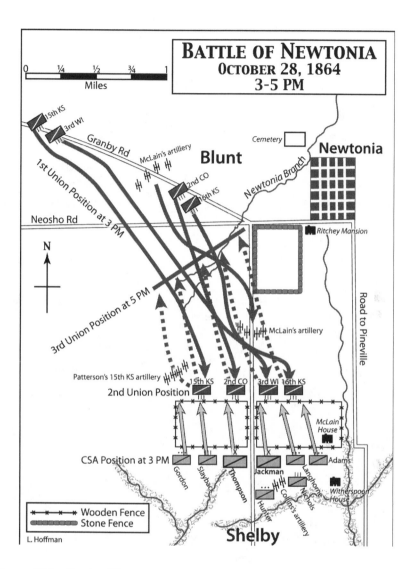

Figure 17.1.   Battle of Newtonia, October 28, 1864, 3 to 5 PM

bugles sounded, and he recalled: "Should I live a century never can I forget the blanched, tired, ragged men around me; they were 'pictures of despair.' There was hurry and confusion throughout the camp, many saddled their worn out steeds and silently stole toward the South; the few remaining, stood silent and aghast, knowing full well what the sudden call had meant." It was a remarkable moment for Price's army and Shelby's division. The constant retreating and food and sleep deprivations had exacted their toll. Making matters worse, in addition to those who did not desert outright, there were hundreds of men who simply refused Shelby's orders to remain dismounted and advance into the open field. Befitting their exhausted and emotionally spent condition, these men were perfectly content to wait for the enemy within the apparent safety of the woods. Thinking the Yankees about to fall upon them, Shelby and Jeff Thompson gave up trying to persuade any more of these men to move. The generals took those who would follow (about two hundred troopers) and immediately marched north about a half mile where they stopped behind a rail fence. They were then at the southern boundary of a farm owned by Thomas McLain. There the Confederates waited for the inevitable onslaught.[15]

Much to Shelby's and Thompson's surprise, however, there was no Yankee attack. Instead, what rushed toward their position were several Confederates who proclaimed the impending Yankee attack a wild rumor. They claimed to have just ridden from Carthage and somehow promised there were no Yankees to be found. For the officers and men who had marched out to resist Blunt, there was great relief as well as an easy willingness to believe this report. Shelby and Thompson did not wait for any further confirmation. They faced the men about and returned to the camps, which were still occupied by hundreds of recalcitrant soldiers and recruits. Thompson and his officers tried immediately to shame those who had not obeyed the order to advance, while also promising to reward those who had answered the call. This could have taken no more than one-half hour, during which time the men ate what little food they had, and some officers, including Thompson, gathered to take a drink of liquor freshly liberated from Newtonia. Thompson never actually got to take his drink as new riders advanced into their camps and shots rang out to the northwest. This time, the men of the division rallied around the pleas of Shelby, Thompson, and the other officers. Shelby quickly went from unit to unit promising to organize a select regiment of cavalry from all those who advanced with him. For Hamp Watts, it was just the right inducement, as he thought immediately "of kindred and friends, and felt how proud mother would be to learn that her boy was a member of 'Shelby's picked regiment.'" For others, including George Cruzen, there was a visceral shame for staying in the camps during the false alarm. Having eaten and rested a bit undoubtedly helped their morale as well. Around 3 PM, most of the men in the division moved to the wall with Slayback, Thompson, and Jackman forming the main line of battle from left to right. Richard Collins's two pieces of artillery stood slightly to the rear and right of the formation supported by Hunter's and Nichols's units from Jackman's brigade.[16]

John C. Wright witnessed Blunt's approach. After ordering a company to the aid of Gunter's rearguard, he climbed to the third floor of the town's mill and cast his binoculars to the west. About one mile out he observed the gradual assemblage of blue coats, which was no doubt Blunt's advance led by McKenny and Ketner. Wright then called the remainder of his regiment, which had been feeding in Mathew Ritchey's cornfield just to the southwest of town, "to horse," and they advanced quickly to the northwest of Newtonia when they ran into the retreating men of Gunter's and Burk's commands. Wright first allowed for the fleeing rearguard to pass through his ranks. He then initiated a counterattack that promptly drove McKenny and Ketner back about one-half mile. This success was short-lived as Wright observed a massing of Yankees another half-mile away on a set of bluffs that overlooked Newtonia and its open fields to the south. James Blunt and the 4th Brigade, commanded by John Ford, had arrived.[17]

Ever aggressive, and perhaps rash, Blunt chose to give battle as soon as possible. However, three factors should have given Blunt cause to go more slowly. First, Blunt was well in advance of his entire army. Accompanying him at the bluffs were only the 2nd Colorado and 16th Kansas of the 4th Brigade and four cannon from William McLain's battery. Blunt's 1st Brigade, now commanded by Lieutenant Colonel George Hoyt as Doc Jennison had taken ill, could be spotted in the distance, but it would still take time to arrive on the field. A second factor that should have troubled Blunt was that straggling had reduced all of his units by at least one-third of their available strength. Third, and most alarming, Blunt had no idea where three of his five brigades were. When Blunt had arrived at Granby an hour earlier, he sent couriers back to find the missing brigades, which, as he later noted, "I supposed were only a short distance in my rear." To his great consternation, Blunt would soon discover those brigades were far away as McNeil and Moonlight continued their rest in the vicinity of Shoal Creek. Fortunately for Blunt, Samuel Curtis had dispatched John Sanborn's brigade once he realized there was no general halt to the army. Unbeknownst to Blunt, Sanborn was, however, about one hour of hard riding in the distance. Despite these problems, James Blunt understood one important reality, which was that Price's army was on the verge of disintegration and all that was needed was one final push. Upon seeing Price's encampment south of the town and soldiers working the mill, Blunt concluded Price was neither ready for, nor expecting, a fight. This was all the information Blunt needed to initiate the attack with only Ford's brigade and McLain's artillery on hand. [18]

Blunt first placed the artillery on the bluffs at the front of his line. In minutes, McLain began firing at Wright's skirmishers to the northwest of the cornfield. This cannonade helped push Wright's troopers back toward, and into, Shelby's line, where they joined many other soldiers from Cabell's and Slemmons's brigades of Fagan's division. As the artillery belched shell toward the mass of Confederates, John Ford ordered his brigade of six hundred men forward in two lines with Ketner's 16th Kansas in front followed by the 2nd Colorado, now commanded by Major Jesse L. Pritchard. Not content to watch the combat, Blunt chose to lead from the front. With revolvers in hand, he and his staff joined Ketner's regiment. It was a decision befitting Blunt's personal bravery and charisma, but it further detached him from the ability to control the battle, especially when it came to monitoring and directing badly needed reinforcements. Regardless, Blunt and the 4th Brigade galloped down the bluffs and toward Jo Shelby's line more than one mile distant. [19]

As the Unionists sped toward the Confederate lines, two new things became readily apparent. First, additional Confederate troops were mobilizing in the woods behind Shelby's position at the fence. Second, there was another rail fence about five hundred yards in front of Shelby's now well-ensconced position. For the Yankee cavalry to press home the attack, they would either have to dismount and negotiate the fence or change into a column of fours to squeeze into a ten-foot-wide lane that bisected the fence and the adjoining fields of Thomas McLain's farm. In reality, Blunt's troopers could do neither, and the charge braked to a halt in front of the second fence line. The battle then turned briefly into a static affair in which both sides pumped rounds at each other from across parallel fences. Given that the combatants were two hundred yards beyond the maximum effective range of a trained shooter with a .58 caliber long rifle, most of the shots fell harmlessly short. This was a particularly fortuitous situation for the Union cavalry, which stayed mounted. For the Confederates, only a few officers, including Jeff Thompson, remained atop their horses. What damage that did occur came from the artillery on both sides. Nevertheless, and despite the inaccuracy of the small-arms fire, things were about to become very perilous for Blunt. Not only did he fail to repeat the shock of the Union cavalry at Mine Creek, but also he was now in danger of being turned on both flanks. As Yankee and Confederate blazed away at each other from across their fences, Shelby augmented his flanks with a detachment led by Major George Gordon on the left and two detachments commanded by captains Maurice Langhorne and R. H. Adams from Thompson's brigade on the right. To the good fortune of the Union, the deployment of these units came about the same time Hoyt's 1st Brigade rode on to the field. Because Blunt was already at the fence line with Ford's brigade, there was no one to give Hoyt any further orders. Hoyt, nevertheless, grasped the tactical situation from the elevated bluffs and ordered his men forward. The 15th Kansas Cavalry and a battery of four howitzers led by Sergeant George Patterson moved to the right of the 2nd Colorado. Lieutenant James Pond's detachment of the 3rd Wisconsin, numbering all of thirty-four effectives, rode to a gap between the 2nd Colorado and the 16th Kansas. Almost simultaneously, McLain redeployed his battery forward in support of the 2nd Colorado. Much like Hoyt's movement, McLain rode without any direct orders from Blunt.[20]

The timely and prescient movements of Hoyt and McLain, although they temporarily stabilized the Union line, could not by themselves save Blunt's command. Despite the effective artillery fire of Patterson and the incessant rattle of Hoyt's breech-loading repeaters, Confederate forces continued to accumulate on the Union right flank. McLain's appearance on Ford's front did little to further that defense as the rifled Parrotts overshot Shelby's main line. The long rounds did, however, create havoc among those Confederates skulking in the woods to the south. For the Confederacy, Richard Collins's artillery fired with greater effect, especially after correcting for a few salvos of canister that fell short and peppered the fence rails above the heads of some of Shelby's prone soldiers. With Blunt's flanks in danger of being turned and Confederate canister falling in their midst, Blunt's cavalry did not stay long at the second, or northernmost, fence. They withdrew about two hundred yards back along their initial path of attack. This sudden retreat inspired Shelby's men to begin their own counterattack. The Confederates clambered up and over their fence and rushed toward the northern fence. Helping to lead the charge was George Collins, a color bearer in Jeff Thompson's brigade. Collins, having taken over for a soldier accused of some recent cowardice, "carried the flag," in Thompson's words, "as high as both hands would reach." Thompson himself remained conspicuously mounted, and as he exhorted the line forward, an enemy bullet struck his horse in the head, showering Thompson with blood. Many within eyesight thought he had been wounded. Still, Thompson and the entire Confederate line continued the advance to the second fence where there was yet little pause in the attack. The rapid pace of the attack owed itself to the actions of officers such as

Colonel Moses Smith of the 11th Missouri, who straddled the second fence and shouted out to his men only to be mortally wounded when hit with three bullets almost simultaneously. No less prominent near this stage of the battle was Major A. V. Reiff, who now commanded Monroe's 1st Arkansas. According to Richard Hinton, Reiff "was an officer of splendid proportions, finely mounted on a white horse, who, bareheaded, and sabre in hand, rode furiously up and down the rebel lines, cheering on the men and exposing himself heedlessly." Reiff's actions, needless to say, attracted great attention among Yankee shooters. But according to Hinton, he "seemed to bear a charmed life" and was never hit.[21]

Given its inspired leadership, the Confederate line continued to advance, although it did move more slowly when Sergeant Patterson's four howitzers, positioned adjacent to the 15th Kansas on Blunt's right, brought a highly effective cannonade on Shelby's left flank. Nevertheless, it was not enough to stop the Confederates. A crisis soon developed within the Union ranks when Blunt ordered a more general withdrawal another three hundred yards to the northwest where the Union left could anchor on the stone wall of Ritchey's cornfield. McLain's battery was to displace first and be followed by the remainder of the cavalry. Amid the chaos of the battlefield, some units did not quite understand Blunt's orders. When McLain limbered his pieces and withdrew abruptly, at least one battalion of the 15th Kansas thought the artillery was abandoning them. Panic ensued, causing the battalion to start a dash to the rear. Only the extreme exertions of a number of staff officers brought the retreat under control and allowed for a steadying of the Union line that ran from Ritchey's cornfield to the southwest. The creation of this line did not, however, stop a steady flow of men from leaving the line and heading further to the rear.[22]

It now approached 5 PM, and the sun began to set in a blood red western sky. With Blunt's small force stretched to its proverbial breaking point, the situation appeared only to get worse. About one-half of the troops were out of ammunition. The lack of ammunition appeared greatest in the 1st Brigade where most of the troopers had expended their initial load of eighty rounds per man. Perhaps more important, Captain McLain decided without orders to withdraw his battery to the foot of the bluffs. He later claimed that his battery was utterly exhausted. In the midst of all this and facing the inexorable Confederate advance, Blunt prepared to withdraw his units one more time. This instance, it would be to the top of bluffs. But miraculously, Blunt would not have to make this retreat. John Sanborn's 3rd Brigade had finally galloped onto the scene.[23]

Sanborn's march to Newtonia was exhausting. In the previous thirty-six hours, he had ridden 104 miles with his supporting artillery and four wagons of ammunition. Sanborn rode just ahead of his battalions and first met Richard Hinton at the foot of the bluffs. Hinton informed Sanborn of the situation and suggested that the general bring his brigade to the Union left flank near the Ritchey cornfield, which at that moment appeared to be the most threatened. Sanborn concurred, wheeled about, and began marshaling his brigade for the attack down the bluffs and into the fields below. He was joined almost immediately by Samuel Curtis, who had followed Sanborn into Newtonia with his staff. The bluffs were not quite a safe place to be as one of Sanborn's aides, Captain C. W. Rubey, was shot from his horse while sitting next to Sanborn. As Sanborn dodged the bullets, he surveyed the field and noted the fences and stone walls about the battle area, especially the walls that enclosed Ritchey's cornfield. He also knew that his brigade's horses, in the words of Rubey, "could not be made to move out of a walk." Hence, Sanborn ordered his men to dismount and attack with the 6th MSM in the lead. Sanborn's artillery, a section of Rodman guns commanded by William C. F. Montgomery, set up just south of the bluffs and opened with supporting fire. On cue, the dismounted troopers rushed forward, and meeting little resistance, kept moving for about one mile. As the scattered volleys of Sanborn's men echoed around Newtonia, darkness enveloped the battlefield, and the Unionists would advance no more. It mattered little, though, because as Lieutenant Colonel John F. McMahan of the 6th PEMM noted: "the enemy had disappeared." Jo Shelby had ordered a withdrawal almost at the same time as Sanborn had begun his attack.[24]

The last hostile shots had therefore been fired in what became known as the Second Battle of Newtonia. Both sides showed little inclination to fight any more on the night of the 28th. Blunt's force had been bloodied, and the two remaining brigades of Moonlight and McNeil would not be up until later in the evening. So it was that Ford's and Jennison's brigades lingered on the battlefield until 9 PM and then withdrew to the town and positions northwest of it. Sanborn's brigade camped east of Newtonia. As for the Confederates, Jo Shelby remained in the vicinity of Thomas McLain's field and Indian Creek woods near to midnight. He and Jeff Thompson then abandoned the field so as to rejoin Price and the rest of the army about seven or eight miles south. William Erwin's 12th Missouri covered that retreat.[25]

Although the battle was over, yet again the wounded had to be treated and the dead buried. For the Union, there were eighteen killed, ninety-five wounded, and one missing for a total of 114 casualties. Union surgeons treated most of the wounded at the Ritchey house. As for the Confederates, there are no reliable numbers. Price's chief medical officer, William McPheeters, noted in his journal that he treated at most twenty-five men at "the hospital." This hospital was probably situated in the McLain farmhouse on the southeastern outskirts of the battle area. The Confederates probably also used the Witherspoon house, located south and west from the McLain residence, as another hospital, but there are no estimates of the number of casualties treated there. Based upon the limited evidence and the type of combat seen at Newtonia, Confederate losses approximated, or were lower than, the Union numbers. However, and regardless of the number of Confederates killed at Newtonia, forty-six wounded men would have to be left behind. There was simply not enough rolling stock to transport these men. McPheeters therefore designated an assistant surgeon from Monroe's 1st Arkansas and a medical student from Lexington to attend to the wounded and solicit mercy from Curtis and Blunt on the 29th. To the credit of the Union generals, it appears they treated these casualties properly, though seventeen of the forty-six men would die shortly thereafter from their wounds. [26]

With the smoke barely cleared from the battlefield, both armies wasted little time in making extravagant claims of victory. In a strange way, both sides were correct. For Sterling Price, it represented a small vindication of Confederate arms. Despite the early mutinous behavior of the men in Shelby's division, those troops eventually rallied under their officers and acquitted themselves well. They nearly drove the enemy from the field. Jo Shelby achieved his objective, which was not so much the annihilation of Blunt's brigades but rather a rearguard action that secured the safety of Price's retreating army. Although James Blunt ultimately led a successful counterattack and held most of the contested field by nightfall, he could not claim his mission accomplished. He pursued Price doggedly with the intention of destroying the Confederate army. While Blunt thus deserves credit for an uncommon tenacity, that tenacity got the better of him. It led to a blind determination to give battle with no actual awareness of the location of supporting brigades and ammunition resupply. James Blunt was, in other words, quite lucky that darkness and General Sanborn intervened when they did. Blunt should have also thanked Price for abandoning the field and clearing the way for many a Yankee to make an unabashed declaration of victory at Newtonia.

Chapter Eighteen

A Land of Starvation

When fighting came to a close at Newtonia, Sterling Price had already been on the march for more than a month. During that time, he and the main body of his army had traveled over one thousand miles and fought in thirteen major engagements and dozens of smaller actions. The impact of all this fighting and marching upon his army had been devastating. But the ordeal was not nearly finished. Indeed, the Confederates had to march yet another four hundred miles through wide stretches of territory that had been burned out and depopulated. It would be a march of misery as the temperatures dropped and the snow fell. Starvation and disease struck the army while it tried to outrun the Yankee pursuit. Hundreds of Confederates would die and hundreds more would desert, leaving Price with a shell of an army intended to liberate Missouri and change the course of the war in the Trans-Mississippi.

At daylight on Saturday, October 29th, the Army of Missouri found itself in a very familiar, and bad, situation. The previous day's combat had ended by ceding the field of battle, and now Price had to steal a march on his dogged pursuer. He would do precisely that in marching twenty-six miles to the southeast through territory that had been ruined in three years of war. By nightfall, Price's numbed Confederates rode through Pineville, Missouri, and encamped on Sugar Creek. Surprisingly, the rearguard and scouts could detect no Union pursuit. Not taking any chances the following day, Price continued his run to the southwest and into Arkansas. He then stopped at Maysville near the border between Arkansas and the Indian Territory. Although the scouts still failed to detect any Yankees near the army, Price was not yet willing to think he was in the clear. He therefore got the army moving early on the 31st and marched twenty-six miles to the Illinois River just inside the Arkansas border. On November 1, Price pushed the army yet another seventeen miles to Cane Hill, or Boonsborough, at which point he finally decided to pause. [1]

The decision to stop was bred not only of the lack of an apparent Yankee pursuit but also because of a steady deterioration of the Confederate army. Three things contributed to the deterioration. First, the weather turned miserable. Temperatures plummeted, and few moments seemed to pass without some mixture of rain, sleet, and snow pelting the poorly clothed men. Second, the road between the Illinois River and Cane Hill was wretched. The terrain was hilly and the roads rocky. Rain made passage more difficult for the exhausted horses and mules. As these animals then died by the score, horse thievery became rampant, which caused even the army chief surgeon, William McPheeters, to stand a two-hour horse guard at night. Third, and most important, the territory they were now passing through was destitute of food and forage. "The country," McPheeters recorded, "has been desolated & almost depopulated by the Yankees & Pin Indians." [2]

Consequently, the men grew hungrier. On October 30, R. L. Brown of Marmaduke's division noted that his unit had not received "anything to eat for ten days but poor beef without salt and occasionally a little parched corn." According to Hamp Watts of D. A. Williams's battalion, "The retreat southward from Newtonia was a famine. The flour first gave out, then the meat, then the medicines." After arriving at Cane Hill, J. H. P. Baker, one of Jackman's surgeons, noted despondently that "our trail is literally strewn with broken down horses, mules[,] wagons & men." He went on to conclude, "This raid reminds me of the children of Israel traveling through the wilderness. But alas! We have no Moses to lead us. No cloud by day[;] no pillar of fire by night." [3]

The accumulation of hardships afflicted all of Price's men, but it hit his most precious commodity the hardest: the new recruits. Not accustomed to the hardships of army life, let alone one with little food, exposure to inclement weather, and incessant marching, the recruits became despondent. Incapacitation often followed. These men, noted Hamp Watts, "suffered more in spirit than in the flesh, and fell out by the wayside to die." Many others chose not to suffer any longer with Price, and they deserted in droves. This problem grew even greater when the army entered northern Arkansas. The proximity to home naturally prompted countless Arkansans, who had been recruited or conscripted at the outset of the campaign, to run away. On October 30th, Price surrendered to reality when he began authorizing wholesale unit leaves. Price proclaimed these leaves as necessary to gain additional recruits and recover men who had already deserted, but the desire to assert order over an impending chaos was palpable. So it was that Sidney Jackman's brigade almost ceased to exist when the units commanded by Schnable, Hunter, and Nichols were, according to Jackman, "given an opportunity of visiting their friends in Northern Arkansas." Price also afforded Alonzo Slayback's and W. O. Coleman's men from Shelby's division the same "opportunity."[4]

With his army disintegrating and no signs of Yankee pursuit, Price stopped at Cane Hill for two days. Here Price continued to shed himself of hungry mouths desperate to go home. Price more than optimistically gave each furloughed unit a mandatory reporting date to the army wherever it might actually be after crossing the Arkansas River to the south. On the 2nd, Price furloughed Thomas Freeman's brigade with a return date of December 15th. On the 3rd, he let Thomas McCray's brigade go with a report date of December 20th. Arch Dobbin's men followed on the 4th with a promise to muster on December 25th. Jeff Thompson later charitably described this process of shedding units as getting the army "down to its running weight." But how the army might "regain" its weight does not appear to have been too great a concern to Sterling Price as all of these units were furloughed to areas north of the Arkansas River. However, what was more important during the stop in Cane Hill was the ability to feed the army that remained. Although unremitting cold, freezing rain, and mud plagued the stop at Cane Hill, the army temporarily alleviated its food scarcity. Cattle, corn meal, and fruit could be found in small quantities.[5]

The time and ability to attempt an extended recuperation at Cane Hill was only possible because Samuel Curtis's army was nowhere to be found. But what had happened to Curtis? The sorry explanation was nothing more than the logical conclusion to the political and personal infighting that had characterized relations within the Union high command in the Trans-Mississippi. Alfred Pleasonton had long since departed the campaign, but he had also planted the information that had the potential to undermine completely the continued pursuit of Price. After Mine Creek, he had sent messages surreptitiously to William S. Rosecrans claiming responsibility for the recent victories and pronouncing the campaign finished. He further staked his claim to the captured prisoners and artillery. It took two days for Rosecrans, who was then trying to catch up with Pleasonton and Curtis, to get the messages at

Warrensburg on October 27th. Lacking any other information from Curtis, Rosecrans issued a series of orders to couriers who had to track down Curtis and the Missouri troops under his control.

Curtis finally received these orders at Newtonia just before he planned to restart his chase of Price at 3 AM on October 29th. The orders were demoralizing. First, Rosecrans had ordered the POWs captured at Mine Creek to Warrensburg and the control of the Department of the Missouri. Second, and more importantly, Rosecrans instructed all of the Missouri-based cavalry to withdraw. Sanborn was to take his brigade to Springfield about fifty miles to the northeast. McNeil, who was then approaching Newtonia, had to move his brigade even further to Rolla some 170 miles to the northeast. Benteen, who also drew near to Newtonia, needed to head to Warrensburg. Curtis was "disgusted" by this news. It was especially galling after having already experienced "a foolish delay at Fort Scott" during and following the battle at the Marmaton River. He correctly believed Rosecrans did not have a complete understanding of the tactical situation, and Curtis immediately sent a message to Rosecrans with such an explanation. Curtis also telegraphed the Army Chief of Staff, Henry W. Halleck, in Washington, D.C., to complain and to state his case for a return of the Missouri cavalry. Curtis sent this message with the full realization that he was at least sixty miles from the nearest telegraph and that there was little hope of intervention. In the meantime, Curtis had no tactical options. He could no longer follow Price once the Missouri cavalry began their separate marches home. Thus, on the morning of the 29th, Curtis turned what was left of his army to the west on a slow march of twelve miles that brought it to Neosho, Missouri, by evening.[6]

That night, the implausible events of the campaign took another strange turn. Near to midnight, Curtis received a message from Halleck reversing Rosecrans's orders withdrawing the Missouri cavalry. According to Halleck's note, the commanding general, Ulysses S. Grant, wanted Curtis to pursue Price to the Arkansas River or at least until Price ran into Union forces in Arkansas, which were also ordered to be on the lookout for the Confederates. Halleck's message was dated the 28th and clearly revealed that time and distance had aggravated a situation already muddled by Pleasonton's intense desire to remove his cavalry from the theater. However, the real surprise in all of this confusion is that Halleck's message of the 28th was actually the third to convey a desire to stay the pursuit. Perhaps the problem for Rosecrans was that Halleck's previous two messages on the 24th and 27th did not bear Grant's imprimatur. Instead, Halleck, as he usually did throughout the war, allowed ambiguity and evasion to creep into his corre-spondence as he tried to avoid any appearance of personal responsibility for issued orders. He therefore couched his instructions to Rosecrans in language that implied the desire to pursue Price came from Major General E. R. S. Canby, who commanded the Department of Western Mississippi, which in-cluded Arkansas. In this way, Rosecrans could legitimately believe that Hal-leck was merely passing on the wishes of a fellow departmental commander and not that of a superior. Whatever may have been Rosecrans's motivations, Samuel Curtis took advantage of the reference to Grant in the message of the 28th, and he rightly concluded Grant's wishes overruled those of Rosecrans. Curtis, who had gone through much of the campaign as a tentative and passive commander, had finally seized control of the situation. Consequent-ly, he immediately sent couriers after the departed Missouri cavalry ordering them to return for the resumption of the chase. When Curtis issued these orders, he did so with the apprehension that those units may well ignore him. Writing to his wife, Curtis realized, "it is doubtful whether the troops of General Rosecrans will take orders from me; or if they do it is doubtful whether they will fully and cordially obey."[7]

As Curtis pondered the reliability of Rosecrans's cavalry, he also knew that his own force had been badly reduced by the rigors and distance of the campaign. He had lost dozens of horses, which left him with about 1,200 individually mounted soldiers. In John Ford's 4th Brigade, for example, no more than five hundred men had horses. The remaining troopers had to be sent back to Kansas City. Because there were so few enlisted and even fewer commissioned officers left with the brigade, the companies had to be consoli-dated. Making matters worse, Curtis had lost track of Price. Without any explicit intelligence, he guessed the Confederates continued their retreat in a southeasterly direction from Newtonia. He therefore ordered Rosecrans's dispersed cavalry to join him at Cassville, about thirty-five miles to the southeast of Neosho. By the time Curtis had all of this sorted out and at-tended to the logistics of continuing the campaign, he got a late start and only made it back to Newtonia by nightfall. He was ready to march again on the morning of the 31st and promptly headed southeast toward Cassville. Upon reaching Gadfly, about fourteen miles outside of Newtonia, he realized that Price had not retreated in that direction. There was simply none of the debris of a fleeing army that had so marked Price's previous course. Curtis now pivoted almost directly south and camped at Keetsville on the evening of the 31st, ordering all of the detached Missouri cavalry to meet him there. Miraculously, and despite having lost most of two days, the Union army was only about forty miles from Price. The next morning, Curtis received some welcome news as Frederick Benteen and his brigade of roughly 1,800 troopers finally caught up with the main body. This now gave Curtis a force of nearly three thousand men. But given Curtis's badly mistaken belief that Price had a force numbering thirty thousand men, although he understood it to be ill-clothed, poorly equipped, and starving, the Union general did not want to get too far ahead of his other desired reinforcements. He proceeded slowly on November 1st, riding only ten miles along the wire road to Pea Ridge, Arkansas. Curtis was now on very familiar ground. In March of 1862 he had defeated another Confederate army, which included Sterling Price, on that spot.[8]

For the Yankees, the march to Pea Ridge was a wretched experience. The same cold and freezing rain that afflicted Price's troops also soaked them. There was little escaping it. At night, some in the 2nd Colorado jammed into nearby log cabins, but numerous others simply endured sleeping in the rain. By morning, there was snow on the ground, making the Yankees even more cold and miserable. In circumstances no less familiar to Price's army, food was hard to come by, and Curtis's commissariat could not keep up with the demand. "Of necessity," wrote William Scott of the 4th Iowa, "every man became an independent forager." Few homes along the route were spared. "The hungry soldiers searched every house, taking up the floor, prying through the loft, sometimes finding a little meal or a piece of pork." All in all, trooper Archer Childers of the 11th Kansas thought November 1st the "most disagreeable day we had on the Price raid."[9]

Samuel Curtis lingered a day at Pea Ridge. He hoped the delay would allow reinforcements and badly needed provisions to catch up to the army. While the provisions eventually arrived, the hope for reinforcement was in vain. As he had anticipated, the Missourians did little to exert themselves in a return to his camp. At the top of the Missouri chain of command, William Rosecrans moved from unhelpful to obstructionist. He was more than miffed by the concerted efforts of Grant, Halleck, and Curtis to appropriate his troops, and he did little to cooperate with Curtis. On November 2, Rosecrans informed Sanborn that Curtis had "no authority to order you in the name of General Grant" and that he should pursue Price only "until you are satisfied he is within the grasp of General Steele's troops." Rosecrans went even further by attempting to strip the Missouri cavalry from Curtis's operational control. He gave it all to Sanborn, who was then at Springfield and 140 miles from Price. Grant theoretically put a stop to these machinations when on November 3rd he forwarded an order from the Secretary of War placing all cavalry in western Missouri under the control of Curtis.[10]

But of course, the machinations did not stop there. This was especially true as it concerned the Missouri brigade commanders. On the morning of the 29th, John McNeil had departed Curtis's army headed to the northeast and Rolla via Springfield. The next day he was encamped nineteen miles outside of Springfield when he received Curtis's recall. The temptation of resupply—and the continued absence from Curtis—proved too much. He finished his ride to Springfield where he spent the next two days reshoeing 1,500 horses before heading back toward Cassville on November 2nd with a portion of the brigade. It then took McNeil four days to make a leisurely ride of less than sixty miles. After looking around the countryside and deeming it too destitute to support his brigade, McNeil telegraphed Rosecrans describing worn-out horses and asking for permission to drop any further attempt to rejoin Curtis. Not surprisingly, Rosecrans concurred. John Sanborn proved even more recalcitrant. When he received Curtis's orders to return, Sanborn was already in Springfield. His first reaction was to telegraph Rosecrans and question the legitimacy of the orders. He then claimed that any further chase was unnecessary, asserting "General Starvation" would pursue Price instead. As with McNeil's assessment of things, Rosecrans concurred, but he did at least sustain Curtis's orders. This was still not enough for Sanborn. On the 31st, he expanded his opposition to pursuit, noting the poor condition of Union horseflesh. More dubious was his assertion that Price's men no longer destroyed any property on their retreat and therefore did not deserve serious pursuit. After the campaign, Sanborn went even further to justify inaction by claiming it was better to leave Price's army alone south of Newtonia where it would remain in a "land of starvation" and then break up and die. For the next several days, Sanborn dawdled, delayed, and moved nowhere. Although on the 31st he recommended sending 1,200 of his freshest troops in a pursuit independent of Curtis, he ultimately sent only four hundred men under Colonel J. J. Gravely on November 5th. This token force was guaranteed to be of no value in hunting Price as Sanborn ordered it merely to "ascertain the course and direction of the enemy and report it to me."[11]

All of this was too late to help Curtis. By November 3rd, he waited no more and departed Pea Ridge for Cross Hollows just fifteen miles distant. Around 10 AM, it started snowing and sleeting as the Yankees plodded through an area of Arkansas that had not been quiet during Price's invasion of Missouri. Aside from the near perpetual guerrilla actions, a large number of Confederates came together under the commands of the guerrilla Buck Brown and the regularly commissioned Colonel William H. Brooks. Colonel Brooks was a native of Michigan who had migrated to Fayetteville one year before the war and became an attorney. In that one year he developed a deep attachment not only to the cause of the South but also to his adopted town of Fayetteville, a thriving prewar settlement of about one thousand people. He spent a good portion of the war recruiting and fighting in vicinity of the town. By late 1864, he saw an opportunity to liberate Fayetteville, which had been occupied since the Battle of Prairie Grove on December 7, 1862. At Fayetteville, Colonel Marcus La Rue Harrison maintained a force of 1,100 Yankees inside fairly substantial entrenchments and outer works. As early as October 28 Brown and Brooks had attacked Fayetteville with a force that Harrison estimated at 1,200 men with two supporting pieces of artillery. While Harrison holed up within his fortifications, the Confederates lay outside for the next few days. When Brooks confirmed that Price was retreating in his direction, the colonel dispatched a request to his fellow Arkansan, James Fagan, that he provide assistance in the liberation of Fayetteville. The request arrived on November 1st as Price entered Cane Hill, which was twenty miles to the southwest of Fayetteville. Despite all of the demoralizing battlefield defeats, the calamitous retreat, and the material deprivation of the army, Price indulged Fagan and Brown. Deeming Fayetteville "of considerable importance to the Federals and its capture . . . of great advantage to the cause," Price ordered Fagan to assist with a force cobbled together from the remnants of Fagan's division assisted by eighty men from Elliot's regiment from Shelby's division. With two pieces of Richard Collins's remaining artillery, the column numbered about five hundred men.[12]

Fagan rode at the head of this force during a snowstorm on November 2nd, and it reached Fayetteville late that evening. Deprivation followed the Confederates as they camped around the town on snow-covered ground. There was no food for men or horses. What followed was not surprising. La Rue Harrison was well entrenched and the Confederate force weak. Fagan's reinforcements were disheartened and small, although Harrison completely exaggerated their numbers to 5,200 men. Beginning at 11 AM, the combined Confederate artillery directed a desultory bombardment upon the town and its fortifications that lasted most of the day and inflicted few, if any, casualties. The most telling feature of the bombardment was scattered rounds that landed in a military hospital and civilian homes that had not been evacuated,

provoking great outrage from Harrison. Aside from the haphazard bombardment, the main Confederate effort consisted of three attempted assaults of the
Yankee lines. The attacks were anemic and did not even involve the entire
force as Wright's regiment failed to enter the fray. Disregarding the exhorta-
tions of some officers, the charges lasted until the men came within range of
the Yankee rifles, at which point the Confederates broke and retreated to a
safer range. By sunset it was all over. Fagan withdrew that evening after
suffering what Harrison claimed was over one hundred casualties in killed,
wounded, and captured. Harrison's numbers were estimations, and certainly
inflated, but there was no doubt that Price's men had suffered yet another
tactical and moral defeat. For his troubles, Harrison's force lost one man
killed and eight wounded. If there was anything positive to come of the
expedition for Confederate arms, Fagan and Brooks had pinned Harrison in
Fayetteville long enough for Freeman, McCray, and Dobbin to move their
furloughed troops unmolested into north central Arkansas. [13]

Fagan's retreat was precipitated by news that Samuel Curtis was marching on Fayetteville. La Rue Harrison had dispatched several messengers to
Curtis, apprising the general of the situation and requesting help. These messengers reached Curtis about midnight on the 3rd, just as he entered camp at
Cross Hollows. Their arrival did not make the tactical situation entirely clear
to Curtis. At the same time he received Harrison's plea for help, he also
received an equally urgent request from Fort Smith "to save them from
Price." Notwithstanding the conflicting information, Curtis decided to drive
first for Fayetteville. He made it to Fayetteville, some eighteen miles distant,
by 11 AM on the 4th. Curtis just missed Fagan, who had himself received
word of the coming Yankee reinforcements. Fagan had begun his movement
back toward Cane Hill and Price much earlier in the morning. Curtis would
not, and could not, take up the pursuit. [14]

The march to Fayetteville had been hard, and Curtis was confused. He did
not know where Price's main body was and could not project its route. He
was also initially unwilling to simply follow Fagan, possibly believing he
might not track back to Price. The presence of large guerrilla bands and the
passage of Price's furloughed Arkansans through the area no doubt contributed to this confusion. Curtis thus remained at Fayetteville until the morning
of the 5th when he decided to march toward Cane Hill and Price's last
reported encampment. Before taking up the march, Curtis received written
confirmation of something else he had already concluded. Neither McNeil
nor Sanborn would be coming to his aid. The general compensated to a very

small degree by appropriating much of La Rue Harrison's cavalry and shoving it to the van of his column. That day's march was not, however, too onerous. Curtis made only eleven miles to Prairie Grove, the site of yet another old battlefield. It was something of an unnerving experience as the men slept near to, and almost on top of, the skulls and bones of the dead long ago unearthed by wolves. However, all was not bad because the men also found plenty to eat for themselves and their horses. Following breakfast the next morning, the army pushed into Cane Hill. Here Curtis found the broken parts of Price's Army of Missouri that could move no more. About one hundred sick, wounded, and exhausted Confederates littered the area, including many who had crawled from their hospital beds and hid in the woods believing they would be slaughtered by the likes of Doc Jennison and James Blunt. But to the surprise of the Confederates, Curtis provided what medicines he could spare and promptly paroled them. Now back on Price's line of retreat, Curtis followed south a trail of military debris, animal carcasses, and beaten-down stragglers. By nightfall he had marched twenty-five miles and even managed to skirmish with some elements of Price's rearguard. Samuel Curtis had somehow defied all of the odds and obstructions and was near to hauling down Price one more time. [15]

Forced now from Cane Hill, Price had an important decision to make. What route would he take to cross the Arkansas River into Confederate-occupied territory? There appeared to be several options. First, he could choose a course to the south and east, crossing the Arkansas River between Fort Smith and Little Rock. Second, he could move almost due south and traverse the river near to Fort Smith. Third, and finally, he could head southwest into the Indian Territory, crossing the Boston Mountains at a gap near present-day Stillwell. He could then follow the Sallisaw Creek until he crossed the Arkansas River between Fort Smith and Fort Gibson. Once across the river in this area, Price could drive for Boggy Depot, which offered some provisioning for the army. Price's initial desire seems to have been to keep marching south toward Fort Smith. Indeed, as late as November 1st he more than optimistically wrote Major General Samuel B. Maxey, who commanded the District of Indian Territory, that he would be "glad to assist you in the taking of Fort Smith." But by November 2nd, he had a change of heart. Price decided, with the encouragement of John B. Clark Jr., to take the far more circuitous route to southern Arkansas by crossing the Arkansas River between forts Smith and Gibson. Despite its additional length and the time needed to make the march, it was the right choice. As Price later explained, the route between forts Smith and Gibson provided the best opportunity to subsist the army. The Indian Territory was level prairie land and contained some beef for the men and grass for the animals. The other routes offered no hope of food, forage, or edible grass. No less vexing, the other routes would take the Confederates through the Boston Mountains, which Price's animals could not surmount. One other factor concerned not only Curtis's pursuit from the north but also the presence of large Union garrisons at Fort Smith and Little Rock. Price realized that any trip through the mountains would be at a slow pace, and it offered plenty of time for the available Union forces to converge on his army. There was thus no real choice. Price would have to detour through the Sallisaw Valley in the Indian Territory.[16]

At an initial glance, the journey through the Sallisaw Valley was breathtaking. As described by Richard Hinton, "On the east the flanks of the Boston Mountains sloped to the valley; their summits, lined and softened by the hazy mist of distance, bounded the horizon miles away. Westward rolled the undulating prairies. The valley was dotted with farms, buildings, and fields." And yet, the beauty of the valley and its promise of abundant food and level roads was a mirage. It was only in comparison to a trek through the Boston Mountains that the territory looked appealing. The reality was that the Army of Missouri would now suffer more than it had at any other point in its campaign. Much like northwestern Arkansas, the region was devastated by war. William McPheeters lamented, "Every house that we passed was either burned or rendered desolate. Not a sign of life was visible." There was no forage for the horses and mules. The livestock had to rely upon grass, which was hardly enough to sustain them. For the men it was no better. A destitute, and generally hostile, Indian population provided little food, and that which they did was usually worthless. In one case, a group of soldiers was able to get some bear meat, but it was so laden with fat that the men chose to grease their boots with it rather than eat it. On those occasions when the troops found wild cattle, the meat had to be eaten without salt or bread. The men particularly bemoaned the lack of salt, and with good reason. Although it obviously enhanced the taste of the meat, salt enabled preservation of the meat. A shortage of salt manifested itself as the army was perpetually beset with gastrointestinal sicknesses that not only inflicted pain and discomfort but also eventually forced scores to fall by the side of the roads. The accumulated result was that just one day out of Cane Hill, one soldier recorded that "a feeling of despondency pervades the army," while another sadly remarked, "our army has been a loose undisciplined herd." It would get still worse.[17]

No matter the suffering of men and beasts, Price had to push the army as much as possible because of Curtis's reappearance at Fayetteville. However, Price could only push so much. On the 4th, he made only fourteen miles. On the 5th it was eighteen miles. And on the 6th the army stretched it to twenty miles to Pheasant Ford on the Arkansas River. This was about twenty-five miles upriver from Fort Smith near where the Sallisaw Creek emptied into the Arkansas River. The crossing site was not without its problems, and it allowed Price's army an opportunity to demonstrate that it had not yet been completely demoralized. The ford itself was not readily accessed from the northern bank, as it stood one-and-one-half miles within the woods. Price posted Fagan's men ahead of the army on the 5th, and they succeeded in chopping a path through the trees that would enable the remainder of the army and its wagons to pass. The ability to get the army through the ford quickly was critical.[18]

Although Price did not know it at the time, it was the place at which Curtis would pursue no more. All of his orders from Washington said so, as did common sense. Since the very beginning of the pursuit, all coordinating instructions and orders named the Arkansas River as the end of Curtis's line of pursuit. No less important, Curtis's men and horses were worn out, albeit certainly not to the degree of Price's army or even what generals Sanborn and McNeil had predicted. It should be noted here that the failure to prevent Price from crossing the Arkansas River should not have depended entirely upon Curtis. In fact, the deeper Price drove into Arkansas and then the Indian Territory, the more Union success depended upon the actions of Union commanders in Arkansas. In this there was nothing but disappointment. As Curtis bore down on Price from the north, Union commanders in Arkansas failed to concentrate their forces or track the Confederates aggressively. It was much the same story as it had been when Price left Arkansas in August headed for Missouri, and responsibility for this lack of aggressiveness fell again on the shoulders of Frederick Steele, who commanded the Department of Arkansas.

Since the beginning of the campaign, General Steele had been a poor bystander. He had allowed Price to travel through Arkansas with near impunity back in August, and he did so again upon Price's return in October and November. It is not that Steele possessed large numbers of men and equipment to deal with Price. At the end of October, Steele showed 17,618 soldiers ready for active duty largely garrisoned in outposts strung along the Arkansas River. He also had his fair share of supply trains to protect and guerrillas to fight behind his lines. But Price's expedition also provided Steele operational breathing space. When Price left the state, he took with him many of the organized Confederate troops then in Arkansas and just about every cavalryman. More significantly, Price also cleaned out a good chunk of the guerrilla population and its primary leadership and dragged that along to Missouri as well. However, as much as this changed the Confederate order of battle in Arkansas and eased Steele's operational needs, it did not prompt the department commander to great action. As Price moved north, Steele looked south, and, in the words of the historian David Demuth, "instituted a campaign of harassment on Confederate camps, forage stations, and supply points south of the Arkansas River."[19]

This was especially true even after Steele received news of Price's difficulties in Missouri. Between October 19th and the 23rd, Steele responded by orchestrating a cavalry drive eighty miles south from Little Rock to Princeton with the simple goals of gathering food and locating Confederate forces. The ensuing operation provoked only small Confederate resistance and gathered up just enough food to sustain the Unionists in their expedition. It also distracted Steele from any serious attempt to concentrate his forces and support Curtis, although that was precisely what E. R. S. Canby, Halleck, and Grant had directed him to do once Price headed south from Kansas City. Things could not have been made more clear to Steele than when Canby sent Steele the following telegram on October 31st: "[Price] should not be allowed to get back by any route through Arkansas or within your reach. Any troops that you may use for this purpose will be replaced on the Arkansas and White Rivers by troops from other points." Steele informed Canby that he was "watching Price's movements closely" and that he had sent some cavalry and infantry to Fort Smith, yet his tactical plan was entirely passive. After providing the reinforcements to Fort Smith, Steele ordered its commander, Brigadier General John M. Thayer, to "draw in his outposts and all public property . . . before Price can reach them, in case he should come that way." The only other significant move Steele made was to send 1,600 cavalry and four pieces of artillery to Lewisburg, about fifty miles up the Arkansas River from Little Rock, to guard against Price's crossing there. On November 4th he promised further to put "all the infantry that can be furnished" in the field once he determined anything concrete about Price's whereabouts. Unfortunately for the Union, he did not look too terribly hard with anything approaching active patrolling. The troops at Fort Smith and Lewisburg remained stuck in place.[20]

Left on his own to continue the chase past Cane Hill, Samuel Curtis pressed as much as possible, with Benteen's brigade once again in the lead. The path was now very easy to follow. The unbroken terrain helped, but it was a path made clear by the disintegrating residue of the Confederate army. All along the trail could be found discarded ammunition, camp equipage, wagons, and broken-down horses and mules. Curtis kept moving past nightfall on November 7th. By 11 PM he had marched thirty miles and was within possible striking distance. But his column was strung out badly, and darkness prevented any further pursuit for the evening. After resting for the night, though without any food, the army started the chase anew at 7 AM with La Rue Harrison and his 1st Arkansas Cavalry in the lead. Daylight revealed the broad expanse of timber skirting the northern bank of the Arkansas River, and the army pressed harder. Aside from a few stragglers, though, there was little Confederate resistance to be found. Price and what was left of his army had crossed the river one day earlier. Upon arrival at the river itself, Curtis's men ran into the stragglers and the freshly cut road through the timber and to the ford. Harrison's cavalry exchanged some gunfire with the disorganized Confederates and promptly shoved them across the river to the southern side. Some of the Unionists splashed to the opposite bank, but they quickly returned as there would be no further pursuit. Harrison instead reported back to Curtis, who rapidly forwarded William McLain's artillery to the bank of the river. At Curtis's direction, McLain's artillerymen discharged thirty-four rounds of shell into the trees on the opposite bank, and into the remaining Confederate stragglers, as a salute to the Union on its national election day. As the sounds of the artillery salvos echoed along the banks of the river, Curtis's hunt for Sterling Price came to an end.[21]

The return of Union forces to Kansas and Missouri did not, however, mean the end of all peril for Price's army. It was very much to the contrary, as few marches during the war exceeded it in privation. In the week following the passage of the Arkansas River, one day blended into the next as the army trudged to the west along the Arkansas River and then to the southwest, skirting the Canadian River. There was little unit cohesion, and in the words of Henry Luttrell the "troops straggle along as they please." From November 8 to 10, the army made short marches averaging slightly more than ten miles each day. A cold rain was constant, as was an ever-increasing hunger. Food and forage almost disappeared. From time to time, wild beef came within the range of the troops, but even then some units got little. This was especially so for those regiments at the rear of the army, which prompted officers and enlisted men to break away from the slow-moving army so that they could forage in its advance. With little available meat, the men took to eating acorns and hickory nuts. The horses and mules suffered no less. They died by the hundreds, turning the army into one long procession of walking skeletons. In Shelby's division, the few remaining healthy horses got rotated into pulling Richard Collins's two pieces of artillery. The army's generals were not immune to the consequences of the famine. Shelby lost his horse to sickness, Jeff Thompson had his mount stolen, and James Fagan gave his horse to a sick soldier. All would have to walk through various sections of the Indian Territory. There was no precise accounting of the loss of mounts in the army, but John C. Wright's regiment provides some measuring point for estimation. Writing on November 8th, Wright noted, "there is not a pack horse or mule in my Regt: more than half of my command is dismounted."[22]

Another consequence of the loss of the livestock was the further erosion of the number of wagons in the army and thus the ability to carry the sick and wounded. Here, again, John C. Wright offers the best accounting of an individual regiment when he informed his brigade commander that he had no wagons and only two ambulances. Given the dearth of transportation, the sick and wounded were left to die by the road and in adjacent fields. For those who witnessed this scene, it was a shattering experience. As recounted by R. L. Brown, "I have often seen men lying by the road side dying from starvation and fatigue with no hand to help and scarcely one to pity, and the poor fellows asked to have sticks piled over him to keep the wolves off him." Among those now falling out were victims of a new terror within the ranks: a smallpox epidemic. As the misery and hunger spread, discipline frayed. Theft became rampant with food, horses, and even wagons becoming the most sought-after commodities.[23]

The remaining wagons in the headquarters trains proved popular targets. Part of the attraction came from rumors that the chief quartermaster, Major Isaac Brinker, had several wagons filled with food and private goods. No less important, these wagons contained an unknown number of blacks. Who these men were is not known. They could have been impressed along the march. They could have been among the large number of teamsters traveling with the army. Or, they could have been the slaves of men in the army. Whatever their nature, they rode in commissary wagons with the small amount of flour the army carried with it. For the sick and hungry soldiers walking alongside the wagons, this was an intolerable situation. Insults and threats rose in intensity, and Jeff Thompson had to tamp down an assault. A similar situation developed on the evening of the 9th when a large number of men determined to attack the headquarters trains in the mistaken belief that the officers were hoarding flour. The posting of a strong guard that night deterred the uprising, but it did not stop them the next morning after the guard had been released. About twenty men charged the breakfast table of some of the officers and, according to William McPheeters, "ate all our breakfast." Given the disappearance of food, it was not long into this stage of the march when the men began eating their horses and mules. On the evening of November 10th even John B. Clark Jr.'s headquarters officers joined the roster of men eating "horse style." In the 10th Missouri, there were not enough sick or dying mules and horses to satisfy the need. Fearing for his own horse, Henry Luttrell began guarding the animal at night to prevent others from eating it. With wolves gathering about the army, William G. Hazen of Monroe's regiment concluded that "we present a pitiable, forlorn aspect." He also remarked that many now openly blamed Sterling Price for their troubles: "G___ d___ old Price, is the almost constant ejaculation from men exhausted in both body and spirit."[24]

For all of Price's responsibility for the disaster that befell his army, he was not remotely the only one to blame. Edmund Kirby Smith had at the outset of the campaign abdicated any role in supporting Price's journey either through Arkansas or Missouri. He did even less to support Price on his way back to Arkansas. As Robert L. Kerby has properly noted, Kirby Smith had at least three ways of supporting Price upon his return. First, he could have directed Samuel Maxey to make a concerted push from the Indian Territory toward Fort Scott, which would have diverted Union forces. Second, he could have used John B. Magruder's infantry in Arkansas to make some kind of offensive along the Arkansas River, which would, once again, pull Union troops from Price. Third, and most doable, would have been to try to establish some type of depot system along Price's retreat that would have alleviated the starvation gripping the army. Instead, Kirby Smith did nothing. Throughout much of Price's expedition, he apparently remained incapacitated by illness, leaving his chief of staff, Brigadier General William Boggs, as the de facto commander of the Confederate Trans-Mississippi. The tragic part of this episode was that Brigadier General Stand Watie's Indian brigade was chomping at the proverbial bit throughout the summer of 1864 to make a raid into Kansas. In August, Boggs conveyed Kirby Smith's approval of the raid with the suggestion that Watie move before October so as to strike while Price was in Missouri. The only problem was that when Watie moved in the middle of September, Price had not yet cleared Arkansas. In this regard, there is some defense for Kirby Smith's failure to support Price. Price had traveled much slower than Kirby Smith probably anticipated, and he had lost communication with Price's army. Consequently, Watie's success in capturing a Union wagon train at Cabin Creek in the Indian Territory occurred much too early to do anything for Price. Kirby Smith would encourage no further action. Even when John Magruder sought approval to move on Little Rock in early October, Kirby Smith would only direct Magruder to hold fast. A series of telegrams flowed between Magruder, Kirby Smith, and Maxey, but there would be no further action to help Price.[25]

Abandoned, Price continued to try to salvage his army. To do so, Price realized he could not keep the army in one piece. In some cases, this meant mass furloughs for the Arkansas units. In other cases, it meant sending units ahead to Boggy Depot and detaching Shelby's division to forage in an area between the Canadian River and its northern fork. Helping matters even further was the simple fact that as the army continued to move south it entered into a more fertile, and friendly, area of the Indian Territory. Wild game and edible grass became more plentiful and the Indians more willing to trade. Surgeon J. H. P. Baker proved a valuable indicator of the quick change in fortune when he described the army on November 12th as "destitute but somewhat encouraged." The condition of the army improved even further when Price's headquarters and Shelby's division finally entered Boggy Depot on the 18th. The men received rations and traded with the Indians, while many an officer dined at a well-stocked table within the town. However, Boggy Depot could not sustain Price for long, and Old Pap decided to depart after only one day. After leaving all of his nonambulatory sick and wounded at the depot, Price pointed his army south toward a crossing of the Red River at Kent's Ferry in Fannin County, Texas. The Confederates marched slowly, averaging a bit more than ten miles per day and crossing the Red River on November 22. About this time, Price finally reestablished contact with Magruder, who provided orders to march to Laynesport, just across the Texas and Arkansas border.[26]

Price and his jaded men would thus travel for another eleven days. This part of the journey was marked by short daily distances, muddy roads, increasingly plentiful food and forage, and a drunken brawl among Price's staff. Rarely did all the brigades travel together or in close proximity. They sometimes took different routes or delayed departures from the various evening campsites. When Price finally brought his men into Laynesport on December 3rd after a march of 1,434 miles, it was a pitiful remnant of the army that entered Missouri back in September with such high hopes of redeeming the state for the Confederacy. Excluding the units that had been furloughed, Price had no more than 3,500 men, and about one-third of those had no weapons. About the only thing left to do, aside from pray that the Union conducted no offensive operations south of the Arkansas River, was to take most of what had been Price's cavalry and convert it into infantry. Price's Army of Missouri ceased to exist, and its odyssey had come to a close.[27]

Chapter Nineteen

Aftermath

Sterling Price's arrival at Laynesport did not close the story of the campaign. There was yet a great deal of unfinished business. Hundreds of Confederate Missourians, long isolated from Price's main body, moved south trying desperately to find and join Price's army. Moving in the opposite direction, worn-out Union troops made a barbarous return march to Kansas and Missouri. Even as these actions took place, over one thousand captured Confederates experienced retribution and a threat of death unlike anything they had seen on the battlefield. And finally, the end of the campaign gave soldiers on both sides the opportunity to engage in bitter public disputes about who either deserved the glory of victory or the responsibility of defeat. Price, himself, would have to face his oldest and most ardent critic, and in so doing it would bring into the open so many of the controversies associated with the expedition and its historical memory.

Some degree of irony characterized Price's retreat to Laynesport. As his army hemorrhaged thousands of men through death, desertion, and furlough, as many as two thousand old soldiers and new recruits stalked the army, trying to join it. These men fell into at least two categories. First, there was a host of soldiers who had become separated from Price either through furlough or battlefield confusion as the army retreated rapidly in the aftermath of the battles around Kansas City. Many of these men eventually made it back to Price, while others remained forever separated and scattered throughout Arkansas, the Indian Territory, and Texas.[1]

The second, and largest, group to pursue Price was cohesive bands of recruits. They varied in size from a handful to several hundred. Colonel

Caleb W. Dorsey led one such large group. Dorsey had entered the state in the spring and successfully gathered several hundred recruits in a cluster of counties north of the Missouri River and near St. Louis. When Price pivoted away from St. Louis early in the campaign, he left Dorsey isolated. Dorsey and his growing gaggle of recruits then crossed the Missouri River in the vicinity of Jefferson City and headed south through central Missouri. Although several of Dorsey's men would be captured and executed along the way and dozens more would desert, the group somehow evaded all manner of EMM and MSM and joined Price in Texas.[2]

Yet another large group was led by Captain Salem H. Ford and a Captain Grooms from Shelby's division. The two captains had entered northwest Missouri in the summer and successfully recruited about two hundred men by the time Price made it to Kansas City. Among the recruits was a black man out of Clay County. However, Ford and Grooms could not link with Price, which then prompted them to cross the Missouri River just to the east of the retreating Confederate army. The group managed to make it into Hickory County before running into the 8th MSM near the town of Quincy on November 1st. In a running battle that lasted nearly two days, the 8th MSM managed to kill at least seven men, including Captain Grooms. Ford ultimately made it to Price in Texas, but with an unknown number of recruits. Years after the war, Ford was incensed to read a Yankee newspaper account of the action in Hickory County that included a claim of one hundred Confederates killed. Point by point, Ford demonstrated the falsity of the Yankee story in his own article in the *Confederate Veteran* magazine and a memoir, but he never quite realized that the two men were arguing over two different actions.[3]

In all probability, the Yankee account referred to Colonel Eli Hodge's body of recruits. A Kentuckian by birth, Hodge recruited in Boone, Audrain, and Howard counties and succeeded in gathering up about 450 men. Once again, the recruits became isolated from the main army when Price made his turn to the south at Kansas City. Somehow, Hodges shepherded the group all the way through the state and to Cassville in Barry County when a detachment of four hundred troopers from the 2nd Arkansas Cavalry (United States) finally caught up to them on October 29th. The Unionists quickly routed Hodges and his recruits, killing fifty and taking thirty-seven prisoners. Displaying considerable resiliency, Hodges managed to gather up the remaining recruits and press on through Arkansas and the Indian Territory, finally reaching Clarksville, Texas, with what Hodge later believed was 225 men. The unit then disbanded with the recruits, joining D. A. Williams's Missouri cavalry.[4]

All told, Price believed as of December 28th that five thousand recruits had made it to his army. But even in this accounting, Price exaggerated the numbers he actually controlled. Most of these recruits had already been detached with the various Arkansas brigades and regiments that had been shed from the army once it had departed Missouri. Given the size of the groups led by Dorsey, Hodge, and Ford, Albert Castel was probably correct when he estimated that between one thousand and two thousand additional recruits would later trickle into the army throughout the winter of 1864 and 1865. Unfortunately for the Confederacy, these numbers were well below the thirty thousand recruits Price had forecast when he lobbied for, and planned, the invasion. Even in the aftermath of the invasion, Price remained fantastically divorced from reality when he proclaimed, "I am satisfied that could I have remained in Missouri this winter the army would have been increased 50,000 men." Price had his chance to remain in the state, and it proved impossible. He also had his chance to recruit, and the men never came in the numbers he either predicted or needed.

The drama and controversy associated with Confederate recruiting were matched to some degree by the return of Curtis's army to Kansas and Missouri. No sooner had Curtis fired his parting shots at Price's stragglers on the Arkansas River than he promptly disbanded the army and cast off the component parts to go their separate ways. For General Blunt and Thomas Moonlight's brigade, that meant a hike down the Arkansas River to Fort Smith and subsequently a ride up the border to Fort Scott. Benteen was to take his brigade "by the shortest route and at his discretion" back to Missouri so that he could report to the Department of the Tennessee. Doc Jennison and his brigade were to retrace the army's route back through the Indian Territory, Arkansas, and Missouri. In practical terms, Jennison would follow Benteen but ride one day later. John Ford and the 2nd Colorado would accompany Curtis to Fort Leavenworth, taking a very roundabout journey through forts Gibson and Scott. All went pretty much as planned save for the itinerary of Moonlight's brigade. Moonlight did indeed march his men to Fort Smith, where they sojourned for a short time before being directed back up the Arkansas River seventy miles to Fort Gibson, where they promptly marched north to Fort Scott, arriving December 7th.[5]

Although the different major units went their separate ways, they shared privation. Much as the journey south had been marked by suffering, so, too, would the journey north. They carried little food with them on the forced march to the Arkansas River, and the men and horses would be largely on their own for the return. Horses, already stressed, found it difficult to find edible grass. In the 11th Kansas, the short ride to Fort Smith found "strong men crying for food" and having "nothing to eat except the buds on the trees." Horses had to be let go, and those men who now walked watched their boots and shoes disintegrate with each step. Even upon their arrival at Fort Smith, Moonlight's troopers found trouble and especially little to eat. Indeed, they had to camp outside the fort to avoid a fight over food inside the fort with garrison troops.[6]

Benteen's and Jennison's brigades commenced an even more distressing journey. They had come through a desolate land and now had to repeat the task, just in a different direction. The men of the 4th Iowa gave apt testimony to the difficulties. With the temperature approaching zero degrees on November 9th, James Vanorsdol witnessed troopers wearing short sleeves, while others walked with rags tied about their feet in the place of shoes. As chronicled by Lot Abraham, the lack of forage and plummeting temperatures exacted a terrible cost among the horses. Day by day, they froze or simply broke down. In an effort to preserve their horses, the troopers dismounted and led the animals on marches averaging sixteen miles per day. It was not until the 12th that the column finally ran into a supply train from Fort Scott when they camped, yet again, on the old battlefield at Prairie Grove. While the area provided little food of its own, this section of northwest Arkansas remained fertile ground for guerrillas. The guerrillas waylaid isolated foragers and shot several of Benteen's and Jennison's men.[7]

The Yankee response was hardly surprising, and it continued to demonstrate a commingling of the savage guerrilla war with Price's campaign. Frederick Benteen burned numerous houses within five miles of his route. Cane Hill was particularly hard hit as it erupted in flames. However, Benteen's reprisals paled in comparison to the work of Doc Jennison. The destruction was such that the *Arkansas Journal*, a Unionist newspaper, concluded: "The blackened chimneys that mark the burial ground of all that was dear to hundreds of once happy families in Northwestern Arkansas, are appropriately termed 'Jennison's tombstones.'" Upon conclusion of the march, one member of Jennison's brigade proudly noted, "Arkansas guerrilla mothers, and sisters use the name of the latter [Jennison] already to frighten unruly children, and by the light of burning houses, and beside the blackening timbers of their homes, wish perhaps that 'dad hadn't been and gone off with

Price or into the brush.'" Although elements of the 14th Kansas, 16th Kansas, 3rd Wisconsin, and two artillery batteries traveled with Jennison, it was only the 15th Kansas that became associated with this war of vengeance. Ironically, for the bulk of the campaign the 15th had performed well, despite scattered incidents of retributive justice. But in marching through Arkansas and into Missouri, the 15th reverted completely in its ways. Two things helped account for this. First, there was Jennison's personal history with, and attachment to, the 15th. Jennison recruited the men of the regiment in the aftermath of Quantrill's massacre at Lawrence, and they were used to following Jennison almost without question, especially if the orders involved the punishment of bushwhackers or their families. Second, and in a related fashion, there was little effective, or at least restraining, leadership in the unit. George H. Hoyt, described by the historian Stephen Z. Starr as "Jennison's devoted shadow and disciple," was sick for much of the journey home and had to ride in an ambulance. Hoyt was physically unable to command the regiment, but neither Hoyt nor Jennison bothered to designate a replacement by orders. Major John M. Laing became the de facto commander at twenty-one years of age, and a poorer selection could not be imagined. The last time Laing was seen in these pages was when he took his battalion on an ignominious flight from combat at the Big Blue on October 22nd. Notorious as a prewar "Redleg," Laing readily followed Jennison's dubious lead and orders, which allowed the 15th to unravel into a mob. Straggling and rogue foraging proliferated as only between 30 and 50 men out of a possible 175 rode in the regimental column. Where Benteen torched Cane Hill, Jennison and Laing followed suit at Prairie Grove and Bentonville, with homes all along the route pillaged and burned to ashes. When not burning homes, Laing accompanied his men into them to loot. On one occasion, he robbed an old woman and her three daughters of their money, clothing, and blankets. He then, according to one witness, emerged from the house and pranced about the yard with a quilt wrapped around his body. Abetting Laing was Lieutenant John L. Thompson, his assistant quartermaster, who systematically engaged in what a later court martial termed "gross misconduct" when he confiscated massive quantities of food, household supplies, and horses for his personal profit.[8]

Theft turned to murder when on November 11, near Cane Hill, two men from the 15th disappeared and another was wounded by bushwhackers. Rumor spread quickly that bushwhackers had killed the missing men. With reports of similar attacks against Benteen's brigade, Jennison grew excited and demanded vengeance on November 12th. He subsequently forced some women from a nearby home and personally demanded that they turn their men over or he would strip them "bare as a bird's arse" and burn down their houses. Shortly thereafter the women produced two men. After brief questioning, Jennison ordered Laing and the 15th to hang them. Jennison and Laing were not the only ones in the 15th to participate in the mayhem. Perhaps worse was Captain Joseph B. Swain, yet another notorious "Red Leg." Swain unleashed his command, Company K, upon the unarmed, and usually female, population of Arkansas and Missouri, and he personally executed a man outside of Prairie Grove on November 15th.[9]

The passage of the 15th and Jennison's brigade back into Missouri seems only to have accelerated the rampage, albeit with less bloodshed. By November 22, Jennison had marched through Newtonia, Sarcoxie, and Dry Fork, stealing everything that could be put in his wagons or forced to walk behind them. By the time Kansas's preeminent Jayhawker crossed Coon Creek, one person observed he had "as many as 200 head of stock cattle, half of them fit for good beef, 200 sheep, 40 or 50 yoke of oxen, 20 or 30 wagons, and a large number of horses, jacks, [and] jennets." No less appalling, "There are cases where the men tore the clothing off of women in search of money, and threatening to burn houses in order to get money is the common practice. They acted worse than guerrillas." When Jennison had arrived back in Kansas, James Blunt had already received reports detailing many of the outrages. Blunt quickly issued general orders withholding all pay for the men of the 15th until an investigation could determine who was responsible for the various depredations. He also took action to reassign Jennison and institute court martial proceedings against several officers. While all of these men awaited trail, Samuel Curtis's civilian cartographer, Lyman Bennett, could only conclude, "If half the atrocities that are told of Col. Jennison are true, he is too much of a barbarian to live."[10]

As was inevitable, all of the accusations involving Jennison became intertwined with the long-simmering political feuds of Kansas. Jennison, a supporter of the Thomas Carney faction in Kansas politics, charged Blunt with being a lackey of Senator James Lane, who wanted revenge on all opponents. He further claimed that Blunt had discriminated against Jennison's brigade throughout the Price campaign by withholding rations, animals, and wagons. To Jennison, Thomas Moonlight, an ally of Blunt and Lane, got everything that should have been his. Jennison even insinuated that Blunt denied him reinforcements at Byram's Ford on October 22 as a matter of political spite.

But what was missing from Jennison's, or any of the other men accused of heinous crimes in the 15th Kansas, was a denial that they had burned or killed. Inevitably, the accused either claimed they had been ordered to commit the crimes or that their actions were justified by precedent and the authority of "drum-head" courts. Jennison himself asserted that one of Blunt's staff officers ordered him, "in the presence of at least ten officers of my brigade . . . to desolate the country from the Arkansas River to Fort Scott, and burn every house on the route." Jennison never produced one witness to corroborate this claim, but neither he nor his officers doubted the morality of such "orders" or their compliant response to them. Regardless, Jennison and the men of the 15th were probably correct in alleging that politics had something to do with the charges. After all, drum-head trials and executions were quite the norm in the border war, and they rarely generated any sort of official disproval from the side executing prisoners. This was especially the case with many of the actors in the Price invasion. John McNeil, for example, was infamous for his massacre at Palmyra. As late as October 29th, William Rosecrans's chief of staff, John V. DuBois, had exhorted Brigadier General James Craig at Warrensburg to "hang every secesh soldier you catch in Federal uniform by military commission or drum-head." On the Confederate side, there was D. A. Williams's execution of six men near Carrolton, and, of course, Timothy Reeves's execution of seven men from the 3rd MSM near Pilot Knob. Even more to the point, the men of the 15th had long practiced summary execution with nary an official complaint. Joseph Swain, for example, had murdered a prisoner at Trading Post on October 25 and then another near Carthage on the 28th, but no one really cared those times. The controversy involving the 15th ran its predictable course when Blunt court martialed Jennison, not for any atrocity, but for a failure to obey orders involving the reorganization of his command at the conclusion of the campaign and the insults Jennison hurled in his direction. The attendant courts martial for Jennison and his subordinate officers in the 15th Kansas lasted through the spring and into the summer, with most getting relatively light punishments. The heaviest punishment went to Joseph Swain, who the court sentenced to life imprisonment. Swain, nevertheless, avoided even that when he escaped transport to prison.[11]

The cases of Jennison and his men attracted little attention beyond the border areas of Kansas, Missouri, and Arkansas. Of far greater interest to Union authorities in Missouri was the prosecution of the state's pro-Confederate population that had been flushed into the open during Price's expedition. It was time for retribution, and the commander of the District of North Missouri, Brigadier General Clinton Fisk, typified the mind-set: "I have taken the necessary steps to procure a carefully prepared list of all who from this district have, during the year 1864, joined themselves to the Confederates under Price, or have been attached to his more intolerable and wicked organizations within the district." Fisk was hardly the only commander to make these lists, and they revealed the extent of Price's recruiting, especially in many counties near the Missouri River. Morgan County, for example, provided 125 men, while Cooper, Lafayette, and Saline counties generated another 611. At the very least, the men on these lists would be jailed if they returned and their families taxed much as pro-Southern Missourians had been since the beginning of the war. But there was a complication. As many of these men did indeed return, they reported being conscripted. General Fisk did not believe there was any ambiguity at all and sneeringly remarked that the returning Missourians were deserters who had been deluded into thinking Price had meant to stay in Missouri. Only upon their return and the attempt to resume a normal life did they, according to Fisk, come up with a "well-told tale of conscription." Many supported Fisk's sense of things. W. A. Wilson of Marshall, for example, testified: "I am satisfied from what I can learn that all the Rebels & Rebel Sympathisers [*sic*] here were of the opinion that Price was going to occupy and hold the State and thereupon concluded that it would be best for them to manifest a willingness . . . to give him their services." In Chariton County, E. J. Turner did not "think many men were forcibly conscripted as they had the opportunity to take me forcibly if they desired. I refused to go & they did not attempt to use force." Perhaps most telling, Unionists were not the only conscription skeptics. John H. Utz of the 1st Missouri Cavalry, and imprisoned at Gratiot Street Prison in St. Louis, wrote in February 1865 that "some of the conscripts whine powerful. . . . The truth is they are not really conscripts but claim this so as to get home."[12]

Despite all of these declarations, there was ambiguity when it came to the claims of conscription. Not surprisingly, the ambiguity often derived from the intersection of the guerrilla war with Price's journey through Missouri. Such was the case involving Theodor Lachance, John Boyer, and Antoine Carron of St. Francis County. At varying times in September and October, all of these men claimed to have been "conscripted" into a group led by Antoine and Joseph Aubochon. The Aubochons, in turn, belonged to a network of guerrillas loosely commanded by the notorious Sam Hildebrand and a Price recruiter named Theodule Rouse. There were major discrepancies in each of the alleged conscript's stories, but the one thing they could all agree upon was that they had been forced by gunpoint into service and that they all fled when they could. The story mattered little to Union authorities because there was, among other things, no evidence of the men ever trying to report what had happened. [13]

Much like everything associated with ferreting out secessionists in Missouri, there was nothing new in the demand that people report secessionist or bushwhacker activity. But by this point in the war, even a simple report of "conscription" sometimes did little to mollify Union authorities. James Criswell discovered this when he reported being conscripted. The provost marshal in Fulton subsequently arrested and sent him off to Gratiot. Hardened by three years of bitter guerrilla war and the prevarications of people who either sought to straddle the fence between Unionism and secessionism or cover their pro-Confederate actions, Yankee officials believed few of the hard-luck stories associated with Price's coming to Missouri. James Meyer of Callaway County could attest to the provost marshal's uncompromising attitude when he claimed to have been conscripted on October 9th. According to Meyer, he remained with his captors for two days when he escaped and went home. "I staid [*sic*] there until the 15th of October 1864 when the rebels came to my house, & upon my refusal to go with them [they] shot me in the left side." The provost marshal rejected Meyer's explanation for his wound and convicted him of violating a previous loyalty oath and abetting the rebels. He was sentenced to ten years in prison. [14]

Ultimately, the provost marshal relied upon old methods to deal with the influx of people accused of either joining Price or collaborating with him. For some, a simple examination proved enough to gain release. However, the provost marshal usually demanded more proof of either loyalism or coercion. The first step in this process was often to publish the names of men who claimed to have been conscripted by Price. The intention was simply to give notice so that anyone could come forward and present information regarding the loyalty of the conscripts. In this fashion, by November 28th the provost marshal of the Department of the Missouri listed 125 men at either the Gratiot or Alton, Illinois, camps that claimed to have been conscripted. At Fort Leavenworth, Federal authorities possessed another one hundred men who had been captured in Arkansas and the Indian Territory. In short order, eyewitnesses, family, friends, and enemies submitted an avalanche of statements about the men. Where the explanations of the accused seemed plausible and the loyalty testimonials strong, Federal authorities allowed some of the prisoners to post bond. The practice originated in 1861 and eventually covered thousands of Missourians suspected of disloyalty, while raising millions of dollars to help cover the state's war expenses. As it had since the beginning of the war, the amount of the bond for those enmeshed in the Price campaign varied according to location and the financial standing of the accused. Charles Scott and Richard D. Shackleford of Saline posted bond of $500 and proclaimed an oath of allegiance in order to gain release and find proof of conscription. In Morgan County, James Livingstone and Mark H. Goode had to post $1,000 and $3,000 bonds respectively so that they could gather proof of conscription and have it forwarded to Jefferson City for adjudication. Over in Callaway County, ten men accused of volunteering for Price were allowed to make a collective bond of $10,000 before appearing at a hearing. [15]

In still other situations, those professing to be conscripted bypassed trying either to post bond or gather proof of the claim. On October 31st, authorities in Jefferson City found themselves with "a number of conscripts from Price's army," who now wanted to enlist for twelve months in the U.S. Army. Given the flexible loyalties of so many Missourians caught up in the war, the desire to switch sides was hardly surprising, especially now that northern prospects of victory looked strong. No less important, the practice of switching sides was not that rare. At various times during the war, both the Union and the Confederacy combed their prison camps for those willing to change uniforms or "galvanize." By December 3rd, the Department of the Missouri allowed some of Price's self-professed conscripts to galvanize when twenty-four men were released in order to enlist in the U.S. Army. Although there are no precise records as to how many of the men caught up in the Price invasion came to change sides, and this would include men who made no claim of conscription, a majority of the prisoners from the invasion eventually came to reside at the Alton and Rock Island, Illinois, prisons where Federal authorities recruited the galvanized 2nd, 3rd, and 5th U.S. Volunteer Infantries. [16]

While the motivation to galvanize may have been rooted in a weak, or even nonexistent, attachment to the Confederacy, what can also not be doubted is that some switched sides due to the unfathomably brutal conditions at Gratiot, Alton, and Rock Island. Even before arriving at these prisons, the captured men from Price's army had experienced an ordeal. For those able to walk after battlefield capture, they were first herded to Fort Leavenworth or Warrensburg from points all along Price's retreat. There would be little food and even less water as the men trudged along in the increasingly bitter cold. The prisoners were eventually shipped by rail or steamboat to Gratiot. To anyone who observed these men along the route, the prisoners presented a sorry spectacle. Their clothing was threadbare and largely torn. They had no hats and few blankets. Nothing distinguished officers from the enlisted, and one Unionist believed the whole collection "the most uncouth looking fellows that could well be gotten together." At the Hermann stop along the Missouri River, there was also time for summary justice. In one trainload, the provost noticed Abner Kirby, who was suspected of recruiting north of the Missouri River in a blue uniform. He was promptly pulled from the mass of prisoners, tied to a stake, and shot by a squad of eight men. Although prisoners had been funneled to Gratiot throughout the campaign, they only began to arrive in large numbers at the beginning of November. On the 6th, two trains brought the biggest contingent to the city at the 14th Street Depot. Union officials orchestrated an exhibition of the arrival, and Wisconsin infantry escorted 620 prisoners through the streets of St. Louis preceded by a band. The curious and the sympathetic gathered by the dozen to watch. One reporter noted: "Their faces were lean, haggard and cadaverous, their cheeks sunken, their faces bowed, and the whole appearance wretched in the extreme." Some could barely walk, and a few lumbered with greasy blankets or carpet remnants around their shoulders. One girl broke down in tears at the sight. [17]

Not all of the Confederates were in such a miserable state. On the 7th, seven senior officers, including Marmaduke, Cabell, and Slemons, arrived in St. Louis and were, according to one dissatisfied reporter, housed temporarily in "one of the best hotels in the city and feasted like lords." The rest of the prisoners were not treated near as well. Although Gratiot lacks the infamy of Union camps such as Douglas, Point Lookout, or Elmira, it deserves to be listed with those hellholes. Gratiot was a large, octagonal stone building originally designed as a medical college. Founded and owned by a secessionist, Gratiot was seized by the Unionists at the outset of the war. Henry Halleck, then commanding the Department of the West, turned it into a prison with the intention of only using it as a transfer point to other, and larger, camps such as Alton in Illinois. Unlike most camps, Gratiot not only housed prisoners of war but also civilian males and females accused of disloyal acts and U.S. soldiers awaiting trial. Henry Halleck unquestionably intended to administer Gratiot in a humane fashion, but the reality was, as the historian Charles Sanders has noted, that Gratiot "joined the lengthening list of Union pens in which southern captives were sickening and dying at an

alarming rate." The chief problem at Gratiot was overcrowding. Its capacity
was five hundred prisoners, but at varying times during the war it bulged
with over 1,200. During the peak periods of overcrowding, which usually
matched the winter months, sickness spread as the men were crowded into
small, damp, and unventilated rooms with little chance of ever making it into
the equally cramped hospital. It was under these conditions that Price's men
entered the prison, and they were crammed into rooms, according to one
inspection, "like a flock of sheep." Shortly thereafter, the prisoners began to
die. In the first two weeks of November, thirty-four died, with pneumonia
being the biggest killer followed by dysentery and measles. During the next
two weeks, another twenty-one died with, once again, pneumonia the leading
cause. By February more than eight hundred men of Sterling Price's army
entered Gratiot, and 134 died.[18]

As wave after wave of prisoners entered Gratiot, so, too, did they leave.
Beginning November 18, contingents of prisoners departed for a variety of
more permanent facilities. The overwhelming number of enlisted men went
to Alton, with smaller numbers destined for Jefferson City, Rock Island,
Camp Chase (Ohio), Camp Morton (Indiana), and even Point Lookout (Maryland). Some officers, designated for exchange, were transferred to Johnson's Island near Sandusky, Ohio. As early as December 7, the provost
marshal had shed Gratiot of 337 prisoners. Unfortunately, the carnage among
the prisoners continued, especially at Alton. The military prison had been
established in February 1862 on the site of the abandoned Illinois State
Penitentiary. Like Gratiot, Alton suffered from overcrowding. With many of
the soldiers jammed into poorly ventilated cells having twenty-eight square
feet of floor space, disease and epidemics once again ran rampant. In three
years' time an estimated 11,760 prisoners inhabited the stone walls of Alton
with at least 1,500 dying. Price's troops just added to the body count. At least
240 of Price's men appear on the prison's dead list. Combining the death toll
from Gratiot and Alton meant that an astounding 32 percent of Price's captured men died in the Union camps.[19]

Although the arrivals and departures of the prisoners in St. Louis received
significant coverage in the local papers, the story of their suffering and death
got little to no attention. Instead, whatever mention the campaign did receive
in its immediate aftermath was confined largely to ugly squabbles over battlefield laurels and politics. Among Union officers, the squabbles were
rooted in the disputes between Curtis and Pleasonton, which eventually
boiled down to dueling accounts of the campaign by subordinates with both

sides minimizing the role of the other. Pleasonton himself issued a report that barely acknowledged Curtis's contribution to victory, while also painting the campaign as finished following Mine Creek. Richard Hinton responded indirectly when he published his book-length history of the invasion in 1865. His account was detailed, and surprisingly accurate, but it was largely from the perspective of Curtis's army and left out much that pertained to the actions of Pleasonton's forces. This never set well with the Missourians who fought with Pleasonton. Chief among them was John Sanborn and his staff officer, C. W. Rubey. On multiple occasions running into the 1890s, Sanborn wrote of the campaign and had little good to say about either Curtis or his army. Rubey was no less caustic when he referred to Hinton's work as an "attempted perversion of history." However, even more vitriolic was the battle waged by John Philips and Frederick Benteen. As both men had served in Pleasonton's command, the division here was between the Missouri State Militia and the volunteer cavalry. Philips's official report touched off the controversy when it gave his brigade the lion's share of credit for the victories at Byram's Ford and Mine Creek. For Benteen, it was all too much. In a December 1864 letter to a newspaper, Benteen declared Philips's report "a well-woven web of unmitigated falsehoods." Philips, as could have been expected, responded with his own letter to a newspaper by referring to Benteen as a "pretentious coxcomb" and a "pert and obsequious subaltern who seemed only ambitious of writing himself into favor with his master." The controversy eventually blew over without a declared winner or the intervention of a higher-command authority.[20]

In Kansas, much more so than in Missouri, politics mingled readily with how the late expedition would be exploited and battlefield glory apportioned. While the Democratic Party was in eclipse in both states, only in Kansas would Republican Party factional politics bring the outcome of the election of 1864 into question. The vacillation of Kansas governor Thomas Carney in calling out the militia and then the outright mutiny of some of those units made Carney look foolish if not traitorous. Carney's bitter rival, Senator James Lane, readily seized upon Price's invasion as an issue when he returned to Kansas in the week preceding the election. In speeches throughout the state, Lane and his slate of candidates reminded voters of Carney's duplicity and their own valor as volunteer aides on the staff on Samuel Curtis. Their claims of bravery eventually centered on Lane's gubernatorial candidate, Samuel J. Crawford, who they portrayed as having ordered and led the Yankee cavalry charge at Mine Creek. But no one exceeded Lane in exaggeration or venom, particularly when the senator told a Mound City audience that Carney's choice for governor, Solon J. Thacher, was a "coward, Copperhead, and a traitor." If the audience did not quite get Lane's message, the senator eventually shouted, "the Governor, the Major General of the State Militia, the Copperhead Thacher, and three or four others, were plotting treason in the camp and these men are more damned and damnable traitors than any in South Carolina."[21]

Lane did not lack for surrogates, as he enlisted recipients of his patronage to make their own presentations and also to distribute copies of the various speeches of Lane, Crawford, and congressional candidate Sydney Clarke. In the face of this onslaught, Carney's faction tried mightily to right their sinking campaign. Thacher had been wounded in combat, they claimed, while Jim Lane hid in a cornfield. The unrepentant Colonel James D. Snoddy, who had attempted to take his regiment of militia back to Kansas, used his newspaper, the *Border Sentinel*, to "keep it before the people that there is not a horse thief, an enlarged murderer, a reckless, lawless, disorganizing criminal in Kansas who is not howling for Lane." Carney's allies even managed to produce an affidavit that quoted Alfred Pleasonton as saying, "If the people of Kansas are indebted to me, tell them to beat Jim Lane." Pleasonton never owned up to the alleged comment, and it really made no difference. Jim Lane's ticket won the election handily. Kansans cast 13,387 votes for Crawford and but 8,448 for Thacher in the race for the governor's chair. The votes were closer in the race for congress, but here, too, Lane's man, Sydney Clarke, emerged victorious.[22]

Things would not end so cleanly for Sterling Price. Given the failure of the expedition, there was bound to be finger pointing and recrimination. When it finally came, no one should have been surprised by the involvement of Governor Thomas C. Reynolds. On November 19, 1864, Reynolds, while at Boggy Depot, dispatched a letter to Edmund Kirby Smith. It was the first such communication that Reynolds had since the beginning of the campaign. The governor had receded into the background of the invasion since the failed attempt to take Jefferson City and had installed him as the true working governor of the state. Since that time, he stayed almost exclusively with Shelby's division and thus avoided Price and his inner circle of friends and allies. For weeks, Reynolds had simmered with disgust over what had become of the invasion of Missouri. All of his hopes for both himself and the Confederacy had been dashed, and he very much wanted to blame Sterling Price for everything that had gone wrong. Adding to his burning hatred of

Price were early reports in the Confederate press that the invasion had been a success. Particularly noxious to Reynolds would have been the Marshall *Texas Republican*, which blared "Bully, thrice Bully, for the Missouri Expedition" and proclaimed: "The Missouri Expedition has turned out far better than could have been expected." When Reynolds got wind of these sentiments, he could no longer contain himself. To Kirby Smith, he wrote: "There may be an attempt to whitewash the *disgracefully* managed expedition" and "I shall handle all concerned without gloves." In what would emerge as a constant refrain, Reynolds hinted that Price and his minions were ready to blame the failure on others, including Kirby Smith, John Marmaduke, and William Cabell. There were others who believed as Reynolds did. Among them was Captain Henry Ewing of Marmaduke's staff. Ewing was particularly concerned that rumors were circulating about Marmaduke being drunk at Mine Creek. With Ewing's encouragement, Reynolds sought then to publish a self-styled and lengthy letter of "vindication" for generals Marmaduke and Cabell. In reality, the vindication rarely touched upon those two officers, let alone any other officer save Sterling Price.[23]

In word after word and line after line, Reynolds vented his anger upon Price. According to Reynolds, Price had bumbled through Missouri and Arkansas, taking the wrong routes, carrying too much baggage, going too slow, and using no maps. Price enforced no discipline and allowed indiscriminate pillaging of Unionists and Confederates alike. Price even permitted his headquarters to become "the scene of public drunken revelry by night." In Reynolds's narrative, Price was nothing more than an old, indolent fool, who cared for nothing but his personal comfort. Even on the retreat from Westport, Price never "left his cushioned ambulance or well sheltered quarters to inspect, visit, or mingle among his faithful troops." It was the type of leadership that, Reynolds believed, left Price with "only puzzled bewildered anxiety" in battle.[24]

Because of the incendiary nature of the letter, Reynolds had some difficulty in getting it into print. More than one newspaper editor refused publication either because they were sympathetic to Price or they simply did not want to air Confederate dirty laundry. Inevitably, though, Reynolds succeeded in getting the *Texas Republican* to print the letter on December 23, 1864. However, before there could be any sort of reaction, Reynolds descended even deeper into a personal vendetta when he attempted to blackmail Price. Of interest to Reynolds was the relationship of Old Pap to his son Edwin. Edwin, it will be recalled, had renounced the Confederacy and received a pardon from Abraham Lincoln in 1862. He had resided in Missouri ever since then. Thomas Reynolds could never understand Edwin's actions and the relationship between the two Prices, and he preferred to believe that Old Pap was engaged in some type of nefarious conspiracy that was ultimately disloyal to the Confederacy. Upon the conclusion of the invasion, Reynolds redoubled his efforts to gather incriminating evidence concerning the Prices. Although he found nothing, he did not let that stop him from trying to bluff the elder Price. Just one day after the publication of his letter, Reynolds attached a copy of the piece and informed Price that he possessed information about Edwin, "his subsequent course, and the communications between you and him." Reynolds announced that he created a "memoir" of the activity and would give it to Jefferson Davis if Old Pap did not resign his military commission.[25]

Reynolds waited in vain for Price to respond to the blackmail. Price, instead, fought back by filing his official report of the invasion on December 28. Predictably, the report was self-serving and generally upbeat, especially when Price claimed to have captured three thousand men, eighteen pieces of artillery, and "large quantities" of horses, quartermaster stores, and small arms. Although Price could legitimately claim to having captured these sorts of things, the assertion was only half the story as Price brought almost none of them back with him to Texas and Arkansas. Perhaps more egregious was Price's further declaration that he destroyed $10 million in Yankee property. Beyond a doubt, Price had demolished much in the way of government property, and he had inflicted a significant amount of damage upon the Iron Mountain Railroad and the Pacific Railroad of Missouri. Hardest hit was the Pacific Railroad, which estimated its property damage at $500,000 and the related loss of business at $200,000. These were near crippling amounts that pushed the company toward bankruptcy and a reliance upon a $700,000 loan from the public credit. Staggering as the losses were, though, they did not get Price close to his proclaimed figure of $10 million.[26]

One other note should be made regarding Price's claims for the expedition. At no point did he make reference to the diversion of Union troops from any other theater of operations as some measure of success. The omission was significant as it continued to demonstrate the disjunction between what Price thought was the purpose of the expedition and what Edmund Kirby Smith considered its purpose. As early as November 16, Kirby Smith was asserting that the expedition was "a success" and primarily "a demonstration in favor of Mobile & our army in Georgia." Kirby Smith may also have been trying to put the best face possible on the disaster, but plainly Sterling Price saw the purpose of the preceding three months very differently.[27]

For as much as Price's report made extravagant claims for the success of the operation, its most subtle accomplishment was diffusing Thomas C. Reynolds's assertion that Price would scapegoat Marmaduke and Cabell. Instead, Price offered nothing but praise. With Price having effectively dismissed the pretext of Reynolds's letter in the *Texas Republican*, many who remained steadfastly loyal to Price blasted Reynolds publicly. Included in this group was Robert Selden, a Price staff officer and the brother-in-law of Kirby Smith. Selden, by virtue of his connection to Kirby Smith, was somebody Reynolds wanted in his own camp. It pained the governor greatly to hear Selden broadcasting that Reynolds had been waiting for three years "to break down Gen. Price." Also coming to Price's defense was the Reverend Benjamin T. Kavanaugh, superintendent of Methodist Army Missions for the District of Arkansas. Kavanaugh penned a vehement attack upon "Little Tommy Reynolds," denying or dismissing all of Reynolds's charges. On January 10, Price himself finally responded. In a sneering card published in the *Shreveport News*, which was soon picked up by other papers, Price referred to Reynolds as the man who "pretends to be the Governor of Missouri." Whether Reynolds wanted it or not, Price also demanded from Kirby Smith a court martial with charges preferred by Reynolds.[28]

The counterattack stung Reynolds. He could not believe the "howl of the old ladies of both sexes" in support of Price. They were "secret Unionists" who could not tell a drum major from a field marshal. However, more so than any other comment dealing with the substance of his critique of Price, what really bothered Reynolds was the dig at the legitimacy of his title as governor. Reynolds sent notes to newspaper editors defending the legality of his office, and he even demanded that Kirby Smith and Jefferson Davis censure Price for the insult. Hypersensitive to any criticism, Reynolds was not terribly impressed by the call of some of his friends that he moderate his attack upon Price. Writing to the editor of a Houston, Texas, paper, Reynolds smugly remarked, "I can only say that when I reperuse [*sic*] my letter, I am astonished by my own moderation." To others who thought the whole affair unseemly, Reynolds proclaimed it was out of necessity that Price be "slaughtered so publicly" because "he would not submit to being quietly turned out to graze." But ultimately there was a subtext to his desire to take down Sterling Price, and it was an attitude about Price that predated the invasion. Ever the dour politician who fancied himself a statesman, Reynolds could never get over the easy charisma of Price, his ability to make friends, and—despite some grumbling—the popularity he maintained with the rank and file even after the calamity of the retreat. Ultimately, Reynolds saw the battle with Price as "a contest between order, discipline, & civil authority on the one hand, and military misrule & and popularity-hunting on the other."[29]

In the dying days of the Confederacy, much of its senior leadership in the Trans-Mississippi found itself focused on Shreveport, Louisiana, where a court of inquiry convened on April 21, 1865. A key distinction with the inquiry was that it was not a court martial. Although Price had requested the court martial, Kirby Smith reduced the proceedings to that of an inquiry. There would be no formal charges against Price, and in this regard it seemed that Kirby Smith was acting to minimize the amount of embarrassment inflicted upon the army, if not Price himself. Having served on a court of inquiry for Major General Earl Van Dorn, Price well understood that courts of inquiry were reserved for those whose reputations needed whitewashing, but he nevertheless acquiesced to Kirby Smith.[30]

The great procedural weakness of courts of inquiry was that they lacked specific charges to frame the investigation. This lack of focus was magnified exponentially in an inquiry exploring 1,400 miles of marching, dozens of engagements, and a bewildering list of accusations covering everything from plundering to a criminal lack of concern for the well-being of the army. Reynolds saw the lack of fixed purpose in the inquiry, and he tried, at least initially, to shape it as he saw fit. He did this most of all by trying to influence the army's judge advocate, Major Oscar M. Watkins. There was at least one meeting, frequent correspondence, and one offer for Watkins to come and stay at Reynolds's house. Watkins was important to Reynolds in that it was the judge advocate's job to present and question witnesses before a panel of two generals and one colonel. Reynolds was determined to get the right men before the court. Ironically, this did not include his own personal testimony because, as Reynolds professed, his "friends" believed "it will give the proceedings more impartiality if others are first examined." The desire of impartiality was a smoke screen as Reynolds wanted instead to get into the courtroom as a consultant to Watkins. This maneuver did not work as the presiding officers refused Reynolds's offer to be a consultant. Thomas C. Reynolds would be neither a witness nor a consultant to the drama he initiated.[31]

Without the governor, the inquiry fell into a fairly predictable pattern as Watkins called witnesses to address criticisms in Reynolds's published "vindication." In what was probably a great surprise to Reynolds, and contrary to the historian Robert L. Kerby's belief that the court "accumulated a mass of evidence substantiating Reynolds' charges . . . ," none of the witnesses provided any information that confirmed Reynolds's allegations of incompetence and negligence. Captain Thomas J. Mackey, Price's chief engineer, was the first witness, and he provided the longest and most comprehensive testimony of the hearing. Mackey affirmed that Price made no serious errors involving the use of terrain, river crossings, map use, march-order disposition, and the utilization of the army's engineers. Mackey also testified at length concerning the Battle of Pilot Knob. Here, too, Price came away with his reputation intact. According to Mackey, Price's plan of battle was reasonable, and it came at the encouragement of his two present division commanders, Marmaduke and Fagan. Just how much Mackey's testimony backfired can be measured by the fact that Watkins tried unsuccessfully to get Reynolds to testify in the middle of Mackey's appearance. The next two witnesses, Major James R. Shaler and Captain T. T. Taylor, both served as inspectors general, and they described the wretched discipline of the army. However, they also noted that the lack of discipline could not be blamed on Sterling Price. The recruits were poor, and Price had no time to instill discipline on the march. Shaler, especially, supported the idea Price did all he could to maintain order with regulations and directives designed to enforce discipline. Price was also able to present himself as an uncompromising disciplinarian when he cross-examined Shaler and had him verify a story that Price complimented Colonel Thomas Freeman for his summary execution of two marauding soldiers.[32]

Jo Shelby was scheduled next to testify, but he never made it to the stand. On May 3, the tenth day of the hearing, Kirby Smith inexplicably ordered the hearing adjourned to May 8th when it would reconvene at Washington, Arkansas. Sensing a conspiracy, Sterling Price was angered by the change of venue and the attendant delay. Following the adjournment, Price issued a statement declaring that all preceding testimony vindicated his honor and any delays were "without warrant and calculated to do him injustice and wrong." It would not, however, take Price too terribly long to discover the actual reason for the change of venue. Before the inquiry had even started, everyone at Shreveport knew that Robert E. Lee had surrendered on April 9th. Word then spread quickly throughout the Trans-Mississippi Confederacy during the court of inquiry. As these Confederates battled the shock and depression associated with the bad news, they struggled also to figure out what next to do. Events moved quickly when on April 29th Kirby Smith received a formal offer to open negotiations for surrender. At that moment, Kirby Smith was of no mind to surrender, but Sterling Price did not trust Kirby Smith in the matter.[33]

Price, who had started the war as a very reluctant secessionist, had now emerged as a leader of the die-hard element of Confederates who pledged never to capitulate. Price thus convened a meeting of several officers and suggested he would arrest Kirby Smith should he open negotiations with a Yankee officer then waiting at the mouth of the Red River. Among those present was a Missouri brigade commander, Colonel Levin M. Lewis. Lewis had political and personal ties to Reynolds, who had once offered to make Lewis a Confederate States senator. Price either did not know this or chose to ignore it. Regardless, Lewis wasted little time in reporting the affair to Reynolds, who then, naturally, reported it to Kirby Smith by letter. Kirby Smith was not surprised, as his own network of informants and spies had already conveyed the information. Kirby Smith adjourned the court of inquiry to move Sterling Price from Shreveport and thus preempt a coup d'état in the last days of the Trans-Mississippi Confederacy. It took Price several days to figure this out. Sometime around May 18th, General Evander McNair, yet another brigade commander, informed Price that the adjournment was nothing more than a ruse to get him away from Shreveport. Highly agitated, Price left Washington for Shreveport almost immediately. Thirty miles from Shreveport, Price received orders from Kirby Smith to remain in Washington. Price ignored these and pressed on to Shreveport, where he found that Kirby Smith had abandoned the city on the 18th and was headed for Houston, Texas. With the Confederacy thus collapsing all around him, Price barreled into Shreveport where he found Colonel S. S. Anderson, Kirby Smith's assistant adjutant general. Old Pap then threatened force if he did not secure copies of the transcripts of the court of inquiry. Anderson eventually complied, and Price could rest easy, perhaps thinking he possessed the testimony that would preserve his reputation.[34]

Over the remaining two years of his life, Price did not have to refer anyone to the transcripts. His postwar exile in Mexico cemented his place as the symbol of a long-suffering pro-Confederate Missouri population. When Price returned to St. Louis in January of 1867, he was greeted warmly and with some degree of reverence. The war had deprived Price, like so many other Missourians, of all his wealth and property. Yet Missouri's Confederates gathered together and provided their one-time chieftain a house until his death several months later. His funeral procession was then reputed to have attracted the largest crowd of spectators up to that point in the history of St. Louis. Most surprisingly, even Thomas Reynolds eventually made his peace with the memory of Price. In speaking to gatherings of Missouri's Confederates, he tried "to make amends for any injustices I may have done in the heat of controversy," and he even joined an association to erect a monument to Old Pap. By February 1887, Reynolds would go so far as to renounce his infamous letter about the campaign, admitting that his charges "were, of course, largely on the authority of others than myself." A little more than one month later, Reynolds committed suicide by throwing himself down an elevator shaft because he feared slipping into dementia.[35]

No matter Reynolds's mea culpa, his interpretation of events would never go away. In some part, the durability of Reynolds's charges was due to the efforts of John Edwards, who published *Shelby and His Men* the same year Price died. In the aftermath of the war, Edwards was by far the most influential writer and interpreter of the war in Missouri. Although he would gain his greatest notoriety in glorifying Confederate bushwhackers and sanctifying Jesse James, Edwards used *Shelby and His Men* to extol Shelby at the expense of Price when describing the expedition of 1864. Edwards was not the most subtle of writers, as he reprinted Reynolds's letter to the *Texas Republican* and lambasted Price as "too slow, too inexperienced, too cautious, and too lymphatic" to lead the expedition. Edwards's narrative steered the reader to the inevitable conclusion that if Jo Shelby had been in charge the campaign would have been a success. While subsequent historians usually avoided the idea of replacing Price with Shelby, their interpretation of the expedition has generally followed Edwards's critique of Price. The critique was, of course, too simplistic. It focused attention on the tactical and operational levels of warfare where, it was assumed, a different battlefield decision or more nimble march would have spelled victory for the Confederacy. Edwards buttressed this perspective by rhetorically downgrading the strategic nature of the campaign to a "Raid," which clearly required the commander to be "iron of frame, lithe of limb, and eager as a blood hound."[36]

In this regard, Edwards was following in the footsteps of Price himself, who in his official report could only describe the success of the expedition by listing people and things captured and destroyed. The unintended consequence of this sleight of hand was that it helped people forget that no Confederate tactical triumph at any of the battles or exaggerated list of material destruction would have changed the strategic result. Price's original strategic goal, with Kirby Smith's passive acquiescence, had been to liberate Missouri and install a pro-Confederate government. As the march through Missouri demonstrated, the state's pro-Southern population simply lacked the numbers to sustain this sort of revolution.

Sterling Price's generalship certainly did not help matters. He was a terribly flawed commander who made several bad decisions in battles and marches from Pilot Knob to Mine Creek. In far too many instances, Price was either absent from a critical point on the battlefield or had failed to coordinate the actions of his subordinate commanders. Nevertheless, Price's flaws have led to an underappreciation of the operational and logistical difficulties he faced. Lacking any support from Kirby Smith, Price led an army filled with conscripts and one-time deserters who had little motivation to serve the Confederate cause. Even more to the point, when there was a desire to serve, there were too few horses and even fewer weapons to go around. It was an ill-trained, poorly clothed, and undisciplined assemblage whose pace through Arkansas and into Missouri was governed not by the horses in the command but by the thousands of dismounted men who walked in the trains. In combat, there were only a few brigades that would consistently prove their worth. The wonder of it all was not so much Price's bad generalship, but rather how he managed to keep this army together for as long as he did. Given the wretched condition of Price's army and the desperate attempt to liberate a state that ultimately did not want to be liberated, it is difficult to imagine another outcome. Whether led by Sterling Price or any other available senior commander, the Missouri expedition of 1864 was truly going to be the Confederacy's last hurrah west of the Mississippi River.

Acknowledgments

I am indebted to a great many people in the creation of this book. The list starts with Bryce Suderow. At a very early stage in my research, he generously shared the results of his own longtime study of the Price expedition. Over the years he pointed me in the direction of countless documents and other researchers interested in the expedition. No less important has been Daniel Smith, chairman of the Monnett Battle of Westport Fund. He willingly shared his time and vast knowledge of the Price expedition in escorting me around many battlefields. He also proved a patient correspondent in going over countless details and controversies. Yet another early guide to the expedition was the late John Spencer, president of the Mine Creek Battlefield Foundation. His willingness to come out on a rainy Sunday afternoon to take me around Mine Creek was critical in helping me to understand that battle. Numerous people fielded countless phone calls and emails about the expedition. They include Arnold Schofield of the Mine Creek Battlefield State Historic Site, Roger Baker of the Cole County Historical Society, Matt Mathews, and Terry E. Justice. Gil Bergman deserves special thanks for several letters and packages that helped clarify the period roads and river fords around Kansas City. His own research into the Confederate artillery of the campaign helped me greatly. Rick Hatcher, longtime friend and the historian at the Fort Sumter National Monument, provided numerous leads and contacts in my study of the Civil War Trans-Mississippi. The manuscript benefited greatly from the review and comments of readers including Michael Barrett of The Citadel, Rod Andrew of Clemson University, and Kenneth Heineman of Angelo State University. James McGhee not only read the

363

manuscript, and thus helped me avoid many errors, but he also provided valued encouragement and research assistance down through the years. Larry Hoffman worked tirelessly and patiently with me to create the book's many maps. I could not have asked for a better cross-country collaborator. The research and writing of this book could not have been accomplished without the generous financial assistance of The Citadel Foundation and its benefactors. The Foundation enabled release time from my teaching duties at The Citadel and subsidized all of the research and map production attendant to the book. Bo Moore, at varying times my department chairman and dean of undergraduate studies, was an important supporter of the project and one who paved the way for the aforementioned release time and financial assistance. Finally, it must be said that this book does not get finished without the patience, support, and love of my wife, Christina.

Abbreviations

AHCA — Arkansas Historical Commission and Archives

BCM — Egbert B. Brown, General Courts Martial, File #LL 2941, RG 153, NA

CAPC — Cyrus A. Peterson Battle of Pilot Knob Research Collection

CF — Citizen File, E. 2636, RG 393, NA

CWN — Civil War Narratives, Kansas State Historical Society

DTR-DofM — Dispatches and Telegrams Received, Department of the Missouri, E. 2706, Vol. 71, RG 393, NA

EdSHELBY — John N. Edwards, *Shelby and His Men; Or, The War in the West* (Cincinnati: Miami Printing and Publishing Company, 1967)

KSHS — Kansas State Historical Society

LCM — Proceedings of a General Court Martial, John M. Laing, in U.S. Congress, Senate Report, 51st Cong., 2nd sess., 1891, Report #2445

LR-DofM — Letters Received, 1861–1867, Department of the Missouri, E. 2593, RG 393, NA

LR-SPC — Letters Received, Sterling Price's Command, Chapter II, Vol. 211, RG 109, NA

LS-HQ-DofK — Letters Sent, Headquarters Department of Kansas, E. 2081, Vol. 138, RG 393, NA

LS-SC — Letters Sent, Shelby's Command, 1864, General and Special Orders, Trans-Mississippi Department, Microfilm 374, Reel 1, David W. Mullins Library, University of Arkansas

LS-SPC — Letters Sent, Sterling Price's Command, Chapter II, Vol. 178 1/2, RG 109, NA

LTS-AofB — Letters and Telegrams Sent, Army of the Border, E. 2121, Vol. 145, RG 393, NA

MCFCM — James McFerran, General Courts Martial, File #LL 2942, RG 153, NA

MCNCM — John McNeil, General Courts Martial, File #NN 3336, RG 153, NA

MHMA — Missouri History Museum Archives

MSA — Missouri State Archives

NA — National Archives

OCI-SPC — Orders and Circulars Issued, Sterling Price's Command, Chapter II, Vol. 209, RG 109, NA

OR War Department, *The War of Rebellion: A Compilation of the Official Records of the Union and Confederate Armies*, 128 vols. Series 1 (Washington: Government Printing Office, 1880–1901)

PME — Price's Missouri Expedition, E. 450. B. 3, RG 109, NA

SHSMO-C — State Historical Society of Missouri-Columbia

SHSMO-KC — State Historical Society of Missouri-Kansas City

SHSMO-R — State Historical Society of Missouri-Rolla

TCRP-LC — Thomas C. Reynolds Papers, Library of Congress

TCRP-MHMA — Thomas C. Reynolds Papers, Missouri History Museum Archives

TMNCF — Two or More Name Citizen File, E. 2637, RG 393, NA

TMNF — Two or More Name File, E. 2635, RG 393, NA

TR-DoK — Telegrams Received, Department of Kansas, E. 2099, Vol. 150, RG 393, NA

TREM — Donal J. Stanton et al., eds., *The Civil War Reminiscences of General M. Jeff Thompson* (Dayton, OH: Morningside Books, 1988)

TRS-AofB — Telegrams Received and Sent, Army of the Border, E. 2124, Vol. 151, RG 393, NA

TS-DofK — Telegrams Sent, Department of Kansas, E. 2085, Vol. 148, RG 393, NA

TSP — Thomas Snead Papers, E. 113, RG 109, NA

Notes

PREFACE

1. Mark A. Lause's *Price's Lost Campaign: The 1864 Invasion of Missouri* (Columbia: University of Missouri Press, 2011) is a recent addition to the literature, but it examines only portions of the first third of the expedition.

2. EdSHELBY; Richard J. Hinton, *Rebel Invasion of Missouri and Kansas . . .* (Chicago: Church and Goodman, 1865).

3. Howard N. Monnett, *Action Before Westport 1864* (Kansas City: Westport Historical Society, 1964; Reprint Edition Niwor: University Press of Colorado, 1995); Lumir F. Buresh, *October 25th and the Battle of Mine Creek* (Kansas City: The Lowell Press, 1977); Bryce A. Suderow, *Thunder in the Arcadia Valley: Price's Defeat, September 27, 1864* (Cape Girardeau: Center for Regional History and Cultural Heritage, 1986); Albert Castel, *General Sterling Price and the Civil War in the West* (Baton Rouge: Louisiana State University Press, 1968); Robert E. Shalhope, *Sterling Price: Portrait of a Southerner* (Columbia: University of Columbia Press, 1971); Robert L. Kerby, *Kirby Smith's Confederacy: The Trans-Mississippi South, 1863–1865* (New York: Columbia University Press, 1972); Deryl P. Sellmeyer, *Jo Shelby's Iron Brigade* (Gretna: Pelican Publishing Co., 2007).

4. This book will use the last name "Kirby Smith," which is what he preferred.

5. The exact number of Price-related prisoners will never be known. However, Sterling Price's assertion in his official report that he lost nearly one thousand men captured approximates the total number of Price's men (1,113) processed through the primary Union collection point at Gratiot Street Prison in St. Louis by March 5, 1865. The compilation of prisoners at Gratiot can be found in the Bryce Suderow Collection, SHSMO-C.

6. Mark E. Neely Jr., *The Civil War and the Limits of Destruction* (Cambridge: Harvard University Press, 2007), 60.

1. STERLING PRICE IS THE STATE OF MISSOURI

1. Jefferson City *Tribune*, October 20, 1925.

2. Thomas C. Reynolds, "Gen. Sterling Price and the Confederacy," 36–39, typescript, TCRP-MHMA.

3. *OR*, 27:2:749–96.

4. Castel, *General Sterling Price*, 8–9; *Missouri Republican*, March 31, 1887.

5. Thomas C. Reynolds to James A. Seddon, TCRP-LC.

6. William C. Davis, *Jefferson Davis: The Man and His Hour* (Baton Rouge: Louisiana State University Press, 1991), 380–81.

7. Frank L. Klement, *Dark Lanterns: Secret Political Societies, Conspiracies, and Treason Trials in the Civil War* (Baton Rouge: Louisiana State University Press, 1984), 64–90; EdSHELBY, 379. David C. Keehn believes the OAK was a successful operation with more than one thousand members in St. Louis alone by the end of 1863. Other than rumor, there is nothing to back the belief. In a similar fashion, Keehn claims, "Price reportedly became the 'Supreme Commander' of the OAK's southern section." Keehn's use of the adverb *reportedly* is telling. There is simply no evidence. See Keehn's *Knights of the Golden Circle: Secret Empire, Southern Secession, Civil War* (Baton Rouge: Louisiana State University, 2013), 171.

8. Thomas C. Reynolds to James Seddon, January 31, 1863, TCRP-LC.

9. Reynolds's doubts about Price can be seen especially in his "Memorandum Relative to the Appointment of Senators from Missouri," ca. 1864, page 30, TCRP-LC; Reynolds, "General Sterling Price and the Confederacy," 58–60, TCRP-MHMA.

10. *OR*, 22:2:782.

11. Castel, 141. Kirby Smith quoted in Kerby, 1.

12. Reynolds, "Gen. Sterling Price and the Confederacy," 72–73, TCRP-MHMA; Reynolds to E. C. Cabell, June 5, 1863, TCRP-LC.

13. Castel, 160; *OR*, 34:2:870.

14. Sterling Price to Thomas Reynolds, Camp Bragg, AR, November [?], 1863, LS-SPC.

15. *OR*, 34:2:817–18.

16. Reynolds, "Gen. Sterling Price and the Confederacy," 91, 103, TCRP-MHMA; Ludwell H. Johnson, *Red River Campaign: Politics and Cotton in the Civil War* (Baltimore: Johns Hopkins, 1958; reprint Kent: Kent State University, 1993), 86–87.

17. *OR*, 34:2:1028–29.

18. *OR*, 34:2:1043–56.

19. Shalhope, 253; Johnson, 170–205; Gary D. Joiner, *One Damn Blunder from the Beginning to the End: The Red River Campaign of 1864* (Wilmington: Scholarly Resources, 2003), 123–35.

20. Thomas A. Belser, *Military Operations in Missouri and Arkansas, 1861–1865* (PhD diss., Vanderbilt University, 1958), 692.

21. Stephen A. Dupree, *Planting the Union Flag in Texas: The Campaigns of Major General Nathaniel P. Banks in the West* (College Station: Texas A&M University Press, 2008), 34; Jeffery S. Prushankin, *A Crisis in Confederate Command: Edmund Kirby Smith, Richard Taylor, and the Army of the Trans-Mississippi* (Baton Rouge: Louisiana State University Press, 2005), *passim* and 136, 138.

22. *OR*, 34:1:478.

23. *OR*, 34:1:538 and 3:826–27, 829.

24. Castel, *General Sterling Price*, 197; *OR*, 34:1:538.

25. *OR*, 34:1:543–45.

26. *OR*, 34:4:642.

27. *OR*, 53:Supplement:998–99 and 34:3:823.

28. *OR*, 34:2:935; Reynolds to S. B. Buckner, June 25, 1864, and Reynolds to E. C. Cabell, July 4, 1864, TCRP-LC.

29. Joseph H. Parks, *General Edmund Kirby Smith C.S.A.* (Baton Rouge: Louisiana State University Press, 1954), 419; *OR*, 41:22:1015 and 34:4:692.

30. *OR*, 39:2:694, 696.

31. *OR*, 41:2:1011, 1020; J. A. Coker, "My Recollections . . . ," p. 8, B.3, F.3, CAPC.

32. *OR*, 41:2:1015 and 1023.

33. *OR*, 41:2:1022.

34. Kirby Smith to Cassie Smith, August 10, 1864, Roll 4, Edmund Kirby Smith Papers, Southern Historical Collection, University of North Carolina, Chapel Hill, NC; *OR*, 41:1:102, 117; Kerby, 329–30.

35. *OR*, 41:1:92–93 and 41:2:1041.

36. William McPheeters Diary, August 1, 2, 3, and 4, Box 18A.9.5, William M. McPheeters Papers, MHMA.

37. Reynolds to Seddon, August 6, 1864, TCRP-LC.

38. *OR*, 41:1:192; Michael Fellman, *Inside War: The Guerrilla Conflict in Missouri during the American Civil War* (New York: Oxford University Press, 1989), 109.

39. Reynolds, "Gen. Sterling Price and the Confederacy," 120, TCRP-MHMA; EdSHELBY, 378; Kerby, 334; Roy Bird, *They Deserved a Better Fate: The Second Kansas State Militia Regiment and the Price Raid, 1864* (New York: Cummings & Hathaway, 1999), 19.

40. Paul Casdorph, *Prince John Magruder: His Life and Campaigns* (New York: Wiley, 1996), 284.

41. *OR*, 41:2:1040.

42. Oates, 143–44; Castel, *General Sterling Price*, 202; Kerby, 335; Scott E. Sallee, "Missouri! One Last Time: Sterling Price's 1864 Missouri Expedition, 'A Just and Holy Cause,'" *Blue and Gray Magazine* 8 (1991): 10–18, 20, 48–62. Price quoted in *OR*, 41:2:1023.

43. E. C. Cabell to Price, August 27, 1864, B. 60, TSP.

44. *OR*, 41:1:116.

45. Kerby, 330.

46. *OR*, 41:1:113–17, 18.

47. EdSHELBY, 381; *OR*, 41:2:1093 and 3:926; E. C. Cabell to Price, August 27, 1864, B. 60, TSP.

2. WE SUSPECT MISSOURI IS THE OBJECTIVE

1. John W. Brown Diary, Film 200a, David W. Mullins Library Microfilm, University of Arkansas, Fayetteville, Arkansas; *Missouri Republican*, February 27, 1886.

2. Jeffery S. Prushankin, "'To Carry Off the Glory': Edmund Kirby Smith in 1864," in *Confederate Generals in the Trans-Mississippi: Essays on America's Civil War*, vol. 1, ed. Lawrence L. Hewitt (Knoxville: University of Tennessee Press, 2013), 70–71; Charles G. Williams, ed., "A Saline Guard: The Civil War Letters of Col. William Ayers Crawford, CSA, 1861–1865, Part II," *Arkansas Historical Quarterly* 32 (1973): 81; Coker, "My Recollections . . . ," B. 3, F. 3, CAPC.

3. EdSHELBY, 444; Don Mc. N. Palmer, *Four Weeks in the Rebel Army* (New London: D. S. Ruddock, 1865), 21; Leo E. Huff, "The Last Duel in Arkansas: The Marmaduke-Walker Duel," *Arkansas Historical Quarterly* 23 (1964): 36–49.

4. *OR*, 41:2:1015–16, 1041; Helen P. Trimpi, "A 'Gallant and Prudent Commander': Major General John S. Marmaduke," in Hewitt, 145; William J. Crowley, *Tennessee Cavalier in the Missouri Cavalry: Major Henry Ewing, C.S.A. of the St. Louis Times* (Homewood: William J. Crowley, 1978), 134; Reynolds to William P. Johnston, August 27, 1863, TCRP-LC.

5. *OR*, 34:1:947 and 2:1065, 1076; William L. Cabell, *Report of the Part Cabell's Brigade Took in What Is Called "Price's Raid" into Missouri and Kansas in the Fall of 1864* (Dallas, 1900), 2; W. F. Slemons to Mattie, August 24, 1864, William F. Slemons Papers, Soldier Letters Collection, Eleanor S. Brockenbrough Library, Museum of the Confederacy, Richmond, Virginia.

6. *OR*, 41:1:679 and 2:1052–53, 1065; John C. Wright, *Memoirs of Colonel John C. Wright* (Pine Bluff: Rare Book Publishers, 1982), 168–70.

7. *OR*, 41:2:1052; Clark to Marmaduke, August 23, 1864, Correspondence of John S. Marmaduke, 1863–1864, RG 109, NA, Microfilm, Reel 1, UARK; EdSHELBY, 478.

8. Charles K. Mills, *Harvest of Barren Regrets: The Army Career of Frederick William Benteen, 1834–1898* (Glendale: Arthur W. Clark Company, 1985), 801; *History of Vernon County, Missouri, Written and Compiled from the Most Authentic Official and Private Sources . . .* (St. Louis: Brown and Company, 1887), 324.

9. Charles D. Gibson and E. Kay Gibson, *The Army's Navy Series*, Vol. 2, *Assault and Logistics: Union Army Coastal and River Operations, 1861–1865* (Camden: Ensign Press, 1995), 601–2; General Orders #7, September 8, 1864, OCI-SPC; Edward Hagerman, *The American Civil War and the Origins of Modern Warfare: Ideas, Organization, and Field Command* (Bloomington: Indiana University Press, 1988), 44–47.

10. Hagerman, 44–47; *OR*, 45:2:65 and 34:3:809; McPheeters Diary, September 7, 1864.

11. *OR*, 41:2:1059; Cabell, 2.

12. E. C. Cabell to Price, August 23, 1864, B. 60, TSP; *OR*, 41:2:1074, 75.

13. E. C. Cabell to Price, August 22 and 23, 1864, B. 60, TSP.

14. McPheeters Diary, August 29, 1864; Circular Nos. 4 and 5, September 1 and 5, 1864, OCI-SPC; William B. Napton, *Past and Present of Saline County Missouri* (Indianapolis: B. F. Bowen and Company, 1910), 185; "Incidents of General Price's Campaign in Arkansas as Related to Me by an Ex-Confederate Soldier," Roberta Falconer Manuscript on General Price's Campaign, 1892, #13, B. 96, Small Manuscript Collection, AHCA.

15. Price to W. S. Boggs, August 15, 1864, LC-SPC and General Order No. 6, Camp No. 11, September 7, 1864, OCI-SPC; Kirby Smith to Price, August 17, 1864, B. 59, TSP.

16. Reynolds to E. C. Cabell, June 5, 1863, and Reynolds to Shelby, March 11, 1865, TCRP-LC.

17. McPheeters Diary, August 28 and 29, 1864; E. C. Cabell to Price, August 23, 1864, B. 60, TSP; *OR*, 41:1:626, 712.

18. Special Order No. 3, August 31, 1864, OCI-SPC; *OR*, 41:1:626 and 2:1090.

19. *OR*, 41:1:622–23 and 2:936–37.

20. *OR*, 41:2:934.

21. Maclean to Marmaduke, September 5, 1864, LS-SPC; *Washington Telegraph*, September 21 and November 30, 1864.

22. *OR*, 41:1:711, 716; Special Order No. 8, September 11, 1864, OCI-SPC; Mary Hannah Johnston Morrow Diary, September 5, 6, and 7, 1864, Series 1, Folder 1, AHCA.

23. McPheeters Diary, September 6 and 7, 1864.

24. Oates, 142; Kerby, 334; Sallee, 10–18, 20, and 48–62; Bird, 25; Shalhope, 56–77; William Wood, "General Sterling Price: The New Mexico Insurrection, 1846–47," *The Magazine of American History* 18 (1887): 333–35.

25. McPheeters Diary, September 4, 1864; Armstrong to Matilda Armstrong, September 6, 1864, James T. Armstrong Papers, Southern Historical Collection.

26. General Orders No. 4, September 1, 1864, OCI-SPC.

27. War Department, *Revised Regulations for the Army of the United States of 1861* (Philadelphia: J. G. L. Brown Printer), paragraph 482; *OR*, 39:1:149, 45:2:538, and 49:2:697; Thomas C. Reynolds, December 17, 1864, "To the Public," 8–9, Typescript, TCRP-MHMA.

28. *Washington Telegraph*, November 30, 1864; Armstrong to Matilda Armstrong, September 13, 1864, Armstrong Papers.

29. McPheeters Diary, September 10, 11, 12, 1864.

30. McPheeters Diary, September 13, 1864; *OR*, 41:1:626–27; Undated clipping, "Deeds of Gallantry," Joseph O. Shelby Scrapbook, Vol. 1, SHSMO-C.

31. Special Orders, #89 through 162, HQ Shelby's Command 1864 and Shelby to Sidney Jackman, September 9, 1864, LS-SC; A. I. Edgar Asbury, *My Experiences in the War, 1861–1865, a Little Autobiography* (Kansas City: Berkowitz and Company, 1894), 27–28.

32. *OR*, 41:2:665; Crowley, 136.

33. Shelby to Belton, May 22, 1864, Box 59, TSP; *OR*, 41:2:1067.

34. Shelby to Thomas R. Freeman, August 19, 1864 (two different letters), Shelby to Sidney Jackman, August 19, 1864, and Shelby to T. H. McCray, September 11, 1864, HQ Shelby's Command, LS-SC.

35. *OR*, 41:1:627 and 2:458, 1036.

36. Francis Coleman Smith, memorandum, Mrs. Frank Fitzgerald Collection, Jackson County Historical Society, Independence, Missouri; EdSHELBY, 254–55; Wright, 184.

37. Armstrong to Matilda Armstrong, September 18, 1864, Armstrong Papers; EdSHELBY, 384; Maclean to William M. Douglas, September 19, 1864, LS-SPC and Special Order No. 10, September 17, 1864, OCI-SPC; *OR*, 41:1:623, 627; McPheeters Diary, September 19, 1864.

38. T. J. Mackey, "A Lady of Arcadia: The Doomed Garrison of Pilot Knob, and How It Was Saved," 319–20, *Yonkers Statesman*, September 19, 1894.

39. Crowley, 136; Entry #10, September 19, 1864, Log, LR-SPC; Bob Dalehite, "Colonel Arch S. Dobbin," *The Independence County Chronicle* 5 (1964): 39–51; Wright, 185–87.

3. TO THE ARCADIA VALLEY

1. *OR*, 34:2:202 and 4:527; 41:3:527; William M. Lamers, *The Edge of Glory: A Biography of General William S. Rosecrans, U.S.A.* (New York: Harcourt, Brace, and World, Inc., 1961), 416–17.

2. Klement, 74–90. Much like David Keehn's study of the OAK, Frank P. Varney's recent study of the relationship between Grant and Rosecrans accepts the rumors of a massive OAK conspiracy. Varney chooses to believe "it is very possible" that the conspiracy never took place because Rosecrans discovered it. See his *General Grant and the Rewriting of History: How the Destruction of General William S. Rosecrans Influenced Our Understanding of the Civil War* (El Dorado Hills: Savas Beatie, 2013), 248.

3. Proclamation, June 14, 1864, B. 90, F. 8, Office of the Adjutant General, RG 133, MSA, Jefferson City, Missouri; J. B. Fuller to Father, June 20, 1864, F. 11, Correspondence,

1864, Jonathan B. Fuller Papers, SHSMO-KC; William Crede to Brother, June 25, 1864, R. 1, F. 6, Crede Family Papers, SHSMO-C; *OR*, 41:1:24, 52; Henry C. Crawford to friends, August 5, 1864, F. 1, Henry Clay and William H. Crawford Papers, SHSMO-C.

4. "Letter of Reminiscence 'To My Daughters,'" E. H. Grabill, F. 547, Civil War Papers, MHMA; *Tri-Weekly Missouri Democrat*, September 23, 1864; *OR*, 41:3:28, 145.

5. "Syphilitic poison" covered in Affidavits, Richard Bachtel, B. 100, F. 2713 and Affidavits, Robert H. Breeze, B. 103, F. 2807, War Claims and Pensions, Benecke Family Papers, SHSMO-C; *OR*, 41:2:178 and 34:4:567.

6. Co. L, 6th EMM, invoices and returns, R. 1, F. 10, Charles W. Rubey Papers, SHSMO-R; Co. I, 35th EMM, Quarterly Return of Clothing . . . and Quarterly Return of Ordnance . . . , September 30, 1864, Captain Reese's [*sic*] Papers, B. 82, F. 2178, Benecke Papers; *OR*, 41:2:967 and 3:528; James Hamilton, "The Enrolled Missouri Militia: Its Organization and Controversial History," *Missouri Historical Review* 69 (1975): 413–32.

7. For one such list, see Roll of Leading and Influential Citizens in the 2nd Sub District of St. Louis, undated, TMNCF.

8. James Craig to B. K. Davis, July 25, 1864, B. 361, Letters Written, Military District, NW MO, March 11, 1862 to April 22, 1865, RG 133, MSA.

9. Franklin Swap, Transcript of Record for September 1864, Part 1, TMNF.

10. *Liberty Tribune* quoted in Bird, 33; G.O. 107, Part 1, B. 12, LR-DofM; John Dryden and William Carron to Rosecrans, July 18, 1864, Part 1, CF and Charles Burkes et al. to Rosecrans, July 7, 1864, Part 1, B. 12, LR-DofM; *OR*, 41:1:38, 44.

11. *OR*, 41:1:307; Statement of Andrew Kirkpatrick, July 25, 1864, and examinations of Green B. Smith, August 2, 1864, Charles S. Hunt, July 23, 1864, Charles Dunn, July 26 and July 27, 1864, and Edward Hoffman, July 14, 1864, B. 4, E. 33, Third Report, September 3, 1864, Colonel J. P. Sanderson, Provost Marshal General, Department of the Missouri, Judge Advocate General, General Court-Martial Records, RG 153, NA.

12. *OR*, 56:907; John N. Edwards, *Noted Guerrillas* (St. Louis: Bryan and Brand and Company, 1877), 283–84; United Daughters of the Confederacy, Missouri Division, Records, R. 22, F. 201, SHSMO-C.

13. Edwin C. McReynolds, *Missouri: A History of the Crossroads State* (Norman: University of Oklahoma Press, 1962), 254; Castel, *Sterling Price*, 199; Ronald D. Smith, *Thomas Ewing, Jr.: Frontier Lawyer and Civil War General* (Columbia: University of Missouri Press, 2008), 234; Edwards, *Noted Guerrillas*, 283–84.

14. "Statement of John T. Wynn . . . ," typescript, November 11, 1903, B. 8, F. 8, CAPC.

15. *OR*, 41:3:62, 143.

16. *OR*, 41:3:46 and 1:307.

17. *OR*, 41:3:75, 88, 113, 140, 224.

18. A. Ferdinand Herning to Rosecrans, February 13, 1864, Miscellaneous Correspondence, Various Counties, B. 724, F. 9, RG 133, MSA; *Tri-Weekly Missouri Democrat*, September 19, 21, and 23, 1864; Henry Klinge Diary, Entry of September 20, 1864, F. 2, translated typescript, Henry Klinge Papers, SHSMO-C.

19. *Tri-Weekly Missouri Democrat*, September 23, 1864; *OR*, 41:1:307–8 and 3:309; *St. Louis Union*, September 28, 1864; William Crede to Brother, September 25, 1864, R. 1, F. 6, Crede Papers.

20. Missouri Adjutant General's Office, "Historical Memoranda of the Third Regiment Cavalry Missouri State Militia," n.d., B. 1, F. 26, CAPC; *OR*, 41:3:309.

21. OR, 41:3:303–4; *Tri-Weekly Missouri Democrat*, September 23, 1864.

22. Monroe J. Miller to wife, September 25, 1864, Monroe J. Miller Papers, MHMA.

23. Suderow, *Thunder in the Arcadia Valley*, 40–43.

24. Among the more original recent studies of Ewing is Ken Heineman's *Civil War Dynasty: The Ewing Family of Ohio* (New York: New York University Press, 2012).

25. *OR*, 41:1:446; H. C. Wilkinson to Cyrus A. Peterson, Letter #15, B. 8, F. 4, CAPC; Amos Stickney to O. D. Greene, July 12, 1864, B. 1, F. 2, CAPC.

26. *OR*, 41:1:446. "Reminiscence of Peter Shrum of Sligo, MO," typescript, n.d., B. 6, F. 1, CAPC; Suderow, *Thunder in the Arcadia Valley*, 47.

27. Special Orders 20, 97, 116, and 157, Headquarters Department of the Missouri and R. G. Woodson's Letter of Resignation, June 26, 1863, B. 93, F. 2, Correspondence of the 3rd MSM, RG 133, MSA; James R. McCormick to John B. Gray, October 17, 1864, B. 7, F. 239, Military Papers, Missouri State Militia, Correspondence, October 1864, Clarence W. Alvord Collection, SHSMO-C.

28. John W. Hendrick to Cyrus A. Peterson, n.d., B. 4, F. 1, CAPC; *OR*, 22:2:678.

29. John W. Hendrick to Cyrus A. Peterson, n.d., B. 4, F. 1, CAPC; *OR*, 22:1:784.

30. Mackey, 320; Armstrong to Matilda Armstrong, September 26, 1864, Armstrong Papers; General Orders, No. 31, September 30, 1864, OCI-SPC; McPheeters Diary, September 24, 1864.

31. Recruiting Papers, AAG's Office, Price's Army, Index of Papers of the Missouri Expedition, B. 60, TSP; *OR*, 41:1:628.

32. Shelby to C. C. Rainwater, January 5, 1888, typescript, B. 6, F. 1, CAPC.

33. *OR*, 41:1:652–53 and 3:360, 407–8, 414, 444–46; EdSHELBY, 385–86; Francis C. Kajencki, *Star on Many a Battlefield: Brevet Brigadier General Joseph Karge in the American Civil War* (Cranbury: Associated University Presses, Inc., 1980), 183.

34. *OR*, 41:1:653; Jane Evans to H. C. Wilkinson, June 30, 1903, B. 3, F. 7 and "Story of P. H. Harrison Hickman," November 6, 1903, B. 4, F. 1, CAPC; George Cruzen, "The Story of My Life," typescript, c. 1930, p. 24, George R. Cruzen Papers, MHMA.

4. GENERAL, MY BRIGADE NEVER FLICKERED

1. Circular No. 10, September 25, 1864, and Special Order No. 16, September 25, 1864, OCI-SPC; Wright, 189–90.

2. *OR*, 41:3:959; Wilkinson to Peterson, Letter #17, B. 8, F. 4, CAPC; Suderow, *Thunder in the Arcadia Valley*, 61–65.

3. Wilkinson to Peterson, Letter #17, B. 8, F. 4, CAPC; *OR*, 41:3:384–85.

4. S. D. Carpenter to Mrs. Ewing, October 4, 1864, and Carpenter to Peterson, August 31, 1904, B. 3, F. 3, CAPC; *OR*, 41:3:385, 386; Suderow, *Thunder in Arcadia Valley*, 73–74.

5. Cyrus A. Peterson and Joseph M. Hanson, *Pilot Knob: The Thermopylae of the West*, 2nd Edition (Independence: Two Trails Publishing Company, 2000), 93–96; Suderow, *Thunder in the Arcadia Valley*, 72.

6. Thomas C. Fletcher, "The Battle of Pilot Knob, and the Retreat to Leasburg," in *War Papers and Personal Reminiscences, 1861–1865. Read Before the Commandery of the State of Missouri Military Order of the Loyal Legion of the United States* (St. Louis: Becktold and Company, 1892), 1:30–33; Carpenter to Mrs. Ewing, October 4, 1864, B. 3, F. 3, CAPC.

7. Carpenter to Mrs. Ewing, October 4, 1864, B. 3, F. 3, CAPC.

8. David Murphy, "Recollections of Pilot Knob, Mo.," 1902, typescript, B. 5, F. 2 and Carpenter to Mrs. Ewing, October 4, 1864, B. 3, F. 3, CAPC.

9. *OR*, 41:1:447.

10. *OR*, 41:1:703.

11. Wilkinson to Peterson, Letter #17, B. 8, F. 4, CAPC; Peterson, 90, 97–98; *Washington Telegraph*, November 30, 1864; Peterson, 97–102.

12. Suderow, *Thunder in the Arcadia Valley*, 90. Suderow (101) believes Wilson was flushed from the mountain after noon. Given Confederate occupation of the western base of the mountain before noon, Wilson likely retreated into the fort much earlier. James Harrison to Thomas Ewing, October 11, 1864, October 16, 1864, and Harrison to Rosecrans, November 17, 1864, Part 1, B. 13, LR-DofM; Louis Fusz Diary, October 2, 1864, Typescript, v. III, Louis Fusz Papers, MHMA.

13. "Reminiscence of Peter Shrum of Sligo, MO," typescript, n.d., B. 6, F. 1, and Wilkinson to Peterson, Letter #17, B. 8, F. 4, CAPC; Suderow, *Thunder in the Arcadia Valley*, 159.

14. *OR*, 41:1:707, 714; Mackey, 322.

15. *OR*, 41:1:708–9.

16. Suderow, *Thunder in the Arcadia Valley*, 99; Wright, 189–90; Cabell, 4–5.

17. Suderow, *Thunder in the Arcadia Valley*, 94; J. A. Coker, "My Recollections . . . ," B. 3, F. 3 and Murphy, "Recollections."

18. Peterson, 106–9, 121–24.

19. Suderow (109–10) writes that Clark made his first charge without Cabell. Clark's report of the battle and the memoirs of Henry C. Luttrell and James H. Campbell contradict this. See *OR*, 41:1:679–80; *Missouri Republican*, October 24, 1885; and James H. Campbell, "Reminiscence of James H. Campbell's Experiences during the Civil War," typescript, pp. 13–16, copy in author's possession.

20. Carpenter to Mrs. Ewing, October 4, 1864, B. 3, F. 3, CAPC.

21. *OR*, 41:1:680; Cabell, 5; *Washington Telegraph*, November 30, 1864.

22. Only six Confederates would actually be executed. Bryce Suderow, "An Eye for an Eye: An Episode from Missouri's Civil War," in Mark J. Crawford, *Confederate Courage on Other Fields* (Jefferson: McFarland & Company, Inc., 2000), 89–134; John W. Hendrick to Peterson, n.d., B. 4, F. 1, CAPC; Wright, 192–93.

23. Coker, "My Recollections" and Wilkinson to Peterson, Letter #17, B. 8, F. 4, CAPC.

24. Wilkinson to Peterson, Letter #17, B. 8, F. 4 and Dalton to Peterson, April 16, 1903, B. 3, F. 4, CAPC; Peterson, 137–39.

25. Wilkinson to Peterson, Letter #17, B. 8, F. 4 and Dalton to Peterson, April 16, 1903, B. 3, F. 4, CAPC; Peterson, 137–39.

26. Birdie H. Cole, "The Battle of Pilot Knob," *Confederate Veteran* 22 (1914): 417; John Darr, "Price's Raid in Missouri," *Confederate Veteran* 11 (1903): 360; Campbell, 15; Wright, 192–94; Coker, "My Recollections"; Mackey, 324.

27. *OR*, 41:1:449; H. B. Milks to Peterson, March 19, 1903, B. 4, F. 8, Biographical sketch of James S. McMurtry, B. 4, F. 7, Thomas Ewing to George Ewing, September 24, 1894, B. 3, F. 9, Willis Cole to Wilkinson, August 1, 1904, and James Copp to Peterson, February 10, 1903, B. 3, F. 3, Wilkinson to Peterson, Letter #19, B. 8, F. 4, CAPC; *Missouri Democrat*, October 3, 1864; Mackey, 325; Walter E. Busch, *Fort Davidson and the Battle of Pilot Knob: Missouri's Alamo* (Charleston: The History Press, 2010), 35, 178.

28. *Missouri Republican*, October 24, 1885.

29. *OR*, 41:1:629.

30. Richard S. Brownlee, "The Battle of Pilot Knob, Iron County, Missouri, September 27, 1864," *Missouri Historical Review* 92 (1998): 296; Suderow, *Thunder in the Arcadia Valley*, 121; *OR*, 41:1:688. Suderow (138) has calculated Cabell's strength at 1,331 men based upon a report in the Unionist *Missouri Democrat* of October 3, 1864. I think this is less reliable than Cabell's own recollection (2) of brigade strength at the outset of the campaign. There are two

possible figures for casualties in Cabell's brigade. Cabell puts them at 275, while the diary of William H. Trader notes ninety-six (see *Washington Telegraph*, November 30, 1864). I use the larger figure if only because a member of Monroe's regiment noted casualties in his regiment that alone reached ninety-six. See William G. Hazen to Alexander R. Hazen, December 21, 1864, Hazen Letter, Typescript Collection, Vol. 2, #434, SHSMO-C.

31. Horatio Beane to Wilkinson, September 13, 1864, B. 2, F. 11 and Carpenter to Mrs. Ewing, October 4, 1864, B. 3, F. 3, CAPC; *Missouri Democrat*, October 14, 1864.

32. C. J. Pitkin, "Reminiscences of Price's Raid," B. 5, F. 5, CAPC; *Missouri Democrat*, October 14, 1864; Wilkinson to Peterson, Letter #21, B. 8, F. 4, CAPC; Wright, 198–99; Reynolds to Trusten Polk, July 3, 1866, TCRP-MHMA. Provost Marshall Bull is in error when he later reported getting orders to form his department on the 27th in *OR*, 41:1:648. See instead General Orders, Numbers 15 and 31, September 30, 1864, OCI-SPC.

33. Murphy, "Recollections."

34. Milks to Peterson, March 19 and April 4, 1903, B. 4, F. 8 and Wilkinson to Peterson, Letter #19, B. 8, F. 4, CAPC; *OR*, 41:1:449.

35. "The Battle of Pilot Knob: By One Who Was There," n.d., SHSMO-C; "Reminiscence of Peter Shrum of Sligo, MO," typescript, n.d., B. 6, F. 1 and Wilkinson to Peterson, Letter #19, B. 8, F. 4, CAPC; *OR*, 41:1:450.

36. Wilkinson to Peterson, Letter #19, B. 8, F. 4, CAPC; *OR*, 41:1:698; *Missouri Republican*, February 27, 1886.

37. *OR*, 41:1:375.

38. Murphy, "Recollections"; Ruben Bennett, "Story of Ruben Bennett," November 18, 1906, B. 2, F. 11 and Wilkinson to Peterson, Letters #19 and 20, B. 8, F. 4, CAPC.

39. *OR*, 41:1:688.

40. *OR*, 41:1:450–51, 680, 694; Edwin A. Carpenter, "A History of the 17th Illinois Cavalry Volunteers," newspaper clippings, 1886, KSHS; Campbell, 17.

41. Milks to Peterson, March 19, 1903, B. 4, F. 8, CAPC.

5. FOR GOD'S SAKE, GIVE ME AUTHORITY TO DO SOMETHING

1. *OR*, 41:1:630.

2. Cabell, 6; *Missouri Democrat*, October 3, 1864; *Washington Telegraph*, November 30, 1864.

3. Cyrus Russell, "A Prisoner during Price's Raid," typescript, F. 5, Russell Family Papers, SHSMO-R. See also *Missouri Democrat*, October 6, 1864.

4. *OR*, 41:3:926.

5. Special Order No. 19, October 1, 1864, OCI-SPC.

6. Gert Goebel, "*Laenger Als Ein Menschleben* in Missouri," chapter 33, page 2, translated by Anna Hesse, typescript, Gert Goebel Collection, MHMA.

7. Goebel, chapter 32, pages 5–7; *OR*, 41:1:680, 698; Historical Memoranda, 54th EMM, *Annual Report of the Adjutant General of Missouri for 1864* (Jefferson City: W. A. Curry, 1865), 310; Ralph Gregory, *Price's Raid in Franklin County, Missouri* (Washington: Missourian Publishing, 1990), 6.

8. Gregory, 15.

9. *OR*, 41:1:630, 680, 688; Statement of Edwin H. Maxfield, January 28, 1865, B. 728, F. 5, RG 133, MSA; *Missouri Republican*, February 27, 1886; Campbell, 19.

10. *OR*, 41:1:630, 680, 688; Statement of Edwin H. Maxfield, January 28, 1865, B. 728, F. 5, RG 133, MSA; *Missouri Republican*, February 27, 1886; Campbell, 19; Historical Memoranda, 34th EMM, 278.

11. General Orders, No. 16, Camp No. 32, October 1, 1864, and General Orders, No. 17, Camp No. 40, October 9, 1864, OCI-SPC and Entry #4, Head Quarters Army in the Field, October 14, 1864, Log, LR-SPC; Donal J. Stanton et al., eds., *The Civil War Reminiscences of General M. Jeff Thompson* (Dayton: Morningside Books, 1988), 238; Goebel, chapter 32, page 8; *Missouri Republican*, April 3, 1886; Bates Frissell to Eliza Frissell, October 29, 1864, B. 3, F. 1864, Frissell Family Papers, MHMA; Carrie Frissell to Sister, October 30, 1864, F. 1, Reppy-Frissell-Drake Family Papers, SHSMO-C.

12. Civilian deaths are derived from subtracting the men reported killed at Union from the total number of county deaths mentioned in Gregory, 19. *Missouri Republican*, February 27, 1886; October 4, 1864, William A. Lyman Diary, Roll 8, vol. xvi, #449–vol. xviii, #552, William A. Lyman Collection, SHSMO-C; *Missouri Democrat*, October 13, 1864; Goebel, chapter 32, page 12; McPheeters Diary, October 2, 1864; *Missouri Democrat*, October 13, 1864.

13. Willard Frissell to Eliza, October 3, 1864, F. 1, Reppy-Frissell-Drake Family Papers.

14. Willard Frissell to Eliza, October 22 and 30, 1864, F. 1, Reppy-Frissell-Drake Family Papers; *Missouri Democrat*, October 3, 1864; Goebel, chapter 32, pages 5 and 7.

15. Goebel, chapter 32, page 8; Gregory, 14; *Missouri Democrat*, October 18, 1864.

16. For claims documents see, generally, B. 442 and B. 476, EMM Manuscripts, RG 133, MSA. Alverson's claim found in B. 476. Other information found in Daniel Whiteside statement of May 14, 1866, B. 11, F. 395, Clarence W. Alvord and Idress Head Collection; A. Johnson to John B. Gray, November 5, 1864, p. 246, B. 364, Ledger of Letters Received, Missouri Adjutant General, RG 133, MSA; J. H. Steger to Major Foster, October 1, 1864, B. 729, F. 2, Miscellaneous Correspondence, EMM, Adjutant General, RG 133, MSA; *OR*, 41:4:11.

17. General Orders 176, HQ Department of the Missouri, September 26, 1864, J. F. Bennett to Gray, September 25, 1864, and EMM Special Orders 167, September 26, 1864, *Annual Report of the Adjutant General of Missouri for 1864*, 44, 49, 50.

18. *OR*, 41:1:310–11, 462 and 3:611, 753, 754; B. B. Haaguna to Gray, October 12, 1864, p. 211, Ledger of Letters Received, Missouri Adjutant General, January through December 1864, B. 364, Adjutant General, RG 133, MSA.

19. Brown's numbers are taken from his report, which contradicts Fisk's later recollection that Brown had only three thousand men total at Jefferson City prior to his arrival.

20. *OR*, 41:3:515, 521.

21. *OR*, 41:1:418 and 3:454–55, 620, 666.

22. Hinton, 345–48; Neely, 42–48.

23. *OR*, 41:1:375–76; John B. Sanborn, "The Campaign in Missouri in September and October, 1864," in *Glimpses of the Nation's Struggle . . . , 1889–1892*, ed. Edward D. Neill, 3rd Series (New York: D. D. Merrill Company, 1893), 152–53.

24. *OR*, 41:1:366, 654 and 3:645; Cruzen, 26.

25. *OR*, 41:1:362, 653–54 and 3:669; *Missouri Democrat*, October 11, 1864; Cruzen, 26–27; *Missouri State Times*, October 15, 1864.

26. *OR*, 41:1:362, 654 and 3:669; *Missouri Democrat*, October 11, 1864; Cruzen, 26–27.

27. *OR*, 41:1:362, 653–54 and 3:667; Sanborn, "The Campaign in Missouri," 154; McPheeters Diary, October 6, 1864.

28. *OR*, 41:3:667–68.

29. *OR*, 41:1:663 and 3:990.

30. Wright, 204–6; *Washington Telegraph*, November 30, 1864; *OR*, 41:1:412, 419; Dino Brugioni, *The Civil War in Missouri: As Seen from the Capital City* (Jefferson City: Summers Publishing, 1987), 118–25.

31. *OR*, 41:1:419.

32. Brugioni, 118–25; *OR*, 41:1:376, 631.

6. D—N THE STATE, I WISH I HAD NEVER SEEN IT

1. The exact parameters of the Boonslick are open to interpretation. For most nineteenth-century Missourians, the Boone's Lick Country consisted of the adjoining territory of the upper Missouri River, including Jackson, Clay, Ray, Carroll, Chariton, Howard, Boone, Cooper, Saline, Callaway, and Lafayette counties.

2. *OR*, 41:1:655, 663; Sanborn, "The Campaign in Missouri," 161–62.

3. *OR*, 41:1:655; Sanborn, "The Campaign in Missouri," 159; Cabell, 7; *Washington Telegraph*, November 30, 1864; Wright, 209.

4. *St. Louis Globe Democrat*, April 4, 1897; *OR*, 41:1:340 and 3:729; J. David Petruzzi, "The Fleeting Fame of Alfred Pleasonton," *America's Civil War* 18 (2005): 22–28.

5. Doris L. Mueller, *M. Jeff Thompson: Missouri's Swamp Fox of the Confederacy* (Columbia: University of Missouri Press, 2007).

6. TREM, 234–38, 246–47; Donal J. Stanton, Goodwin F. Berquist Jr., and Paul C. Bowers, "Missouri's Forgotten General: M. Jeff Thompson and the Civil War," *Missouri Historical Review* 70 (1976): 237–58; Samuel T. Gill, "Liberator Unmercifully Hounded," *America's Civil War* 1 (1988): 38–39.

7. *OR*, 41:1:655, 663–64; TREM, 240–41; Historical Memoranda, Provisional EMM, Boonville, *Annual Report of the Adjutant General of Missouri for 1864*, 376; *The Central Missourian*, October 17, 1927; EdSHELBY, 402–3; *History of Howard and Cooper Counties, Missouri* . . . (St. Louis: National Historical Company, 1883), 767–68, 772–74.

8. *OR*, 41:1:681; Sanborn, "The Campaign in Missouri," 162; *Missouri Republican*, February 27, 1886; F. F. Basham, Reminiscences of the War between the States, UDC Mary Lee Chapter #87, AHCA.

9. Lizzie Thompson to Beverly Thompson, November 1, 1864, Lizzie Thompson Letter, SHSMO-C; McPheeters Diary, October 10, 1864; *OR*, 41:1:631, 664, 712; *Missouri Republican*, February 27, 1886; Francis Coleman Smith, Memorandum, n.d., Mrs. Frank Fitzgerald Collection.

10. TREM, 242; Benjamin Duval to Fagan, October 12, 1864, PME; *Missouri Democrat*, November 8, 1864.

11. Albert Castel and Thomas Goodrich, *Bloody Bill Anderson: The Short, Savage Life of a Civil War Guerrilla* (Mechanicsburg: Stackpole Books, 1998), 111–15; *History of Howard and Cooper Counties, Missouri* . . . , 767–68, 772–74.

12. Castel and Goodrich, 114–15, 120; *OR*, 41:1:632; *History of Howard and Cooper Counties, Missouri* . . . , 773; *The Central Missourian*, November 8, 1927; *Missouri Democrat*, November 8, 1864.

13. Cabell, 8; McPheeter's Diary, October 11, 1864; *OR*, 41:1:631–32.

14. *OR*, 41:1:382–83, 387–88, 402, 407, 414, 655, 673, 681, and 3:1001–2, 1006; Sanborn, "The Campaign in Missouri," 163–66; Wright, 210–12; *Washington Telegraph*, November 30, 1864.

15. McPheeters Diary, October 11 and 12, 1864; Sanborn, "The Campaign in Missouri," 163–66; *OR*, 41:1:387–88, 674 and 3:817; *The National Tribune*, December 31, 1925.

16. Sanborn, "The Campaign in Missouri," 163–66; *OR*, 41:1:387–88, 674 and 3:817; *The National Tribune*, December 31, 1925.

17. *OR*, 41:1:632; Proclamation of John W. Taylor, October 1, 1864, Typescript, B. 9, F. 2, CAPC.

18. *OR*, 41:1:632; *Missouri Democrat*, October 6, 1864; Special Order 164, September 10, 1864, HQ Shelby's Command, LS-SC.

19. *Salisbury Democrat*, n.d., c. 1905, News Clippings, 1904–1905, B. 81, F. 2131, Benecke Family Papers; *OR*, 41:2:719, 774 and 3:206, 547; Daniel T. Rickman, "Events in the Trans-Mississippi Department," *Confederate Veteran* 21 (1913): 71; Special Order 3, September 20, 1864, HQ Shelby's Command, LS-SC; Special Order 23, October 12, 1864, OCI-SPC.

20. *OR*, 41:1:612–14; Johnathan Fairbanks and Clyde E. Tuck, *Past and Present of Green County Missouri: Early and Recent History and Genealogical Records of Many of the Representative Citizens* (Indianapolis: A. W. Bowen, 1915), 889–93; EdSHELBY, 419.

21. *OR*, 41:2:719, 774 and 3:206, 547; Rickman, 71; Special Order 3, September 20, 1864, HQ Shelby's Command, LS-SC; Special Order 23, October 12, 1864, Orders and Circulars Issued, SPC.

22. *OR*, 41:1:443–45 and 3:522, 1012; Napton, 200–1; Fairbanks, 25; Wiley Britton, *The Civil War on the Border*, Vol. 2 (New York: G. P. Putnam's Sons, 1899; reprint, Ottawa: Kansas Heritage Press, 1994), 458–59. One more Unionist, Captain William Beaty, was executed separately a short time later by the bushwhacker Archie Clements.

23. S. K. Turner and S. A. Clark, *Twentieth Century History of Carroll County Missouri*, Vol. 1 (Indianapolis: B. F. Bowen, 1911), 300–7; Cruzen, 27–28; *History of Clay and Platte Counties, Missouri . . .* (St. Louis: National Historical Company, 1885), 731; Thomas W. Westlake Memoirs, MSS, pages 36–82, F. 8, Watson-Westlake Family Papers, SHSMO-C.

24. The figure of 2,500 recruits is my estimate. At the conclusion of the campaign, Union authorities in the various counties compiled lists of men who joined Price. Extant lists can be found for Lafayette, Saline, and Cooper counties. These counties averaged two hundred recruits each. One near-contemporary estimate had between five hundred and seven hundred men joining from Howard County. See List of Names for Lafayette, Saline, and Cooper Counties, E. 2804 and 2805, Part 1, RG 393, NA and *History of Howard and Chariton Counties, Missouri* (St. Louis: National Historical Company, 1883), 274.

7. YOU ARE HOME BOYS, AND I DO NOT WANT TO HURT YOU

1. James M. Denny, "The Battle of Glasgow," *Boone's Lick Heritage* 3 (1995): 4–9; McPheeters Diary, October 13 and 14, 1864; *OR*, 41:1:632, 645, 656 and 3:1007, 1010, 1011; EdSHELBY, 404.

2. *OR*, 41:1:420–22 and 3:708, 757, 759, 790–91, 819.

3. G. A. Holloway to Samuel R. Curtis, October 5, 1864, Part 1, TR-DoK; *OR*, 41:1:434–36; Britton, 2:452–53; Samuel S. Curtis, *A Cruise on the Benton: A Narrative of Combat on the Missouri River in the Civil War* (Waynesboro: M & R Books, 1967), 1–4.

4. "The Battle of Glasgow," F. 1864, Glasgow, Howard County Papers, MHMA.

5. *OR*, 41:1:436–38, 696; *Fort Smith New Era*, December 3, 1864.

6. EdSHELBY, 406–7; S. C. Turnbo, "Stories of the Ozark," 3 vols., manuscript, B. 33, William E. Connelley Collection, KSHS; *OR*, 41:1:656–57, 681, 689 and 3:1013; *Missouri Democrat*, October 21, 1864.

7. *OR*, 41:1:430–31, 438–39; "The Battle of Glasgow," F. 1864, Glasgow, Howard County Papers, MHMA.

8. One report in the *Missouri Democrat* of October 21, 1864, claimed Confederate losses of fifty men killed and seventy-five wounded. The number seems more than exaggerated. *History of Howard and Chariton Counties, Missouri*, 289–90; *OR*, 41:1:430–31, 438–39, 681–82.

9. *OR*, 41:1:682.

10. *OR*, 41:1:664.

11. *OR*, 41:1:664–65 and 3:1012, 1013; TREM, 242–43.

12. *OR*, 41:1:364, 665 and 4:1000; TREM, 244.

13. R. B. Coleman, "Various Small Fights in Missouri," *Confederate Veteran* 14 (1906): 120; *OR*, 41:1:665 and 4:1000; TREM, 244–45.

14. William S. Rosecrans pronounced the paroles illegal and ordered the men to return to the front. *OR*, 41:1:359–60, 364–65, 388, 665–66 and 4:42, 45, 86, 1000; TREM, 244–46.

15. *OR*, 41:3:726, 755–56; *Documents Exhibiting the Organization, Conditions, and Relations of the Pacific Railroad of the State of Missouri* (New York: Baker, Godwin, and Company, 1853), 52.

16. *OR*, 41:1:462–63; Henry C. Fike Diary, October 3–9, 1864, Henry C. Fike Papers, SHSMO-C.

17. *OR*, 41:1:320–23; George Swain to Carrie Swain, October 9 and 10, 1864, George Swain Collection, Chicago History Museum; Henry Klinge Diary, October 4–15; Henry C. Fike Diary, October 12–14, 1864.

18. *OR*, 41:1:310 and 4:3, 10; Winslow's Memoirs, Episode 6:3, Edward Francis Winslow Papers, Special Collections Department, University of Iowa Libraries, Iowa City, Iowa.

19. Thomas S. Cogley, *History of the Seventh Indiana Cavalry Volunteers . . .* (LaForte: Herald Company, 1876), 125; Winslow Memoirs, Episode 6:4, 5; *Missouri Democrat*, October 18, 1864; *OR*, 41:1:327, 334, 2:934 and 3:62, 187, 211.

20. *OR*, 41:1:320–22, 327–28; 334; George P. Walmsley Sr., *Experiences of a Civil War Horse-Soldier* (Lanham: University Press of America, 1993), 108–10; Byron C. Bryner, *Bugle Echoes: The Story of the Illinois 47th* (Springfield: Phillips Bros., 1905), 146; Lot Abraham Diary, October 10, 1864, Papers of Lot Abraham, 1842–1921, University of Iowa Libraries.

21. *OR*, 41:1:311, 320–22, 328 and 3:783; Walmsley, 110; A. T. Bartlett, "Reminiscences of Dr. A. T. Bartlett . . . ," typescript, n.d., B. M-19 (4A.4.5.), p. 44, A. T. Bartlett Papers, MHMA; Lot Abraham Diary, October 13, 1864; William Forse Scott, *The Story of a Cavalry Regiment: The Career of the Fourth Iowa Veteran Volunteers from Kansas to Georgia, 1861–1865* (New York: G. P. Putnam's Sons, 1893), 317–18; Winslow's Memoirs, Episode 6:11.

22. *OR*, 41:1:657 and 4:40, 41; Walmsley, 110.

23. *OR*, 41:1:388, 3:891 and 4:40, 41, 46; Sanborn, "The Campaign in Missouri," 169–71; *Illustrated Atlas Map of Saline County, MO* (St. Louis: Missouri Publishing Company, 1976), 19.

24. *Washington Telegraph*, November 30, 1864; *OR*, 41:1:633, 682 and 3:1013–14; McPheeters Diary, October 17, 1864; Clark to McClean [*sic*], October 17, 1864, PME.

25. "To the Friends of the Confederacy . . . ," Camp No. 45, October 15, 1864, LS-SPC; McPheeters Diary, October 13–16, 1864, with quote taken from October 14.

26. Maclean to Marmaduke, Camp No. 44, October 14, 1864, LS-SPC; *Washington Telegraph*, November 30, 1864; Ben C. Truman, *The Field of Honor: Being a Complete and Comprehensive History of Duelling [sic] in all Countries . . .* (New York: Fords, Howard, and Hulbert, 1884), 372. The *Telegraph* identifies Belding as Major Reiden.

27. *OR*, 41:4:1003.

28. W. A. Wilson to Jeanette, December 11, 1864, B. 20, F. 472, Correspondence, August–December 1864, Abiel Leonard Papers, SHSMO-C; EdSHELBY, 416–17; Wright, 214–15.

29. *Texas Republican*, December 23, 1864; *OR*, 41:1:653; *Missouri State Times*, October 15, 1864; Historical Memoranda, Morgan County Provisional EMM in *Annual Report of the Adjutant General of Missouri for 1864*, 376; TREM, 266; Lisbon Applegate to William Herford Jr., November 25, 1864, B. 3, F. 80, Lisbon Applegate Collection, SHSMO-C; Entry #3, Headquarters Army in the Field, Camp #45, October 16, 1864, Log, LR-SPC and William Bourne to Fagan, October 17, 1864, PME.

8. MEN OF KANSAS, RALLY!

1. Robert Collins, *General James G. Blunt: Tarnished Glory* (Gretna: Pelican Publishing Company, 2005); Monnett, 42.

2. Blunt to H. Z. Curtis, August 10, 1863, and Blunt to Carney, July 25, 1863, Thomas Moonlight Collection, KSHS; *OR*, 53:565; Albert Castel, *A Frontier State at War: Kansas, 1861–1865* (Ithaca: Cornell University Press, 1958), 83–85; James G. Blunt, "General Blunt's Account of His Civil War Experiences," *Kansas Historical Quarterly* 1 (1931–1932): 219, 221, 249.

3. *OR*, 41:3:528.

4. *Leavenworth Times*, August 7, 1864; Charles Robinson to Sara Robinson, February 28 and October 1, 1864, Charles and Sara T. Robinson Collection, Microfilm Edition, KSHS.

5. *OR*, 41:1:523 and 3:234–35, 279, 290–91; Curtis to George Sykes, September 15, 1864, TS-DofK; *Kansas City Journal*, September 15, 1864; "Price's Invasion," *The Congregational Record* 6, nos. 10, 11, 12 (October, November, December 1864): 109–17, 121–29; Richard Cordley, *Pioneer Days in Kansas* (Boston: The Pilgrim Press, 1903), 241; Carney to Rosecrans, August 29, 1864, LR-DofM.

6. *OR*, 41:3:369, 370, 593–94.

7. *Leavenworth Times*, October 4, 1864; *OR*, 41:3:651.

8. Curtis to Owner of New Steamer, October 7, 1864, and Curtis to J. L. Thomas, October 8, 1864, TS-DofK; *OR*, 41:3:528; *Leavenworth Daily Times*, September 6, 1864; *Border Sentinel*, September 30, 1864.

9. *OR*, 41:1:606; Ford to C. S. Charlot, October 5, 1864, and Ford to Curtis, October 7 and 9, 1864, Part 1, TR-DoK; Douglas R. Cubbison, "Look Out for Hell Some Place Soon: The 2nd Colorado Cavalry in Missouri, February–September, 1864," *Military History of the West* 32 (2002): 1–6; General Orders 2, Headquarters Station Kansas City, October 4, 1864, F. 7, Robert T. Van Horn Papers, SHSMO-C; Curtis to Van Horn, October 8, 1864, TS-DofK.

10. *OR*, 41:1:606; Ford to C. S. Charlot, October 5, 1864, and Ford to Curtis, October 7 and 9, 1864, TR-DoK.

11. *Leavenworth Times*, October 5 and 6, 1864; *OR*, 41:3:650.

12. *Leavenworth Times*, October 5 and 6, 1864; *OR*, 41:3:693–94.

13. *Leavenworth Times*, October 7, 1864; *OR*, 41:1:468 and 3:675, 713, and 768; Charles Robinson to Sara Robinson, October 9, 1864, Robinson Collection; *Leavenworth Conservative*, October 7, 8, 1864; James C. Horton, "Personal Narrative: Peter D. Ridenour and Harlow W. Baker, Two Pioneer Kansas Merchants," *Transactions of the Kansas State Historical Society, 1907–1908* 10 (1908): 613; Cordley, 244.

14. *OR*, 41:1:469.

15. *OR*, 41:1:471, 3:724, 764, and 4:242–43; Charles Robinson to Sara Robinson, October 9, 1864, Robinson Collection; Curtis to Sykes, November 21, 1864, LS-HQ-DofK.

16. *OR*, 41:1:470; *Leavenworth Conservative*, July 17, 1862; Albert Castel, "Civil War Kansas and the Negro," *The Journal of Negro History* 51 (1966): 125–38; Roger D. Cunningham, "Welcoming 'Pa' on the Kaw: Kansas's 'Colored' Militia in the 1864 Price Raid," *Kansas History* 25 (2002): 86–101.

17. *OR*, 41:1:471.

18. *OR*, 41:1:469.

19. Erasmus Manford, *Twenty Five Years in the West* (Chicago: E. Manford Publisher, 1867), 320; "Price's Invasion," *The Congregational Record*, 116; J. S. Sands to Hiram Hill, October 27, 1864, Box 1, Hiram Hill Collection, KSHS; Cordley, 244; *OR*, 41:1:543; *Leavenworth Times*, October 12, 15, 16, 1864.

20. *Report of the Adjutant General of the State of Kansas for the Year 1864* (Leavenworth: P. H. Hubbell & Company, Book and Job Printers, 1865); *OR*, 41:4:61; James W. Steele, *The Battle of the Blue of the Second KSM, October 22, 1864; The Flight; The Captivity; The Escape* (Chicago: W.T.P.A, 1895), 16.

21. Bird, 50; George T. Robinson to R. Delafield, August 31, 1864, B. 13, LR-DofM; Topeka *Journal*, November 2, 1934; General Orders 2, 3, 4 in Orders, Etc., of Maj. Andrew Stark, B. 4, F. 5, Military History Collection, KSHS; Cordley, 246, 250.

22. Bird, 52; *Leavenworth Times*, October 10 and 16, 1864; "Price's Invasion," *The Congregational Record*, 117; General Orders dated October 12, 13, and 15, 1864, in Orders, Etc., of Maj. Andrew Stark, B. 4, F. 5, Military History Collection, KSHS; *OR*, 41:3:822.

23. *OR*, 41:1:472, 543, 572, 614.

24. *OR*, 41:1:472, 543, 572, 614.

25. Blunt to Stanton, November 14, 1863, Moonlight to F. J. Weed, January 23, 1864, and Moonlight to Carney, August 22, 1864, Thomas Moonlight Collection.

26. *Border Sentinel*, October 14, 1864.

27. Hinton, 60; Samuel J. Reader, "The Civil War Diary of Samuel J. Reader . . . ," transcript, KSHS, *passim*, but especially pages 4–8; Henry G. Hodges to Curtis, October 13, 14, 16, and 17, 1864, TS-DofK and John Williams to Curtis, October 13, 1864, J. M. McNutt to Curtis, October 13, 1864, TRS-AofB; Muster Roll, Company A, 2nd Regt. Kansas State Militia, 1864, Kansas Adjutant General, Miscellaneous Bound Volumes, Rng. 31-Sec 02-Shelf 02-Box 01, KSHS.

28. Kyle S. Sinisi, *Sacred Debts: State Civil War Claims and American Federalism, 1861–1880* (New York: Fordham University Press, 2003), 132–70.

29. Curtis to wife, October 13 and 14, 1864, typescripts, Samuel Ryan Curtis Papers, Western Americana Collection, Yale University Library, New Haven, Connecticut; "Special Field Orders," October 16–18 in Part 1, LTS-AofB.

30. Curtis to wife, October 13 and 14, 1864, Curtis Papers; Curtis to wife, October 15, 1864, LTS-AofB; *OR*, 41:1:531–32; Curtis, *passim*.

31. Samuel J. Crawford, *Kansas in the Sixties* (Chicago: A. C. McClurg and Company, 1911), 142–43.

32. Charles Robinson to Sara T. Robinson, October 16, 1864, Robinson Collection; Cordley, 245; *Leavenworth Times*, October 18, 19, 20, and 27, 1864; Castel, *A Frontier State at War*, 190–91.

33. *Leavenworth Times*, October 12, 20, 1864; *OR*, 41:4:23, 60–61, 96, 120, 147–48; Carney to Curtis, October 16, 1864, and T. A. Davies to Curtis, October 18, 1864, TRS-AofB.

34. *OR*, 41:1:596–97, 3:898 and 4:57–58; William A. Mitchell, *Linn County, Kansas: A History* (La Cygne: La Cygne Journal, 1928), 86–87; *Border Sentinel*, December 23, 1864.

35. Cordley, 246; "Price's Invasion," *The Congregational Record*, 121; Hinton, 62–63; *OR*, 41:4:19, 59, 94. There is a minor discrepancy concerning these troops. According to Hinton's book published in 1865, the first two regiments across were the 4th and 19th. I use, instead, the regiments listed in Deitzler's report (*OR*, 41:1:615) written in December 1864: the 12th and the 19th. The 4th probably crossed on October 18.

36. *Leavenworth Times*, October 18 and 20, 1864.

37. *OR*, 41:1:473 and 4:120, 144, and 148.

38. Hinton, 81; Reader, 8; Hinton to John Williams, October 21, 1864, TR-DoK; Jenkins, 142–43; Cunningham, 97.

39. *OR*, 41:4:143; Hinton, 90–91.

9. A BEAUTIFUL AND EXCITING SCENE

1. Blunt, 253; *OR*, 41:1:573 and 4:88; George S. Grover, "The Price Campaign of 1864," *Missouri Historical Review* 7 (1912): 167–81; Matthew C. Hulbert, "Constructing Guerrilla Memory: John Newman Edwards and Missouri's Irregular Lost Cause," *Journal of the Civil War Era* 2 (2012): 59; R. Fuller (?) to Daughter, October 20, 1864, PME.

2. *OR*, 41:1:573 and 4:88; Grover, 167–81; R. Fuller (?) to Daughter, October 20, 1864, PME.

3. *OR*, 41:1:583 and 4:118.

4. Hinton, 84–85; Grover, 167–81; H. E. Palmer, "My Recollections of Stirring Events Which Happened Forty Years Ago," pp. 4–8, 14, CWN.

5. *OR*, 41:1:573; Sanborn, "The Campaign in Missouri," 172.

6. *OR*, 41:1:633; Jones to Shelby, October 18, 1864, PME.

7. *OR*, 41:4:110. For wagon inflation see Buresh, 56; D. Alexander Brown, "The Battle of Westport," *Civil War Times Illustrated* 5 (1966): 7; Monnett, 93; EdSHELBY, 427, 435; Sallee, 20; Gill, 37; William E. Connelley, *Wild Bill and His Era: The Life and Adventures of James Butler Hickock* (New York: The Press of the Pioneers, 1933), 79.

8. *OR*, 41:1:573, 633, 657, 666; TREM, 247; *Kansas City Journal*, November 24, 1881; Cruzen, 28.

9. *National Tribune*, January 31, 1907; *Kansas City Journal*, November 24, 1881; *OR*, 41:1:573–74 and 582; R. Fuller (?) to Daughter, October 20, 1864, PME.

10. Palmer, 8; Grover, 171.

11. *OR*, 41:1:573, 582, 591; William E. Connelley, *The Life of Preston Plumb, 1837–1891* (Chicago: Browne and Howell, 1913), 184; McPheeters Diary, October 19, 1864.

12. *Kansas City Journal*, November 26, 1881; William E. Connelley, *A Standard History of Kansas and Kansans*, 5 vols. (Chicago: Lewis Publishing Company, 1918): 2:756–57.

13. *OR*, 41:1:574, 582–83, 591–92; R. Fuller (?) to Daughter, October 20, 1864, PME; *National Tribune*, January 31, 1907; *Kansas City Journal*, November 26, 1881; Connelley,

Kansas and Kansans, 2:756–57; *Leavenworth Daily Standard*, November 26, 1881; Grover, 167–81; Palmer, 9–13; Hinton, 84–91.

14. *OR*, 41:1:388 and 646; Sanborn, "The Campaign in Missouri," 173.

15. Sanborn, "The Campaign in Missouri," 174; Wright, 227–28; Sallee, 57.

16. TREM, 248; *Washington Telegraph*, November 30, 1864; McPheeters Diary, October 20, 1864; *Missouri Republican*, March 6, 1886; *OR*, 41:1:633, 646.

17. *Kansas City Journal*, November 24, 1881; Blunt, 255; *OR*, 41:1:592, 682; Hinton, 92.

18. *OR*, 41:4:144–45.

19. The 11th Kansas operated without two companies. Company G acted as Curtis's escort, while Company L remained in Kansas at Fort Riley. *OR*, 41:1:574, 592; Blunt, 255; Kip Lindberg and Matt Matthews, "'The Eagle of the 11th Kansas': Wartime Reminiscences of Colonel Thomas Moonlight," *Arkansas Historical Quarterly* 62 (2003): 34–35; Palmer, 14–15.

20. Hinton, 93; Palmer, 14–15.

21. *OR*, 41:1:682.

22. *OR*, 41:1:592–93, 682.

23. *OR*, 41:1:682, 690.

24. *OR*, 41:1:574, 580, 607; Blunt, 256.

25. *National Tribune*, March 29, 1883; Grover, 172; *OR*, 41:1:476; Blunt, 256; Lindberg and Matthews, 35.

26. *OR*, 41:1:543, 592, 607; Bryce Suderow, ed., "McLain's Battery and Price's 1864 Invasion: A Letter from Lt. Caleb Burdsal, Jr.," *Kansas History* 6 (1983): 29–45; Hinton, 95–96. My placement of the 16th Kansas follows the reports of Moonlight and Ford, while disregarding Hinton's assertion that the 16th operated to the right of Moonlight. Ford, especially, seems definitive as he noted he was ordered to move Walker to the far left.

27. Suderow, ed., "A Letter from Lt. Caleb Burdsal, Jr.," 42; Campbell, 21–22.

28. Campbell, 23; John Ballard Draper, *William Curtis Ballard: His Ancestors and Descendants* (N.P., 1979), 69–76 (hereafter referred to as *Ballard Diary*); Jesse Ellison to W. L. Skaggs, March 22, 1915, Jesse Ellison Letters, William L. Skaggs Collection, AHCA; *OR*, 41:1:683.

29. *OR*, 41:1:657, 666, 683.

30. Cruzen, 28–29; Blunt, 256–57.

31. Blunt, 256; Suderow, ed., "A Letter from Lt. Caleb Burdsal, Jr.," 44; Palmer, 16; Grover, 173–74; *OR*, 41:1:607–8. There is no evidence to support the then contemporary rumor (*Leavenworth Daily Times*, November 5, 1864) that Todd and Smith killed each other with shots fired simultaneously. Similarly, the preponderance of evidence is that Todd died in this particular engagement and not later at the Court House Square in Independence as George Grover would recollect. Grover would also get the time of Smith's death wrong when he stated that it occurred about 10 AM. Smith, of course, was still in Independence with the rest of Blunt's division. For the different accounts, and places, of Todd's death, see: Virginia H. Asbury, "An Anomaly of Written History," *Confederate Veteran Magazine* 22 (1914): 138; Cubbison, 20; and Cruzen, 28–29.

32. *OR*, 41:1:575; Archer S. Childers, "Longest March in the War. . . ," Archer S. Childers, Miscellaneous Collections, page 6, KSHS; EdSHELBY, 421.

33. Clipping, Mrs. Robert Hill to Mrs. Kate Doneghy, October 23, 1864, in "R. F. Crews One of the Survivors of the Battle of Westport," reprinted in *Kansas City Star*, December 7, 1923, Scrapbook, John S. Marmaduke Chapter, United Daughters of the Confederacy, Vol. 1., SHSMO-C; McPheeters Diary, October 21, 1864.

34. *Kansas City Journal*, October 22, 1864; *OR*, 41:1:646, 692, 697, 699; William G. Cutler, ed. *History of the State of Kansas*, 2 vols. (Chicago: A. T. Andreas, 1883), 1:197, 199.

35. Reynolds to Kirby Smith, February 11, 1865, TCRP-LC.

36. EdSHELBY (421) claims that Marmaduke lost three.

10. I CAN STOP PRICE AT THIS CROSSING

1. George Swain to Carrie Swain, October 27, 1864, George Swain Collection.

2. *OR*, 41:1:597 and 3:869; Hinton, 122–24; Cunningham, 86–101.

3. H. A. Seiffert to Andrew C. McMaken, November 11, 1864, B. 24, F. 3, Lighton Family Papers, KSHS.

4. *OR*, 41:1:480, 526, 575, 593, 608. Howard Monnett (72) errs in stating that Blunt "overlooked" Hinkle's Ford and placed Moonlight at Simmons. Blunt's report shows that he did indeed order Moonlight to Hinkle's Ford. Moreover, Curtis believed Moonlight to be at Hinkle's (*OR*, 41:4:192). My placement of the fords, and the troops, tends to follow Hinton, 122–27. Confusion with the dispositions started with inaccurate maps created by Curtis's chief engineer, George Robinson, and then got repeated by an army contract cartographer, Lyman Bennett, after the war. Clarification of the fords and distances can be found in *An Illustrated Historical Atlas Map: Jackson County, MO* (Philadelphia: Brink, McDonough, 1877; reprint, Jackson County Historical Society, 1976), 53. The proper route of the Independence to Westport Road is also revealed by the map produced by William M. Lewis for the *Kansas City Journal*, June 15, 1923. See U.S. Army Corps of Engineers, *Blue River Channel Project, Kansas City, Missouri*, 9, 12–17, 29, 34.

5. Hinton, 124; Grover, 167–81; J. J. Jones, "The Battle of Westport," n.d., manuscript, Jackson County Historical Society.

6. Curtis to Rosecrans, October 20, 1864, LR-DofM; *OR*, 41:1:479 and 4:146.

7. *Leavenworth Daily Standard*, December 4, 1881; Moonlight, 36–37; Blunt, 257; *Indiana True Republican*, n.d., James Hanway Scrapbooks; Reader, 9; Childers, 5.

8. *OR*, 41:1:634, 658.

9. TREM, 249; *OR*, 41:1:658, 666–67, 675.

10. *OR*, 41:1:526, 562 and 4:190–91, 192, 193.

11. *OR*, 41:1:480, 658, 666, 675; Hinton, 131; TREM, 243; MCFCM, 80; Connelley, *Kansas and Kansans*, 2:758–59.

12. There is no evidence to substantiate Monnett's (79) claim that Alonzo Slayback's cavalry exploited the lower ford. There is also no evidence to support Paul Jenkins's assertion in *The Battle of Westport* (Kansas City: Franklin Hudson Publishing Company, 1906), 77, that Fagan's division was involved in the initial breach of Byram's Ford. *OR*, 41:1:480, 658, 666, 675; Hinton, 131; Cruzen, 29.

13. *OR*, 41:1:480–82; *Leavenworth Daily Standard*, December 4, 1881; Palmer, 19.

14. *OR*, 41:1:544 and 4:191; Palmer, 19.

15. *Leavenworth Daily Standard*, December 4, 1881; *OR*, 41:1:667; Hinton, 125–27; P. I. Bonebrake, "Recollections of the Second Day's Fight in the Battle of Westport," 72, CWN.

16. *Leavenworth Daily Standard*, December 4, 1881; *The Commercial Press* (Pultneyville, New York), October 1864.

17. Guilford G. Gage, *The Battle of the Blue of the Second Regiment* . . . (Chicago: WTPA, n.d.), 39–40; *Kansas City Journal*, November 24, 1881; Cruzen, 30.

18. Levi Williams, "My Recollections of the Battle of the Blue . . . ," 2 and Henry M. Greene, "My Big Blue Experience," 1, CWN; Bonebrake, 71; Reader, 11; Gage, 40–41.

19. LCM, 21.

20. Gage, 40–41; Greene, 1; John Kemp, "What I Remember of the Battle of the Blue, and Incidents Connected with It," 1, CWN; Williams, 3.

21. S. B. Miles, "Reminiscences of the Battle of the Big Blue," December 12, 1896, CWN; *OR*, 41:1:658, 667; Bonebrake, 72; J. H. P. Baker Diary, October 22, 1864, Miscellaneous Document, SHSMO-C.

22. Williams, 4; Bonebrake, 72.

23. Cruzen, 30–31; H. D. Rice, "Reminiscences of the Battle of the Blue . . . ," CWN.

24. Williams, 5; Greene, 1–3; Theodore B. Mills to G. G. Gage, June 14, 1895, and "The Battle of the Blue of the Second Regiment of the K.S.M.: Narrative of G. G. Gage," 3–4; Kemp, 2.

25. *OR*, 41:1:566–67; *Kansas City Star*, July 10, 1898; William E. Connelley, *The Life of Preston Plumb, 1837–1891* (Chicago: Browne and Hall Company, 1913), 190; Bonebrake, 72.

26. LCM, 11–14, 15–16, 17–20, 21; *OR*, 41:1:566–77. Laing was later acquitted of a charge of cowardice.

27. *OR*, 41:1:635.

28. Sallee, 57.

29. *OR*, 41:1:312 and 4:157–59; Wright, 227–28.

30. *OR*, 41:1:336, 371; Wright, 219–20; Sanborn, "The Campaign in Missouri," 176; MCFCM, 176.

31. *OR*, 41:4:183; Wright, 220; MCFCM, 76.

32. *OR*, 41:1:336, 371, 379, 383, 403; Cabell, 10; Frederick M. Woodruff, ed., "The Civil War Notebook of Montgomery Schuyler Woodruff," *Missouri Historical Bulletin* 29 (1973): 182; MCFCM, 76; Sanborn, "The Campaign in Missouri," 177.

33. *OR*, 41:1:336, 371, 379, 403, 635; Starr, 333; Sanborn, "The Campaign in Missouri," 177; *National Tribune*, April 17, 1890, April 14, 1898, September 15, 1904; Clipping, Mrs. Robert Hill to Mrs. Kate Doneghy, October 23, 1864, in "R. F. Crews One of the Survivors of the Battle of Westport," reprinted in *Kansas City Star*, December 7, 1923; Ples H. Morgan, Reminiscences of the War between the States, UDC Mary Lee Chapter #87, AHCA; *Annual Report of the Adjutant General of Missouri: For the Year Ending December 31, 1865* (Jefferson City: Emory Foster, 1866), 385; Wright, 221; Darr, 361; Cabell, 10.

34. Sanborn, "The Campaign in Missouri," 177; *OR*, 41:1:683; Winslow's Memoirs, Episode 6:13–14.

35. *OR*, 41:1:346–47, 359, 371; MCFCM, 36–38, 43, 51, 58, 68–71, 91–92, 114–15, 133, 194–95, 221, 240; BCM, 90. McFerran was subsequently tried for cowardice—as well as for the poor handling of his regiment on the 23rd—and acquitted.

36. *OR*, 41:1:346–47, 359, 371; MCFCM, 36–38, 43, 51, 58, 68–71, 91–92, 114–15, 133, 194–95, 221, 240; Winslow's Memoirs, Episode 6:14–15.

37. *OR*, 41:1:346–47, 359, 371; MCFCM, 36–38, 43, 51, 58, 68–71, 91–92, 114–15, 133, 194–95, 221, 240.

38. BCM, 160, 286; *OR*, 41:1:683; MCFCM, 66, 200, 204. Winslow (Episode 6:15) did not believe the claims of a lack of ammunition.

39. Scott, 320; Winslow's Memoirs, Episode 6:17–18; Diary of James Boyle, October 22, 1864, typescript, Collection BG C4998, Vol. XVII, Iowa Historical Archives, Des Moines, Iowa.

40. *Ballard Diary*, 69–76; *OR*, 41:1:683; BCM, 72; *Missouri Republican*, March 6, 1886.

11. A DESPERATE STAND AT BRUSH CREEK

1. *OR*, 41:1:615.

2. Hinton, 145.

3. *Leavenworth Weekly Times*, March 10, 1914; *Topeka Journal*, November 2, 1934; Cordley, 250–52; Lathrop Bullene, *The Life of Lathrop Bullene* (Privately published, 1916), 38–40.

4. *OR*, 41:4:195; Walter E. McCourt, *The Geology of Jackson County* (Rolla: McCourt, 1917), 1–15; Jonathan B. Fuller to Father, October 24, 1864, F. 11, Jonathan B. Fuller Papers, SHSMO-C.

5. *OR*, 41:1:593–94, 616; Hinton, 152; *Report of the Adjutant General of the State of Kansas, 1861–1865*, vol. 1 (Topeka: Kansas State Printing Company, 1896), 232–43.

6. *Leavenworth Daily Standard*, December 4, 1881.

7. Fuller to Father, October 24, 1864, F.11 and Fuller Journal, October 23, 1864, F.1, Fuller Papers; Wright, 224; *OR*, 41:1:667; Jenkins, 91, TREM, 250; Cruzen, 31. Where the sources disagree, my placing of Confederate units follows the battle report of Jeff Thompson and the memoirs of John Wright, both of which complement each other. Howard Monnett's placement of McCray's brigade along the Harrisonville Road just south of Brush Creek (97 and 100) is unsubstantiated by any contemporary source or suggestion.

8. Fuller to Father, October 24, 1864, F. 11 and October 23, 1864, Fuller Journal, F.1, Fuller Papers; *OR*, 41:1:585, 593–94; Hinton, 154–55; Suderow, ed., "McLain's Battery," 44; Cruzen, 31; TREM, 250.

9. Most evidence points to the gun simply shattering contrary to the Union belief that they hit the gun with a well-aimed shot. Wright, 251; *OR*, 41:1:667.

10. Suderow, ed., "McLain's Battery," 44.

11. Hinton, 155; Moonlight, 37; *OR*, 41:1:594; *Leavenworth Daily Standard*, December 4, 1881; Wright, 224.

12. *OR*, 41:1:585, 608, 667; TREM, 250; Cruzen, 31.

13. *OR*, 41:1:576, 585, 598, 609; Mitchell, 88.

14. Hinton, 157; *OR*, 41:1:576, 585, 598; TREM, 250; October 23, 1864, Fuller Journal, F.1, Fuller Papers.

15. *OR*, 41:1:667; TREM, 250; Shalhope, 256. Federal gun tubes included Henry Barker's four, Daniel Knowles's two, McLain's six, James Dodge's six, H. F. Douglas's six, P. H. Minor's two, and Gustavus Zesch's two.

16. *OR*, 41:1:485, 576, 598–99; Charles P. Deatherage, *Early History of Greater Kansas City . . .* vol. 1 (Kansas City: Interstate Publishing Company, 1927), 553; *Leavenworth Daily Times*, October 26, 1864. Blunt misspoke in his official report by placing the Confederate incursion on his left flank. Richard Hinton (158–59) almost confuses the matter beyond all recognition by placing the 5th and 19th KSMs on opposite ends of the Union line where they repulsed separate flanking maneuvers. There was, however, only one Confederate probe of Curtis's line, and it was on the Union right. James Ford, on the Union left, makes no mention of a Confederate flanking attempt and the attendant reinforcement of the 19th KSM, as does Charles Blair.

17. *OR*, 41:1:485–86; Hinton, 160; Monnett, 103–4; Bonebrake, 76.

18. Hinton, 165; Jenkins, 140–43.

19. Suderow, ed., "McLain's Battery," 44; Wright, 225. John Edwards in his campaign to deify Shelby probably invented his comment that Shelby "strongly advised against it" (Ed-

SHELBY, 438). Wright makes no mention of Shelby's protest, which would have been out of character for Wright to miss an opportunity to impugn Fagan.

20. Jeff Thompson and James Ford imply that the attack took place before Blunt moved the Army of the Border to the north of Brush Creek. Doc Jennison and John C. Wright place the attack after Curtis orders the general advance. Richard Hinton gets the best of all worlds by describing McGhee's attack twice: once before the Union retreat and once afterward! My estimation of 11:30 is supported by the recollection, albeit well after the fact, of William S. Shepherd, a trooper in the 15th Kansas. See Westport Historical Society, ed., *The Battle of Westport: October 21–23, 1864* (Kansas City: Westport Historical Society, 1996), 65; Cruzen, 31; Wright, 225; Hinton, 156, 161; Suderow, ed., "McLain's Battery," 44; *Kansas City Star*, October 23, 1925; *OR*, 41:1:585–86, 608.

21. Wright, 225; Hinton, 156, 161; Suderow, ed., "McLain's Battery," 44; *OR*, 41:1:585–86, 608; H. A. Seiffert to Andrew C. McMaken, November 11, 1864, B. 24, F. 3, Lighton Family Papers; Service Record, J. M. McGehee, McGehee's Regiment, Arkansas Cavalry, http://www.fold3.com/image/271/219829731/, accessed November 19, 2013.

22. Seiffert to McMaken, November 11, 1864, Lighton Family Papers; Stanton, 250. Historians have inflated the casualties for this affair. Monnett (108) is typical in reporting twenty-five Confederate KIA and one hundred prisoners. Monnett (and Hinton, 161) seem to rely upon Jennison's report for the prisoners (*OR*, 41:1:586). While the KIA figure represents a reasonable guess, the number of prisoners is certainly Jennison's wishful thinking. Fred Lee has concluded there were thirty-four in his *The Battle of Westport: October 21–23, 1864*, Special Publication Number One (Kansas City: Westport Historical Society, 1976), 23. This number is close to the twenty-seven listed by name in the 2nd Colorado's Francis M. Gordon Diary. See Gordon Diary, *Civil War Diaries, 1864–1867*, vol. 2, SHSMO-C.

23. *OR*, 41:1:667; TREM, 250–51; Cruzen, 31–32.

12. REBELS, REBELS, FIRE, FIRE!

1. BCM, 24–25, 39, 72, 171, 189, 212.

2. BCM, 188–98, 198–99.

3. BCM, 8, 10, 12, 28, 63, 72, 93, 128–29, 153–57; MCFCM, 9–23; *OR*, 41:1:349. There was controversy about when Brown received his orders. Brown claimed 5:30, while other evidence pointed to 4:30. Given what will soon be seen as Brown's complete inactivity between 4:30 and 5:30, it stands to reason he received them at the later time.

4. BCM, 41, 43, 153–54, 171, 189, 190, 198, 232, 248, 251; *Kansas City Star*, October 23, 1923; MCFCM, 65.

5. BCM, 14, 24, 26, 98, 287–95; MCFCM, 56, 81, 86; Lazear to wife, August 11, 1864, F. 8, Bazel F. Lazear Papers, SHSMO-C; James H. Baker and George E. Lewis, ed., *History of Colorado*, vol. 4 (Denver: Linderman Company, Inc., 1927), 302–7.

6. BCM, 34, 57, 72, 194, 270, 271.

7. BCM, 33–38, 65, 71–74, 88, 192–97, 216, 218, 233, 234, 259–64; *Kansas City Star*, August 28, 1941.

8. MCFCM, 78–79, 323, 327; Winslow's Memoirs, Episode 6:13–14; *OR*, 41:4:204; Edward G. Longacre, *The Cavalry at Gettysburg: A Tactical Study of Mounted Operations during the Civil War's Pivotal Campaign, 9 June–14 July 1863* (Rutherford: Fairleigh Dickin-

son University Press, 1986), 91, 161–62; BCM, 11, 73; Arthur Candenquist, "Did Anybody Really Know What Time It Was?" *Blue and Gray Magazine* 8, no. 6 (1991): 32–35.

9. Scott, 322.

10. Pleasanton was mistaken when he recollected the time at around 7 AM (BCM, 12). C. F. Little corroborates Pleasanton's timing (BCM, 157), but most other testimony indicates it was closer to 8 AM. See, for example, BCM, 44, 63, 85. Not surprisingly, there was even one observer who placed the time at 9 AM. He wore a watch, but admitted it was fast (BCM, 116).

11. BCM, 44, 63, 74, 85, 237–38, 260; *OR*, 41:1:328, 684, 688.

12. BCM, 237–38; Winslow Memoirs, Episode 6:21; Scott, 322; Campbell, 24; *OR*, 41:1:350–51, 693.

13. *OR*, 41:1:330, 350–51, 361, 363; BCM, 101, 217, 238; Scott, 323–24; Walmsley, 111; Winslow's Memoirs, Episode 6:22–23; John F. Philips, "Diary of Acting Brigadier General John F. Philips . . . ," *The Annals of Kansas City* 1 (1923): 267–71; Scott, 323–24. The exact ordering of 4th and 7th MSMs is not clear. Philips's report has the 7th MSM on the left, while Kelly's report places the 4th at the "extreme left" of the line.

14. *OR*, 41:1:330–31, 351, 363; Winslow's Memoirs, Episode 6:24; Mills, 179; Scott, 324; Walmsley, 111.

15. *OR*, 41:1:363; Scott, 324; Jenkins, 127; Frederic A. Culmer, ed., "Brigadier Surgeon John W. Trader's Recollections of the Civil War in Missouri," *Missouri Historical Review* 48 (1952): 330.

16. *Sedalia Advertiser*, December 24, 1864; *OR*, 41:1:324, 330; Scott, 324; BCM, 103–4.

17. *OR*, 41:1:330, 361, 363, 692, 696, 697, 696; Jenkins, 128; Lurton Dunham Ingersoll, *Iowa and the Rebellion* (Philadelphia: J. B. Lippincott, 1866), 410, 427; Monnett, 115; Earl J. Hess, *The Rifle Musket in Civil War Combat: Reality and Myth* (Lawrence: University Press of Kansas, 2008).

18. Scott, 325; Walmsley, 111; Philips, 269; Sanborn, "The Campaign in Missouri," 181; *OR*, 41:1:337, 390; BCM, 44–45. Winslow's Memoirs (Episode 6:23) include an uncorroborated claim of an early, and unsuccessful, assault by Sanborn at Byram's Ford.

19. *OR*, 41:1:658–59, 676.

20. *OR*, 41:1:390, 676; Sanborn, "The Campaign in Missouri," 182–83; MCFCM, 235–36, 247–49; Gene Greer, "Up and in Line at Day Break: Considable Skemish," *White River Valley Historical Quarterly* 1 (1964): 1–15.

21. Sanborn, "The Campaign in Missouri," 183; *OR*, 41:1:676.

22. *OR*, 41:1:586, 609; Hinton, 164.

23. Hinton, 162.

24. *OR*, 41:1:331, 334, 335, 351, 667; TREM, 250–51; Scott, 326–27.

25. *OR*, 41:1:594, 668; TREM, 251–52; Alonzo Slayback to Thompson, December 8, 1867, M. Jeff Thompson Papers, Manuscripts Collection 72, Manuscripts Department, Howard-Tilton Memorial Library, Tulane University, New Orleans, LA; Cruzen, 33.

13. LOST OPPORTUNITY AT HART GROVE CREEK

1. There is a brief mention of the correct route in the *errata* listing of the revised edition of Monnett (xxxiv).

2. MCNCM, 238–40, 332; Fletcher Pomeroy Diary, October 1864, typescript, page 242, KSHS.

1127

3. *OR*, 41:1:634–36; Cabell, 10; Wright, 227.

4. MCNCM, Affidavit, E. G. Manning, July 7, 1865, Defense Statement of John McNeil, and pages 67–68, 83, 87, 97, 162–64, 220, 254, 295, 296, 344; OR, 41:1:372.

5. MCNCM, 16–17, 100.

6. *OR*, 41:1:635–36; Cabell, 10; Kemp, 2; MCNCM, 185, 332, and E. G. Manning's affidavit.

7. MCNCM, 17, 90, 92, 184, 186–87, 200–3, 259, 269–70, 293, 299–300, 318–21, 336–38.

8. MCNCM, 17, 90, 184, 186–87, 200–3, 259, 293, 299–300, 336–38; Fletcher Pomeroy Diary, 242.

9. MCNCM, 82, 301–4, 336.

10. McPheeters Diary, October 23, 1864; *OR*, 41:1:587, 594; Dispatches Received per Messengers, McKenney, One Mile South of Little Santa Fe and McKenney, Four Miles South of Little Santa Fe, TRS-AofB; Sanborn, "The Campaign in Missouri," 183; Edwin A. Carpenter, *History of the 17th Illinois Cavalry Volunteers* (N.P., 1886); Jacob Gantz, *Such Are the Trials: The Civil War Diaries of Jacob Gantz*, edited by Kathleen Davis (Ames: Iowa State University Press, 1991), 75.

11. *OR*, 41:1:337, 491–92; Hinton, 174–77; Curtis to wife, October 30, 1864, Curtis Papers; Blunt, 260.

12. Fuller to Father, October 24, 1864, F. 11 and Journal 1851–1867, October 23, 26, 1864, F. 1, Fuller Papers; Theodore B. Mills to G. G. Gage, June 14, 1895, CWN; *Kansas City Western Journal of Commerce*, October 25 and 26, 1864.

13. *Kansas City Star*, October 25, 1925, and October 24, 1937; Fred Lee, *Gettysburg of the West: The Battle of Westport, October 21–23, 1864* (Independence: Two Trails Publishing, 1996), 47, 52–53; *Kansas City Western Journal of Commerce*, October 25, 1864; *Leavenworth Daily Times*, October 26, 1864; George Swain to Carrie Swain, October 27, 1864, Swain Collection.

14. David Heidler et al., eds., *Encyclopedia of the American Civil War* (New York: W. W. Norton, 2002), 2093; Monnett, 123–24; Phillip Katcher, *Civil War Day by Day* (St. Paul: Zenith Press, 2007), 162; http://www.nps.gov/abpp/battles/mo027.htm , accessed August 14, 2009. Albert Castel dissented from Monnett's figures when he postulated there were one thousand Confederate casualties, using the estimation of an anonymous staffer in Fagan's division. See Castel, *General Sterling Price*, 236. A very good, but little noted, commentary on the casualties can be found in Fred Lee, ed., *Battle of Westport: October 21–23, 1864* (Kansas City: Westport Historical Society, 1976), 23. Suderow's notes and compilations can be found in the Bryce A. Suderow Collection, SHSMO-C.

14. MUSKETRY LIKE SWARMS OF LIGHTNING BUGS

1. TREM, 252; Edwin A. Carpenter, *History of the 17th Illinois Cavalry Volunteers*, chapter xxix; Hinton, 183–85; James H. Campbell, "Reminiscence of James H. Campbell's," 25.

2. McPheeters Diary, October 24, 1864; Hinton, 187; Blunt, 260; *OR*, 41:1:636.

3. Bird, 104, 111; Ellen Williams, *Three Years and a Half in the Army; Or, History of the 2nd Colorado* (New York: Fowler and Wells Company, 1885), 6–7; "The Civil War Diary of Samuel J. Reader," 13–14.

4. Cruzen, 22; Hinton, 183, 190; *Leavenworth Daily Times*, November 9, 1864; Campbell, 25; *Border Sentinel*, October 28, 1864; Mitchell, 153, 176, 306–7.

5. Mitchell, 118–19, 308–9.

6. Scott, 328; Pomeroy Diary, October 24–25, 1864; Philips, 269; Carpenter, *History of the 17th Illinois*, chapter xxix; Hinton, 185–88; Cabell, 10–11; *OR*, 41:1:493, 587, 599, 609. Cabell asserts he fired the prairie on the 23rd. There is no other reliable evidence of this. John Darr's account (359–62) written in 1903 is largely derived from Cabell's memoir. However, Scott's more contemporaneous memoir places the event on the 24th with additional commentary about its effectiveness.

7. Blunt, 260; Hinton, 187–88; Ellen Williams, 111. Buresh (70) takes the Union command to task for not employing local men from within the ranks to explain the area topography. However, according to Colonel Edward R. Smith of the 6th KSM (Mitchell, 88), this is precisely what Blunt did on the evening of the 24th.

8. Mitchell, 88.

9. *OR*, 41:1:493; Blunt, 260–61; Mitchell, 88; Sanborn, "The Campaign in Missouri," 185. Buresh (70) criticizes Curtis for not trying to turn Price downriver from Trading Post. Here, again, the same problems attached to any such crossing as they did to one upriver from Trading Post.

10. Sanborn, "The Campaign in Missouri," 187; John B. Sanborn, "Battles and Campaigns of September, 1862, Read March 13, 1900," 5th Series of *Glimpses of the Nation's Struggle . . . , 1897–1902* (St. Paul: Review Publishing Company, 1903), 266; Hinton, 193–96; Frederick M. Woodruff, ed., "The Civil War Notebook of Montgomery Schuyler Woodruff," *Missouri Historical Society Bulletin* 29 (1973):183.

11. Sanborn, "The Campaign in Missouri," 187; Sanborn, "Battles and Campaigns," 266; Hinton, 193–94.

12. *OR*, 41:1:413, 495; Hinton, 193–94; Sanborn, "The Campaign in Missouri," 187.

13. Sanborn, "The Campaign in Missouri," 187; Vanorsdol, 62.

14. Scott, 329.

15. Sanborn, "The Campaign in Missouri," 186–87; Hinton, 197–200; Scott, 329–30; Williams, *Three Years*, 113–14.

16. Sanborn, "The Campaign in Missouri," 186–87; Hinton, 197–200. The only quantification of casualties in the action at the mounds occurs in Williams, *Three Years*, 110. The author claims that the men of the 2nd Colorado killed six Confederates and wounded several others on the skirmishing on the night of the 24th.

17. Sanborn, "The Campaign in Missouri," 186–87; Hinton, 197–201; Williams, *Three Years*, 114.

18. Hinton, 201.

19. Sanborn, "The Campaign in Missouri," 189; James Campbell to Charles Campbell, November 9, 1864, Campbell Collection; Hinton, 201–2.

20. *Border Sentinel*, October 21, 1864; *Leavenworth Daily Times*, November 9, 1864; *Pleasonton Observer*, November 19, 1881; Moonlight, 38; Edward Moore Richards, "'Price's Raid,' Personal Reminiscences of the American Civil War, Kansas, October 1864," *Irish Sword* 7 (1966): 235; *OR*, 41:1:594.

21. *Border Sentinel*, October 21, 1864; *Leavenworth Daily Times*, November 9, 1864; *Pleasonton Observer*, November 19, 1881; Moonlight, 38; *OR*, 41:1:579, 594, 622; Childers, 7.

22. *OR*, 41:4:243; Childers, 7; *Pleasonton Observer*, November 19, 1881; Mitchell, 311.

23. *Border Sentinel*, October 21, 1864; *Leavenworth Daily Times*, November 9, 1864; *Pleasonton Observer*, November 19, 1881; Moonlight, 38; Hinton, 223–24; *OR*, 41:1:594 and 4:319; Childers, 8; Richards, 236–37.

24. *OR*, 41:1:594, 636; Moonlight, 38; *Border Sentinel*, December 16, 1864; *Leavenworth Daily Times*, November 9, 1864. The Leavenworth paper asserted that the militia collected eighteen to twenty prisoners by the end of the day.

25. *OR*, 41:1:636.

15. I DON'T GIVE NO QUARTERS NOR WILL I ASK ANNY

1. *OR*, 41:1:636; Cabell, 10–11; *Missouri Republican*, March 13, 1886; McPheeter's Diary, October 25, 1864.

2. *OR*, 41:1:404, 684, 691; Sanborn, "The Campaign in Missouri," 191; Hinton, 202–5; Crawford, 155–56; Williams, *Three Years*, 114–15; Buresh, 82–83; Campbell, 25; *Missouri Republican*, March 13, 1886.

3. *OR*, 41:1:404, 684, 691; Sanborn, "The Campaign in Missouri," 191; Hinton, 202–5; Crawford, 155–56; Williams, *Three Years*, 114–15; Buresh, 82–83; Sanborn, "Battles and Campaigns," 267.

4. *OR*, 41:1:332, 351, 494, 691; Sanborn, "The Campaign in Missouri," 191; Culmer, 332; Cabell, 11. Buresh (84) claims that Benteen's and Philips's brigades crossed the Marais des Cygnes a few miles north of Trading Post and rode south along the river before turning onto what was the Old Military Road. There is no evidence to support the assertion. Indeed, Major Theodore Weed of Curtis's staff notes that they crossed at Trading Post (*OR*, 41:1:494).

5. *OR*, 41:1:646.

6. *OR*, 41:1:636–37; William B. Lees, "When the Shooting Stopped, the War Began," in *Look to the Earth: Historical Archaeology and the American Civil War*, ed. Clarence R. Geier, Jr. and Susan E. Winter (Knoxville: University of Tennessee Press, 1994), 39–59; Campbell, 25; Buresh, 90.

7. *OR*, 41:1:684; *Missouri Republican*, March 13, 1886; Mitchell, 308; Cabell, 11; Marmaduke to My Dear and Antique Friend, May 26, 1865, F. 1865, Kennelly Family Papers, MHMA.

8. *OR*, 41:1:352, 691, 694, 696; Cabell, 11; Wright, 229–30; *Ballard Diary*, 69–76. There are several points to make about these dispositions. First, there is some dispute concerning the number of Confederate lines. Most references, such as Colton Greene and John Philips, note three. Richard Hinton (206) goes as far as to say that there were six lines in the Confederate center. Second, there is little direct evidence about the locations of either Slemons or Dobbin. The assumption is that with Dobbin's artillery on the far left, Dobbin himself must also be on the far left. John C. Wright, in fact, recollected his regiment of Slemons's brigade on the far left of the line. Third, the placement of Freeman's brigade is no less difficult. The direct primary accounts are muddled with the most explicit placement by Lieutenant Curtis Ballard being to the right of the 7th Missouri. This cannot be. If so, Freeman's brigade would be right in the middle of Clark's brigade. Making matters worse, Ballard placed his regiment just to the right of Slemons. I believe Ballard was confused, and this would have ramifications for assessing subsequent blame for the collapse of the Confederate lines. One other account demonstrates the fog of battle and the troubles lower-ranking soldiers had in identifying troop placements beyond their own company. Lieutenant John Bennett of Jeffers's 8th Missouri recalled a CSA line with McCray on the right, Slemons on the left, and Clark Jr. in the center. See his edited diary in James E. McGhee, ed., *Campaigning with Marmaduke: Narratives and Roster of the 8th Missouri Cavalry Regiment CSA* (Independence: Two Trails Publishing, 2002), 25–26.

9. *OR*, 41:1:352, 691, 694; Cabell, 11; Wright, 229–30; Gil Bergman, "Probable Alignment of the Confederate Artillery at the Battle of Mine Creek, October 25, 1864," Mine Creek Battlefield Museum, Pleasanton, Kansas. My rendition of the artillery places the James Rifle in the center. There is no reason to believe that T. J. Williams, who now commanded Harris's battery, swapped his James Rifle for Dobbin's remaining Woodruff gun.

10. *OR*, 41:1:351–52, 361, 560; Sanborn, "The Campaign in Missouri," 192–93; Lazear to wife, November 7, 1864, F. 10, Bazel Lazear Papers, SHSMO-C; Scott, 333; Buresh, 105; Hinton, 207.

11. *OR*, 41:1:332, 352, 361; Scott, 332–33; Cogley, 211; Crawford, 160.

12. *OR*, 41:1:332, 352, 361; Scott, 332–33; Cogley, 211; Crawford, 160; Unidentified and undated clipping, "General Jo. O. Shelby," Joseph O. Shelby Scrapbook; Walmsley, 112; William Lyman Diary, October 25, 1864, Lyman Collection; Lazear to wife, November 7, 1864, F. 10, Lazear Papers; William L. [last name not legible] (Co G, 10th MO Cav) to Herman Crede, November 15, 1864, Roll 1, F. 16, Crede Family Papers.

13. *Missouri Republican*, March 13, 1886; Kip Lindberg, "Chaos Itself: The Battle of Mine Creek," *North and South* 1, no. 6 (1998): 74–85.

14. *OR*, 41:1:332, 352, 361; Lazear to wife, November 7, 1864, F. 10, Lazear Papers; Scott, 332; Hinton, 208; Walmsley, 112; Philips, 270; *Missouri Republican*, March 13, 1886.

15. *OR*, 41:1:332, 352, 361; Lazear to wife, November 7, 1864, F. 10, Lazear Papers; Scott, 333–34; Hinton, 210.

16. *OR*, 41:1:332, 692, 694, 696, 699; Scott, 333–35; *Missouri Republican*, March 13, 1886.

17. *OR*, 41:1:332 and 4:290; *Missouri Republican*, March 13, 1886; Jenkins, 70, 125; MCFCM, 121; BCM, 239; Mills, 79; Jason Marmor, *Prelude to Westport: Phase I Archaeological Survey of a Portion of the Big Blue Battlefield in Kansas City, Jackson County, Missouri...* (Laramie: TRC Mariah Associates, Inc., 1997), 34.

18. *OR*, 41:1:692, 694, 696, 699; *Missouri Republican*, March 13, 1886; Wright, 229–31; *Ballard Diary*, 69–76; *Washington Telegraph*, November 30, 1864.

19. John C. Leach Diary, Typescript, Mine Creek Battlefield State Historic Site Museum; *Pleasanton Enterprise*, March 28, 1935; Marmaduke to "My Dear and Antique Friend," May 26, 1865, F. 1865, Kennelly Papers; Mark A. Plummer, "Missouri and Kansas and the Capture of General Marmaduke," *Missouri Historical Review* 59 (1964): 93.

20. McGhee, *Campaigning with Marmaduke*, 38.

21. Wright, 232; Clement A. Evans, ed., *Confederate Military History*, vol. x (Atlanta: Confederate Publishing Company, 1899), 286; Cabell, 11–12; *OR*, 41:1:335.

22. *OR*, 41:1:352; Curtis, 13; Wright, 231; William L. [last name not legible] (Co G, 10th MO Cav) to Herman Crede, November 15, 1864, Roll 1, F. 16, Crede Papers.

23. *OR*, 41:1:700; Buresh, 138, 227.

24. *OR*, 41:1:352; Britton, 2, 502–3; Wright, 232–33; Scott, 336–37; Philips, 270; Sanborn, "The Campaign in Missouri," 195; Greer, 1–15.

25. My casualty figures are based on the meticulous work of Buresh (222–33). Differing accounts of the casualties can be found in Lindberg, 84; Suderow to Fred Lee, September 24, 1973, Suderow Collection; Scott, 337–39; Hinton, 225; *Leavenworth Conservative*, November 9, 1864.

16. WE ALL EXPERIENCED TRIBULATION THIS DAY

1. *OR*, 41:1:527 and 4:238; Hinton, 215–16.

2. Buresh, 152–54; Mitchell, 307–11; *Leavenworth Conservative*, October 28, 1864.

3. Mitchell, 307–11.

4. Walmsley, 114–15.

5. Lyman G. Bennett Diary, January 5, 1865, F. 7, January 1–October 4, 1865, Lyman G. Bennett Collection, SHSMO-R.

6. *OR*, 41:1:372, 391, 580; Sanborn, "The Campaign in Missouri," 195; Blunt, 261; Buresh, 141–42.

7. *OR*, 41:1:372, 392, 413; Scott, 338; Hinton, 220–27; Sanborn, "The Campaign in Missouri," 196. Sanborn's already small brigade was further reduced by the detachment of J. J. Gravely's 8th MSM as prisoner guards.

8. James Hanway to Brother, November 6, 1864, *Indiana True Republican*, James S. Hanway Scrapbook; EdSHELBY, 440, 447.

9. *OR*, 41:1:636–37, 659, 700.

10. EdSHELBY, 447; Lindberg, 84. It is impossible to determine the precise location of Price when he ran into Marmaduke's and Fagan's refugees. However, Kip Lindberg probably errs when he places Price and Shelby near to Mine Creek. There simply was not enough time for either general to have made that ride in the short time since they received Marmaduke's courier.

11. Hinton, 223–24; EdSHELBY, 440; T. F. Robley, *History of Bourbon County, Kansas to the Close of 1865* (Fort Scott: Press of the Monitor Book and Print Company, 1894), 191–92; *OR*, 41:1:594; Moonlight, 38.

12. *OR*, 41:1:636–37, 659–60; TREM, 253–56; Hinton, 220–30; Sanborn, "The Campaign in Missouri," 196. Sanborn asserts that Confederates claimed to have used unarmed men to compose one of their lines. I think Sanborn was mistaken as he confused the action of Tyler's brigade later at the Marmaton River with that of the Little Osage.

13. *OR*, 41:1:636–37, 659–60; TREM, 253–56; Hinton, 220–30; Sanborn, 196.

14. TREM, 255–56; Hinton, 220–30; *OR*, 41:1:405, 637.

15. TREM, 255–56; Hinton, 220–30; Cruzen, 33; *OR*, 41:1:405, 637.

16. J. W. Halliburton, "That Charge," *Confederate Veteran* 28 (1920):264; TREM, 255–56; Hinton, 220–30; *OR*, 41:1:405, 637; Sanborn, "The Campaign in Missouri," 196.

17. There is controversy over the location of the crossing site and its attendant battlefield. The Missouri Department of Natural Resources has placed a marker 6.3 miles from the Kansas border marking both the battlefield and river crossing. Patrick Brophy's *Fire and Sword: A Missouri County in the Civil War* (Nevada: Bushwhacker Books, 2008), 182–83 contains a map and narrative supporting this location. The evidence does not sustain the placement. Buresh (174–75, 182) is more likely correct that the battle and crossing occurred just inside the Kansas side of the border. There are no primary accounts that confirm a Missouri location. Although a Charlow Branch stream did empty into the Marmaton near the alleged Missouri site, the terrain at the Missouri site and the route depicted on Brophy's map are simply not compatible with the two contemporary battle maps created by A. Konig of the 2nd Colorado and Jacob Miller of the 3rd Wisconsin. Miller's map accompanied page 502 of Samuel Curtis's official report. The only near contemporary source to specify a location, and it is within Kansas, is Robley (191). Much of my thinking on this issue was shaped by correspondence with Mr. Daniel Smith and analysis of the Township 25, South Range 25 East, Plat Map in *An Illustrated Historical Atlas of Bourbon County, Kansas* (Philadelphia: Edwards Brothers, 1878).

18. Sanborn, "The Campaign in Missouri," 197; EdSHELBY, 455; Crawford, 166; *History of Vernon County*, 325; TREM, 256–57; Hinton, 232–33.

19. Buresh, 175–76; EdSHELBY, 452; Hinton, 234; *OR*, 41:1:660, 691. Hinton noted four Confederate lines. This observation seems more the product of the structure of individual brigades rather than distinct lines spread over a mile in width.

20. Charlot represents the linguistic corruption of Sharlow, the name of a nearby hamlet and one-time post office.

21. Buresh, 175–76; EdSHELBY, 452; Hinton, 234; *OR*, 41:1:502, 660, 691.

22. *OR*, 41:1:700.

23. *OR*, 41:1:333, 660, 676–77; Scott, 339–41; Hinton, 234–35; EdSHELBY, 453–54. There is some evidence to suggest that the detachment of the 7th Indiana split off from the rest of Simonson's command and joined Benteen's assault. Cogley (128) claims that "the regiment" made two charges at the Marmaton.

24. Hinton, 236–37; Crawford, 172–73; *OR*, 41:1:338, 339, 502–3 and 4:286.

25. Hinton, 236–37.

26. Hinton, 236–37; Crawford, 172–73; *OR*, 41:1:338, 339, 502–3; Curtis to Wife, October 30, 1864, Curtis Papers.

27. Hinton, 236–37; Carpenter, chapter XXX; Crawford, 172–73; Scott, 341; *OR*, 41:1:338, 339, 502–3; Blunt, 261.

28. General Orders No. 22, Headquarters Army of Missouri, October 25, 1864, Shelby Testimony, Proceedings of a Board of Survey Convened at Clarksville, Texas, November 29, 1864, PME; EdSHELBY, 455; *Ballard Diary*, 69–76; TREM, 258; Campbell, 27; Carpenter, chapter XXX; *History of Vernon County*, 326; Bennett Diary, January 8, 1865; Sanborn, "The Campaign in Missouri," 197–98; Hinton, 238–39; Henry to Rosecrans, November 8, 1864, LR-DofM; *OR*, 41:4:274, 278.

29. *History of Vernon County*, 326–27; *Ballard Diary*, October 26, 1864; Shelby Testimony, Proceedings of a Board of Survey; TREM, 258; R. L. Brown, "Army Journal, 1864: Price's Raid," October 25, 1864, typescript, F. 392, Civil War Papers, MHMA.

17. THERE IS NOT AN ENEMY IN A HUNDRED MILES

1. *Missouri Republican*, March 13, 1886; TREM, 259; Baker Diary, October 26, 1864; McPheeters Diary, October 26, 1864.

2. *OR*, 41:1:637; Hinton, 262; Cruzen, 34; Wright, 234–35; Orson Davis, Lauchlan Maclean, Henry W. Tracy, Jo Shelby Testimonies, Proceedings of a Board of Survey and Circular No. 13, October 25 [*sic*], 1864, OCI-SPC.

3. *OR*, 41:1:507, 637; Bonebrake, 73; Reader, 16–17; Gage, "Narrative," 5; Wright, 236; Hinton, 275; Kemp, 3; B. F. Dawson to Colonel of the 2nd KS Malitia [*sic*] from Topeka, October 14, n.d., 1:22, CWN.

4. *OR*, 41:1:637; *Missouri Republican*, March 20, 1886; Brown Journal, October 27, 1864; TREM, 259.

5. *OR*, 41:1:338, 342, 504, 505 and 4:286–88; Crawford, 175; *History of Vernon County*, 327; Hinton, 254–55; James P. Mallery, *"Found No Bushwhackers": The 1864 Diary of . . .*, edited by Patrick Brophy (Nevada: Vernon Historical Society, 1988), 44.

6. *OR*, 41:1:338–39, 342, 504, 505 and 4:286–88; Curtis to wife, October 26, 1854, Curtis Papers; Hinton, 254–60; Crawford, 175; Philips Diary, October 26, 1864.

7. Moonlight, 38; *OR*, 41:1:339, 352–53; Philips Diary, October 26, 27, 1864; Hinton, 259–61.

8. *OR*, 41:1:338–39, 342, 352, 504, 505 and 4:286–88; F. W. Benteen to Curtis, 1100 hours, October 27, 1864, Dispatches Received per Messengers, TRS-AofB; Hinton, 254–60; Crawford, 175; Philips Diary, October 26, 1864.

9. Hinton, 262–63; Ward L. Schrantz, *Jasper County, Missouri in the Civil War* (Carthage: The Carthage Press, 1923), 225–26.

10. An excellent treatment of the Second Battle of Newtonia can be found in Larry Wood's *The Two Civil War Battles of Newtonia* (Charleston: The History Press, 2010). However, Wood's narrative does not incorporate the memoirs and perspective of John C. Wright. See Wright, 236.

11. Brown, "Army Journal," October 25, 1864; *Springfield Missouri Patriot*, August 24, 1865; *OR*, 41:1:637–38; TREM, 260; EdSHELBY, 459–60.

12. *OR*, 41:1:507.

13. *OR*, 41:1:507, 540, 577, 609; Hinton, 262–63.

14. Wright, 236–37.

15. Kemp, 3; Undated clipping, "Shelby at Newtonia," Joseph O. Shelby Scrapbook; Cruzen, 34; TREM, 260–61.

16. Undated clipping, "Shelby at Newtonia," Joseph O. Shelby Scrapbook; Cruzen, 34; TREM, 260–61; *OR*, 41:1:577, 661, 669; EdSHELBY, 456.

17. Wright, 237–38; Hinton, 266–67.

18. *OR*, 41:1:587–88, 609–10; Hinton, 264–65; Blunt, 262–63; *Leavenworth Daily Conservative*, November 5, 1864.

19. *OR*, 41:1:587–88, 609–10; Hinton, 264–65; Blunt, 262–63; *Leavenworth Daily Conservative*, November 5, 1864; Wright, 238; *Washington Telegraph*, November 30, 1864; F. F. Basham, Reminiscences of the War between the States.

20. *OR*, 41:1:587–88, 590, 609–10, 661, 669, 677; Hinton, 266–67; *Leavenworth Daily Conservative*, November 5, 1864; TREM, 261–62. There is a possibility that John C. Wright's regiment formed on the Confederate right with Adams's and Langhorne's units. See Wright, 238.

21. *OR*, 41:1:661, 669; Hinton, 267, 269; *Leavenworth Daily Conservative*, November 5, 1864; Cruzen, 34; TREM, 262–63. Monroe had been elevated to command the remnants of Cabell's brigade.

22. Hinton, 268.

23. Hinton, 270, 274; *OR*, 41:1:508.

24. *OR*, 41:1:392, 405, 408, 411; Sanborn, "The Campaign in Missouri," 200. There are differing accounts of just how far Sanborn attacked before stopping. Sanborn claimed three miles, while his regimental commanders (William Mitchell and John McMahan) noted one mile in their official reports. Private Taylor Bray of the 6th Provisional EMM also notes one mile in his diary (Greer, 1–15). In light of the geography of the battlefield and Confederate reports/reminiscences, one mile seems the correct distance. See also Hinton, 270–71; Sanborn, "Battles and Campaigns," 271.

25. *OR*, 41:1:610, 647; Greer, 1–15; McPheeters Diary, October 28, 1864.

26. Hinton, 272, 277; EdSHELBY, 458; *OR*, 41:1:554. Union casualties can be broken down as follows: 15th Kansas: ten killed, twenty-nine wounded, one missing; 16th Kansas: two killed and thirteen wounded; 3rd Wisconsin: eleven wounded; 2nd Colorado: one killed and five wounded.

18. A LAND OF STARVATION

1. *OR*, 41:1:638.

2. TREM, 265; McPheeters Diary, October 29, 30, 31, and November 1, 1864. Pin Indians were pro-Union Cherokees.

3. Brown, "Army Journal," October 30, November 1, 1864; Unidentified and undated clipping, "Shelby at Newtonia," Joseph O. Shelby Scrapbook.

4. Baker Diary, October 30 and 31, 1864; Unidentified and undated clipping, "Shelby at Newtonia," Joseph O. Shelby Scrapbook; *OR*, 41:1:661, 677.

5. *OR*, 41:1:647 and 4:1020; TREM, 264; Brown, "Army Journal," October 30, November 1, 1864; *Washington Telegraph*, November 30, 1864; William G. Hazen to Alexander R. Hazen, December 21, 1864, William G. Hazen Letter, SHSMO-C; *Missouri Republican*, March 20, 1886; Cruzen, 35. Freeman had orders to depart on October 31st, although it appears he did not leave until November 2nd.

6. *OR*, 41:1:338–39, 342, 352, 504, 505, 510–11 and 4:277, 286–88; Hinton, 254–60; Crawford, 175; Sanborn, "The Campaign in Missouri," 200. Philips was only one day's ride out of Fort Scott when Rosecrans ordered him to Warrensburg on the 28th. See Philips Diary, October 27–28, 1864.

7. *OR*, 41:1:511–13, 4:219, 274; Curtis to My Dear Wife, October 30, 1864, Curtis Papers; Halleck to Rosecrans, October 31, 1864, TRS-AofB.

8. *OR*, 41:1:511–14, 610 and 4:356; Irving W. Stanton, *Sixty Years in Colorado: Reminiscences and Reflections of a Pioneer of 1860* (Denver, 1922), 116; Gantz, 77; Williams, *Three Years*, 125–26.

9. *OR*, 41:1:511–14, 610 and 4:356; Stanton, *Sixty Years*, 116; Gantz, 77; Williams, *Three Years*, 125–26; Hinton, 282–83; Scott, 343; Childers, 10.

10. *OR*, 41:4:402–5, 419, 420.

11. *OR*, 41:1:374 and 4:334, 350–53, 404–5, 419, 420, 442, 476; Hinton, 281.

12. *OR*, 41:1:399–400, 638; Williams, *Three Years*, 127; Russell L. Mahan, *Fayetteville, Arkansas in the Civil War, 1860–1865* (Bountiful: Historical Byways, 2003), 38, 112; Hinton, 284–87. Robert R. Mackey, *The Uncivil War: Irregular Warfare in the Upper South, 1861–1865* (Norman: University of Oklahoma Press, 2004), 63; EdSHELBY, 461.

13. *OR*, 41:1:400, 515; Wright, 242–43; Hinton, 286; EdSHELBY, 461; Williams, *Three Years*, 127.

14. *OR*, 41:1:515–16 and 4:421; Williams, *Three Years*, 127, 130; Hinton, 289–90; Gantz, 77.

15. *OR*, 41:1:515–16 and 4:421; Williams, *Three Years*, 127, 130; Hinton, 289–90; Gantz, 77; Childers, 11; Hinton, 289–90.

16. Maclean to Maxey, November 1, 1864, and Maclean to Fagan, November 2, 1864, LS-SPC; *OR*, 41:1:638–39, 685.

17. Hinton, 290–91; McPheeters Diary, November 5, 1864; Baker Diary, November 5, 1864; Brown, "Army Journal," November 5, 1864.

18. *OR*, 41:1:647 and 4:649; Fagan to Maclean, November 5, 1864, PME.

19. David O. Demuth, "Federal Military Activity in Arkansas in the Fall of 1864 and the Skirmish at Hurricane Creek," *The Arkansas Historical Quarterly* 38 (1979):140–43; *OR*, 41:4:340, 341, 425, 426.

20. Demuth, 140–43; *OR*, 41:4:340, 341, 425, 426; Hinton, 304.

21. *OR*, 41:1:516–17; Hinton, 291–93; Gantz, 78.

22. *OR*, 41:1:647; *Missouri Republican*, March 20, 1886; EdSHELBY, 464; John D. Bennett Diary, November 10, 11, 1864, in McGhee, *Campaiging with Marmaduke*, 28; *Washington Telegraph*, November 30, 1864; James T. Armstrong to Matilda Armstrong, November 13, 1864, James T. Armstrong Papers; *Ballard Diary*, 69–76; TREM, 264–66; Wright to W. A. Crawford, November 8, 1864, B. 1, F. 1, CAPC.

23. TREM, 264–66; McPheeters Diary, November 7–11, 1864; Brown, "Army Journal," November 10, 17, 1864; Baker Diary, November 7–11, 1864; Cruzen, 35.

24. EdSHELBY, 462–63; Wright to W. A. Crawford, November 8, 1864, B. 1, F. 1, CAPC; *Washington Telegraph*, November 30, 1864; James T. Armstrong to Matilda Armstrong, November 13, 1864, Armstrong Papers; *Ballard Diary*, 69–76; TREM, 264–66, McPheeters Diary, November 7–11, 1864; Brown, "Army Journal," November 10, 17, 1864; Baker Diary, November 7–11, 1864; Cruzen, 35; William G. Hazen to Alexander B. Hazen, December 21, 1864, Hazen Letter.

25. Kerby, 352–58.

26. *OR*, 41:1:639, 647–48, 705; W. W. Alston to Price, November 30, 1864, B. 60, TSP and Alston to Price, December 3, 1864, LS-SPC; McPheeters Diary, November 10–December 3, 1864; Baker Diary, November 13, 1864; TREM, 266–67.

27. *OR*, 41:1:640 and 4:1112–13; Castel, *General Sterling Price*, 252.

19. AFTERMATH

1. Schrantz, 219–21; *Salisbury Democrat*, n.d., in B. 1, F. 2131, Benecke Collection; *History of Callaway County, Missouri* (St. Louis: Press of Nixon-Jones Printing Company, 1884), 724.

2. *OR*, 41:1:911–12 and 4:513; James E. McGhee, *Guide to Missouri Confederate Units, 1861–1865* (Fayetteville: University of Arkansas Press, 2008), 163–64, 169; Coshow to J. W. Allen, January 30, 1908, Civil War Papers, MHMA.

3. *OR*, 41:1:894–95; Salem H. Ford, "Recruiting in North Missouri," *Confederate Veteran* 19 (1911): 335; S. H. Ford, "Reminiscences of S. H. Ford," March 8, 1909, typescript, pages 29–30, SHSMO-C; *Kansas City Star*, April 17, 1908.

4. *OR*, 41:1:406; Unidentified and undated clipping, "Col. Eli Hodge Died this Morning 4. A.M.," Scrapbooks, vol. 2, John S. Marmaduke Chapter, UDC, SHSMO-C; UDC, Records of Missouri Confederate Veterans, Eli Hodge, R. 16, F. 139, SHSMO-C; McGhee, *Guide*, 116.

5. *OR*, 41:1:529; Stanton, *Sixty Years*, 120–2; Childers, 13–20.

6. Lot Abraham Diary, November 8–10, 1864; Scott, 344–45; Vanorsdol, 65; Childers, 13–16.

7. Scott, 344–45; Vanorsdol, 65; Lot Abraham Diary, November 8–12, 1864.

8. Lot Abraham Diary, November 12, 1864; *Leavenworth Daily Times*, November 24, 1864; Hinton, 262, 310; Starr, 78; General Orders, No. 77, March 20, 1865, Headquarters Department of the Missouri, in author's possession; LCM, 5–28; O. A. Curtis Court Martial Proceedings, #OO657, pages 15, 32–42, 109, RG 153, NA.

9. LCM, 5–29; LCM, 32–42, 109; General Orders, No. 77.

10. *OR*, 41:4:798, 892–93; Lyman Bennett Diary, January 1, 1865.

11. *OR*, 41:4:894; Charles R. Jennison Court Martial Proceedings, #MM1731, *passim* and 42–44, RG 153, NA; General Orders, No. 77.

12. *OR*, 41:1:424; W. Wayne Smith, "An Experiment in Counterinsurgency: The Assessment of Confederate Sympathizers in Missouri," *Journal of Southern History* 35 (1969): 361–80; E. 2804 and 2805, Part 1, RG 393, NA; Joel Potts Proceedings, January 20, 1865, and John L. Austin Proceedings, January 13, 1865, B. 675, Civil War Cases, 1862–1865, RG 133, MSA; W. A. Wilson to Jeanette, December 11, 1864, B. 20, F. 472, Abiel Leonard Papers and Testimonial of E. J. Turner, B. 83, F. 2200, Testimonials, 1864–1865, Benecke Papers, SHSMO-C; W. H. Utz, *Biographical Sketches of the Bartlett Marshall Duncan and Henry Utz Families* (W. H. Utz, 1936), 54.

13. *OR*, 41:1:434; Gustavus to George Shinn, Chief Examination Bureau, December 28, 1864, and the statements of John Boyer, October 24, 1864, Theodor Lachance, November 21, 1864, Antoine Carron, November 15, 1864, Case of Joseph Aubochon, Antoine Aubochon, Charles Lachance, and Theodule Boyer, Part 1, E. 2792, Charges of Disloyalty, RG 393, NA.

14. Statement of George Criswell, February 17, 1865, R. 9, F. 193, James Rollins Papers, SHSMO-C; James Meyer Proceedings, January 12, 1865, B. 675, Civil War Cases, 1862–1865, RG 133, MSA.

15. William E. Parrish, *A History of Missouri: Volume III, 1860 to 1875* (Columbia: University of Missouri Press, 1973), 67; *Missouri Democrat*, November 28 and 30, 1864; List of Prisoners Received and Remaining at Military Prison, Fort Leavenworth, Kansas, January 2, 1865, transcript, Suderow Collection; Special Orders No. 295, Joseph Darr, Acting Provost Marshal General, HQ Dept. Mo., November 16, 1864, Darr to Swap, November 29, 1864, and Statement of Bond, Otho McCracken, William Trimble, John Robinson, Walter Robinson, Samuel Trimble, Greif Byanham, James Craig, William Miller, William Gray dated November 29, 1864, TMNCF.

16. Conklin to Headquarters, Dept. Missouri, October 31, 1864, DTR-DofM; Department of Missouri and Special Orders 393, HQ, Office of the Provost Marshal General, Department of the Missouri, December 3, 1864, Provost Marshal General, Part 1, E. 2803, Records Relating to Prisoners and Gratiot Prison, RG 393, NA; Charles W. Sanders, *While in the Hands of the Enemy: Military Prisons of the Civil War* (Baton Rouge: Louisiana State University, 2005), 275–77.

17. George J. Mook to Sister Emma, November 9, 1864, George J. Mook Papers, MHMA; Crowley, 145; *Border Sentinel*, November 4, 18, 1864; *Missouri Democrat*, November 7, 1864.

18. Crowley, 145; Sanders, 62–63; Semi-Monthly Reports of Gratiot St. Prisoners who have Died at the U.S. Prison Hospital, Nov 1–15 and Nov 16–31, 1864, Provost Marshal General, Records Relating to Prisoners at Gratiot Prison; *OR*, Series 2, 7:1115; Lonnie R. Speer, *Portals to Hell: Military Prisons of the Civil War* (Mechanicsburg: Stackpole Books, 1997), 134, 179; Louis S. Gerteis, *Civil War St. Louis* (Lawrence: University Press of Kansas, 2001), 188–201.

19. Speer, 323; Alton in the Civil War, Database, http://www.altonweb.com/history/civilwar/confed/index.html, accessed November 14, 2013.

20. Sanborn, "The Campaign in Missouri," *passim*; Sanborn to J. J. Lutz, July 12, 1895, John Lutz Papers, KSHS; *St. Louis Globe-Democrat*, April 4, 1897; *Missouri Democrat*, December 14, 28, 1864.

21. *Fort Smith New Era*, November 5, 1864; *Leavenworth Daily Times*, November 3, 4, 1864; *The Border Sentinel*, October 28, 1864; Castel, *A Frontier State at War*, 200–1.

22. *Fort Smith New Era*, November 5, 1864; *Leavenworth Daily Times*, November 3, 4, 1864; *The Border Sentinel*, October 28, 1864; Castel, *A Frontier State at War*, 200–1; Clarke to My Dear Sister, November 27, 1864, B. 8, F. 44, Sidney Clarke Collection, Carl Albert Research Center, The University of Oklahoma, Norman, Oklahoma.

23. Reynolds to Kirby Smith, November 19, 1864, December 16, 1864, Reynolds to Ewing, December 21, 1864, TCRP-LC; Ewing to Reynolds, December 8, 1864, TCRP-MHMA; *Washington Telegraph*, November 16, 1864; *Texas Republican*, November 18, 1864, December 23, 1864; Castel, 259.

24. *Texas Republican*, December 23, 1864.

25. *Texas Republican*, December 23, 1864; *Galveston Tri Weekly News*, February 3, 1865; *OR*, 4:1123.

26. *OR*, 41:1:640; *History of the Pacific Railroad of Missouri from Its Inception to Its Final Completion* (St. Louis: Democrat Book and Job Printing House, 1865), 23–24.

27. Kirby Smith to Mother, November 16, 1864, Kirby Smith Papers.

28. *OR*, 41:1:625–40 and 48:1:1318; Reynolds to Selden, January 7, 1865, TCRP-LC; *Shreveport News*, January, 10, 1865; *Galveston Tri Weekly News*, February 3, 1865; *Texas Republican*, February 17, 1865; Stephen Chicoine, *The Confederates of Chappell Hill, Texas: Prosperity, Civil War, and Decline* (Jefferson: McFarland and Company, 2005), 96.

29. Reynolds to Henry Ewing, January 16, 1865, Reynolds to Kirby Smith, January 18, 1865, Reynolds to Jefferson Davis, January 18, 1865, Reynolds to Waldo P. Johnston, January 21, 1865, Reynolds to E. H. Cushing, January 23, 1865, February 22, 1865, Reynolds to Mosby Parsons, January 28, 1865, Reynolds to George Vest, February 25, 1865, TCRP-LC.

30. EdSHELBY, 518.

31. Reynolds to Watkins, March 27, 30, April 5, 15, 1865, TCRP-LC.

32. *OR*, 41:1:701–29; Kerby, 360.

33. *OR*, 41:1:726–28; Kirby Smith to Governor, '65, Kirby Smith Papers.

34. *OR*, 41:1:726–28; Kirby Smith to Governor, '65, Kirby Smith Papers.

35. Gerteis, 327; Castel, 277–79; Reynolds to Snead, February 16, 1887, B. 3, F. 15, Thomas L. Snead Papers, MHMA; *Missouri Republican*, March 31, 1887.

36. EdSHELBY, 465, 476–77; Lause, 188.

Bibliography

ARKANSAS HISTORY COMMISSION AND ARCHIVES (LITTLE ROCK)

Reminiscences of the War Between the States, UDC Mary Lee Chapter #87
F. F. Basham
Ples H. Morgan
Roberta Falconer Manuscript on General Price's Campaign
Mary Hannah Johnston Morrow Diary
William L. Skaggs Collection

CHICAGO HISTORY MUSEUM

George Swain Collection

IOWA HISTORICAL ARCHIVES (DES MOINES)

Diary of James Boyle

JACKSON COUNTY HISTORICAL SOCIETY (INDEPENDENCE)

Mrs. Frank Fitzgerald Collection
J. J. Jones, "The Battle of Westport," Manuscript

KANSAS STATE HISTORICAL SOCIETY (TOPEKA)

Archer S. Childers, Miscellaneous Collections

Newspaper Clippings, 1886, Edwin A. Carpenter, "A History of the 17th Illinois Cavalry Volunteers"
William E. Connelley Collection
James Hanway Collection
Hiram Hill Collection
Kansas Adjutant General, Miscellaneous Bound Volumes
John Lutz Papers
Military History Collection
Civil War Narratives: P. I. Bonebrake; B. F. Dawson to Colonel of the 2nd KS Malitia [*sic*]; G. G. Gage; Henry M. Greene; John Kemp; S. B. Miles; Theodore Mills to G. G. Gage; H. E. Palmer; H. D. Rice; Levi Williams
Orders, Etc., of Maj. Andrew Stark
Thomas Moonlight Collection
Fletcher Pomeroy Diary
"The Civil War Diary of Samuel J. Reader"
Charles and Sara T. Robinson Collection, Microfilm Edition

LIBRARY OF CONGRESS (WASHINGTON)

Thomas C. Reynolds Papers

MINE CREEK BATTLEFIELD MUSEUM (PLEASANTON)

Gil Bergman, "Probable Alignment of the Confederate Artillery at the Battle of Mine Creek, October 25, 1864"
John C. Leach Diary

MISSOURI HISTORY MUSEUM ARCHIVES (ST. LOUIS)

A. T. Bartlett Papers
Civil War Papers (MHS collection title)
George R. Cruzen Papers
Frissell Family Papers
Gert Goebel Collection
Louis Fusz Papers
Howard County Papers
Kennelly Family Papers
William M. McPheeters Papers
Monroe J. Miller Papers
George J. Mook Papers
Cyrus A. Peterson Battle of Pilot Knob Research Collection
Thomas C. Reynolds Papers
Thomas L. Snead Papers

MISSOURI STATE ARCHIVES (JEFFERSON CITY)

Office of the Adjutant General, Record Group 133

MUSEUM OF THE CONFEDERACY, ELEANOR S. BROCKENBROUGH LIBRARY (RICHMOND)

William F. Slemons Papers

NATIONAL ARCHIVES (WASHINGTON)

RG 109, War Department Collection of Confederate Records
Price's Missouri Expedition, E. 450. B. 3
Letters Received, Chapter II, Vol. 211, Sterling Price's Command
Letters Sent, Chapter II, Vol. 178 1/2, Sterling Price's Command
Orders and Circulars Issued, Chapter II, Vol. 209, Sterling Price's Command
Thomas Snead Papers, E. 113, B. 59
RG 153, Judge Advocate General, General Court-Martial Records
Egbert B. Brown, File #LL 2941
O. A. Curtis, File #OO 657
Charles R. Jennison, #MM 1731
James McFerran, File #LL 2942
John McNeil, File #NN 3336
Provost Marshal General, Department of the Missouri
RG 393, Records of the U.S. Army Continental Commands, 1821–1920
E. 2081, Vol. 138. Letters Sent, Headquarters Department of Kansas
E. 2085, Vol. 148. Telegrams Sent, Department of Kansas
E. 2099, Vol. 150. Telegrams Received, Department of Kansas
E. 2121, Vol. 145. Letters and Telegrams Sent, Army of the Border
E. 2124, Vol. 151. Telegrams Received and Sent, Army of the Border
E. 2593, Letters Received, 1861–1867, Department of the Missouri
E. 2635, Two or More Name File
E. 2636, Citizen File
E. 2637, Two or More Name Citizen File
E. 2706, Vol. 71. Dispatches and Telegrams Received, Department of the Missouri
E. 2792, Charges of Disloyalty
E. 2803, Records Relating to Prisoners at Gratiot Prison
E. 2804, List of Men Who Left Missouri to Join the Forces of . . . Sterling Price
E. 2805, List of Men Who Left Missouri to Join the Forces of . . . Sterling Price

THE STATE HISTORICAL SOCIETY OF MISSOURI (COLUMBIA)

Clarence W. Alvord and Idress Head Collection
Lisbon Applegate Collection
J. H. P. Baker Diary

Benecke Family Papers
Henry Clay and William H. Crawford Papers
Crede Family Papers
Henry C. Fike Papers
Jonathan B. Fuller Papers
Salem H. Ford, "Reminiscences of S. H. Ford"
Francis M. Gordon Diary, Civil War Diaries, 1864–1867
William G. Hazen Letter
Henry Klinge Papers
Bazel F. Lazear Papers
Abiel Leonard Papers
William A. Lyman Collection
Reppy-Frissell-Drake Family Papers
James Rollins Papers
Joseph O. Shelby Scrapbook, Vol. 1
Bryce A. Suderow Collection
"The Battle of Pilot Knob by One Who Was There"
Lizzie Thompson Letter
United Daughters of the Confederacy, John S. Marmaduke Chapter, Scrapbooks
United Daughters of the Confederacy, Records of Missouri Confederate Veterans
Robert T. Van Horn Papers
Watson-Westlake Papers

THE STATE HISTORICAL SOCIETY OF MISSOURI (KANSAS CITY)

Jonathan B. Fuller Papers

THE STATE HISTORICAL SOCIETY OF MISSOURI (ROLLA)

Lyman G. Bennett Collection
Charles W. Rubey Papers
Russell Family Papers

TULANE UNIVERSITY, HOWARD-TILTON MEMORIAL LIBRARY (NEW ORLEANS)

M. Jeff Thompson Papers

UNIVERSITY OF ARKANSAS, DAVID W. MULLINS LIBRARY, SPECIAL COLLECTIONS (FAYETTEVILLE)

John W. Brown Diary
Correspondence of John S. Marmaduke, 1863–1864, Records of the War Department, Collection of Confederate Records, RG 109, Microfilm, Reel 1

General and Special Orders, Trans-Mississippi Department, Microfilm 374, Reel 1
Lighton Family Papers

UNIVERSITY OF IOWA LIBRARIES, SPECIAL COLLECTIONS DEPARTMENT (IOWA CITY)

Papers of Lot Abraham
Edward Francis Winslow Papers

UNIVERSITY OF NORTH CAROLINA, WILSON LIBRARY SOUTHERN HISTORICAL COLLECTION (CHAPEL HILL)

James T. Armstrong Papers
Edmund Kirby Smith Papers

UNIVERSITY OF OKLAHOMA, CARL ALBERT RESEARCH CENTER (NORMAN)

Sidney Clarke Collection

YALE UNIVERSITY LIBRARY, WESTERN AMERICAN COLLECTION (NEW HAVEN)

Samuel Ryan Curtis Papers

AUTHOR'S POSSESSION

Campbell, James H. "Reminiscence of James H. Campbell's Experiences During the Civil War"
General Orders, No. 77, March 20, 1865, Headquarters Department of the Missouri

NEWSPAPERS

The Border Sentinel (Mound City)
The Central Missourian (Boonville)
The Commercial Press (Pultneyville, New York)
Fort Smith New Era
Galveston Tri Weekly News
Jefferson City Tribune
Kansas City Journal
Kansas City Star
Leavenworth Conservative

Leavenworth Daily Standard
Leavenworth Daily Times
Leavenworth Times
Missouri Democrat (St. Louis)
Missouri Republican (St. Louis)
Missouri State Times (Jefferson City)
The National Tribune (Washington)
Pleasanton Enterprise
Pleasonton Observer
Sedalia Advertiser
Shreveport News
Springfield Missouri Patriot
St. Louis Globe Democrat
St. Louis Union
Texas Republican
Topeka Journal
Tri-Weekly Missouri Democrat (St. Louis)
Washington Telegraph
Western Journal of Commerce (Kansas City)
Yonkers Statesman

ARTICLES AND BOOK CHAPTERS

Asbury, Virginia H. "An Anomaly of Written History." *Confederate Veteran Magazine* 22 (1914): 138.

Blunt, James G. "General Blunt's Account of His Civil War Experiences." *Kansas Historical Quarterly* 1 (1931–1932): 211–65.

Brown, D. Alexander. "The Battle of Westport." *Civil War Times Illustrated* 5 (1966): 6–11, 40–42.

Brownlee, Richard S. "The Battle of Pilot Knob, Iron County, Missouri, September 27, 1864." *Missouri Historical Review* 92 (1998): 1–30.

Candenquist, Arthur. "Did Anybody Really Know What Time It Was?" *Blue and Gray Magazine* 8, no. 6 (1991): 32–35.

Castel, Albert. "Civil War Kansas and the Negro." *Journal of Negro History* 51 (1966): 125–38.

Cole, Birdie H. "The Battle of Pilot Knob." *Confederate Veteran* 22 (1914): 417.

Coleman, R. B. "Various Small Fights in Missouri." *Confederate Veteran* 14 (1906): 120.

Cubbison, Douglas R. "Look Out for Hell Some Place Soon: The 2nd Colorado Cavalry in Missouri, February–September, 1864." *Military History of the West* 32 (2002): 1–6.

Culmer, Frederic A., Ed. "Brigadier Surgeon John W. Trader's Recollections of the Civil War in Missouri." *Missouri Historical Review* 48 (1952): 323–34.

Cunningham, Roger D. "Welcoming 'Pa' on the Kaw: Kansas's 'Colored' Militia in the 1864 Price Raid." *Kansas History* 25 (2002): 86–101.

Dalehite, Bob. "Colonel Arch S. Dobbin[s]." *The Independence County Chronicle* 5 (1964): 39–51.

Darr, John. "Price's Raid in Missouri." *Confederate Veteran* 11 (1903): 359–62.

Demuth, David O. "Federal Military Activity in Arkansas in the Fall of 1864 and the Skirmish at Hurricane Creek." *The Arkansas Historical Quarterly* 38 (1979): 131–45.

Denny, James M. "The Battle of Glasgow." *Boone's Lick Heritage* 3 (1995): 4–9.

Fletcher, Thomas C. "The Battle of Pilot Knob, and the Retreat to Leasburg." In *War Papers and Personal Reminiscences, 1861–1865. Read Before the Commandery of the State of Missouri Military Order of the Loyal Legion of the United States.* Vol. 1. St. Louis: Becktold and Company, 1892.

Ford, Salem H. "Recruiting in North Missouri." *Confederate Veteran* 19 (1911): 335.

Gill, Samuel T. "Liberator Unmercifully Hounded." *America's Civil War* 1 (1988): 34–41.

Greer, Gene. "Up and in Line at Day Break: Considable Skemish." *White River Valley Historical Quarterly* 1 (1964): 1–15.

Grover, George S. "The Price Campaign of 1864." *Missouri Historical Review* 7 (1912): 167–81.

Halliburton, J. W. "That Charge." *Confederate Veteran* 28 (1920): 264.

Hamilton, James. "The Enrolled Missouri Militia: Its Organization and Controversial History." *Missouri Historical Review* 69 (1975): 413–32.

Horton, James C. "Personal Narrative: Peter D. Ridenour and Harlow W. Baker, Two Pioneer Kansas Merchants." *Transactions of the Kansas State Historical Society, 1907–1908* vol. 10 (1908): 589–621.

Huff, Leo E. "The Last Duel in Arkansas: The Marmaduke-Walker Duel." *Arkansas Historical Quarterly* 23 (1964): 36–49.

Hulbert, Matthew C. "Constructing Guerrilla Memory: John Newman Edwards and Missouri's Irregular Lost Cause." *The Journal of the Civil War Era* 2 (2012): 58–81.

Lindberg, Kip. "Chaos Itself: The Battle of Mine Creek." *North and South* 1, no. 6 (1998): 74–85.

Lindberg, Kip and Matt Matthews, ed. "'The Eagle of the 11th Kansas': Wartime Reminiscences of Colonel Thomas Moonlight." *Arkansas Historical Quarterly* 62 (2003): 1–41.

Petruzzi, J. David. "The Fleeting Fame of Alfred Pleasonton." *America's Civil War* 18 (2005): 22–28.

Philips, John F. "Diary of Acting Brigadier General John F. Philips . . ." *The Annals of Kansas City* 1 (1923): 267–71.

Plummer, Mark A. "Missouri and Kansas and the Capture of General Marmaduke." *Missouri Historical Review* 59 (1964): 90–104.

"Price's Invasion." *The Congregational Record* 6, nos. 10, 11, 12 (October, November, December 1864): 109–17, 121–29.

Richards, Edward Moore. "'Price's Raid,' Personal Reminiscences of the American Civil War, Kansas, October 1864." *Irish Sword* 7 (1966): 234–40.

Rickman, Daniel T. "Events in the Trans-Mississippi Department." *Confederate Veteran* 21 (1913): 71.

Sallee, Scott E. "Missouri! One Last Time: Sterling Price's 1864 Missouri Expedition, 'A Just and Holy Cause.'" *Blue and Gray Magazine* 8 (1991):10–18, 20, 48–62.

Sanborn, John B. "Battles and Campaigns of September, 1862." In *Glimpses of the Nation's Struggle . . . , 1897–1902.* 5th Series. St. Paul: Review Publishing Company, 1903.

Sanborn, John B. "The Campaign in Missouri in September and October, 1864." In *Glimpses of the Nation's Struggle . . . , 1889–1892,* edited by Edward D. Neill. 3rd Series. New York: D. D. Merrill Co., 1893.

Smith, W. Wayne. "An Experiment in Counterinsurgency: The Assessment of Confederate Sympathizers in Missouri." *The Journal of Southern History* 35 (1969): 361–80.

Stanton, Donal J. et al. "Missouri's Forgotten General: M. Jeff Thomson and the Civil War." *Missouri Historical Review* 70 (1976): 237–58.

Suderow, Bryce. "An Eye for an Eye: An Episode from Missouri's Civil War," in *Confederate Courage on Other Fields*, by Mark J. Crawford, 89–134. Jefferson: McFarland & Company, Inc., 2000.

Suderow, Bryce, ed. "McLain's Battery and Price's 1864 Invasion: A Letter from Lt. Caleb Burdsal, Jr." *Kansas History* 6 (1983):29–45.

Williams, Charles G., ed. "A Saline Guard: The Civil War Letters of Col. William Ayers Crawford, CSA, 1861–1865, Part II." *Arkansas Historical Quarterly* 32 (1973): 71–93.

Wood, William. "General Sterling Price: The New Mexico Insurrection, 1846–47." *The Magazine of American History* 18 (1887): 333–35.

Woodruff, Frederick M., ed. "The Civil War Notebook of Montgomery Schuyler Woodruff." *Missouri Historical Bulletin* 29 (1973):163–88.

BOOKS

An Illustrated Historical Atlas Map: Jackson County, MO. Philadelphia: Brink, McDonough, 1877; reprint, Jackson County Historical Society, 1976.

An Illustrated Historical Atlas of Bourbon County, Kansas. Philadelphia: Edwards Brothers, 1878.

Annual Report of the Adjutant General of Missouri for 1864. Jefferson City: W. A. Curry, 1865.

Annual Report of the Adjutant General of Missouri: For the Year Ending December 31, 1865. Jefferson City, MO: Emory Foster, 1866.

Asbury, A. I. Edgar. *My Experiences in the War, 1861–1865, a Little Autobiography*. Kansas City: Berkowitz and Company, 1894.

Baker, James H. and George E. Lewis, ed. *History of Colorado*. Vol. 4. Denver: Linderman Company, Inc., 1927.

Bird, Roy. *They Deserved a Better Fate: The Second Kansas State Militia Regiment and the Price Raid, 1864*. New York: Cummings & Hathaway, 1999.

Britton, Wiley. *The Civil War on the Border*. Vol. 2. New York: G. P. Putnam's Sons, 1899; reprint, Ottawa: Kansas Heritage Press, 1994.

Brophy, Patrick. *Fire and Sword: A Missouri County in the Civil War*. Nevada: Bushwhacker Books, 2008.

Brugioni, Dino. *The Civil War in Missouri: As Seen from the Capital City*. Jefferson City: Summers Publishing, 1987.

Bryner, Byron C. *Bugle Echoes: The Story of the Illinois 47th*. Springfield: Phillips Bros., 1905.

Bullene, Lathrop. *The Life of Lathrop Bullene*. Privately published, 1916.

Buresh, Lumir F. *October 25th and the Battle of Mine Creek*. Kansas City: The Lowell Press, 1977.

Busch, Walter E. *Fort Davidson and the Battle of Pilot Knob: Missouri's Alamo*. Charleston: The History Press, 2010.

Cabell, William L. *Report of the Part Cabell's Brigade Took in What Is Called "Price's Raid" into Missouri and Kansas in the Fall of 1864*. Dallas, 1900.

Carpenter, Edwin A. *History of the 17th Illinois Cavalry Volunteers*. n.p., 1886.

Casdorph, Paul. *Prince John Magruder: His Life and Campaigns*. New York: Wiley, 1996.

Castel, Albert. *A Frontier State at War: Kansas, 1861–1865*. Ithaca: Cornell University Press, 1958.

Castel, Albert. *General Sterling Price and the Civil War in the West.* Baton Rouge: Louisiana State University Press, 1968.

Castel, Albert and Thomas Goodrich. *Bloody Bill Anderson: The Short, Savage Life of a Civil War Guerrilla.* Mechanicsburg: Stackpole Books, 1998.

Chicoine, Stephen. *The Confederates of Chappell Hill, Texas: Prosperity, Civil War, and Decline.* Jefferson: McFarland and Company, 2005.

Cogley, Thomas S. *History of the Seventh Indiana Cavalry Volunteers . . .* LaForte: Herald Company, 1876.

Collins, Robert. *General James G. Blunt: Tarnished Glory.* Gretna: Pelican Publishing Company, 2005.

Connelley, William E. *The Life of Preston Plumb, 1837–1891.* Chicago: Browne and Hall Company, 1913.

Connelley, William E. *A Standard History of Kansas and Kansans.* 5 vols. Chicago: Lewis Publishing Company, 1918.

Connelley, William E. *Wild Bill and His Era: The Life and Adventures of James Butler Hickock.* New York: The Press of the Pioneers, 1933.

Cordley, Richard. *Pioneer Days in Kansas.* Boston: The Pilgrim Press, 1903.

Crawford, Samuel J. *Kansas in the Sixties.* Chicago: A. C. McClurg and Company, 1911.

Crowley, William J. *Tennessee Cavalier in the Missouri Cavalry: Major Henry Ewing, C.S.A. of the St. Louis Times.* Homewood: William J. Crowley, 1978.

Curtis, Samuel S. *A Cruise on the Benton: A Narrative of Combat on the Missouri River in the Civil War.* Waynesboro: M & R Books, 1967.

Cutler, William G., ed. *History of the State of Kansas.* 2 vols. Chicago: A. T. Andreas, 1883.

Davis, William C. *Jefferson Davis: The Man and His Hour.* Baton Rouge: Louisiana State University Press, 1991.

Deatherage, Charles P. *Early History of Greater Kansas City . . .* Vol. 1. Kansas City: Interstate Publishing Company, 1927.

Documents Exhibiting the Organization, Conditions, and Relations of the Pacific Railroad of the State of Missouri. New York: Baker, Godwin, and Company, 1853.

Draper, John Ballard. *William Curtis Ballard: His Ancestors and Descendants.* n.p., 1979.

Dupree, Stephen A. *Planting the Union Flag in Texas: The Campaigns of Major General Nathaniel P. Banks in the West.* College Station: Texas A&M University Press, 2008.

Edwards, John N. *Noted Guerrillas.* St. Louis: Bryan and Brand and Company, 1877.

Edwards, John N. *Shelby and His Men: The War in the West.* Cincinnati: Miami Printing and Publishing Company, 1967.

Evans, Clement A., ed. *Confederate Military History* Vol. X. Atlanta: Confederate Publishing Company, 1899.

Fairbanks, Jonathan and Clyde E. Tuck. *Past and Present of Green County Missouri: Early and Recent History and Genealogical Records of Many of the Representative Citizens.* Indianapolis: A. W. Bowen, 1915.

Fellman, Michael. *Inside War: The Guerilla Conflict in Missouri during the American Civil War.* New York: Oxford University Press, 1989.

Gage, Guilford G. *The Battle of the Blue of the Second Regiment . . .* Chicago: WTPA, n.d.

Gantz, Jacob. *Such Are the Trials: The Civil War Diaries of Jacob Gantz.* Edited by Kathleen Davis. Ames: Iowa State University Press, 1991.

Gerteis, Louis S. *Civil War St. Louis.* Lawrence: University Press of Kansas, 2001.

Gibson, Charles D. and E. Kay Gibson. *The Army's Navy Series, Vol. 2. Assault and Logistics: Union Army Coastal and River Operations, 1861–1865.* Camden: Ensign Press, 1995.

Gregory, Ralph. *Price's Raid in Franklin County, Missouri.* Washington: Missourian Publishing, 1990.

Hagerman, Edward. *The American Civil War and the Origins of Modern Warfare: Ideas, Organization, and Field Command.* Bloomington: Indiana University Press, 1988.

Heidler, David et al., eds. *Encyclopedia of the American Civil War.* New York: W. W. Norton, 2002.

Heineman, Kenneth J. *Civil War Dynasty: The Ewing Family of Ohio.* New York: New York University Press, 2012.

Hess, Earl J. *The Rifle Musket in Civil War Combat: Reality and Myth.* Lawrence: University Press of Kansas, 2008.

Hewitt, Lawrence L., ed. *Confederate Generals in the Trans-Mississippi: Essays on America's Civil War.* Vol. 1. Knoxville: University of Tennessee Press, 2013.

Hinton, Richard J. *Rebel Invasion of Missouri and Kansas . . .* Chicago: Church and Goodman, 1865.

History of Callaway County, Missouri. St. Louis: Press of Nixon-Jones Printing Company, 1884.

History of Clay and Platte Counties, Missouri . . . St. Louis: National Historical Company, 1885.

History of Howard and Cooper Counties, Missouri . . . St. Louis: National Historical Company, 1883.

History of the Pacific Railroad of Missouri from Its Inception to Its Final Completion. St. Louis: Democrat Book and Job Printing House, 1865.

History of Vernon County, Missouri, Written and Compiled from the Most Authentic Official and Private Sources . . . St. Louis: Brown and Company, 1887.

Illustrated Atlas Map of Saline County, MO. St. Louis: Missouri Publishing Company, 1976.

Ingersoll, Lurton Dunham. *Iowa and the Rebellion.* Philadelphia: J. B. Lippincott, 1866.

Jenkins, Paul B. *The Battle of Westport.* Kansas City: Franklin Hudson Publishing Company, 1906.

Johnson, Ludwell H. *Red River Campaign: Politics and Cotton in the Civil War.* Baltimore: Johns Hopkins, 1958; reprint Kent: Kent State University, 1993.

Joiner, Gary D. *One Damn Blunder from the Beginning to the End: The Red River Campaign of 1864.* Wilmington: Scholarly Resources, 2003.

Kajencki, Francis C. *Star on Many a Battlefield: Brevet Brigadier General Joseph Karge in the American Civil War.* Cranbury, NJ: Associated University Presses, Inc., 1980.

Katcher, Phillip. *Civil War Day by Day.* St. Paul: Zenith Press, 2007.

Keehn, David C. *Knights of the Golden Circle: Secret Empire, Southern Secession, Civil War.* Baton Rouge: Louisiana State University, 2013.

Kerby, Robert L. *Kirby Smith's Confederacy: The Trans-Mississippi South, 1863–1865.* New York: Columbia University Press, 1972.

Klement, Frank L. *Dark Lanterns: Secret Political Societies, Conspiracies, and Treason Trials in the Civil War.* Baton Rouge: Louisiana State University Press, 1984.

Lamers, William M. *The Edge of Glory: A Biography of General William S. Rosecrans, U.S.A.* New York: Harcourt, Brace, and World, Inc., 1961.

Lause, Mark A. *Price's Lost Campaign: The 1864 Invasion of Missouri.* Columbia: University of Missouri Press, 2011.

Lee, Fred. *The Battle of Westport: October 21–23, 1864.* Special Publication Number One. Kansas City: Westport Historical Society, 1976.

Lee, Fred. *Gettysburg of the West: The Battle of Westport, October 21–23, 1864.* Independence: Two Trails Publishing, 1996.

Lees, William B. "When the Shooting Stopped, the War Began." In *Look to the Earth: Historical Archaeology and the American Civil War*, edited by Clarence R. Geier Jr. and Susan B. Winter, 39–59. Knoxville: University of Tennessee Press, 1994.

Longacre, Edward G. *The Cavalry at Gettysburg: A Tactical Study of Mounted Operations during the Civil War's Pivotal Campaign, 9 June–14 July 1863*. Rutherford: Fairleigh Dickinson University Press, 1986.

Mackey, Robert R. *The Uncivil War: Irregular Warfare in the Upper South, 1861–1865*. Norman: University of Oklahoma Press, 2004.

Mahan, Russell L. *Fayetteville, Arkansas in the Civil War, 1860–1865*. Bountiful: Historical Byways, 2003.

Mallery, James P. *"Found No Bushwhackers": The 1864 Diary of Sgt. James P. Mallery, Company A, Third Wisconsin Cavalry, Stationed at Balltown, Mo.* Edited by Patrick Brophy. Nevada: Vernon Historical Society, 1988.

Manford, Erasmus. *Twenty-Five Years in the West*. Chicago: E. Manford Publisher, 1867.

Marmor, Jason. *Prelude to Westport: Phase I Archaeological Survey of a Portion of the Big Blue Battlefield in Kansas City, Jackson County, Missouri . . .* Laramie: TRC Mariah Associates, Inc., 1997.

McCourt, Walter E. *The Geology of Jackson County*. Rolla: McCourt, 1917.

McGhee, James E., ed. *Campaigning with Marmaduke: Narratives and Roster of the 8th Missouri Cavalry Regiment CSA*. Independence: Two Trails Publishing, 2002.

McGhee, James E. *Guide to Missouri Confederate Units, 1861–1865*. Fayetteville: University of Arkansas Press, 2008.

McReynolds, Edwin C. *Missouri: A History of the Crossroads State*. Norman: University of Oklahoma Press, 1962.

Mills, Charles K. *Harvest of Barren Regrets: The Army Career of Frederick William Benteen, 1834–1898*. Glendale: Arthur W. Clark Company, 1985.

Mitchell, William A. *Linn County, Kansas: A History*. La Cygne: La Cygne *Journal*, 1928.

Monnett, Howard N. *Action Before Westport 1864*. Kansas City: Westport Historical Society, 1964; Reprint Edition Niwor, CO: University Press of Colorado, 1995.

Mueller, Doris L. *M. Jeff Thompson: Missouri's Swamp Fox of the Confederacy*. Columbia: University of Missouri Press, 2007.

Napton, William B. *Past and Present of Saline County Missouri*. Indianapolis, IN: B. F. Bowen and Company, 1910.

Neely, Jr., Mark E. *The Civil War and the Limits of Destruction*. Cambridge: Harvard University Press, 2007.

Oates, Stephen B. *Confederate Cavalry West of the River*. Austin: University of Texas Press, 1961.

Palmer, Don Mc. N. *Four Weeks in the Rebel Army*. New London: D. S. Ruddock, Printer, 1865.

Parks, Joseph H. *General Edmund Kirby Smith C.S.A.* Baton Rouge: Louisiana State University Press, 1954.

Parrish, William E. *A History of Missouri: Volume III, 1860 to 1875*. Columbia: University of Missouri Press, 1973.

Peterson, Cyrus A. and Joseph M. Hanson. *Pilot Knob: The Thermopylae of the West*. 2nd Edition. Independence: Two Trails Publishing Company, 2000.

Prushankin, Jeffery S. *A Crisis in Confederate Command: Edmund Kirby Smith, Richard Taylor, and the Army of the Trans-Mississippi*. Baton Rouge: Louisiana State University Press, 2005.

Report of the Adjutant General of the State of Kansas, 1861–1865. Vol. 1. Topeka: Kansas State Printing Company, 1896.

Report of the Adjutant General of the State of Kansas for the Year 1864. Leavenworth: P. H. Hubbell & Company, Book and Job Printers, 1865.

Robley, T. F. *History of Bourbon County, Kansas to the Close of 1865*. Fort Scott: Press of the Monitor Book and Print Company, 1894.

Sanders, Charles W. *While in the Hands of the Enemy: Military Prisons of the Civil War*. Baton Rouge: Louisiana State University, 2005.

Schrantz, Ward L. *Jasper County, Missouri, in the Civil War*. Carthage: The Carthage Press, 1923.

Scott, William Forse. *The Story of a Cavalry Regiment: The Career of the Fourth Iowa Veteran Volunteers from Kansas to Georgia, 1861–1865*. New York: G. P. Putnam's Sons, 1893.

Sellmeyer, Deryl P. *Jo Shelby's Iron Brigade*. Gretna: Pelican Publishing Company, 2007.

Shalhope, Robert E. *Sterling Price: Portrait of a Southerner*. Columbia: University of Columbia Press, 1971.

Sinisi, Kyle S. *Sacred Debts: State Civil War Claims and American Federalism, 1861–1880*. New York: Fordham University Press, 2003.

Smith, Ronald D. *Thomas Ewing, Jr.: Frontier Lawyer and Civil War General*. Columbia: University of Missouri Press, 2008.

Speer, Lonnie R. *Portals to Hell: Military Prisons of the Civil War*. Mechanicsburg: Stackpole Books, 1997.

Stanton, Donal J. et al., eds. *The Civil War Reminiscences of General M. Jeff Thompson*. Dayton: Morningside Books, 1988.

Stanton, Irving W. *Sixty Years in Colorado: Reminiscences and Reflections of a Pioneer of 1860*. Denver, 1922.

Starr, Stephen Z. *Jennison's Jayhawkers: A Civil War Cavalry Regiment and Its Commander*. Baton Rouge: Louisiana State University Press, 1973.

Steele, James W. *The Battle of the Blue of the Second KSM, October 22, 1864; The Flight; The Captivity; The Escape*. Chicago: W.T.P.A, 1895.

Suderow, Bryce A. *Thunder in the Arcadia Valley: Price's Defeat, September 27, 1864*. Cape Girardeau: Center for Regional History and Cultural Heritage, 1986.

Truman, Ben C. *The Field of Honor: Being a Complete and Comprehensive History of Duelling [sic] in all Countries . . .* New York: Fords, Howard, and Hulbert, 1884.

Turner, S. K. and S. A. Clark. *Twentieth Century History of Carroll County Missouri*. Vol. 1. Indianapolis: B. F. Bowen, 1911.

Utz, W. H. *Biographical Sketches of the Bartlett Marshall Duncan and Henry Utz Families*. W. H. Utz, 1936.

Vanorsdol, James. *Four Years for the Union*. n.p., 1888.

Varney, Frank P. *General Grant and the Rewriting of History: How the Destruction of General William S. Rosecrans Influenced Our Understanding of the Civil War*. El Dorado Hills: Savas Beatie, 2013.

Walmsley, Sr., George P. *Experiences of a Civil War Horse-Soldier*. Lanham: University Press of America, 1993.

Watts, Hamp B. *The Babe of the Company: An Unfolded Leaf from the Forest of Never To-Be-Forgotten Years*. Fayette: Democrat-Leader Press, 1913.

Westport Historical Society, ed. *The Battle of Westport: October 21–23, 1864*. Kansas City: Westport Historical Society, 1996.

Williams, Ellen. *Three Years and a Half in the Army: History of the 2nd Colorado*. New York: Fowler and Wells Company, 1885.

Wood, Larry. *The Two Civil War Battles of Newtonia*. Charleston: The History Press, 2010.

Wright, John C. *Memoirs of Colonel John C. Wright*. Pine Bluff: Rare Book Publishers, 1982.

U.S. GOVERNMENT DOCUMENTS

U.S. Army Corps of Engineers. Blue River Channel Project, Kansas City, Missouri, Independence-Westport Road Crossing and Other Oregon/Santa Fe Trail Alternatives, National Register Assessment. 1994.

U.S. Congress, Senate Report, 51st Cong., 2nd sess., 1891, Report #2445. Proceedings of a General Court Martial, John M. Laing.

War Department. Revised Regulations for the Army of the United States of 1861. Philadelphia: J. G. L. Brown Printer.

War Department. The War of the Rebellion: A Compilation of the Official Records of the Union and Confederate Armies. 128 Volumes. Washington: Government Printing Office, 1880–1901.

UNPUBLISHED DISSERTATION

Belser, Thomas A. "Military Operations in Missouri and Arkansas, 1861–1865." PhD dissertation, Vanderbilt University, 1958.

INTERNET SOURCES

Alton in the Civil War, Database, http://www.altonweb.com/history/civilwar/confed/index.html, accessed November 14, 2013.

CWSAC, Battle Summaries, Westport, http://www.nps.gov/abpp/battles/mo027.htm, accessed August 14, 2009.

Service Record, J. M. McGehee, McGehee's Regiment, Arkansas Cavalry, http://www.fold3.com/image/271/219829731/, accessed November 19, 2013.

Index

Index

295, 309–310, 311, 313–136, 326, 330,
341, 342, 346, 349, 350–352, 367n5,
387n22, 391n24; Confederate treatment
of Union, 66, 81, 206, 261, 308–309;
galvanized Confederates, 350–344;
squabble over Mine Creek prisoners,
291–292, 309–310, 311, 326; Union
taken, xv, xvi, 58, 63, 66, 73, 81, 95,
117, 121, 137–138, 206–207, 249, 257,
261, 296, 308–309, 356; Union
treatment of Confederate, xv, 63, 81,
97, 104, 124, 230, 286, 291, 341, 342,
346, 349, 350–352. *See also* Alton
Military Prison; Gratiot Street Prison
Pritchard, Maj. Jesse L., 318
Pulliam's Farm, 63

Quantrill, William C., 54, 55, 60, 117, 133,
158, 164, 344–345
Quincy, Missouri, 342

Race, Pvt. Merrick D., 206
railroads. *See* Hannibal and St. Joseph
Railroad; Iron Mountain Railroad;
North Missouri Railroad; Pacific
Railroad; Southwest Branch of the
Pacific Railroad
Rapley, Maj. William F., 144
Rathbun, Cpt. George S., 122–123
recruits and recruiting (Confederate), 1, 3,
20, 34, 36, 53, 63–65, 79, 82, 94, 96,
187, 193, 249, 272, 282, 294, 297; as an
objective of the invasion, 17, 23;
Confederate attempts to sort, 95, 121;
conscripts, xv, 27, 30, 95, 100,
121–123, 128, 145, 256–257, 347–350,
362; desertion among, 309, 325;
distribution of recruits among units, 45,
176; frustrations in recruiting to the
Boonslick, 121–122; ill discipline and a
lack of training among, 44–45, 46, 65,
125, 127, 359; incapacitation of, 324;
individual and group efforts to join
Price's army, 124–125, 341–343; lack
of weapons among, 44, 45, 123, 127,
246, 274, 298–299, 301; poaching of
recruits, 45; Price's anticipation of
recruiting in Missouri, 9, 10, 17, 91, 93,
343; Price's exaggeration of, 343;

recruiters and recruiting officers, 46,
51, 54, 56, 122–125, 198; recruiting in
the Boonslick, 121–122, 124–125, 127,
134, 138, 143, 173, 174, 378n24;
Shelby's efforts to recruit in Arkansas,
30, 43–45, 46. *See also* blacks; Brooks;
Dorsey; Ford; Freeman; Hodge;
Perkins; Rathbun; Searcy; Slayback;
Tyler; D. A. Williams
Red River Campaign, 10–12, 14, 28–29,
30, 31–32, 33, 40, 57
Redd, Capt. Oliver F., 243
Reeves, Col. Timothy, 62, 63–64, 81, 346
Reiff, Maj. A. V., 320
Reynolds, Gov. Thomas C., 5, 15, 16, 17,
19–20, 23, 36, 50–51, 87, 94, 114, 117,
190; as military advisor to Kirby Smith,
8–9, 11, 13, 21; background and
personality, 4; brokers deal regarding
Price, 7; criticism of Price's
generalship, 41–42, 145; distrust of
Sterling Price, 5–6, 9, 20; his peace
with Price's memory, 360–361; policy
toward Sterling Price, 7; post-invasion
quarrel with Price, 341, 354–361
Richwoods, Missouri, 87, 95, 99, 102, 103
Ridenour, Peter, 156
Ritchey, Mathew H., 317, 320–322
Roberts, Lt. Cyrus M., 207
Robinson, Col. C. H., 160
Robinson, Gov. Charles, 148, 150, 164
Robinson, George, 384n4
Rocheport, Missouri, 123, 129
Rock Island Prison Barracks, 350, 352
Rock Mountain, 60, 76, 82
Rolla, Missouri, 50, 58, 87, 89, 90, 101,
104, 326, 329
Rollins, Cong. James S., 129
Rosecrans, Maj. Gen. William S., 49, 56,
57, 96, 97, 101, 151, 153, 156, 167,
181, 197, 213, 217, 236, 346; and Pilot
Knob, 59, 72, 73, 74, 81, 86;
background of, 49; belief in OAK
conspiracy, 50–51, 54–55, 60, 371n2;
controversies involving Curtis, 303,
326–327, 329, 396n6; co-ordination of
pursuit of Price from Jefferson City to
Lexington, 117, 129, 130, 138, 139,
141, 179, 379n14; defense of St. Louis